Assessment of Children and Youth with Special Needs

FIFTH EDITION

Libby G. Cohen
University of Southern Maine

Loraine J. Spenciner
University of Maine at Farmington

PEARSON

Boston Columbus Indianapolis New York San Francisco Upper Saddle River
Amsterdam Cape Town Dubai London Madrid Milan Munich Paris Montreal Toronto
Delhi Mexico City São Paulo Sydney Hong Kong Seoul Singapore Taipei Tokyo

Vice President and Editorial Director:
 Jeffery W. Johnston
Executive Editor: Ann Castel Davis
Editorial Assistant: Andrea Hall
Marketing Manager: Krista Clark
Project Manager: Kerry Rubadue
Operations Specialist: Michelle Klein
Senior Art Director: Jayne Conte
Text Designer: Aptara®, Inc.

Cover Designer: Karen Noferi
Cover Art: Zhu Qing
Media Producer: Autumn Benson
Media Project Manager: Noelle Chun
Full-Service Project Management: Aptara®, Inc.
Composition: Aptara®, Inc.
Printer/Binder: RR Donnelley/Harrisonburg
Cover Printer: RR Donnelley/Harrisonburg
Text Font: StoneSerif

Credits and acknowledgments for materials borrowed from other sources and reproduced, with permission, in this textbook appear on the appropriate page within the text.

Every effort has been made to provide accurate and current Internet information in this book. However, the Internet and information posted on it are constantly changing, so it is inevitable that some of the Internet addresses listed in this textbook will change.

Photo Credits: Quanlin Huang, p. iii (top) Zhu Qing, cover, p. iii (bottom); Kali9/E+/Getty Images, p. 3; Dragon Images/Shutterstock, p. 18; Robert Kneschke/Shutterstock, p. 35; Monkey Business Images/Shutterstock, pp. 51, 73, 211 Zurijeta/Shutterstock, p. 85; ZouZou/Shutterstock, p. 103; Lisa F. Young/Shutterstock, p. 129; Creatas/Thinkstock, pp. 163, 285; Moodboard/Getty Images, p. 191; Eyecandy Images/Thinkstock, p. 230; Fuse/Thinkstock, p. 248; Moodboard/Thinkstock, p. 270; Vladgrin/Shutterstock, p. 301; Bikeriderlondon/Shutterstock, p. 315; iStock/Thinkstock, p. 343.

Copyright © 2015, 2011, 2007 by Pearson Education, Inc. All rights reserved. Printed in the United States of America. This publication is protected by Copyright and permission should be obtained from the publisher prior to any prohibited reproduction, storage in a retrieval system, or transmission in any form or by any means, electronic, mechanical, photocopying, recording, or likewise. To obtain permission(s) to use material from this work, please submit a written request to Pearson Education, Inc., Permissions Department, One Lake Street, Upper Saddle River, New Jersey 07458 or you may fax your request to 201-236-3290.

Library of Congress Cataloging-in-Publication Data
Cohen, Libby G.
  Assessment of children and youth with special needs/Libby G. Cohen, University of Southern Maine, Loraine J. Spenciner, University of Maine at Farmington.—Fifth edition.
    pages cm
  ISBN 978-0-13-357107-3
  1. Psychological tests for children. 2. Child development—Testing. 3. Youth—Psychological testing.
  4. Adolescence. 5. Behavioral assessment of children. 6. Behavioral assessment of teenagers.
  7. Educational tests and measurements. I. Spenciner, Loraine J. II. Title.
  BF722.C638 2015
  371.26—dc23
                                                                                    2013045250

ISBN 10:   0-13-357107-6
ISBN 13: 978-0-13-357107-3

THE COVER IMAGE, *Holding the Umbrella for You*, is a watercolor and an accompanying poem which is part of a series of one hundred paintings and poems that were completed by Zhu Qing over a period of one hundred days, painting a picture each day. Zhu Qing is a senior student at Beijing University of Technology in Beijing, China. She hopes that through her paintings the world will become a little bit more kind.

Original text in Chinese。
〈为你打伞〉
下雨了
街上的下伞
大的小的
各种各样
但是我信心
让你一眼看见
舒把
我为你
打的伞

Translated:
Holding the Umbrella for You
It's raining
Umbrellas in the street
Large and small
But I have the confidence
To make you see easily
The one umbrella
I am holding for You

Preface

New to This Edition

The purpose of the fifth edition of *Assessment of Children and Youth with Special Needs* is to present future and experienced educators and other professionals with an up-to-date understanding of contemporary perspectives on the assessment of children and youth. This edition expands previous coverage of both traditional and contemporary assessment approaches. The text explains various assessment approaches in detail that can be implemented by teachers and other professionals and discusses individual tests at length

New to this edition is:

- To enhance affordability and portability, this exciting new edition is available as a Pearson eText. With the eText students can easily take and share notes, highlight, and search for key concepts.
- A pedagogical strategy to assist the reader in understanding and reflecting on the content material was added. *Pause and Consider* sections, embedded within the chapters, provide thought-provoking questions, encouraging the reader's active involvement. These sections also support the reader's use of suggested resources to discover additional information.
- The Snapshots features reflect increased diversity in schools, relevance, and the readers' involvement.
- In addition, this edition includes a new classroom-based assessment cycle, including the characteristics of classroom assessment and the approaches that teachers use.
- Expanded discussions of classroom assessment practices will assist the reader in developing a greater understanding of the role of the special educator in inclusive settings and in response to intervention (RTI) schoolwide assessment practices, which are implemented to assess and monitor all children's academic work, behaviors, and progress.
- Furthermore, a new section on interpreting assessment information (Chapter 7) provides the reader with numerous examples of how to interpret class-room assessment approaches, observations, and standardized assessments.
- Each chapter now includes the latest information on assessment tests, tools, measures, techniques, and approaches with an emphasis on assessment approaches, such as curriculum-based assessment and informal tools that class-room teachers can use.

Upon completing this textbook, the reader should have acquired knowledge, understanding and skills related to the special education assessment process, including referral for special education services, response to intervention, assessment timelines, eligibility requirements, monitoring, and evaluating student progress. The reader should be able to discuss various approaches to assessing academic and behavioral concerns and be able to compare and contrast specific approaches and implement them. Given assessment information, the reader should be able to interpret the assessment results and explain the results to peers. The reader should be able to describe how to use and interpret assessment information, write assessment reports, tailor interventions, and evaluate students' progress.

Major topics covered in this edition include the following:

- **Response to intervention** This chapter (Chapter 2) describes the essential components of response to intervention (RTI). The reader follows examples of the use of RTI for students who experience difficulty in literacy (reading, written language, and/or spelling), mathematics, and behaviors. The chapter discussion includes examples describing when RTI becomes a prereferral for special education services.

- **In-depth considerations of recent research on assessment practices** Becoming a professional involves understanding how special educators and other school personnel use research findings to inform assessment practices. Many of the chapters in this new edition contain summaries of important research findings. For example, in Chapter 2, we learn that, based on the research, curriculum-based measurement is a highly effective assessment practice for monitoring and evaluating progress for students with disabilities.

- **Universal design and assistive technology** Universal design concepts applied to assessment practices hold much promise, allowing many children and youth with disabilities to demonstrate what they know and can do alongside peers without disabilities. For other students, the use of assistive technology devices allows access to the same assessment material as their peers without disabilities. Throughout this new edition, various chapters embed discussions of how special educators are applying universal design, accommodations, and assistive technology in practice.

- **Accommodations and modifications** This edition expands previous discussions of the use of accommodations and modifications in assessment activities. Chapter 1 includes examples of typical accommodations and modifications used during the assessment process.

- **The role of families in the assessment process** Enhanced emphasis on the role of families in the assessment process helps the reader understand both federal mandates and best practices. Chapter 4 provides an expanded discussion of professional activities and the importance of being responsive to the diversity of families. The reader is encouraged to consider relevant research such as parent involvement and the perception of special education services. Chapters 10, 11, and 14 describe contemporary approaches to assessing reading, writing, spelling, and mathematics and suggest ways that educators can share this information with peers and family members and implement approaches that help to assess academic progress.

- **Students with diverse cultural and linguistic backgrounds** Following the lead of previous editions, the fifth edition of *Assessment of Children and Youth with Special Needs* contains strands that run through most chapters. The reader will find that the responding to diversity strand has been expanded and updated to include best practices. Chapters 2 and 3 provide up-to-date information on implementing a range of assessment approaches in schools. Chapter 13 discusses the changing demographics of the school population and the new challenges of assessing oral language skills when students are learning English as a second or third language.

- **Contemporary approaches to the assessment of mathematics and literacy** Readers will be able to explain and implement various approaches to the assessment of reading, writing, spelling, and mathematics. Readers will be able to convey ways in which standardized achievement tests, curriculum-based assessment, curriculum-based measurement, progress monitoring, and performance-based and informal approaches can be used in the assessment of literacy.

- **Standardized instruments, with the latest updates** Each content area chapter, including reading, written language, oral language, and mathematics, includes updated standardized assessments. Additional chapters on topics including cognitive development, behavior, young children, and youth in transition also provide the reader with descriptions of the most recent editions of relevant assessment instruments.

- **Curriculum-based assessment and curriculum-based measurement** The fifth edition provides the reader with an in-depth foundation of curriculum-based measurement (CBM), beginning in Chapter 2. Chapters 10, 11, 12, and 14 illustrate the use of these assessment approaches in various areas of the curriculum.

- **Interpreting tests and writing reports** Interpreting assessment information is a key skill for special educators and other professionals working with children and youth with disabilities. Chapter 7 provides an expanded discussion of interpretation, with new examples of assessment information and Web-based resources.
- **Assessment of young children** Chapter 17 in this edition contains a complete update of standardized instruments appropriate for screening young children and determining eligibility for services. The chapter includes a new section on contemporary assessment approaches and discusses how parents are involved in the assessment process *and* ways that parents provide information to team members.
- **Transition assessment** The transition chapter, Chapter 18, has been revised and updated to include recent research. Readers should be able to explain the purposes of transition assessment and ways in which students' transition needs and preferences are assessed. Person-centered planning and self-determination are emphasized.

Organization

Several themes appear throughout the book. Each chapter begins with a set of objectives. We hope that the reader will use these objectives as guideposts in learning. Each chapter contains an *Overview* section that discusses theories, perspectives, and conceptual frameworks. Features called *Tests-at-a-Glance* provide brief information about specific standardized assessment instruments; *Snapshots* examine individual students and teachers so that the reader may deepen understanding and involvement in the examples. *Research-Based Practices* describe research findings, *Pause and Consider* involve the reader in understanding and reflecting upon the material, and *Responding to Diversity* considers issues of sensitivity and responsiveness to students and the uniqueness of their families. Key points from each chapter are summarized.

Acknowledgments

We dedicate this book to current and future teachers—we admire and respect you for your dedication to improving the lives of children and youth. We extend our sincere appreciation to the many people who helped and supported us in the development of this book. Thank you to our reviewers, who provided thoughtful and insightful reviews for the fifth edition: Jeanette W. Farmer, Marshall University Graduate College; Merridi Haskell, Arizona State University; Kathryn Klingler Tackett, George Mason University; and Joel Shapiro, Green Mountain College.

Special thanks to colleagues, educators, and friends at the National Institute of Education, Singapore, and the University of Maine at Farmington, who have shared their passions, skills, and knowledge with us. We appreciate the comments by Mel Christensen and her commitment as a future educator. We greatly fully acknowledge the assistance from Guanglei Chen. Deep thanks to Ann Davis and Kerry Rubadue for their support of this fifth edition.

We are especially grateful to our families, Les, Seth, Gaby, Jay, Amy, Dave, Dina, Ben, and Marina. We appreciate your continued support and good humor.

Brief Contents

PART I   **Foundations of Assessment**   1
Chapter 1   Understanding Assessment   3
Chapter 2   Response to Intervention   18
Chapter 3   Assessment Framework   35
Chapter 4   Involving Families   51

PART II   **Assessment Skills**   71
Chapter 5   Reliability and Validity   73
Chapter 6   Developing Technical Skills   85
Chapter 7   Test Interpretation and Report Writing   103

PART III   **Behavior**   127
Chapter 8   Observing, Interviewing, and Conferencing   129
Chapter 9   Behavior   163

PART IV   **Achievement**   189
Chapter 10   Achievement: Overall Performance   191
Chapter 11   Reading   211
Chapter 12   Written Language   230
Chapter 13   Oral Language   248
Chapter 14   Mathematics   270
Chapter 15   Performance-Based, Authentic, and Portfolio Assessments   285

PART V   **Special Considerations**   299
Chapter 16   Intelligence   301
Chapter 17   Young Children   315
Chapter 18   Youth in Transition   343

Contents

PART I Foundations of Assessment   1

Chapter 1 Understanding Assessment   3

Overview   3

Assessment in the Classroom   4
- Why Do Teachers Assess?   4
- Response to Intervention   5

Individuals With Disabilities Education Improvement Act   5
- Who Is Eligible for Special Education?   5
- Multidisciplinary Teams   6
- The Individualized Education Program   8
- Special Considerations for Young Children   9
- Transition Services   10
- Procedures for Ensuring the Rights of Students and Families   10

Elementary and Secondary Education Act   11
- Assessment Requirements   11
- Alternative Assessments   13

Family Educational Rights and Privacy Act   14

Professional Standards   15
- Confidentiality   15

Responding to Diversity   15

Research-Based Practices   16

Summary   16

Questions for Reflection   17

References   17

Chapter 2 Response to Intervention   18

Overview   18

Introduction to Response to Intervention   18
- Response to Intervention Basics   18
- Universal Screening   19
- High-Quality Evidence-Based Instruction   19
- School–Parent Connections   19
- Progress Monitoring   20
- Multitiered Interventions   21
- Responding to Diversity   25

Implementing RTI   26
- Assessment of Student Performance   26
- Curriculum-Based Measurement   27

        Reading 28
        Written Language 28
        Spelling 30
        Mathematics 30
        Behavior 31
Emerging Issues 33
Summary 33
Questions for Reflection 33
References 34

Chapter 3 — Assessment Framework 35

Overview 35
Classroom-Based Assessment Cycle 35
Special Education Assessment Framework 38
Special Education: Assessment Questions, Purposes, and Approaches 39
    Assessment Questions 39
    Assessment Purposes and Approaches 40
Responding to Diversity 44
Universal Design and Assessment Practices 46
Assessment of Assistive Technology Needs 46
    Approaches to Assistive Technology Assessment 48
Summary 49
Questions for Reflection 49
References 49

Chapter 4 — Involving Families 51

Overview 51
Understanding More About Families 52
Responding to Diversity 53
    Aspirations 53
    Assistance 55
    Authority of the School 55
    Child Rearing 55
    Communication 55
    Disability 55
    Family Structure 56
    Legal Status 56
    Literacy and Language 56
    Meetings and Support Groups 56
    Parental Roles 56
    Transient Status 57

Federal Legislation and the Role of Parents   57
    Guaranteed Rights   57
The Assessment Process for Families of Young Children   57
    Initial Questions and Decisions   58
    Screening Questions and Decisions for Families   59
The Assessment Process for Families of Children and Youth   59
    Addressing Parent Questions and Concerns   59
    Referral and Decisions for the Team   60
    Questions and Decisions in Determining Eligibility   60
    Questions and Decisions in Planning Services   62
    Questions and Decisions in Monitoring Services   62
    Questions and Decisions in Evaluating Services   63
Techniques for Listening to and Understanding Parent Perspectives   64
    Interviews   65
    Family Stories   67
    Parent–Teacher Conferences   67
Summary   68
Questions for Reflection   69
References   69

PART II Assessment Skills   71

Chapter 5 Reliability and Validity   73

Overview   73
Reliability   73
    Approach 1: Using Correlation Coefficients   74
    Approach 2: Variances or Standard Deviations of Measurement Errors   78
    Approach 3: Item Response Theory (IRT)   79
    Factors That Influence Reliability   79
Validity   79
    Content Validity   80
    Criterion-Related Validity   80
    Construct Validity   81
Validity of Test Interpretations   82
    Consequential Validity   82
Responding to Diversity: Fairness in Assessment   82
    Equity   83
    Nonbiased Assessment   83
    Linguistic Diversity   83
    Consideration of Adverse Consequences   83
Summary   84
Questions for Reflection   84
References   84

Chapter 6 Developing Technical Skills 85

- Overview 85
- Standardized Tests 85
- Standardization Sample 85
- Norm-Referenced Tests 86
- Criterion-Referenced Tests 86
- Distinguishing Norm-Referenced Tests From Criterion-Referenced Tests 87
- Scales of Measurement 87
  - Nominal Scale 87
  - Ordinal Scale 87
  - Interval Scale 88
  - Ratio Scale 88
- Frequency Distribution 88
- Normal Curve 89
  - Skewed Distributions 89
- Measures of Central Tendency 89
  - Mean 89
  - Median 91
  - Mode 91
  - Standard Deviation 91
- Types of Scores 91
  - Raw Scores 91
  - Percentage Scores 92
  - Derived Scores 92
  - Scores of Relative Standing 94
  - Basal and Ceiling Levels 96
  - Growth Scores 97
- Standard Error of Measurement and Confidence Intervals 97
  - Standard Error of Measurement 97
  - Confidence Intervals 97
- Scoring Guidelines 98
- Completing the Test Record Form 98
  - Biographical Information 98
  - Chronological Age 98
  - Calculating Raw Scores 98
  - Transforming Raw Scores to Derived Scores 98
  - Graphing Scores 99
  - Interpreting Test Performance 99
  - Behavioral Observations 100
  - Observations of the Environment 100
  - Discussion of Results 100
- How Should Assessment Approaches Be Evaluated? 101
- Summary 102
- Questions for Reflection 102
- References 102

Chapter 7 — Test Interpretation and Report Writing   103

Overview   103
Interpreting Assessment Information   103
  Introduction   103
  Classroom Assessment   104
  Observations   104
  Standardized Assessments   105
  Hypothesis Generation   107
  Examiner Bias   108
  Using Professional Knowledge   108
General Principles for Report Writing   109
Synthesizing Information   110
Writing the Report   114
Evaluating the Report   115
Types of Assessment Reports   115
  Reports of Observations   116
  Progress Reports   116
  Individual Test Reports   119
Sharing Assessment Results With Others   122
  Family Members   123
  Students   123
National and Statewide Assessments   123
Summary   125
Questions for Reflection   125
References   125

PART III   Behavior   127

Chapter 8 — Observing, Interviewing, and Conferencing   129

Overview   129
Observations   129
Planning Observations   130
  Observation Questions   131
  Defining an Event or Behavior   131
  Location   131
  Documentation   131
  Accuracy   132
  Multiple Observations   132
  Integration   132
Observing the Student   132

Types of Observations 133
Anecdotal Record 134
Running Record 135
Event Recording 136
Duration Recording 138
Intensity Recording 139
Latency Recording 140
Interval Recording 140
Category Recording 141
Rating Scales 141
Checklists 144

Increasing Technical Skills in Conducting Observations 144
Understanding More About Reliability 144
Errors of Omission 144
Errors of Commission 145
Errors of Transmission 145
Observer Drift 145
Reactivity 145
Understanding More About Validity 145
Developing Informal Norms 145

Observing the Classroom Environment 149
Physical Environment 149
Learning Environment 151
Social Environment 152

Interviews 158
Steps in Conducting Student Interviews 159
Questionnaires 159

Conferencing and Collaborating 160
Conferencing 160
Collaborating 161

Summary 161

Questions for Reflection 162

References 162

Chapter 9 Behavior 163

Overview 163

Adaptive Behavior 164
Supports 164

Standardized Instruments Evaluating Adaptive Behavior 165
Adaptive Behavior Assessment System Second Edition 165
Vineland Adaptive Behavior Scales, Second Edition 166

Problem Behaviors 168

Responding to Diversity 169

Assessing Supportive Environments   170
   Physical Environment   170
   Learning Environment   170
   Social Environment   171

Classroom Problem Behaviors Within an Intervention Context   171
   Ecological Assessment   171

Assessment Questions, Purposes, and Approaches   174
   Functional Behavioral Assessment   174

Standardized Instruments for Assessing Problem Behaviors   182
   Behavior Assessment System for Children, Second Edition   182
   Burks' Behavior Rating Scales, Second Edition (BBRS 2)   183
   Child Behavior Checklist System (CBCL)   184
   Conners Third Edition   186

Summary   187

Questions for Reflection   187

References   187

PART IV Achievement   189

Chapter 10 Achievement: Overall Performance   191

Overview   191
   Responding to Diversity   191

Curriculum-Based Assessment   192
   Developing a Curriculum-Based Assessment Instrument   193

Criterion-Referenced Tests   194
   Teacher-Developed Criterion-Referenced Tests   194

Connecting Instruction With Assessment: Alternative and Informal Assessment   195

Assessment Approaches   196
   Probes   196
   Error Analysis   197
   Oral Descriptions   197
   Written Descriptions   197
   Checklists and Questionnaires   198
   Interviews   198
   Conferences   199
   Digital Media, Such as Journals, Blogs, Tweets, Online Communications   199
   Performance-Based Assessment   199
   Portfolios   199
   Exhibitions   200
   Self-Assessment   200
   Peer Assessment   200

Observing the Student in Various Environments   201

Standardized Instruments   201
Steps in the Development of a Standardized Achievement Test   201
Benefits   202
Disadvantages   202

Steps and Purposes of Standardized Achievement Testing   203
Screening   203
Determining Eligibility   203
Program Planning   203
Monitoring Progress   203
Program Evaluation   203

Group Tests   203
Benefits   204
Disadvantages   204

Individual Achievement Tests   204
Kaufman Test of Educational Achievement, Second Edition   204
Wechsler Individual Achievement Test-III   205
Wide Range Achievement Test 4   206
Woodcock-Johnson Tests, Normative Update, Tests of Achievement   208

Summary   210
Questions for Reflection   210
References   210

Chapter 11 Reading   211

Overview   211
Assessment Principles   211
Connecting Assessment With Instruction   212
Progress Monitoring   212
Curriculum-Based Assessment   212
Curriculum-Based Measurement   212
Comparison of Progress-Monitoring Measures   216
Criterion-Referenced Assessment   216

Informal Assessment Approaches   216
Probes   216
Error Analysis   217
Cloze Procedures   217
Think-Alouds   217
Retelling   218
Oral Descriptions   218
Written Descriptions   218
Checklists and Questionnaires   219
Interviews   222
Conferences   222
Students' Journals, Notebooks, and Blogs   222
Performance-Based Assessments   222
Portfolios   223
Exhibitions   223
Self-Assessment   224
Peer Assessment   224

Standardized Instruments   225
  Gray Oral Reading Tests–Fifth Edition   225
  Test of Reading Comprehension–Fourth Edition   226
  Woodcock Reading Mastery Test—Revised/Normative Update   226

Summary   228

Questions for Reflection   229

References   229

Chapter 12 | Written Language   230

Overview   230

Connecting Assessment With Instruction   231

Curriculum-Based Measurement   232
  Curriculum-Based Measurement of Written Language   232
  Curriculum-Based Measurement of Spelling   233

Criterion-Referenced Assessment   233
  Formal Measures for Monitoring Progress   234

Informal Approaches   234
  Probes   234
  Error Analysis   234
  Oral Descriptions   235
  Written Descriptions   236
  Checklists and Questionnaires   236
  Interviews   236
  Conferences   236
  Digital Media   239
  Performance-Based Assessment   239
  Self-Assessment   240
  Peer Assessment   240

Scoring   241
  Holistic Scoring   241
  Analytic Scoring   243
  Anchor Papers   244

Standardized Instruments   244
  Oral and Written Language Scales, Second Edition (OWLS-II LC/OE and RC/WE)   244
  Test of Written Language, Fourth Edition   245
  Test of Written Spelling, Fifth Edition   247

Summary   247

Questions for Reflection   247

References   247

Chapter 13 | Oral Language   248

Overview   248

Understanding Speech and Language Disorders   249
  More About Speech Disorders   249
  More About Language Disorders   249

Oral Language Assessment 249
    Form 250
    Content 251
    Use 251
Assessment Questions, Purposes, and Approaches 252
    Language Samples 253
    Mean Length of Utterance 253
    Language Probes 255
    Curriculum-Based Measurement 256
Observing the Student Within the Environment 256
    Physical Environment 256
    Learning Environment 256
    Social Environment 257
Standardized Tests of Oral Language 259
    Clinical Evaluation of Language Fundamentals, Fifth Edition 259
    Preschool Language Scale, Fifth Edition 263
    Test of Adolescent and Adult Language, Fourth Edition 264
Concerns About Standardized Tests of Oral Language 265
    Receptive Language 265
    Expressive Language 266
Responding to Diversity 266
Students With Severe Communication Disorders 267
    Augmentative or Alternative Communication (AAC) Systems 267
    Assessment for AAC 267
Summary 268
Questions for Reflection 268
References 269

Chapter 14 | Mathematics 270

Overview 270
Connecting Assessment With Instruction 271
    Probes 271
    Error Analysis 271
    Oral Descriptions 273
    Written Descriptions 273
    Checklists and Questionnaires 273
    Interviews 274
    Conferences 274
    Student Journals, Diaries, and Blogs 275
    Self-Assessment 275
    Peer Assessment 276
Criterion-Referenced Assessment 276
Curriculum-Based Measurement 276
    Suggestions for Accommodations When Using CBMs
        in Mathematics 278
    Formal Measures for Monitoring Progress 278

Performance-Based Assessment   279
    Portfolios   279
    Exhibitions   280

Observing the Student Within the Classroom Environment   280
    Physical Environment   280
    Learning Environment   280
    Social Environment   280

Standardized Instruments   281
    KeyMath 3 Diagnostic Assessment   281
    Test of Mathematical Abilities, Third Edition   282

Summary   283

Questions for Reflection   283

References   284

Chapter 15   Performance-Based, Authentic, and Portfolio Assessments   285

Overview   285

Performance-Based Assessment   286

Authentic Assessment   287

Portfolio Assessment   288
    Contents of a Portfolio   289
    Organizing the Portfolio   289
    Portfolios Support Students' Learning   289
    Using Technology   290

Exhibitions   290

Responding to Diversity   291

Developing Scoring Systems   292
    Rubrics   292
    Analytic Scoring   292
    Holistic Scoring   294
    Benchmarks   294

Ensuring Technical Adequacy   294
    Reliability   294
    Consistency and Stability   295
    Consequential Validity   295
    Fairness   296
    Improving Reliability and Validity   296

Using Performance-Based, Authentic, and Portfolio Assessment   296
    Considerations About Using Performance-Based Assessments   297

Summary   298

Questions for Reflection   298

References   298

PART V Special Considerations 299

Chapter 16 Intelligence 299

Overview 301
Intelligence Tests as Samples of Behavior 301
Responding to Diversity 302
Standardized Instruments 302
  Batería III Woodcock-Muñoz 302
  Comprehensive Test of Nonverbal Intelligence-II 303
  Detroit Tests of Learning Aptitude, Fourth Edition 304
  Kaufman Assessment Battery for Children, Second Edition 305
  Stanford-Binet Intelligence Scale, Fifth Edition 306
  Test of Nonverbal Intelligence, Fourth Edition 307
  Wechsler Intelligence Scale for Children, Fourth Edition Integrated 308
  Wechsler Intelligence Scale for Children, Fourth Edition (WISC-IV Spanish) 312
  Woodcock-Johnson III, Normative Update, Tests of Cognitive Ability 312
Summary 314
Questions for Reflection 314
References 314

Chapter 17 Young Children 315

Overview 315
Screening 316
  Choosing Appropriate Standardized Screening Instruments 317
  Standardized Screening Instruments 318
  Planning the Screening Procedure 322
  Limitations of Screening 324
Comprehensive Developmental Assessment 325
  Arena Assessment 327
Standardized Assessments 327
  Assessment, Evaluation, and Programming System for Infants and
    Children, Second Edition 327
  Battelle Developmental Inventory, Second Edition 329
  Bayley Scales of Infant and Toddler Development®, Third Edition 330
  Carolina Curriculum for Preschoolers With Special Needs,
    Second Edition 331
Considerations Regarding the Assessment of Young Children 334
Responding to Diversity 335
Linking Assessment With Classroom Activities 335
  Teaching Strategies GOLD 336
  The Work Sampling System®, Fifth Edition 337
  Using Early Childhood State Standards 338
Working With Families 340
  Transition and Assessment 340

Summary 341
Questions for Reflection 341
References 342

Chapter 18 — Youth in Transition 343

Overview 343
    Legal Requirements 344
Transition Assessment 345
    Purposes of Transition Assessment 345
    Involving Families 346
Person-Centered Planning 346
Self-Determination Skills 347
Assessment Instruments 349
    Job and Career Interests 349
    Reading-Free Vocational Interest Inventory 2 349
    Adaptive Behavior and Life Skills 351
Connecting Assessment With Instruction: Performance-Based Assessment 351
Summary 352
Questions for Reflection 352
References 352

Glossary 353

Name Index 360

Subject Index 363

PART I
Foundations of Assessment

 **CHAPTER 1** Understanding Assessment

 **CHAPTER 2** Response to Intervention

 **CHAPTER 3** Assessment Framework

 **CHAPTER 4** Involving Families

1 Understanding Assessment

Chapter Objectives

After completing this chapter, you should be able to:

- Discuss the purposes of assessment and some of the different assessment approaches that teachers use today.
- Explain the general requirements for assessment of students with disabilities as mandated by federal laws.
- Discuss professional knowledge and skills related to assessing students with disabilities.

Overview

A teacher shares concerns with another teacher about a new student in the classroom. A mother calls to discuss questions that were raised during a meeting about her child. Questions and concerns such as these are examples of typical occurrences in a school day. Teachers and other professionals who work with students with disabilities not only raise questions but also must work with others to respond to concerns and make decisions about students. They must be able to observe, collect, record, and interpret information about students with disabilities. As members of a school team, they plan, monitor, implement, and evaluate **individualized education programs (IEPs)**.

This chapter discusses U.S. federal laws that relate to the assessment of children and youth with disabilities. Federal legislation has had profound effects on assessment practices and the education of students with disabilities. Because this is an area that continues to change, we will examine resources that regularly provide updated information.

Sections of this chapter begin themes that you will learn more about throughout this text:

- Each chapter contains an Overview, which discusses perspectives and conceptual frameworks.
- Snapshots are intended to involve you with individual students and special educators to deepen your understanding.
- Research-Based Practices describe content important for educators and other team members to consider during the assessment process.
- Responding to Diversity considers issues of sensitivity and responsiveness to students and the uniqueness of their families.
- Tests-at-a-Glance provide brief information about specific standardized assessment instruments.

Assessment in the Classroom

Why Do Teachers Assess?

Assessment is a global term for observing, gathering, recording, and interpreting information to answer questions and make instructional decisions about students. Assessment is an integral aspect of instruction. It enables educators to gather and interpret information about students and to make decisions and provide information about what individual students can and cannot do and about what they know and do not know. Assessments also help to determine individual students' strengths and needs, assist in setting goals, and guide instruction. Schoolwide assessments help administrators and school board members determine the success of school programs and the progress of students. The assessment process is conducted according to legal mandates and best professional practices.

Let's look more closely at some of the reasons that educators use assessment in the classroom. First, assessment guides classroom instruction. Teachers collect information about what students already know and can do. They use a variety of informal assessments, such as asking students to complete a written questionnaire or respond orally to questions or to share ideas about what they know during a class discussion.

Second, assessment measures student progress toward achieving academic standards and behavioral goals and objectives. Teachers gather assessment data by using both informal and formal assessments. For example, a teacher may develop an assessment for a lesson or unit. Teachers often work individually with students to not only gather information about what they can do but also to discuss with them how they arrived at specific answers or selected good choices in managing behaviors. To learn more about how one primary teacher uses this informal assessment to measure progress toward academic standards, visit the Education Northwest site at **http://educationnorthwest.org/common-core/assessing-mathematical-understanding**. As you explore this site, consider how the teacher is collecting assessment information.

In addition to ongoing assessment, teachers also use end-of-year assessments to measure student progress in meeting academic standards. These formal assessments, which may be completed online, allow teachers to track individual student achievement as well as compare student progress. Other types of assessments given at the end of the year involve specialized tests for some students with disabilities. For example, a student who is learning to read and write in Braille will take a test to assess his or her progress in Braille literacy.

Third, assessment provides information about individual student and group progress. By analyzing the assessment results, educators can track student progress and achievement trends of individuals or groups of students by grade or by school. When results indicate a lack of progress, educators can identify the steps needed to reverse these trends.

Assessment is a major instructional tool in education today. The term **assessment approach** describes the way information is collected for making an educational decision. In addition to quizzes, tests, and exams, teachers use other assessment approaches such as portfolios or presentations to provide regular feedback to students regarding their performance and to give them opportunities to improve. Teachers connect instruction with assessment and use this information to change, modify, and evaluate teaching and learning activities.

Teachers also use assessment approaches to answer questions regarding student achievement, abilities, behavior, development, and skills. Is the student demonstrating expected achievement levels? If not, what types of interventions does the student need? Are the interventions effective, and is the student making progress? If not, is there a possibility that the student has a disability? Should the student be referred for further assessment? By observing, collecting, and recording information, classroom teachers work with other educators and school personnel to interpret the information, answer questions, and make decisions about students.

Response to Intervention

Response to intervention (RTI) is a process of identifying students who are experiencing difficulties and providing specific interventions to address areas of concern before children fail. This multistep process usually begins with the general education teacher, who implements high-quality instruction in the classroom and monitors closely each student's progress. When a student experiences difficulty, the next step occurs. Here the classroom teacher or content area specialist, such as a reading or behavior specialist, provides additional instruction, using one or more research-based interventions. These educators also monitor student progress by collecting student performance data.

For many students, intervention will be successful. Other students may need additional interventions and make progress in small steps or not at all. Educators will continue to collect data while monitoring student performance regarding the interventions. When students do not respond to these interventions, the students' performance data provides documentation and evidence that students may have significant learning or behavior problems, such as specific learning disabilities, attention deficit hyperactivity disorder, or serious emotional disturbance. In Chapter 2, you will read much more about the RTI process and the various steps involved.

Thus, the process of identifying students who may be eligible for special education services is often based on the student's response to research-based interventions. Questions about students with disabilities bring assessment to another level. Assessment in the field of special education involves not only these general assessment aspects but legal aspects, too. Is the student eligible for special education services? Federal and state laws specify assessment requirements that must be followed during the prereferral, referral, and assessment processes. The following section examines the federal mandates regarding assessment practices. These mandates address how the assessment process should be conducted. Special educators and other personnel working with students with disabilities must comply with these requirements and also use best professional practices.

Individuals With Disabilities Education Improvement Act

Children and youth with disabilities have been able to receive special education services in their local schools since 1974 when Federal Legislation (PL 94-142) was passed by Congress. Since then, this legislation has been revised and reauthorized several times. In 2004, the reauthorization (PL 108-446) was known as the **Individuals with Disabilities Education Improvement Act (IDEA) of 2004**. Sometimes the acronym IDEA is written to include the term *improvement*: IDEiA.

The revised law provides a new emphasis on improving results for students with disabilities. IDEA specifies special education services for children and youth ages 3 through 21 and early intervention services for infants and toddlers, birth through age 2. IDEA ensures that all children and youth with disabilities, beginning at age 3, have available to them a free and appropriate public education (FAPE) that emphasizes special education and related services designed to meet their unique needs and prepare them for further education, employment, and independent living (20 USC Sec. 602(d)(1)(A)).

IDEA includes mandated requirements relating to the assessment process that teachers and test examiners must know and understand. These requirements form the legal basis for identifying and providing services to children and youth with disabilities.

Who Is Eligible for Special Education?

To be eligible for special education services, students must meet the eligibility description of one of the categories of disability identified in IDEA and listed in Figure 1.1. IDEA guarantees

Autism
Deaf-blindness
Deafness
Developmental delay
Emotional disturbance
Hearing impairment
Intellectual disability
Multiple disabilities
Orthopedic impairment
Other health impairment
Specific learning disability
Speech or language impairment
Traumatic brain injury
Visual impairment (including blindness)

FIGURE 1.1 • Disabilities Related to Qualifying Children and Youth for Special Education and Related Services

Source: 20 USC Sec. 3(A).

that children and youth with disabilities have the right to special education services if their disability adversely affects their educational performance and if these special services would allow them to benefit from the education program.

IDEA encourages schools to provide interventions, or targeted assistance, to students as soon as their academic or behavioral difficulties become apparent. IDEA further suggests that educators collect information regarding intervention effectiveness. Prior to this emphasis on early intervention, many students, were overidentified as having learning disabilities. Thus, to address possible overidentification of students, IDEA urges schools to identify students who are experiencing difficulties as soon as possible and to provide effective teaching strategies and positive behavioral interventions. When the data indicate a student's lack of response to the various interventions implemented, the student is referred to a multidisciplinary team. Some of these students may have disabilities.

Multidisciplinary Teams

As members of a multidisciplinary team, teachers and other professionals who assess children and youth suspected of having disabilities represent various disciplines, depending on the needs of the student. For example, individuals may come from the fields of medicine, occupational therapy, physical therapy, psychology, social work, **speech** and language pathology, or therapeutic recreation in addition to general education and special education. A student's parent(s) also provides important information to the assessment process. This multidisciplinary team, often referred to as an **IEP team** (IEP stands for *Individualized Education Program*), is responsible for planning, developing, monitoring, and evaluating specialized instruction and related services for a student with a disability. This team may also be known as the special services team or other term as defined by state regulations.

Team members use a variety of assessment tools and strategies to gather relevant functional, developmental, and academic information, including information provided by the parent. They select assessment and other **evaluation** materials in the language (such as English, Spanish, Mandarin, or Thai) and form (such as print, Braille, or American Sign Language) most likely to yield accurate information on what the child knows and can do academically, developmentally, and functionally. When the student's IEP team meets, the team must include an individual who can interpret the assessment results and instructional implication. As a result of assessments, the multidisciplinary team determines whether the student has a disability.

Another function of the IEP team is to determine whether the child or youth needs accommodations or modifications to be successfully involved and make progress in the general curriculum and to achieve IEP goals. **Accommodations** are changes to the education program and assessment procedures and materials that do not substantially alter the instructional level, the content of the curriculum, or the assessment criteria. An accommodation for a writing assessment, for example, might consist of changes in the format of materials, such as using a tablet or laptop rather than paper and pencil.

Accommodations also include changes to the classroom arrangement, scheduling, or timing, for example, giving a student extra time to complete the assessment. On the other hand, **modifications** refer to changes or adaptations made to the educational program or assessment that alter the level, content, and/or assessment criteria. For example, a modification to an assessment might include reading a condensed version of the paragraph or completing half of the assessment items.

The purpose of making accommodations and modifications is to reduce the impact that certain student characteristics, such as distractibility or short-term memory deficits, have on test performance. Accommodations and modifications should respond to the needs of the student, and test administrators should document and describe them in the testing report. Although two students may have the same disability, such as a learning disability, the accommodations and modifications each student may need can differ.

When the IEP team determines that a student needs an accommodation or modification, this is written into the student's IEP. When a student receives accommodations or modifications during the instructional program, the student is also eligible to receive similar accommodations or modifications during assessments. However, even when the IEP team recommends an accommodation or a modification, not all accommodations or modifications are permitted on certain standardized assessments or on some state assessments. For example, the publisher of an assessment test specifies in the examiner's manual that using an accommodation or modification to the assessment may cause the results to be invalid. In the case of statewide assessments, individual states usually develop a state list of acceptable accommodations allowable. Table 1.1 describes frequently used accommodations and modifications.

TABLE 1.1 • Frequently Used Accommodations and Modifications

Type of Accommodation or Modification	Example of Accommodations	Examples of Modifications
Presentation mode	• Test is administered individually rather than in a group. • Examiner reads items out loud (except when student is tested in reading). • Student takes a computer-administered form of the test. • Large-print forms are used. • Braille form of the test is used. • Test directions and items are signed. • A specific examiner may be chosen who is able to develop (or who already has) rapport with the student.	• Examiner uses prompts or cues.
Location of the test administration	• Test is administered in an area with reduced distractions. • Test is administered while the student is using special furniture. • Test is administered in a space that has special lighting.	
Response mode	• Teacher or helper marks the responses as indicated by the student. • Student indicates responses on paper that has lines or a grid. • Student uses a communication device. • Time limits for responding are extended or modified.	• Student is allowed to use a calculator for mathematics calculation. • Examiner accepts key-word responses instead of complete sentences required by the test. • Student is allowed to use a spell checker, specialized software, or dictionary for writing test.
Test content	• Number of items per page is reduced, but student completes all test items. • Use of bilingual glossaries and dictionaries (for English-language learners).	• Fewer test items are presented.
Test format	• Test items are magnified.	• Key words in the test directions are highlighted or color-coded. • Test items are reworded. • Pictures or graphics are substituted for words.

The Individualized Education Program

Each child or youth who receives services must have an IEP. An IEP team develops the written IEP using the results of a comprehensive assessment. This document includes annual goals based on academic standards or behavioral expectations that the student will meet. For students who will be working toward alternative achievement standards and who will be taking alternate assessments, the IEP includes short-term objectives, or benchmarks. **Alternate assessments**, such as student portfolios with photographs and work that students have completed, enable students with persistent academic problems and students with severe or significant disabilities to participate in general large-scale assessments.

According to the federal legislation, the IEP team conducts a reevaluation not more frequently than once a year, unless the parent and school personnel agree otherwise, and at least once every 3 years, unless the parent and school personnel agree that a reevaluation is unnecessary (20 USC Sec. 614(a)(2)). The team begins by reviewing existing assessment information. Using the review and input from the parents, the team determines whether additional assessment is needed. Figure 1.2 illustrates the assessment information required on the IEP.

---

(1) A statement of the child's present levels of academic achievement and functional performance, including how the child's disability affects the child's involvement and progress in the general education curriculum.
   (a) For preschool children, as appropriate, how the disability affects the child's participation in appropriate activities.
   (b) For children with disabilities who take alternate assessments aligned to alternate achievement standards, a description of benchmarks or short-term objectives.

(2) A statement of measurable annual goals, including academic and functional goals, designed to—
   (a) Meet the child's needs that result from the child's disability to enable the child to be involved in and make progress in the general education curriculum.
   (b) Meet each of the child's other educational needs that result from the child's disability.

(3) A description of how the child's progress toward meeting the annual goals described in clause (2) will be measured and when periodic reports on the progress the child is making toward meeting the annual goals (such as through the use of quarterly or other periodic reports, concurrent with the issuance of report cards) will be provided.

(4) A statement of the special education and related services and supplementary aids and services, based on peer-reviewed research to the extent practicable, to be provided to the child, or on behalf of the child, and a statement of the program modifications or supports for school personnel that will be provided for the child—
   (a) To advance appropriately toward attaining the annual goals.
   (b) To be involved in and make progress in the general education curriculum in accordance with clause (1) and to participate in extracurricular and other nonacademic activities.
   (c) To be educated and participate with other children with disabilities and nondisabled children in the activities described in this subparagraph.

(5) An explanation of the extent, if any, to which the child will not participate with nondisabled children in the regular class and in the activities described in subclause.

(6) A statement of any individual appropriate accommodations that are necessary to measure the academic achievement and functional performance of the child on state- and district-wide assessments consistent with section 612, and if the IEP team determines that the child shall take an alternate assessment on a particular state- or district-wide assessment of student achievement, a statement of why—
   (a) The child cannot participate in the regular assessment.
   (b) The particular alternate assessment selected is appropriate for the child.

(7) The projected date for the beginning of the services and modifications described in clause (4) and the anticipated frequency, location, and duration of those services and modifications.

FIGURE 1.2 • Assessment Information Required in the IEP

Source: 20 USC Sec. 614(d)(1).

To help reduce paperwork, IDEA offers states an opportunity to develop multiyear IEPs. This allows IEP teams to engage in long-term planning by developing an IEP, not to exceed 3 years, which is designed to coincide with natural **transition** points for the student. Schools must provide parents with informed consent and assurances that a multiyear IEP is optional.

Special Considerations for Young Children

Over the years, teachers and professional organizations have voiced concerns over (1) the potential detrimental effects of labeling a child at a young age, (2) the lack of adequate assessment tools for young children, and (3) the belief that some of the disability categories, such as intellectual disabilities, used with older children may not be appropriate (Figure 1.1). Thus,

SNAPSHOT
Samantha

Six-year-old Samantha and her family recently moved to a new city where her mother enrolled Samantha in the local school and shared the following information about her daughter with school personnel. Several months after Samantha was born, the pediatrician noticed a delay in her motor development and referred Samantha to a pediatric neurologist, who diagnosed Samantha as having mild cerebral palsy. The family was referred to a regional program for early intervention, where the IFSP team determined that she was eligible for services because of her developmental delay. The family received home-based services until she was 3, when she transitioned to a community-based inclusive preschool program.

Recently, the parents took Samantha for a follow-up visit to the neurologist. The doctor discussed concerns with the parents about additional developmental delays that Samantha was experiencing. Upon being informed of this, Samantha's mother provided written consent to have her records forwarded to the new school.

Shortly after Samantha was enrolled in her new school, the IEP team convened to discuss Samantha's records, including past assessment results and her current education program. The team members who were present included the building principal, Samantha's first-grade teacher, the special education teacher, the occupational therapist, and Samantha's parents. They recommended additional assessments because they wanted further information about Samantha's functioning before making any educational decisions.

Samantha's first-grade teacher, Linda Skillings, shared her observations of classroom work. Linda felt that Samantha often experienced difficulty at the classroom math center, such as writing numerals and using manipulatives. Although most of the students could complete this work independently, Samantha usually needed extra support from the teacher aide. Her teacher had recommended Samantha for more intensive math work with the math specialist; but even in a small group, she observed that Samantha had difficulty with tasks. The math specialist wondered if these difficulties were affecting her level of attention, and John Xihu, the special educator, asked, "Do you think Samantha is mainly experiencing attention difficulties or are the problems associated with understanding math concepts?" As the team discussed these questions and others, they realized that there was a need to collect more information about Samantha's difficulties.

John volunteered to conduct several classroom observations during both large- and small-group math activities. He would observe and record the teacher dialogue as well as Samantha's behaviors of attention and inattention. Because Samantha's parents had already signed release forms for further assessment, John did not need to obtain parent permission before he could begin the observations. Linda suggested several days that would be convenient for John to make the classroom observations, and then they identified a time the following week to meet to discuss the assessment results.

Because of the increased expectations of written language in first grade, coupled with concerns regarding motor delay, the occupational therapist agreed to see Samantha for an initial evaluation of her fine motor skills. Once her evaluation was complete, the occupational therapist would examine the results and write up an assessment report. She would make arrangements to share this with Samantha's parents and then present the findings to the team.

Pause and consider
- What do you think was the team's rationale behind recommending additional assessments?
- Considering assessment, what would be your role as a special educator?

> **Transition services** means a coordinated set of activities for a child with a disability that—
>
> - Is designed to be within a results-oriented process that is focused on improving the academic and functional achievement of the child with a disability to facilitate the child's movement from school to postschool activities, including postsecondary education, vocational education, integrated employment (including supported employment), continuing and adult education, adult services, independent living, or community participation;
> - Is based on the individual child's needs, taking into account the child's strengths, preferences, and interests; and
> - Includes instruction; related services; community experiences; the development of employment and other postschool adult living objectives; and, when appropriate, acquisition of daily living skills and functional vocational evaluation.

FIGURE 1.3 • Definition of Transition Services

Source: 20 USC Sec. 602(34).

all children from birth through 2 years receive services under the eligibility term **developmental delay**. Although young children vary greatly in their rate of development, this term reflects a significant delay in one or more areas of development, including physical, cognitive, communication, social or emotional, or adaptive development.

Eligibility for early intervention services is determined by an **early childhood multidisciplinary team (ECT)**. The ECT includes parents, the family service coordinator, and team members from various disciplines. This team assesses and develops an **individualized family service plan (IFSP)** for children age birth through 2 years and their families. Similar to the IEP team, the ECT also monitors and evaluates the IFSP. Compared to an IEP, the IFSP also includes information about the child's level of functioning. However the outcomes and services focus on the child and needs of the family as they relate to the child's development.

Transition Services

When a student with a disability reaches age 16, or earlier if the IEP team determines the need to make decisions about the student's future plans, preparation for transition begins. The IEP team discusses and begins planning the **transition services** (Figure 1.3) that the student will need during the transition to postsecondary education, employment, and/or community living. Transition services and assessment are further described in Chapter 18. Transition needs are based on the individual student, taking into account the student's preferences and interests. Beginning no later than the first IEP that is in effect when the student is 16, the team writes a description of the need(s) for transition services. From this point forward, the IEP must include

- Appropriate measurable postsecondary goals based on age-appropriate transition assessments related to training, education, employment and independent living skills, where appropriate
- Transition services needed to assist the student in reaching those goals, including courses of study
- Beginning not later than 1 year before the student reaches the age of majority under state law, a statement that the student has been informed of the student's rights under this title, if any, that will transfer to the student on reaching the age of majority under Section 615(m)

Procedures for Ensuring the Rights of Students and Families

IDEA specifies procedures that ensure the protection of parents' and children's rights during the assessment process and the delivery of services. These procedures, called **due process requirements**, specify that:

- Parents must receive written notice whenever there is a proposal to initiate or change the identification, evaluation, or educational placement of their child.

- Parents have the right to review their child's records regarding the assessment and educational placement.
- Parents may obtain an independent evaluation of their child by a qualified examiner who is not employed by the school. The evaluation is at no cost to the parent and is paid for by the public school.
- Due process also ensures that parents, schools, or agencies have a right to an impartial hearing conducted by a hearing officer when disagreements occur. A hearing can be requested by either a parent or a school district.

IDEA requires the school to obtain informed written consent from the parent before his or her child is assessed. **Informed consent** is a process that involves (1) presenting information so that it can be easily understood, (2) providing alternatives, (3) identifying risks and benefits, and (4) accepting or consenting to the information proposed. Figure 1.4 illustrates a school district form for obtaining parent consent. Informed consent is also required before the team develops a comprehensive multiyear IEP. The only exceptions to these requirements are if the school can demonstrate that it has taken reasonable measures to obtain parent consent and the student's parent failed to respond, if the parental rights have been terminated, or if the whereabouts of the parents are unknown.

Elementary and Secondary Education Act

Originally passed in 1965, the Elementary and Secondary Education Act, the nation's general education law, continues to be reauthorized by Congress with the goal of improving academic performance for *all* students. In 2001, the reauthorization of this act, known as **No Child Left Behind (NCLB) Act** of 2001, stressed accountability through scientifically based research practices and regular and ongoing assessment of student progress. Updates regarding changes in NCLB Act can be checked at the U.S. Department of Education Web site: ed.gov (Search for "No Child Left Behind").

Led by the National Governors Association Center for Best Practices and the Council of Chief State School Officers, teachers, administrators, and content experts developed Common Core State Standards. Updates can be checked at **http://www.nga.org/cms/center** and **http://www.ccsso.org/**. Within each academic area, these standards describe what students should know and be able to do at each grade level. Assessments, aligned with the Common Core, provide valuable information to educators regarding student progress and instruction. Typically, assessments are Web based and allow educators to query the assessment data to determine the achievement trend of a specific student or a group of students. This use of assessment data is referred to as data-driven decision making and can be defined as a process that involves systematically collecting and analyzing data to guide practices that will improve student progress and achievement. When assessment data indicates that one or more students are experiencing difficulties, educators modify instruction or provide supplemental instruction.

Assessment Requirements

The NCLB Act overlapped assessment activities in some states with additional requirements. These requirements specified that schools were required to assess student achievement annually in reading/language arts and math for students in grades 3 through 8 and at least once during grades 10 through 12. Science achievement must be assessed at least once in grades 3 through 5, 6 through 9, and 10 through 12. Assessments must be aligned with state content and achievement standards. Students with disabilities must have reasonable accommodations, when appropriate.

When the IEP is developed, the team identifies how the student will be assessed. Most students with disabilities participate in the annual assessment, or they take the regular assessment with accommodations. When the IEP team determines that a student with a disability

Point Street School District
CONSENT TO CONDUCT INDIVIDUAL ASSESSMENT(S)

Name: _Loren Sinkinson_ Date of Birth: _2/21/xx_

School: _Point Street_ Grade: _7_

Date: _September 12, xxxx_

The following is a description of the methods to be used to evaluate your child. You will be notified and given the opportunity to review and obtain copies of evaluation summaries or other reports to be discussed at the multidisciplinary team meeting. At this meeting, we will explain the results of the evaluation and discuss its significance to your child's education program. If you have any questions about these procedures, please call the special education director at 111-1111, and we will discuss them with you.

Description of Evaluation

☑ 1. *Academic testing* is designed to determine what the student's academic progress is within specific academic areas. The student's achievement will be compared to the achievement of students in this school and students throughout the country. Commonly used tests include Wechsler Individual Achievement Test—Third Edition, Woodcock-Johnson Test of Achievement-III NU, and curriculum-based assessments. Other: _____

☐ 2. *Intellectual testing* involves the individual administration of intelligence tests. These tests are designed to measure different types of abilities, such as what the student can do. Commonly used tests include Wechsler Intelligence Scale for Children IV (WISC-IV) and the Kaufman Assessment Battery for Children, Second Edition. Other: _____

☑ 3. *Observation* is designed to assist the team in relating test data to the student's classroom performance in academic, social, and behavioral areas as compared to others in the classroom.

☐ 4. *Speech/language testing* is designed to determine the student's communication skills in articulation, voice, fluency, expressive language, and receptive language. Commonly used tests include Clinical Evaluations of Language Fundamentals-5, Goldman Fristoe Test of Articulation-2, Peabody Picture Vocabulary Test IV, and the Oral and Written Language Assessment II. Other: _____

☐ 5. *Psychological evaluation* is designed to assess cognitive, personality, and/or behavioral function. Commonly used evaluation methods include parent and child interviews, personality inventories, and projective tests. Other: _____

☑ 6. Additional assessments are designed to collect essential information on health, social, or developmental history; behavior (may be completed by an interview with the parents, school personnel, or the child); or sensory assessments in vision or hearing. Commonly used instruments include Vineland Adaptive Behavior Scale II (Vineland-II) or the Adaptive Behavior Assessment System-II (ABAS-II). Other: _____

I understand the nature of, and the reasons for, the evaluations checked above as well as the statement of procedural safeguards attached to this consent form. I further understand the additional testing areas not indicated on this form will require prior written notice before administration.

A withdrawal of parental consent after the initial evaluation or initial placement in special education shall be considered a request to change the student's program and placement. As such, the IEP Team shall convene and consider the parent's request. If the IEP Team disagrees with the parent's request, Point Street School District may use the mediation process or initiate a hearing to override the parent's withdrawal of consent.

I do give consent for such evaluations: _Janet Sinkinson_
Parent Signature
September 17, xxxx
Date

FIGURE 1.4 • Point Street School District Form: Consent to Conduct Individual Assessment(s)

SNAPSHOT

Tad Farnsworth, Special Educator

Tad Farnsworth is a special educator with dual certification in special education and mathematics at Highlands Middle School. As a member of the seventh-grade team, he meets weekly with the three seventh-grade mathematics teachers to discuss student progress and plan instruction. Several students have IEPs, including Sal Springer, a 12-year-old, who has a learning disability. Last year, Tad Farnsworth, provided additional special education instruction in the resource room to Sal and the other students with learning disabilities. They finished the year working on using tables and graphs to represent relationships and to communicate information to supplement the ongoing instruction in this area in the regular classroom.

In September, when the IEP team met for Sal's annual review, they discussed his progress last year and the continuing needs for this year. His parents provided their input and observations, too. The team decided that Sal would participate in the regular math class with additional support from the special educator, within the math classroom.

Pause and consider:
- What do you think was the rationale behind this decision of recommending regular classroom mathematics with support from the special educator?
- How would providing instruction in the regular classroom change your role as a special educator in planning instruction? In assessing student progress?

As Tad listened to the team recommendations, he was not surprised with the recommendation to return Sal to the regular classroom to receive math instruction. Sal's math achievement had continued to improve the previous year, and the school was working to ensure that all students with disabilities had access to the general education curriculum. Tad also thought about how his role would be changing this year. He would still be a member of the seventh-grade team, but rather than providing separate math instruction, he would be coteaching with one of the regular education teachers in the seventh-grade math classroom. He would work closely with his colleague in preassessing student knowledge, planning instruction, and monitoring student progress. He also would provide assistance to Sal and other students with IEPs in the classroom. As a result of this collaboration, Tad would know the material and the math content that would be covered. He could prepare outlines or graphic organizers that would help not only Sal but other students as well. If he observed that Sal (or other students) experienced difficulty with new math vocabulary, he could prepare additional resources and provide additional small-group instruction when needed. He would work closely with his coteacher in assessing student learning or a regular basis. He could offer to prepare quizzes that were directly linked to classroom instruction. He could assist in analyzing the results and identify specific problem areas based on the assessment data.

Tad's thoughts returned to the meeting as the IEP team discussed the Common Core assessments that would be administered this year and whether Sal would need accommodations to participate in these assessments. The team agreed that Sal should take the grade-level assessments with accommodations. His IEP includes the following description of accommodations that Sal needs for assessments. *"Sal will take the District Assessment in a quiet room and will be allowed two additional breaks beyond those allowed for other students."*

Pause and consider:
- Using Table 1.1, review the types of accommodations for assessments. Knowing that Sal has a learning disability, what other accommodations might the team want to consider?
- After making your decision, review the research on the Web to see if you can locate information regarding the effectiveness of your accommodations.

is unable to participate in the state- and districtwide assessments, the student must take an alternate assessment.

Alternate Assessments

Alternate assessments are based on modified achievement standards for students with persistent academic disabilities. These students are not likely to reach grade-level achievement standards at the same pace as students without disabilities because of their disability. The Elementary and Secondary Education Act caps the number of students with disabilities who can take these alternate assessments at 2 percent of the total student population. For students with significant intellectual disabilities, states use alternate assessments for alternative

---

Point Street School District
IEP TEAM DECISION FORM FOR ALTERNATIVE ASSESSMENT

Name: _Keith Parker_ Date of Birth: _5/01/xx_

School: _Point Street_ Teacher: _Ms. Bryant_ Age: _9_

Date: _September 12, xxxx_

The IEP team for _Keith Parker_ has determined that he should participate in the state alternative assessment for students with disabilities because:

✓ His present level of functioning significantly affects his participation and completion of the general education curriculum.
✓ His specially designed instruction focuses on extended curriculum standards.
✓ His difficulty is primarily the result of his disability and not related to any of the following:
  ○ Excessive absence from school
  ○ Social factors
  ○ Cultural factors
  ○ Environmental factors

FIGURE 1.5 • Point Street School Alternate Assessment Documentation Form

achievement standards. Students with significant intellectual disabilities who use alternate assessments cannot equal more than an additional 1 percent of the total school population.

The IEP team makes decisions on the abilities and progress of each individual student. A student may take a grade-level assessment in mathematics, for example, yet need to take an alternate assessment in reading. The decisions made by the IEP team must be based on individual student needs, not the type of disability or the setting where the student receives special education services. Each year, the IEP team reviews assessment and accommodation options. If the student takes an alternate assessment, the IEP must identify the alternate assessment and include a statement describing why the student cannot participate in the regular assessment (with appropriate accommodations). Depending on state requirements, the IEP team must document the alternate assessment decision-making process (Figure 1.5).

For students with disabilities, providing alternate assessment options based on modified achievement standards allows students to demonstrate their achievement. However, some educators worry that students who do not need them may be given alternate assessments based on modified achievement standards. Furthermore, students who are not held to the same high grade-level achievement standards may become part of a cycle of low expectations. What do you think?

Family Educational Rights and Privacy Act

The **Family Educational Rights and Privacy Act (FERPA)** (PL 93-380), commonly referred to as the Buckley amendment, states that no educational agency may release student information without written consent from the student's parents. This consent specifies which records to release, the reasons for such release, and to whom. The agency should then send a copy of the released records to the student's parents.

FERPA allows families and students over 18 years of age access to and the right to inspect any of their records from any education institution, including preschool, elementary and secondary schools, community colleges, and colleges and universities that accept federal money. Parents also have the right to challenge and correct any information contained in these records. Professionals will want to ensure that they file only materials relevant to the student in the student's folder. Irrelevant information about the personal lives of families or information that is at best subjective and impressionistic has no place in a family's record.

In 2011, the U.S. Department of Education published the final amendments to the regulations for implementing the Family Educational Rights and Privacy Act. The *Federal Register* notice can be accessed at federalregister.gov/a/2011-30683.

Professional Standards

Special educators not only hold high standards for their students but also adhere to high professional standards for themselves. For teachers entering the field of special education, the Council for Exceptional Children (CEC) sped.org developed a set of 4 professional standards and related elements: the CEC's Initial Preparation Standards for Special Educators (NCATE approved 2012). Standard 1 focuses specifically on assessment knowledge and skills. Many colleges and universities expect teacher candidates to be able to demonstrate their work toward the CEC Professional Standards. Special educators who conduct assessments should be able to discuss and demonstrate these professional standards.

Other organizations such as the Interstate New Teacher Assessment and Support Consortium (InTASC) **http://www.ccsso.org/resources/programs/interstate_teacher_assessment_consortium_(intasc).html** also have released standards for new teachers. The InTASC standards address what beginning general education teachers and special education teachers need to know and be able to do when teaching students with disabilities.

In addition to demonstrating knowledge and skill standards, special educators develop a high level of competence and integrity as they engage in professional activities. All individuals who administer tests should have the training and experience necessary and should follow professional standards and ethical procedures. They should not attempt to evaluate students whose age, disability, linguistic, or cultural backgrounds are outside the range of their academic training or supervised experience. Special educators use objective professional judgment and demonstrate ethical practices.

Confidentiality

Professionals who are involved with the gathering of information about a student have both a legal and an ethical responsibility to maintain the information and use it appropriately. These individuals need to agree that the shared information is for the purposes of enabling the family and assisting the student through individualized educational services. Information about a particular student should be discussed only with those professionals who have a legitimate interest in the information and with whom the parent has consented to share information.

Responding to Diversity

In addition to assessment practices, CEC's Initial Preparation Standards for Special Educators (NCATE approved 2012) address becoming aware of and understanding one's own diversity and the diversity of others. For example, Standard 1, Foundations, lists as one of the key elements of knowledge:

- *Beginning special education professionals understand how language, culture, and family background influence the learning of individuals with exceptionalities.* (sped.org, p. 2)

In the past many students with diverse backgrounds were placed in separate programs and classrooms, away from the general education classroom. In many cases, individual students did not have disabilities. School districts were sued when these practices came to light, and some of these court cases went as far as the U.S. Supreme Court. Knowing the history of the discipline of education helps us be aware of the injustices of these historical practices so that these mistakes will not be repeated. For example, in the past standardized test items were often biased in favor of the majority. Today, test developers must ensure that test times are not biased toward any one group of students. You can learn more about these decisions and others at the Supreme Court **supremecourt.gov/default.aspx** Use the Supreme Court Web site search bar to locate special education decisions.

During your studies, you will learn more about responding to diversity and developing a sensitivity and openness to learning. Sensitivity involves concern and respect for others; it begins by learning about yourself, your beliefs, and your family heritage. Sensitivity grows by meeting other people, listening to who they are, and discovering their traditions, beliefs, and values. Sensitivity deepens over time through working with families, acknowledging and appreciating their special strengths and unique qualities.

Research-Based Practices

IDEA describes the use of scientifically based research practices with students with disabilities, including early identification and referral and prereferral procedures. In addition, IDEA describes the use of research-based interventions, curricula, and practices. Researchers have contributed and advanced knowledge on teaching, learning, and assessing students with special needs. Sometimes professionals refer to scientifically based research practices as evidence-based practices. Whichever term you use describes best practice, providing educators with assurance of the effectiveness of what they do.

When considering evidence-based practices, educators must consider effective practices that are relevant to today's students, who bring an array of experiences to the classroom. For example, one student may be homeless and living in a community shelter with few materials for completing class projects; another student, who is learning English as a second language, must spend time after school translating for family members who wish to make doctors' appointments, read a bus schedule, or purchase groceries.

Finding more about research-based practices can involve a search of your university library databases, such as ERIC or Academic Search Premier. Many Web sites also maintain information on research-based practices. You might begin with one of the following:

- What Works Clearinghouse (**http://ies.ed.gov/ncee/wwc/**) identifies current research studies on effective practices and intervention.
- ERIC/OSEP Special Project (**http://www.hoagiesgifted.org/eric/osep-sp.html**) disseminates federally funded special education research at this Web site.
- National Center for Research on Evaluation, Assessment, and Student Testing (**http://www.cse.ucla.edu/products.html**) focuses on the development of scientifically based assessment approaches.

Summary

- Teachers use assessments to answer many types of questions: Is the student demonstrating expected achievement levels? If not, what types of interventions does the student need? Are the interventions effective, and is the student making progress? If not, is there a possibility that the student has a disability? Should the student be referred for further assessment? Is the student eligible for special education services?

- IEP teams use assessment to answer many questions about a student suspected of having a disability, to plan, and to monitor the student's program. IDEA requires specific assessment information in the IEP, including the student's present level of academic achievement and functional performance; a statement of measurable annual goals and a description of how the student's progress toward meeting the annual goals will be measured; and accommodations, modifications, and supports necessary to attain the annual goals and measure the academic achievement and functional performance
- During the assessment process, IDEA specifies procedures that ensure the protection of parents' and children's rights. These procedures are called due process requirements.
- The Elementary and Secondary Education Act, also known as No Child Left Behind Act, requires schools to assess all students on a periodic basis. When the IEP team determines that a student with a disability is unable to participate in the state- and districtwide assessments, the student must take an alternate assessment.
- The Council for Exceptional Children's Professional Standards for Initial Teacher Certification provides guidance regarding the knowledge and skills that special educators need to be able to demonstrate. Of the 10 Standards, Standard 8 focuses on assessment knowledge and skills.

QUESTIONS FOR REFLECTION

1. Make a list of all the new terms in this chapter. Write definitions for each term using your own words.
2. State departments of education maintain extensive Web sites. Locate your state department and explore resources related to special education and assessment practices. Share your findings with your classmates.
3. List what has been helpful to you in developing sensitivity toward others, and identify the ways that have been most effective. Share your list, and discuss your findings with the class.
4. Check with your state department of education about what accommodations for students with disabilities are permitted for state- and districtwide assessments. What types of alternate assessments allow students with disabilities to demonstrate their achievement?
5. FERPA applies to any student who attends a school that receives federal funds. How do these regulations apply to your college or university?

REFERENCES

Council for Exceptional Children. (2012). Initial CEC preparation standards for special educators (NCATE approved 2012). Retrieved from http://www.cec.sped.org/Standards/Special-Educator-Professional-Preparation/CEC-Initial-and-Advanced-Preparation-Standards?sc_lang=en

Individuals with Disabilities Education Improvement Act of 2004. (2004). (20 USC).

2 Response to Intervention

Chapter Objectives

After completing this chapter, you should be able to:

- Describe the essential components of response to intervention (RTI).
- Compare and contrast the different tiers of intervention.
- Discuss why teachers use RTI in the classroom.
- Describe the characteristics of curriculum-based measurement (CBM) and how educators use CBMs to monitor student progress.
- Discuss emerging issues with RTI.

Overview

Classroom teachers are usually the first to observe when a student is having problems. Based on their knowledge and expectations of what children or youth in their classrooms should know and be able to do, these educators can identify students before they get too far behind. Classroom teachers often can be successful in increasing student achievement, reducing behavior problems, and preserving student self-esteem when they reach students early and begin an intervention process.

In classrooms today, educators know that response to intervention (RTI) assists children and youth who are experiencing difficulties in reading, writing, and/or mathematics or are displaying inappropriate behaviors. This chapter begins by examining the rationale for using an RTI process and typical schoolwide efforts that take place during the year. Next, we look at the essential components within the general education classroom, including high-quality classrooms, tiered instruction, family involvement, and school-based teams. We examine why and how teachers use RTI in different areas of the curriculum or to support positive student behaviors and how this system interfaces with special education services. Last, we address emerging issues in the field.

Introduction to Response to Intervention

Response to Intervention Basics

Response to Intervention Basics (RTI) is an intervention process that is aimed at improving educational outcomes for all students. This systematic process for teaching and assessing students consists of ongoing data collection, documenting, and monitoring of student performance. Educators examine the data and use the results in planning and assessing instruction. When assessment data indicates that a student is not making progress, educators adjust instruction using evidence-based practices. By improving the quality of instruction based on monitoring of student progress, RTI can reduce the number of inappropriate referrals to special education while improving the quality of instruction for diverse learners in the general education classroom. Thus, RTI can be conceptualized as a general education initiative with direct implications for children with disabilities (Griffiths, Parson, Burns, VanDerHeyden, & Tilly, 2007).

Universal Screening

Today, many states have districtwide processes that may be known under a different term, such as Ohio's Intervention-Based Assessment Model, Pennsylvania's Instructional Support Teams, or Minneapolis Public Schools' Problem-Solving Model. As a districtwide process, RTI incorporates **universal screening**, a procedure that occurs two or three times during the year to identify students who are experiencing difficulties with age-appropriate skills. In elementary school, universal screening often focuses on literacy and mathematics. For students in middle and secondary school, universal screening also includes information that predicts poor adjustment, difficulties with transitions, and dropping out of school. To see examples of universal screening, visit the National Center on Response to Intervention at **rti4success.org/essential-components-rti/universal-screening**.

Universal screening provides school personnel with a snapshot of information about each student on a periodic basis. This ongoing process provides early identification for students who are at risk. When a student is identified, the general classroom teacher may make instructional adjustments or refer the student for more intensive instruction.

High-Quality Evidence-Based Instruction

In the general education classroom, teachers provide high-quality instruction for all students and make changes to the classroom environment to improve overall student performance. For example, a teacher considers various ways to arrange the classroom to encourage small-group work or reflects on the assignment of students to small groups that would best promote learning. In implementing RTI, classroom teachers not only work to create positive classroom environments and ensure that all students benefit from instruction, but they also monitor students' progress.

Teachers use only interventions that have a strong research base in terms of effectiveness. Studies show that RTI makes a real difference for many children and youth (Fuchs, Fuchs, & Compton, 2012; Greenwood et al., 2011; Mahdavi & Beebe-Frankenberger, 2009). The many students who succeed through RTI often reduce the number of referrals for special education services.

Selecting research-based interventions involves identifying information that describes the materials, the frequency and duration of the instruction, and how performance will be monitored. Implementing the intervention involves accurately following the specific procedures that the intervention requires for successful service delivery. Educators want to ensure **intervention fidelity**. Intervention fidelity, or treatment fidelity, means that the procedures and process are carried out consistent with how they were designed and that they are delivered consistently to all students over time. Excellent resources for information about research-based intervention can be found at the Web sites of What Works Clearing House (ies.ed.gov/ncee/wwc/) and RTI Action Network (**http://www.rtinetwork.org/Learn/Research/ar/ResearchReview**).

School–Parent Connections

Teachers communicate regularly with parents through teacher conferences, weekly e-mails, or other ways to let parents know how their child is progressing. When a student is experiencing difficulty, the teacher may arrange an informal conference or invite the parents to the RTI school meeting, where members discuss more intensive instruction. This instruction targets the area(s) in which the student is experiencing difficulty and provides students with opportunities to be successful.

To address classroom teachers' questions and concerns, an RTI team comprised of school personnel meets on a regular basis, sometimes as frequently as weekly. Schools may include a special educator on the school team at different points; some schools may do so in the beginning, and some schools may wait until later in the RTI process. For example, the RTI school team may consist of a core team that includes an administrator, curriculum specialists, general classroom teachers, the family member, and a special educator who can share knowledge of interventions and teaching strategies. When a student's performance indicates the need for more intensive instruction, other members, such as a reading specialist, school psychologist, or social worker, are added to the team. In contrast, other RTI school teams may begin with an enhanced core of 10 or more individuals who bring individual areas of expertise in academic areas and special education, as well as behavior management. The core team may be subdivided into smaller teams, depending on the concerns and the intensity of the interventions.

Progress Monitoring

When a student is referred for more intensive interventions, the school team (Figure 2.1) identifies how often (frequency) the student will receive the intervention and how long

FIGURE 2.1 • RTI Team Membership

(duration) it will last. Each student's response to the intervention is carefully monitored by assessing the student's progress, sometimes weekly. **Progress monitoring** is a process of regularly assessing student performance on general outcomes measures during RTI and making instructional decisions based on the data. Educators examine the data carefully to determine if instruction is effective or if adjustments need to be made, such as a change in instructional strategy, adjustment in instructional time (frequency), use of more concrete hands-on materials, or the size of the instructional group.

When a student does not demonstrate progress, even with intensive levels of intervention, school personnel notify the parent(s) of the continued concerns and explain that there will be a referral to special education services. The referral includes documentation of the intervention efforts that have been implemented and the assessment results. This documentation of the various interventions implemented and the resulting performance of the student provides valuable information during consideration of the student's eligibility for special education services.

Individuals with Disabilities Education Improvement Act (IDEA) discusses the increasing intensity and frequency of interventions used in RTI as a model to determine whether a student can succeed. When a student continues to experience difficulty after the implantation of documented interventions, then the student may in fact have a disability and need specially designed instruction. IDEA suggests, but does not mandate, that RTI can be used to determine eligibility for special education services under the eligibility category of learning disability and requires each state to develop a process for determining whether a learning disability exists (34 C.F.R. Sec. 300.307(a)).

Multitiered Interventions

RTI is often described as a **multitiered intervention system**. This continuum of support allows educators to provide academic and behavior interventions to meet the needs of all learners. Each tier provides a different type of intervention focus and an increasing level of intensity of instruction. Teachers use **data-based decision making (DBDM)** to determine the level of intervention needed and the effectiveness of the intensity of instruction. Models of RTI describe various numbers of tiers; the most common is the three-tier model.

Tier 1

Tier 1 focuses on activities in the general education classroom (Table 2.1), where all students receive high-quality evidence-based curriculum and instructional strategies. Professional learning communities within the school, including teachers, administrators, parents, and community members, often examine research on effective schools and best practices. Then they discuss how they will implement high-quality instruction. For example, a group of educators became concerned when they were reviewing the data across grade levels on student achievement in mathematics. They found that some subgroups of students showed few gains. Why might this be so? In an effort to gain a better understanding, they examined current research findings regarding math curriculum and achievement of diverse learners.

At the Tier 1 level, teachers need to know if there is a difference in the effectiveness between various instructional approaches before identifying the curricula to be used in the classroom. As professional learning communities examine high quality evidence-based curriculum, they identify research-based interventions to determine preferred strategies and approaches for students with and without disabilities. They also examine and compare student results from their school with regional and national data. Some learning community members may take advantage of professional development workshops, online learning opportunities, or self-study to learn more about instructional strategies that support student learning and positive behaviors.

TABLE 2.1 • Overview of the RTI Tiers		
RTI Step	**Instruction Group**	**Instruction Focus**
Tier 1	General education whole class	High-quality evidence-based curriculum Research-based instructional strategies Student progress monitoring through assessment Overall classroom environment School–parent connections
Tier 2	Small group	Intensive research-based instruction on specific area of difficulty Frequency (amount of time and number of days per week) and duration (how many weeks) are specified Monitoring of student progress through assessment
Tier 3	Individual	Intensive research-based instruction Intervention focuses on identified individual need(s) Frequency, duration, and curriculum are specific to increase the likelihood of student responding Monitoring of student progress through assessment

Whole-class instruction also provides numerous opportunities such as projects, performances, and class discussions for monitoring performance. Monitoring of general outcomes also may be in the form of regular quizzes. General education teachers use information from these sources to make adjustments in instruction. For example, as part of daily reading instruction and progress monitoring, the classroom teacher identifies students who require more intensive instruction. Figure 2.2 illustrates Jinsu's performance on a quiz that his teacher gives weekly to the class. Notice that the horizontal line indicates time, or the number of weeks of instruction, whereas the vertical line represents the number of correct student responses. In this case, the vertical axis shows the number of words Jinsu read correctly. When the teacher constructed this graph, the highest total number of possible correct responses was 35. This number was used as the upper number on the graph; thus, this graph could be used to measure performance for each student in the class.

By looking at the graph, you can see that Jinsu's performance does not increase over a 10-week instruction period, although a series of interventions were implemented. Her performance is lower than the expected goal after this amount of instructional time. Her teacher will make arrangements to meet with Jinsu's parents to discuss her performance and make suggestions for more frequent and intensive instruction (Figure 2.2). Here, the general education teacher has the primary responsibility for identifying students who are at risk for learning and behavioral difficulties and for referring these students to a more intensive level of intervention, Tier 2. Students also may be identified for Tier 2 through schoolwide universal screening, which was described previously.

Tier 2

Tier 2 focuses on providing small-group instruction that is targeted to the specific area in which the student is experiencing difficulty. When Tier 2 intervention continues in the regular education classroom, the general education teacher or inclusion teacher, a special educator who coteaches with the general educator, is responsible for instruction (Bender & Shores, 2007). The small groups are homogenous in that students with similar skill levels are grouped together. A small group in reading, for example, could consist of four children who receive instruction on **phonemic awareness**. In addition to targeted daily instruction, student progress is monitored regularly, as in Tier 1. Bender and Shores (2007) recommended that student progress be monitored on a daily basis and that Tier 2 intervention be provided for a 6- to 8-week period so that students have enough time to demonstrate progress.

Jinsu receives reading instruction in the general education classroom. Since September, her teacher has monitored each student's work on a weekly basis. This graph illustrates Jinsu's progress in oral reading. Her teacher, Mrs. Bigelow, is planning to meet with Jinsu's parents to discuss concerns about her progress. Following is part of a monologue that illustrates what Mrs. Bigelow might say.

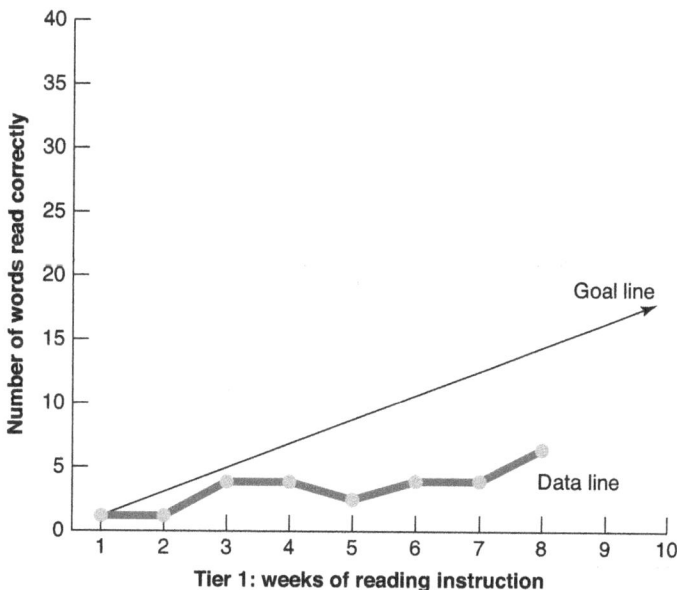

"Good afternoon, Mr. and Mrs. Li. I am very pleased to meet you now. I want to share with you some information about Jinsu's reading progress. She is a delightful student who works very hard. As you know, we have been trying several interventions to help increase her reading achievement. I think this graph will help me explain. Each week, I monitor her progress by asking her to read a short selection out loud. We call this a "1-minute reading passage." As you can see by the graph, each of her weekly scores is indicated. The upper line, called a goal line, represents how many words per minute she should be reading, if she were on grade level. We expect first-grade students to increase the number of words that they are able to read each week. For the first 4 weeks, Jinsu made some progress. At that point we began a more intensive phonics intervention, but her progress continued to be very slow. For Jinsu to meet expected grade level, I believe we need to provide her with additional reading instruction. In our school, we refer to this as "Tier 2 Reading Groups." This would mean that she would still receive instruction in her classroom, but in addition, she would receive biweekly reading instruction with our reading specialist, who works with small groups of children."

FIGURE 2.2 • Jinsu's Tier 1 Graph

Typically, Tier 2 instruction is implemented by a trained professional rather than the general education teacher. Students receiving Tier 2 support in reading could receive instruction from a reading or learning specialist, for example. When the RTI team identifies interventions that involve the student's placement in another class, the parent must be notified and provide permission for this placement (Bender & Shores, 2007).

During Tier 2 interventions, school professionals determine realistic goals for the student. When a student exceeds expectations, these goals are adjusted; when a student's performance indicates that the goal will not be reached, the instructional interventions are adjusted. Throughout this period, student performance is monitored, and the results are tracked by graphing the data. Later in this chapter, we will look more closely at how teachers graph student data. At the end of the intervention period, students who are making adequate progress return to their classrooms and continue Tier 1 intervention. If students show some progress, the RTI school team may decide to make adjustments to Tier 2 interventions and continue this level of intervention. When students make limited progress, the team contacts the parents and obtains consent to refer the student to the last level. Figure 2.3 illustrates this multistep decision process.

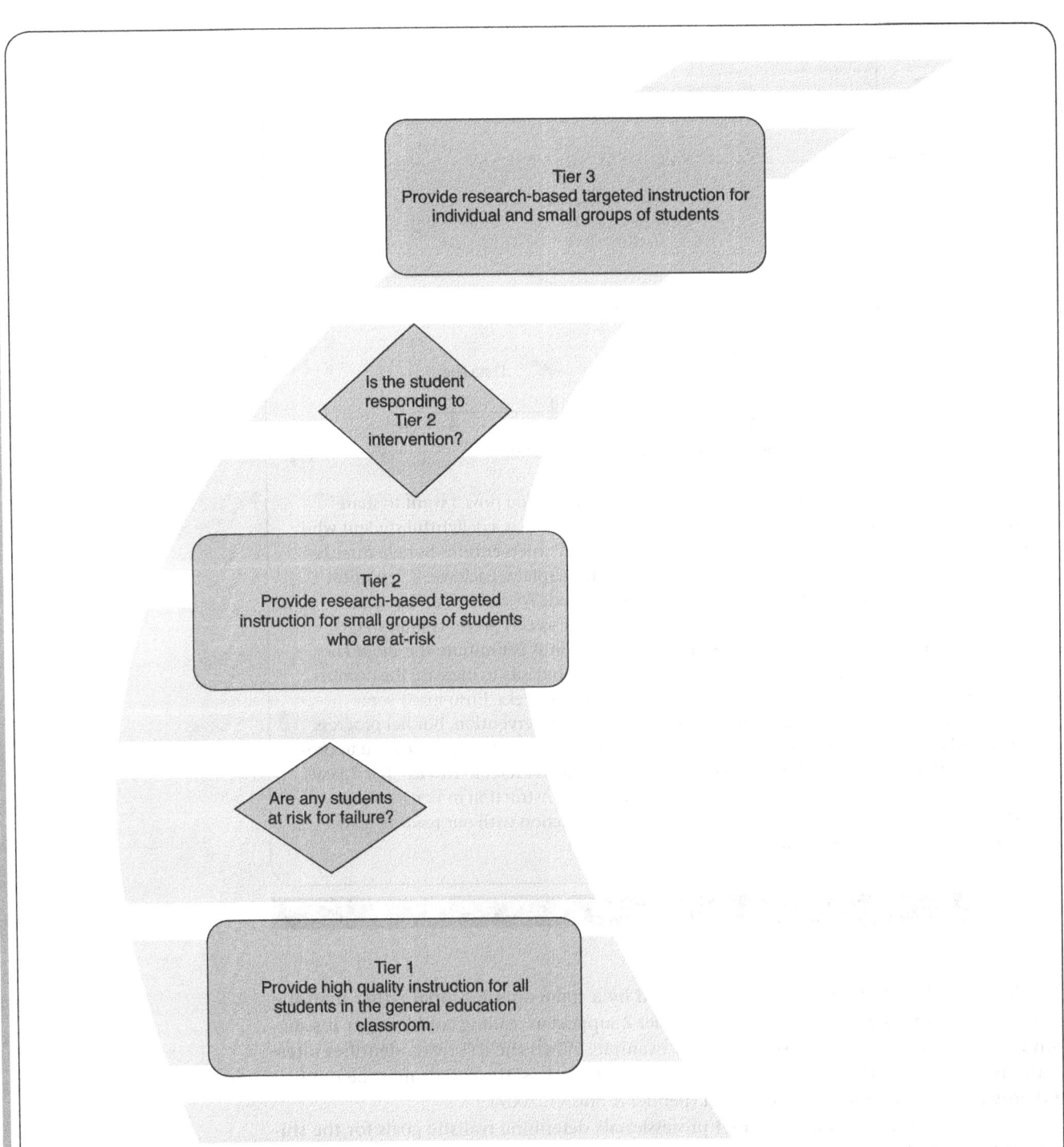

FIGURE 2.3 • Questions and Decisions in the RTI Multistep Model

Tier 3

When the RTI school team determines that the student continues to demonstrate inadequate progress, they recommend that the student moves to Tier 3, or the most intensive level of intervention. At this level, curriculum specialists or behavioral specialists provide intensive interventions. Students work in small groups and/or individually with highly trained professionals. Instruction is more frequent and for longer periods of time during the school day, and student progress is monitored on a regular basis. If students show some progress, the RTI school team may recommend adjustments to Tier 3 interventions.

When students show limited or no progress, school personnel will complete a referral to special education services. Educators and specialists gather additional information, including direct observations of the student and sometimes parent observations. Parents can also provide medical history and early developmental history, if they have not done so previously. In addition, all the information from Tiers 1 and 2 is reviewed, and additional assessment procedures (such as cognitive and achievement assessment) are considered. A student who is referred to special education receives a full evaluation to determine eligibility for services. The Individualized Education Program (IEP) team considers the results of the assessment and, if the student is eligible, creates an IEP. In Chapter 3 you will read more about this assessment framework.

For many students with disabilities, the RTI process provides opportunities to increase progress through multiple interventions, data collection points, and assessments. Although many students can demonstrate increased achievement, other students will not be able to do so, perhaps because of the characteristics of a disability, individual strengths and challenges, inadequate curriculum, lack of prior experiences, or other reasons. The data collected during RTI provides valuable evidence in documenting continued low performance despite interventions. This documentation is particularly important in making decisions about students with difficulties in learning. When a school uses RTI and refers a student to special education services, the IEP team uses the RTI documentation and the student's lack of response as part of the data documenting the presence of a specific learning disability or other disability.

Responding to Diversity

RTI has the potential to reduce the continued overrepresentation in special education of children who are culturally and linguistically diverse. Yet along with this promise, there are some concerns. Is the prereferral process sensitive to cultural and linguistic diversity? Garcia and Ortiz (2006) identified several key aspects of high-quality instruction that can be implemented during Tier 1: (a) instructional practices that promote proficiency in first and second languages/dialects; (b) teachers' use of culturally responsive pedagogy and culturally responsive curricula for literacy development, academic content, and social skills; and (c) teachers' focus on building positive relationships with culturally and linguistically diverse families and communities. After implementing RTI for the first year, classroom teachers in an urban elementary school reported that they had a better understanding of "when" to refer English language learners for special education services (Greenfield, Rinaldi, Proctor, & Cardarelli, 2010).

When implementing interventions, teachers can consider the extent to which instructional interventions have proven successful with diverse students. In other words, teachers should have assurance of the extent to which the evidence-based instruction has been validated with students who are English language learners. As schools implement tiered support systems, some researchers urge that schools consider supports that are needed to ensure the success of all students (O'Connor & Freeman, 2012). Students who are culturally and linguistically diverse may require different Tier 1 and Tier 2 interventions (Harry & Klingner, 2007). When working with elementary children with reading difficulties, Linan-Thompson (2006) found that the most successful instruction:

- Explicitly and systematically builds language skills during reading instruction
- Explicitly teaches letter/sound correspondences, word patterns, and spelling rules

SNAPSHOT

Mark Paolucci, High School Special Educator

My colleagues and I at Hillsdale High School utilize Response to Intervention (RTI). This fall I am a member of our Professional Learning Community (PLC) and our Core Team. The PLC consists of all 10th-grade teachers. Once a week, we meet to review and discuss the types of interventions that are being used for particular students. As each of us provides input, such as observations and classroom assessments, the team leader documents the data. Then the team leader takes this information to our Core Team, where members provide additional suggestions.

The Core Team includes some of the curriculum specialists, such as the literacy coordinator and math consultant, social worker, behavior specialist, special educator, and administrator. Students receiving Tier 2 or Tier 3 interventions work with one or more members of the Core Team. The targeted skills are in mathematics, language arts, and positive behavior. During Tier 2 students are placed in one or more small classes: Math Seminar, Language Arts Seminar, or Exploration Forum. When a student first moves to Tier 2, the student is given an assessment, and the data is used as baseline information. For example, the assessments in the language arts class use reading passages as the baseline. The student reads for 3 minutes and then answers questions that assess comprehension, understanding parts of speech, decoding, and reading fluency. The assessments in math target mathematical comprehension and calculation. The students participate in daily small-group instruction in addition to their regular class in math or reading. Student progress is observed and monitored weekly. Each student's progress is charted and the data is compared to the student's baseline data. If a student is not responding as expected, the teacher will try one or more types of interventions. When a student does not demonstrate progress after 1 to 2 months, then the Core Team may move the student to a Tier 3 level.

Tier 3 has a more focused and intense curriculum with specified intervention methods targeted to the individual student needs. This tier includes an extended class time with individualized attention. The teacher usually involves the student in setting goals and graphing progress.

Each Wednesday, after school, the Core Team meets to examine and discuss individual students' progress—or lack of progress—and provide additional suggestions tailored to these individual students. If a Tier 3 plan has been implemented and documented as unsuccessful, the Core Team will then choose to make a referral for special education services. This requires further evaluations to see if the student qualifies.

Pause and consider:
- What might be some advantages for having a special educator on the school's professional learning committee?
- On the core team?
- What types of expertise could the special educator contribute to the team?

- Introduces skills in isolation and practice in context
- Builds vocabulary and emphasizes the relationships between and among words to build oral language skills
- Includes story retells that target both comprehension and language development

Implementing RTI

Assessment of Student Performance

Assessment of student performance allows educators to target instruction to specific skills and knowledge that the student is lacking. In each of the tiers of intervention, assessment and data collection are integral parts of the RTI process. The data allow teachers to make adjustments in using methods of instruction, incorporating instructional strategies, or introducing manipulatives, for example. Assessment data also provide teachers with evidence that a student can return to a less-intensive level of instruction or needs a more intensive level to be successful. We refer to teachers using assessments to provide recurring information as formative evaluation. Formative evaluation refers to an evaluation that is ongoing during the period of program implementation.

Formative evaluation approaches are usually informal assessments that are linked closely to the curriculum. **Curriculum-based assessment (CBA)**, which is discussed in Chapter 10, is one broad approach. Closely associated with CBA, **curriculum-based measurement (CBM)** has a strong research base and is often used in formative evaluation. Schoolwide application of CBM is particularly promising when all children are screened with CBM, and this approach is used to monitor student performance during RTI (Griffiths et al., 2007).

Curriculum-Based Measurement

CBM is an assessment approach that links instruction with assessment and emphasizes repeated, direct measurement of student performance. CBMs are directly aligned with the curriculum; that is, the CBM incorporates the same content that is covered during instruction, and students are expected to respond the same way during the assessment as they do during instruction. Generally, CBMs are technically adequate. The results of CBMs are reliable, and they measure the content that they are expected to measure. CBMs are very useful when teachers use them to observe trends in student performance.

One of the most common examples of CBM is a weekly spelling test. The teacher selects words that students use frequently. During the week, students may use the words in various writing and reading activities. Then at the end of the week, the students have a test. The number of correctly written words is totaled, and each student receives a score.

In reading and mathematics, teachers may refer to CBMs as probes. According to Fuchs and Fuchs (2009a), each probe has different test items, but the probe assesses the same skills at the same level of difficulty (p. 2). A student's score is based on accuracy and sometimes speed, as in math calculations or early reading. Each score is graphed, and by examining the trend of scores, the teacher easily determines if the student is making progress.

Teachers can create graphs of student performance using many types of software, apps, and online resources. One such tool is Create a Graph (nces.ed.gov/nceskids/createAgraph). Graphs are set up with specific information, such as individual days or weeks on the horizontal axis and the number of correct student responses on the vertical axis (Figure 2.4). The student scores on each CBM are plotted on the graph. These scores may be connected by lines

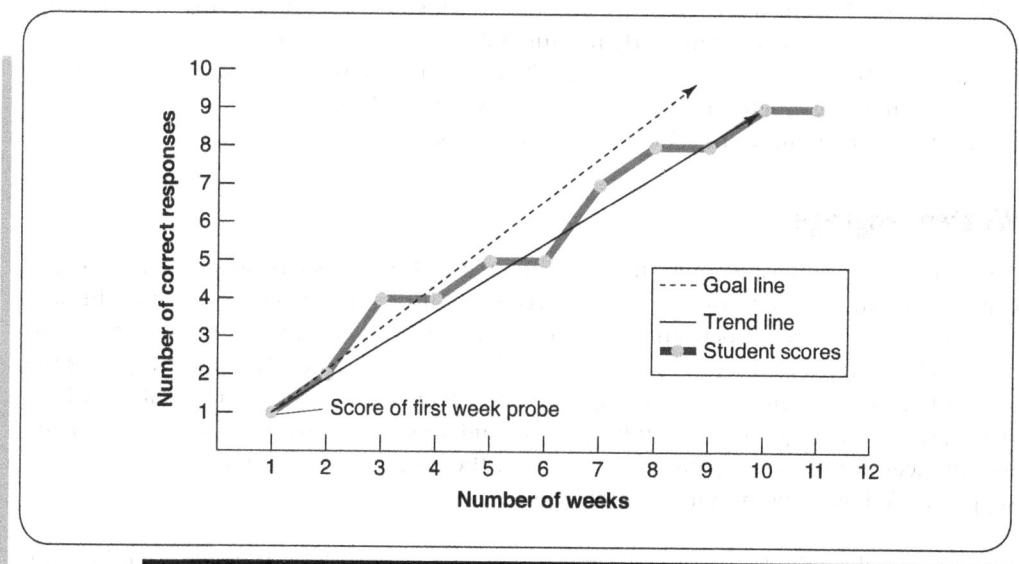

FIGURE 2.4 • Graphing Student Performance

to better indicate the trend in student performance. Computer software programs and online resources often include a **goal line**, also referred to as an **AIM line**. A goal line is represented on a graph and shows the rate of progress that a student must make to meet the level of expected performance. The expected performance could be for the class or for the student's IEP. As the student's performance data are collected, an average of the student's scores can be computed and then also represented on the graph. This **trend line**, sometimes referred to as **growth rate**, represents the average performance of the student over time and is represented by the slope on the graph. By comparing the student's trend line with the goal line, teachers can make decisions regarding the student's rate of progress. When the distance between the student's growth rate and the goal line is increasing, the teacher will consider referring the student to more intensive instruction.

There are numerous resources for obtaining CBM materials, which usually include directions for administering, test items or tasks, scoring directions, and ways to compare student performance with same-age peers. For example, many Web-based resources allow educators to view or download CBMs for free or low cost. Other sites provide online CBMs with data management. In addition to Web tools, numerous commercial software programs allow teachers to input student data and generate various graphs, saving teachers' time. Let's look more closely at some examples of how teachers use CBM during the intervention process.

Reading

Early literacy is a major component of the curriculum in the primary grades. If we asked an early elementary teacher to identify typical skills in beginning reading, these skills probably would include phonemic awareness, such as identifying initial and final sound; sound blending; and sound segmentation. In sound segmentation, a teacher might say, "I am going to say a word, and I want you to tell me all the sounds in the word. Let's try one together. If I say, 'pan' you would say, 'p/a/n.'" Other beginning reading skills include **phonics**, **reading fluency**, comprehension, and vocabulary. Early **reading comprehension** involves identifying information from stories, such as being able to answer who, what, and when questions; identifying the main idea; and answering questions about the characters and the events that took place.

Knowing the components of early reading are critical when identifying test items to include in a CBM. Specific test items and the assessment of student performance assist the teacher in pinpointing one or more of the specific skills where the student is experiencing difficulty and allow the teacher to track the student's progress over time. Probably one of the most popular CBMs for assessing early reading skills is the Dynamic Indicators of Basic Early Literacy Skills (DIBELS; dibels.uoregon.edu). This assessment tool can be used for both screening and monitoring progress in the early elementary grades. In the Snapshot about Celia, you will read more about how one school used this process.

Written Language

Assessing written language begins in early elementary school or as soon as a student is able to compose a phrase containing a few words. Assessment of student skills continues through grade 12. CBM of student performance consists of a high-interest probe or story starter and can be administered to the whole class or to an individual student. Choosing a topic for the probe or story starter involves selecting a topic to which students can relate or about which they have some background. Depending on the student's ability, the student is asked to write in sentences or to write in paragraphs based on the prompt. For example, a teacher might supply the following prompt in the sixth-grade class:

> *The school administration is considering a dress code for our school. What do you think? Provide a rationale for adopting such a code or for opposing the code.*

> **SNAPSHOT**
>
> ### Celia and the RTI Process
>
> Celia followed expected levels of development as a young child and on beginning kindergarten, she participated in the schoolwide universal screening, which included DIBELS, a CBM for assessing early reading skills, discussed previously. Celia's performance fell within the low average for children beginning kindergarten, but she was not identified as needing additional intervention at that time.
>
> **Pause and consider:**
> - To implement universal screening, an individual school may use DIBELS or another screening tool. What universal screening procedures are used in your local schools? How might you locate this information?
> - What does the research say about DIBLES or another universal screening tool?
>
> During the kindergarten year, her classroom teacher provided high-quality, early literacy instruction to all the children that included phonemic awareness and phonics learning activities. Each child's performance was monitored by weekly assessment of knowledge of letter sound and letter blending. Celia's performance indicated that she was making progress but not to the extent of other children in the class.
>
> Her teacher discussed the concerns with her parents, who were anxious for Celia to receive additional help if she needed the assistance. Together they met with the RTI school team to discuss the next steps. The team decided to implement additional classroom interventions at the Tier 1 level. These included (a) checking to make sure all children were attending before beginning instruction and (b) decreasing the amount of visual distractions such as hanging mobiles in the classroom. These classroom interventions helped Celia maintain attention. The classroom teacher continued to monitor Celia's performance on weekly quizzes.
>
> After 4 weeks had passed, Celia's performance continued to show little improvement, and the RTI school team reconvened to discuss next steps. The members decided that the next level of intervention (Tier 2) should be implemented. Celia would join a small group of children to work with the reading specialist outside her classroom, in addition to her regular classroom instruction. This small-group intensive instruction was offered 30 minutes daily. By the end of her kindergarten year, Celia demonstrated progress with the small-group instruction and told her teacher that she liked working with the three other children.
>
> In first grade, Celia continued to make progress, and she was not identified as needing further intervention until second grade. In October of that year, her teacher found her falling behind the other children in both reading and written expression. Tier 2 interventions included working with the reading specialist and participating in a second-grade writers' program. The writers' program included a research-based approach to supplemental instruction and practice within the general classroom. Celia's performance was monitored weekly through CBM. Working in small groups for reading and writing, Celia was able to make progress over the next 2 months, but her overall performance fell short of the goals for children in second grade. The team decided to continue the Tier 2 interventions and increase the amount of time Celia worked with the reading specialist. Monitoring of her performance was changed to a biweekly basis. She continued to make small gains. As the end of the school year approached, her classroom teacher recommended her for the summer reading program. Celia enjoyed this 8-week program very much.
>
> The following September, when Celia entered third grade, her teacher observed that her reading and written language performance were below grade level and that she was falling further behind her peers. At this point, the RTI school team, which included Celia's parents, decided to complete a referral for special education services. Celia's folder contained detailed information about each of the interventions that had been implemented and data from her performance. Although she had received numerous evidence-based interventions and made small gains, her performance suggested that her continuing difficulties in reading and written language may be the result of a learning disability. The IEP team will identify additional information and other assessments to assist in this determination.

The teacher provides each student with a written copy of the prompt and also reads the prompt aloud. The students have 1 minute to think about what they want to write, and then they begin writing. According to Fuchs and Fuchs (2009b), students in mid-elementary grades should be given 3 minutes to write. Students in late elementary grades should be given 5 minutes to write, and middle- and high-school students should be given 7 minutes to write.

There are a number of different ways to score written expression. Cusumano (2007) identifies the following:

1. Count the total number of words written (TWW). Spelling and other errors are ignored.
2. Count the total number of words spelled correctly (WSC). Grammatical and other errors are ignored.
3. Count the number of correct word sequences (CWS). Correct word sequences are adjacent word pairs that are correct in spelling, grammar, punctuation, and **syntax**.

Knowing about the student's needs in written language will affect what type of scoring method the teacher selects. The educator may take into consideration the student's current level of performance and the grade-level goals (or individualized goals identified on the student's IEP). After deciding on the scoring method, the teacher will use the same method throughout the program year to monitor the student's progress.

Spelling

Student performance in spelling is typically monitored through weekly spelling quizzes. Students are given a list of new spelling words each week and, at the end of the week, take a spelling quiz, either as a class or individually. During the quiz, the teacher dictates each word, usually repeating the word and using it in a sentence. Students are given about a minute to write the word on lined paper.

Once the student's scores are tabulated, they are graphed, and the teacher plans targeted instruction. Graphs provide important feedback to the teacher. When the graph shows that the student is not progressing from week to week, the teacher will need to conduct a careful analysis of the student's work and pinpoint area(s) of difficulty. Then the teacher will need to make decisions. Does the material need to be retaught? What teaching strategies might be helpful? What materials could be used?

Mathematics

CBMs in mathematics sample an array of skills; some of the skills would be above the student's current skill level, and some would be below. For example, at the beginning of instruction, a resource room teacher might administer a broad CBM on concepts and applications that includes several items each on geometry, number and operations, place value, and data analysis. These items represent skills that students are expected to have already mastered.

The student's performance on this CBM helps inform instruction and allows the teacher to identify skills that the student has mastered, skills that need review, and skills that need to be taught. At the end of each week of instruction, the teacher administers a CBM over the material covered that week. In subsequent CBMs, the teacher uses alternative forms with the same number of items and the same types of problems representing the same level of difficulty, but with different numerals. These CBMs are a direct measure of the instructional goals and are very sensitive to changes in learning. By analyzing the student's performance on the CBM, the teacher can calculate the correct items as well as examine the items that were incorrect. Once the data are obtained and graphed, the teacher compares student progress to the expected growth rate of students. The teacher also examines the items that the student did not answer correctly. These items provide valuable additional information. For example, if the student missed items involved in converting decimals to fractions, the teacher analyzes the student's work to determine patterns of error. Are there consistent patterns? Does the student understand the concept? Does the student understand the procedure for converting decimals? These answers will lead the teacher in developing an instructional plan. The teacher will decide whether the instruction focuses on the concept, a learning strategy, or a fact to be taught.

Teachers seeking additional materials can find a number of free and low-cost resources for CBMs for mathematics. Web-based tools include AIMSweb (Math and Reading; **http://www.aimsweb.com**), STAR Math (and Reading; **http://www.renlearn.com**), and mCLASS (**http://www.mclassdirect.com**). Researchers at the Iris Center (iris.peabody.vanderbilt.edu) have developed numerous CBM materials for mathematics *and* for reading and written language.

Behavior

Students with problem behaviors present challenges for teachers today. RTI uses evidence-based practices to intervene and teach new skills or redirect students to support positive behaviors. Similar to the interventions of academic difficulties, teachers use the same tiered approach to addressing problem behaviors and to monitoring and documenting student performance.

As part of schoolwide efforts, schools adopt universal interventions for all children. These preventative measures often include schoolwide:

- Discipline plans
- Social skills instruction
- Conflict resolution instruction
- Bullying prevention skills

In the general education classroom, teachers not only provide instruction in these areas, but they also may work with other school professionals to support these schoolwide efforts. For example, the school social worker or guidance counselor may come to the classroom for a period of 4 weeks to teach a Monday/Wednesday class period on self-control and social responsibility.

When classroom teachers identify students who continue to present behavior problems, they notify the school team. Often these same students demonstrate academic problems as well. In these cases, the RTI school team will discuss ways to link behavior and

Research-Based Practices — **Does Curriculum-Based Measurement Really Work?**

CBM was first described by Deno in the mid-1980s. Since then, much has been written about this assessment approach, and hundreds, if not thousands, of research studies have been conducted. CBMs work well within an RTI framework for monitoring progress of students who are consistently low performing (Anderson, Cheng-Fei, Alonzo, & Tindal, 2011). These assessments are effective ways to inform teachers that there is a need for additional or different forms of instruction (Stecker, Fuchs, & Fuchs, 2005; VanDerHeyden & Burns, 2005) and to set goals and monitor progress (Christ, Zopluoglu, Long, & Monaghen, 2012). The use of graphed analysis of students' CBM scores helps teachers plan more effective programs (Cusumano, 2007; Graney, Missal, Martinez, & Bergstrom, 2009).

Research studies indicate that several critical practices can enhance achievement for students with disabilities (Stecker et al., 2005). Systematic data collection and using data are two important practices. One finding indicates the importance of using systematic data collection as opposed to a sporadic collection of data. A second finding is that teachers must use the data to inform teaching and make instructional changes, if necessary. This includes the use of an analysis of student data to pinpoint areas of difficulty and then using this analysis to adjust instruction accordingly. These researchers also explored teacher use of goal setting. Findings indicate that when teachers use goal setting and (a) adjust goals upward when progress is higher than expected and (b) adjust instruction when progress is lower than expected, they positively enhance the achievement of students with disabilities.

> ### SNAPSHOT
> ### Tier 2 Intervention for Diego
>
> Diego lives with his mother and five brothers in a small southwestern town. At home, the family speaks Spanish, and English is Diego's second language. In school, he is an active sixth grader who has difficulty sitting still and paying attention to the teacher. During breaks, he often engages in rowdy play with other students, and sometimes these activities lead to fighting in the corridor and in the classroom.
>
> Diego's teacher discussed her concerns and frustrations with the RTI school team. The teacher also contacted Diego's mother by phone. His mother was not able to come to school to meet with the teacher, but she did share that she too is having difficulty controlling Diego at home. As the oldest child, she expects him to help her with the care of his younger brothers and to assist in getting the meals when she is at work.
>
> Working with the classroom teacher, the RTI school team identified some strategies to address Diego's problem behaviors. The school social worker described the small group that he was beginning so that he could provide social skills training and self-management for identified students, and the team agreed that Diego should be included. The students meet in a small conference room during homeroom period twice a week. The school psychologist discussed appropriate reinforcements for Diego and a strong reward system for displaying positive behaviors. Last, the team decided to identify an adult mentor for Diego through the community/school support representative.
>
> Diego's performance was monitored daily through systematic observations. Before the interventions were in place, his behaviors continued to be disruptive and occurred five to six times each day. The team worked to implement the recommendations within a few days' time as his performance was monitored. At the end of the first week, his problem behaviors had decreased to two and three times daily. After a second week, the problem behaviors rarely occurred.
>
> **Pause and consider:**
> - What information would you suggest that the teacher gather during the phone conversation with Diego's mother?
> - What other information about the family and the community might be important?
> - How might the team integrate this information into their plan?

academic interventions. The school psychologist often participates on the school team when there is a discussion of behavioral interventions. The team discusses various supports that could be implemented by the general education teacher in the classroom, such as a behavior checklist or classroom behavior monitoring sheet. In addition, the classroom teacher may begin implementing specific reinforcement when the student demonstrates positive behaviors. The teacher also contacts the parents and establishes a communication plan between home and school.

During intervention for problem behaviors, the team typically uses a problem-solving approach. They consider questions such as: What purpose is the behavior serving? Is the student trying to avoid a task? Is the student communicating a need? Often, the school team initiates a **functional behavioral assessment** to assist in the problem-solving procedure. A functional behavioral assessment is a systematic process of gathering information that identifies the causes of and interventions for addressing problem behaviors. Later in this book (Chapter 9), we will examine this type of assessment in detail.

During behavioral interventions, the teacher or other school professional monitors the student's performance and graphs the data. Monitoring student performance often involves a series of systematic observations, such as recording specific events or behaviors during a prespecified interval of time. In Chapter 8, you'll learn more about systematic observations and their usefulness.

Emerging Issues

RTI holds much promise for children who are experiencing difficulties. Yet the more we learn about RTI, the more we begin to understand the work ahead. For example, when students do not respond to Tier 1 or Tier 2 intervention, how many interventions should we try? For how long? Compton (2006) discussed *nudges* such as: What should the *nudge* be? When should the *nudge* be given? How long should *nudging* continue?

A second issue involves the implementation of interventions and *intervention fidelity*. Remember, that *intervention fidelity* means that the intervention was implemented as planned and that it was delivered consistently to all students over time. As school teams identify research-based interventions, how will the teams ensure intervention fidelity? In a review of the literature, researchers (Smith, Daunic, & Taylor, 2007) write that the practice of reporting intervention fidelity is limited in many studies. This lack of information creates difficulties when trying to establish evidence-based practices. Much work lies ahead in applied education research for the next generation of young researchers, whose work will improve the lives of children and youth.

Summary

- Response to intervention (RTI) is a systematic model for teaching and assessing students with ongoing data collection, charting, and monitoring of student performance.
- Beginning in the general education classroom, RTI addresses both academic and behavioral concerns among students.
- RTI involves a series of tiers of intervention, with increasing frequency and intensity of interventions.
- Student progress is monitored carefully using CBM.
- RTI reduces the number of inappropriate referrals for special education services.
- When a student demonstrates continued lack of response to the interventions, the student is referred to a multidisciplinary team to determine the need for special education services.

QUESTIONS FOR REFLECTION

1. Create a graphic or text handout that illustrates the essential components of RTI.
2. Working with a small group of peers, identify the questions that you have regarding the role and responsibilities of a special educator in RTI.
3. After completing question 2, make plans to interview a special educator about this teacher's involvement in RTI, and record the results of your interview. Share your findings with the class.
4. Visit the Web site of the National Center on Response to Intervention, and select one or two resources to review. Prepare a one-page summary of your findings to share with others.
5. Conduct a Web search to locate sites that have helpful information and resources for educators who are using RTI. Create an annotated bibliography of your findings. You might start with one or more of the following sites:

- Equity Alliance (**http://www.equityallianceatasu.org/**)
- National Center on Response to Intervention (**www.rti4success.org**)
- National Center on Student Progress Monitoring (**http://www.studentprogress.org/**)
- OSEP Technical Assistance Center on Positive Behavioral Interventions and Supports (**http://www.pbis.org/**)
- Research Institute on Progress Monitoring (**http://www.progressmonitoring.org/**)
- The Access Center Improving Outcomes for All Students K–8 (**http://www.k8accesscenter.org/index.php**)

REFERENCES

Anderson, D., Cheng-Fei, L., Alonzo, J., & Tindal, G. (2011). Examining a grade-level math CBM designed for persistently low-performing students. *Educational Assessment, 16*(1), 15–34. doi:10.1080/10627197.2011.551084

Bender, W. N., & Shores, C. (2007). *Response to intervention: A practical guide for every teacher.* Thousand Oaks, CA: Corwin Press.

Christ, T. J., Zopluoglu, C., Long, J. D, & Monaghen, B. D. (2012). Curriculum-based measurement of oral reading: Quality of progress monitoring outcomes. *Exceptional Children, 78*(3), 356–373.

Compton, D. L. (2006). How should "unresponsiveness" to secondary intervention be operationalized? It is all about the nudge. *Journal of Learning Disabilities, 39,* 170–173.

Cusumano, D. L. (2007). Is it working? An overview of curriculum based measurement and its uses for assessing instructional, intervention, or program effectiveness. *The Behavior Analyst Today, 8*(1), 24–34.

Fuchs, D., Fuchs, L. S., & Compton, D. L. (2012). Smart RTI: A next-generation approach to multilevel prevention. *Exceptional Children, 78*(3), 263–279.

Fuchs, L. S., & Fuchs, D. (2009a). Using curriculum based measurements in response to intervention framework: Introduction to using CBM. Retrieved from the National Center of Response to Intervention Web site at http://www.rti4success.org/images/stories/cbmModules/introtocbmmanual_5-21-09.doc

Fuchs, L. S., & Fuchs, D. (2009b). Using curriculum based measurements in response to intervention framework: Introduction to using CBM for progress monitoring in written expression and spelling. Retrieved from the National Center of Response to Intervention Web site at http://www.rti4success.org/images/stories/cbmModules/writtenexpressionmanual_5-21-09.doc

Garcia, S. B., & Ortiz, A. A. (2006). Preventing disproportionate representation: Culturally and linguistically responsive pre-referral interventions. Retrieved from http://www.rti4success.org/images/stories/pdfs/pre-referral_brief.pdf

Graney, S. B., Missal, K. N., Martinez, R. S., & Bergstrom, M. (2009). A preliminary investigation of within-year growth patterns in reading and mathematics curriculum-based measures. *Journal of School Psychology, 47*(2), 121–142.

Greenfield, R., Rinaldi, C., Proctor, C., & Cardarelli, A. (2010). Teachers' perceptions of a response to intervention (RTI) reform effort in an urban elementary school: A consensual qualitative analysis. *Journal of Disability Policy Studies, 21*(1), 47–63. doi:10.1177/1044207310365499

Greenwood, C. R., Bradfield, T., Kaminski, R., Linas, M., Carta, J. J., & Nylander, D. (2011). The response to intervention (RTI) approach in early childhood. *Focus on Exceptional Children, 43*(9), 1–22.

Griffiths, A. J., Parson, L. B., Burns, M. K., VanDerHeyden, A., & Tilly, W. D. (2007). *Response to intervention: Research for practice.* Alexandria, VA: National Association of State Directors of Special Education.

Harry, B., & Klingner, J. (2007). Discarding the deficit model. *Educational Leadership, 64*(5), 16–21.

Individuals with Disabilities Education Improvement Act (Pub. L. No. 108-446). (2004). 20 U.S.C.Secs. 1400 et. seq. Washington, DC: U.S. Government Printing Office.

Linan-Thompson, S. (2006). Response to intervention and EL learners: Questions and some answers. Retrieved from http://www.rti4success.org/images/stories/pdfs/rti_cec_06.pdf

Mahdavi, J. N., & Beebe-Frankenberger, M. E. (2009). Pioneering RTI systems that work. *Teaching Exceptional Children, 42*(2), 64–72.

Mellard, D. F., & Johnson, E. (2008). *RTI: A practitioner's guide to implementing response to intervention.* Thousand Oaks, CA: Sage.

O'Connor, E. P., & Freeman, E. (2012). District-level considerations in supporting and sustaining RtI implementation. *Psychology in the Schools, 49*(3), 297–310. doi:10.1002/pits.21598

Stecker, P. M., Fuchs, L. S., & Fuchs, D. (2005). Using curriculum-based measurement to improve student achievement: Review of research. *Psychology in the Schools, 42*(8), 795–819.

3 Assessment Framework

Chapter Objectives

After completing this chapter, you should be able to:

- Describe the classroom-based assessment cycle, including the characteristics of classroom assessment and the approaches that teachers use.
- Identify and discuss a framework for understanding assessment procedures in special education.
- Discuss assessment purposes and approaches that team members use when a student is referred to the evaluation team for special education services.
- Describe assessment practices used in determining assistive technology (AT) devices and services and why special educators must assess student needs.

Overview

This chapter begins by examining teaching and assessment practices in the general education classroom. We'll examine various types of classroom-based assessments and the cycle that teachers follow in planning instruction and assessing student progress. Then we examine a framework for understanding classroom-based assessment and the intersection with response to intervention (RTI) and special education. We'll look at the questions that guide the process of collecting information and the purposes of the assessment process. Selecting assessment approaches, or ways of assessing student skills and knowledge, begins with a careful consideration of the assessment questions and purposes. Throughout this text, you will find detailed discussions of specific questions, purposes, and approaches.

Classroom-Based Assessment Cycle

What kinds of questions might a teacher have? At the beginning of the year, a teacher may wonder,

> "What skills did the students retain from last year?"
> "What special interests or talents do the children have?"

Several weeks into the school, a teacher may ask,

"Is my instruction effective?"
"Are the students making progress?"
"How should I handle this student's behavior problems?"

Learning how to select assessment approaches, or different types of assessments, and using the assessment information appropriately is an essential skill. Assessments can focus on answering questions regarding academic or behavior concerns and physical or developmental factors. All educators must be able to observe, collect, record, and interpret information about students. They use assessment information in planning instruction and in monitoring progress of student achievements.

In the classroom, the teacher begins with planning instruction based on curriculum standards (goals or objectives). Then the teacher implements lessons and various activities to assist learning. In the following phase, the teacher assesses student progress. Often this assessment is brief, designed to provide the teacher with information concerning student achievement and the effectiveness of the instruction. Next, the teacher analyzes and evaluates assessment information, adjusting instruction as necessary, and then plans for instruction based on the assessment results and students' progress. For example, a teacher might decide to reteach a math lesson using additional visuals and a graphic organizer. Figure 3.1 illustrates

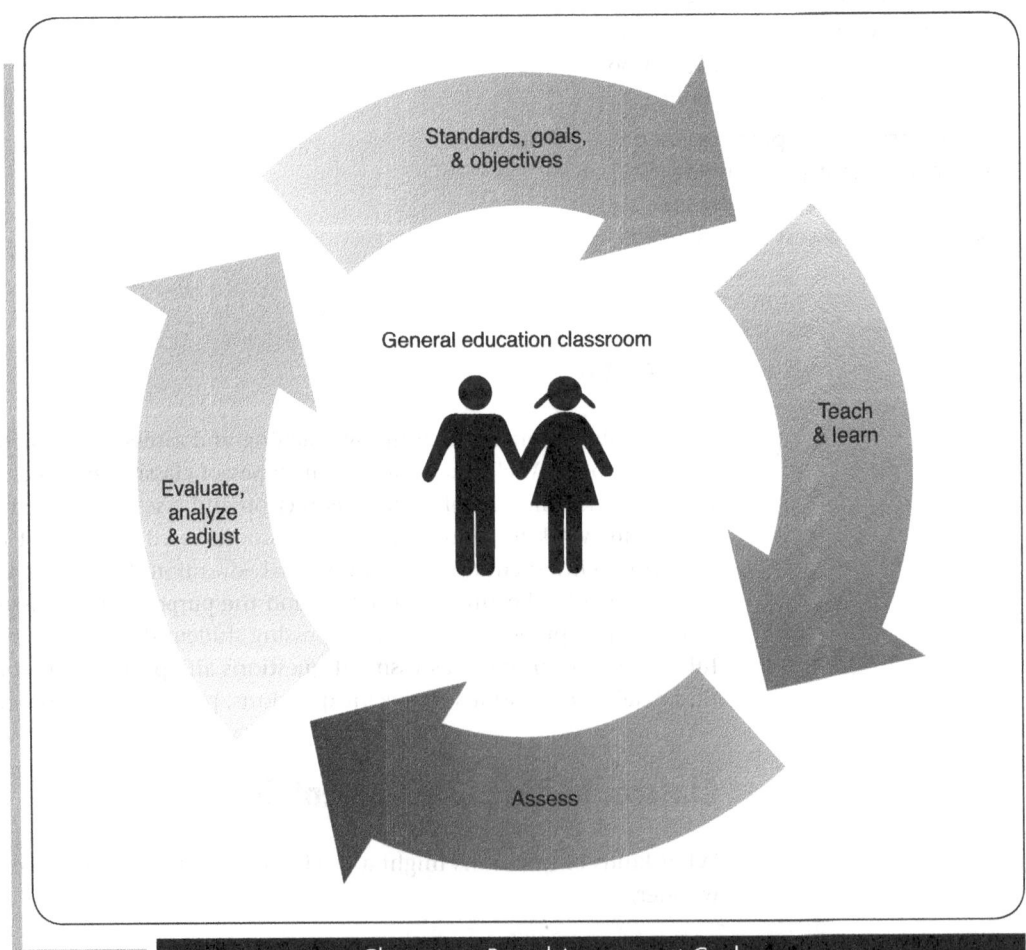

FIGURE 3.1 • Classroom-Based Assessment Cycle

that this process is an ongoing cycle where the teacher uses assessment to measure student progress and guide classroom instruction (Figure 3.1).

We can refer to this classroom-based assessment cycle as formative assessment. Teachers use formative assessments frequently to examine the data, and make adjustments in instructional content or teaching methods if needed. Let's take a closer look at some typical questions: "Are the students making progress?" and "Is my instruction effective?" Teachers use many different types of assessment approaches to gather information to answer these questions. Following are some examples.

- Consider the curriculum standards (goals or objectives). The National Council for Teachers of Mathematics (NCTM, 2012) suggests that teachers write the test first. Before starting a new unit or chapter, write a test that covers the main topics. By doing so, the assessment will guide how the topics are covered.
- Review from the start. Provide review exercises every day. Use warm-ups to tie together topics day-to-day and to review topics covered last week that will appear on an upcoming test. These review exercises will show the teacher on which topics students may need extra instruction. (NCTM, 2012)
- Create the One-Minute Paper. A few minutes before the end of class, distribute small pieces of paper, and ask the students to respond to the following question: "What was the most important information you learned in class today?" Students hand in their brief responses as they leave the classroom. This assessment technique allows a teacher to obtain information regarding student understanding of specific subject content and to use this input to help plan future classes. If the teacher finds that most of the students are unable to complete the question, then the teacher will need to consider how to modify instruction to be more effective.

    Alternately, the One-Minute Paper question can ask older students to write about "The most important information that I learned and what I understood the least" or "What I learned from completing my homework assignment" or "What I enjoyed the most about the chapter reading." This approach allows the teacher to see not only how students understand the material but also if they are using vocabulary related to the content (University of Delaware, 2012).
- Try paraphrasing. Use this approach to quickly assess student understanding of new terms and concepts. During last few minutes of class, ask students to create their own definitions of concepts introduced or vocabulary words reviewed. Students submit their answers, and the teacher reviews to determine what terms students are having difficulty in understanding and what concepts may need to be retaught during the next class.
- Explore 50 CATS. This is an entire collection of techniques for quickly assessing knowledge and skills of older students. The CATS (Classroom Assessment Techniques), by Angelo and Cross, focuses on both the learning that is taking place in the classroom and how learning can be improved. For many examples, visit: **http://pages.uoregon.edu/tep/resources/newteach/fifty_cats.pdf**
- Employ Web-based tools. These tools provide immediate assessment data. Web sites such as ASSISTments are free online platforms where teachers can write and select questions. Students can receive feedback as well as tutoring. Teachers can receive immediate reports on students' learning (ASSISTments, 2012).

Teachers use a variety of other ways to answer questions about student learning and achievement in the general education classroom (Table 3.1). For example, teachers conduct conferences, read student journals, and provide opportunities for students to create portfolios or exhibitions of their work. Teachers develop quizzes and tests. Some of these assessments, such as short answer or essay tests, may ask students to compare, analyze, or synthesize

TABLE 3.1 • Examples of Classroom-Based Assessment Approaches

Assessment Questions	Assessment Approaches
Is my instruction effective? Are students making progress?	One-Minute Paper Checklists Curriculum-based assessment
Why is student having difficulty understanding mathematics?	Observation Error analysis Conference
Does the student meet grade-level expectations in reading?	Norm-referenced assessment Performance assessment Exhibitions
Has the student's behavior improved?	Interview Checklists Student journals

specific information. Other tests, such as multiple choice or matching, only require students to recognize the correct answer. In subsequent chapters, we'll examine these and other assessment approaches in more detail.

During response to intervention (RTI) tiered instruction, educators provide increasing levels of interventions while tracking student progress. Curriculum-based measurement, one of the most powerful assessment approaches, is closely aligned with the curriculum content taught. Perhaps you remember learning in Chapter 2 how curriculum-based measurement allows a teacher to pinpoint what students understand and where students are experiencing continuing difficulty.

For many students, we know that the RTI process can be successful and that after a period of intensive intervention, students can succeed. However, sometimes students continue to experience learning or behavior difficulties, even after intensive interventions. You'll remember from the previous chapter that when a student does not respond to an intervention, a teacher documents the interventions tried and how the student responded. When the student does not demonstrate progress, even after intensive interventions, the teacher completes the documentation and makes a referral for special education assessment.

Special Education Assessment Framework

A special education assessment framework, as illustrated in Figure 3.2, provides a way for us to think about assessment practices in general education and when students require special education services. The general education classroom depicts the assessment cycle that we discussed in the previous section. Some students may leave the general classroom to receive RTI services for a short period of time. When a student does not succeed even with intensive intervention, the student is referred for further assessment. Although the referral for special education assessment often comes as a result of RTI, sometimes a referral comes directly from parent or teacher concerns. When the referral is received, team members discuss the questions that teachers have about the student, what interventions have been tried, and what difficulties the student continues to experience. Team members often base further assessment on these identified questions.

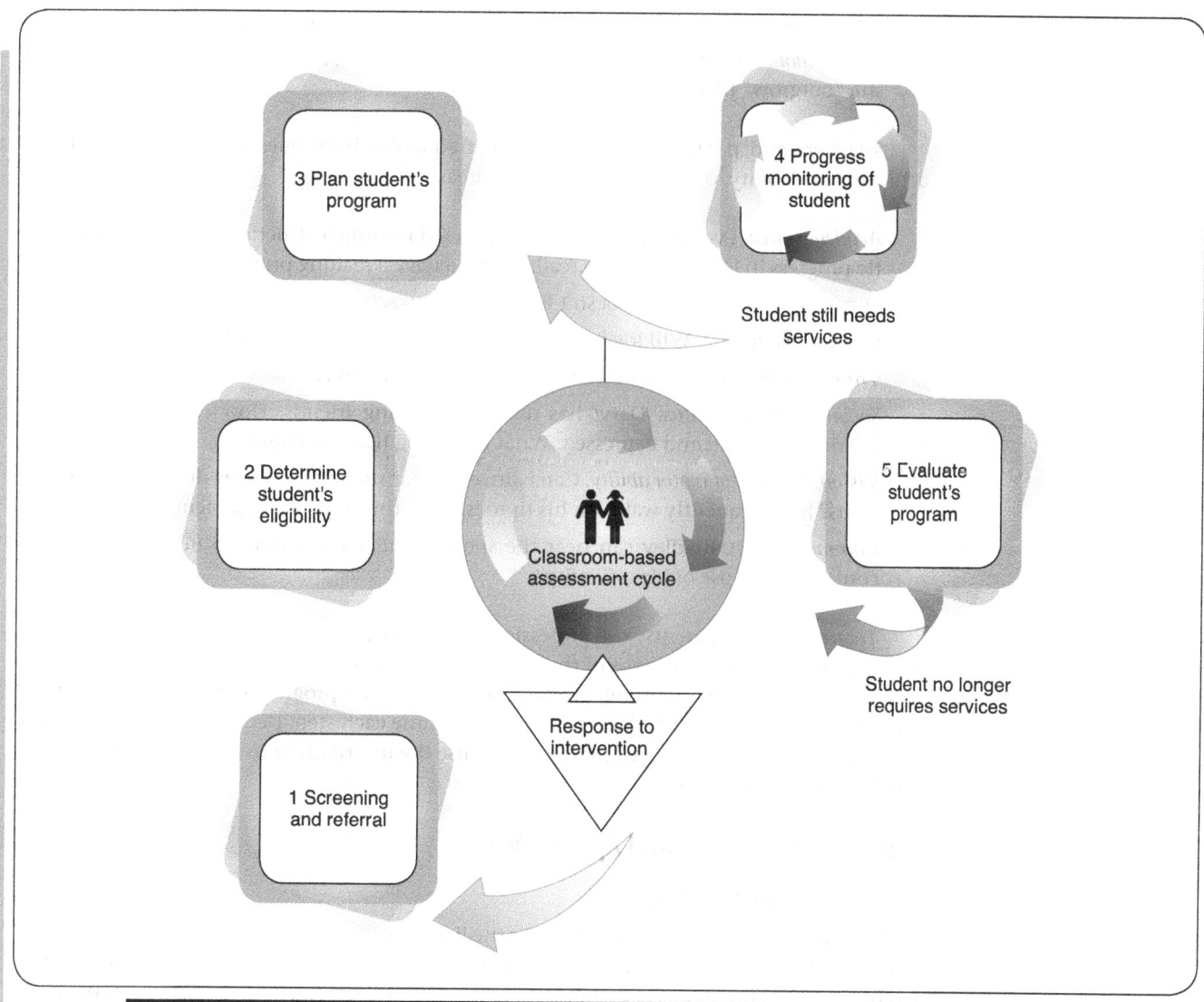

FIGURE 3.2 • Special Education Assessment Framework

Special Education: Assessment Questions, Purposes and Approaches

Assessment Questions

What types of questions do teachers and parents have?

Teachers of young children and parents wonder if the child is developing typically in one or more of the following developmental areas:

Communication development. Should Jaleh be talking more now that she is 4 years old?

Cognitive development. Is Katie experiencing difficulty performing many activities that the other children can do quite easily?

Physical development. Does Sammy have difficulty seeing? Hearing? Does he have problems with fine and gross motor activities?

Adaptive development. Should Luis be able to feed himself and take care of toileting needs?

Social-emotional development. Sonia has difficulty getting along with other children. Will she "outgrow" this?

Teachers and parents of older children frequently have questions about a student's achievement, ability, or skills in one or more areas:

Academic area. Even after participating in tiered reading instruction, Elliott has made little progress in learning how to read. Does he have a reading problem?

Overall achievement. Why doesn't Bill do better in school?

General intelligence. Will Joy be able to learn how to compute a math problem?

Transition. What transition service needs does Chris have?

Social-emotional status. Daryl has difficulty making friends. How can he be helped? Sabrina seems sad and depressed. What is causing this behavior?

Vision, hearing, or motor ability. Can Norweeta hear students speaking during class discussions? Joey frequently walks on his tiptoes. Does this indicate a problem?

Communication. Bradley can hear the speaker but doesn't seem to understand. What could be the cause of his difficulty?

Team members, parents, and professionals ask many questions and make decisions during each of the assessment steps in the process of universal screening and referral, determining eligibility, program planning, progress monitoring, and program evaluation. Let's follow the assessment framework in Figure 3.2 as we examine each step. Decision points, illustrated by each phase or step, allow team members to use the information to make decisions regarding the needs of the student.

Assessment Purposes and Approaches

Step 1. Screening and Referral

Children who are entering public school for the first time or transferring to a new school require screening. Several individuals, such as the special education teacher or general education teacher, speech and language pathologist, and a physical therapist or occupational therapist, typically conduct the screening, which involves various approaches. For children first entering school, the screening team may use a commercially published assessment instrument, for example, an instrument specifically designed to screen kindergarten children. Team members also may complete an informal observation of the child at play and a developmental checklist of specific skills, such as knowledge of colors, number concepts, and numeral identification.

For students who are transferring to a new school, an educator often begins by reviewing past work, school records, and test scores of the incoming student or by asking the new student and parents a set of questions. If the student has previously received special education services, the review includes information about a student's current individualized education program (IEP) from the sending school. In the classroom, teachers observe and collect information about the student's work and performance. Teachers may observe that the student is having trouble seeing a tablet screen, understanding and following directions, working with others, reading, comprehending, or calculating.

Sometimes a student is referred directly to the team by a health care provider, social worker, or school nurse for consideration. For example, a student who returns to school after receiving a traumatic brain injury in an accident has special needs concerning processing of information that require specialized instruction. Thus, some students may be referred directly because of newly identified disabilities and the adverse effect that the condition has on achievement in the general education classroom.

The purpose of **screening** is to determine whether students may have disabilities and to refer them for further assessment. Screening is designed to assess large numbers of students efficiently and economically. Universal screening as part of schoolwide intervention helps in identifying students who may benefit from more intensive interventions than those provided in the general education classroom. For example, classroom teachers administer a brief reading test or the school nurse arranges for students to have regular vision and hearing screenings. Based on the information collected during screening, evaluators decide whether or not to refer the student for tiered intervention or further assessment. In the following Snapshot, we follow Cory, an elementary school student who is experiencing some academic difficulties.

Teachers document their concerns in a written **referral**. For children entering school for the first time, the referral often comes from the screening process. For students already enrolled in school, teachers consult with the RTI team and then complete referrals for students who have a documented lack of progress even after receiving increasingly intensive levels of intervention through the RTI process (Figure 3.3). Parents utilize referrals, too. They may have concerns about their child when they see their child in relation to other children in the neighborhood or when they compare their child to their knowledge about growth and development.

REFERRAL DECISIONS   The IEP team receives the written referral form. Based on the referral information about the student, the team recommends specific assessment approaches or assessment instruments to be used in **determining eligibility** for special education services.

Step 2. Determine Student's Eligibility

To determine student eligibility for special education services, the assessment questions focus on the following questions: "Does the student have a disability? What disability does the student have? Is there an adverse effect on learning? Does the student meet the criteria for services?" The purpose of this step is to examine the assessment information to make a determination regarding the student's eligibility for special education and related services according to state and federal guidelines for children and youth as outlined in Individuals with Disabilities Education Improvement Act (IDEA) of 2004.

As specified in IDEA, a multidisciplinary team conducts assessment for the purposes of eligibility for special services. Thus, a student's assessment covers all areas related to the suspected disability, including, if appropriate, health, vision, hearing, social and emotional status, general intelligence, academic performance, communication, and motor abilities. For example, a student who is nonverbal may have a multidisciplinary evaluation that includes meeting with (1) an audiologist to determine the extent, if any, of a hearing loss; (2) a speech and language pathologist to assess understanding of language (receptive language) and communication skills; (3) a special educator to assess academic and functional skills; (4) a vocational rehabilitation counselor to identify interests and abilities; and (5) a psychologist to determine intellectual functioning. The team will use various approaches, including, for example, observations, commercial instruments, and performance assessments. The team will ask the student's parent(s) to provide information, too. Together these individuals view and analyze the assessment information, with all contributing expertise from their respective disciplines and perspectives.

Team members share the assessment information during the IEP meeting and determine the student's eligibility to receive special education and related services. As active members of the team, parents may have questions and collect various types of information, such as medical records or developmental history as well as behaviors observed in the home and community.

Because the team bases its decisions on assessment information and data analysis, they must choose and use appropriate assessment approaches carefully. Evaluators must have

SNAPSHOT

Cory

Cory is a fifth-grade student at Memorial School. Although he has never been referred for special education services, Cory has had some difficulty in past years. School has been in session only a few weeks this fall, and already his teacher, Joanne Leslie, has become increasingly concerned about his lack of academic progress and his difficulty in organizing his work. Cory is very distractible in class and has a short attention span. Because his reading, language arts, and math skills are weak, he has difficulty in keeping up with assignments.

From a meeting with last year's teacher, Ms. Leslie knew that Cory had participated in small-group intensive interventions for both reading and mathematics instruction. According to the fourth-grade teacher, his distractibility and short attention span continued to interfere with his achievement, and Cory showed little progress, despite the intensive interventions. Ms. Leslie examined the documentation of Cory's interventions and learned that the teacher felt that he should be referred for further assessment, but the parents wanted to wait to see if summer school could provide Cory with the extra help that he needed. Ms. Leslie also examined Cory's most recent achievement scores. Compared to other students in fifth grade, Cory's reading and math scores were low. After consulting with Cory's parents, who agreed with the concerns, she completed a referral form for special education services (see Figure 3.3).

Pause and consider:
- If you were Cory's teacher, what other information could you add to this referral?
- What questions might you ask Cory's parents?
- What questions would you ask Cory?

Memorial School
Referral Form

Student's name: Cory Young
Date of Birth: 9/17/xx
Grade: 5
Teacher: Ms. Leslie
Parent/guardian: Joseph Davis
Other parent/guardian: _____
Address: Harris Lane
Phone: 222-2222
Columbia

Person making referral/position: Joanne Leslie, Classroom Teacher
Person accepting referral/position: Crystal Kane, Special Education Administrator
Parent notification of referral: September 5, xxxx by phone (Joanne Leslie, classroom teacher)
Date of consent for evaluation received: September 10, xxxx

1. Described below are the reasons for the referral (attach separate page if necessary):
   Cory has a lot of difficulty organizing his work, and he is highly distractible. His reading and math skills are below grade level. His written work is weak—mechanics, storyline, and topic development below average.

2. Described below are the interventions that were implemented and the student's response to the intervention.
   Last spring Cory participated in intensive small-group instruction in corrective reading and in corrective mathematics. Cory began attending small-group instruction twice a week for one month. During that time, he made little progress. His schedule was changed to daily small-group instruction until the end of the school year. His distractibility and short attention span interfered with his achievement, and Cory showed little progress.
   During the summer Cory attended the 6-week summer school offered by the school district. He participated in daily small-group instruction in both reading and math. During this time, the records indicate that he made little progress.

3. Described below are other alternative strategies that were implemented and why they were not successful.
   Cory was assigned alternative seating, near the teacher; this placement seemed to agitate him.

4. Described below are the procedures, tests, records or reports that were used as part of the basis for this referral.
   Iowa Tests of Basic Skills: Reading 3.0, Language arts 2.8, Spelling 2.5, Mathematics 3.1. A portfolio of Cory's work is available for review.

5. Described below are any other factors that are relevant to this referral and/or other school personnel knowledgeable about this referral (principal, nurse, social worker, school counselor, Title I teacher, etc.)
   Cory wears glasses inconsistently. Cory's family is proud of their Native American heritage and speaks their native language in the home.

FIGURE 3.3 • Cory's Referral Form

appropriate training, take responsibility in evaluating the adequacy of the approach, follow professional standards and ethical principles, and be knowledgeable about the limitations of specific approaches. In the chapters that follow, we will discuss these approaches in more detail.

Step 3. Plan Student's Program

In **program planning**, the assessment questions focus on "What should be included in the student's IEP? If behavior impedes learning, what strategies, including positive behavioral interventions, should the team write in the plan? What supplemental aids, services, and assistive technology (AT) does the student need? What types of accommodations and/or modifications should team members make to the curriculum? Where should instruction begin? What supports for school personnel does the student need?" The purposes are to (1) determine the student's current level of functioning and (2) plan the instructional program. Much of the information gathered in Step 3 will be useful in planning the instruction and developing realistic goals.

WHAT SHOULD PROGRAM PLANNING INCLUDE? Program planning includes assessing the student's current level of functioning and determining where instruction should begin. Team members will also discuss the frequency and duration of specialized instruction. Members of the IEP team identify the special education and related services they will include in the student's program. They determine if the student needs one or more assistive technology devices to access the general education curriculum. The team plans accommodations and/or modifications to the curriculum and to the classroom environment. Team members utilize student observations, curriculum-based assessments, commercially published criterion-referenced tests, standardized tests, and checklists, as well as other assessment approaches.

CONNECTING ASSESSMENT WITH INSTRUCTION Connecting assessment with instruction is part of both program planning and Step 4, **individual progress monitoring**. Connecting assessment with instruction provides rich, ongoing information about a student's current level of achievement, which allows the teacher to make informed decisions regarding the student's instructional program. A teacher uses this type of assessment in planning daily teaching and learning activities to address the special needs of students. Connecting assessment with instruction is one of the most important aspects of the assessment process. In later chapters we will examine a variety of assessment approaches that link instruction with assessment.

Step 4. Progress Monitoring of Student

The purposes of this step are to determine (1) if the student is making progress and (2) whether to modify instruction if the student is not making progress. Teachers should assess the student's progress frequently. Information from this assessment step allows the IEP team members to modify interventions, teaching procedures, or materials if the student's progress is lagging.

Step 5. Evaluate Student's Program

Program evaluation is a process used to assess (1) the progress the student has made and (2) the overall quality of *the* school program. To evaluate the student's progress, the IEP team focuses on the student's IEP. They ask, "Is the student meeting the goals of the IEP?"

To address the overall evaluation of special education services, the questions focus on the achievement, as a group, that students accomplished in the program; the degree of satisfaction with the program as expressed by teachers, administrators, and parents; and the effectiveness of the program. The following subsections examine these two types of evaluation questions in more detail.

STUDENT EVALUATION This type of assessment helps evaluators make decisions about the success of the instructional program for individual students. The IEP team reviews the student's IEP *at least* annually to address any lack of expected progress, the results of any reevaluation, information about the student provided to or by the parents, or the student's anticipated needs (20 USC Sec. 614(d)). For children receiving services under an individualized family service plan (IFSP), family and evaluators must review the program every six months (or more frequently, if appropriate) and conduct the full evaluation annually.

IDEA requires a reevaluation of the student's performance and educational needs at least every three years, or more frequently if conditions warrant a reevaluation or if the child's parent or teacher requests a reevaluation. The team reviews existing assessment information, including (1) evaluations and information provided by the parent(s); (2) current classroom-based, local, or state assessments and classroom-based observations; and (3) observations by teachers and related services providers (20 USC 1414 Sec. 614(c)), and considers the following questions: "Does the student continue to need special education and related services? What is the student's present level of performance and educational need? Does the student need any additions or modifications to the special education and related services to meet the annual goals?" On the basis of the review, and with input from the student's parents, the team decides what additional information it needs and what assessment approaches to use.

PROGRAM EVALUATION   Program evaluation involves evaluating the overall services provided to groups of students or to programs, such as a school's special education services. Educators should examine the success of programs offered to students to replicate strong programs and to refine or change programs that are not effective. Evaluation questions include: "Is the program successful? Are goals being met? Do parents feel satisfied with the services?" Information is collected in a variety of ways, including aggregating assessment results of students who participate or have participated in the program; asking teachers, students, and parents to complete checklists or rating scales; interviewing current students in the program and their parents; or asking graduates of the school or program and their employers to complete questionnaires.

Responding to Diversity

Students and their families have diverse cultural, ethnic, racial, and linguistic backgrounds and come from different geographic regions of origin and from different gender, disability, and economic groups. They bring with them various perspectives, values, knowledge of native languages, and attitudes about the roles and responsibilities of the family, society, education, and professionals. The experiences, knowledge, and attitudes that students bring to the classroom can affect assessment practices and students' performance.

Sometimes perspectives and school expectations seem to work in opposing directions. For example, educational expectations of the classroom developed by members of the majority culture may tend to focus on the individual work of the student, whereas the educational expectations held by other families place importance on group affiliation rather than individual accomplishment. These diverse perspectives also may conflict with aspects of special education services and assessment practices in which assessment focuses on building student independence and individualizing intervention services.

To address these concerns, special educators must develop expertise in assessment. For example, assessing English-language learners takes special skills on the part of the educator conducting assessment. The teacher must consider the student's native or home language and proficiency in English. In selecting testing materials and procedures, the teacher must examine for appropriateness.

Bunch, Shaw, and Geaney (2010) examined performance-based assessments and language demands that fifth-grade English language learners encounter. They found that performance assessments may present barriers with regard to students' abilities to demonstrate their scientific knowledge and skills. However, these researchers also wondered if the language involved

> **TABLE 3.2** • Assessment Requirements for an English Language Learner Who Has a Disability or Is Suspected of Having a Disability
>
> **Planning the Assessment**
> What is the student's native or home language? Native language refers to the language normally used by the student or, in the case of a child, the language normally used by the parents of the child.
>
> **During the Assessment Procedure**
> Assessment materials or procedures are selected and administered in the child's native or home language or other mode of communication, unless it is clearly not feasible to do so. No single procedure should be the sole criterion for determining an appropriate educational program for a child. Standardized tests that the child takes must:
>
> (i) have been validated for the specific purpose for which they are used;
> (ii) be administered by trained and knowledgeable personnel; and
> (iii) be administered in accordance with any instructions provided by the producer of such tests.
>
> Materials and procedures used to assess a child with limited English proficiency are selected and administered to ensure that they measure the extent to which the child has a disability and needs special education, rather than measure the child's English language skills.
>
> **IEP Meeting**
> The IEP team must consider the language needs of the student as those needs relate to the child's IEP.
>
> The school must take whatever action is necessary to ensure that the parent understands the proceedings at the IEP meeting, including arranging for an interpreter for parents who are deaf or whose native or home language is other than English.
>
> *Source:* 20 USC Sec. 602; 612.

in performance assessments might present opportunities for students to demonstrate a wider variety of language skills compared to teacher-made tests and other assessments.

IDEA specifies assessment requirements to ensure that assessment procedures are fair for children who are English language learners (Table 3.2). Teachers and other professionals should be aware that translating a test into another language does not mean that its content,

Research-Based Practices: English Language Learners and Special Education

Identifying learning and other disabilities in English language learners is a complex and difficult task. Jennifer Samson and Nonie Lesaux (2009) wondered if more children who are English language learners are identified as needing special education services than children whose first language is English. They also were interested in examining classroom predictors of learners who receive special education services in the early elementary grades. Their findings indicated that for children in kindergarten and first grade who receive special education services, English language learners were underrepresented, but in third grade, these children were overrepresented in all disability categories. The most significant predictors of placement in special education were the child's language minority status, teacher readings of language and literacy skills, and reading proficiency level.

With over- and underreferral problems of students who are English language learners in schools today, many professionals feel that children are not being accurately identified. Research findings such as this and other studies provide evidence for the need for collaboration among bilingual education teachers, general education teachers, and speech and language pathologists (Linan-Thompson & Ortiz, 2009).

When children who are English language learners are referred to special education services, IEP team members must use only assessment tools that are validated for use with students who are English language learners. Other considerations for teachers include (1) assessing students in their first language as well as in English (if they speak English) and (2) becoming familiar with the cultural norms of students with whom they work (Shore & Sabatini, 2009).

difficulty, reliability, and validity are the same. A word in one language can have a different meaning, a different frequency of use, and a different difficulty level when translated into another language (American Educational Research Association, American Psychological Association, and National Council on Measurement in Education, 1999).

Universal Design and Assessment Practices

Universal design is a concept that helps educators think broadly about assessment practices and how we can effectively gather information concerning a broad range of knowledge and skills. According to IDEA and the Assistive Technology Act of 2004, "[t]he term 'universal design' means a concept or philosophy for designing and delivering products and services that are usable by people with the widest possible range of functional capabilities, which include products and services that are directly usable (without requiring assistive technologies) and products and services that are made usable with assistive technologies" (20 USC Sec. 602(35); 29 USC Sec. 3002). IDEA supports the use of the principles of universal design in developing and administering assessments and instruction. In developing assessments, such as classroom-based assessments, teachers would consider the flexibility of materials, the ways that students could demonstrate achievement, and the responses required of students. Web-based assessments, such as large-scale assessments that measure achievement in the Common Core areas of mathematics and English language arts are good examples of assessments that incorporate aspects of universal design. For example, when a student takes a Web-based exam, the student can choose the font size to view the test items or whether to read the text on the screen or listen to the text using text to speech. Table 3.3 illustrates other examples of universal design in assessment. At the U.S. Department of Education Web site, **http://www.osepideasthatwork.org/udl/assessment.asp**, you can learn more about additional ways to evaluate an assessment for universally designed test items.

Assessment of Assistive Technology Needs

Although using universal design principles in assessment and instruction will be effective for many students, some students have disabilities that require a more individualized approach to learning, accessing the general education curriculum, and demonstrating achievement. For a student with specific needs, an AT device can mitigate some of the challenges that the

TABLE 3.3 • Examples of Universal Design Components in Assessments

Visuals or graphics	Visuals are clearly defined and labeled. Contrast between colors is adequate.
Text	Text consists of commonly used words (except vocabulary being tested). Text vocabulary and complexity is appropriate for grade level.
Computer-based assessments	Navigation and response selection can be made by using a mouse click or keyboard. Student can return to test items.

Adapted from Thompson, S. J., Johnstone, C. J., Anderson, M. E., & Miller, N. A. (2005). *Considerations for the development and review of universally designed assessments* (Technical Report 42). Minneapolis, MN: University of Minnesota, National Center on Educational Outcomes. Retrieved December 22, 2013, from the World Wide Web: http://education.umn.edu/NCEO/OnlinePubs/Technical42.htm

disability presents. **Assistive technology** (AT) helps individuals with disabilities to learn, be independent, communicate, and lead productive lives. According to IDEA, a student can receive AT devices and services if specifically included in the IEP.

AT encompasses a wide range of low-tech to high-tech devices to assist students in instructional, learning, and assessment activities. On the one hand, computers and tablets, software, and apps provide easy-to-use features to obtain and use information; on the other hand, many inexpensive materials, often found in the school supply room, are waiting to be used. For example, graph paper helps a student with a learning disability keep proper place value during a math assessment. Another student uses a headset to keep distracting noises to a minimum. AT can improve students' learning, independence, self-esteem, functional life skills, communication, and quality of life (Scherer, Craddock, & Mackeogh, 2011).

Each time the IEP team meets, members consider whether or not a student needs AT to access the general education curriculum. Ideally, team members come prepared to discuss the student's performance and ways that AT can allow the student to participate more fully or more efficiently in classroom activities. Figure 3.4 illustrates a teacher-developed form that a special educator and other team members could complete to help the IEP team in this discussion.

An **assistive technology service** assists students with disabilities in selecting, acquiring, and using AT devices. AT services can include evaluation of AT needs; purchase or lease of AT devices; selection, design, and customization; coordination of other services and therapies with AT; training for students, family members, educators, and others in using AT; and the

---

Student's name: _Ann Lee Chase_

Grade: _3_

Background information: _Ann was diagnosed with cerebral palsy. She receives physical and occupational therapy once a week and consultation services from her special education teacher, who meets regularly with her classroom teacher._

Academic Area	Classroom Teacher Expectations	Student's Level of Performance	Low- to High-Tech AT Suggestions
Mathematics	Students complete mad minute work sheets daily.	Ann has difficulty stabilizing the worksheets and in managing her pencil to record answers in the small answer squares.	Use tape to help stabilize the worksheets Use a pencil grip Enlarge math sheet
Reading	Students progress individually through level reading books; teacher works with all students in small groups daily.	Ann has physical difficulty managing her book.	e-Book and digital copy of text
Science	Students conduct small-group research using the classroom computer.	Ann has difficulty using the computer keyboard, locating the correct key, and selecting it.	Large print, high-contrast stickers for keyboard Enlarged keyboard
Social studies	Students read 2 to 3 pages of their book independently.	Ann has physical difficulty managing her textbook and locating the correct pages.	e-Book and digital copy of text

FIGURE 3.4 • Classroom Expectations and Student Needs for Assistive Technology

> ## SNAPSHOT
> ### Rose Martinez
>
> Rose Martinez works at a high-performing K–8 elementary school in Arizona. Over 80 percent of the students are eligible for free/reduced price lunches, and students who are English language learners comprise 40 percent of the students. Despite these challenges, the teachers and administration are dedicated to helping all students reach high levels of achievement.
>
> Rose and other special educators, along with regular educators, belong to grade-level teams and meet regularly to ensure that all students are working toward meeting curriculum standards. The teachers hold themselves accountable to identify and address inadequate student performance. In-class instruction and intensive interventions are designed to meet the needs of individual students. When a student with a disability has difficulty accessing the general education curriculum despite classroom accommodations, the IEP team discusses the student's possible needs for AT devices and services. An AT assessment is conducted by several members of the team, who may then recommend specific AT for the student.
>
> **Pause and consider:**
> - With what types of AT devices are you familiar?
> - What examples of AT services can you identify?
> - What are the features of commonly used technologies that could support students in their learning (e.g., remembering, translating, speaking, communicating, text messaging)?
>
> Assessment is an ongoing process. Teachers use various methods of monitoring student performance in the classroom. For example, in the lower grades, students use individual white boards to write their responses and then hold up the boards to indicate their answers. This gives teachers the opportunity to immediately address student confusion. Older students use clickers, individual handheld devices, to register their responses to teacher questions. Dana, a student with cerebral palsy, uses a tablet to enter his answers. Student responses are visible on the data projector. The teacher uses the technology to help keep student attention, check for understanding, and modify instruction based on how students respond.

use of AT in students' homes if the IEP determines that AT is needed to receive the benefits of appropriate education.

Assessment of AT needs includes not only looking at specific devices but at services as well. Assessment should include gathering information about what services are needed, who will provide them, and when they will be provided. For example, identifying and obtaining the device or software also should include training on how to use the item. Not only will the student need to know how to use the device but, depending on the age of the student, others such as the student's teacher and parent also will need to know how the device works and how to charge the device, if needed. Because training is considered an AT service, this should be written into the student's IEP as well.

Approaches to Assistive Technology Assessment

Educators use different approaches to identify AT devices that will best assist a student. During the assessment process, team members identify why a student is having difficulty accessing the general education curriculum. They brainstorm technology ideas, obtain devices for the student to try, and then select the preferred device(s), software, and apps. Assessment of technology needs is really a continuous process, as a students' technology needs change over time, as school and educational demands increase, and as technology develops and proliferates.

In practice, let's follow one IEP team to learn how their school conducts AT assessments. This team is considering Ann Lee's annual IEP review. Ann Lee is a third-grade student who has cerebral palsy. Both her general education and special education teachers are concerned that she is having difficulty in both using the classroom materials and accessing science and social studies content. In preparation for the team meeting, the teachers worked together to complete the form that the school uses when discussing a student's need for AT services and devices (Figure 3.4).

The IEP plan includes both low-tech and high-tech devices, software, and apps. As the team gathers to discuss her evaluation, they review and discuss the suggestions. Ann's classroom teacher volunteers to try several of these ideas with Ann to see what the student prefers and which ones work best.

Pause and consider:
- As you examine this form (Figure 3.4), consider how the information would be helpful to you if you were Ann's special educator.
- What AT suggestions could you add to Ann Lee's plan?

Summary

- An assessment framework guides our understanding of assessment, a global term for observing, gathering, recording, and interpreting information to answer questions and make instructional and legal decisions about students.
- Educators use assessment to guide classroom instruction and to measure student progress, to determine student strengths and areas of weakness, and to identify progress and achievements.
- When a student is referred to the team because of a possible disability, the student progresses through an assessment process to determine eligibility, plan, monitor progress, and evaluate the special education services.
- During the assessment process, team members seek to answer questions about the student using various assessment approaches.
- For students who are English language learners, team members must develop special competencies in assessment practices.
- Special educators assess student needs for AT and thus assist the IEP team in identifying and evaluating appropriate devices and services for students with disabilities.

QUESTIONS FOR REFLECTION

1. If you were a member of Cory's IEP team (see Cory's Snapshot), what additional information would you want to know?
2. Make a list of various assessment approaches that you have experienced. Which approaches were the most effective for you? Why?
3. In preparing to administer assessments, which steps do you think might take the most preparation? What additional considerations might be important?
4. After reviewing the definition of universal design in this chapter, brainstorm with a small group of peers regarding your own experiences. Identify a list of examples that you feel illustrate the principles of universal design.
5. Interview a special educator to learn how technology is used with students with disabilities. Share your findings with your peers.

REFERENCES

American Educational Research Association, American Psychological Association, and National Council on Measurement in Education. (1999). *Standards for educational and psychological testing.* Washington, DC: American Educational Research Association.

ASSISTments. (2012). Formative assessments that assist. Retrieved from assistments.org/

Bunch, G. C., Shaw, J. M., & Geaney, E. R. (2010). Documenting the language demands of mainstream content-area assessment for English learns: Participant structures, communicative modes and genre in science performance assessments. *Language & Education: An International Journal, 24*(3), 185–214.

Individuals with Disabilities Education Improvement Act (Pub. L. No. 108-446). (2004). 20 USC- Secs. 1400 et. seq. Washington, DC: U.S. Government Printing Office.

Linan-Thompson, S., & Ortiz, A. A. (2009). Response to intervention and English-language learners: Instructional and assessment considerations. *Seminars in Speech & Language, 30*(2), 105–120.

National Council of Teachers of Mathematics. (2012). Testing. Retrieved from nctm.org/resources/content.aspx?id=6332

Samson, J. F., & Lesaux, N. K. (2009). Language-minority learners in special education: Rates and predictors of identification for services. *Journal of Learning Disabilities, 42*(2), 148–162.

Scherer, M. J., Craddock, G., & Mackeogh, T. (2011). The relationship of personal factors and subjective well-being to the use of assistive technology devices. *Disability & Rehabilitation, 33*(10), 811–817. doi:10.3109/09638288.2010.511418

Shore, J. R., & Sabatini, J. (2009). *English langauge leaners with reading disabilities: A review of the literature and the foundation for a research agenda.* ETS RR-09-20 Princeton, NJ: Educational Testing Service.

Thompson, S. J., Johnstone, C. J., Anderson, M. E., & Miller, N. A. (2005). *Considerations for the development and review of universally designed assessments* (Technical Report 42). Minneapolis, MN: University of Minnesota, National Center on Educational Outcomes. Retrieved December 22, 2012, from the World Wide Web: http://education.umn.edu/NCEO/OnlinePubs/Technical42.htm

University of Delaware. (2012). Classroom assessment. Retrieved from cte.udel.edu/instructional-topics/classroom-assessment.html

4 Involving Families

Chapter Objectives

After completing this chapter, you should be able to:

- Define the term *family* and describe areas that are important to consider in working with families.
- Identify the important issues in being responsive to family diversity.
- Describe the role of families in the assessment process as outlined by federal law.
- Use techniques for listening to and understanding parents.
- Discuss important components of conferencing with parents.

Overview

Educators work closely with family members in identifying student strengths and needs, planning the education program, and assessing progress. Within each family, adult members may have similar or very different priorities for their children. They may wish to be involved in their child's program in a variety of ways. Family members are often at different points in their understanding and acceptance of their child's disability. For example, one parent wants to assist the team by sharing medical reports and discussing the child's diagnosis; another parent looks to team members for help and explanations. In working with families, you will need to identify the extent to which families wish to be involved in their child's assessment process and in the development of the individualized program as well as the preferred methods of home and school communication.

Working with diverse family groups involves many skills: listening carefully, understanding and being responsive to various perspectives, sharing meaningful information, and planning together to develop an appropriate education program. Each family unit is unique. The uniqueness of families includes diverse aspects such as culture, disability, economic level, ethnicity, family structure, gender, geographic region of origin, language, and race. Professionals who work with families must be sensitive and responsive to all elements of diversity. This chapter will give you a foundation in these skills.

Understanding More About Families

Our definition of the term **family** continues to undergo changes. Today, the term reflects our understanding of the increasing diversity of family patterns and structures. Although there continues to be much debate regarding the definition, many agree that a family consists of two or more individuals who may or may not be related but who have extended commitments to each other.

Although families can include many or only a few members, each family unit is affected by four major factors (Erwin, Shogren, Soodak, Turnbull, & Turnbull, 2011). The first component, a family's interaction system, is the center of the model and involves the interactions of individual family members on a daily and weekly basis. These can include adult and adult; parent and child; child and child; and extended family, friends, neighbors, and professionals.

The second component, family functions, includes financial considerations, recreation, and educational or vocational choices. Certain functions are more important to some families than to other families because of personal desires or cultural traditions. For example, some families feel that they should eat at least one meal a day together; other families may not view this activity as essential.

The third component, family characteristics, includes the individual characteristics of family members and the uniqueness of the family unit, as well. For example, the number of family members, their cultural background(s), and their economic level all affect family distinctiveness. A child's disability, including any special challenges the child's disability presents, affects the family, too.

Finally, families, like individuals, have life cycles. Progressing through a lifetime, an individual experiences a series of transitions. Similarly, all families go through periods of transition as the family unit's needs and interests change. For example, a young family's immediate needs may be finding a job and a place to live. The family may be coping with concerns that are interrelated problems, including poverty, illiteracy, and lack of job skills. Young children can make physical and emotional demands, just when parents would rather spend time finding friends for themselves or perhaps someone to assist with child care. Often families of children with disabilities have difficulty finding reliable child care and may experience social isolation as well.

As children grow older, the role of parents shifts. Families in this stage become more involved in their children's schooling and planning for their future. Families of various backgrounds approach these changing roles differently. Family traditions may lead to tensions as parents develop an understanding of their own parenting roles. As children move into adulthood, families will experience other challenges and needs, such as accepting decisions of adult children and encouraging them in their chosen vocations.

For families that include a child with a disability, there will be additional considerations at each of these stages. Families with a young child with special needs frequently must adjust a dream about their child's future. The child they envisioned running and skipping may never walk, hear, or speak. Grandparents who had looked forward to the birth of a grandchild may also need help in their acceptance of the infant with special needs. Later on, families with a teenager find that they have to arrange for continued supervised child care. They will need to find time to attend team meetings at school and to meet with their child's teacher. Eventually, families with a young adult must make decisions regarding independent housing and moving from the familiar education system to a new service system. Rehabilitative services, which often have different criteria for eligibility, will replace educational services. Eventually, families need information about guardianship, estate planning, and wills.

In many ways, the basic life cycle experience is common, but the family unit that includes a child with special needs faces additional demands. Furthermore, different expectations for the child and different concerns during the family life cycle frame different perspectives for families who have recently moved to this country, who come from poverty, who speak a home language different from the majority group, or who represent a nondominant group.

> **Research-Based Practices** **Parent Involvement in and Perception of Special Education Services**
>
> Because parents are considered equal team members by the school in providing information about their children, participating in educational decision making, and developing their children's individualized education programs (IEPs), some researchers have wondered about parents' perception of their involvement. One researcher (Lo, 2008) investigated the experiences of Chinese American families and IEP teams. Out of 15 parents who reported on their team meetings, she found that 12 parents were dissatisfied and had minimal participation. Parents reported several reasons for lack of participation, including a language barrier, poor interpretation services, and disrespect by professionals. Each of these reasons is most unfortunate for both parents and educators who hope to build collaborative home–school partnerships and positive learning experiences for students.

Responding to Diversity

Educators, other school personnel, and service providers who work with families and children with disabilities begin by developing an understanding of the family. These professionals know that assumptions by members of the dominant group may not be appropriate or relevant to members of less-dominant groups. For example, in the early grades, educators work toward early identification of children who experience difficulties in learning and connect them with early intervening services to address and remediate these difficulties. Most parents are willing to have their child receive intervention and additional instruction. For some families, though, these special services may not be so readily received. Difficulties in learning, in some traditional cultures, are attributed to laziness or lack of adequate parenting or may be viewed as an unwanted reflection on the family and their ancestors. Thus, some families are reluctant to discuss their child's problems and feel shame in acknowledging the presence of learning and behavioral difficulties. Parents who are culturally and linguistically diverse may understand their child's disability from a non-Western perspective. For example, some parents view autism spectrum disorder not from a deficit point of view but rather as a different state of being (Tincani, Travers, & Boutot, 2009). Educators often work with members of the family's community, such as a community club or a religious group, to help parents feel part of the team.

Cultural heritages, values, and beliefs also may dramatically affect the family's perception of and participation in the assessment process (Artiles & Bal, 2008; Mandell et al., 2009), development of the intervention, and plans for the future. Other aspects of diversity may affect a family's cooperation. One group of researchers (Tincani et al., 2009) was interested in how culture and linguistic diversity affects identification of students with autism spectrum disorder. After an extensive review of the research, these researchers recommend that assessment should be strength based and should include the student's preferences and skills as well as critical features of the family system. Table 4.1 summarizes the important considerations when interacting with families and developing sensitivity to diversity. To learn more about some of these considerations described, visit the National Center for Cultural Competence at http://nccc.georgetown.edu/

Aspirations

A family's hopes for their child may range from appropriate to elevated or depressed expectations. Family aspirations have an impact on the levels of involvement that families choose: from making the referral for assessment, to participating in the assessment process, to helping

TABLE 4.1 • Considerations in Responding to Family Diversity	
Area of Consideration	**Issues in Being Responsive to Diversity**
Aspirations	A family's hopes for the child may range from appropriate aspirations to elevated or depressed expectations.
	Family aspirations affect the level of involvement families choose in making the referral, in participating in the assessment process, and in helping to develop a plan of services. Family aspirations are influenced by culture, economic level, gender, or geographic regional expectations.
Assistance	Family members may actively seek help, or they may view needs and concerns as private matters. Family views are influenced by one or more aspects of diversity.
Authority of the school	Some families wish to participate in parent–professional partnerships. Families from some cultural communities naturally defer to authority.
Child rearing	Families approach child rearing from various perspectives, including independence, communication, and physical contact.
Communication	Some families use an assertive style in their verbal communication that assists them in referring their child and in entering the service system. Other families naturally defer to authority figures and do not pursue issues.
	Some families use nonverbal communication, including eye gaze and gestures, to communicate important wants or needs.
	Communicating takes on a special significance for some groups. Finishing a conversation is more important than being on time.
	Communication that involves technology may be a barrier for some families.
Disability	A disability may be viewed as shameful, or the person with a disability may be viewed as having a second-class status.
	A disability can present social or physical barriers. These barriers may be perceived, or they may be actual barriers of access.
	Issues of acceptance involve one or more of the following groups: parents, extended family, or community.
Family structure	The child's family may consist of a single parent, a grandparent(s), two mothers, or two fathers.
Legal status	Families may lack knowledge of their rights.
	Families with illegal status often fear government authorities or school officials.
Literacy and language	Family members may not have literacy skills in their own language or in English.
	Information and materials are seldom available in the family's native language.
	Translators may not be available.
	Standardized instruments often lack a representative norming sample.
	Examiners may not be familiar with aspects of diversity.
Medical practices	Medical practices differ and can cause misinterpretation between families and school personnel.
Meetings and support groups	The format of group discussions can cause difficulty for families of some communities.
Parental roles	In many cultures, the person who makes the decisions is the principal male family member.
Transient status	Families that are homeless or move frequently have difficulty entering the service system.

develop a plan for services. Certain cultural or regional expectations can also influence family aspirations. For example, residents in some regions place a high value on family and community. A family from this region may hope that, after completing school, their child will join the family business.

Assistance

The family may actively seek help from others, or the family may view its needs and problems as private matters to be addressed only within the family. For example, families in some areas place a high value on personal independence and self-sufficiency. They may be reluctant to ask for additional assistance or be ashamed to request help.

Authority of the School

Cultural beliefs, such as feelings about school authority in decision making (Erwin et al., 2011) or respect for authority (Chen, 2011), often affect the level and type of involvement family members choose. Some families have difficulty with the joint decision-making process of parents and professionals working together. They consider professionals as authority figures to be respected and obeyed. Such family members may try to avoid confrontation in discussions, or they may reject school authority altogether.

Child Rearing

Families approach child rearing from various perspectives, too. In some families, there is much close physical contact between mother and child, and communication is characterized more by touch than by vocal stimulation. Other families spend much time talking and singing to their children. Some families do not encourage their children to participate in gross motor activities because of safety concerns. Other families of young children promote independent exploration and travel.

Communication

Communication involves active listening and responding to both verbal and nonverbal communication. Being sensitive and responsive to family diversity includes appreciating that family groups may have unique communication patterns. For example, some regional and cultural groups support and value assertiveness in making needs and wishes known to others; some groups view assertiveness as rude and avoidable.

Communication styles can help or hinder family members' efforts to seek services. For example, to receive services, family members have to make an initial referral, make follow-up phone calls, complete paperwork, and deal with a service system with various requirements and eligibility procedures. The variety of communication and interpersonal skills needed to negotiate the service system can create barriers for some families in obtaining services.

Some family groups have unique nonverbal communication patterns—for example, avoiding eye contact with elders to signify respect. The art of communication may take on a special significance to some groups. For instance, a focus on relationships rather than on tasks can mean it is more important to continue a conversation with a friend than it is to be on time for an appointment to discuss a child's assessment.

Disability

Perceptions of disability encompass a range of emotions for family members: embarrassment and shame, guilt and blame, grief and acceptance. Some groups may view a person with a disability as having lower status or as a significant being. Family members may believe that there are social or physical barriers because their child has a visible disability. Parents may lack knowledge about their child's disability and have difficulty in locating information to develop realistic expectations. Various issues relating to the acceptance of the disability involve the parents, the extended family, and the community. The extended family's perceptions and the cultural community's acceptance of the disability often influence and impact the immediate family.

Family Structure

Various family structures contribute to the rich diversity of the classroom. Some children may live with a grandparent or other close relative. Other children may have gay or lesbian parents or come from a family with a single parent. When the school community values and accepts a choice of family structures, children learn tolerance and understanding.

Legal Status

Families may lack knowledge of their rights regarding services for their children. Parents who have an illegal status commonly fear government and school officials and are reluctant to have their children assessed.

Literacy and Language

Some family members may not have the ability to speak, read, or write English. Other family members may have poor literacy skills in their native language. Even families who have strong literacy skills may be limited by the availability of materials in their native languages or dialects. Identifying translators and their availability is critical for families so that they can participate in the assessment process. The challenge of translating exact meanings between languages is often difficult. For families who speak a dialect different from the translator's, this challenge sometimes becomes a barrier.

When family members participate in the assessment process, they find that few standardized assessment instruments are written in languages other than English. This may be true of a parent questionnaire as part of a screening or a parent form of a behavior rating scale. In addition, many standardized instruments do not include representative samples from cultural, racial, ethnic, and linguistic groups. To compound the problem, examiners can lack familiarity with family diversity.

Meetings and Support Groups

Support groups are often helpful for family members who would like assistance. A group may be as informal as a listserv, blog, chat, or other technology resource. The majority of today's parents have searched for both information and support on the Internet.

Other parents prefer local or regional meetings, although the group discussion format may be difficult for some parents. Approaches that are beneficial for support groups (Chen, 2011) include the development of culturally competent group facilitators (who have a familiarity with the family's ethnic history and culture), the involvement of community leaders, outreach using conationals (individuals from the same country of origin), and repeated personal contact. These ethnic networks can help the family with the resources and procedures, for example, in the education of their child with a disability. For single heads of households, ethnic networks can substitute for the familial or community network that existed in their country of origin.

Parental Roles

In many cultures, the person who makes the decisions is the principal male family member. This could be the father, grandfather, uncle, or brother-in-law. Although the mother or other female family representative might attend all meetings regarding the child, she may refuse to make any decisions or sign any papers. The male figure may never attend any of the meetings, yet the decisions are his to make. This decision-making process can be frustrating to the team; however, if the team has knowledge of the parental roles beforehand, additional attempts can be made to accommodate the male family member's schedule.

Transient Status

Understanding and being responsive to diversity is a complex process that involves working with various perspectives that family members hold, including families who are transient, such as migrant workers and other workers who frequently travel for their jobs. Some families move frequently from one residence to another, and some can be homeless for periods of time. In these cases, even locating children and providing continuing services is important. The skills involved require educators to be thoughtful and reflective in practice. You must exercise care and not promote or reinforce stereotypes by making generalities about cultural background, ethnicity, language, or economic level, for example. A key point to remember when interacting with families is to *ask*. Asking families to determine preferences and needs avoids stereotypical assumptions as well as careless regard for family heritage.

Federal Legislation and the Role of Parents

Federal legislation that regulates the provision of services to children and youth with disabilities emphasizes the importance of families. One of the most important aspects of this legislation is the defining of parent and guardian rights. Individuals with Disabilities Education Improvement Act (IDEA) of 2004 describes these rights under the broad term *due process*. Due process refers to the legal safeguards professionals must follow during the assessment process and the delivery of services. These safeguards protect the rights of families and their children.

Guaranteed Rights

School personnel must notify the child's parent(s) or guardian of any assessment procedure (*right of notice*) and provide consent (*right of consent*) for the assessment of their child. Before the assessment process begins, school personnel must send the parents a written form that describes the types of assessments to be conducted. The parent provides consent by signing and returning the form. However, the parent can revoke consent at any time during the assessment process by notifying the school. The parent can request that a full assessment of all areas associated with the disability be completed. This assessment must include multiple measures and must be conducted by a multidisciplinary team (*right of evaluation*). Parents may request a reevaluation or obtain an independent evaluation if there are any questions or concerns regarding the evaluation (*right to an independent evaluation*). Table 4.2 describes these and other important rights.

The Assessment Process for Families of Young Children

In this section, we will examine some of the questions and decisions that parents make concerning the assessment of young children. Early childhood teachers and other professionals who work with families of young children provide services within the context of **family-centered practices**. Family-centered practices require that teachers and therapists attempt to create opportunities for families to acquire the knowledge and skills necessary to strengthen family functioning. Thus, families are not merely recipients of services but rather active participants in the assessment, implementation, and evaluation of special services. Parents of

TABLE 4.2 • Rights of Parents and Guardians According to IDEA

Right of Parents and Guardians	Definition
Beginning the Assessment Process	
Right of notice	The parent must receive a notification of the proposed assessment in the family's native language or principal mode of communication.
Right of consent	The parent must give consent before the child is assessed to determine eligibility for special education services.
Right of evaluation	The assessment must include multiple measures and be conducted by a multidisciplinary team.
Right to an independent evaluation	The parent has a right to request an evaluation by an independent evaluator if there are questions or concerns regarding the child's evaluation conducted by school personnel.
Using the Assessment Information	
Right of participation	The parent must be invited to participate in the writing of the child's educational plan (or an individualized family service plan [IFSP] or an individualized educational program [IEP]).
Right of notice	The parent must receive a notification of the proposed changes in the education program, which must be in the family's native language or principal mode of communication.
Right of access	The parent must be allowed access to all educational records.
Right to confidentiality	The educational records are confidential. The parent must give consent to have the child's records released to other institutions or agencies. The parent has the right to refuse disclosure of information contained in the records to other professionals or agencies.
Right to a hearing	The parent has the right to a hearing with an impartial hearing officer. The parent has a right to present evidence and to cross-examine school staff.
Right to mediation	The parent has the right to a process, called mediation, that attempts to resolve differences with school personnel before going to a hearing.
Right to resolve differences	If the parent is not satisfied with the decision of the hearing officer, a second step, the right to appeal to the state court system, can be implemented.

young children frequently have questions about their children's development and the ability to do well in school. Some parents have questions about their children's behavior.

Initial Questions and Decisions

During the early years of a child's growth, parents and other family members may develop concerns about their child's development. In fact, parents are often the first to question or observe areas of difficulty for their child, such as happened in the Snapshot of Juan and his family. Parents sometimes share their concerns with someone close to their child, often a teacher or child care provider.

Teachers and child care personnel should listen to parents and encourage discussions about their children. They should inform parents about neighborhood screening activities and encourage them to have their children screened periodically. Assisting parents and other adults to become aware of screenings, programs, and services for children with special needs is called **Child Find**.

Preschool teachers, public health nurses, social workers, and doctors are some of the professionals involved with Child Find. Personnel from state agencies who work with children and families conduct a variety of Child Find activities throughout the year. For example, radio and television announcements, e-Newsletters, or newspaper articles describe community screenings and dates when screenings will be held. Brochures distributed in public places explain ways to observe a young child's development and list common questions that arise for parents. These materials also contain information about community screenings. Families with questions about their children may decide to take advantage of these free screenings, or families may decide to discuss their concerns with a primary medical provider.

Screening Questions and Decisions for Families

Parents can share their observations and concerns during screening. A social worker, nurse practitioner, or educator usually meets with the parent(s) to discuss his or her questions and concerns and to record information about the child's development. The assessment question is: Does this child have a problem that requires further assessment? Parents usually complete a checklist or parent report form concerning various milestones in their child's development. Many standardized screening tools provide a parent report form as an integral part of the screening profile. You can read more about these instruments in Chapter 17.

If there are concerns after collecting information about the child, the screening team forwards the results to a team of professionals known as the early childhood team or the IEP team. The **early childhood team** consists of the parents, the family service coordinator, and representatives of various disciplines who assess, design, implement, monitor, and evaluate early intervention services. The team makes decisions regarding eligibility and services for children from birth through age 2 and, in some states, for children ages 3 to 5 or children ages 3 to 9. This team invites the child's parent(s) to participate, and together, they decide what additional assessment information is necessary. Once the assessment information is complete, the team meets to determine if the child is eligible for special education services.

SNAPSHOT
Juan

Juan was born 3½ months premature and is now 4 years old. He lives at home with his father, grandmother, and two younger brothers. Every day his grandmother takes him for a ride in his red wagon when she goes down to the corner store. He enjoys watching the activities at a construction site along the way. His grandmother and his father have some concerns about Juan's development. He was slow to walk and talk, and his speech is still difficult to understand. He prefers to play alone or to watch cartoons on television.

His grandmother shared her concerns with a neighbor who works at the community child care center. The staff at the center had recently completed an in-service workshop on child development. The neighbor listened sympathetically and then suggested that the grandmother could take Juan to the child center for a free community screening on the first Monday of the month.

The Assessment Process for Families of Children and Youth

Addressing Parent Questions and Concerns

Once children begin school, parents may share their concerns with their child's teacher. Depending on the particular problem, they may decide to involve other school professionals or family members. For example, Mrs. Balinsky is worried about her daughter's grades. She remembers with pride how Alexandra put a puzzle together when she was only 2 years old. Later, in elementary school, she always brought home report cards with As. But now, in ninth grade, Alexandra seems to have lost interest in schoolwork and good grades. She is barely passing English language arts and mathematics this first marking period. Why could there be such a change in Alexandra? Mrs. Balinsky decides to contact the school with her questions and concerns.

After Mrs. Balinsky shares her concerns with the homeroom teacher, they decide to involve the school counselor as well as Alexandra's other teachers. Using a problem-solving approach, they plan one or more interventions. During the implementation of the intervention(s), the teacher or, when appropriate, the parent carefully records its effectiveness. If the first intervention is not successful, the team will identify and implement additional interventions and record the results.

During the child's school career, teachers will contact parents regarding their concerns or parents can contact school personnel with their questions, as Alexandra's mother did. Teachers should encourage parents to discuss any questions or concerns that they have throughout the school year. Teachers can assist parents by asking informal questions such as "What would be helpful for me to know about Alexandra?" or leading questions such as "Tell me what Alexandra likes to do at home."

Referral and Decisions for the Team

In Chapter 2, we discussed the various tiers of intervention provided to students prior to referral for special education services. When questions about a student persist, the team completes a written referral form and forwards the referral to the coordinator of the special services team. This team consists of the student's parents, school personnel, and the student, when possible. The team may be known as the IEP team or child study team.

The special services team receives the formal referral delineating the type of interventions and the outcomes. The special services team makes decisions regarding assessment procedures and develops an assessment plan. This plan describes questions the team is trying to answer about the student's special needs, the tests and procedures the team will use, and the individuals who will complete the assessments. The parent or guardian must sign a written permission before the assessment process begins. As team members, parents contribute information to this process. They may provide copies of medical records and/or educational reports. Parents frequently add observations of the student at home and in the community. They also assist the team in gathering information by using informal tools such as checklists, rating scales, or video recordings.

Questions and Decisions in Determining Eligibility

In this step of the assessment process, the team addresses the following question: Does the student meet the criteria for a disability? Does the disability have an **adverse effect** on educational performance? Does the student need specially designed instruction to learn and to develop? These are the questions that parents and other team members must answer.

The IEP team plans an individual assessment to determine if the child has a disability and to determine what the educational needs of the child are. The child is assessed in all areas related to the suspected disability including, if appropriate,

- Health
- Vision
- Hearing
- Social and emotional status
- General intelligence
- Academic performance
- Communication
- Motor abilities

The information collected during the assessment process determines the decisions regarding eligibility for special education services. Parents provide helpful information and a unique perspective. Parents can provide information informally through discussions or contribute information on a standardized instrument. There are numerous instruments that solicit parent information as part of the profile. Throughout this text, you'll find examples of how parents provide valuable information to the assessment process.

SNAPSHOT

Jimmy's Mother

Jimmy's mother contacted his teacher at Bennington Elementary School to discuss her concerns about her son. Ten-year-old Jimmy seems to struggle with completing his homework, she explained. After supper, he looks forward to watching his favorite television program before beginning his assignments. After the program finishes, Jimmy sits down to work on the couch; yet his mother has noticed that he gets up frequently and wanders around the house to find an assignment, a pencil, or a book. He becomes distracted easily and often forgets what he has set out to find. He rarely finishes his work before bedtime. After listening to these concerns, Jimmy's teacher, Jon Parker, explained that he, too, had become increasingly concerned about Jimmy's work in class.

Pause and consider:

- If you were the special educator on this team, what other strategies could you suggest?
- Jimmy's mother is anxious to collaborate with school personnel, but other parents may not be able to do so. What might be some reasons?

After listening to the parent's concerns, Jon discussed the school's **Student Assistance Team (SAT)** and explained that the team met on a regular basis to provide assistance to students and teachers. Jimmy's mother expressed an interest in attending the team meeting.

Within a couple of weeks, arrangements were made for Jimmy's mother to attend. At the meeting, Jimmy's mother and teacher shared their concerns. The team worked to devise an intervention plan for Jimmy. Some examples of strategies that they discussed included teaching Jimmy a self-monitoring strategy when doing his homework and creating a list of incentives. Figure 4.1 shows an example of one of the materials, a parent–student monitoring sheet that Jimmy, his teacher, and his mother developed.

As a result of their discussions, Jimmy's mother agreed to let him work at the kitchen table because other family members usually watch television or use the family computer in the living room each evening. She agreed to remind him of the time they have set for evening homework. Jimmy's teacher suggested she can assist Jimmy in organizing his materials. The SAT agreed that she would help him decide where to keep school supplies such as pencils, highlighters, and paper. During the homework hour, Jimmy agreed to record his progress on the monitoring sheet. If he receives six checks out of a possible seven areas, he can choose a previously agreed-upon reward.

Perhaps for Jimmy, these interventions will address the problem, and the assessment process will end. However, when **assistance team** members think that a student requires more extensive remediation, they provide a formal referral to the special services team.

Jimmy's Daily Homework Check

September 13

Six checks for extra hour of TV

	Parent checks	Comments
Quiet area for homework	_____	
Study hour starts at 7:30 P.M.	_____	
School supplies available	_____	

	Jimmy checks	Comments
Working on homework 1 to 15 minutes	_____	
Working on homework 16 to 30 minutes	_____	
Working on homework 31 to 45 minutes	_____	
Working on homework 46 to 60 minutes	_____	

FIGURE 4.1 • Parent–Student Monitoring Sheet

Questions and Decisions in Planning Services

If the team decides that the student is eligible for special services, the next step involves questions and decisions regarding the student's program and writing the IEP. One of the rights of parents is to participate with other team members in planning the special education services that their child will receive. During the IEP meeting, the team addresses several questions: What types of special education services does the student need? Where should the student receive the services? How should planners coordinate and evaluate the services?

Team members may decide to place the student in the general education classroom with the special education teacher providing consultation services. On the other hand, some parents may question whether their child will receive as much support in the regular classroom as in the resource room. Parents and other team members will need to discuss these difficult questions and make decisions based on the assessment process. In addition to planning special education services, the team will make decisions about the types of related services that will be provided, as illustrated in Table 4.3.

Questions and Decisions in Monitoring Services

Once the plan is in place, communication between home and school is very important in monitoring services. The assessment questions during this step include the following: Is the student making progress? Does the program need to be modified? Teachers and parents monitor student progress by observing the student's work and behavior or by completing informal assessments. For example, parents, as well as the student's teachers, can use a logbook to

---

TABLE 4.3 • Related Services for Children and Youth Under IDEA 2004

- Transportation.
- Speech-language pathology.
- Audiology services.
- Interpreting services.
- Psychological services.
- Physical therapy.
- Occupational therapy.
- Recreation, including therapeutic recreation.
- Social work services.
- School nurse services designed to enable a child with a disability to receive a free appropriate public education as described in the individualized education program of the child.
- Counseling services, including rehabilitation counseling.
- Orientation and mobility services.
- Medical services (except that such medical services shall be for diagnostic and evaluation purposes only) as may be required to assist a child with a disability to benefit from special education, and including the early identification and assessment of disabling conditions in children.
- Exception: Related services do not include a medical device that is surgically implanted, or the replacement of such device.

Source: P.L. 108-446, 20 USC 1401, Sec. 602 (26).

> October 5 Jenny had an appointment with the doctor this afternoon. The doctor told us that she wants to change the dosage of her medication. This morning Jenny began the increased amount. The doctor said it may take her a few days to adjust.
>
> Mrs. Williams

FIGURE 4.2 • Entry From a Traveling Logbook

enter comments about daily or weekly progress. Figure 4.2 illustrates information provided by the parent. These informal tools that parents utilize are helpful to the team in monitoring the student's individualized program.

Questions and Decisions in Evaluating Services

Evaluating the special education services that students with disabilities receive involves two types of decision making: First, the team addresses questions regarding the student, and second, school personnel focus on questions regarding the overall program. Parents should have the opportunity to assist in both types of evaluations.

Evaluating Student Gains

Parents must receive written notification of each IEP meeting concerning their child. The team addresses questions regarding whether the student is making gains or if the program needs changing. Team members review the part of the IEP form that lists the annual goals and objectives, if appropriate, and discuss the student's progress. Teams need to consider whether the student still requires special education service(s) to benefit from the education program. Parents may actively participate in the evaluation of student gains by completing checklists, videotapes, parent reports, or other recording sheets. Let's examine some specific examples of information that parents share during team meetings:

- A father shares information with the team regarding his son's behavior after school and on the weekend, while the teacher shares information regarding her observations of the student in the lunchroom and on the playground.
- A grandmother records information about homework habits and other behaviors at home.
- A mother and special education teacher report information that they have compiled together, using observations of the student.

The Three-Year Review

The IEP team must reevaluate students every three years, or more often if the parent(s) or school personnel believe it is necessary. The IEP team meets to review existing evaluation data and identifies what additional data is needed. Once team members gather additional assessment information, they reconvene to discuss the results. Based on the reevaluation assessment information, team members make a decision about the student's eligibility for special education. If the team makes the decision that the student is no longer eligible, then the student exits the special services system. If the team makes the decision that the student continues to be eligible for special services, then the next step is to write the new IEP.

May 15

Dear Parent,

We are evaluating your child's reading program this spring, and we would appreciate your help. Please take a few minutes to answer the following questions. If possible, please return this letter in the enclosed stamped envelope by Friday.

Thank you,
Sandy Files, Third-Grade Teacher/Resource Room
W. G. Willard School

	Yes	Sometimes	No
1. My child brings home books from the school library.	____	____	____
2. My child likes to read out loud to other family members.	____	____	____
3. My child enjoys reading activities at school.	____	____	____
4. I feel that my child is making progress in reading.	____	____	____
5. My child completes homework assignments in a reasonable amount of time.	____	____	____
6. Please add additional comments or suggestions.			

Thank you for your help.

FIGURE 4.3 • A Teacher-Developed Program Evaluation Form

Evaluating the Education Program

As consumers, parents can contribute valuable information in this assessment step because they are most familiar with the day-to-day operation of the program. Parents commonly provide feedback to educators through the use of informal instruments, such as the teacher-made questionnaire illustrated in Figure 4.3.

To improve education programs, local school districts may develop Web-based program evaluation questionnaires that parents complete. Figure 4.4 illustrates a form that is designed for parents to provide feedback regarding their child's special education program.

Techniques for Listening to and Understanding Parent Perspectives

Parents and other family members have a wealth of knowledge about their children. Some people are more comfortable in sharing this information by filling out a checklist or online form. Others prefer a more personal approach. In reaching out to parents and other adults in the family, begin by using the terms Mr., Mrs., or Ms. to address the individual. Later, you may ask the parent how he or she wishes to be addressed. Some family members enjoy talking

Web-based parent questionnaire
Please indicate your level of agreement by clicking on the circle next to your choice.

	Strongly Agree	Moderately Agree	Don't Know	Moderately Disagree	Strongly Disagree
1. I feel welcome at IEP meetings.	⊙	⊙	⊙	⊙	⊙
2. During the meeting, team members encourage me to contribute information regarding my child's development or behaviors that I observe.	⊙	⊙	⊙	⊙	⊙
3. I feel that my contributions to the IEP team are valued by team members.	⊙	⊙	⊙	⊙	⊙
4. When my child has an assessment, the examiner explains the scores and the results to me.	⊙	⊙	⊙	⊙	⊙
5. I feel comfortable asking questions if I do not understand the assessment information.	⊙	⊙	⊙	⊙	⊙
6. My child is receiving the services that are described in the IEP.	⊙	⊙	⊙	⊙	⊙
7. If I have questions about my child's achievement in school, I know whom to contact.	⊙	⊙	⊙	⊙	⊙
8. I am pleased with the special education services that my child receives.	⊙	⊙	⊙	⊙	⊙

FIGURE 4.4 • Special Education Services Program Evaluation for Parents of Children With Disabilities

to others to share descriptive information. Begin with the acknowledgment that you want to hear what parents are saying. Careful listening ensures that your own biases do not overshadow what parents are relating to you. Listening to families requires key skills, including sensitivity and respect.

Interviews

The interview format allows different family members to talk and to share their individual perspectives. An interview that involves a face-to-face meeting may be easier for some family members, whereas an interview conducted over the telephone may better fit other family members' needs. Like other forms of assessment, the interview should be responsive to diversity. Create a positive tone by your respect, acceptance, support, and warmth. Set aside your own beliefs and judgments. You will need to focus on listening carefully and not let personal bias be a source of error.

Be sensitive in your probing. Respect parents' right to share only the information that they wish. Some parents are not ready to discuss some areas initially, or they do not want to confront a topic at certain periods of time. Conducting an interview with the family (Friend & Cook, 2013) includes several steps: planning the interview, meeting the family, and completing the interview.

Planning the Interview

When you contact the family, be sure to state the purpose of your visit; for example, "I'd like to visit with you and Alexandra's father to talk further about your concerns." Decide on a mutually convenient place and time. Some families prefer a meeting in their home because they feel more comfortable talking about their concerns in familiar surroundings. Other families prefer meeting in the home due to a strong sense of duty or cultural tradition about entertaining a guest in their home. Some families are more comfortable meeting in a community setting, perhaps a quiet coffee shop or at the school.

Many professionals find it helpful to prepare a few questions in advance. Prepared questions can help family members in "getting started." As you think about the types of questions that would be helpful, consider the wording of the questions and the type of answer that might result.

For example, a question such as, "Could you tell me about some of the difficult times during the day for Alexandra?" encourages an extended response. Leading questions such as, "Tell me more about . . . ," are helpful too. Asking "What time of day is most difficult for Alexandra?" will likely lead to a word or phrase response, whereas "Is getting ready for school in the morning a difficult time for Alexandra?" will probably result in a minimal response (yes or no). These latter types of questions serve to stop or limit discussion.

Meeting the Family

Four important aspects help ensure that the interview will go well. The first is to acknowledge each family member who is present and to thank each person for taking the time to be there. Next, establish rapport with family members by showing a genuine interest in what they have to say. Third, repeat the purpose of the visit. "I know that you have some concerns about Alexandra, and I hope that from our visit I can better understand them." Finally, help family members clarify important points by asking questions and rephrasing statements.

Completing the Interview

Remember that family members have many obligations and that they have probably made special arrangements to be present. Generally, interviews should not exceed an hour in length. Conclude the interview by summarizing the discussion and thanking each of the family members present. After the interview, record notes that you wish to remember. These notes could include information about the student, such as pending changes in medication

SNAPSHOT

Melissa Reynolds, Parent

I still remember the assessment process that we went through at the Family Pediatric Center. Our son was between 2 and 3 years of age and had been receiving speech therapy but had still not started speaking and was beginning to express himself behaviorally. We arrived early in the morning, took a lunch break, then finished by 2 p.m. My husband and I were pretty confident parents but there were moments during that day when we were shaken and apprehensive. Our son only had speech and language delays, and we as parents were hit with fears for his development and his future.

In one of the sessions, the professional asked us questions about our parenting then would say it back to us in an accusatory manner: "So, your son is capable of feeding himself, and yet sometimes, you help him?" I am not sure if that was the exact quote, but I remember feeling naked and vulnerable to the core. Later our son was determined to be eligible for speech therapy and occupational therapy services, and he was referred to a specialized clinic that could check his hearing.

Pause and consider:
- Do you think the interview question is an example of an interview technique? How might you reword? How might you be more responsive to the parent?
- If you were working with a family who had newly arrived from another country, what might you do or not do differently?

SNAPSHOT

La Donna Harris, a Comanche Woman

(This snapshot is an excerpt from her speech, given a few years ago at the first Comanche training session [Harris, n. d.].)

I am the daughter of Lily Tabbytite, the granddaughter of Wakeah, and the great-granddaughter of Kotsepeah, who was the daughter of Maria, a Spanish captive. My grandfather was Tabbytite, son of Hohwah and Tsa-ee.

I do this so that you will know how we are related; if not by blood, then by extended family, the "Indian Way." It not only shows our relationship, but it shows me how I should behave toward you. Tribal governments and tribal societies were built on relationships and kinships; how you were related showed you the etiquette of how you should behave to one another. In a tribal society, one would never openly criticize a relative. There were other ways of doing it. There were only certain people that could do the criticism or the correcting—not necessarily criticism—but they could show you the way to behave properly. When we try to make tribal societies work like Western societies, sometimes it doesn't fit and creates a lot of stress in our community.

The first time that I went to tribal council, I remember Edgar Monetachi. Because he was such an eloquent speaker, people would ask him to speak for them, even if they disagreed with his position. He had a responsibility to those relatives and talked for them because he had the power and medicine to be able to be a good speaker.

It was always amazing to me when kaku and papa would go downtown to Walter's and we would run into an old Comanche lady. The old lady would call me sister or daughter and they would chat for a while. Afterward, I'd say, "I didn't know that we were related to her" and kaku would trace it back to some wonderful thing that happened between families that made us kin—not between her and that other old lady, but between families. Those relationships made me feel strong and gave me a feeling of belonging to everybody....

Pause and consider:

- What are some important themes in this family story?
- How might these themes affect the assessment process?

or times when the student is expected to be absent. Value judgments of the family or individual members are not appropriate to include in these notes.

Family Stories

Sharing a family story can be the easiest and the least intimidating assessment technique for family members. Family stories represent events and people that are important to the family. Family stories often include valuable information regarding how others in the household relate to the child with special needs. By listening to family stories, you learn about the family's cultural values and practices, attitudes, habits, and behaviors. Family stories provide a good idea of how families see themselves and how they want others to see them.

Parent–Teacher Conferences

Parent–teacher conferences can be effective ways to share information with parents and to learn more about the student from the parent's perspective. In addition to sharing and receiving information, parents and professionals can develop a rapport and a better ability to cooperate in preventing and solving problems (Erwin et al., 2011). However, the key to successful conferences is planning. The teacher typically has a limited amount of time scheduled for meetings. Parents, too, often have made several special arrangements to come to the school at the scheduled conference time.

Planning the Conference

Planning the conference consists of notifying the parent(s) and preparing the conference agenda. Notify the parents of the date and purpose of the conference. Many schools routinely schedule conference days at the beginning of the year and send written notices. If the meeting is to be an IEP conference, a written notice must be sent prior to the meeting.

Families generally appreciate a follow-up telephone call, text message, e-mail, or other form of communication. However, be sure to ask the parent whether you have called at a convenient time. If not, ask when a better time would be for you to call back. The telephone conversation allows the parent to ask questions about the conference and to decide on which family members should attend. Families may want to decide whether the student with a disability should be present at the conference.

Planning the conference also includes identifying the agenda items. Notify other professionals who are working with the student and who may not be aware of the scheduled conference. For example, the speech therapist, occupational therapist, or physical therapist may want to be present.

Review the student's folder and gather samples of the student's work. Plan a tentative agenda of areas or items to be covered. Consider where you will be meeting. Several chairs placed at a small round table look inviting and less threatening than chairs placed around your desk.

Conference Time

To establish rapport, talk informally with parents and other family members before beginning the conference. Express your gratitude to family members for making arrangements to attend the conference. Have an interpreter or translator present for family members, if needed.

Begin with the student's accomplishments. Provide examples of student work or share classroom anecdotes. Discuss areas of growth and areas of concern. Encourage parents to ask questions or to make comments. Ask for clarification when you are unsure of the information that family members have shared. Use good communication skills, including jargon-free language. Remember, body posture and head nods, as well as the words you speak, are important ways of showing your interest in what family members have to say.

At the close of the conference, summarize the important points. End the meeting on a positive note, and thank family members again for coming.

Completing Postconference Activities

After the conference is over, two activities need attention. First, teachers should record a brief summary of the conference as soon as possible after the meeting. These notes should include the date, the participants, highlights of the meeting, and any decisions made. These notes are particularly important if there is a due process hearing at some future time. If the conference was an IEP or IFSP meeting, teachers must mail a copy of the minutes of the meeting to the parents.

Second, whether or not the student attended the conference, set aside time to talk about the meeting with the student. Briefly summarize the meeting and any decisions that were made. Answer any questions the student may have about the conference.

Summary

- Parents have an important role in the assessment process.
- Family priorities probably change over time. Always check to see if family members feel that the information they have provided in the past is current.
- Involve families to the extent that they wish to be involved in the assessment process and accept the wishes of family members concerning their levels of participation. Individual family members can differ in their preferences: One member may be more comfortable in just talking; another family member may prefer to provide information by completing a questionnaire or a rating scale.
- Be open to issues in working with families different from your own. Family diversity can include issues of culture, disability, economic level, family structure, gender, geographic region or origin, and race. Avoid stereotypical assumptions.
- Work to become familiar with families in your community. When in doubt, ask families to determine preferences and needs.

QUESTIONS FOR REFLECTION

1. Discuss several reasons for including parents (or other family members) in the assessment process.
2. Consider your own family within the family systems framework described in this chapter. How would you describe the interaction system? Your family characteristics? How would you describe your family in terms of the family life cycle?
3. Make arrangements to interview a parent. In thinking about your conversation, did the parent identify family needs and priorities for the child? Did the parent mention resources important to the functioning of the family? Which interview questions were most helpful? What questions might you include in another interview?
4. Contact a parent organization in your community or call the office of your state parent organization for children with disabilities. What information is available regarding families and their involvement in the assessment process?
5. Begin a list of resources to help you become responsive to diversity. What Web sites would you recommend? What families in your area would be willing to be a resource?

REFERENCES

Artiles, A. J., & Bal, A. (2008). The next generation of disproportionality research: Toward a comparative model in the study of equity in ability differences. *Journal of Special Education, 42*, 4–14.

Chen, D. (2011). *Developing cross-cultural competence: A guide for working with children and their families* (4th ed.) In E. W. Lynch, & M. J. Hanson, (Vol. Eds.). Baltimore, MD: Paul H. Brookes.

Erwin, E. J., Shogren, K. A., Soodak, L. C., Turnbull, A. P., & Turnbull, H. R., III. (2011). *Families, professionals, and exceptionality: Positive outcomes through partnerships and trust* (6th ed.). Upper Saddle River, NJ: Pearson Merrill Prentice Hall.

Friend, M., & Cook, L. (2013). *Interaction: Collaboration skills for school professionals* (7th ed.). Boston: Pearson, Allyn & Bacon.

Harris, L. (n.d.). Summarized version of the speech given by La Donna Harris at the first Comanche training session. Unpublished manuscript.

Lo, L. (2008). Chinese families' level of participation and experiences in IEP meetings. *Preventing School Failure, 53*(1), 21–27.

Mandell, D. S., Wiggins, L. D., Yeargin-Allsopp, M., Carpenter, L. A., Daniels, J., Thomas, K. C., et al. (2009). Racial/ethnic disparities in the identification of children with autism spectrum disorders. *American Journal of Public Health, 99*, 493–498.

Tincani, M., Travers, J., & Boutot, A. (2009). Race, culture, and autism spectrum disorder: Understanding the role of diversity in successful educational interventions. *Research & Practice for Persons with Severe Disabilities, 34*(3/4), 81–90.

PART II
Assessment Skills

 **CHAPTER 5** Reliability and Validity

 **CHAPTER 6** Developing Technical Skills

 **CHAPTER 7** Test Interpretation and Report Writing

PART II

5 Reliability and Validity

Chapter Objectives

After completing this chapter, you should be able to:

- Define reliability and validity.
- Describe the application of the types of reliability and validity.
- Explain why assessment approaches should be responsive to diversity.

Overview

Reliability and validity, two closely related concepts, are central to an understanding of assessment. This chapter continues the discussion on responding to diversity. Being responsive to diversity means that assessment procedures are fair. Fairness in assessment indicates that assessment methods are equitable; free of bias; adapted for students with disabilities; sensitive to diverse groups of students; and considerate of contemporary views of growth and development, aptitude, cognition, learning, behavior, and personality.

Reliability

Reliability indicates the consistency or stability of test performance and is one of the most important considerations when selecting tests and other assessment tools. A test must be constructed so that examiners can administer the test with minimal errors and can interpret the performance of students with confidence.

The assessment process is subject to error from many sources. Errors in measurement can stem from the testing environment, the student, the test, and the examiner. Sources of error in the testing environment include the following:

- Noise distractions
- Poor lighting
- Uncomfortable room temperature

Sources of error associated with the student include the following:

- Hunger
- Fatigue
- Illness
- Difficulty in understanding test instructions
- Difficulty in understanding or interpreting language used

Sources of error stemming from the test include the following:

- Ambiguously worded questions
- Biased questions
- Different interpretations of the wording of test questions

An examiner who is not prepared or who incorrectly interprets administration or scoring guidelines contributes to measurement errors. Sources of error associated with test administration include the following:

- Unclear directions
- Difficulty in achieving rapport
- Insensitivity to student's culture, language, preferences, or other characteristics
- Ambiguous scoring
- Errors associated with calculation or computation of scores
- Errors associated with recording information about the student

Reliability information that is reported in test manuals should be carefully considered. Although some books and journal articles report evaluations of tests, tests are not given "seals of approval." To be useful, they must meet certain standards. Three professional organizations—the American Educational Research Association, the American Psychological Association, and the National Council on Measurement in Education (1999; http://www.apa.org)—have published *Standards for Educational and Psychological Testing,* which provide criteria for evaluating tests, testing practices, and the effects of test use on individuals. The *Standards for Educational and Psychological Testing* describes reliability and provides a departure from more traditional thinking about reliability. Reliability signifies the consistency of such measures when a test or measure is repeated on certain individuals or groups.

Test developers convey reliability of assessment instruments in various ways. They are responsible for reporting evidence of reliability. Test users and consumers must use this evidence in deciding the suitability of various assessment instruments. Although no one approach is preferred, educators should be familiar with all the approaches to judge the usefulness of instruments. These approaches include (1) one or more correlation coefficients, (2) variances or standard deviations of measurement errors, and (3) technical information about tests known as **item response theory (IRT)**.

Approach 1: Using Correlation Coefficients

Traditionally, reliability has been described as the stability or consistency of test performance. The teacher needs to know that a student's test performance is stable over time and over different test items that have similar objectives. Of course, it is impractical and unnecessary for a student to take a test every day. If a teacher administers a test to a student on a given day, that teacher wants to have some assurance that the student, if retested on the following day, will score about the same on both tests. Or if a student takes one form or version of a test, the teacher needs to know that the test scores of the student, if that student is taking a similar form of a test, will be about the same.

This type of reliability also provides an estimate of the consistency of test results when administering a test under similar conditions. This consistency or agreement is described by means of a **correlation coefficient**. Some test manuals use the term *reliability coefficient* in place of the term *correlation coefficient*. To understand this type of reliability, it is useful to know about the concepts of correlation and correlation coefficients.

Correlation

A **correlation** indicates the extent to which two or more scores vary together. It measures the degree to which a change in one score has a relationship with a change in another score. For example, in general, the higher a student's intelligence score, the higher will be the student's score on a vocabulary test. Usually, students with higher intelligence quotient (IQ) scores tend to have higher vocabulary scores, and students with lower IQ scores will probably have lower vocabulary test scores. IQ and vocabulary level correlate with each other. However, examiners must use caution when interpreting relationships—just because two scores correlate does not mean that one score causes a change in the other score. The correlation between shoe size and reading achievement is an example of a strong correlation but lack of causation. As shoe size increases, reading achievement may also increase, but this is pure coincidence—a person's shoe size has nothing to do with how well that person reads.

Correlation Coefficient

A correlation coefficient measures the correlation, or relationship, between tests, test items, scoring procedures, observations, or behavior ratings. A correlation coefficient quantifies a relationship and provides information about whether there is a relationship, strength of the relationship, and the direction of the relationship. The symbol for correlation coefficient is a lowercase *r*. Test developers conduct research studies to determine correlation coefficients and report these coefficients in test manuals.

Strength of a Relationship

The value of a correlation coefficient can vary from +1.00 to −1.00. The closer the correlation coefficient is to 1.00, either +1.00 or −1.00, the stronger the relationship. The closer the correlation coefficient is to 0.00, the weaker the relationship. For example, a coefficient of .89 is stronger than a coefficient of .15 because .89 is closer to 1.00, just as a coefficient of −.54 is stronger than a coefficient of −.45 because −.54 is closer to −1.00.

Direction of a Relationship

The presence of a plus (+) or minus (−) sign determines the direction of a correlation. A plus sign indicates that a relationship is positive; a negative (minus) sign indicates that a relationship is negative. When positive correlation coefficients are written, the plus sign is usually omitted. When one test score increases as another test score increases, the relationship is positive. In a positive relationship, the scores either increase together or decrease together. However, when one test score decreases while the other test score increases, the relationship is negative. The relationship between IQ and vocabulary achievement is a positive relationship because both of these variables usually increase together.

Positive Relationship

If there were a perfect relationship between IQ level and vocabulary achievement, the correlation would be expressed as either +1.00 or 1.00. If for every increase in IQ score, there is a corresponding increase in vocabulary scores, the relationship between IQ and vocabulary level would be perfect, and the resulting correlation coefficient would be 1.00. However, because there are so many other variables that influence both IQ and vocabulary achievement, this relationship will never be a perfect 1.00. Figure 5.1 illustrates this relationship.

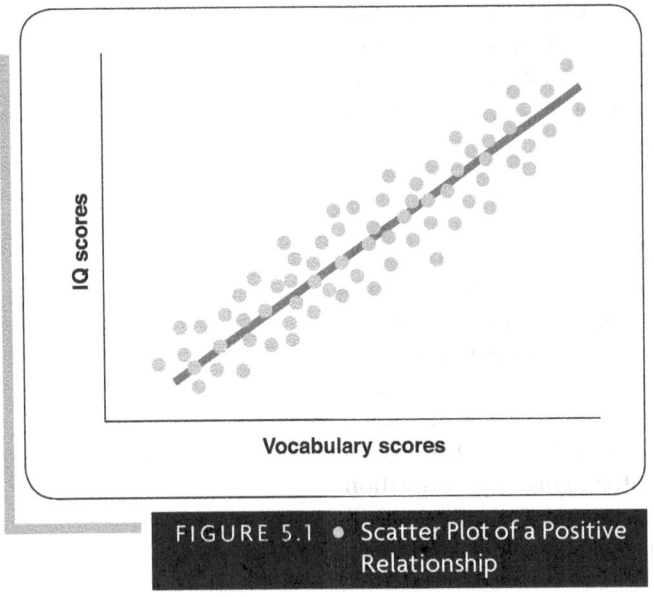

FIGURE 5.1 • Scatter Plot of a Positive Relationship

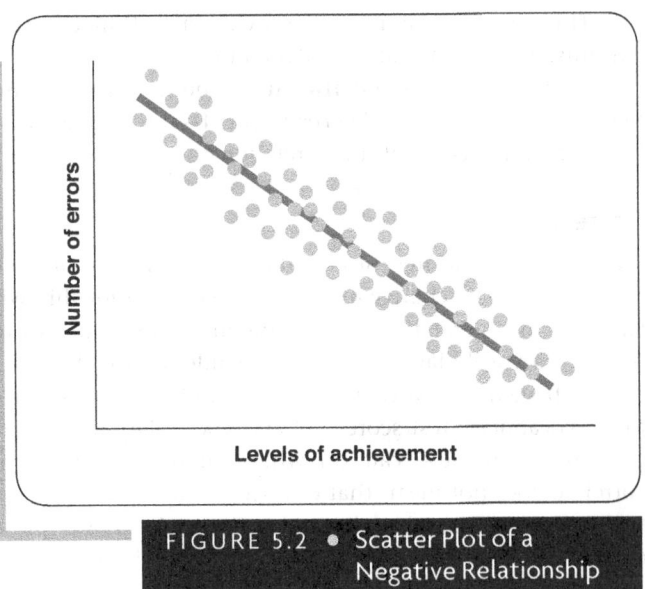

FIGURE 5.2 • Scatter Plot of a Negative Relationship

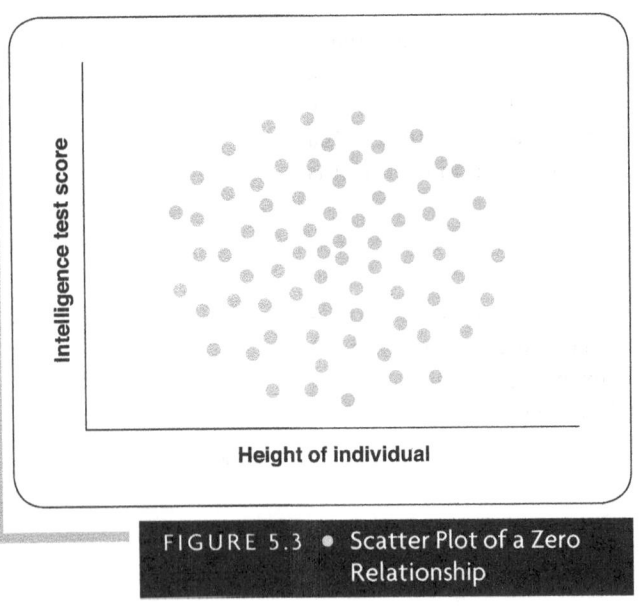

FIGURE 5.3 • Scatter Plot of a Zero Relationship

Negative Relationship

A perfect negative relationship is indicated by −1.00. The relationship between level of achievement and the number of errors made is a negative relationship. As the achievement increases, the number of errors that an individual makes decreases. Figure 5.2 illustrates this relationship.

Zero Relationship

The relationship between an individual's score on an intelligence test and the height of that individual is zero. When arranged on a **scatter plot**, most of the intelligence test scores and the height measurements are not associated with each other; the scores do not vary with each other. Figure 5.3 illustrates this relationship.

Applying Correlation Coefficients to Reliability

In test manuals, a lowercase r designates a reliability or correlation coefficient. For example, when a test manual reports that $r = .92$, the reliability for the test is .92. Because .92 is close to a perfect correlation coefficient of 1.00, a teacher can have confidence that the test has adequate reliability. For guidance in evaluating correlation coefficients, Nitko and Brookhart (2003) recommend that when making major educational decisions, a reliability coefficient of at least .90 is the preferred standard.

Types of Reliability That Involve Correlation Coefficients

The traditional view of reliability conceptualizes five types of reliability: test-retest, alternate form, split-half, internal consistency, and **interscorer/interobserver/interrater reliability**. For these types of reliability, it is incumbent on test publishers to report information fully in test manuals. Test publishers should tell how they obtained the samples of students, individuals, or observations from which they determine their reliability coefficients. Interpretations of total test scores, subscores, or combinations of scores should include stated relevant reliabilities. Similarly, when tests have both long and short versions, test publishers must report reliabilities of each version based on separate independent administrations of each version.

TEST-RETEST RELIABILITY **Test-retest reliability** can be obtained when administering the same test to the same student twice by correlating the scores on the first and second administrations and obtaining a reliability coefficient. This coefficient is a measure of the stability of the test score. Because the same test is administered twice, test developers need to state the time interval between the two administrations of the test. Too short an interval will inflate the reliability coefficient. When the time interval is too long, a student may experience developmental changes that affect the reliability coefficient.

There are several drawbacks to this type of reliability. Having seen the test items and the directions for taking the test over two test administrations, for example, the student may obtain a higher test score on the second testing.

ALTERNATE FORM RELIABILITY **Alternate form reliability** is also known as equivalent form or parallel form reliability. Frequently, there is a need for two forms of a test that contain different test items but that evaluate the same knowledge and skills. This procedure is especially useful when pretesting and posttesting students. The two forms have different designations. For example, some forms are designated A and B; others may be labeled X and Y or L and M.

Like test-retest reliability, alternate form reliability has several disadvantages. It is difficult to develop two parallel forms of a test. In addition, as with test-retest reliability, a shorter interval between test administrations can inflate the reliability coefficient and the effect of practice on similar test items.

SPLIT-HALF RELIABILITY **Split-half reliability** is measured by administering a test to a group of students, dividing the total number of test items in half to form two tests, and correlating the scores on the two halves of the test. For example, suppose a test has 20 items. We could administer the entire test to a group of students and then divide the test into two halves, each containing 10 items. We can use different methods to break a test into two halves: by separating the first half from the second half or by separating the even-numbered items from the odd-numbered items. We can then correlate the items on the two halves to determine the relationship between the scores from the first half of the test and the scores from the second half.

Dividing a test into a first half and a second half can cause problems in determining the reliability. Fatigue, practice effect, failure to complete the test, and print quality can all affect the reliability coefficient (Nitko & Brookhart, 2006). Assuming random order of the test items, we could divide the test by odd-even items or by balancing the halves. Balancing halves could involve item length, response type, or another characteristic that is appropriate for the test. The most appropriate method of splitting the halves of a test depends on the test and the testing situation (Nitko & Brookhart, 2006).

With the split-half procedure, the test is administered only once. Therefore, this procedure gives reliability coefficients that are a measure of internal consistency, not of the temporal stability of test performance.

INTERNAL CONSISTENCY RELIABILITY **Internal consistency reliability** is similar to the split-half method. Internal consistency reliability is an estimate of the homogeneity or interrelatedness of responses to test items. Students take this test only once. Usually test developers use one of the Kuder-Richardson formulas to find the average coefficient by calculating all the possible split-half coefficients. The more similar the test items are to each other, the higher is the reliability coefficient. Like split-half reliability, internal consistency reliability does not provide an estimate of the stability of the test over time.

SNAPSHOT

Prentice Dillon and Erin Gates

After all the students left school for the day, Prentice Dillon, a special education teacher, decided that he wanted to review the teachers' test booklet and digital resources for a test that the school district had recently decided to use for assessing students' overall achievement. He read the beginning sections that described how the test should be administered. Okay so far. Dillon began the section that described the reliability of the test. He read that test reliability indicates the consistency or stability of test performance. The section that described internal consistency reliability said, "The reliability coefficient for the composite scores (which are derived from several subtest scores) is $r = .92$. This is greater than the reliability coefficients for the subtest scores." Prentice asked himself, "Why were the reliability coefficients of the composite scores higher than the reliability coefficients of the individual subtests?" Prentice decided to see what Erin Gates, another teacher in his building, knew about this test.

Pause and consider:
- How you reply to Prentice's question about why composite scores have higher reliability coefficients than the coefficients for the individual subtests?
- Can you suggest additional questions about testing that Prentice could ask Erin?

Erin explained that it is not unusual for composite scores to have higher reliability coefficients than individual subtests because test developers use more test items to calculate the reliability coefficients associated with composite scores than with individual subtests. Composite scores, in general, show higher reliability coefficients than do individual subtests.

The advantage of using internal consistency instead of the split-half method is that internal consistency provides the average of all split-half correlations—all possible ways of dividing the test into two halves. The split-half method allows only one division of the test in half. The Snapshot of Prentice Dillon and Erin Gates illustrates how teachers consider this type of reliability.

INTERSCORER/INTEROBSERVER/INTERRATER RELIABILITY Interscorer/interobserver/interrater reliability is a measure of the extent to which two or more scorers, observers, or raters agree on how to score a test. **Interscorer/interobserver/interrater reliability** is important when errors in scoring or differences in judgment can affect the test outcomes. This type of reliability should be reported when:

1. There is a possibility that errors can be made in computing the test score(s).
2. A test item can have more than one answer.
3. A response to a question can have more than one interpretation.
4. Observations are made about the behaviors of one or more students.
5. Interviews are used to collect information.

Approach 2: Variances or Standard Deviations of Measurement Errors

The true score is the score an individual would obtain on a test if there were no measurement errors. The obtained score is the actual score that a student obtains on a test. This is the best estimate we have of a student's performance.

If all testing conditions were perfect and there were no errors of measurement, the obtained score and the true score would be the same. But because error is always present, the true score cannot be known. However, an individual's true score can be measured by using the formula $X = T + E$, where the student's obtained or observed score, X, equals the true score, T, plus the errors that are associated with measurement, represented by E, the error score. **Standard error of measurement (SEM)** is especially important when evaluators need to make immediate decisions with limited information.

Examiners should report the SEM for derived scores, including standard scores, grade or age equivalents, and percentile ranks. SEM is of special concern when using cut scores. **Cut scores** are prespecified scores that determine how to select or classify students. Typically, evaluators may select or classify students who score at or below a prespecified cut score, such as 30, for special education or labeling. When using cut scores, test publishers must specify the measurement error associated with each cut score. SEM is also important to consider when making score comparisons, such as between achievement and ability and when interpreting score profiles.

Approach 3: Item Response Theory (IRT)

Technical information about tests is known as IRT. IRT involves a statistical calculation that determines how well the instrument differentiates between individuals at various levels of measured abilities or characteristics. If test publishers, authors, and researchers choose to demonstrate reliability using IRT, they should provide sufficient information in test manuals. Test publishers should clearly and comprehensively describe the procedures they used to determine reliability.

Factors That Influence Reliability

Several factors can affect the reliability of a test (Nitko & Brookhart, 2006):

1. Test length. Generally, the longer a test is, the more reliable it is.
2. Speed. When a test is a speed test, reliability can be problematic. It is inappropriate to estimate reliability using internal consistency, test-retest, or alternate form methods. This is because not every student is able to complete all the items in a speed test. In contrast, a power test is a test in which every student is able to complete all the items.
3. Group homogeneity. In general, the more heterogeneous the group of students who take the test, the more reliable the measure will be.
4. Item difficulty. When there is little variability among test scores, the reliability will be low. Thus, reliability will be low if a test is so easy that every student gets most or all of the items correct or so difficult that every student gets most or all of the items wrong.
5. Objectivity. Objectively scored tests, rather than subjectively scored tests, show a higher reliability.
6. Test-retest interval. The shorter the time interval between two administrations of a test, the less likely that changes will occur and the higher the reliability will be.
7. Variation with the testing situation. Errors in the testing situation (e.g., students misunderstanding or misreading test directions, noise level, distractions, and sickness) can cause test scores to vary.

Validity

Validity is the most important consideration when developing, evaluating, and interpreting tests. Reliability is a prerequisite of validity. A test must demonstrate reliability before test developers or test users can consider evidence of validity. A test that is reliable is not necessarily valid. Validity conveys the degree to which evidence and theory confirm the interpretation of test scores as described by the test developers. Additional information about validity can be found in the *Standards for Educational and Psychological Testing* (**http://www.apa.org**).

To establish validity of a test and of test interpretations, test developers usually gather evidence in multiple forms over a period of time. The determination of validity is the obligation of both the test developer and test user. Test developers should provide information about validity in test manuals. Ultimately, it is incumbent on the test user to review the evidence and determine the extent to which a test is valid and the interpretations of the test are valid. The test user should consider the process used to construct the instrument, the score reliability, test administration procedures, scoring procedures, the standards-setting process, and the extent to which the test is fair. We describe fairness in detail later in this chapter.

Traditionally, validity has several aspects: content, criterion-related (which includes concurrent and predictive validity), and construct. A correlation coefficient (r) commonly represents criterion-related and construct validity. From our discussion of reliability, you will recall that r is also a measure of reliability. Therefore, it is important that users pay attention to whether the r values refer to reliability or validity.

Content Validity

Content validity measures the extent to which the test items reflect the content domain of a test. Content validity is the most important type of validity for achievement tests because achievement tests typically measure content knowledge such as reading, writing, mathematics, science, and social studies.

An estimate of the content validity of a test is obtained by thoroughly and systematically examining the test items to determine the extent to which they reflect and do not reflect the content domain. In general, a panel composed of curriculum experts and specialists in tests and measurements evaluate content validity by determining the extent to which the test items reflect the test objectives. Test developers should provide information about the experts who reviewed the test content.

Most norm-referenced tests represent the curricula that are taught in various geographic regions of the United States. A **norm-referenced test (NRT)** is a measure that compares a student's test performance with that of similar students who have taken the same test. In addition, scores from standardized tests can be used to make interpretations about an individual student's performance on several tests. Because these tests are so broad, they may inadequately represent the curricula in many schools. Thus, as a rule, test users must ensure the content validity of NRTs before a test user can be confident that a particular test is appropriate in this respect.

Criterion-Related Validity

Criterion-related validity refers to the extent to which scores from one test, instrument, or measure relate to scores from another test, instrument, or measure. When determining criterion-related validity, test developers compare their test with another outcome or criterion: another test, school grades, or observations. If test developers use this type of validity, they should report their findings in the test manuals.

When assessing the criterion-related validity of a test, it is important to verify the criterion measure's validity as well. Concurrent and predictive validity are two types of criterion-related validity.

Concurrent Validity

Concurrent validity is the extent to which the results of two different tests administered at about the same time correlate with each other. To obtain concurrent validity, test developers administer two different tests within a brief interval and calculate the correlation between the scores from the tests. This method of estimating validity is especially useful when constructing a new test.

Suppose a test publisher wanted to develop a new way to test the hearing abilities of students. The publisher would administer this new test and also a standard hearing test. Next, the publisher would establish concurrent validity by examining the relationship between the scores from the two tests. The test publisher wants to know the extent to which a known instrument and a new test measure the same objectives. If the new test correlates highly with the established instrument, the test publisher can conclude that the new test is valid and that it has an acceptable level of concurrent validity.

Predictive Validity

How accurately can current performance predict future performance or behavior? Predictive validity is the standard for forecasting student performance or behavior from a test score.

Be careful not to confuse concurrent validity with predictive validity. There are some important differences. Whereas concurrent validity is a measure of the extent to which two sets of test scores relate to each other, predictive validity is an estimate of the extent to which one test accurately predicts future performance or behavior. When scores on one test accurately predict performance on another test or criterion, we can say that there is high predictive validity.

Construct Validity

Construct validity is the extent to which a test measures a particular trait, construct, or psychological characteristic. Examples of constructs include reasoning ability, spatial visualization, reading comprehension, sociability, and introversion.

Construct validity is the most difficult type of validity to establish. Test developers need a long period of time and numerous research studies before verifying construct validity for a particular test. The establishment of construct validity can be compared to a detective's search for clues, accumulating evidence. The clues assist the test developer in determining the consistency of the evidence in the interpretation of construct validity. If the evidence falls into a systematic pattern, then test developers and test examiners can have confidence in the validity of the construct. Prentice Dillon and Erin Gates continue their conversation in the next Snapshot.

SNAPSHOT

Prentice Dillon and Erin Gates

Prentice continued reading the booklet and online resources about the new test that his school district had adopted. After finishing the reliability section, he decided to turn to the validity section. The manual said, "The achievement subtests were correlated with the subtests that relate to intelligence, and the coefficients ranged from .20 to .65." Prentice knew that coefficients that approach 1.00 indicate that there is a very close relationship. But when evaluating the validity of a test, what did correlations between .20 and .65 mean?

Pause and consider:
- How would you reply to Prentice's question about the interpretation of validity coefficients?
- In addition to Erin, where could he find answers to his question? Suggest online resources where he could find additional information about reliability and validity.

Erin Gates was still in her classroom when Prentice asked if she could help him understand validity. Erin explained that the authors of the test booklet were presenting evidence for the construct validity of their test. Construct validity is the extent to which a test measures a particular trait, construct, or psychological characteristic, such as achievement and intellectual abilities. In determining construct validity, the booklet describes the construct, indicating how it differs from other constructs.

Erin told Prentice that the correlations between .20 and .65 indicate that there is, in fact, some relationship between achievement and cognitive ability because achievement and intellectual abilities are actually different, but not totally separate, constructs. In fact, if the correlations were close to 1.00, for example, .90, .93, or .95, it would mean that the achievement subtests and the cognitive subtests were too closely related and that they were measuring the same constructs!

Validity of Test Interpretations

The interpretation of test results can have profound **consequences** for students, families, and educators. Thus, test developers and publishers should provide validity information for each proposed interpretation and use of test scores, subtests, subscores, score differences, and test profiles (American Educational Research Association et al., 1999). Test developers and publishers should also provide evidence of validity, including the statistics they used to conduct analyses, the composition of samples they used to collect the data, and the conditions under which they collected the data, for each proposed interpretation.

Test users, such as teachers, psychologists, and administrators, should evaluate the evidence to determine the extent of support for the proposed interpretations. If evidence is unavailable or inconsistent, test developers and publishers should disclose this information to test users. Similarly, if a test user would like to use a test in a way for which validity evidence is lacking, the user should refrain from using the test until developers and publishers can provide sufficient evidence.

Consequential Validity

Consequential validity describes the extent to which an assessment instrument promotes the intended consequences (Linn & Baker, 1996). Test publishers use consequential validity to describe performance-based assessments. Performance-based assessment, which we discuss in Chapter 15, provides information about how a student can apply knowledge in real-life, real-world settings rather than simply accumulating isolated bits of knowledge. Domains such as dance and music have long used performance-based assessments to evaluate students. Performances are far more appropriate for evaluating how students dance or play musical instruments than are multiple-choice questions.

One of the primary reasons for using performance-based assessments is to improve student learning. Consequential validity reflects the extent to which performance-based assessment improves student learning. Factors that can affect student learning positively, and thus impact consequential validity, include school improvement activities, instructional improvements, staff development activities, levels of student achievement, and accountability systems (Linn & Baker, 1996).

Responding to Diversity: Fairness in Assessment

Assessment has a great influence on curriculum, instruction, classroom, and school organization and on educational and career opportunities for students. Fairness in assessment means that all assessment approaches, including standardized tests, performance assessment, portfolio assessment, and informal measures, are free from bias and that methods of student assessment are equitable and sensitive to diverse student populations. Assessment should be fair to all students to avoid limiting students' present education and their future opportunities (Gipps & Stobart, 2009). Fairness in assessment means that assessment methods reflect the following:

- Equity
- Nonbiased assessment
- Linguistic diversity
- Accommodations and modifications for students with disabilities
- Sensitivity to diverse student populations
- Consideration of contemporary views of growth and development, aptitude, cognition, learning, behavior, and personality

- Availability and use of assistive technology
- Consideration of possible adverse consequences of any applicable assessments to students

Equity

Differences in test results may be due to differences in educational opportunities, resources, or cultural expectations. This is especially true when considerations about culture, ethnicity, race, language, geographic region of origin, gender, disability, or economic status are a concern. Equity in assessment means that assessment is approached in a fair, impartial, and just manner. Assessment tools must be more than reliable and valid. Valid assessments arise only when the assessment is fair. Fair assessments mean that all students have access to and can participate in a variety of assessment approaches.

Nonbiased Assessment

Assessment tools must be nonbiased. When groups know approximately the same amount of material but one group scores consistently higher than other groups on a test, it may indicate test bias. For example, a test may portray individuals in stereotypic ways in test problems that contain references applying to only males, to only middle-class individuals, to only a particular culture, or to topics that carry status with only those groups. When evaluating student behavior in such tests, one must realize that some behaviors considered aberrant for one group may be proper for another group.

Linguistic Diversity

There are important considerations when testing students who are nonnative speakers of English or who speak languages other than English. Translation of an assessment tool or use of an interpreter is not always appropriate (American Educational Research Association et al., 1999).

Translation alone does not ensure that an assessment procedure is comparable in content, difficulty level, reliability, or validity to the original version. Both the language dominance and language proficiency of test takers should be considered (American Educational Research Association et al., 1999). **Language dominance** refers to the individual's preferred language. **Language proficiency** refers to level of expertise in a language. A student who may be bilingual, or even trilingual, may have different levels of proficiency in speaking, reading, and writing. Test administrators should determine the language proficiency of the students and administer tests in the language in which the student is most proficient.

When recommending a test for use with linguistically diverse test takers, test developers and publishers should provide the information for appropriate test use and interpretation. When translating a test from one language or dialect to another, test administrators need to establish the test's reliability and validity for the uses intended in the linguistic groups they will test.

Consideration of Adverse Consequences

Some students do not perform well on assessments simply because they lack the background or experiences with certain methods of assessment. Teachers can try to ameliorate this by providing all students with instruction and practice in the assessment approaches that are used in evaluations.

Assessment developers and users must actively avoid assessment approaches, instruments, and techniques that may have adverse consequences on groups that currently are targets of discrimination or have previously been the targets of discrimination. Proper assessment assists in providing learning opportunities for students rather than in placing students in tracks or limiting educational opportunities (National Forum on Assessment, 1995).

Summary

- Test developers and publishers should provide information about reliability and validity.
- Teachers, test examiners, and administrators should review tests and test manuals, booklets, and online information and satisfy themselves that each test has acceptable levels of reliability and validity.
- Fairness in assessment means that assessment approaches and tests should be reliable and valid.
- Fairness also means that bias has been minimized, that the assessment is equitable, and that the measures are sensitive to diverse students and populations.

QUESTIONS FOR REFLECTION

1. Visit a Web resource that contains information about tests and assessments, such as **http://www.pearsonassessments.com**. Compare reliability and validity information about several tests.
2. The director of testing has asked you to evaluate the reliability and validity of a test that is being considered for purchase. What standards of reliability and validity will you use when evaluating this test?
3. Gina, who recently moved to this country from Guatemala, may have a learning disability. Which aspects of reliability and validity must the teacher and test examiner consider when deciding which tests to use when assessing Gina?

REFERENCES

American Educational Research Association, American Psychological Association, and National Council on Measurement in Education. (1999). *Standards for educational and psychological testing*. Washington, DC: American Educational Research Association. (Also see apa.org)

Gipps, C., & Stobart, G. (2009). Fairness in assessment. In C. Wyatt-Smith & J. Cumming (Eds.), *Educational assessment in the 21st century* (pp. 105–118). London: Springer.

Heumann, J., & Warlick, K. R. (2000). *Memorandum: Questions and answers about provisions in the Individuals with Disabilities Education Act amendments of 1997 related to students with disabilities and state and district-wide assessments*. Office of Special Education and Rehabilitative Services, Office of Special Education Programs, August 24.

Linn, R. L., & Baker, E. L. (1996). Can performance-based student assessments be psychometrically sound? In J. B. Baron & D. P. Wolf (Eds.), *Performance-based student assessment: Challenges and possibilities* (pp. 84–103). Chicago: University of Chicago Press.

National Forum on Assessment. (1995). *Principles and indicators for student assessment systems*. Cambridge, MA: National Center for Fair and Open Testing.

Nitko, A. J., & Brookhart, S. (2006). *Educational assessment of students* (5th ed.). Upper Saddle River, NJ: Prentice-Hall.

6 Developing Technical Skills

Chapter Objectives

After completing this chapter, you should be able to:

- Describe norm-referenced and criterion-referenced assessment.
- Discuss the advantages and disadvantages of using various types of test scores when interpreting test performance.
- Compare a range of ways to present and interpret test scores.
- Describe how to evaluate the usefulness of tests.

Overview

This chapter discusses scoring, interpreting, and reporting test performance and describes standardized assessment tests, scores, scoring procedures, and norms. In the following chapters, we will return to these topics and discuss their application to **assessment strategies** and approaches.

Standardized Tests

Standardized tests are tests in which a test manual prescribes administration, scoring, and interpretation procedures that must be strictly followed by the test examiner. Examiners must follow exact administration procedures when using standardized tests. Failure to follow these procedures compromises the reliability, validity, and interpretation of the test results. Standardized norm-referenced tests can be both individual and group administered.

Standardization Sample

When a norm-referenced test is administered to a student, the teacher can compare the performance of that student with the scores obtained by the sample of students who participated in the normative sample during the development of the test. A **standardization sample** is a subgroup of a large group that is representative of the large group. When test publishers develop a test, it is this subgroup that is actually tested. The **population** is the larger group from which the sample of individuals is selected and to which individual comparisons are made regarding test performance. *Normative sample* or *norm sample* are other terms for the standardization sample.

The standardization sample must represent the population of students who will be taking the test. The standardization sample should include, in appropriate proportion, students from various geographic regions of the country; males and females; students who represent various racial, ethnic, cultural, and linguistic populations; and students from various economic strata. Information may even include the occupational categories and educational levels of the parents of the students.

The best way for a test publisher to determine the appropriate proportions of representative groups (e.g., males, females, race, ethnicity, native language) that should be included in the standardization sample is to refer to the most recent census data and base the selection of the standardization sample on those percentages. For example, a test that is to be used with students from Cambodia or from Central America should include appropriate samples of these student groups in the standardization group. If the test is to be administered to students who are nonnative speakers of English and who come from various backgrounds, the test publisher must provide appropriate information concerning the administration and interpretation of test performance (American Educational Research Association, American Psychological Association, and National Council on Measurement in Education, 1999).

Norm-Referenced Tests

A **norm-referenced test** is a standardized test that compares a student's test performance with that of a sample of similar students who have taken the same test. After constructing a test, the test developers administer it to a standardization sample of students using the same administration and scoring procedures for all students. This makes the administration and scoring "standardized." The test scores of the standardization sample are called *norms*, which include a variety of types of scores. Norms are the scores obtained by the standardization sample and are the scores to which students are compared when they are administered a test.

Once test developers standardize a norm-referenced test, examiners can administer it to students with similar characteristics to the norm group and can compare the scores of these students with those of the norm group. Norm-referenced standardized tests can use local, state, or national norms as a base. Because of the comparison of scores between a norm group and other groups of students, a norm-referenced test provides information on the relative standing of students.

When assessing students with disabilities, evaluators should employ caution before making comparisons or interpretations stemming from established norms. It is possible to use typical norms when making interpretations that draw from the relative performance of the students with disabilities and from the general population of students. However, when making comparisons or interpretations that use level or degree of disability, normative data should come from the sample population to which comparisons are made.

Test manuals should provide sufficient details about the normative group so that test users can make informed judgments about the appropriateness of the norm sample (American Educational Research Association et al., 1999).

Criterion-Referenced Tests

Instead of comparing a student's performance to a norm group, criterion-referenced tests measure a student's performance with respect to a well-defined domain such as reading or mathematics. Whereas norm-referenced tests discriminate between the performance of individual students on specific test items, **criterion-referenced tests** provide a description of a student's knowledge, skills, or behavior in a specific range of test items. This specific range is referred to as a *domain*. Test items on criterion-referenced tests frequently correspond to well-defined instructional objectives.

Criterion-referenced tests, instead of using norms, provide information on the performance of a student with respect to specific test items. The results of criterion-referenced tests are not dependent on the performance of other students, as are norm-referenced tests. Examples of criterion-referenced tests include the *BRIGANCE* series.

Distinguishing Norm-Referenced Tests From Criterion-Referenced Tests

Several characteristics distinguish norm-referenced tests from criterion-referenced tests. Performance on a criterion-referenced test provides information on whether the student has attained a predetermined achievement or behavioral criterion. Although it is possible for a test to be both norm-referenced and criterion-referenced, professionals must use caution when interpreting the results of these tests because it is difficult to combine both types of tests in one instrument.

Another distinction is the breadth of the content domain the test covers (Salvia, Ysseldyke, & Bolt, 2013). Typical norm-referenced tests survey a broad domain, whereas criterion-referenced tests usually have fewer domains but more items in each domain. Criterion-referenced tests typically sample the domain more thoroughly than do norm-referenced tests.

Criterion-referenced tests are very helpful in making instructional planning decisions. Because criterion-referenced tests frequently cover a more restricted range of content than do norm-referenced tests, they can provide more information about a student's level of performance.

Scales of Measurement

Evaluators can estimate student performance using test scores based on different types of measurement scales. The description of a student's performance depends on the test's measurement scale. There are four different measurement scales: nominal, ordinal, interval, and ratio.

Nominal Scale

A **nominal scale** represents the lowest level of measurement. It is a naming scale. Each value on the scale is a name, and the name does not have any innate or inherent value. Hair color and students' names are examples of nominal scales. Although there are numerals on football uniforms, there is no inherent rank or value to the numerals. A numeral is just associated with the name of the football player. A teacher may use a nominal scale to distinguish among groups 1, 2, and 3. The numbers 1, 2, and 3 have no intrinsic value; they are simply labels for the groups. Because nominal scales merely represent names, they have limited usefulness. They cannot be added, subtracted, multiplied, or divided. They are rarely used in reporting test performance.

Ordinal Scale

An **ordinal scale** is the next level of measurement. An ordinal scale orders items in a scale or continuum. Ordering students according to class rank is an example of an ordinal scale (Table 6.1). The Snapshot called Activity Levels also provides an example of an ordinal scale.

TABLE 6.1 • Ordinal Scale

Student	Rank
Jean	10
Mia	9
Mura	8
Melissa	7
Chris	6
Ruth	5
Lisa	4
Mei	3
Dan	2
David	1

SNAPSHOT

Activity Levels

Suppose a teacher is observing a student with a high activity level. The teacher wants to rank the activity level of the student from 1 to 10, with 10 being the most active and 1 the least active, like this:

Activity level	1	2	3	4	5	6	7	8	9	10
Classroom										
Playground										

The distance between each of the ranks 1, 2, 3, and so forth, is not equal. That is, the same increase in activity may not be required, in the teacher's judgment, to raise a ranking from 3 to 4 as from 7 to 8. Because of this limitation, ordinal scales cannot be added, subtracted, multiplied, or divided.

Pause and consider:
- Why would ordinal scales be seen as misleading when ranking students' activity levels?
- Suggest alternative approaches for measuring students' activity levels.

Interval Scale

An **interval scale** is similar to an ordinal scale, but it has several important advantages. Interval scales order items on a scale or continuum, as do ordinal scales, but unlike ordinal scales, the distance between the items is equal. Because of this characteristic, interval scales can be added, subtracted, multiplied, and divided.

Interval scales have another interesting characteristic. Interval scales may include a zero point but do not have a true or rational zero. For example, a Fahrenheit scale is an equal interval scale; there is an equal distance between the degrees of temperature. The zero point, however, was arbitrarily established by Daniel Fahrenheit when he developed the temperature scale. Intelligence quotient tests also base their scores on equal interval scales. Although there is an equal distance between the scores, an IQ of zero cannot be measured.

Ratio Scale

A **ratio scale** has all the characteristics of ordinal and interval scales, and in addition, it has an absolute zero. Height and weight measurements are examples of ratio scales. Teacher-developed tests, such as classroom spelling or mathematics tests, frequently use the ratio scale as a base. The total number of test items that a student answers correctly, or the raw score, is based on a ratio scale. Some observation and rating scales are also ratio scales. Because the ratio scale has an absolute zero, the scores adapt to mathematical operations. If we are recording the number of times students raise their hands, we may conclude that one student exhibits this behavior two or three times more than another student.

Frequency Distribution

A **frequency distribution** is a way of organizing test scores according to how often they occur. To create a frequency distribution, arrange the test scores in a column from high to low. Next to each test score, record the number of individuals who received that score on the test (Table 6.2). Next, construct a graph (Figure 6.1).

TABLE 6.2 • Frequency Distribution

Score	Frequency Distribution
100	3
90	2
80	5
70	4
60	6
50	5
40	2
30	1

Total number of students: 28

Normal Curve

Frequency distributions can have different shapes. The shape represents groupings of students' scores. In a **normal curve** most scores fall in the middle, and fewer scores occur at the ends of the distribution. The normal curve is a symmetrical, bell-shaped curve (Figure 6.2).

There has been considerable debate about whether human characteristics are distributed in a normal curve. Although there is some evidence that physical characteristics such as height and weight are distributed normally, there has been active discussion about whether other characteristics, such as intelligence, development, and achievement, are normally distributed. Although it is less likely that the performance of small groups of children will distribute normally on a specific characteristic, the test results from large norm samples will probably be more normal in appearance.

Skewed Distributions

Sometimes, the majority of scores occur at one end of the curve. These scores show a **skewed distribution**. Positively skewed distributions contain only a few high scores, with the majority of scores occurring at the low end. Negatively skewed distributions have few scores at the low end and a majority of scores at the high end. When distributions are either positively or negatively skewed, the measures of central tendency—that is, the mean, median, and mode—shift. Figure 6.3 shows the placement of the mean, median, and mode in skewed distributions.

Measures of Central Tendency

Measures of central tendency describe the typical test performance of a group of students using a single number. The number that results from the calculation of a measure of central tendency represents the typical score obtained by the group of students. The mean, mode, and median are measures of central tendency. In the Snapshot, teachers Brendan Strout and Ken Brown decide when to use measures of central tendency.

Mean

The **mean**, or the average score, is the most frequently used measure of central tendency. To compute the mean, add all of the scores and divide by the total number of scores (Table 6.3).

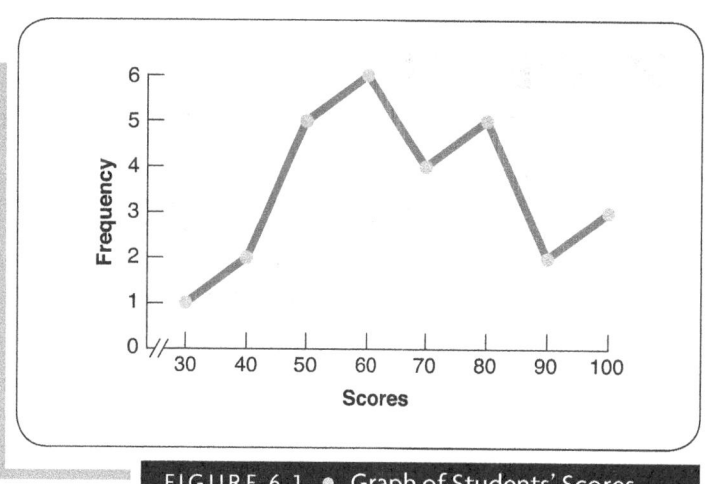

FIGURE 6.1 • Graph of Students' Scores

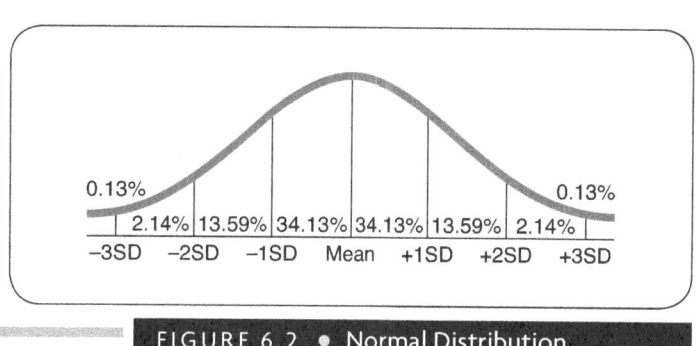

FIGURE 6.2 • Normal Distribution

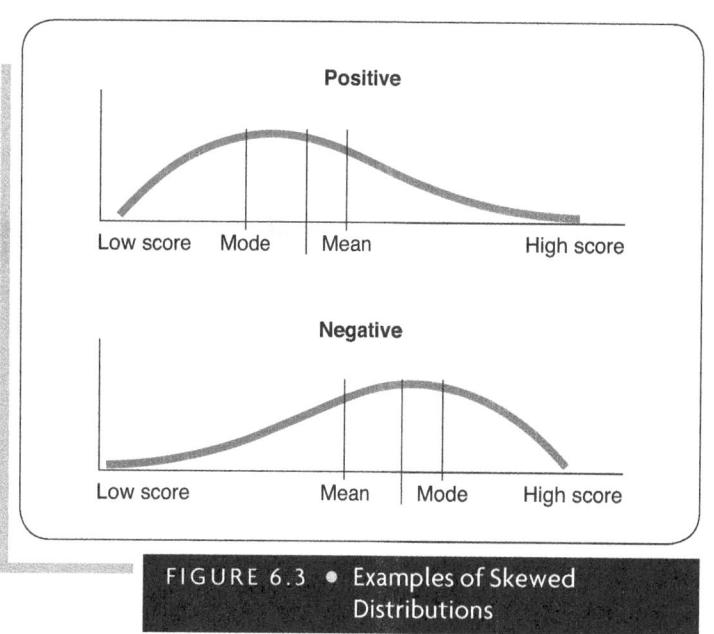

FIGURE 6.3 • Examples of Skewed Distributions

SNAPSHOT

Deciding When to Use Measures of Central Tendency

Brendan Strout, the special education consultant at Washington School, was preparing to meet with Ken Brown, a sixth-grade classroom teacher. Brendan was examining the test scores of a group of students from Ken's classroom. Brendan wanted to be able to describe the performance of the students to assist Ken in making instructional decisions. Here are the scores of Ken's students:

90
82
81
80
79
75
75
75
20

Brendan summarized the scores in three ways:

1. By calculating the mean, or average: adding up all of the scores and dividing by 9, the total number of scores.

90
82
81
80
79 Median
75
75 Mode
75
20

$657 \div 9 = 73$. This is the mean, or average, score.

2. Next, Brendan arranged the scores from high to low and found the score that separates the top 50 percent of students who took the test from the bottom 50 percent of students. This score is 79 and is the median.
3. Finally, Brendan found the score that occurred the most often in the group of scores. This score is 75 and is the mode.

Pause and consider:
- Which measure of central tendency—the mean, median, or mode—should Brendan use in his discussion with Ken?
- What are your reasons for your answers?
- Where could you find additional information on this topic?

In the Snapshot, we asked: Which measure of central tendency—the mean, median, or mode—should Brendan use in his discussion with Ken? *Answer:* Brendan should use the median score of 79 because most of the scores in the class cluster around this score. The score represents the division between the top 50 percent of students and the bottom 50 percent of students. The mean score of 73 should not be used. Notice how this score was strongly influenced by the bottom score of 20.

TABLE 6.3 • Finding the Average (Mean)

Score	Frequency	Frequency × Score
100	1	100
98	2	196
90	2	180
85	4	340
70	6	420
50	5	250
42	3	126
30	2	60
25	1	25
Number of scores: 26		Sum of scores: 1697

$$\frac{\text{Sum of scores}}{\text{Number of scores}} = \text{Mean}$$

$$\frac{1697}{26} = \text{Mean}$$

$$\text{Mean} = 65.26$$

Because all the scores in a distribution are taken into account when the mean is calculated, extreme scores affect the mean.

Median

Another measure of central tendency is the median. It is the point on a scale above which and below which 50 percent of the cases occur. The **median** is an excellent measure of central tendency when most of the scores cluster together but a few scores lie at the extreme ends of a distribution. The median score in Table 6.3 is 70.

Mode

The **mode** is the score that occurs most frequently. In a distribution of scores, the mode is the most commonly occurring score. However, a distribution of test scores can have more than one mode. If a teacher wants to know which test or test item students most frequently answer correctly, the teacher would look at the mode. However, educators use the mode infrequently because it is not very helpful when describing the performance of an individual child or of a group of students. In a normal distribution, the mean, median, and mode all occur at the same point (Figure 6.2).

Standard Deviation

The **standard deviation (SD)** tells the degree to which various scores deviate from the mean. It is a unit of measurement, just as an inch and a foot are units of measurement. Scores can be expressed by the number of standard deviation units that they deviate from the mean.

The standard deviation is useful when comparing several sets of scores. It can be helpful when interpreting the test performance of one student or a group of students. When comparing scores, the larger the standard deviation, the more variable is the performance; the smaller the standard deviation, the less variable is the performance of the students. In a normal distribution, the percentage of scores that can be expected to fall within the first, second, and third standard deviations above or below the mean are shown in Figure 6.2. For example, when a group of scores distributes normally, 34.13 percent of the scores can be expected to occur between the mean and the $+1$ SD, and 34.13 percent of the scores also occur between the mean and -1 SD. Approximately 13.59 percent of the scores fall between the $+1$ SD and $+2$ SD, and 13.59 percent of the scores fall between the -1 SD and -2 SD. Just over 2 percent (2.14) of the scores occur between the second and third standard deviations, and 0.13 percent of the scores occur beyond the third standard deviation.

For most tests, publishers provide information about the mean and the standard deviation in test manuals. You will not have to calculate the standard deviation. For example, the *Wechsler Intelligence Scales* have a mean of 100 and a standard deviation of 15. This represents that approximately 34.13 percent of students have intelligence quotients (IQs) between 100 and 115. Similarly, approximately 68.26 percent of students have IQs between 85 and 115.

Types of Scores

There are many ways of reporting test performance. A variety of scores can be used when interpreting students' test performance.

Raw Scores

The **raw score** is the number of items a student answers correctly without adjustment for guessing. For example, if there are 15 problems on a mathematics test, and a student answers

11 correctly, then the raw score is 11. Raw scores, however, do not provide us with enough information to describe student performance.

Percentage Scores

A **percentage score** is the percentage of test items answered correctly. These scores can be useful when describing a student's performance on a teacher-made test or on a criterion-referenced test. However, percentage scores have a major disadvantage: We have no way of comparing the percentage correct on one test with the percentage correct on another test. Suppose a child earned a score of 85 percent correct on one test and 55 percent correct on another test. The interpretation of the score is related to the difficulty level of the test items on each test. Because each test has a different or unique level of difficulty, we have no common way to interpret these scores; there is no frame of reference.

To interpret raw scores and percentage-correct scores (to make comparisons), it is necessary to change the raw or percentage score to a different type of score. Evaluators rarely use raw scores and percentage-correct scores when interpreting performance because it is difficult to compare one student's scores on several tests or the performance of several students on several tests.

Derived Scores

Derived scores are a family of scores that allow us to make comparisons between test scores. Raw scores are transformed to derived scores. Developmental scores and scores of relative standing are two types of derived scores. Scores of relative standing include percentiles, standard scores, and stanines.

Developmental Scores

Sometimes called age and grade equivalents, **developmental scores** are scores that have been transformed from raw scores and reflect the average performance at age and grade levels. Thus, the student's raw score (number of items correct) is the same as the average raw score for students of a specific age or grade. Age equivalents are written with a hyphen between years and months (e.g., 12-4 means that the age equivalent is 12 years, 4 months old). A decimal point is used between the grade and month in grade equivalents (e.g., 1.2 is the first grade, second month).

Developmental scores can be useful (Sattler, 2008). Parents and professionals easily interpret them and place the performance of students within a context. Because these scores are so easy to misinterpret, parents and professionals should approach them with extreme caution. There are a number of reasons for criticizing these scores.

For a student who is 6 years old and in the first grade, grade and age equivalents presume that, for each month of first grade, an equal amount of learning occurs. But from our knowledge of child growth and development and theories about learning, we know that neither growth nor learning occurs in equal monthly intervals. Age and grade equivalents do not take into consideration the variation in individual growth and learning.

Teachers should not expect that students will gain a grade equivalent or age equivalent of one year for each year that they are in school. For example, suppose a child earned a grade equivalent of 1.5, first grade, fifth month, at the end of first grade. To assume that at the end of second grade the child should obtain a grade equivalent of 2.5, second grade, fifth month, is not good practice. This assumption is incorrect for two reasons: (1) The grade and age equivalent norms should not be confused with performance standards, and (2) a gain of 1.0 grade equivalent is representative only of students who are in the average range for their grade. Students who are above average will gain more than 1.0 grade equivalent a year, and students who are below average will progress less than 1.0 grade equivalent a year.

A second criticism of developmental scores is the underlying idea that because two students obtain the same score on a test, they are comparable and will display the same thinking, behavior, and skill patterns. For example, a student who is in second grade earned a grade equivalent score of 4.6 on a test of reading achievement. This does not mean that the second grader understands the reading process as it is taught in the fourth grade. Rather, this student just performed at a superior level for a student who is in second grade. It is incorrect to compare the second grader to a child who is in fourth grade; the comparison should be made to other students who are in second grade (Sattler, 2008).

A third criticism of developmental scores is that age and grade equivalents encourage the use of false standards. A second-grade teacher should not expect all students in the class to perform at the second-grade level on a reading test. Differences among students within a grade mean that the range of achievement actually spans several grades. In addition, developmental scores are calculated so that half of the scores fall below the median and half fall above the median. Age and grade equivalents are not standards of performance.

A fourth criticism of age and grade equivalents is that they promote typological thinking. The use of age and grade equivalents causes us to think in terms of a typical kindergartner or a typical 10-year-old. In reality, students vary in their abilities and levels of performance. Developmental scores do not take these variations into account.

A fifth criticism is that most developmental scores are interpolated and extrapolated. A normed test includes students of specific ages and grades—not all ages and grades—in the norming sample. **Interpolation** is the process of estimating the scores of students within the ages and grades of the norming sample. **Extrapolation** is the process of estimating the performance of students outside the ages and grades of the normative sample.

DEVELOPMENTAL QUOTIENT A **developmental quotient** is an estimate of the rate of development. If we know a student's developmental age and chronological age, it is possible to calculate a developmental quotient. For example, suppose a student's developmental age is 12 years (12 years $\times$ 12 months in a year = 144 months) and the chronological age is also 12 years, or 144 months. Using the following formula, we arrive at a developmental quotient of 100.

$$\frac{\text{Developmental age 144 months}}{\text{Chronological age 144 months}} \times 100 = 100$$

$$\frac{144}{144} \times 100 =$$

$$\frac{1}{1} \times 100 =$$

$$1 \times 100 = 100$$

But suppose another student's chronological age is also 144 months and that the developmental age is 108 months. Using the formula, this student would have a developmental quotient of 75.

$$\frac{\text{Developmental age 108 months}}{\text{Chronological age 144 months}} \times 100 = 75$$

$$\frac{108}{144} \times 100 = 75$$

Developmental quotients have all the drawbacks associated with age and grade equivalents. In addition, they may be misleading because developmental age may not keep pace with chronological age as the individual gets older. Consequently, the gap between developmental age and chronological age becomes larger as the student gets older.

Scores of Relative Standing

PERCENTILE RANKS A **percentile rank** is the point in a distribution at or below which the scores of a given percentage of students fall. Percentiles provide information about the relative standing of students when compared with the standardization sample. Look at the following test scores and their corresponding percentile ranks.

Student	Score	Percentile Rank
Delia	96	84
Jana	93	81
Pete	90	79
Marcus	86	75

Jana's score of 93 has a percentile rank of 81. This means that 81 percent of the students who took the test scored 93 or lower. Said another way, Jana scored as well as or better than 81 percent of the students who took the test.

A percentile rank of 50 represents average performance. In a normal distribution, both the mean and the median fall at the 50th percentile. Half the students fall above the 50th percentile and half fall below. Percentiles can be divided into quartiles. A quartile contains 25 percentiles or 25 percent of the scores in a distribution. The 25th and the 75th percentiles are the first and the third quartiles. In addition, percentiles can be divided into groups of 10 known as deciles. A decile contains 10 percentiles. Beginning at the bottom of a group of students, the first 10 percent are known as the first decile, the second 10 percent are known as the second decile, and so on.

The position of percentiles in a normal curve is shown in Figure 6.4. Despite their ease of interpretation, percentiles have several problems. First, the intervals they represent are unequal, especially at the lower and upper ends of the distribution. A difference of a few percentile points at the extreme ends of the distribution is more serious than a difference of a few points in the middle of the distribution. Second, percentiles do not apply to mathematical calculations. Last, percentile scores are reported in one-hundredths. But because of errors associated with measurement, they are accurate only to the nearest 0.06 (six one-hundredths). These limitations require the use of caution when interpreting percentile ranks. Confidence intervals, which are discussed later in this chapter, are useful when interpreting percentile scores.

STANDARD SCORES Another type of derived score is a **standard score**. *Standard score* is the name given to a group or category of scores. Each specific type of standard score within this group has the same mean and the same standard deviation. Because each type of standard score has the same mean and the same standard deviation, standard scores are an excellent way of representing a child's performance. Standard scores allow us to compare a child's performance on several tests and to compare one child's performance to the performance of other students. Unlike percentile scores, standard scores function in mathematical operations. For instance, standard scores can be averaged. In the Snapshot, teachers Lincoln Bates and Sari Andrews discuss test scores. Figure 6.4 compares standard scores with the other types of scores we have discussed. As is apparent, standard scores are equal interval scores. The different types of standard scores, some of which we discuss in the following subsections, are

1. *z*-scores: have a mean of 0 and a standard deviation of 1.
2. *T*-scores: have a mean of 50 and a standard deviation of 10.
3. Deviation IQ scores: have a mean of 100 and a standard deviation of 15 or 16.

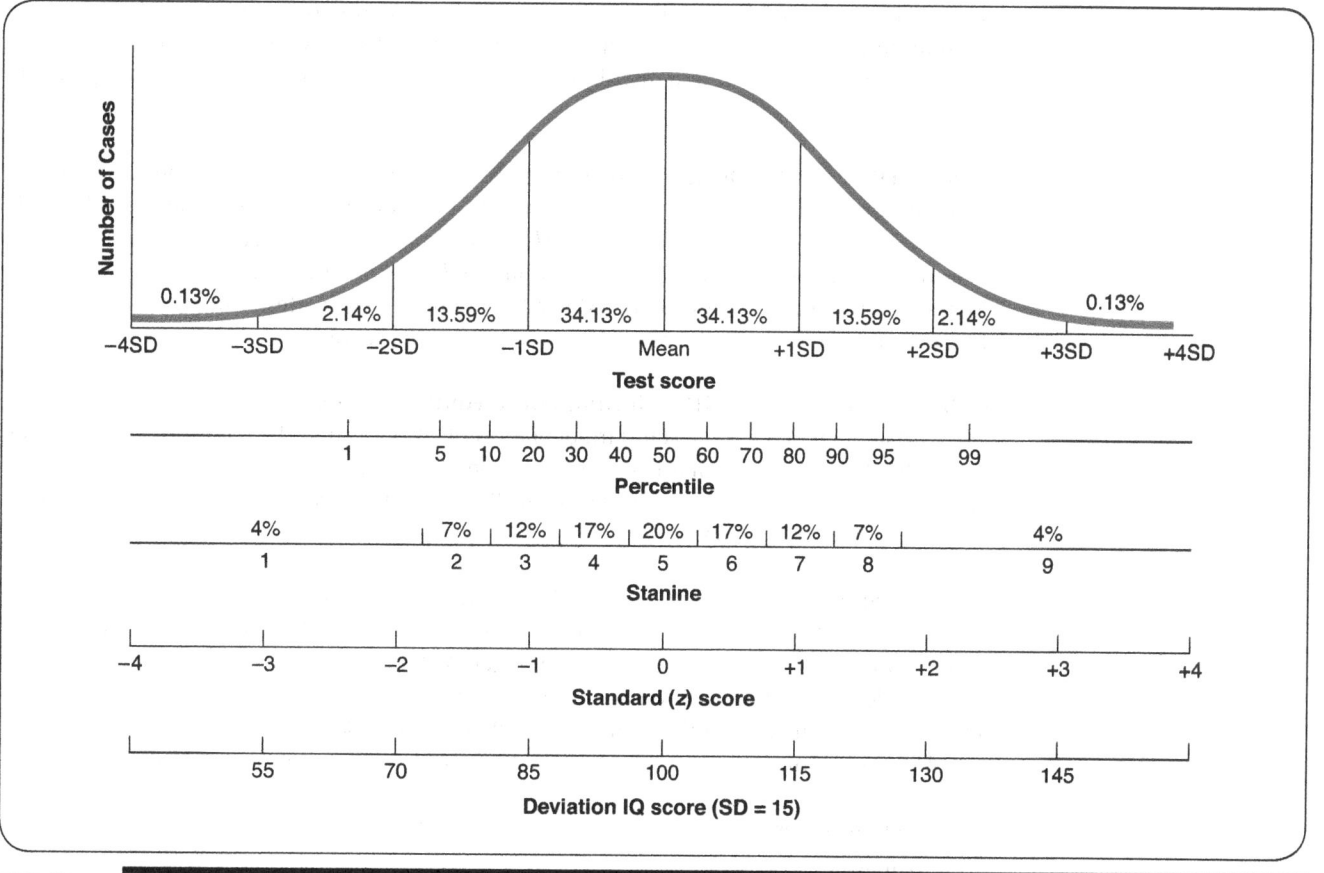

FIGURE 6.4 • Normal Curve With Types of Scores

SNAPSHOT

A Conversation Between Lincoln Bates and Sari Andrew

Just after school started in September, Lincoln Bates, a seventh-grade teacher of mathematics, reviewed last spring's test results for Karen Anderson, one of his students. He noticed that the results were reported using several types of scores:

Student's Name: Karen Anderson
Age: 13 years, 5 months
Teacher: J. Plante
Grade: 6

Subtest	Grade Equivalent	Age Equivalent	Percentile Rank
Mathematics	4.1	9–6	9
Reading comprehension	10.2	13–0	75
Spelling	6.4	12–0	45

Lincoln was unsure how to interpret Karen's scores on the mathematics achievement subtest. He decided to ask Sari Andrews, the school's test examiner. Lincoln said, "I'm not sure how to interpret the age equivalent and grade equivalent scores. Even though I used to teach fourth grade, I don't think that Karen approaches mathematics in the same way that a typical fourth grader does."

Pause and consider:
- Provide an explanation for Lincoln about Karen's age and grade equivalent scores.
- Where would you find additional information on these types of scores?

Sari explained, "Just because Karen earned a grade equivalent of 4.1 in mathematics does not mean that her thinking, behavior, and skill patterns are the same as other students who are in the fourth grade. The same holds true for her age equivalent score of 9–6. Age and grade equivalent scores can be misleading. I prefer to use percentile rank or standard scores as a way of interpreting her performance." What do you think?

4. Normal curve equivalents: have a mean of 50 and a standard deviation of 21.06.
5. Stanines: standard score bands divide a distribution of scores into nine parts.
6. Percentile ranks: point in a distribution at or below which the scores of a given percentage of students fall.

DEVIATION IQ SCORES **Deviation IQ scores** are frequently used to report the performance of students on norm-referenced standardized tests. The deviation scores of the *Wechsler Intelligence Scale for Children—IV* and the *Wechsler Individual Achievement Test—II* have a mean of 100 and a standard deviation of 15, and the *Stanford-Binet Intelligence Scale—V* has a mean of 100 and a standard deviation of 16. Many test manuals, Web sites, and resources provide tables that allow conversion of raw scores to deviation IQ scores.

NORMAL CURVE EQUIVALENTS **Normal curve equivalents** (NCEs) are a type of standard score with a mean of 50 and a standard deviation of 21.06. When the baseline of the normal curve is divided into 99 equal units, the percentile ranks of 1, 50, and 99 are the same as NCE units. One test that does report NCEs is the *Battelle Developmental Inventory—2*. However, NCEs are not reported for some tests.

STANINES **Stanines** are bands of standard scores that have a mean of 5 and a standard deviation of 2. As illustrated in Figure 6.4, stanines range from 1 to 9. Despite their relative ease of interpretation, stanines have several disadvantages. A change in just a few raw score points can move a student from one stanine to another. Also, because stanines are a general way of interpreting test performance, caution is necessary when making classification and placement decisions. As an aid in interpreting stanines, evaluators can assign descriptors to each of the 9 values:

9—very superior

8—superior

7—very good

6—good

5—average

4—below average

3—considerably below average

2—poor

1—very poor

Basal and Ceiling Levels

Because test authors construct tests for students of differing abilities, many tests contain more items than are necessary. To determine the starting and stopping points for administering a test, test authors designate basal and ceiling levels. (Although these are really not types of scores, basal and ceiling levels are sometimes called rules or scores.) The **basal level** is the point below which the examiner assumes that the student could obtain all correct responses, and therefore, it is the point at which the examiner begins testing.

The test manual will designate the point at which testing should begin. For example, a test manual states, "Students who are 13 years old should begin with item 12. Continue testing when three items in a row have been answered correctly. This is the basal level. (In other words, for this test, the basal point is the third test item in a row that was answered correctly.) If three items in a row are not answered correctly, the examiner should drop back a level."

Let's look at the example of a student who is 9 years old. Although the examiner begins testing at the 9-year-old level, the student fails to answer correctly three items in a row. Thus, the examiner is unable to establish a basal level at the suggested beginning point. Many manuals instruct the examiner to continue testing backward, dropping back one item at a time, until the student correctly answers three items. Some test manuals instruct examiners to drop back an entire level, for instance, to age 8, and begin testing. When computing the student's raw score, the examiner includes items below the basal point as items answered correctly. Thus, the raw score includes all the items the student answered correctly plus the test items below the basal point. The **ceiling level** is the point above which the examiner assumes that the student would obtain all incorrect responses if the testing were to continue; therefore, it is the point at which the examiner stops testing. "To determine a ceiling," a manual may read, "discontinue testing when three items in a row have been missed."

A false ceiling can be reached if the examiner does not carefully follow directions for determining the ceiling level. Some tests require students to complete a page of test items to establish the ceiling level.

Growth Scores

Growth scores are used to describe students' learning, progress and performance over time (O'Malley, Murphy, McClarty, Murphy, & McBride, 2011). Growth scores refer to changes in students' proficiency from one year to the next, changes in performance over several points in time, or predicted performance in the future. There are various types of growth scores, and they can be interpreted in different ways. Growth scores have some limitations, and various statistical models are applied when calculating these scores.

Standard Error of Measurement and Confidence Intervals

Standard Error of Measurement

The administration of a test is subject to many errors. Errors can occur in the testing environment, the examiner may make errors, the examinee may not be exhibiting the best performance, and the test itself may not able to evoke the best performance from the student. All these errors contribute to lowering the reliability of a test.

The **standard error of measurement (SEM)** is related to reliability and is very useful in the interpretation of test performance. The SEM is the amount of error associated with individual test scores, test items, item samples, and test times. A **true score** is the score an individual would obtain on a test if there were no measurement errors. (The obtained score is the score that a student gets on a test.) Figure 6.5 shows the distribution of the SEM around the estimated true score. If examiners expect that the reliability or the SEM will differ for different populations, SEMs should be reported for each population taking the test.

When the SEM is small, we can be more confident of a score; when the SEM is large, there is less confidence in the score. Thus, it follows that the more reliable a test is, the smaller the SEM and the more confidence we can have. The less reliable a test, the larger the SEM and the more uncertainty we have in a score.

Confidence Intervals

Although educators can never know a student's true score, we can use the concept of **confidence intervals** to give us a range within which the true score can be found. Because it is inadvisable to present a student's score as an exact point, the concept of confidence intervals is an important one to use when reporting a student's test score.

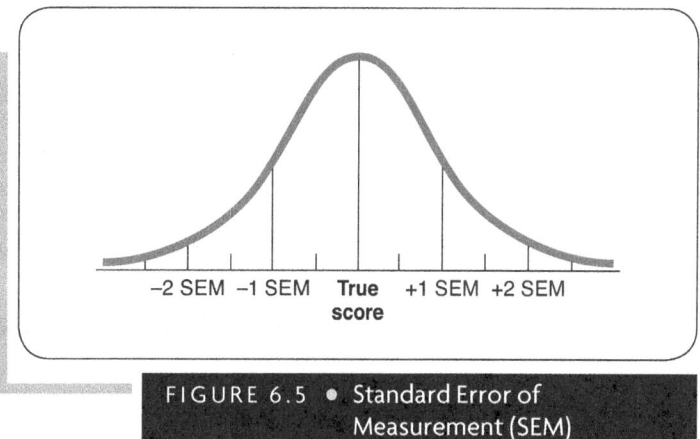

FIGURE 6.5 • Standard Error of Measurement (SEM)

We can determine the probability that a student's score will fall within a particular range. Three equivalent terms can describe this range: band of error, confidence interval, and confidence band. The lower the probability, the less confidence we have that a score falls within a particular range. For instance, we can be 50, 68, 90, 95, 98, or 99 percent confident that a student's true score can be found within a range of scores. The percentage of confidence that is chosen depends on the preference of the test examiner. However, we prefer to use 90 percent level or higher.

Scoring Guidelines

After you have administered the test, you must carefully score it. If you have used a standardized test, you must use the specific procedures for scoring described in the test manual. Score the test as soon as possible after you have administered it. Be sure to allot sufficient time so that you do not feel rushed. Scoring must be accurate. Check all calculations carefully. Software programs and Web sites that will calculate the test scores for you are available for many measures. These resources can be very helpful in avoiding errors.

Completing the Test Record Form

Biographical Information

The test record form contains a section for the examiner to complete biographical information about the student. Usually, this section is on the front of the test record form. The form, in general, asks for the following information: student's name, gender, name(s) of parent(s), home address, home telephone number, grade in school, age when tested, date of birth, student's homeroom teacher, name of school, and examiner's name. If the student needs to use corrective lenses or a hearing aid, the examiner should note this also.

Chronological Age

Often it is necessary to calculate the student's **chronological age**, the precise age of the student in years and months. If testing took place over several days, use the first test date to calculate the chronological age. Figure 6.6 shows the steps in calculating chronological age.

Calculating Raw Scores

The raw scores are the number of items that the student answered correctly. Directions for computing the raw score may vary from one test to another. Within each subtest you will need to add the total number of items the student answered correctly. Each test will have its own system for indicating the student's correct and incorrect answers. Following the directions given in the test manual or on the test record form, the examiner will designate the correct answers by marking either a plus sign (+) or by designating points (e.g., 1, 2, or 3 points) for each correct answer. When calculating the raw score, the examiner will need to follow the test manual directions for calculating basal and ceiling scores.

After calculating the raw scores, the examiner writes these scores on the test form and transfers them to the section that summarizes the student's scores. For many test forms, this section is on the front of the test form.

Transforming Raw Scores to Derived Scores

Calculating derived scores allows educators to make comparisons among test scores. Developmental scores and scores of relative standing are two types of derived scores. We prefer to

Example 1
Begin with the right column and subtract days, then months, and finally years. In this example, no borrowing is required.

	Year	Month	Day
Test date	2014	6	15
Birth date	1999	3	13
Chronological age	15	3	2

Example 2
If the day for the test date is smaller than the day for the birth date, it is necessary to borrow one month (30 days) from the month column and add the 30 days to the day column. When borrowing one month, always borrow 30 days.

	Year	Month	Day
Test date	2014	6̶	3̶
	1999	5	33
Birth date	1995	3	13
Chronological age	15	2	20

Example 3
If the month for the test date is smaller than the month for the birth date, it is necessary to borrow one year (12 months) from the year column and add the 12 months to the month column.

	Year	Month	Day
Test date	2014	2̶	15
	2013̶	14	15
Birth date	1999	3	13
Chronological age	14	11	2

In general, chronological age is reported in days and months. If the number of days exceeds 15, add 1 month. If the number of days is equal to or is smaller than 15, do not change the months. An online chronological age calculator can be found at **http://www.pearsonassessments.com**

FIGURE 6.6 • Three Examples of Calculating Chronological Age

use scores of relative standing: percentiles, standard scores, and stanines. Test manuals have norm tables that allow the examiner to convert raw scores to one or more types of derived scores. Some test manuals contain tables for age and grade norms for tests conducted during the fall, winter, or spring; other test manuals will have norm tables for tests administered at any time during the year. You may need to use more than one of the norm tables in the test manual. The section of the test form that summarizes the student's scores will indicate which type of derived score to use.

Graphing Scores

Many test record forms allow the examiner to plot a graph or profile of the student's test scores. For some measures, software programs and Web sites are available to plot graphs and profiles. A graph allows the examiner to depict test scores visually and assists in the interpretation of test performance. When developing a graph by hand, the examiner transfers the student's scores to the designated section of the test record form, connects the points, and creates a graph. Some record forms also allow bands of error to be plotted.

Interpreting Test Performance

Conclusions and interpretations about a student's performance based on the results of one test, measure, or observation are limited. A student's performance on only one measure indicates a narrow slice of information about the student. Because many sources of variability and error are present in any assessment situation and because many of the assessment approaches have limitations, we recommend that examiners use several different sources of assessment data. Sources of assessment data include standardized measures; portfolio assessment; performance-based assessment; interviews with family members, teachers, and the student; and observations in the classrooms, on the playground, in the cafeteria, and in the student's home, if appropriate.

When making interpretations about a student's performance, include observations of the behavior of the student and observations of the environment. Chapter 7 provides an in-depth discussion about the test interpretation process.

Behavioral Observations

In this section, the student's behavior during formal and informal testing is described. The examiner will want to note whether the student was cooperative, distractible, attentive, tired, shy, or exhibited other behaviors. What was the student's behavior at the beginning of the testing? During the testing? At the end? To a certain extent, the testing situation is artificial, and examiners must consider this when drawing conclusions about a child's behavior (Sattler, 2008). A child's behavior can vary in different settings and with different examiners. Systematic observations, as discussed in Chapter 8, can be important sources of information. The following list relating to appearance and behaviors is a starting point for discussion (Sattler, 2008):

- Physical appearance
- Reactions to test session and to the examiner
- General behavior
- Typical mode of relating to the examiner
- Language style
- General response style
- Response to failures
- Response to successes
- Response to encouragement
- Activity level
- Attitude toward self
- Attitude toward the examiner and the testing process
- Visual-motor ability
- Unusual habits, mannerisms, or verbalizations
- Examiner's reaction to the child

Observations of the Environment

Note any factors in the environment, such as interruptions, excessive noise, or unusual temperature, that may affect the student's test performance and behavior. Approaches to assessing the environment are discussed in Chapter 8.

Discussion of Results

When reporting the results of standardized tests, use the same types of scores throughout. Most professionals prefer standard scores, percentiles, or stanines. Report two or more types of scores, such as standard scores and percentiles. If a graph of the student's performance is available, be sure to use it.

How Should Assessment Approaches Be Evaluated?

We have discussed many concepts in this chapter. It is important for you to understand these concepts when using a test. Table 6.4 can be helpful when determining the adequacy of assessment approaches.

Before using individual tests, professionals would do well to consult independent reviews. Numerous resources are available that provide independent evaluations of tests. The Internet provides a wealth of information. The Buros Center for Testing Web site (**http://www.unl.edu/buros**) and Test Reviews Online (**http://marketplace.unl.edu/buros/**) have information about test reviews. Many journals and other online sources contain reviews of

---

TABLE 6.4 • Evaluation of a Test or Other Assessment Approach

Name of Assessment Test or Approach _____

Author(s) _____

Publisher _____ Date of Publication _____

About the Assessment Test or Approach
1. Purpose(s)
2. Extent to which individual items or tasks match the purpose(s)
3. Length of time for test administration
4. Group or individual

About Administration Requirements
1. Education and experience required for the examiner
2. Additional training requirements

About the Student
1. Considerations/adaptations for disability
2. Considerations/adaptations for language
3. Considerations/adaptations for culture/race/ethnicity

About the Technical Aspects
1. Norms, goals, standards, outcomes. If relevant, indicate
   a. Type
   b. Age, grade, language, culture, gender
   c. Representativeness
   d. Relevance of sample to student(s) tested
   e. Method of selection of sample
   f. Date of development of norms, goals, standards, outcomes
2. Reliability. What are the coefficients, and how were they determined?
   a. Test-retest
   b. Alternate form
   c. Split-half
   d. Internal consistency
   e. Interscorer/interrater/interobserver

3. Validity: What is the justification for each type of validity?
   a. Content
   b. Concurrent
   c. Predictive
   d. Construct
   e. Consequential validity

About the Results and Aids to Interpretation
1. Types of scores
2. Interpretation aids

About Fairness
1. Is the norm or comparison group appropriate?
2. Are considerations made for race, culture, gender, language, socioeconomic status, or disability?

About the Usefulness of This Test or Approach
1. Is it appropriate for the student(s)?
2. Is it fair?
3. Is it technically adequate?
4. Report from an independent source (*The Mental Measurements Yearbooks*, *Tests in Print*, *Test Critiques*, journal article, or Internet)

Conclusions
1. Overall strengths
2. Overall weaknesses
3. Summary and recommendations

About References
1. List of references consulted
2. List of other sources consulted

tests. Journals that may be of particular interest to special educators include *Assessment for Effective Intervention, Diagnostique, Exceptional Children, Journal of Early Intervention, Journal of Learning Disabilities, Journal of Reading, Journal of School Psychology, Journal of Special Education, Remedial and Special Education,* and *Topics in Early Childhood Special Education.*

Summary

- When using standardized, norm-referenced tests, educators must determine whether they are measuring consistent student performance and whether tests measure what the authors describe as the purpose of the tests.
- Test resources should provide information about technical aspects of tests, including the development of norms and test scores.
- Teachers, test examiners, and administrators should review tests carefully before using them to satisfy themselves that each test has acceptable levels of reliability and validity.
- Professionals should apply the technical concepts we have discussed in this and previous chapters to assessment approaches, procedures, and techniques.

QUESTIONS FOR REFLECTION

Select several tests and compare the standardization samples. Compare and contrast the development of two tests based on these descriptions. How closely does the norm sample of each test represent students in the community in which you live? What conclusions can you make?

1. What are the advantages of using norm-referenced tests? Disadvantages?
2. Several different types of test scores are discussed in this chapter. Which ones do you prefer to use? Why?
3. Annie received a score of 64 and a confidence interval of ±4 on an achievement test. How can the special education teacher use the concept of confidence intervals to explain Annie's performance to her family?
4. Imagine that you have recently attended a professional development workshop on testing and assessment and have been asked to share what you have learned in 10 minutes. What topics should you discuss relating to the technical adequacy of tests? Why did you choose each of these topics?

REFERENCES

American Educational Research Association, American Psychological Association, and National Council on Measurement in Education. (1999). *Standards for educational and psychological testing.* Washington, DC: American Educational Research Association.

O'Malley, K. J., Murphy, S., McClarty, K. L., Murphy, D., & McBride, Y. Y. (2011). Overview of student growth models. http://www.pearsonassessments.com/research

Salvia, J., Ysseldyke, J., & Bolt, S. (2013). *Assessment in special and inclusive education.* Belmont, CA: Wadsworth.

Sattler, J. (2008). *Assessment of children: Cognitive foundations.* LaMesa, CA: Author.

7 Test Interpretation and Report Writing

Chapter Objectives

After completing this chapter, you should be able to:

- Discuss the process of analyzing and interpreting assessment data.
- Discuss how assessment information is synthesized.
- Describe the process of hypothesis generation.
- Explain the general principles that guide the development of assessment reports.
- Explain considerations in sharing reports with the student and family members.
- Discuss the use of technology-generated test results and reports.

Overview

Educators use a variety of assessment approaches to answer questions about a student's behavior or performance. This chapter introduces you to the process that special educators use once they have gathered the information. Analyzing, interpreting, and synthesizing assessment information takes skill and practice. The interpretation of assessment results requires the practitioner to engage in a series of analyses that lead to one or more explanations of the student's performance and behavior. Then, the practitioner synthesizes this information into a written report with recommendations that becomes part of the student's record.

Interpreting Assessment Information

Introduction

Teachers interpret a variety of assessment information. We'll begin by examining classroom-based assessments and student observations; then, we'll examine standardized assessments. No matter what type of assessment data is gathered, educators must keep in mind that an assessment is just a brief snapshot in a moment of time. To ensure an accurate interpretation of a student's progress and achievements, educators and other practitioners will need to collect data from multiple sources over a period of time.

Classroom Assessment

Teachers use a variety of assessment approaches to plan instruction and monitor student progress. For example, one special educator gives weekly spelling tests. Each test consists of 10 vocabulary words chosen from those that the student has had difficulty in writing correctly during the previous week. After the student completes the quiz, the teacher adds up the items that were answered correctly to find the total number of correct items. This total is the raw score. One of the students, Danni, received a score of 8/10, which means on this day she wrote 8 out of the 10 words correctly. Sometimes the teacher will convert this raw score into a percentage; in this case, we can say that Danni received an 80 percent on her spelling test. Using raw scores, we can report the total number correct or convert the score into a percentage correct.

Pause and consider:
- Now it's your turn: In Danni's science class, the teacher gave the students a 15-question quiz. Danni received a score of 7.
- How would you calculate the percentage and interpret the results?

Observations

Observations of student behaviors provide a rich resource of information. There are many different types of observations that we'll learn more about in the following chapter. Here, let's examine one example. Earlier in the month, a special education teacher conducted several observations of Jason, who had been hitting and kicking other children, especially during circle and transition times. After the observations, the special educator and general education teacher sat down to examine the data (frequency of the behaviors) and brainstorm some strategies that could be used to reduce the occurrence of these behaviors. These strategies included the use of visual prompts using schedule strips that provide the student with illustrations of alternative, positive behaviors, increased proximity of the teacher assistant, and use of verbal and physical prompts when necessary. The teachers also discussed the need to teach the other children how to respond to Jason's behaviors. After two weeks, the special educator completed another observation and collected the following information:

> Observation notes (October 21): As children were lining up to come inside after recess, Jason attempted to push the student ahead. Teacher assistant prompted "Hand down" and provided Jason with a small object to hold. Jason complied. Five minutes later when the children were waiting for circle to begin, Jason raised his hand to hit the child beside him. Teacher assistant used the visual prompt showing Jason sitting at circle and said "Hand down," and Jason complied. After circle was over, and children were transitioning to small-group reading, Jason started to raise his hand to strike another child and then put his hand down, upon seeing that the teacher was watching.

The special education teacher wrote the following interpretation:

> This student continues to struggle with the behavior (striking), though we have seen an overall reduction of attempts/instances. The suggested techniques seem to be working. The most difficult time for this student continues to be when waiting at circle and when transitioning to and from an activity.

Pause and consider:
- Now it's your turn. We learned in this example that the teachers also discussed the need to teach the other children how to respond to Jason's behaviors. If you were part of the discussion, what might you suggest?
- How would you collect information to see if your ideas are working?

Standardized Assessments

Standardized assessments provide educators with information not only about how the student did but also about how the student's performance compares with other students of the same age and grade who took the assessment. Once the student completes the asssessment, the examiner educator may use hand scoring or technology-generated scoring to obtain the results. If the assessment is hand scored, the practitioner begins by scoring each area of the assessment, double-checking any mathematical calculations. For example, a standardized mathematics test could include operations (addition, subtraction, multiplication, and division), fractions, and word problems. The examiner calculates the raw scores for each area and then finds the student's composite score. A **composite score** represents the student's overall performance. It is derived by combining the results of two or more contributing tests according to a specific formula. A composite score is very useful in interpreting assessment results because it allows the examiner to examine the student's overall performance in an academic area, development, or behavior. For example, one standardardized achievement test includes the following composite scores:

- Reading total = Reading Subtest 1 + Reading Subtest 2 + Reading Subtest 3
- Mathematics total = Mathematics Subtest 1 + Mathematics Subtest 2

Most educational test publishers report composite scores as standard scores with a mean and a standard deviation. You will need to check the manual to determine the mean and standard deviation of a specific test. Many educational assessments use composite scores with a mean of 100 and a standard deviation of 15. To locate the composite score, the examiner uses a table in the examiner's manual, scoring software, or app that automatically generates composite scores.

Let's look more closely at an example of interpreting an assessment for a student who received a composite score of 86 (based on a mean = 100 and a standard deviation = 15). When we interpret composite scores, we examine the score and consider how many deviations the score is from the mean. A beginning teacher might start to interpret the score by saying, "The student received a total score of 86, which is within 1 standard deviation of the mean or within the average range." However, we know that individual test scores and test items contain some degree of error, or standard error of measurement. We would remind our colleague that we always use confidence intervals when we report test scores. (To review these concepts, see Chapter 6). Test developers publish information about confidence intervals in tables, often the same tables used to locate composite scores. Usually the test developer provides more than one type of confidence level to use. Let's return to our example and reword our colleague's attempt by including the following information, "The student obtained an overall total score of 86, with a confidence interval of 82–90. We can be quite certain (95 percent confident) that his score falls within this average range." Sometimes we simply write 86+/4. Another way of saying this would be, "The student's composite score was 86, with her true score falling in the range of 82–90 at the 95 percent confidence interval."

Pause and consider:
- Now it's your turn. How would you explain a composite score of 108 and a 90 percent confidence interval of 104–112 (based on a mean = 100 and a standard deviation = 15)?

Sometimes standardized tests also include the use of scaled scores to report student results. A **scaled score** is derived from raw scores according to a mathematical scaling process. Usually the standardized test reports the mean and standard deviation of these scores. For example, in one standardized assessment, the examiner's manual states that scaled scores have a mean of 10 and a standard deviation of 3. Scaled scores enhance test interpretation because scaled scores from one test may be compared with scaled scores from a second test. Sometimes scaled scores can be helpful in developing the student's individualized education program (IEP) or in evaluating progress toward goals. However, we usually use caution in reporting scaled scores, as sometimes a student's scaled score is based on only a few test items within a subdomain.

Let's look at a detailed example of using both composite and scaled scores. Emily received a composite score of 76+/−4 at the 95 percent confidence level on an assessment that measures social skill development. This area includes two subdomains: Leisure and Friendship. For each of the subdomains, the test yields scaled scores. Emily received a scaled score of 4 in Leisure and 5 in Friendship. We would interpret these results as follows:

> Emily received a composite score of 76 (mean = 100 and standard deviation = 15, which falls within the range of 72–80 at the 95 percent level of confidence. This places her in the low average range. Within the subdomain areas she received a score of 4 in Leisure and a score of 5 in Friendship (mean = 10 and standard deviation = 3). These scores indicate that she is approximately 1.5–2 standard deviations below the mean, suggesting she has very low skills compared to her peers. Because Emily's leisure and social skills needed for engaging in play and recreational activities function in the below average range, she may need supports at school and in the community to help her engage in activities.

Pause and consider:

- Now it's your turn. How would you explain a composite score in mathematics of 89+/−4 (based on a mean = 100 and a standard deviation = 15) and scaled scores of 8 in multiplication and division and 11 in addition and subtraction (based on a mean = 10 and a standard deviation = 3)?

Standardized tests also provide other types of scores for interpreting student performance in comparison with other students of the same age and grade. A percentile rank provides information about the student's relative standing to other students. For example, Emily, who took the social skill assessment described earlier, received a percentile rank of 12 in the Friendship area. This area consists of questions that focus on a variety of skills including, for example, greeting friends, beginning and maintaining conversations, and discussing appropriate topics with peers and adults. To interpret the percentile rank, we would say that the student scores the same as or better than 12 percent of the other students of her same age who took the test. In talking with the student's parents about the test results, we would include some practical interpretations. For example, we might report,

> Emily has beginning skills that allow her to build friendships at school and in the community. Her skills are the same as or better than 12 percent of other students who are the same age; this means that 88 percent of students scored higher than Emily. Because her social skills needed to interact with peers, initiate and maintain relationships with others, express and recognize emotions, and help others are in the very low range, she will need instruction and supports in these areas.

We would explain that the student's scores are based on one assessment, and we would discuss whether these results are confirmed by additional assessment information of how the student functions in the community, at home, and at school. If so, then this information indicates that this is an area that needs to be strengthened.

> **Pause and consider:**
> - Now it's your turn: How would you explain the following information?
>   *Total Composite Score = 96; Overall Percentile Rank = 48 (based on a mean = 100 and a standard deviation = 15)*
> - Write a few sentences to describe how you would report these results to the student's parent.

We have seen that percentile ranks, scaled scores, and composite scores help build a picture of student performance. Now let's examine how the examiner uses a process of analysis for each assessment administered and then synthesizes and interprets the results:

1. *Overall test performance.* Analyze the student's overall performance and consider an interpretation of the full-scale or total score performance.
2. *Subtest performance.* Analyze the student's performance in each area assessed. List the areas that indicate strong student performance as well as areas that indicate student weaknesses.
3. *Compare the subtest performance on all tests.* Consider each subtest and the skills, knowledge, or behaviors that it measures. Compare the shared abilities across assessments. Identify relative areas of student strengths and needs. If a student's score on one test looks different from a score on a different test, the practitioner will need to consider possible reasons for the discrepancy. Use of multiple sources of data, often known as triangulation, helps the practitioner in developing accurate interpretations.
4. *Integrate the student's relative strengths and needs.* Compare all the assessment data, including the results of observations, interviews, and conferences, with more formal assessments such as norm-referenced, curriculum-based, or criterion-referenced assessments. Continue to build the picture of student performance by integrating the student's relative strengths and needs across multiple forms of assessment data (Flanagan & Kaufman, 2009; Frick, Barry, & Kamphaus, 2010).

Hypothesis Generation

When interpreting the results of testing, we prefer the process described as **hypothesis generation** (Flanagan & Kaufman, 2009) or integrative interpretation (Frick et al., 2010). In test interpretation, a hypothesis is an explanation of a student's performance and behavior based on the collected assessment data. In generating a hypothesis, the examiner uses assessment information from multiple sources. For example, a special educator works with the team to assist a classroom teacher who has a student with problem behaviors. The special educator completes a set of classroom observations and a student interview while the classroom teacher completes daily notes. The school nurse reviews the student's medical history. Optimally, these professionals meet with other team members to review the assessment information and to develop a hypothesis regarding the present problem behaviors. As the team reviews the assessment information, several hypotheses emerge. One hypothesis relates to the referral questions; other hypotheses may relate to levels of achievement, behavior, cognitive ability, communication, development, functioning, motor development, or sensory functioning.

When the team asks another member or a specialist, such as a psychologist, to conduct a comprehensive assessment, the examiner will integrate information obtained from interviews with teachers, therapists, support staff, the student, and family members with information obtained from behavioral observations of the student. Flanagan and Kaufman (2009) cautioned that hypotheses are not facts and that, later, they may prove to be artifacts. Hypotheses are informed assumptions; when evidence does not substantiate hypotheses, further investigation is necessary. The test data may need reanalysis, or the examiner and the team may have to collect additional data to generate new or modified hypotheses.

Examiner Bias

Examiner bias can arise in the interpretation of assessment results. Examiners need to be aware of the types of biases in order to identify and control them. Bias colors how the data will be viewed and interpreted. Bentzen (2009) describes two levels of potential bias. At one level is the personal bias and perspective of the examiner: The examiner brings individual experiences, abilities, attitudes, and knowledge to the interpretation process; sometimes these experiences or attitudes interfere with the careful, objective interpretation of information. We can begin by examining our own beliefs and attitudes, becoming aware of any personal bias that we may hold. We can follow up by learning more about culture, traditions, and beliefs of others.

The second level of bias is the result of formal training and includes bias shaped by theory, conceptual framework, or philosophy. For example, a teacher trained in a developmental approach may hold a different perspective in understanding child behavior than a teacher trained in a behavioral approach. These biases affect how each teacher interprets a situation, event, behavior, and ultimately, the assessment results.

Using Professional Knowledge

To interpret test results, the examiner must understand the purpose of the test itself, how it is administered, and what the test scores mean. In our discussion of norm-referenced tests and standardization samples in Chapter 6, you learned that a standardized test can be administered to students with characteristics that are similar to the norm group and that the examiner can compare each student's score with those of the norm group. In interpreting test results, the examiner must consider the norm sample of a test instrument; if the characteristics of the student tested are not similar to those of the norm group, the examiner will need to explain how this affects the test scores. The test scores of students who have characteristics different from the norm sample cannot be compared with the test scores of the students who participated in the standardization of the instrument.

Examiners should have an understanding of test scores and be able to explain them to others. For example, an examiner may be called on to explain the difference between a percentile rank and a percentage-correct score or to clarify misperceptions about a grade equivalent score and explain the results using nontechnical terms.

In interpreting assessment information, the examiner must be a keen observer of behavior, context, culture, and environmental conditions that adversely affect students' performance. In the following chapter, we will examine the effects of the physical, learning, and

---

Research-Based Practices | Test Bias and Fairness

Today the problem of disproportionality among African American students in special education continues to persist in the United States. Vallas (2009) discussed the problem by examining a variety of possible causes, including bias in assessment, referral, and the lack of cultural responsiveness among school personnel. Ford and Helms (2012) discussed strategies for overcoming barriers in standardized assessments for African American children and youth. Even though publishers claim that revisions of standardized assessments are more culturally sensitive and recently normed instruments use standardization samples that reflect the cultural diversity of the current population in the United States, there remain concerns that these assessments are unfair.

Perhaps some of these difficulties will be addressed by the changes that many schools are making in how students with learning disabilities or emotional-behavior problems are identified. More and more practitioners are transforming practices by using a response to intervention (RTI) process to identify children and youth who are at risk for academic and behavior problems (Fuchs, Fuchs, & Compton, 2012). School psychologists report conducting fewer psychoeducational assessments (Sullivan & Long, 2010). By providing students with early intervention and supports to promote positive behaviors, researchers are finding decreases in problem behaviors (Benner, Nelson, Sanders, & Ralston, 2012; Froiland, 2011) and increased use of the RTI model in identifying students with learning disabilities (O'Donnell & Miller, 2011).

social environments on performance. Observations of the environment and of the student will add valuable information. As the examiner synthesizes assessment results, the observations may corroborate information obtained during formal testing, or these observations may help to explain why a student's score was unexpectedly low.

Interpreting assessment information requires a wide range of knowledge concerning child and adolescent growth and development as well as disability. Examiners need professional knowledge of classroom curriculum and pedagogy, and a solid understanding of statistics is essential in interpreting test scores. Knowledge of special education, related services, state regulations, and federal law is essential in clarifying the information.

General Principles for Report Writing

Once the examiner has interpreted the assessment information, the results are synthesized and organized into an assessment report. One of several different types of assessment reports is used, depending on the assessment question(s) and the purpose for the assessment. Later in this chapter we will examine examples of some different types of assessment reports.

We will begin by looking at the general principles for report writing. In writing the report, the examiner makes sure that general statements about the student's performance or recommendations can be supported by the assessment data. The following general principles guide the development of a well-written report.

- *Organize the Information.* Organize the information systematically. Present information in sections with appropriate headings. Discuss recommendations at the end of the report; do not insert them in the body of the document.
- *Relate Only the Facts.* Report only factual information. Do not include unsubstantiated information. When including information from other sources, such as other assessment reports, mention the date when the source was written and the name of the author(s).
- *Include Only Essential Information.* Write about the facts, and avoid extraneous information about the student or family. Although your report must be comprehensive, some information is not essential; you will need to make judgments about whether what you have learned is appropriate for the report. Use only information that contributes to an understanding of the student, the test results, and recommendations.
- *Improve What We Say.* As professionals, we must uphold high ethical standards, including what we say and how we write. Figure 7.1 describes points to consider and ways to improve. We use people-first language to refer to students with disabilities and the special education services that they receive. We also know that some disability groups have other preferences. To determine how to refer to a group of individuals, we can ask the individuals involved. For example many people who are deaf, prefer to use a capital noun to refer to the group, as in *the Deaf* or a *Deaf person*. Some racial, ethnic, and cultural groups have changed preferences over time. Today, naming a nation or region of origin is preferred, such as *Mexican American* or *Guatemalan*. We use specific terms to describe conditions, rather than talk in general terms. For example we would say, "Adolescents who are at risk *for dropping out of school.* . . . Finally, we use the terms *boy* and *girl* to refer to children under 12 years of age, and *young men* or *young women* or *male adolescent* or *female adolescent* for youth ages 13–17 (APA, 2010, p. 75–76).
- *Present Accurate Information.* Make sure that the information is accurate. The examiner must always verify that the test scores were copied correctly from the test to the report. Be sure that there are no misinterpretations about performance due to inaccurate calculations or inaccurate copying.
- *Include Any Reservations.* Incorporate, and discuss, any reservations about the assessment process and its effect on the results. Reservations may include observations of the student that indicate the results are not accurate or do not reflect the student's best abilities. Record any interruptions or other disturbances in the environment that may have

> 1. Use people-first langague. Generally, say the student first then the disability. Children *with learning disabilities* or students *who receive special education services.*
> 2. Be sensitive to labels. Respect preferences. Some groups representing people with disabilties prefer to use the disability term first. *Deaf* students.
> 3. Use words that are free from bias. When describing racial and ethnic groups of students, describe them by their nation or region of origin: *Mexican* American children or *Chinese* children.
> 4. Use terms that are specific rather than making a broad statement: Children who are at-risk *for early reading difficulties.*
> 5. Use terms to refer to specific age groups:
>   - Under age 12: use *boy* and *girl*
>   - Between 13 and 17: use *young man* or *male adolescent; young female* or *female adolescent*
>   - 18 and over: use *man* or *woman*

FIGURE 7.1 • Reducing Bias: Guidelines for What We Say and Write

Adapted from American Psychological Association (2009), 71–77.

affected the results, and note the limitations in technical adequacy of the instrument(s) for students with characteristics that the norming sample does not represent.

- *Avoid Technical Jargon.* Use clear, understandable language. Avoid discussion of the formulas used to measure discrepancies or of the theoretical perspectives of various experts. Technical jargon can make the report confusing or ambiguous. How could the language in the following excerpt be simplified?

  > Tony has dual diagnostic deficits that affect expressive and receptive language, articulation, internal regulation, and cognition. A coexisting diagnosis can be made of Attention-Deficit Hyperactive Disorder and mental retardation. This diagnosis is strongly suggested by biological maternal history of ethanol abuse, apparently during the gestational period, and Tony's striking physiognomy.

- *Write Clearly.* Work to develop report-writing skills. Use the writing process to create a working draft. Reread and rewrite the working draft. Check the draft by using the grammar and spell-checkers. Avoid ambiguous language. Use a checklist like that found in Table 7.1 to ensure that you have included all the necessary information.

Synthesizing Information

Graphs allow us to illustrate assessment information in meaningful ways. They synthesize data in a visual format that allows us to easily compare data from one or more assessments. Graphically displayed data enhance understanding and serve to highlight findings that may be embedded in an assessment report.

Two commonly used types of graphs are

1. *Pie charts:* Pie charts display a circular graph cut into segments. This type of graph is most useful in displaying percentages of data when the examiner wants to illustrate parts of a whole.
2. *Bar graphs:* Bar graphs display rectangular sets of information with the length proportional to the amount of information represented. Bar graphs are most useful in displaying frequency counts or plotting trends over time.

TABLE 7.1 • A Checklist for Evaluating an Assessment Report		
Report Section	**Yes**	**No**
A. Identifying information		
1. Is the information complete?	_____	_____
2. Is the information accurate?	_____	_____
B. Reason for referral		
1. Is the reason for referral clearly described?	_____	_____
2. Is the source of the referral included?	_____	_____
3. Does the reason for referral provide a reason for conducting the assessment?	_____	_____
C. Background information		
1. Is this section complete?	_____	_____
2. Are any of the descriptions vague?	_____	_____
3. Can some information be omitted?	_____	_____
D. Behavioral observations		
1. Are the observations clearly described?	_____	_____
2. Are any of the descriptions vague?	_____	_____
3. Does this section help the reader to visualize the student's behavior?	_____	_____
E. Assessment approaches used		
1. Are the sources of information identified?	_____	_____
F. Discussion of results		
1. Does the discussion relate to the referral questions?	_____	_____
2. Is this section organized around themes?	_____	_____
3. Are the themes discussed separately, including references to appropriate tests and assessment procedures?	_____	_____
4. Are strengths and needs described?	_____	_____
G. Summary		
1. Does this section restate the major themes and how the testing addressed the reasons for referral?	_____	_____
2. Is this section too long?	_____	_____
H. Recommendations		
1. Do the recommendations logically follow from the rest of the report?	_____	_____
2. Can the recommendations be implemented?	_____	_____
3. Are recommendations for a variety of settings included?	_____	_____
4. Are the recommendations understandable?	_____	_____
I. General evaluation		
1. Is the writing clear?	_____	_____
2. Has the report been proofread?	_____	_____
3. Have the spelling, grammar, and punctuation been checked?	_____	_____
4. Are the sections of the report identifiable?	_____	_____
5. Has technical language been minimized?	_____	_____
6. Is there any bias?	_____	_____

SNAPSHOT

Analyzing and Interpreting Assessment Information

Spencer Lanley, a special educator at Summit Middle School and a member of the school's student assistance team, has been asked by team members to conduct several classroom observations. The team has been working with an eighth-grade teacher who was concerned about Cindy, a student with a learning disability. Initially, the teacher had brought her concerns to the team because she was worried about Cindy's progress in mathematics. She had explained, "I'm really concerned about Cindy's participation in the classroom. All of the interventions we have tried just don't seem to be working. It doesn't seem that Cindy is paying attention or getting any work accomplished."

First, Spencer defined "math-related activities" as looking at the teacher during the class lesson, working with paper and pencil on math problems, and discussing solutions to the math problems with peers. Then he collected data over a period of 3 days. The data analysis indicated that Cindy engaged in several behaviors during the class period: She was out of her seat, out of the classroom, looking around the room, and engaged in math-related activities.

The three pie charts in Figure 7.2 allow comparison of Cindy's behavior on each day of observation. The pie graph depicts the percentage of time that Cindy was engaged in each of the behaviors during math class. The bar graph (Figure 7.3) compares each behavior over the 3-day period.

Pause and consider:
- Which type of graph do you think best displays the data in answer to the observation question? Your answer should take into account the original assessment question!
- You can find our answer at the end of the Summary Section of this chapter.

The pie chart is the recommended way to display data in answer to the observation question because it allows the viewer to see how Cindy spends her time during the entire math class. If the observation question had been concerned with increasing or decreasing a behavior, then the bar graph would have been the recommended choice.

Spencer remembered an assessment class that he had taken in college and how the instructor had discussed the importance of comparing a target student to one or more students about whom the teacher has no concerns. He learned that a variation of the bar graph allows comparison of several students. He decided that this could provide additional information regarding whether the target student's behavior is atypical. Figure 7.4 compares Cindy's engagement in math-related activities with three other students across the different days. Spencer carefully analyzed this information. By looking at day 1, he saw that, although Cindy wasn't engaged as long as Tanya and Maria, her level

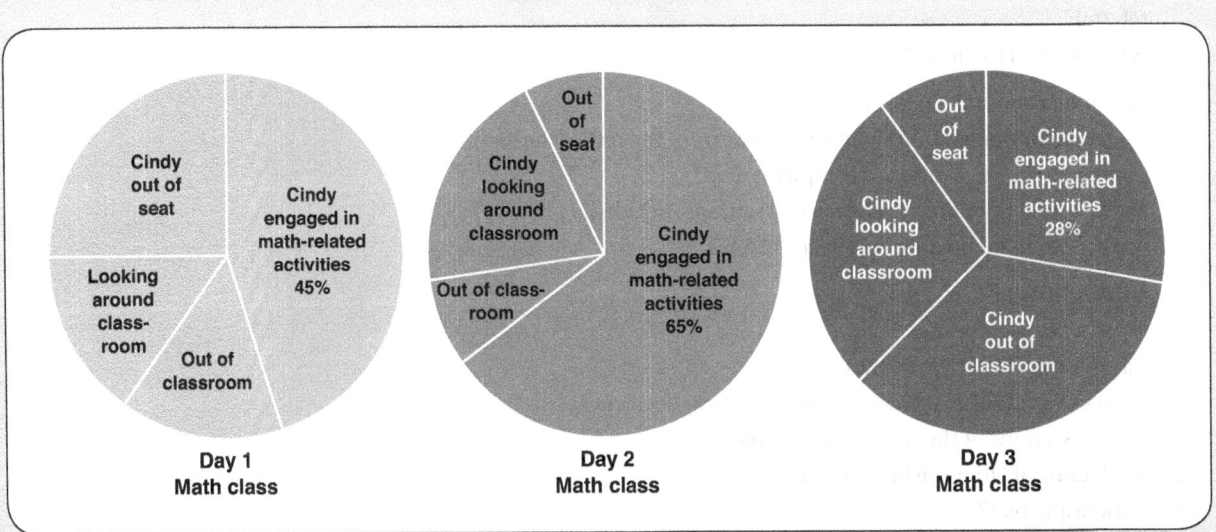

FIGURE 7.2 • Data Presentation in Pie Charts

(Continued)

SNAPSHOT Continued

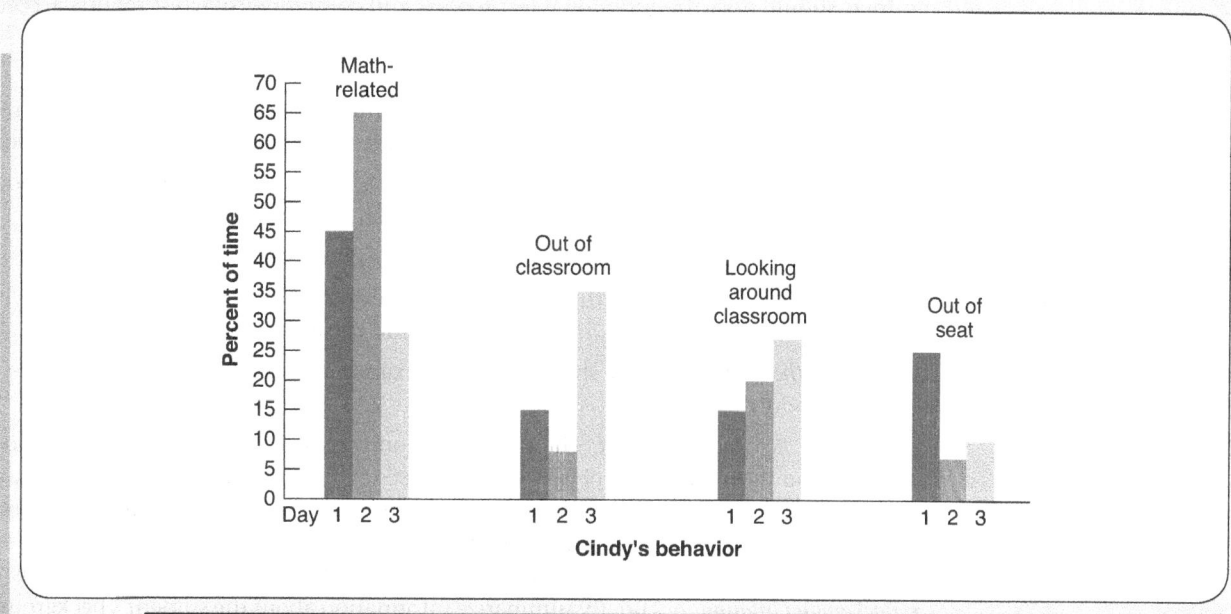

FIGURE 7.3 • Data Presentation in a Bar Chart

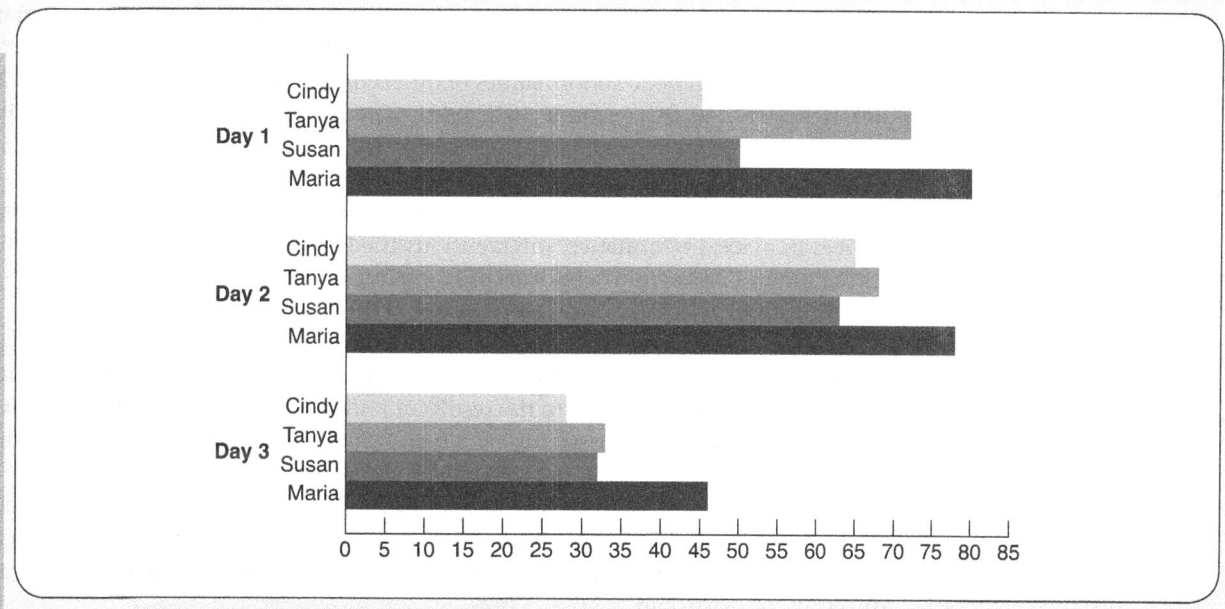

FIGURE 7.4 • Percentage of Engagement in Math-Related Activity for Four Students Over 3 Days

of engagement was similar to Susan. Day 2 provided evidence that Cindy and the other students were engaged for a high percentage of the time, and Cindy's behavior on the third day didn't seem to be much different from the other students, except Maria.

Spencer planned to show the charts to Cindy's teacher and other team members. By working together, they will identify some teaching strategies and materials that will help the classroom teacher enhance learning opportunities for these students.

Writing the Report

Examiners should organize individual test reports and comprehensive test reports according to the following areas:

- *Identifying Data.* School records, the referral form, interviews with family members or teachers, records of administered tests, and so forth, are standard sources for this information.

    About the student: Include the student's name, address, phone number, chronological age in years and months, birth date, and gender.

    About the parents: Include the names and addresses of parents or guardian.

    About the school: Include the student's grade level; the school's name, address, phone number, and director or principal's name; and the teacher's name.

    About the testing: Include the name of the examiner, the date of testing, and the date the report was written.

- *Reason for Referral/Assessment.* The second section contains a summary of the reasons for referral and the name of the person who initiated the referral or the reasons for the current assessment. Throughout the report, be sure to address directly the reasons and make sure the conclusions and recommendations refer to them. As the report develops, its central themes will be the assessment questions and the extent to which the testing addressed these issues.

- *Background Information.* Briefly summarize information about the student's background—the student's education, family history, medical care, and previous assessment results. Medical history can include a description of any unusual medical problems, diagnoses, extended hospital stays, continuing medical care, general health, and the results of vision and hearing testing. Some students have experienced early and prolonged medical interventions; some of these students may have had extended hospital stays and received extensive care for genetic abnormalities or other conditions. Their medical folders can be quite lengthy, and the examiner will need to judge which information is pertinent. Extensive discussion of a student's medical history may bias the reader to think that the child has a severe disability or may be unusually difficult to manage.

    Facts such as dates of attendance, regularity of attendance, type of placement or services in place, performance, interventions tried, and results of previous educational testing are available from school records, interviews, and home visits. A summary of child care experiences, depending on the age of the student, is also important.

    Details of familial and/or cultural background can be useful, but use this type of information carefully and judiciously, and only when it is relevant and helps to explain student behavior related to the results of testing. Knowledge about the family and cultural background is customarily obtained from interviews with the student, family members, teachers, and other professionals and through a home visit.

- *Observations of the Environment.* The description of the classroom environment includes the physical setting and the learning and social environments. Chapter 8 discusses important environmental factors and suggests ways to gather information about these aspects of the classroom.

- *Behavioral Observations.* The report includes a description of student behavior during testing. The examiner will want to observe whether the student was cooperative, distractible, attentive, tired, or shy or exhibited other types of behavior. How did the student approach the testing situation? What was the student's behavior at the beginning of the testing? During the testing? At the end? This section reports any observations conducted in the classroom, playground, cafeteria, or other setting.

    Systematic observations can be an important source of data. Methodical observations help in understanding student behavior and learning strategies and can also inform us about intervention strategies. Nevertheless, observations about behavior in the testing situation may not be generalizable to other settings. Testing assesses a narrow sample of behavior. To a certain extent, the testing situation is artificial. A student's behavior can vary in different settings and with different examiners. These factors must be considered when interpreting results and drawing conclusions about a student's behavior.

In writing the report, practitioners often begin with a physical description of the student. The student's reaction to the practitioner and the demands of the test situation are important to include, too. Other information in this section, often relevant to an overall picture of the student, involves the student's level of activity, interest, and effort.

The report includes a list of the tests and other assessments, both formal and informal, that teachers and others conducted to collect the assessment data. These could include work samples and student interviews, for example. All assessments are briefly described in terms of the purpose of the assessment and the achievement or behavior areas assessed.

When discussing the results, begin by discussing the student's overall performance. When the assessment report focuses on individual tests, discuss the student's total scores or composite scores and provide an interpretation of the meaning of the scores. This should provide a picture of the student's current level of functioning. Use the same types of scores throughout the section. Standard scores, percentiles, or stanines are preferable. Always include the confidence intervals when reporting standard scores. You may decide to report two or more types of scores, such as standard scores and percentiles. Some examiners like to report scores in a table format within the discussion of the results.

Next, consider each subtest and the skills, knowledge, and behaviors measured. Discuss the areas that indicate strong student performance as well as areas that indicate student weaknesses. Analyze each test separately; then synthesize the results.

Compare the shared abilities across all assessments given. Integrate the student's relative strengths and needs by discussing student performance across test data, including both formal and informal assessments. Include one or more hypotheses regarding student performance or behavior.

The summary section should be brief. Summarize the major points that have been discussed, and synthesize the results. Report the current level of functioning, and indicate areas of relative strength and need. Answer the referral questions. Restate the one or more hypotheses that emerged.

Finally, the report includes specific recommendations. These recommendations logically stem from the information in the assessment report. Suggest realistic, practical recommendations for implementation. Develop recommendations for the student in a variety of settings, including school, home, and community. Do not include specific goals in the assessment report; these are to be written in the IEP during the team meeting. The Snapshot about Gina illustrates an example of a comprehensive assessment report.

Evaluating the Report

Writing a report is an important way to communicate assessment findings. A report helps you to organize the results of testing systematically, to analyze a student's performance, and to make recommendations. Reports should be written clearly using correct grammar and spelling. Table 7.1 illustrates a checklist for use when reviewing the adequacy of assessment reports.

Types of Assessment Reports

Assessment reports are written for a variety of purposes, and the information they contain varies accordingly. In the following section, we will look at examples of reports written to (1) summarize a series of observations and synthesize the observational data, (2) report student progress over a period of time, (3) describe the results of administering an individual test, and (4) integrate and interpret the results of a comprehensive assessment.

Reports of Observations

A teacher typically writes a report providing a synthesis of several observations conducted on a student. Conducting multiple observations helps to ensure an accurate sample of student behavior. The written report organizes the information the teacher collected from all the observations.

How to Write an Observation Report

Examiners should complete a written observation as soon as possible after the final observation. Observation reports include the following information:

1. *Student information:* Name, date of birth, age, grade, and teacher's name.
2. *Dates of observations:* Date and time period of each observation.
3. *Purpose(s) for conducting the observations:* The observations may focus on the learning environment or on the student. Clearly state the purposes of the observations and define the events or behaviors in observable terms.
4. *Setting(s) in which the observations took place:* Note the specific setting, such as "Mrs. Turner's second-grade classroom" or "upper-level playground."
5. *Description of the environments:* The classroom environment includes physical, learning, and social aspects.
6. *Behavioral observations:* Be sure to relate only observed information. Do not interpret or make judgments.
7. *Discussion:* Summarize your observations of the environment and the student's behavior. Include your interpretation of the assessment data.
8. *Recommendations:* State realistic suggestions for implementing progress or improvement.

The Snapshot about John Diamond illustrates an observation report written by the special education consultant.

Progress Reports

Progress reports are summaries of the advances a student makes during a specific time period and provide a link to the IEP, which requires periodic monitoring of student progress. Progress reports must relate information about the student with reference to these goals and intended outcomes of the IEP. Teachers can prepare these reports to accompany a report card at the end of the marking period or to provide an update of information to family and other team members. One example of a progress report is a checklist (see Figure 7.5).

Second Marking Period	In Progress	Mastered
1. Uses correct punctuation to end a sentence.		×
2. Uses correct form of *you're* and *your*.	×	
3. Uses commas in a series correctly.		×
4. Correctly places apostrophe in contractions and possessives.	×	
5. Uses correct form of *their*, *there*, and *they're*.	×	
6. Uses correct form of adjectives.	×	

FIGURE 7.5 • Progress Report

SNAPSHOT

Observation Report on John Diamond

The special education consultant, Marilyn Philbrick, was asked to observe an eighth-grade student, John, in his regular classroom. At the time, John was receiving speech therapy and had been referred to the school psychologist because the team was concerned with John's aggressive behavior. According to the eighth-grade teacher, "He is always in motion. He frequently hits and pushes other students, and he is verbally abusive."

Marilyn met with John's teacher to discuss John's problem behaviors more fully. The meeting helped to clarify the behaviors that were of concern and to plan the best time and place to conduct the observations. Marilyn decided to develop her own observation instrument that would allow her to collect information about the behaviors of concern and the frequency of their occurrence.

After completing her observations, Marilyn wrote an observation report that summarized the findings. She also developed a graph to help explain the observation data. A copy of the graph (Figure 7.6) and one of her data sheets (Figure 7.7) that she developed to help explain her data followed her written report.

Observation Report

Name: John Diamond

Birth Date: 9/21/xx

Age: 13 years, 2 months

Grade: 8

Teacher: Dara Hall

Dates of Observations: 11/1/xx; 11/4/xx; 11/8/xx

Observer: Marilyn Philbrick

Purpose of Observations: The assessment team requested classroom observations because of concerns regarding John's behavior problems. Specific concerns include his out-of-seat behavior, hitting and pushing other students, and verbally abusing others. The purpose of the observations was to determine the degree to which John actually engages in the behaviors of concern.

Setting: Students change classes for each subject. Three observations were conducted over a 2-week period; John was observed in mathematics and language arts classes and during the lunch period. Each observation consisted of 30 minutes and took place between 9:00 and 11:00 a.m.

Observations of the Environment: The classrooms are designed for small-group work, with student desks clustered in groups of four. Students are not assigned a particular desk but are free to choose where to work. The classrooms consisted of 20 to 23 students with one teacher and occasional other support staff.

Behavioral Observations: The results of the observations indicate that John did indeed display many aggressive behaviors. John pushed and poked other students five to six times during each of the observations; less frequently (three to four times each observation), he hit and swore at other students and occasionally (two times each observation) swore at the teacher. These behaviors usually occurred when students were changing classes.

At other times (five to six times each observation), John joined the other students in laughter, volunteered answers, helped a student who was having difficulty with finding materials, and participated in activities willingly.

Discussion: John engages in pushing, hitting, and poking other students, as well as swearing at others, including the teacher. These observations indicate that the teacher continually has to watch him closely and frequently has to intervene on behalf of the other students.

John's problem behaviors are most apparent when he is listening without being able to be active, when the general noise level in the classroom begins to escalate, and when he is anticipating transition.

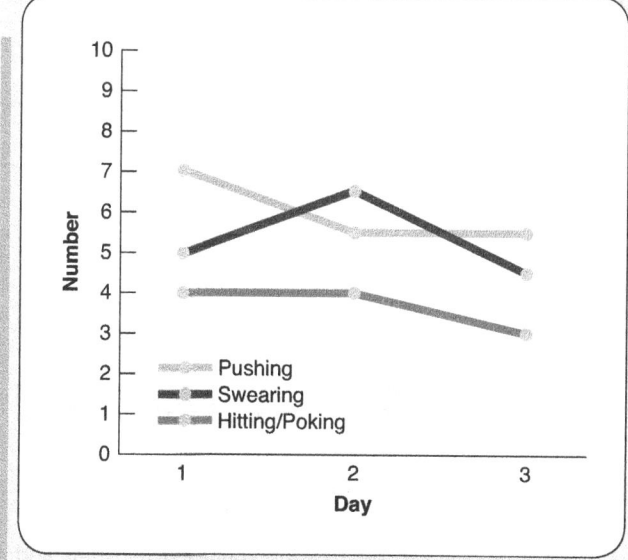

FIGURE 7.6 • Teacher-Developed Graph

(Continued)

SNAPSHOT Continued

Name: John				Date: November 1
Key: p=push h=hit s=swear				
Two-minute interval	Total behaviors			Comments
	p	h	s	Math class
00–02				Teacher goes over assignment for following day. John asks questions to clarify.
02–04				
04–06	||		|||||	Class changes at 9:05 Behavior occurs during transition and in hallway.
06–08	||	||||		Hits and pokes the boy behind him.
08–10				Other occurrences? –unable to follow John closely during this period.
10–12		||		Language arts class begins at 9:12.
12–14					Helps student find materials.
14–16				Volunteers to assist teacher.
28–30				

FIGURE 7.7 • Teacher-Developed Data Sheet

Aggression was especially high during transition, with no instances occurring during a spelling activity in which the teacher directed the whole class, and each student was actively engaged. Few aggressive behaviors occurred during small-group math manipulative activities. Both spelling and math were structured and required him to be more involved.

John appears to be a happy youngster, laughing and participating in activities willingly, but he shows little self-control or regard for his effects on others.

(Continued)

SNAPSHOT Continued

Recommendations: The contextual factors, such as transition activities, whole-class instruction, and small-group activities, and their influence on John's behavior need to be carefully analyzed. John appears to benefit from structured learning activities that include active student participation. Classroom noise, especially during transitions, should be monitored because this may have an adverse effect on his behavior. Positive behavior management strategies should be shared with his teacher and other support staff in the classroom.

Pause and consider:
- Now that you have read the observation report of the special education consultant, Marilyn Philbrick, summarize the original assessment question and the process that she used to gather data.
- Review the data sheet (Figure 7.7) and graph (Figure 7.6) she developed. Do you agree with her conclusions? What additional information would be helpful?

Individual Test Reports

Individual test reports, such as the Snapshot of Gina's Assessment Report, describe the test results and the examiner's interpretation of student performance. Usually, these reports are shared at the team meeting and become part of the student's permanent record. Individual reports of tests present a limited account of a student's performance; thus, they may be combined later into a comprehensive assessment report to provide more complete information on the student.

Each member of the team who conducts an assessment of the student must complete a written test report. At the team meeting, reports by several examiners, such as the special education teacher, the school psychologist, the physical or occupational therapist, or the speech and language pathologist, are considered.

Today professionals have access to many different types of technology-generated reports. For example, not only could a report summarize individual student performance, but it also could interpret the performance with recommendations of specific skill areas that the teacher should reteach.

Or a teacher could use a technology-generated report that interprets the assessment data of a student suspected of having a disability. Software, Web sites, templates, and apps allow the examiner to input the student's raw scores and then receive a detailed printout of the composite and scaled scores as well as an interpretation. The technology also may provide additional information, including behavioral objectives for each item answered incorrectly and a parent letter.

One of the advantages of using technology-generated reports is that scoring and computation errors can be minimized. Table 7.2 provides a checklist for evaluating technology-generated reports. What do you think might be other advantages? On the other hand, what might be some disadvantages?

TABLE 7.2 • Evaluation Form for Technology-Generated Scoring and Report Writing

1. Name of assessment:
2. Ease of data input:
3. Test results reported:
   Standard scores____ with confidence intervals____
   Stanines__
   Percentiles__
   Other_____
4. Quality of the report: Does the report contain technical jargon? Does the report contain any generalizations that may bias the report?
5. Cross-referencing: Does the report include the student's IEP information?

SNAPSHOT

Gina's Assessment Report

Larry Kahn is one of the special education consultants for the Allen School District. He recently completed a comprehensive assessment of Gina A., a first-grade student. Gina was referred to the assessment team by her teacher, Maria Gordon, who was troubled about her high level of activity and her lack of skills, among other concerns. The assessment report follows.

After completing the written report, Larry contacted Gina's foster parents to arrange for a convenient time to share the report with them. He wanted an opportunity to go over the report prior to the team meeting to allow the family an opportunity to ask questions and to discuss specific areas in more detail. During Gina's team meeting, he will present the results and recommendations contained in the report, then file a copy of the report in the office of student records.

Confidential Report of Special Education Evaluation
Office of Special Services
14 Main Street
Allen,_____
Telephone: 200–299–2000

CONFIDENTIAL REPORT

Name: Gina Anderson
Date of Birth: 11/10/xx
Age: 7.2
Foster Parents: Keith and Diane Anderson
Address: 1 Hill Road, Allen, ____

School: Allen Elementary School
Grade: 1
Evaluation by: Larry Kahn, M.S.,
Date of Evaluation: 05/10/20xx

Referral Information and Purpose for Assessment: Gina was referred by her teacher because of problems of extreme activity within the classroom, developmental concerns, and a history of physical abuse. The purpose of this assessment is to provide further information to the IEP team to assist in eligibility for special services and educational program planning.

Relevant Background Information: Gina has been in foster care since the age of 4, when she was exposed to inappropriate behaviors at home, neglect, and abuse. Her foster parents are very involved in her education and recreational activities in the community. Her biological mother, who has a history of abuse, is completing a prison sentence. Her brother, Paul, is living with a paternal grandmother. Her father has infrequent contact with Gina and her brother.

According to Mrs. Anderson, there are significant difficulties at home involving Gina's activity level, "... she always seems to be going ... has great difficulties settling down at night and sleeping. She is strong willed and overreacts much of the time to suggestions or requests from me or my husband."

Observation of the Environment: Gina is currently in an inclusive first grade—that is, the classroom includes some children who have disabilities and some children who do not. There are 18 children in the classroom, with a teacher and an aide. The classroom is divided into four learning centers: math, science, reading, and community studies. There is much activity in the room as the children, teacher, and aide move about. Children's pictures and drawings cover the walls. The room appears to be stimulating and busy.

Behavior Observation: Informal testing and achievement testing were begun in a quiet corner of the classroom so that Gina could get used to the examiner before going to the examiner's office for further testing. The child was very reluctant to participate in the testing, and her behavior was consistently negative during the testing session. Gina repeatedly questioned why she was being asked to complete test items and several times

FIGURE 7.8 • Gina's Assessment Report

(Continued)

SNAPSHOT Continued

she refused to try an item. Testing sessions were very brief because of her refusal to participate, which was compounded by her short attention span. She could attend to a task for a few seconds but then was distracted by pictures on the wall, sounds from the radiator, and other background noise. She had to be coaxed to focus on the tasks. She was very distracted by all the test materials and touched everything throughout the session.

Tests and Interviews: The following tests were administered: The *Wechsler Intelligence Scale for Children—Fourth Edition (WISC—IV)* measures intellectual ability and the *Wechsler Individual Achievement Test—Second Edition (WIAT—II)* measures achievement skills and problem solving. Both of these assessments have a mean of 100 and a standard deviation of 15. The *Child Behavior Checklist,* which measures children's competencies and behavior/emotional problems, was completed by both Gina's teacher and her foster parents. Interviews were also conducted with Gina's foster parents and with her teacher. Gina was observed three different times in her classroom.

Discussion of Results: Gina's performance on the *WISC—IV* indicates that she is functioning well within the average range of intellectual ability. Her full scale score of 101 ± 5 places her within the average range (85–115). Her scores on each of the individual scales also fell within the average range, with a relative strength in verbal comprehension (112 ± 6).

On the *Wechsler Individual Achievement Test—II*, Gina achieved a total composite score of 80 ± 4. This places her in the low average range. Gina shows relative strengths in mathematics with a standard score of 96 ± 7. Both written and oral language scores fell within the low average. Gina's reading score of 75 ± 4 indicates an area of weakness.

WISC—IV Composite Scores Summary

Score	Composite Scale	95% Confidence Interval	Percentile Rank	Qualitative Description
Verbal Comprehension (VCI)	112	106–118	79	High Average
Perceptual Reasoning (PRI)	92	85–100	30	Average
Working Memory (WMI)	102	94–109	55	Average
Processing Speed (PSI)	91	83–101	27	Average
Full Scale (FSIQ)	101	96–106	53	Average

WIAT—II Composite Scores Summary

Composites	Composite Score	95% Confidence Interval	Percentile Rank
Reading	75	71–79	5
Mathematics	96	89–103	39
Written Language	82	74–90	12
Oral Language	81	70–92	10
Total	80	76–84	9

FIGURE 7.8 • *(Continued)*

(Continued)

SNAPSHOT Continued

On the *Child Behavior Checklist,* Gina scored in the high range of externalizing behaviors: attention problems, 80th percentile; delinquent behavior, 70th percentile; and aggressive behavior, 77th percentile.

Summary: Overall, it appears that Gina's short attention span and distractibility interfere with the formal testing. Her performance in verbal comprehension and oral language is not consistent. Observations confirmed that Gina performs somewhat better in the first-grade classroom than on the formal testing. However, when Gina's performance is compared with children of her age, she performs below her age peers. Classroom observations also indicate that Gina is reluctant to comply with requests made by her teacher and that she rarely cooperates with other children. She has a constant need for limit setting.

Recommendations: Gina needs intensive intervention services, including support in reading, consistent setting of limits, expectations for more age-appropriate behavior, and an environment with a great deal of structure.

Counseling and behavior management strategies should be offered to the foster family to help them deal with the negative behaviors, short attention span, and distractibility.

Please do not hesitate to contact me with questions or concerns by calling my office at xxx-xxxx ext. xxx or e-mailing larrykahn@xxx.k12schools

_____

Larry Kahn, M.S.
Special Education Teacher

The parent/guardian has received a copy of this report at least 3 days prior to the IEP Team Meeting at which the evaluation will be discussed.

Date sent: 12/10/xx.
By whom: Larry Kahn

FIGURE 7.8 • *(Continued)*

Educators must use technology-generated reports judiciously. Because most of these programs yield a report based on a single test, they do not integrate information from other sources, such as additional assessments, observations, and interviews. As special educators, we must use multiple sources of information. In addition to observations and test data, we consider contextual factors that affect student behavior and achievement, interviews, work samples, and other types of information. Professional judgment and the ability to integrate various sources of information are skills that can be developed with time and experience. As part of professional training, practitioners must acquire knowledge of technology-based test interpretations and learn how to use and evaluate them. Equally important, future practitioners also need opportunities to work beside experienced mentors to guide their analysis and integration of assessment data into high-quality assessment reports.

Sharing Assessment Results With Others

Chapter 1 discusses the Family Educational Rights and Privacy Act (also known as the Buckley amendment). The Buckley amendment allows families access to their records held at any educational agency that accepts federal money, including a public school. Family members have a right to all assessment information, and you should provide a copy of the report to the family members on their request.

The Buckley amendment also protects students and families from the illicit sharing of assessment information. Before the school can release assessment information to other agencies or individuals outside the school system, the parent must sign a written consent form. The consent form specifies which records to release, to whom, and the reason for the release. A copy of the records to be released must be sent to the student's parents or guardian.

Family Members

Share assessment results and recommendations with parents or the guardian as soon as possible after you have completed the report. Look over the test results, and make sure that you can explain the test scores. You will want to be sensitive so that your comments are not misunderstood or misinterpreted because family members may be very anxious about the assessment results, speak other languages, or have various personal and cultural perspectives about disabilities. It is good practice to plan the topics you will be covering and what you want to say. Using descriptive terms to interpret test scores is helpful for parents and other team members. Lyman (1998) suggested the following scale:

Percentile Ranks	Descriptive Terms
96 or above	Very high; superior
85–95	High; excellent
75–85	Above average; good
25–75	About average; satisfactory or fair
15–25	Below average; fair or slightly weak
05–15	Low; weak
5 or below	Very low; very weak

Students

Students usually are anxious to know, "How did I do?" When students pose this question during the test, the examiner should offer a neutral response. For example, "I can see that you are trying hard." Upon completion of the assessment, the student may ask or expect you to explain some of the general results, depending on the age of the student, the student's interest in the testing situation, and your knowledge of the student. In some instances, your explanation may need to be a delicate balance between not discouraging the student, on the one hand, and helping the older student accept certain limitations and appreciate what can be accomplished on the other. Thus, you might say, "You may have to study more than other students do if you want to get good grades."

National and Statewide Assessments

Knowing how to interpret and use information from national and statewide assessments assists special educators in talking with other educators and parents. These tests usually feature common elements that describe individual and group scores. If the assessment is norm-referenced, the report allows comparison of the student to other groups of students who took the same test. If the assessment is criterion-referenced, then the report states how many questions

TABLE 7.3 • Categories of Scores

Type	Description	Interpretation
Standard score (SS)	This score allows comparison of the student to a group of other students. Standard scores have a mean of 100 and a standard deviation of 15. Scores falling between 85 and 115 are average.	A student received a score of 55, which is over 2 standard deviations below the mean, placing the student in the considerably below-average range.
Grade equivalent (GE)	This score indicates the grade and month of the school year for which the score is average.	A student who is in the seventh grade and was tested in September scored 7.1. The score would be interpreted as average.
National percentile rank (NPR)	This score compares the student's score to the percentage of the norm group that performed at or below the student's score.	A student received a score of 39, which is interpreted as the student scored the same as or better than 39 percent of the students of the same age who took the same test.
Normal curve equivalent (NCE)	This score allows comparison of the student to a group of other students. This score has a mean of 50 and a range of 0–99.	A student received an NCE of 49, which means that the student scored about average for students of the same age who took this test.
National stanines (NS)	This score ranges from 1 to 9, with a score of 5 representing an average score.	A student received a score of 1, which means that the student scored significantly below average.

the student attempted and how many were answered correctly in each curriculum area. Table 7.3 illustrates typical scores from national and statewide assessments. You can find out more about national assessments for the Common Core Standards at Partnership for Assessment of Readiness for College and Careers (PARCC) **http://www.parcconline.org/** and Smarter Balanced Assessment Consortium at **http://www.smarterbalanced.org/** Other Web-based assessment resources, such as the Northwest Evaluation Association (NWEA) at **http://www.nwea.org/** are assessment systems aligned with the Common Core. The NWEA site is an example of how systems can provide group data to the school leadership team regarding school achievement goals as well as class and individual student reports.

Studying a specific student's score or the score of a group of students provides helpful information for linking assessment with instruction. For example, Laura Chamberlain, a special educator, examined the printout of the mathematics assessment results for Jamie, a student who receives math instruction in her resource room. Jamie had received a composite score of 25 (national percentile rank [NPR]) and the following NPRs on the math subtests: computation, 49; probability, 15; data analysis, 20; and geometry, 8. Laura began thinking: How am I teaching the content of each of these areas? What materials am I using? Am I spending too much time on one area? How am I asking Jamie to demonstrate what he knows?

As Laura considered the instructional time with Jamie, she thought about other methods for teaching and learning activities that would help Jamie master concepts. Laura decided that she needed additional assessment information to pinpoint Jamie's difficulties. Planning ongoing assessment and instruction for Jamie would allow careful monitoring of his progress and provide Laura with information to adjust instruction such as reteaching or analyzing content to manageable units when needed.

Summary

- Analyzing and interpreting assessment information takes practice and a solid base of professional knowledge. Beginning teachers should follow the guidance that has been provided in this chapter.
- Some individuals may have the opportunity to work with experienced mentors during the assessment process. A mentorship could include time to discuss interpretations of assessment information and to review and examine drafts of the assessment report.
- Educators organize and synthesize assessment information into a written report. Depending on the assessment question and purpose of the assessment, the report could address observations of the student, a progress report of student achievement, an individual test report, or a comprehensive assessment report.
- The assessment report could include one or more hypotheses based on assessment data that addresses the original questions about student performance or behavior.
- Care must be taken when interpreting low scores. Students often live up—or down—to our expectations. The report shared with family members and later filed in the student's records can have an impact on how the family and teachers perceive the student in years to come.
- The use of technology to support report writing continues to evolve. Our challenge will be to use our skills as professionals and our skills as thoughtful human beings to determine what is accurate, sensitive, and appropriate.

Answers to questions from the Snapshot called Analyzing and Interpreting Assessment Information:

- The pie chart is advantageous because it depicts the whole period of time available for mathematics and how Cindy spent this time during three different days.
- The bar graph is advantageous because it allows us to see the type of individual activities in which Cindy was engaged.

QUESTIONS FOR REFLECTION

1. After reading the observation report in the Snapshot on John Diamond (pp. 117–119), consider the contextual factors and their effect on his behavior. What other recommendations could you suggest to the team?
2. Discuss how the hypothesis-generation approach can be useful in interpreting Gina's test performance.
3. Use the checklist in Table 7.1 to evaluate Gina's evaluation report. (See the Snapshot on pp. 120–122.)
4. Search for and evaluate technologies that can be used to generate assessment reports. Use the criteria in Table 7.2 to appraise the usefulness of this report. What additional criteria do you feel are important in deciding the usefulness of the program?

REFERENCES

American Psychological Association. (2009). *Publication manual of the American Psychological Association*, 71–77.

Benner, G. J., Nelson, J., Sanders, E. A., & Ralston, N. C. (2012). Behavior intervention for students with externalizing behavior problems: Primary-level standard protocol. *Exceptional Children, 78*(2), 181–198.

Bentzen, W. R. (2009). *Seeing young children* (6th ed.). Albany, NY: Delmar.

Flanagan, D. P., & Kaufman, A. S. (2009). *Essentials of WISC—IV assessment* (2nd ed.). Indianapolis, IN: Wiley.

Ford, D. Y., & Helms, J. E. (2012). Overview and introduction: Testing and assessing African Americans: "Unbiased" tests are still unfair. *Journal of Negro Education, 81*(3), 186–189.

Frick, P. J., Barry, C. T., & Kamphaus, R. W. (2010). *Clinical assessment of child and adolescent intelligence* (3rd ed.) New York: Springer Science+Business Media, Inc.

Froiland, J. (2011). Response to intervention as a vehicle for powerful mental health interventions in the schools. *Contemporary School Psychology, 15*, 35–42.

Fuchs, D., Fuchs, L. S., & Compton, D. L. (2012). Smart RTI: A next-generation approach to multilevel prevention. *Exceptional Children, 78*(3), 263–279.

Lyman, H. B. (1998). *Test scores and what they mean* (6th ed.). Boston: Allyn & Bacon.

O'Donnell, P. S., & Miller, D. N. (2011). Identifying students with specific learning disabilities: School psychologists' acceptability of the discrepancy model versus response to intervention. *Journal of Disability Policy Studies, 22*(2), 83–94. doi:10.1177/1044207310395724

Sullivan, A. L., & Long, L. (2010). Examining the changing landscape of school psychology practice: A survey of school-based practitioners regarding Response to Intervention. *Psychology in the Schools, 47*(10), 1059–1070. doi:10.1002/pits.20524

Vallas, R. (2009). The disproportionality problem: The overrepresentation of black students in special education and recommendations for reform. *Virginia Journal of Social Policy & the Law, 17*(1), 181–208.

PART III
Behavior

 **CHAPTER 8** Observing, Interviewing, and Conferencing

 **CHAPTER 9** Behavior

8 Observing, Interviewing, and Conferencing

Chapter Objectives

After completing this chapter, you should be able to:

- Provide a rationale for planning and conducting observations.
- Compare and contrast the use of various documenting techniques, including anecdotal records, running records, event recordings, duration recordings, intensity recordings, latency recordings, interval recordings, category recordings, rating scales, checklists, and questionnaires.
- Plan and conduct observations of students.
- Describe concerns relating to reliability and validity of observations.
- Plan and conduct interviews.
- Identify skills used in conferencing and collaborating with others.

Overview

This chapter focuses on several informal ways special educators gather information to help answer assessment questions. First, by observing and recording a student's behavior, the teacher collects valuable information about the student's functioning. Second, observing the classroom environment provides insight about the physical, learning, and social environments. Finally, gathering information from students themselves, their parents, and teachers provides valuable insights. Whether individuals come together in a single room or in a virtual space, participants share information, concerns, and ideas. Even though these assessment approaches are considered informal, each involves careful preparation and a range of skills.

Observations

Observing students and their environments allows educators to gather information to answer questions such as: How independently is the student functioning? Does the student use age-appropriate skills? Does the student socialize with students without disabilities in a nonstructured setting? What factors in the classroom environment provide guidelines for appropriate behavior? Does the learning environment support the student's special needs? How does the classroom environment encourage collaboration and a feeling of well-being among students?

As an assessment approach, **observation** involves a systematic process of gathering information by looking at students and their environments. The observer may record student behaviors, interactions, language, or responses of peers or teachers, for example. Observations may be conducted by special educators and general educators, as well as parents, therapists, and other related services providers.

For students with or at risk for disability, the Individuals with Disabilities Education Act (IDEA) requires observations to be part of an initial assessment and included in reevaluation of the student. In fact, observations of the student and the environment provide valuable information in helping to answer the questions during each phase of the assessment process:

1. Screening
   - Is there a possibility of a disability?
2. Determining eligibility
   - Does the student have a disability?
   - What disability does the student have?
   - Does the student meet criteria for services?
   - What are the student's strengths and weaknesses?
   - In what areas is the student having difficulty?
3. Program planning
   - What is the student able to do and not do?
   - What is the student able to understand and not understand?
   - Where should instruction begin?
   - Should assistive technology be considered?
4. Progress monitoring
   - What is the pace of instruction?
   - What does the student know before and after instruction?
   - What strategies does the student use for learning?
5. Conducting evaluations
   - Has the student met the individualized education program (IEP) goals?
   - Has the instructional program been successful?
   - Has the student made progress?
   - Has the instructional program achieved its goals?

In addition to gathering information about students, observers can gather information about the environment. This information can be useful in answering questions about the physical arrangement or other aspects of the classroom. Using a systematic process, an observer can collect information about the use of student groupings, teacher expectations, classroom procedures, and many other aspects of the learning and social environments.

Planning Observations

Planning observations involves identifying the assessment question(s), defining the event or behavior to be observed, specifying the location(s) for the observations, and deciding the type of observation to use in collecting observation data. In addition, you must consider what steps to take to ensure that the information being collected is accurate and is representative of the student. A good observation actually consists of a series of several observations of the student over a period of a few days or longer. You must analyze and synthesize the observation information with other assessment information. The following subsections examine each of these areas in more detail.

Observation Questions

Observations can help answer assessment questions. The observation may focus on the environment or on one or more students. Because many activities are going on in a classroom at one time, the observer should have a clear focus on the information that will be collected. Identifying one or more assessment questions before the observations occur permits the observer to focus on the key areas. The questions should be stated clearly, in terms that can be observed. For example, one special educator wanted to know how Tia functions in the regular education classroom. The special educator will need to further refine what question(s) and answer(s) will yield the information that will be most helpful. For example, compared to the other students, how long does it take Tia to start on her work? Does she require prompting? If so, what type of prompt does the teacher use? How long does she stay engaged when working with a small group of students?

Defining an Event or Behavior

To define an event or behavior, educators develop a description of the behavior (or event) that can be observed. Defining a behavior or an event in precise, descriptive, and observable terms helps the observer know when to record the occurrence of the behavior. A detailed description also helps ensure that the documentation is reliable. For example, one special educator was interested in answering the question, "How much time is the student engaged during class time?" To observe "engaged behavior," the teacher began by developing a description of what "engagement" would look like. Here is definition of the behavior that the teacher wrote:

> Engagement: looking at the teacher, responding orally to class discussions, using math materials to solve problems, or completing a worksheet.

Because individual educators may define the term *engagement* to include various behaviors, agreeing on a clear definition enables everyone to know the specific behaviors being observed.

Location

Observations take place in the classroom, cafeteria, playground, other school settings, or the home. Teachers and parents can usually observe students without disrupting routines. However, when an observer is not typically part of the setting, the presence of the outsider can change aspects of the environment or of the students' behavior. To address this concern, a teacher may set up a digital camera/recorder in the classroom for a specified time period. This can be quite helpful in gathering and documenting students' performance, behaviors, and social interactions.

Documentation

There are various ways of collecting and recording information: anecdotal records, running records, event recording, duration recording, intensity recording, latency recording, interval recording, category recording, rating scales, checklists, and questionnaires. During the planning stage, teachers carefully select the recording technique that will be the most effective one in answering the assessment question(s). Later sections of this chapter examine each of these techniques.

Accuracy

Gathering information takes skill and practice. Some of the important considerations include the following: Are your observations accurate? Are your findings consistent with what you might observe tomorrow? Do your findings agree with others who conduct the same observation? Other sections of this chapter discuss methods of ensuring accuracy and consistency when using observation assessments.

Multiple Observations

Teachers can collect observation information over a period of time; that is, observations can take place on several different occasions. Completing multiple observations helps ensure that the data was not an unusual occurrence on the day of the observation. Frequency increases reliability and, as the information is synthesized, trends become apparent.

Integration

Observation data should be integrated with other assessment information that has been gathered. This involves carefully reviewing all the assessment information and synthesizing the results. Chapter 7 describes a process for integrating assessment information.

Observing the Student

Conducting observations of a student is one of the best ways for obtaining specific information to answer an assessment question. Accurate observations create a picture of the uniqueness of the student. Some of the areas to consider in planning an observation include the following.

Work Habits
- Time
    - How long does it take the student to get started?
    - How long is the student able to stay on task?
- Levels of assistance needed
    - What can the student do independently?
    - How frequently does the student need prompting?
    - What types of prompts (physical, verbal, gestural) are helpful?
- Reinforcements used
    - What types of reinforcement are effective?
    - How does the student react to the reinforcement?

Interactions with Others
- Other students
    - Does the student use a variety of ways to communicate?
    - Do other students communicate with the student?
    - Does the student socialize with other students?
- Teacher
    - Does the student have a variety of ways to communicate?
    - Can the teacher communicate with the student?
    - Is the student given opportunities to demonstrate competence?

Facial Expression and Affect
- Eye contact: Does the student make eye contact with others?
- Affect: Does the student have appropriate affect?

Body Movements
- Independent skills: Does the student have independent mobility skills?
- Quality of movement: Is the quality of gross and fine motor responses refined (not jerky)?

Adaptive Skills
- Independent skills

    Can the student eat independently?
- Appropriate skills

    Does the student use appropriate grooming skills?

    Does the student dress in an age-appropriate manner?

Participation in Play and Games
- Level of participation

    Does the student participate in unorganized play (free time, recess)?

    Does the student understand the rules of the game?

    Does the student play cooperatively?

Types of Observations

Several different types of observations are available for documenting information. The assessment question influences the type of observation and the documentation (Table 8.1). Let's examine some typical assessment questions and ways of recording observation data. In our discussions, we'll also look at some of the advantages and disadvantages of these various approaches.

TABLE 8.1 • Assessment Questions and Type of Observation

Assessment Question	Type of Observation
How independently is the student functioning?	Anecdotal record Latency recording Category recording Rating scale Checklist
How does the student communicate with peers?	Anecdotal record Running record Duration recording Rating scale Checklist
Does the student socialize with students without disabilities in a nonstructured setting?	Running record Event recording Interval recording Category recording

Anecdotal Record

An **anecdotal record** is a brief narrative description of an event or events that the observer considered was important to document. Anecdotal records are recorded after the events have occurred, usually in the form of notes. The writer records the date, time, and place of the event and, as accurately as possible, describes the event as it took place, including verbal and nonverbal cues and direct quotations. The observation should be as objective as possible, describing only what the observer saw and heard. Interpretive comments should not be part of the description of the episode.

Let's consider the following question, which was referred to the student assistance team. Leo's parent had contacted school personnel to let them know that their physician planned to change Leo's level of medication and wanted to monitor any side effects, both at home and at school. The parent asked if the classroom teacher could observe any changes in behavior over the next two weeks, such as restlessness, sleepiness, or lack of attention. The student assistance team met to plan aspects of the observation. The team decided that the classroom teacher should complete a daily anecdotal record. Figure 8.1 is an example of the anecdotal record that Leo's classroom teacher logged.

There are several advantages to maintaining anecdotal records:

1. Observers can record unanticipated events.
2. Observations record actual behavior in natural settings.
3. The technique provides a check on other types of assessment.

However, this technique has several disadvantages:

1. The recording of anecdotal records depends on the memory of the observer.
2. Bias may occur if the observer selects only certain aspects or incidents to record.
3. The technique may not describe specific behaviors completely.
4. Validating narrative recordings is difficult because typically there is only one individual who has completed these observation notes.
5. The recording of the behavior can be time-consuming.

Date: October 15   Time Period: 1:00–1:50

Student: Leo B.   Class activity: Science

Leo worked in a small group with two other students for the first part of the period. The group used the classroom computer in locating information about bats for their presentation next week. Leo typed in much of the search information on the computer and worked well with the other two students. However, when they returned to their desks, he had trouble settling down. He asked to go to the bathroom twice, broke his pencil three times, and then spent the remainder of the class period with his head on the desk.

Comment:
Leo seems to be very interested in this topic. Today was the first time he has worked for a steady 20 minutes. Is it the topic or use of computer? Or medication change?

Tomorrow I'll try having his group use other materials for searching for information.

FIGURE 8.1 • An Anecdotal Record

6. Records of several anecdotal observations may be difficult to summarize (Beaty, 2010; Miller, Linn, & Gronlund, 2013; Sattler, 2008).

Table 8.2 provides tips for recording anecdotal records.

Running Record

A **running record**, sometimes called a continuous record, is a description of events written as they occur. Unlike an anecdotal record, in which the observer records events sometime after they occur, a running record describes events while they are taking place. A running record provides a rich description of events and is helpful in analyzing the behavior of students. Unlike the anecdotal record, which is a selective record of events, the running record includes everything that is observed; it is a comprehensive, detailed account of events.

Here's an example: A special education teacher was gathering information about Sami's progress in preparation for the annual IEP meeting. One of the questions that the team was likely to raise was how Sami functioned in homeroom. The special education teacher decided to use a running record to gather information about Sami's interactions with other students during this time (see Figure 8.2).

TABLE 8.2 • Tips for Recording Anecdotal Records

Complete your anecdotal record as soon as possible.

Record only what you observed.

Include specific notes for:
- Any unexpected or unusual behaviors
- Events leading up to the behavior
- Events that followed the behavior

Complete multiple observations before drawing conclusions.

Date: May 10   Student: Sami G.

Period: Homeroom   Focus: Sami's interactions with other students during free time

Time	Event	Observer comments
7:45	Sami enters the room with two other students. One student grabs Sami's hat and turns it around backward. Sami grins and says "haaay."	Students entering the classroom. Several students seated; about 15 students standing around.
7:47	Sami wanders toward the back of the classroom and stops at JR's desk.	
7:48	JR asks, "How's the man?"	
7:49	Sami gives him a high-five.	
7:50	The homeroom teacher enters and asks everyone to take their seats.	
7:52	Sami heads for his desk but stops to watch Joe and Mark arm wrestle.	About 7 of the 25 students are milling around. Sami is the only student not in his seat.
7:55	The teacher again asks everyone to take their seats.	
7:56	Sami makes his way to his desk and sits down. He looks at Jen (sitting to his left) and asks her if she watched HBO last night.	
7:59	The teacher takes attendance and asks students to indicate if they are taking hot lunch. Sami raises his hand.	
8:05	Bell for first period rings.	

FIGURE 8.2 • A Running Record

When recording information, the observer must carefully describe the events. It is much better to provide a factual, detailed account than to be judgmental. Factual accounts are less likely to be influenced by observer bias. The observer strives to write not only accurate but also detailed descriptions of the observed events. Instead of simply recording, "the student sat in his seat," the observer can write "squirmed in his seat," "slumped in the chair," or "sat rigidly."

Beaty (2010) describes several disadvantages of running records:

1. Writing a running record can be time-consuming.
2. Recording all observable events is difficult; some details may be overlooked.
3. This technique is useful when observing individual students but is difficult when observing a group or groups of students.

One of the major disadvantages of anecdotal records and running records is that they are subject to observer bias and judgment. In addition, although they can provide rich descriptions of events, it is difficult to quantify behaviors. For these reasons, other types of recording systems have been developed.

Event Recording

Event recording, sometimes known as frequency recording or event sampling, is a procedure in which the observer records a behavior each time it occurs during a given period. For example, if an observation lasts for 20 minutes, the observer records each occurrence of the behavior during the 20-minute period. The observer must pay close attention to the student and precisely tally the number of times that the behavior occurs. Before beginning event recording, the observer must carefully define the behavior to be observed, including a description of the beginning of the behavior and the end of the behavior, so that there is no ambiguity about whether the behavior occurred. Event recording is useful for behaviors that occur very frequently or very infrequently.

Several procedures are effective for recording events. The simplest one is a tally. Each time the behavior occurs, a line is drawn on the page, and then the lines are totaled:

$$\text{IIII IIII II}$$

Observers use event recording to answer questions about students with disabilities. For example, an IEP team wondered if accommodations to the classroom environment had helped Pedrico feel more comfortable in volunteering in class. An event recording was used to gather this information (see Figure 8.3). The first observation occurred during a 20-minute period when the class was discussing a book that they had been reading. During this time, Pedrico volunteered by raising his hand on four different occasions. According to the observer's comments, Pedrico loses interest and becomes distracted when the teacher does not call on him. We might recommend that, in conducting subsequent observations, the observer plan to include a comparison child. This would allow a comparison of Pedrico's performance with that of another student to see if his behavior is typical of same-age peers.

In monitoring another student's IEP, the IEP team wondered to what degree the regular classroom environment was providing opportunities for Tia to communicate with her peers. The teacher aide completed event recordings over a period of 10 days to document Tia's communication with peers during her daily schedule (see Figure 8.4).

Sometimes teachers wish to know the rate of behavior over time. With event recording, they can calculate the rate of occurrences of the behavior. This is helpful when observation times vary, when evaluating behaviors before and after an intervention, or when comparing the behaviors of various students. For example, suppose the teacher is using a teaching strategy to decrease Stacy's disruptiveness in class and wants to judge its effectiveness. Two

Date: December 1 **Student:** Pedrico G.

Observation questions: Does Pedrico participate in class discussions?

Class activity: Reading **Behavior observed:** Volunteers by raising his hand or by responding to teacher-directed questions

Observer: Jake Orone

Time	Frequency	Comments
:00		Beginning of class discussion.
:05	I	P. immediately raises hand and teacher calls on P. After P.'s comment, teacher says, "That's an interesting idea about why the author chose to open the story with a flashback. What do other people think?"
:10		P. stares out the window. Is he distracted by the noise of the dump truck outside?
:15	IIII	P. raises his hand to each of the next four questions but teacher does not call on him.
:20		P. plays with pencil, doodling on paper.

FIGURE 8.3 • An Event Recording: Pedrico's Participation in Class Discussion

---

Student: Tia B.

Date: Weeks of September 5 through September 16

Assessment question: Is the general education classroom providing opportunities for Tia to communicate with her peers?

Behavior: Communication (verbal communication)

Observer: T. Morrill, personal aide

Schedule	Time	9/5	9/6	9/7	9/8	9/9	9/12	9/13	9/14	9/15	9/16
*Homeroom	7:30–7:45	0	0	0	1	1	0	2	0	1	0
*Art/music rotation	7:50–9:00	1	0	0	0	1	1	0	0	1	2
Functional life skills	9:10–10:20	3	0	1	2	1	0	1	3	2	0
*Physical education	10:30–11:40	2	1	3	1	2	3	3	0	2	3
*Cafeteria/lunch	11:50–12:20	0	0	1	2	1	0	2	2	1	1
Vocational training	12:30–1:50	2	0	1	2	3	1	1	3	2	2
Leisure	2:00–2:20	1	0	0	1	1	1	2	1	2	2
Prepare for departure/Bus	2:30–2:45	1	1	2	3	2	0	3	2	3	3

*General education settings

FIGURE 8.4 • An Event Recording: Tia's Communication With Peers

months ago, an observer counted that Stacy engaged in shouting 30 times during a 15-minute period. To obtain a rate of occurrence, divide the number of occurrences of the behavior by the length of time observed. The calculation follows:

$$\frac{N}{T} = \text{Rate of occurrence}$$

where N = the number of occurrences of the behavior
 T = the length of time of the observation

$$\frac{30 \text{ occurrences}}{15 \text{ minutes}} = 2 \text{ occurrences of shouting per minute}$$

In a recent observation, Stacy engaged in shouting 15 times during a 10-minute observation. What is the rate of occurrence? Would you say that there has been an improvement in Stacy's behavior? See page 162 to find the answer.

Event recording has several advantages (Beaty, 2010; Sattler, 2008):

1. The behavior or event remains intact, thus facilitating analysis.
2. It is possible to monitor behaviors that occur infrequently.
3. It is possible to record changes in behavior over a period of time.

Despite the advantages, event recording also has several disadvantages (Beaty, 2010; Sattler, 2008):

1. Because the event is taken out of context, it may be difficult to analyze events that preceded the behavior.
2. Patterns of behavior may remain undetected.
3. Reliability between observers is difficult to establish.

Duration Recording

Duration recording is a measure of the length of time a specific event or behavior persists. For example, in developing instructional goals, the teacher wants to know how long a tantrum or behavioral outburst lasts or how long a student works independently. Duration recording is an effective technique to use when it is important to know the length of time the behavior or event lasted rather than whether it occurred.

Before the observer begins a duration recording, precise definitions for the beginning and ending of the behavior(s) must be set. For example, the definition of when independent work begins could be when the student begins to look at the material, when the student picks up the pencil, or when the student actually touches the laptop keyboard. Once the observer has determined how to define the beginning and ending of a behavior or event, a timer that indicates seconds can measure the length of the behavior.

Besides simply recording the duration of a behavior or event, teachers may wish to further analyze the data. The observer can determine the percentage of time a behavior or event occurs, for example during a week, or calculate the average length of the behavior or event, such as under 30 seconds. Finding the percentage of time that the behavior or event occurs is called the **percentage duration rate**. To calculate the percentage duration rate, the observer divides the total duration of the behavior or event by the total time of the observation and multiplies this answer by 100 to obtain a percentage.

$$\frac{d}{t} \times 100$$

where d = the total duration of the behavior or event
 t = the total length of the observation period

> Date: October 12 Class:
> Student: Ian B. Observer:
> Purpose: To observe Ian working independently
>
> | Time: | Comments: |
> |---|---|
> | 10:00–10:08 | works independently |
> | 10:08 | asks for help in reading paragraph |
> | 10:15 | returns to seat |
> | 10:16 | drops pencil, gets up to sharpen pencil |
> | 10:20 | returns to seat |
> | 10:22 | starts working |
> | 10:23–10:27 | works independently |
> | 10:28–10:30 | glances around room |

FIGURE 8.5 • A Duration Recording

Let's see how Ian's special educator used percentage duration rate to help in planning his program. One of Ian's IEP goals was to increase his ability to work independently. The special educator, using a timer, observed Ian for a 30-minute interval and recorded the information (see Figure 8.5). The duration recording showed that Ian worked independently during two time periods of 8 minutes and 4 minutes for a total duration of 12 minutes.

To calculate the percentage of time that Ian worked independently during this time period, the numbers are inserted into the formula:

$$\frac{12}{30} \times 100 = 40 \text{ percent of the observation period}$$

This observation data indicates that, during a 30-minute period, Ian worked independently 40 percent of the time. Ian's special education teacher finds this information helpful in planning and monitoring instruction. After completing several other observations with similar results, his teacher decided to give Ian a choice of which assignments to complete first. After several weeks, the teacher will complete additional observations to see if this strategy increased Ian's ability to work independently.

Intensity Recording

Intensity recording is a measure of the degree of a behavior. The degrees are usually defined as high, medium, or low, so the observer's judgment can be very subjective and unreliable. Before using an intensity recording, the teacher must specify the ways in which the various levels differ. For example, Carlos's IEP team wanted to know if the teaching strategies for including students with and without disabilities were enabling him to generalize the skills to other settings. The team asked the special education teacher to observe Carlos's behavior on the playground during informal play and games. The teacher decided not to use event recording because the information needed (level of involvement) went beyond whether Carlos simply participated in outdoor games with students without disabilities. The teacher defined the degrees of involvement in the following ways:

High involvement: The target student participated fully in the activity and showed great interest through interactions with other students, body language, and general overall affect.

Medium involvement: The target student joined the other students in the activity but showed little interest in the progression of the activity, either by lack of interactions or affect.

Low involvement: The target student primarily watched the other students, occasionally shouting words of encouragement or adding comments to the activity.

No involvement: The target student ignored the activity.

Using these descriptors, the teacher was able to complete an accurate, reliable recording.

Latency Recording

Latency recording is a measure of the amount of time between a behavior or event (or request to begin the behavior) and the beginning of the prespecified or **target behavior**. For example, suppose we want to know the length of time that elapsed between the moment Darcy was encouraged to respond and when she began speaking. Using a timer, the observer can determine the amount of time that elapses between the initiation of the request and when Darcy begins the requested behavior.

Latency recording can be difficult to measure. The observer must carefully define the **stimulus** behavior (the behavior that actually signals the request to initiate behavior), the beginning of the target behavior, and the end of the target behavior. Sometimes educators use a variation of latency recording to record the time between the initial request and the completion of the behavior.

Interval Recording

Interval recording is an observational technique that involves the recording of specific events or behaviors during a prespecified time interval. Interval recording is effective for behaviors that are visible and occur frequently. The period of observation is divided into equal time segments, and in each time slot the observer records the presence or absence of the behavior. Generally, the length of the time interval ranges from 5 seconds to 30 seconds. During each interval, the observer records whether the behavior has occurred. The observer proceeds from one interval to the next until the end of the observation period.

An easy way to begin an interval recording is to use a low-cost app or Web template and cloud computing, where the data can be saved directly. Having data stored in this way not only eliminates reentering data but also allows for easy retrieval of information from previous observations. These tools usually allow you to determine the length and number of intervals. For example, if the observer will be observing for 10 minutes, there will be twenty 30-second intervals; for a 20-minute observation period, there will be forty 30-second intervals.

Educators should use a combination of interval and event recording for behaviors that occur frequently. Let's examine why a teacher might select this technique. The top section of Figure 8.6 illustrates an interval-event recording during fifteen 1-minute time intervals to collect information about a student's disruptive behavior, defined as "poking others with a pencil, name-calling, and swearing." Here, the educator recorded the number of disruptive behaviors (events) that the target student, Sheena, and a typical student, Angela, displayed during each minute (interval) of the 15-minute observation period. The bottom section of Figure 8.6 shows the same information scored as an interval-only recording. By looking at both recordings, you can see that interval-only scoring does not provide information about the increase in disruptive behaviors during the latter part of the observation period—only the presence of the behavior. By examining the interval-event recording, you can see a sudden increase in the behaviors after 9 minutes. Interval-only recording is not as sensitive to the difference between the two students. In minutes 7, 11, 13, and 15, both students participated in disruptive behavior, but by examining the interval-event scoring, you can see that the target student's disruptive behavior was more frequent during each of these time intervals than was that of the typical student.

One-Minute Interval-Event Recording

Student	1	2	3	4	5	6	7	8	9	10	11	12	13	14	15	Total Number of Disruptive Behaviors During Observation Period
Sheena	0	0	II	I	III	I	I	I	II	IIII	IIII	III	IIII	IIII	III	33
Angela	0	0	0	0	0	0	I	0	0	0	I	0	I	0	I	4

One-Minute Interval-Only Recording

Student	1	2	3	4	5	6	7	8	9	10	11	12	13	14	15	Percent of Intervals in Which Disruptive Behaviors Were Observed
Sheena	0	0	X	X	X	X	X	X	X	X	X	X	X	X	X	87%
Angela	0	0	0	0	0	0	X	0	0	0	X	0	X	0	X	27%

FIGURE 8.6 • A Comparison of the Sensitivity of Interval-Event and Interval-Only Recording

Sometimes it is difficult for the observer to continue to observe while recording. Proceeding from one interval to the next can be especially demanding when the observation interval is very brief, the behavior to be observed is complex, or the observer is recording the behaviors of a number of students. To help alleviate this problem, the observer can establish a recording interval. With this technique, the student is observed for a time interval, such as 30 seconds, and then the observer records the data during the next 30-second time interval. The observer then proceeds from one interval to the next, observing, recording, and so on as illustrated in Figure 8.7. This type of recording, for example, can be helpful in comparing the behavior of a student who displays hyperactive behavior with the behavior of other students.

Category Recording

Category recording is a system of recording behavior in discrete groupings. Figure 8.8 shows two observation instruments that use category recording. Category recording can be as simple as using two categories (e.g., on-task and off-task) or complex enough to contain many categories (e.g., uses words to express needs, raises hand to signal teacher for help, regards speaker, complies with requests). As with other types of observations, the behaviors must be discrete, be carefully defined, and have an observable beginning and end.

Rating Scales

Rating scales can help to evaluate the quality of the behavior of one student or many students. In other words, **rating scales** measure the degree to which a student exhibits a prespecified behavior. Figure 8.9 illustrates a teacher-developed rating scale to measure student behaviors. The teacher intended to increase reliability by using **descriptors**. Descriptors

One-Minute Intervals

	:00	:30	1:00	1:30	2:00	2:30	3:00	3:30	4:00	4:30
Student	O	R	O	R	O	R	O	R	O	R
Anna		x		x		x		x		
Maria				x		x				
Nan		x				x				x

O = Observe   R = record data   X indicates on-task behavior

FIGURE 8.7 • Comparison of On-Task Behavior (First 5 Minutes of a 20-Minute Recording Interval Form)

Student's name: Rebecca

Two-Category Instrument

Two-Minute Intervals	0:00–2:00	2:00–4:00	4:00–6:00	6:00–8:00	8:00–10:00	10:00–12:00	12:00–14:00	14:00–16:00	16:00–18:00	18:00–20:00
On-task	X				X	X	X	X		
Off-task		X	X	X					X	X

Four-Category Instrument

Two-Minute Intervals	0:00–2:00	2:00–4:00	4:00–6:00	6:00–8:00	8:00–10:00	10:00–12:00	12:00–14:00	14:00–16:00	16:00–18:00	18:00–20:00
Uses words to express needs	X		X				X	X		
Raises hand to signal teacher for help	X	X						X		
Regards speaker		X	X	X		X		X		
Complies with requests			X				X			

FIGURE 8.8 • Category Recording

Behavior	1	2	3	4
Student participates in small-group activity.	Student regards others who are talking.	Student regards others who are talking and participates in group discussion.	Student uses materials to assist in group activity and all of #2.	Student evaluates own role in group activity and all of #3.
Student shows respect for personal boundaries.	At school, student keeps hands to self.	At school, student maintains personal space when speaking with others and keeps hands to self.	Student identifies behavior appropriate to the environmental setting (school, home, community) and all of #2.	Student displays behavior appropriate to the setting (school, home, community).

FIGURE 8.9 • An Example of Descriptors in a Rating Scale

SNAPSHOT

Rebecca's IEP Team

Let's visit with Rebecca's team as they plan several classroom observations. First, they discuss the purpose of the observation while one team member records the information:

> Rebecca is a 17-year-old student who attends the Essential Skills Program at Central High School. One of her IEP goals focuses on increasing prosocial behavior skills. The purpose of the observation is to collect information regarding the IEP goals in preparation for the annual review.

Team members begin by identifying some of the prosocial skills she has been learning. They note that one impediment has been Rebecca's angry outbursts. The team asks the special education teacher if she could observe Rebecca's angry outbursts. "What do you mean by 'angry outbursts'?" one member asked. The team works on the definition until they decide on: Angry behavior is defined by screeching and screaming as well as hitting other students.

"But let's not get sidetracked," interjected the special educator. "We want to focus on the prosocial skills that Rebecca is developing and look for ways that she can increase these skills. After some discussion, the team agrees. The member who was taking notes wrote:

> Rebecca's behavior to be observed includes prosocial skills such as using eye contact, greeting others, listening when other students are talking, and offering to help.

Next they discussed where the observations will occur. Observations of the student may take place in any number of settings. They decided that the observations of Rebecca will be conducted in the classroom and in the cafeteria. Some of the details that they hope to include are

- The arrangement of tables
- The types of assistance from other students
- The types of assistance from teachers or cafeteria monitors
- The methods Rebecca uses to approach other students
- The initiations of other students talking to Rebecca

Next the team discussed the technique of recording behavior. They knew that a direct observation such as this example may focus on the target student or on the target student interacting with other students. Several observations are necessary to ensure consistency or reliability of results. After completing each observation, they wanted to obtain feedback from the classroom teacher. "How typical was today's class?" "In what ways was it different?"

Finally, the team discussed who would conduct the observations and write the report, integrating the results with other information about the student.

Pause and consider:

- What recording technique do you think the team chose?
- Provide a rationale for your answer. Use the information in Table 8.1 to help you.

provide detailed information regarding each of the levels of the rating scale. These scales are useful when they are combined with other types of assessment, such as with data obtained from interval recording, event recording, and the results of other assessment approaches. Although rating scales can be useful, they have been criticized as being impressionistic, lacking interrater reliability, and being affected by the subjectivity of the observer (Sattler, 2008).

Checklists

A **checklist** consists of several characteristics or behaviors arranged in a consistent manner that allows the evaluator to check the presence or absence of the characteristic or behavior. Rating scales help to evaluate the degree or frequency of an item or a behavior, but checklists usually require a simple yes or no response. Some checklists provide space for comments or descriptions.

Checklists are easy-to-use templates that a teacher creates, downloads, or modifies. The following guidelines are helpful when developing checklists (Beaty, 2010; Miller et al., 2013):

1. Checklist items should be brief, yet detailed and easily understood.
2. The items should be nonjudgmental.
3. The procedure for indicating the presence or absence of each item should be specified.

Increasing Technical Skills in Conducting Observations

Understanding More About Reliability

Reliability is an important concern when discussing direct observations. Reliability is the consistency or stability of the observations. Educators and other team members plan that the behaviors observed are representative of the student. On the day of the observation, the observer should enter the classroom quietly and find a location where data can be collected as unobtrusively as possible. During the observation period, the observer should check the accuracy of the observations against the criterion or definition of the behavior being observed. Observations should be conducted precisely and systematically.

Reliability of observations can be compromised when conditions change or when an observer neglects to record information. Observation recording errors affect the accuracy of observations, so let's examine the sources of error so that this understanding will help reduce the possibility of their occurrence.

Errors of Omission

To leave out information that is helpful or important to understanding a student's behavior is an **error of omission**. Sometimes an observer makes an error of omission that is critical to the understanding of the student's behavior. Let's consider the observations that Jon's teacher planned and conducted. Jon is a 10-year-old student with autism. He has a number of self-abusive behaviors, including biting his wrists and banging his head. His teacher, concerned that the incidence of these behaviors is increasing, decided to conduct a series of classroom observations.

The first observation was conducted during lunch in the cafeteria. The teacher recorded this observation in terms of the number of minutes that Jon was in the cafeteria before he began the self-abusive behavior (that is, latency recording). Jon was observed as he entered the cafeteria and chose a seat at one of the tables. Another student sat down beside him at the table. Jon quickly opened his lunchbox and began eating while the observer was momentarily distracted when two students briefly obstructed the view. Suddenly, Jon began to slap his head with his hand, and the behavior escalated until the teacher assistant noticed the self-abuse and went over to speak to Jon.

Unfortunately the observer's view was blocked at the same moment that a student sat down next to Jon. Missing part of the sequence of events, even by a temporary distraction, jeopardizes the observer's understanding of Jon's behavior. In this case, the student who joined Jon may have sat too close or acted in a way that disturbed Jon. Perhaps Jon's abusive behavior was a communication attempt in response to the other student. Errors of omission can result from simply missing behaviors that occur.

Errors of Commission

Including information that did not actually occur is an **error of commission**. Errors of commission frequently occur when the observer is not able to take complete notes during the observation but must rely on memory to record the information at a later time.

Errors of Transmission

An **error of transmission** occurs when observers record behaviors in an improper sequence. Because many behaviors relate to each other, and the order in which they occur is important, take precautions to guard against this type of error. Recording the time at which you observe a particular behavior or recording the number of times that a particular behavior begins or ends can reduce errors of transmission.

Observer Drift

Observer drift occurs when the observer shifts away from the original objectives of the observation. For example, a teacher is recording on-task behaviors when she notices that the student is subtly disrupting another student. The observer begins to note these disruptions, neglecting to continue to collect data regarding on-task behaviors. Usually, the observer is not aware of this alteration. To prevent this phenomenon from occurring, you need to periodically check the established purposes and criteria for conducting the observation.

Reactivity

Reactivity refers to the adjustments that individuals make in behaviors during an observation. Teachers may alter their instructions, give additional prompts, or increase the amount of feedback when someone is observing them. Students may improve behavior because of the "visitor," or they put on a good "show." These changes in behavior are threats to the accuracy of an observation. Taking photos and videos may also increase reactivity.

Understanding More About Validity

The validity of observational measures is a very important concern. Validity is the extent to which an instrument measures what it is intended to measure. Although there is some evidence of validity for some observational instruments, the validity of many instruments is either unsubstantiated or questionable. As a discriminating consumer, carefully check the instructor's manual and other documentation that comes with a commercial observation instrument to see what information the publisher has included about the instrument's validity.

Developing Informal Norms

Developing informal norms helps observers evaluate the behavior that they observe. The behavior of one or more typical students in the group can serve as the norm or comparison group for the target student who is to be observed. In this instance, the other students in the group are known as the norm group, and the student who is to be observed is referred to as the target student. Without informal norms, it is difficult to determine if the target student's behavior is atypical or abnormal.

One way of establishing an informal norm sample is to ask the teacher to identify a student whose behavior is typical or representative of the behavior of the students in the group. By watching the behavior of the typical student, the observer can use the scan-check technique Figure 8.10) to compare the typical student's behavior with that of the target student.

Student: Ben **Observer:** D. Southard
Age: 10–8 **Date:** November 12
School: North **Teacher:** Blesson
Reason for Observation: To determine the extent that Ben's behaviors differ from his peers'
Activity Observed: Social studies class
Observation Technique Used: Interval recording, 1 min. intervals

Behavior Codes		Grouping Codes		Teacher and Peer Reaction Codes	
T	On-task	L	Large group	AA	Attention to all
O	Off-task	S	Small group	A+	Positive attention to target student
		O	One-to-one	A–	Negative attention to target student
				NA	No attention to target student

Time	Target Student Behavior	Percent of Students Engaged in On-Task Behavior During Group Scan	Anecdotal Notes	Group	Teacher	Peer
9:15	O			L	NA	NA
9:16	O	80%	making faces	L	A–	A+
9:17	O		making faces	L	A–	A+
9:18	T	70%		L	NA	NA
9:19	T		plays with pencil	L	NA	NA
9:20	T	80%		L	NA	NA
9:21	T		teacher praise	L	A+	NA
9:22	O	90%	pokes student in front	L	AA	NT
9:23	O		argues with student	L	A–	A+
9:24	O	80%	argues with teacher	L	A–	A+
TOTAL	4/10					
Percent of time	40%	80%				

FIGURE 8.10 • Scan-Check Recording Sheet

SNAPSHOT

Timmy

Timmy is an active 8-year-old boy who has been referred to the IEP team. Timmy's teacher is concerned about Timmy's lack of attention and engagement in the classroom. During the team meeting, members decided that they need additional information about Timmy's functioning to determine how much he participates in classroom activities. Observing Timmy's performance during instructional time would provide information about his engagement during more focused activities and assist in planning intervention strategies.

Working together, the special educator and regular educator defined *engagement* as "looking at the speaker (teacher or other student), following directions, and using materials to complete assignments." Next they refined the observation question: "What percentage of time does Timmy spend appropriately engaged (e.g., listening, looking at the speaker, following directions, and using materials to complete assignments) in activities as compared to the typical student?"

The special educator completed two 20-minute classroom observations on October 3 and October 10. Using an interval recording, she recorded either the presence (X) or absence (0) of engaged behavior for both Timmy and the typical student at the beginning of each 2-minute interval. The data is illustrated below.

October 3: Interval Recording Data on Timmy, Language Arts/Spelling

2-Minute Time Intervals	Timmy	Comparison Student	Observer Comments
1:00	X	X	Teacher introduces spelling words.
1:02	X	X	
1:04	X	X	
1:06	0	X	Timmy crumples his paper and tears off small pieces, throwing them on the floor.
1:08	0	0	Timmy distracts other students by whispering loudly while doodling on his desk with a pencil.
1:10	0	0	Timmy continues to distract other students with whispering and low-pitched noises. Teacher is helping other students.
1:12	X	X	Teacher hands Timmy new piece of paper and encourages him to write spelling words.
1:14	0	X	Timmy whispers loudly and makes faces.
1:16	0	X	Continues to complain.
1:18	0	X	Teacher assistant moves to Timmy.
Total	4 out of 10	8 out of 10	
Percentage	40% engagement	80% engagement	

SNAPSHOT Continued

October 10: Interval Recording Data on Timmy, Language Arts/Spelling

2-Minute Time Intervals	Timmy	Comparison Student	Observer Comments
1:00	X	X	Teacher asks students to get their writing notebooks.
1:02	0	X	All students but Timmy have retrieved their notebooks from the literacy shelf.
1:04	0	X	Timmy is still looking for his notebook and starts to speak to himself in an audible whisper.
1:06	X	X	Teacher tries to help find the notebook. Both Timmy and the teacher search the shelves.
1:08	0	X	Teacher locates notebook inside Timmy's desk.
1:10	0	0	Timmy distracts other students by scraping his chair on the floor, then he throws a small piece of paper at another student and says the student's name.
1:12	X	X	Teacher hands Timmy a pencil and encourages him by telling him that she enjoyed his last entry in the journal. Timmy starts the assignment.
1:14	0	X	Timmy breaks pencil (on purpose?) by snapping it over his knee. He plays with the broken pieces.
1:16	0	0	Distracts other students as he complains about the assignment. He avoids the teacher's looks.
1:18	X	X	Teacher helps Timmy write one idea in his notebook by helping him formulate his thoughts.
Total	4 out of 10	7 out of 10	
Percentage	40% engagement	70% engagement	

OBSERVATION RESULTS: Timmy was observed for two 20-minute periods on two consecutive Mondays. During the first observation, he was observed during the introduction of new spelling words and an assignment that followed. The second observation included a writing activity that students were to complete independently on the class blog. There were 18 students, the classroom teacher, and classroom aide present during each of the observations.

SUMMARY OF THE RESULTS: Timmy was engaged 40 percent of the time during the first observation and 40 percent of the time during the second observation. The comparison student was engaged 80 percent and 70 percent, respectively. Both students were engaged at the beginning, but Timmy quickly became disengaged. During both observations, his complaining distracted the comparison student.

INTERPRETATIONS AND RECOMMENDATIONS: These results reinforce the initial impression that Timmy is not engaging in activities at the level that might be considered typical in this classroom. Although the comparison student and Timmy both became disengaged at similar points, Timmy was not

> **SNAPSHOT** Continued

able to reengage in his work without teacher assistance. For example, Timmy worked on the assignment for the first 55 seconds and then began to look at other students and around the room until he was redirected by the teacher. The comparison student worked on the assignment and, despite several interruptions, returned to his work without a reminder. Timmy appears to be easily frustrated when completing written assignments. His lack of organization interferes with his work. Yet he is able to refocus with adult support.

These observations suggest that the classroom teacher should

1. Work with Timmy to find an appropriate place for his books, pencils, markers, and tablet. Ensure that Timmy puts away materials in the same place every day.
2. Develop and review Timmy's daily schedule with him. Prepare him for transitions.
3. Ensure that Timmy has little downtime by giving him structured, directed assignments because he responds to these types of assignments.
4. Keep extra pencils and other consumable materials available for Timmy and other students.
5. Provide adult support before Timmy becomes frustrated. For example, the teacher could ask the classroom aide to monitor Timmy's behavior at the beginning of a new activity and provide support so that he can start and complete the activity successfully. During assignments, the teacher should monitor Timmy's independent work and provide direction at the first indication of frustration.
6. Seat Timmy near the teacher because he responds to prompts and praise.
7. Establish a system that reinforces positive behaviors such as putting materials away and completing an assignment.
8. Assign tasks and activities that are at Timmy's academic level to reduce frustration.
9. Keep his assignments brief so that his attention can be kept focused on the assignments.

Do you agree with the special educator's interpretation of the data? What other ideas could you suggest? Share your ideas.

Pause and consider:

- You are working with Timmy's IEP team as they seek to determine how much he participates in activities in the general education classroom. Develop an assessment question that addresses the teacher's concern.
- Define the behavior in terms that can be observed.
- Determine how you would collect your observation data and create an appropriate form.

Observing the Classroom Environment

Teachers assess the needs of individual students within the context of the classroom environment. "What can I do to help Timmy, a student with disabilities, feel like he is included in our classroom?" "How can we assist Boyanna in becoming more independent?" The interaction of student learning and behavior is complex. The classroom environment can affect learning and behavior adversely, or the environment can be structured to promote positive behaviors, enhance positive conduct, and build self-esteem.

Three aspects of the classroom environment affect the student's learning and behavior: the physical environment, the learning or instructional environment, and the social environment. Checklists and classroom sketches are the most common ways of gathering information about the classroom environment. The following subsections examine ways teachers can use software and apps to create tools for observing these three aspects of the classroom environment.

Physical Environment

The physical environment consists of seating arrangements, lighting, noise level, distractions, temperature, overall atmosphere, and general layout of the classroom. Some of the areas to consider in planning an observation of the physical environment are listed in Table 8.3. What other areas can you suggest that would be important in observing the physical environment?

TABLE 8.3 • Observing the Physical Environment

Suggested Areas to Observe	Assessment Questions
1. Seating	• **Positioning** Does the height and size of the chair give the student proper support? Are the student's feet supported (either resting flat on the floor or supported by a footrest)? Is the student seated in close proximity to other students?
2. Lighting	• **Lighting intensity** Is the degree of lighting appropriate? Is the board or screen free from glare that might make reading difficult?
3. Noise	• **Minimum noise level** Is the noise level of student work groups appropriate?
4. Distractions	• **Sight** Does the room have displays that are visually distracting? • **Sound** Is there noise distraction (such as a clock ticking or a radiator pinging)? • **Events and activities** Are there activities in the room that are distracting to the student?
5. Climate	• **Temperature** Is the temperature level of the classroom comfortable?
6. Classroom	• **Ambiance** Is the ambiance of the classroom warm and accepting?
7. General layout	• **Layout of the room; type and placement of furniture, equipment, and materials** Are all areas of the classroom accessible to the student? Are classroom materials accessible to the student? • **Amount and type of space** Is there enough space to meet the student's needs? Is there an accessible place to store adapted materials and equipment? Can the student easily move between areas of the room?

The amount and arrangement of physical space affects student functioning. For example, grouping desks in sets of three or four encourages students to discuss and share ideas. The placement of furniture, equipment, and materials is critical for students with disabilities. Furniture and adaptive equipment need to maximize the students' potential for independent participation. The availability of accessible space allows a student with a physical disability full-classroom access. Differences in texture or color of carpeting between centers enable a student who is blind or has multiple disabilities to increase orientation and independent travel (mobility) skills. An organized environment helps all students learn appropriate storage of materials. Accessible storage of materials assists students with disabilities in locating and using materials independently.

Figure 8.11 illustrates a draw program for creating a classroom sketch to illustrate the physical layout of a kindergarten classroom. The sketch helped the teaching team to think

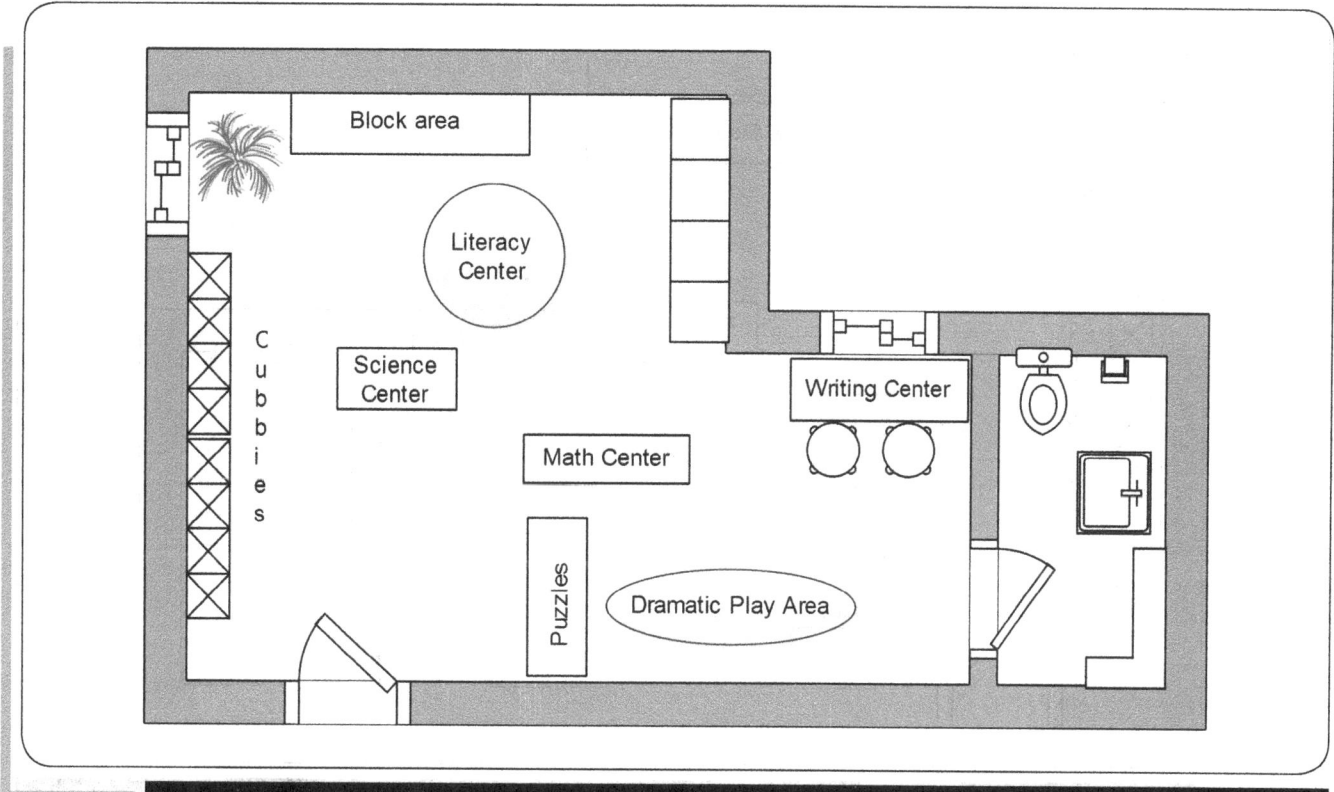

FIGURE 8.11 • Teacher-Made Drawing of a Kindergarten Classroom

about the classroom layout and how they might improve learning opportunities. The teachers decided to try moving the science and mathematics center closer to the block area to allow children to use the blocks in various mathematics and science activities. The teachers also discussed how the location of adjacent areas contributed to difficulties that they had experienced during circle time. They decided to move the circle area away from the block area, which was distracting for two students. They changed the center of the room to accommodate space for circle activities and added individual carpet squares to the area to help children understand individual space and reduce the likelihood of disruptive behavior. Figure 8.12 represents the rearranged environment.

Sometimes teachers involve their students in designing the environment. **Makerspaces** are designed by children to enhance learning. Sometimes referred to as DIY (Do It Yourself), these spaces encourage students to think about various aspects of space. Makerspaces can encourage students to create, invent, and learn!

Learning Environment

What are the expectations of the classroom? How can the classroom be adapted to accommodate the students' learning needs? The learning or instructional environment consists of the teaching strategies that the teacher uses and the materials that are available for student use. Observing the learning environment involves examining the instructional materials as well as the methods of instruction. Table 8.4 illustrates some of the areas to consider in planning an observation of the learning environment.

As we know, teacher expectations, teaching methods, and student requirements often differ from one classroom to the next. These differences vary from the materials and equip-

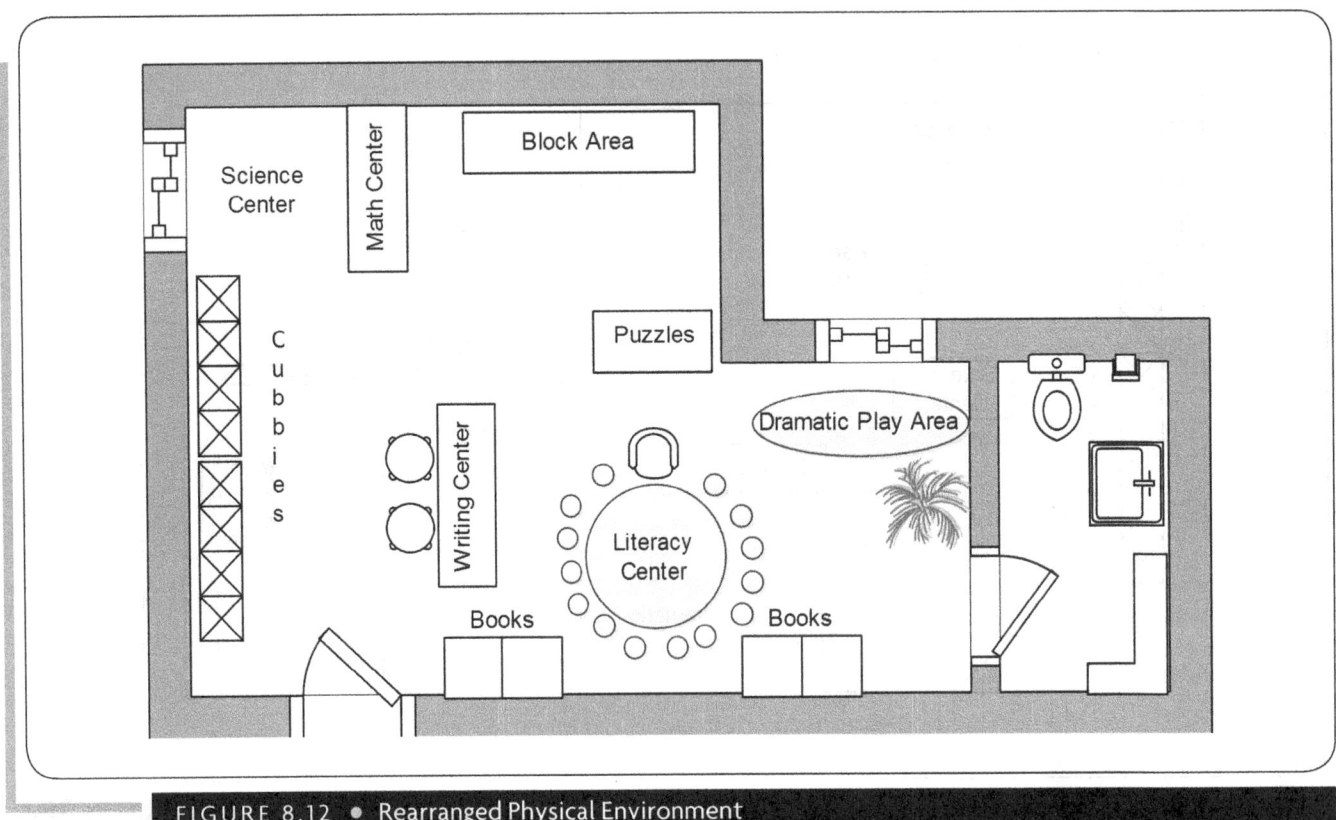

FIGURE 8.12 • Rearranged Physical Environment

ment that are available to assist students in their work, to the teaching methods that may require different skills from the students.

The classroom examples in the snapshot called Stoney Brook Elementary and Lincoln High Learning Environments illustrate the variety of teaching methods, materials, and demands that students may encounter in the same grade. Students with disabilities at Stoney Brook or Lincoln High may experience difficulties in one or more of these classrooms.

Social Environment

The social environment consists of the general classroom ambiance as well as the relationships among students and between students and teachers. Positive social environments assist students in managing frustration, resolving conflict, and developing respect and appreciation for individual differences. Teachers who foster positive social environments have zero tolerance for bullying behaviors, which continue to plague many of our schools. According to a recent data analysis of the Health Behavior in School Children: WHO Cross-National Survey, bullying increases among children who watch television frequently, lack teacher support, have themselves been bullied, attend schools with unfavorable environments, have emotional support from their peers, and have teachers and parents who do not place high expectations on their school performance (Barboza, Schiamberg, Oehmke, Korzeniewski, Post, & Heraux, 2009) Some of the areas to consider when assessing the social environment are listed in Table 8.5.

After carefully considering the areas to observe in the environment, one special educator developed a checklist that included many of the areas that we have just discussed. In addition to each of the areas, she also included space for observer comments because observers sometimes gather information that should be noted, but there is no space for it on the form. Table 8.6 illustrates this checklist.

TABLE 8.4 • Observing the Learning Environment

Suggested Areas to Observe	Assessment Questions
1. Materials	• **Variety** Do students have access to a variety of materials? • **Format** Is the format of materials appropriate?
2. Manipulatives	• **Availability and appropriateness** Are appropriate manipulatives available?
3. Learning activities	• **Instructional methods** Does the teacher use a variety of instructional methods? • **Opportunities to make choices** Does the classroom teacher provide students with opportunities to make choices during learning activities? • **Opportunities to share ideas** Are student comments and questions respected and encouraged?
4. Instructional demands	• **Clear instructions for completing the assignments** Does the teacher provide clear instructions and check for student understanding before students begin learning activities and assignments? • **Assignments that are appropriate in difficulty and in length** Are students assigned work that is appropriate in difficulty and length? • **Learning activities and assignments that are relevant to the students** Do students perceive that the work is useful? Can students use a variety of materials?
5. Modifications	• **Changes in furniture, equipment, or materials** Is there easy and convenient access to furniture and equipment? Can students use the materials, or is there a need for accommodations or modifications?
6. Grouping	• **Grouping of students** Do students complete some work independently? Can students work with a peer? Do students have opportunities to work cooperatively with others?
7. Instruction	• **Adjustments** Are the instructional strategies appropriate, or is there a need for revision? Is there a variety of instructional methods in use? • **Pace of instruction** Is the pace of instructional delivery appropriate? • **Adequate levels of assistance** Does the teacher (or teaching assistant) provide prompts and other types of assistance on an as-needed basis to students? Is assistance faded as soon as possible?
8. Expectations	• **Demands placed on students** Are the teacher's expectations appropriate?
9. Student involvement	• **Teacher support** Does the teacher encourage student involvement? Is the student actively involved in learning activities? Does the student participate in classroom discussions? • **Peer support** Do other students interact with the student? Does the student interact with other students?

TABLE 8.4 • (Continued)

Suggested Areas to Observe	Assessment Questions
10. Assessment	• **Tools** Does the teacher use a variety of assessment approaches in assessing student instructional needs and progress? • **Format** If appropriate, does the teacher implement alternative formats? • **Feedback** Does the teacher give students feedback and suggestions for improvement?
11. Curriculum	• **Curriculum reform and standards** Does the curriculum reflect recent reform, standards, and contemporary views?
12. Schedule	• **Predictability of the daily schedule** Does the classroom teacher follow a regular schedule? Is the schedule posted for students to see? Is there a minimum of interruptions?
13. Transitions	• **Preparation and follow-through** Does the teacher prepare students for the transition from one activity to another? Does the teacher provide time for students to transition?

TABLE 8.5 • Observing the Social Environment

Suggested Areas to Observe	Assessment Questions
1. Teacher–student interactions	• **Respect for oneself and others** Are all students valued for themselves? Does the teacher expect students to respect others? • **Supportive social environment** Does the teacher know how to communicate with students with disabilities? • **Interactions** Are interactions warm and friendly? Does the teacher encourage students to interact appropriately with the teacher?
2. Behavioral interventions	• **Positive behavioral supports** Does the teacher use positive teaching strategies in helping students learn appropriate behavioral expectations? • **Behavior management** Are behavior management strategies effective? Are expectations of behavior posted in the classroom?
3. Peer interactions	• **Student-to-student interactions** Do students know how to communicate with students with disabilities? Do students interact appropriately with each other? Are students courteous, respectful, and supportive of learning?
4. General atmosphere	• **Positive classroom climate** Does the teacher have high expectations for all students? Is there an atmosphere of enthusiasm and support for students? Does the student appear to be comfortable in the social environment? • **Distractions** Are distractions kept to a minimum?

TABLE 8.6 • Teacher-Made Checklist for Observing the Classroom Environment

Student's Name: Joe   Date: 10/19   Time: 9:15
Observer: Mr. T.   Location: classroom

Physical environment	Always	Sometimes	Never
1. Seating Is the student seated properly?	X		

Suggestions for improvement:

	Always	Sometimes	Never
2. Lighting Is the lighting appropriate?	X		

Suggestions for improvement:

	Always	Sometimes	Never
3. Noise Is the noise level appropriate?		X	

Suggestions for improvement: When group activities are underway, the noise level of the classroom tends to rise. Teacher should monitor.

	Always	Sometimes	Never
4. Distractions Is the student distracted by activities in the room?		X	

Suggestions for improvement: Joe should be seated in an area away from the door where distractions will be minimized.

	Always	Sometimes	Never
5. Temperature Is the temperature of the room appropriate?	X		

Suggestions for improvement:

	Always	Sometimes	Never
6. General classroom surroundings Does the student appear to be comfortable in the environment?		X	

Suggestions for improvement:

Learning environment	Always	Sometimes	Never
1. Materials Are a variety of reading materials available?	X		

Suggestions for improvement: All materials should be provided in both text and digital formats.

	Always	Sometimes	Never
2. Curriculum Does the reading/writing curriculum reflect contemporary views of reading and writing?	X		

Suggestions for improvement:

TABLE 8.6 • *(Continued)*

Learning environment	Always	Sometimes	Never
3. Activities Is instruction oriented toward the use of various reading and writing materials?	X		

Suggestions for improvement:

	Always	Sometimes	Never
4. Instructional Demands Are the instructional demands appropriate for the student?		X	

Suggestions for improvement: Although Joe has difficulty blending sounds together to form words, he is capable of keeping up with his peers. Instructional demands should be appropriate in keeping with his abilities.

	Always	Sometimes	Never
5. Modifications Have modifications been made to instruction to accommodate the learning needs of the student?		X	

Suggestions for improvement:

	Always	Sometimes	Never
6. Assessment Are a variety of assessment tools used to provide feedback to the student? Is information collected on the student's progress and performance?	X		

Suggestions for improvement:

	Always	Sometimes	Never
7. Materials If grouping is used, is it appropriate?		X	

Suggestions for improvement: Joe should be grouped with students who can actively engage Joe in group discussions during projects.

	Always	Sometimes	Never
8. Curriculum Are teacher expectations appropriate?		X	

Suggestions for improvement: Teacher expectations should be high. Although it may take Joe longer to complete assignments, he is able to achieve at a high level.

	Always	Sometimes	Never
9. Activities Is the student actively involved in reading and writing activities?	X		

Suggestions for improvement:

	Always	Sometimes	Never
10. Instruction Is instruction matched to the assessed needs of the student? Are a variety of instructional methods used?	X		

TABLE 8.6 • (Continued)

Learning environment	Always	Sometimes	Never
Suggestions for improvement:			
11. Pace of instruction Is the pace of instruction appropriate?	X		
Suggestions for improvement:			
12. Schedule Is the student's schedule appropriate?		X	
Suggestions for improvement: Joe may need a longer time than his peers to change classrooms.			
13. Transitions Are transitions made smoothly?		X	
Suggestions for improvement: Planning for transitions should occur. Joe may need extra time to take out and put away materials.			

Social environment	Always	Sometimes	Never
1. Teacher–Student Interactions Are interactions warm and friendly?	X		
Suggestions for improvement:			
2. Disruptions Are disruptions kept to a minimum?	X		
Suggestions for improvement:			
3. Behavioral interventions Are behavioral interventions effective and appropriate?	X		
Suggestions for improvement:			
4. Peer interactions Are peer interactions appropriate?		X	
Suggestions for improvement: Due to Joe's reading difficulties, he is reluctant to initiate peer interactions. A circle of friends should be convened.			
5. General Atmosphere Does the student appear to be comfortable in the social environment?		X	
Suggestions for improvement: Some students seem to be uncomfortable with Joe. With his permission, the teacher could be asked to explain Joe's disabilities to the students. Joe can also be encouraged to share his feelings with the students.			

SNAPSHOT

Stoney Brook Elementary and Lincoln High Learning Environments

Stoney Brook Elementary School has three fourth-grade classrooms. The school district has adopted the state curriculum framework for English language arts. Among other areas, all fourth graders must demonstrate competency in researching and writing a paper about a topic of their interest. The fourth-grade teachers approach the teaching of skills in researching information in different ways. In one classroom, the teacher invites an author to come in and talk with students. The author shares resource materials and shows how his or her information was researched. The author's enthusiasm for writing sparks the children's interest. In a second classroom, the teacher makes arrangements to take the students to the library, where the school librarian gives them a tour of the library's resources and discusses ways to find information using various technologies, search engines, and databases. Later, the children are divided into small work groups and return to the library to use the materials. In the third classroom, the children already use various technologies daily to search for information on the Internet. Their teacher encourages them to use their skills independently in locating information for their individual papers.

The English teachers at Lincoln High use the state curriculum framework for secondary English language arts. They approach student learning in different ways, use a variety of teaching strategies in the classroom, and hold different expectations for student achievement. In the first classroom, the teacher plans learning activities around projects that last from a few weeks to several months. The teacher encourages students to work together in small groups and plans conference meetings with individual students several times a week to monitor student progress.

Next door, in another classroom, the teacher relies primarily on the textbook to provide the curriculum content. Students complete daily assignments from textbook readings. Each class begins with a lecture that reviews the previous reading and provides some supplemental information. The teacher requires students to take notes. The teacher assesses student learning by giving short-answer tests that cover the textbook and classroom lectures.

Pause and consider:
- Identify components of the learning environments in two of the classrooms at Stoney Brook Elementary School. Compare and contrast the two environments. Which do you prefer? Why?
- At Lincoln High School, you learned about two other classrooms and the learning environments supported by the teachers. What other elements might be important to consider in assessing the learning environment?

Interviews

Interviewing students, parents, colleagues, or other professionals is another approach that helps in answering assessment questions. The interview allows a face-to-face meeting in which participants discuss and share their individual perspectives.

Interviewing consists of asking the right questions and listening carefully to what the other person is saying. This skill demands that you know yourself and not let your own biases overshadow what is being told to you. If you use this technique, you must want to hear what the other person is saying. Being a good listener is a complex skill that calls for sensitivity and respect for others. Skillful interviewing requires training and practice.

The interview makes certain assumptions about the give and take of the communication process between individuals. Professionals need to be sensitive to assumptions that members of the dominant group hold about this communication process; these assumptions may not be the same for members of less dominant groups.

An interview usually follows a series of steps, beginning with planning the interview. The special educator contacts the individual and states the purpose of the meeting. The purpose may be to follow up on a student referral: "I'd like to sit down and talk further about your concerns about Sharda." The special educator suggests that they find a convenient time and meeting place: "Do you have some time in the next few days that we could meet?"

Because information shared during the interview may be confidential in nature, take care to find a meeting place that can ensure confidentiality. Locations that are public gathering spots, such as the cafeteria or teachers' lounge, are not appropriate.

Beginning the interview involves establishing rapport with the individual. Some interviewers spend a few minutes talking about a shared activity of mutual interest before sitting down to work. Acknowledge the fact that the individual has set aside time for the meeting. Begin the interview with broad questions and gradually ask more specific and focused questions (Nitko & Brookhart, 2011).

In conducting the interview, show a genuine interest in what the individual has to say. Create a positive tone by your respect, support, and warmth. Ask questions and rephrase statements to help clarify important points. Many professionals find it helpful to prepare a few questions in advance. As you think about the types of questions that would be helpful, consider the wording of the questions and the type of answers that may result. Open-ended questions are usually more helpful. For example, ask, "What have you tried to address these behavior problems?" or "What are you thinking about doing?" Too often the interviewer may not take the time to listen and fully understand. The interviewer may jump to finding a solution, "Have you tried to address this problem by . . . ?" This line of questioning may produce single-word responses and a sense of frustration. Listen not only to hear but also to understand what the individual is saying. Generally, interviews should not exceed an hour in length. Conclude the interview by summarizing the discussion.

Interviews with students are helpful both when students are having academic difficulties and when students are doing well. The interview provides information about a student's perspective in a wide variety of areas and is especially productive in giving insight into the student's overall patterns of behavior (Salvia & Ysseldyke, 2013) and self-concept. Student interviews are helpful in making adjustments to the classroom environment.

Interviews should be used with caution, however, because they can present difficulties for students with disabilities and for students who are English language learners. The interview technique requires skills in understanding and speaking the language of the interviewee. For example, an interviewer can inadvertently cut off students with processing difficulties, who may take longer to compose a response. Students who are not proficient in English can experience difficulty, even when a translator is present. The translator may or may not be proficient in the student's dialect, or the student may misinterpret the translation because the nuances in the language do not transfer.

Steps in Conducting Student Interviews

Whitcomb and Merrell (2012) described the following steps in conducting a student interview:

1. Begin by asking generally for the student's reasons for having the interview. Allow time for discussion of the student's interests and attitudes.
2. Lead the discussion toward a specific probing of the problem. For example, the interviewer might ask the student to describe what happens just before the student gets involved in a fight.
3. Ask the student to describe his or her behavioral assets.
4. Obtain the student's perspective on what positive and appropriate behaviors the student can marshal, as well as a description of likes and dislikes.
5. Use this information, along with other assessment information, to develop a plan for addressing the problem behavior.

Questionnaires

Questionnaires consist of a set of questions designed to gather information. Educators and other professionals design questionnaires to collect various types of information and to assist

---

Student Questionnaire

Name _____

Date _____

Teacher _____

Grade _____

1. What assignments have you enjoyed most so far this year? Why were they enjoyable?
2. Did you work alone or with others on these assignments?
3. How did you demonstrate what you learned?
4. If your parent or other relative were coming to school to see your work, what work would you show them?
5. What work would you probably not show them?

FIGURE 8.13 • Student Questionnaire

---

in answering questions. Sometimes the use of a questionnaire is preferred over an interview or conference. For example, students who have difficulty with spoken English may be more comfortable answering a written question. Busy professionals may prefer completing information at a time that is convenient to them.

This section focuses on questionnaires developed for the purpose of gathering information about the student. For example, a special education teacher who is working with a student with problem behaviors might ask the general education teacher, parents, and others who know the student well to complete a questionnaire about the student's behavior at school, at home, and in the community.

Special educators can use questionnaires to ask students about their learning preferences. Using the information, a teacher can work toward improving the learning environment. Figure 8.13 illustrates a teacher-made questionnaire to be completed by the student. Do you think the questionnaire would provide helpful information to you, if you were the teacher?

Conferencing and Collaborating

Conferencing

Conferencing involves meeting with parents, teachers, therapists, or professionals in other agencies to share information, concerns, and ideas regarding common issues. Planning the conference takes some time and thought. Find a time and location that is convenient for each person. Consider, too, the diversity of today's families. As you prepare for the conference, be sure to know the correct names of each parent, grandparent, or guardian. Take time to think about how you will begin the discussion. Beginning on a positive note can set the tone for a productive meeting! Talk about the strengths of the student. Then, consider the concerns and how you will describe them.

During the conference, identify and clarify the situation. Describe the areas of concern: "I understand that Roberto has been having a difficult time. Could you describe what has been happening?" Ask questions or restate what has been said if you are unsure of the issues. Determine the history and the frequency of the problem (Friend & Cook, 2013; Heward, 2013).

Assist participants to work together to brainstorm a list of interventions, recording each idea using a large chart (during face-to-face meetings) or note box on the screen during a videoconference. This written record assists the generation of additional ideas, as no suggestion is rejected. The process allows participants to feel that they are making progress identifying possible solutions.

Next, make decisions by building consensus among those involved. Develop a timeline by writing down the activities and interventions that will be tried and when. Clarify the responsibilities of each member and schedule a follow-up meeting (Friend & Cook, 2013). Finally, thank each person for participating. Ending on a positive note creates a feeling of goodwill among participants. In future meetings, share ideas of good experiences and solutions that have worked.

Research-Based Practices Assessment Approaches

Not only educators but also professionals from other disciplines regularly use direct observations and interviews to gather information about students and their environments. For psychologists, the assessment of students with social, behavioral, and emotional disabilities has changed over the last few years. No longer do psychologists just administer intelligence tests, achievement tests, tests of perceptual-motor performance, or projective measures such as *Draw-A-Person*. According to a survey conducted by Shapiro and Heick (2004), over 1,000 members of the National Association of School Psychologists reported increased use of direct instruction, structured interviews, and rating scales. In fact, over 60 percent of the respondents indicated that they used these approaches frequently in addition to more traditional assessments.

Collaborating

Collaborating is a more active process than simply meeting with others to discuss common issues. Collaboration involves a commitment on an individual's part to work cooperatively with others toward a common goal.

Building expertise in conferencing and collaborating begins with good interpersonal skills. Some individuals seem to have strong interpersonal skills; others need to develop and practice these faculties. Professionals improve interpersonal competence by working with others who demonstrate a strong commitment to teamwork and collaboration. Let's examine some of the characteristics of effective interpersonal skills.

- Individuals with strong interpersonal skills communicate in a positive, genuine manner.
- Interpersonal skills involve both verbal and nonverbal communication. Verbal communication refers not only to the spoken words but also to the tone and pitch the speaker uses. Nonverbal communication consists of facial expression, body language, and gestures.
- Effective listeners do not interrupt. Knowing all the answers is not important—or possible. Working together to create solutions is critical.
- Speakers use everyday language and eliminate the use of jargon. The field of special education is filled with numbers and acronyms. Professionals from other disciplines may not be familiar with many of the terms that special educators use frequently.

Summary

- Through carefully planned observations, educators can gather a wealth of information about students and their environments and answer various types of assessment questions.
- Depending on the assessment question, observers use different recording techniques, including anecdotal records, running records, event recordings, duration recordings, intensity recordings, latency recordings, interval recordings, and category recordings.
- In conducting observations, the examiner needs to be aware of the sources of error that affect the accuracy of observations.
- Reliability refers to the consistency of observations. Observers can ensure reliability by taking steps to address factors such as observer drift, reliability checks, predetermined expectations, or student and setting characteristics.
- Validity, or the extent to which the observation measures what it is intended to measure, must be considered when planning the observation and defining the behavior.
- By using observation data, educators can develop informal norms.
- Interviewing, another assessment approach, involves the careful selection of questions and being a good listener.

- Conferencing consists of planned meetings with parents, teachers, therapists, or other professionals to share information, concerns, and ideas.
- Collaborating, a more active process than conferencing, involves commitments to work cooperatively with others toward a common goal.

Answer to Question:

On page 138, we asked if Stacy's behavior had improved after a two-month interval. The answer is:

$$\frac{15 \text{ occurrences}}{10 \text{ minutes}} = 1.5 \text{ occurrences per minute}$$

This represents an improvement.

QUESTIONS FOR REFLECTION

1. Design a form that teachers can use to collect information about the intensity of a student's behavior.
2. Revisit the Snapshot about Timmy.
   a. What other information about Timmy and the teacher can you gather by studying the observation data sheets?
   b. Do you agree with the special educator's interpretation of the data? Share your ideas.
3. Select either Stoney Brook Elementary or Lincoln High from the Snapshot called Stoney Brook Elementary and Lincoln High Learning Environments. Develop two or more assessment questions about the learning environment described. Next, carefully review the teacher-made checklist (see Table 8.6). Would this checklist help you gather information to answer your assessment question? What other area(s) would you suggest adding?
4. Consider the interviews in which you have participated. What skills can you identify that were helpful during the interview process?

REFERENCES

Barboza, G. E., Schiamberg, L. B., Oehmke, J., Korzeniewski, S. J., Post, L. A., & Heraux, C. G. (2009). Individual characteristics and the multiple contexts of adolescent bullying: An ecological perspective. *Journal of Youth & Adolescence, 38*, 1, 101–121.

Beaty, J. J. (2010). *Observing development of the young child* (7th ed.). Boston: Pearson.

Friend, M., & Cook, L. (2013). *Interactions: Collaboration skills for school professionals*. Boston: Pearson.

Heward, W. L. (2013). *Exceptional children: An introduction to special education* (9th ed.). Boston: Pearson.

Miller, M. D., Linn, R. L., & Gronlund, N. E. (2013). *Measurement and assessment in teaching* (11th ed.). Boston: Pearson.

Nitko, A. J., & Brookhart, S. M. (2011). *Educational assessment of students* (6th ed.). Boston: Pearson.

Salvia, J., & Ysseldyke, J. (2013). *Assessment in special and inclusive education* (12th ed.). Independence, KY: Cengage Learning.

Sattler, J. (2008). *Assessment of children* (5th ed.). La Mesa, CA: Author.

Shapiro, E. S., & Heick, P. F. (2004). School psychologist assessment practices in the evaluation of students referred for social/behavioral/emotional problems. *Psychology in the Schools, 41*(5), 551–561.

Whitcomb, S., & Merrell, K. W. (2012). *Behavioral, social, and emotional assessment of children and adolescents* (4th ed.). Florence, KY: Routledge Taylor & Francis Group.

9 Behavior

Chapter Objectives

After completing this chapter, you should be able to:

- Define and describe examples of adaptive behaviors.
- Define and describe examples of common problem behaviors.
- Consider behavior within an intervention context by assessing the physical, learning, and social environments of the classroom.
- Describe the process for conducting a functional behavioral assessment.
- Compare standardized instruments that assess adaptive behaviors and compare standardized instruments that assess problem behaviors.

Overview

This chapter considers two categories of behaviors: (1) behaviors that are essential for students to function successfully from day to day and (2) behaviors that students must have to be productive members of society. The first category of behaviors, often referred to as adaptive behaviors, is associated with intellectual disabilities and other developmental disabilities. Adaptive behaviors cover a wide range of skills, such as dressing or preparing a snack or simple meal. No single instrument measures the entire adaptive behavior domain. In fact, standardized instruments reflect different views of adaptive behavior and the skills involved.

Later in this chapter, we examine the second category. Students with some disabilities, such as oppositional defiant disorder or other emotional or mental health difficulties, often display problem behaviors. Special educators and other team members assess these behaviors and develop plans, often referred to as positive behavior support plans, to identify instructional procedures and data collection to monitor progress. This second section of the chapter discusses common problem behaviors and how various classroom environments,

TABLE 9.1 • Adaptive Behavior Skills	
Adaptive Behavior	**Examples of Skills**
Conceptual	Reads functional words Writes words and phrases Identifies coins and makes change
Social	Works appropriately with others Follows classroom rules Initiates personal greetings
Practical	Prepares simple meals Showers and dresses independently Uses public transportation

such as the physical, learning, and social environments, affect these behaviors. Some students may do well in one setting and yet have difficulty performing the same task or skill in a different setting.

Adaptive Behavior

Adaptive behavior consists of a variety of conceptual, social, and practical skills that individuals learn to function in their everyday lives (American Association on Intellectual and Developmental Disabilities [AAIDD], 2008). The concept of adaptive behavior is most closely associated with intellectual disabilities. For students who are in school, the assessment of adaptive behavior plays a part in determining whether a student is found eligible for special education services under the Individuals with Disabilities Education Act (IDEA) categorical term *intellectual disabilities*. The student must demonstrate significant limitations in intellectual functioning and in adaptive behavior skills on standardized measures that are normed on people with and without disabilities. Assessment of a student's adaptive behavior includes a variety of skills, as seen in Table 9.1.

Supports

Assessment of adaptive behavior must include the assessment of supports needed for the individual to participate in the environment. **Supports** are resources and strategies necessary to promote the development, education, interests, and personal well-being of a person with intellectual disability. (AAIDD, 2008) When assessing a student's supports, the AAID (**http://www.aaidd.org**) recommends that team members examine the following areas:

- Human development
- Teaching and education
- Home living
- Community living
- Employment
- Health and safety
- Behavior
- Social
- Protection
- Advocacy

After gathering information about a student's needs, special educators use this assessment information to plan various instructional activities and implement supports to improve the student's functioning and to promote self-determination and advocacy. For example, a special educator develops learning activities that allow the student to practice making appropriate decisions with peers. Later, the student applies these skills on a classroom field trip.

Based on the assessment information, the student may also receive related services such as occupational therapy, physical therapy, or speech and language therapy. For example, a speech and language pathologist works with the special educator to identify strategies to help teach new vocabulary. In another instance, an occupational therapist works with a

> **Research-Based Practices** — **Adaptive Behavior and Achievement of Students with Developmental Disabilities**
>
> Research studies show that when teachers teach students how to use learning strategies (such as self-monitoring) or use teaching strategies (such as peer tutoring), students with disabilities can improve adaptive behaviors. For students with developmental disabilities, self-management strategies and decreasing **maladaptive behaviors** are important for success in the general education classroom.
>
> Researchers (McDonnell, Thorson, Disher, Mathot-Buckner, Mendel, & Ray, 2003; Palmer, Heyne, Montie, & Abery, 2011) explored the use of teaching strategies and supports in inclusive classroom settings with both students with developmental disabilities and students without disabilities. In the classroom, the students with developmental disabilities received a number of different supports, such as curriculum and instructional adaptations, embedded instruction, parallel instruction, circles of friends, peer tutoring, and direct instruction. Teachers used both large- and small-group instruction, cooperative learning, and coteaching between general and special educators. At the end of the school year, the results indicated that students with developmental disabilities had made significant gains in adaptive behavior, as measured by standardized instruments, parent interviews, and personal accounts.

student to promote fine motor skills that would allow the student to use the apps on her cell phone.

Standardized Instruments Evaluating Adaptive Behavior

The instruments in this section have the specific purpose of assessing adaptive behavior. Many other tests besides these assess adaptive skills and behavior. In the following subsections, we will examine the most common tools.

Adaptive Behavior Assessment System Second Edition

The *Adaptive Behavior Assessment System, Second Edition* (*ABAS II®;* Harrison & Oakland, 2003) is a norm-referenced assessment of adaptive behavior for children and adults, ages birth to 89 years. This assessment measures 10 adaptive skill areas, including communication, community use, functional academics, school living/home living, health and safety, leisure, self-care, self-direction, social, and work. According to the authors, these skill areas comprise the three general areas of adaptive behavior—conceptual, social, and practical—identified by AAIDD. The *ABAS II* includes Spanish-language Parent and Teacher Forms.

ADMINISTRATION   Multiple forms allow parents, teachers, family members, and the individual to provide information. Skill items are scored on a rating scale, with 0 (is not able), 1 (never when needed), 2 (sometimes

> **TESTS-at-a-GLANCE**
>
> **Adaptive Behavior Assessment System, Second Edition (ABAS II®)**
>
> http://www.pearsonclinical.com/education/products/100000449/adaptive-behavior-assessment-system-second-edition-abassecondedition.html?Pid=015-8004-507&Mode=summary
>
> - **Publication Date:** 2003
> - **Purpose:** Assesses adaptive behavior skills.
> - **Age/Grade Levels:** Birth through 89 years.
> - **Time to Administer:** 15 to 20 minutes.
> - **Technical Adequacy:** The standardization sample should be updated to reflect changes in student demographics according to the most recent Census.
> - **Suggested Use:** Identifying areas of strengths and areas of limitations, as well as monitoring student progress. This instrument provides rating scales that may be used by the individual, parents, teachers, and others to assess skills associated with adaptive behavior.

when needed), and 3 (always when needed). A separate column allows the informant to indicate if the item required a guess. Approximate time to complete is 15 to 20 minutes.

SCORING Norm-referenced scaled scores are available for each of the skill areas (mean = 10, standard deviation = 3), and standard scores are available for the composite areas (mean = 100, standard deviation = 15). Confidence intervals of 90 percent and 95 percent may be calculated.

STANDARDIZATION For children birth to 5 years, the standardization sample consisted of 2,100 individuals. For children 5 years through adult, the sample consisted of 5,270 individuals who were representative of the 2000 U.S. Census in terms of sex, race/ethnicity, geographic regions, and parent education level.

RELIABILITY Internal consistency reliability coefficients for the overall general adaptive composite are in the high .90s for all age groups. Reliability coefficients for the skills areas range from .91 to .98. Test-retest reliability coefficients for the general adaptive composites are in the .90s. Interrater reliability coefficients on the general adaptive composites (teacher form) are .91 for students between ages 5 and 9 and .87 for students between ages 10 and 21. On the parent form, the interrater reliability coefficients for the general adaptive composites are .83 to .85 for both age groups.

VALIDITY The manual reports clinical validity studies to support the use of the *ABAS II* to assist in identifying mental retardation. Mean scores of almost 30 individuals with intellectual disabilities ranged from 55 to 73 points, which was significantly lower than the matched control groups, where individuals' scores ranged from 95 to 101. There were significant differences between the mean general adaptive composite scores of individuals with mild and moderate mental retardation.

SUMMARY The *Adaptive Behavior Assessment System, Second Edition*, is a well-designed norm-referenced rating scale that is aligned with *the Diagnostic and Statistical Manual, Fourth Edition-TR* adaptive skill areas and incorporates the AAIDD guidelines for evaluating the three composite areas of adaptive behavior: conceptual, social, and practical. The standardization sample was based on the 2000 U.S. Census data and will need to be updated to reflect changes in student demographics in schools today. Scoring software may be purchased separately.

Vineland Adaptive Behavior Scales, Second Edition

The *Vineland Adaptive Behavior Scales, Second Edition* (*Vineland-II*; Sparrow, Cicchetti, & Balla, 2005), measures personal and social skills from birth to adulthood. This instrument assists in identifying and classifying intellectual disabilities and other disorders such as autism, Asperger syndrome, and other developmental delays. The *Vineland-II* includes four forms; the first three also are available in Spanish:

1. Survey Interview. This consists of open-ended questions that the examiner uses in talking with the parent or caregiver.
2. Parent/Caregiver Rating Form. A parent or caregiver completes a rating scale on the content covered in the Survey Interview. This provides an alternative format to the interview.
3. Expanded Interview. This includes more comprehensive information helpful for planning a student's specialized education program and may be used as a follow-up to the Survey Interview.
4. Teacher Rating Form. This questionnaire, appropriate for children ages 3 through 21, is completed by the student's teacher.

The *Vineland II* measures the following domains and subdomains:

Communication
Receptive
Expressive
Written

Daily Living Skills
Personal
Domestic
Community

Socialization
Interpersonal Relationships
Play and Leisure Time
Coping Skills

Motor Skills
Fine
Gross

Maladaptive Behavior (Optional)
Internalizing
Externalizing
Other

> **TESTS-at-a-GLANCE**
>
> **Vineland Adaptive Behavior Scales, Second Edition (Vineland-II)**
> http://www.pearsonclinical.com/psychology/products/100000668/vineland-adaptive-behavior-scales-second-edition-vineland-ii-vinelandii.html?Pid=Vineland-II&Mode=summary
>
> - **Publication Date:** 2005
> - **Purposes:** Identifies adaptive and maladaptive behaviors.
> - **Age/Grade Levels:** Birth to age 90.
> - **Time to Administer:** 20 to 60 minutes.
> - **Technical Adequacy:** The standardization sample will need to be updated to reflect changes in student demographics.
> - **Suggested Use:** Identifying adaptive and problem behaviors in students. Useful for determining eligibility, program planning, and program monitoring.

According to the examiner's manual, the first three broad domains (Communication, Daily Living Skills, and Socialization) correspond to the three broad domains of adaptive functioning recognized by the AAIDD.

ADMINISTRATION   Survey Interview and Parent/Caregiver Rating Forms take 20 to 60 minutes.

SCORING   Domain and adaptive behavior composite scores are reported as standard scores (mean = 100; standard deviation = 15). Percentile ranks, adaptive levels, and age equivalents may also be reported. Subdomain scores are reported as scaled scores (mean = 15; standard deviation = 3), percentile ranks, adaptive levels, and age equivalents.

STANDARDIZATION   Norms are representative of the 2000 U.S. Census.

RELIABILITY AND VALIDITY   According to the authors, the *Vineland-II* is a reliable and valid instrument; considerable research documents the usefulness of this instrument.

SUMMARY   The *Vineland Adaptive Behavior Scales, Second Edition*, consists of four forms, also available in Spanish, that aid in diagnosing intellectual disabilities and other disorders. The instrument measures the following domains: communication, daily living skills, socialization, motor skills, and maladaptive behavior (optional). The standardization sample was based on the 2000 U.S. Census data and will need to be updated to reflect changes in student demographics in schools today.

SNAPSHOT

Jean's Assessment Results

"I'm concerned about Jean," remarked Mr. Chen, referring to Jean, a 14-year-old student who is in Mr. Chen's homeroom. She is currently identified as having a language disability and an intellectual disability. According to her school records, Jean was administered the *Wechsler Individual Intelligence Scale-IV (WISC-IV)* last year and obtained a Full Scale IQ of 66 (1st percentile). The *Vineland Adaptive Behavior Scales-II* were administered to evaluate Jean's adaptive behavior and to review areas of concern. Jean's mother and her special education teacher were the respondents. Jean's scores on the *Vineland-II* revealed her to be functioning well below the average range when compared to other 14-year-old students. The scores are reported in standard scores where the mean equals 100 and the standard deviation equals 15. The Adaptive Behavior Composite was 76 (±3) at the 90 percent confidence interval. Her skill domain scores were

Domain	Standard Score	90% Confidence Interval
Communication	69	±6
Daily Living Skills	68	±7
Socialization	71	±4
Motor Skills	55	–

Areas of noted concern were the student's tendency to be withdrawn and having poor concentration and attention.

Pause and consider:
- Consider Jean's overall score, the Adaptive Behavior Composite Score of 76 (±3) at the 90 percent confidence interval. How would you interpret this score?
- Examine the domain scores. How would you explain the results to other team members? Provide some examples of the skill areas assessed in each domain.

In a conference with Jean's teachers, Jean's mother expressed great concern regarding Jean's future. She noted that Jean has "few friends in the neighborhood" and prefers to play with her 6-year-old sister. In thinking about Jean's future, her mother believes that Jean would be able to get a job at a local motel as a housekeeper. She does admit, however, that Jean has generally low levels of skill in this area.

The special education teacher explained that Jean is currently doing well in an applied occupations course where students explore various job settings. She often talks about her favorite course, an inclusive art media class. Her specialized instruction focuses on functional literacy, applied mathematics, and community living skills. She is continuing to develop skills across these areas.

Jean stated that she liked being around young children. This led the team to discuss possibilities of her enrolling in a child care course with work experience as a teacher's aide in the community child care program. Members of Jean's IEP team began to brainstorm a list of supports that would help to promote Jean's interests.

Problem Behaviors

Problem behaviors in the classroom include antisocial behavior, aggression, withdrawal behavior, delayed social skills, and difficulties with interpersonal relationships. The term **externalizing behaviors** refers to a broad array of disruptive and antisocial behavior, whereas the term **internalizing behaviors** includes social withdrawal, anxious or inhibited behaviors, or somatic problems. Educators, school counselors, and school psychologists can measure and change behaviors in the classroom on a number of dimensions (White & Haring, as cited in Alberto & Troutman, 2013). A behavior can occur many times or only occasionally (frequency); a behavior can last a long or a short time (duration); upon the request of the adult or another student, a behavior can occur immediately or after a period of time (latency); a behavior can be described (topography); a behavior can be performed strongly or weakly (intensity); and a behavior can occur in one or more locations (locus).

Along each of these dimensions, cultural expectations dictate a range of behavior. "Typical" behaviors may differ, depending on the expectations of the group members, culture, family, societal expectations, and other considerations. Observers can identify

> ### SNAPSHOT
> #### Mr. Norford's Seventh-Grade Class
>
> Andy has difficulty sitting still; he plays with his pencil, shuffles his feet, and jingles the coins in his pocket. Mr. Norford describes his activity level, or frequency of behavior, as high. When Andy becomes upset, he reacts strongly. He becomes angry, shouts, and quickly resorts to pushing and shoving. The intensity of his behavior is also high.
>
> Shelly is an average student. When she becomes upset, she becomes sullen and uncooperative. She refuses to talk with the teacher or to other students. Mr. Norford describes Shelly's level of activity as low, but her intensity is high. Her behavior may be overlooked more readily than Andy's behavior. Shelly's problem behavior may not be as disruptive to the classroom as Andy's problem behavior, but it is disruptive to her learning.
>
> Kenichi enrolled in the middle school last spring, soon after his family moved to this country from Japan. Kenichi had no difficulty understanding English because he had studied the language for several years. Over the past few months, Mr. Norford has observed that he has become very quiet and rarely speaks in class. Walking between classes and in the cafeteria, Kenichi is usually seen alone. His teacher believes that he is experiencing periods of sadness and depression for many days at a time. The frequency of Kenichi's behavior often is low and the intensity of his behavior is weak. Mr. Norford has observed these behaviors in several locations.
>
> #### Pause and consider:
> - Consider students with whom you have worked. What problem behaviors have you noted that could be described as high in both frequency and intensity?
> - What problem behaviors have you noted that could be described as low in frequency but high in intensity? Low in both frequency and intensity?

atypical behavior by comparing the individual's behavior with that of members of the comparison group.

In the classroom, students exhibit a range of behavioral dimensions. Students with problem behaviors of high frequency or behaviors that have a strong intensity are easily identifiable. Students who exhibit low frequency or low levels of intensity of behavior are often equally needy; however, observers may not identify these students as easily because problem behaviors in students who are quiet, withdrawn, or depressed may go unnoticed. You can read more about one teacher's observation of his students in the Snapshot called Mr. Norford's Seventh-Grade Class.

Responding to Diversity

Expectations of society, schools, and teachers contribute to or compound problem behaviors in the classroom. Some behaviors may be tolerable or acceptable as the norm in the community, yet these behaviors may not be tolerable to the school or acceptable to the classroom teacher. Teacher expectations also differ widely. The teacher's tolerance for activity level and intensity level affects whether the teacher refers the student for special education services or whether the teacher handles behavior concerns in the classroom.

A student's disability can hasten the development of problem behaviors. For example, a student with Tourette's syndrome develops multiple motor and one or more vocal tics over time. These symptoms occur many times throughout the day, although not necessarily simultaneously. Sometimes the student develops patterns of verbal outbursts, such as words and phrases that are inappropriate. The student is not able to repress these outbursts, and medication may not control the problem satisfactorily. The problem behaviors contribute to decreases in the student's self-concept and self-esteem and affect the development of social skills and interpersonal relationships.

Disabilities in communication can foster problem behaviors. Students with disabilities who have difficulty communicating quickly learn to use behaviors that attract another's attention. Some attention-seeking behaviors are appropriate; others are antisocial, aggressive, or inappropriate.

Assessing Supportive Environments

Physical Environment

A teacher can positively affect the physical environment by creating a structure and a set of expectations for student behavior. The structure consists of predictable classroom routines, where students know the daily schedule and what activities follow one another. The teacher posts the schedule in the classroom using a format that students can understand. For example, the teacher may use both text and pictures in a poster and display it on the wall, as a screen saver on classroom technology devices, and on students' personal devices, which can provide alerts for upcoming activities.

The teacher also discusses behavioral expectations with the students, perhaps involving them in developing a list of the positive behaviors that each student will demonstrate in class. The teacher then posts the behavioral expectations in highly visible places to serve as a reminder to the students.

Learning Environment

Successful educators use a variety of strategies to create positive learning environments. Clear classroom guidelines or rules, specific teacher praise, and ignoring minor student

---

Research-Based Practices | **The Role of Auditory Processing and the Development of Language and Problem Behaviors**

Researchers are investigating relationships between atypical auditory processing, such as difficulty in remembering what the teacher had said first, and the development of language (Benasich & Fitch, 2012), whereas others are investigating the role auditory processing plays in behavior problems and low achievement. For example, researchers Kathy Rowe, Ken Rowe, and Jan Pollard observed that children with learning disabilities and attention difficulties frequently exhibited problems with auditory processing. The children had trouble following directions as well as difficulties in reaching developmental and literacy milestones.

The researchers found that many of the students responded to simple interventions that changed the way verbal information was presented. This made a significant difference in reducing special education referrals, in addition to strengthening literacy skills. The interventions implemented by the teachers included the following:

1. Attracting the child's attention.
2. Speaking slowly, using short sentences, maintaining eye contact, and providing visual cues (waiting for students to comply with instructions).
3. Pausing between sentences and repeating when necessary.
4. Using visual cues (such as a blank look or a shrug of the shoulders), and repeating instructions as needed.
5. Creating hearing, listening, and compliance routines for students (Rowe, Rowe, & Pollard, 2004).

provocations assist in promoting positive behaviors while decreasing problem behaviors (Gable, Hester, Rock, & Hughes, 2009). Effective teachers carefully plan interesting learning activities within the student's academic instructional level. Classroom interruptions are kept to a minimum.

Social Environment

Classroom teachers employ strategies that affect students' behavior and help them build skills in working with others. These strategies allow students to build relationships with their peers by creating an environment that promotes skills in communication, conflict resolution, and respect for others. During a visit to the classroom, the observer may note teachers using one or more of these strategies. Classroom strategies that are effective in promoting social relations among students with and without disabilities include the following:

1. Teachers actively facilitate social interactions. Teachers plan and work to facilitate social exchanges between students. They place students in cooperative groupings and encourage collaborative problem solving. Teachers create opportunities for peer tutoring and assign students to various classroom roles of assisting and helping others. Teachers structure the classroom schedule so that students have opportunities to develop social relationships.
2. Teachers involve students in the responsibility for social inclusion of all students.
3. Teachers build a feeling of community in the classroom. Teachers work to create a climate of concern for others among students.
4. Teachers model acceptance.

Classroom Problem Behaviors Within an Intervention Context

Assessing behavior problems in the classroom occurs within the context of interventions. When a behavior problem first occurs, the classroom teacher often begins by considering questions about the classroom such as: What strategies are most effective for creating a supportive learning environment? What classroom management strategies are in place? The teacher customarily confers with the IEP team, behavioral specialist, or special education consultant to develop and implement management strategies to address problem behaviors that progress in intensity. This process can involve implementing one or more different strategies over a period of weeks. Educators refer to this process as response to **intervention** (RTI), which you may remember from Chapter 2. Figure 9.1 illustrates a behavior management observation form that a special education teacher developed when conferring with classroom teachers.

Ecological Assessment

Ecological assessment is an assessment approach that allows teachers to gather information about a student through observations and other assessment approaches in more than one setting. Assessment involves examining classroom management strategies and other aspects of the learning environment, as well as observing strategies that teachers use to help students build skills in working with others and becoming productive members of the classroom. Assessment also involves observing the student, such as you learned about in Chapter 8. Observations allow the teacher to examine the problem behavior to determine the function that it serves for the student. By analyzing and interpreting this information, teachers and other team members are able to develop one or more hypotheses regarding student performance and behavior. This information will form the basis for developing recommendations for intervention.

◀ **POINT STREET SCHOOL** ▶
Behavior Management

Student's Name _____ Date _____ Time _____
Observer _____
Teacher _____
Location _____

Characteristic

1. **Classroom Guidelines**
   Are behavior guidelines posted in the classroom?
   Are guidelines written in positive terms describing the behavior expected of students?
   ✔ Suggestions for improvement:

2. **Student Understanding**
   Does the student understand the classroom guidelines for behavior?
   ✔ Suggestions for improvement:

3. **Teacher Reinforcement**
   How does the teacher react when the student behaves appropriately?

   Does the teacher use:
   _____ social reinforcers
   _____ activity reinforcers
   _____ tangible reinforcers
   _____ edible reinforcers
   ✔ Suggestions for improvement:

4. **Teacher Interventions**
   How does the teacher react when the student behaves inappropriately?

   Does the teacher:

   _____ ignore some behaviors
   Explain:

   _____ use directives
   Explain:

   _____ use contingency contracts
   Explain:

   _____ teach pro-social skills
   Explain:

   ✔ Suggestions for improvement:

FIGURE 9.1 • Point Street School Classroom Observation Form

5. **Classroom Consequences**
   What consequences does the teacher use when the student behaves inappropriately?

   ✔ Suggestions for improvement:

6. **Classroom Consistency**
   Is the teacher consistent in managing the student's behavior?
   Is the management of the student's behavior consistent with that of all students in the classroom?

   ✔ Suggestions for improvement:

FIGURE 9.1 • *(Continued)*

SNAPSHOT

Classroom Behaviors Within an Intervention Context

Let's visit Joe Wing's classroom where we will learn more about some of the classroom management difficulties that a first-year teacher is experiencing. His class consists of 23 students; three students have been identified as having disabilities. He is concerned about one of these students, Mark D., and how to help him. Joe worries if he is meeting Mark's needs and decides to ask the special education consultant, Russ Sanford, for help.

Joe describes his concerns: "During class time, Mark never seems to pay attention. When I call on him, he is usually on the wrong page of our book. He rarely knows the answer to my questions. I don't think he has ever participated in class discussions, and he is very disruptive when others are talking. Here are some observations and notes that I have kept."

Russ Sanford listened carefully as Joe talked about his student. Together they examined the observation data and notes that the teacher had kept over the past month. This information led Russ to wonder if the teacher may be having difficulty with managing student behaviors. Russ thought about how he could lead the conversation away from focusing on the student to a more general discussion of classroom management strategies. When there was a pause in the conversation, he asked, "When Mark or some other student disrupts class, what strategies have you found that work well in dealing with this behavior?" The two teachers spent some time talking about strategies and Joe's apparent frustrations. As the discussion proceeded, Joe expressed an interest in reviewing his classroom management plan and translating his expectations into procedures and rules. Together the educators made some changes based on the following principles for behavior management:

1. Establish clear guidelines for the expected classroom behavior for students. Ideally, these guidelines are clearly visible in the classroom as a reminder to students.
2. State rules, or guidelines, in terms of what the student should do so that the behavioral expectations are clear. ("We listen when another student is talking.")
3. Provide positive reinforcement to students engaged in appropriate classroom behavior.
4. Use directive statements to tell students how to act correctly and responsibly. ("Holly, if you don't want Mark to push the back of your chair, you need to use words to tell him to stop.")
5. Teach prosocial skills such as:
   a. How to ask for help
   b. How to join a group of students engaged in an activity
   c. How to join a group discussion
   d. How to make friends
6. Provide consequences for students who disregard behavior guidelines.
7. Be consistent with all students in their management of classroom behavior.

Pause and consider:

- After reading about Joe Wing's classroom, how would you describe his behavior management in the classroom and the effect on student behavior?
- Examine Figure 9.1, the Point Street School Classroom Observation Form. What items would yield helpful information to Joe? What other items would you suggest adding?

Assessment Questions, Purposes, and Approaches

If the student's problem behavior continues, even after implementing the various tiers of response to intervention, the teacher notifies the student's parents and completes a referral to the individualized education program (IEP) team. For serious and recurring behavior problems, the IEP team usually recommends a **functional behavioral assessment (FBA)**.

Functional Behavioral Assessment

When a student's behavior continues to interfere significantly with participation, performance, or achievement, teachers, school psychologists, counselors, and other team members need to gather additional information to better understand the function of these behaviors. This assessment, referred to as an FBA, is a systematic process of gathering information that identifies the causes of and interventions for addressing problem behaviors.

To comply with IDEA requirements, teachers need to know how to conduct FBAs. If a student with behavior problems receives disciplinary action—for example, for carrying a weapon to school or possessing illegal drugs—IDEA requires the IEP team to meet within 10 days to begin an FBA plan. If a behavior plan is already in place, the team must review the plan and revise it, if necessary, to address the behavior.

Typically, an FBA examines the physical environment, the learning environment, and the social environment in which the student's problem behaviors occur. The assessment includes both indirect and direct assessment approaches, such as a review of the student's records, interviews with the teachers (and other significant adults), a student interview, and direct observations of the student on several different occasions. These multiple approaches allow teachers and other professionals to gather information from a variety of perspectives concerning the problem behaviors.

Problem behaviors usually serve a function for the student, such as gaining attention from adults or peers. The function is usually appropriate (most of us like attention), but the behavior itself is not appropriate (such as acting out in class). An FBA involves identifying (1) the behavior and the function that it serves; (2) specific triggers, or **antecedents**, such as events or actions that preceded the behavior (for example, a teacher-directed lesson); (3) the events or actions that occur after the behavior, or consequences (such as other students laughing), that help maintain the behavior; and (4) developing an intervention plan.

Conducting an FBA

Team members work together by following a sequence of steps for conducting an FBA (Figure 9.2). In the following sections, we describe these individual steps.

1. *Verify the Seriousness of the Problem Behavior.* Because an FBA is time consuming, the IEP team begins by verifying the seriousness of the problem. Team members usually begin by discussing whether the student's behavior significantly differs from that of other classmates and what management strategies have been tried in the past. They discuss how the behavior is affecting the student's learning as well as the learning of classmates. Let's sit in on Trish's team meeting, where the teacher is discussing her frustration with Trish.

    > I just don't know what to do anymore. Trish is so wise with me and the assistant teacher. She talks back to me and makes wisecracks. Sometimes her language is really inappropriate. She often refuses to work and puts her head down. Yesterday she turned over her chair, screamed at another student, and stomped out of class. I had to call the assistant principal to go after her, after she ran down the hall. I am really afraid her behavior is escalating, and someone is going to get hurt.

> 1. Verify the seriousness of the problem behavior.
> 2. Define the problem behavior in observable terms.
> 3. Collect assessment information using multiple approaches, including review of student's records; teacher, parent, and student interviews; and direct observations.
> 4. Analyze assessment information and examine possible functions of the problem behavior.
> 5. Establish a hypothesis to determine possible functions of the behavior.
> 6. Develop and implement behavior intervention plan.
> 7. Monitor and evaluate the behavior intervention plan.

FIGURE 9.2 • Steps in Performing a Functional Behavioral Assessment

2. *Define the Problem Behavior in Observable Terms.* Defining the problem behavior allows teachers and other members to pinpoint the concerns and to plan assessment approaches. Team members develop a definition of the problem behavior in terms that are observable. Describing the behavior in this way helps to ensure accurate, reliable observations. For example, Trish's team has concerns about the student's "aggressive" behavior; the team needs to agree on how they will know if a student is aggressive. By developing a definition of *aggression* that is observable, such as "physically hitting or verbally abusing another person," observers will be able to see and record the behavior whenever it occurs. Many times a teacher refers a student because of vague concerns. In these cases, the teacher or other team member needs to observe the student's behavior across several different settings to help in defining the behavior. These initial observations often involve watching and recording two or three students at the same time, including typical peers as well as the student who has been referred to the IEP team. Conducting observations on several students simultaneously allows the observer to determine how different the behavior of the student in question is from the behavior of others. Sometimes initial observations indicate that several students have similar problems, and the greater difficulty is one of classroom management, rather than individual student behavior.

When the referred student is a newcomer to this country, team members need to take into account possible differences in behavioral expectations that are an integral part of family expectations, prior school experiences, or cultural beliefs. In these instances, parents can be a valuable source of information to assist team members in their understandings of these expectations and beliefs. Team members may identify a school or community member who is knowledgeable about the student's background to serve on the IEP team as an additional resource person. In large school districts, a pool of language interpreters and cultural brokers assist IEP teams. A **cultural broker** is an individual within the community, typically identified by community members because of the individual's knowledge, skills, and wisdom concerning ethnic, racial, or cultural matters. In the schools, a cultural broker may act as a family or student advocate.

3. *Collect Assessment Information Using Multiple Approaches.*
    a. *Reviewing the Student's Records.* The student's cumulative records provide a starting place to gather information about medical history, school attendance, achievement, assessments, IEPs and behavior management plans, and past disciplinary actions. By reviewing the student's records, a team gleans additional information about medications, patterns of truancy, prolonged difficulties with achievement, positive behavioral intervention, strategies, and supports described in previous behavior management plans or trends in disciplinary referrals. One or more of these areas can contribute to the current behavior problem.

b. *Interviewing.* Structured interviews not only provide information about the student from others who know the student but also provide information from the student's perspective. Sometimes the IEP team selects a commercial interview tool, or they may decide to construct a structured interview with questions that they have identified. A team member experienced in interviewing techniques, such as the school social worker or school psychologist, usually conducts the structured interviews.

   i. *Teachers.* Teachers and teacher assistants can provide information about how the target student interacts socially with other students and adults in the classroom. They can address questions about the settings and conditions where they have observed the behaviors. They can describe possible events that may trigger behaviors and the interactions that typically take place following the behavior.

   ii. *Parents.* Parents provide yet another perspective. Parents can share their own family's expectations regarding their child's behavior and school performance. They can provide information about their child's behavior difficulties in the past and the types of interventions that were attempted and were successful. They can describe complications or changes in the family structure that the student experiences at home, including parents' unemployment, death of a family member, birth of siblings, and divorce, all of which create additional stressors on family members. The structured interview might include the following questions:

   - Have there been any changes at home or new events in your student's life recently?
   - Does your child experience any problems that you are aware of?
   - Do you think your child is interested in school this year? Why or why not?
   - Do you think that the academic work is too easy or too hard? Could you explain?

   iii. *The Student.* The student can provide valuable information in identifying the motivational factors supporting inappropriate behavior. Figure 9.3 depicts the interview with Trish.

   After reading the transcript of the interview, what information did you find relevant to the problem behavior?

   The information gathered from reviewing student records and interviewing can be helpful in preparing to conduct direct observations of the student. Through the interviews, the teacher may be able to identify and define the target behaviors, identify and define potential antecedents and consequences that may be observed, and gain an understanding of the student's strengths (Cooper, Heron, & Heward, 2007).

   Although functional interviews often yield valuable information, team members are aware, too, that the information may be influenced by individual perspectives. The teacher may have preconceived ideas about the student and the reasons for the problem behaviors. Although these ideas are recorded as part of the teacher interview, they may not be representative of the actual situation. Or the parent may deny that a problem exists by not responding in full to the interview questions. Or the student may misrepresent thoughts and feelings during the structured interview because of embarrassment or shame.

c. *Conducting Observations.* You learned earlier about the various methods of recording observation data. These same methods—event recording, duration recording, intensity recording, latency recording, interval recording, and category recording—are useful when conducting direct observations as part of an FBA. Recall that each method has particular strengths, depending on the assessment question. For example, event recording is useful when our question involves "how often" or "how frequently" (see Figure 9.4). In conducting observations, team members gather information not only about occasions when the student displays problem behaviors but also occasions

School Social Worker: Is there anything that is happening at home that is bothering you?

Student: No.

School Social Worker: Is there something new at school that is bothering you?

Student: Not really . . . Well, we're getting a lot of homework this year.

School Social Worker: Does it bother you?

Student: No, I mean, well . . . it takes a lot of time and I have a part-time job now.

School Social Worker: Let's talk a little about what happened in class today. What was the teacher doing right before you made the comments that made the other students laugh?

Student: I don't know, I think he was giving some directions.

School Social Worker: Do you remember what he was asking everyone to do?

Student: Well, when he talks so much it's very hard to follow everything. Like he tells us five things and I'm still back on the first.

School Social Worker: Do you remember what you were thinking right before you made the comments?

Student: I was just so mad and frustrated!

School Social Worker: When you make noises and comments in class, what usually happens afterward?

Student: Everyone laughs and gives me high fives.

School Social Worker: How does that make you feel?

Student: Pretty cool, I guess. . . .

FIGURE 9.3 • Functional Interview With a Student

Event recording helps answer questions such as the following:
- How many times does (student) . . . ?
- How frequently does (student) . . . ?
- How often does (student) . . . ?
- At what rate does (student) . . . ?

Duration recording helps answer questions such as this:
- How long does (student) . . . ?

Intensity recording helps answer questions such as the following:
- To what degree does (student) . . . ?
- To what level does (student) . . . ?

Latency recording helps answer questions such as this:
- Given a request, how long does it take (student) to begin . . . ?

Interval recording helps answer questions such as these:
- What amount of time does (student) . . . ?
- What percent of time does (student) . . . ?

FIGURE 9.4 • How to Select an Appropriate Observation Recording Method

	Time Intervals									
Behaviors	1 min	2 min	3 min	4 min	5 min	6 min	7 min	8 min	9 min	10 min
Recess										
-Sept 8	0	0	×	×	+	+	+	+	+	+
-Sept 10	+	+	+	+	×	×	×	+	+	+
-Sept 11	0	0	0	0	×	0	0	0	×	×
-Sept 12	0	0	0	0	0	+	+	+	+	+
Total on-task behaviors	1	1	1	1	1	2	2	3	4	3

Key:
Observations conducted during recess on Sept 8, 10, 11, and 12
+ = on-task, appropriate behaviors
0 = verbally aggressive behaviors
× = physically aggressive behaviors

FIGURE 9.5 • Sample Scatter Plot

when the student maintains appropriate behavior. Because one observation represents only a snapshot of the student, the team collects multiple observations to produce more accurate and reliable information. Observations may also include one or more comparison students.

Observers may use specific forms, such as a scatter plot, to record observation data. A scatter plot is a type of interval recording form that the observer uses to record single behaviors or a series of behaviors during the observation period. Scatter plots are useful for initial and follow-up observations to identify patterns of behavior that relate to specific contextual conditions (Center for Effective Collaboration and Practice, 2001a). Figure 9.5 is a scatter plot conducted on Trish during several recess periods over a span of four days. The observer collected information about her on-task and appropriate behaviors and off-task, inappropriate behaviors on the playground. Based on this data of Trish's recess behaviors, can you identify a pattern of behaviors?

An antecedent-behavior-consequence (ABC) recording form provides a way to record the problem behavior within a contextual condition. These forms are used when an observer wants to organize descriptive information so that classroom conditions that trigger and maintain behavior can be identified. Three columns on the form allow the observer to record the antecedent events, the behavior, and the consequences that followed the behavior. ABC recording sheets can come in various formats and can record various aspects of the behavior, such as the frequency, duration, intensity, or latency of the behavior. Figure 9.6 illustrates an example of an ABC recording form.

After studying the information recorded in the ABC observation of Trish, what data did you find relevant to the problem behavior identified by the team?

d. *Rubrics*. In later chapters, we will examine rubrics as types of assessment scales used to measure performance. Rubrics are useful tools in FBA, too, when the assessment question concerns the degree of intensity or severity of a behavior, such as disruptive outbursts. To identify the severity of a behavior, the team develops descriptions of the different levels of intensity, assigning a numeric score or categorical label to each

Student: Trish Observer: Carraway

Grade: 8 Teacher: Hershorn Class: Math

Behavior observed: _____ *Aggression* defined as physically touching (or attempting to touch) a person in a harmful way or verbally abusing another person

Interval Time (5-minute intervals)	Classroom Activity	Antecedent	Behavior	Consequence	Comments
0:00–0:05	Transition	Buzzer rings signaling the transition to period 2	Trish slowly wanders into class with other students	Students are talking No one talks to Trish	Trish looks like she has been crying
0:05–0:10	Teacher greets students and discusses homework	Trish looks at teacher briefly	Looks through backpack	Teacher, "Trish, I need your eyes up here" "I'm finding my #$@$ work"	
0:10–0:15	Review of homework	Teacher reminds Trish to use language for the classroom	Slams her backpack on the floor	Teacher, "I don't want to see that again" Some students smirk	Trish makes a face behind her hand and then puts head down on desk
0:15–0:20		Asks students to take a 5-minute stretch break	Trish scrapes her chair back and stands with other students, stretching	Teacher ignores	
0:20–0:25	Lesson review: fractions	Teacher distributes materials and paper to each student; reviews how to use materials	Trish takes her materials out of the box		The other students take materials out and begin arranging them
0:25–0:30	Direct instruction	Representing fractions	Trish and others make fractions using shapes	Teacher moves around room, commenting on student work "Trish, good job"	
0:30–0:35	Direct instruction	Representing factions	Trish leans over to neighbor and whispers	Student replies "I'm not sharing with you" Teacher ignores	Trish mumbles under her breath
0:35–0:40		Student to Trish, "You're minding your own business"	Trish screams and kicks student's chair	Teacher moves closer Trish stops kicking	
0:40–0:45	Practice	Students work independently with materials, teacher moves around classroom	Trish has head down on desk	Teacher ignores	Does Trish understand what to do, as the lesson progresses to independent practice?
0:45–0:50	Collects materials Homework assignment	Teacher shows students Web-based assignment	Trish sits up and glances at teacher several times	Ignores	Is her behavior indicating an interest here?
0:50–0:55	End of period	Teacher dismisses students	Trish makes loud sounds as she gets up	Teacher ignores; several students laugh	
0:55–1:00	End of period	Teacher talking and laughing with several students	Continues loud sounds	Teacher ignores	

FIGURE 9.6 • Sample ABC Recording Form

Rating Scale	Intensity of Behavior
1	Slow to comply but responds to verbal prompts from authority figure
2	Initial refusal but complies from authority figure (may require with physical assist)
3	Defiance of teacher or other authority figures; may leave classroom and building
4	Complete refusal to comply; disrupts other students by shouting or name calling
5	Disrupts other students by throwing objects or running around the classroom with intent to hit others.
6	Displays weapon with intent to hurt others

FIGURE 9.7 • Rubric for Measuring the Severity of Disruptive Behavior

level. Figure 9.7 illustrates a rubric that measures the severity of disruptive behavior. When the team uses detailed descriptions and examples for each of the different levels, they increase the reliability of the rubric.

4. *Analyze Assessment Information and Examine Possible Functions of the Problem Behavior.*

Analyzing data involves studying and synthesizing the results of all the information collected, while looking for patterns of behavior. The team considers key questions such as:

- What student behaviors occurred under different antecedent conditions?
- Did the behavior in question occur under one or more than one antecedent condition?
- What consequences occurred after the behavior in question?

As the team examines the collected information, they look for recurring instances of the problem behaviors. They work to synthesize information across the multiple assessment approaches by asking:

- How does the information from the interviews corroborate or confirm the ABC observations?
- Based on the review of student records, what other factors may be contributing to the behavior?

To help in synthesizing all the information, they use a process called triangulation. **Triangulation** is the process of drawing conclusion(s) based on an analysis of multiple sources of data. A data triangulation chart (see Figure 9.8) allows team members to record the multiple sources of data that they have collected and to visually compare the information. Using the data triangulation chart, team members can develop deeper understandings of the behavior and the function that it serves.

5. *Establish a Hypothesis to Determine Possible Functions of the Behavior.* After analyzing the data, team members develop one or more possible explanations for the student's behavior. Let's return to the IEP team that is working with Trish. Using information from the direct observations, including the scatter plots of her playground behavior, discipline records, and interviews, the team developed the following hypothesis:

> Trish knows how to respond appropriately, based on the four playground observations. In fact, much of the time she engages in appropriate behavior. She is more verbally aggressive than physically aggressive. When she calls other children names, pushes and shoves others, grabs the ball, and hits other children, she usually gets her way. In addition, she

> Point Street School Data Triangulation Chart
>
> Student: __Trish__   Date: __9-26–10/18__
>
> | Source 1 | Source 2 | Source 3 |
> |---|---|---|
> | ABC Observation | Interview Student | Scatter Plot |
> | Trish yells and screams at the teacher when teacher requests her to do something. She uses inappropriate language and gestures. She screams and kicks chairs of other students when they don't comply with her requests. During instructional time, Trish often keeps her head on the desk. She produces little academic work during class time. | Trish talks about her part-time (volunteer) job and "a lot" of homework. She reports that her teacher "talks a lot" and that it is difficult for her to follow what the teacher says. She says that she gets mad and frustrated in class. | Trish engages in both appropriate and inappropriate peer interaction on the playground. She experiences the most difficulty in participating in organized games. |
>
> *Interpretation:*
> 1. Precipitation events: *Classroom teacher requests and organizes games on the playground.*
> 2. Maintaining consequences: *Trish often gets a reaction from other students. When teacher addresses the behaviors, they tend to escalate. Teacher often ignores her positive and problem behaviors.*
> 3. Function: *Trish's behavior often allows her to get her way with others or to avoid classroom work.*

FIGURE 9.8 • Point Street Triangulation Chart

receives individual attention from her teachers and the playground supervisors when she engages in inappropriate behavior. In Trish's case, the team feels that Trish's behavior serves as an attempt to join her classmates and also to receive attention from adults.

6. *Develop and Implement the Behavior Intervention Plan.* After completing the FBA, team members develop the student's behavior intervention plan, which may be referred to as a positive behavior support plan. Educators and other team members teach students social, communication, and other skills to replace problem behaviors. Let's return once more to Trish's team.

> As part of her behavior intervention plan, the special education teacher will help Trish learn more appropriate replacement behaviors. Replacement behaviors are appropriate behavior substitutes for the undesirable behavior. The teacher will provide instruction in social skills training, helping Trish to learn different strategies for joining a group of peers. In addition, the team will ask the playground supervisors and her teachers to begin a conscious effort to recognize Trish for appropriate behavior.

Her behavior intervention plan also must address her problem behaviors in the classroom.

Examine the sources of data (teacher report, student interview, and one of the ABC observations), and share your ideas.

7. *Monitor and Evaluate the Behavior Intervention Plan.* A student's behavior intervention plan needs reviewing on a regular basis, at least annually. Problem behaviors can appear and quickly escalate if left unattended. When problem behaviors resurface, team members recognize that the original plan may not be working and reconvene to discuss the student's current needs.

Standardized Instruments for Assessing Problem Behaviors

Standardized instruments for assessing problem behaviors usually are in the form of rating scales or checklists designed to be completed by school psychologists, teachers, parents, or the students themselves. Instruments that assess problem behaviors focus on one or more specific areas. The choice of an instrument depends on the presenting questions and concerns. The following subsections describe several of these instruments in more detail.

Behavior Assessment System for Children, Second Edition

The *Behavior Assessment System for Children, Second Edition* (BASC 2; Reynolds & Kamphaus, 2005) is a set of rating scales and forms to understand behaviors and emotions of children and adolescents, 2 years through 21 years 11 months. The materials allow for multiple collections of data from the perspectives of the individual, home, and school and include Teacher Rating Scales (TRS), Parent Rating Scales (PRS), Self-Report of Personality (SRP), Student Observation System (SOS), and Structured Developmental History (SDH). Parent and student forms are also available in Spanish. The rating scales describe positive and negative behaviors. The teacher or parent indicates how often the student displays each of these behaviors by answering Never, Sometimes, Often, or Almost always. The phrases are grouped into different scales, with each scale relating to a specific area of behavior:

activities of daily living	functional communication
adaptability	hyperactivity
aggression	leadership
anxiety	learning problems
attention problems	social skills
atypicality	somatization
conduct problems	study skills
depression	withdrawal

ADMINISTRATION Administration takes approximately 10 to 20 minutes (teacher and parent forms) and 30 minutes for the SRP. For students and parents who have difficulty reading, the items are available on CD.

STANDARDIZATION Norms are based on the 2000 U.S. Census.

SCORING This instrument reports assessment results in *T*-scores (mean equals 50, standard deviation equals 10) and percentiles for both the general population

---

> **TESTS-at-a-GLANCE**
>
> **Behavior Assessment System for Children, Second Edition (BASC 2)**
>
> http://www.pearsonclinical.com/psychology/products/100000658/behavior-assessment-system-for-children-second-edition-basc-2.html?Pid=PAa30000
>
> - **Publication Date:** 2005
> - **Purpose:** Provides multiple forms to gather information about behavior and emotions of children and adolescents.
> - **Age/Grade Levels:** 2 years through 21 years 11 months.
> - **Time to Administer:** 20 to 30 minutes.
> - **Technical Adequacy:** The standardization sample will need to be updated to reflect changes in student demographics.
> - **Suggested Use:** The *BASC 2* provides information from various perspectives (student, teacher, parent) on a range of behaviors typically seen in the classroom. Rating scales are available in both English and Spanish and on an audio CD.

and clinical population. Scoring may be completed by hand or with the BASC 2 ASSIST™ Plus software, which is purchased separately. The *BASC 2* also offers software for conducting observations.

RELIABILITY AND VALIDITY   Both reliability and validity are adequate.

SUMMARY   The *BASC 2* is a comprehensive assessment system designed for use with children and youth from 2 years through 21 years 11 months. The system consists of various rating scales and other forms that are completed by the examiner, parent, teacher, and student. These multiple sources of information provide a variety of perspectives on behaviors and emotions. The standardization sample was based on the 2000 U.S. Census data and will need to be updated to reflect changes in student demographics in schools today.

Burks' Behavior Rating Scales, Second Edition (BBRS 2)

The *Burks' Behavior Rating Scales, Second Edition* (*BBRS 2*; Burks & Gruber, 2006) identifies the nature and severity of behaviors in children from prekindergarten through grade 12 (ages 4 through 18 years). The *BBRS 2* is available in both a teacher and parent form.

ADMINISTRATION   The parent and teacher complete the *BBRS 2* by indicating on a 5-point scale how often the behavior is seen in the child. Each form contains 100 items that describe behaviors considered atypical. According to the examiner's manual, time to complete the scale is 10 to 15 minutes.

STANDARDIZATION   The *BBRS 2* was normed on a sample of 2,864 individuals, representative of the U.S. population according to region, gender, ethnicity, and parent education level. Separate samplings of teachers and parents included 1,481 teachers and 1,383 parents.

SCORING   Both teacher and parent forms have the same test questions but each form has distinct test norms. The *BBRS 2* produces seven scale scores:

- Disruptive behavior
- Attention and impulse control problems
- Emotional problems
- Social withdrawal
- Ability deficits
- Physical deficits
- Weak self-confidence

RELIABILITY AND VALIDITY   The author conducted a study on a clinical sample that included 860 individuals. This study demonstrated internal consistency, retest reliability, and content validity. The revised edition (*BBRS 2*) includes two new scales to test response validity: the *I*-scale for inconsistent responding and the *F*-scale for possible overstatement of problem behavior.

SUMMARY   The *Burks' Behavior Rating Scales, Second Edition*, provides a quick way to evaluate problem behaviors in children from 4 through 18 years of age. The second edition includes several positive additions, including a reduction in the number of test items and a reduction in

> **TESTS-at-a-GLANCE**
>
> **Burks' Behavior Rating Scale, Second Edition (BBRS 2)**
> http://www.wpspublish.com/store/Search?Q=Burks%20Behavior%20Rating%20Scales%E2%84%A2%2C%20Second%20Edition%20(BBRS%E2%84%A2-2)
>
> - **Publication Date:** 2006
> - **Purpose:** Provides a quick way to assess problem behavior in children and youth.
> - **Age/Grade Levels:** 4 years through 18 years.
> - **Time to Administer:** 10 to 15 minutes.
> - **Technical Adequacy:** Reliability and validity studies are adequate.
> - **Suggested Use:** Uses multiple perspectives (parent and teacher) to evaluate problem behaviors in children and youth.

the number of scales used to categorize behaviors, as well as two new scales to increase response validity.

Child Behavior Checklist System (CBCL)

The *Child Behavior Checklist System* (*CBCL System*; Achenbach & Rescorla, 2000, 2001; McConaughy & Achenbach, 2001b) consists of various behavior checklists and report forms for gathering information about children and youth from 1 year 6 months to 18 years and about young adults from 18 years through 30 years. The *CBCL System* conceptualizes emotional or behavioral problems as external and internal behavioral clusters. The *System* includes several *Diagnostic and Statistical Manual* (*DSM*; 2000) oriented scales that are consistent with *DSM* diagnostic categories. Although the *CBCL* is entitled a "checklist," the instruments are really rating scales because they require the observer to rate items on a numerical scale. These forms have been translated into over 60 languages and are available from the publisher. Published reports describe the use of the *Child Behavior Checklist System* from 50 cultures. The *CBCL* consists of three age levels, each with its own technical manual and scoring system:

Ages $1^{1}/_{2}$ through 5

1. *Child Behavior Checklist for Ages $1^{1}/_{2}$–5* (*CBCL/$1^{1}/_{2}$–5*; Achenbach & Rescorla, 2001). This checklist consists of 99 items and is designed for the parent or other caregiver to complete. The *CBCL/$1^{1}/_{2}$–5* includes the Language Development Survey (LDS) for identifying language delays. Similar to the checklist for older children, scores on this instrument can convert to percentile ranks and *T*-scores. A Spanish version is available.
2. *Caregiver–Teacher Report Form/$1^{1}/_{2}$–5* (*C–TRF*; Achenbach, 2000). This form obtains ratings by child care providers and early childhood teachers on 99 items and descriptions of problems or concerns. Similar in layout to the *Child Behavior Checklist for Ages $1^{1}/_{2}$–5*, the forms allow the examiner to compare responses.

Ages 6 through 18

3. *Child Behavior Checklist for Ages 6–18* (*CBCL/6–18*; Achenbach, 2001a). This scale is designed for the parent to complete and consists of two sections: competence items and problem items. A student's score converts to percentile ranks and *T*-scores. This checklist has adequate technical characteristics. A Spanish version is available.
4. *Teacher's Report Form for Ages 6–18* (*TRF*; Achenbach, 2001b). This scale is similar to the *CBCL/6–18* and is designed for completion by the teacher. The *Teacher's Report Form* consists of three main areas: academic performance, adaptive functioning, and behavioral/emotional problems. Percentiles and *T*-scores can be calculated.
5. *Youth Self-Report for Ages 11–18* (Achenbach, 2001c). This rating scale is for youth ages 11 through 18 years of age. Students must have at least fifth-grade reading ability, or the teacher can administer the items orally. Test items are similar to those in the *CBCL/6–18*. Scores can convert to percentile ranks and *T*-scores. A Spanish version is available.

TESTS-at-a-GLANCE

Child Behavior Checklist System (CBCL)

Young children http://www.aseba.org/preschool.html

School age http://www.aseba.org/schoolage.html

- **Publication Date:** 2000, 2001
- **Purposes:** Assesses behavior in terms of internal and external behavior clusters. School-related areas include academic functioning, adaptive characteristics, and behavioral/emotional problems.
- **Age/Grade Levels:** Consists of two different rating scales, one designed for children ages 1 year 6 months through 5 years, and the second designed for students ages 6 years through 18 years. For adults ages 18 through 59 years, there is an Adult Behavior Checklist.
- **Time to Administer:** 10 to 45 minutes, depending on the amount of information to be recorded.
- **Technical Adequacy:** Reliability and validity studies adequate.
- **Suggested Use:** Measures behaviors from multiple perspectives, including the student, parent, and teacher. Rating scales are available in Spanish. Many of the forms have been translated into other languages and are available from the publisher.

6. *Direct Observation Form for Ages 6–11* (Achenbach, 2009). This assessment consists of writing a narrative description of the student's behavior during a 10-minute classroom or recess observation. The observer also rates on-task behavior at ten 1-minute intervals. At the end of the 10-minute observation, the observer then rates various problem behaviors.
7. *Semistructured Clinical Interview for Children and Adolescents* (*SCICA*; McConaughy & Achenbach, 2001a). The *SCICA* uses a protocol of questions and probes for interviewing students ages 8 through 18 years. The examiner also completes an observation of the student, and the student completes a self-report form. Administration time is 60 to 90 minutes; this instrument should be completed by an experienced interviewer.

Ages 18 through 59

8. *Adult Behavior Checklist for Ages 18–59* (*ABCL/18–59*; Achenbach, 2003a). The *ABCL/18–59* is an upward extension of the *Child Behavior Checklist for Ages 6–18*. Parents, partner or spouse, and others who know the adult well complete this form, which has 126 items that describe specific behavioral and emotional problems.
9. *Adult Self-Report Form for Ages 18–59* (*ASR/18–59*; Achenbach, 2003b). The *ASR/18–59* is an upward extension of the *Youth Self-Report*. In addition, there are three other areas concerning adaptive functioning as youth move to adulthood: education, job, and spouse (or partner). These sections are answered only by individuals who have attended secondary or postsecondary institutions, have been employed, or who have lived with a spouse or partner within the past 6 months. An additional section provides open-ended questions regarding physical problems, disabilities, concerns, and strengths.

ADMINISTRATION The various forms take 10 to 45 minutes to complete, depending on the amount of information to be recorded.

STANDARDIZATION For the *CBCL/6–18*, the norming sample consisted of 1,753 children, ages 6 through 18 years. The sample was stratified by age, gender, geographic region, urban/suburban/rural, socioeconomic status, and ethnicity. For the *CBCL/1½–5*, 700 children participated in the normative sample.

SCORING Scoring may be completed by hand or by the Assessment Data Manager (ADM) software, which can be purchased separately.

RELIABILITY For the *CBCL/6–18*, adequate reliability coefficients are reported for interrater, test-retest, and internal consistency. For the *CBCL/1½–5*, small studies were completed that suggest moderate to adequate reliability. Additional studies are needed.

VALIDITY The manual provides evidence of construct validity for the *CBCL/6–18*. Reported criterion-related validity between the *CBCL* and the *Conners' Rating Scales* and the *Revised Behavior Problem Checklist* is .82 and .81, respectively. Evidence of content validity, criterion-related validity, and construct validity is presented for the *CBCL/1½–5*.

SUMMARY The *CBCL* is a comprehensive assessment system designed for use with children and youth from

---

TESTS-at-a-GLANCE

Conners 3™ (Conners 3rd Edition™)

http://www.pearsonassessments.com/HAIWEB/Cultures/en-us/Productdetail.htm?Pid=Conners_3&Mode=summary

- **Publication Date:** 2008
- **Purposes:** Assesses behavior with a focus on ADHD and comorbid disorders.
- **Age/Grade Levels:** Ages 8 through 18 years.
- **Time to Administer:** Short scales take 10 minutes to administer; the long scales take approximately 20 minutes.
- **Technical Adequacy:** Adequate test-retest studies and internal consistency reliability. Interrater reliability is low. Validity is adequate.
- **Suggested Use:** Measuring student behavior from the perspectives of the parents, teachers, and the individual.

1 year 6 months through 30 years of age. The system consists of various instruments that are completed by the examiner, parent, teacher, and student. These multiple sources of information provide a variety of perspectives on the problem behaviors.

Conners 3™ (Conners 3rd Edition™)

The *Conners 3*™ (*Conners 3rd Edition*™; Conners, 2008) is designed to provide a thorough assessment of attention-deficit hyperactivity disorder (ADHD) and other disorders such as oppositional defiant disorder and conduct disorder. Designed to be used with children and youth ages 6 to 18 years, this assessment consists of multiple components in both paper and computerized format. *Conners 3* comes in both full-length and short versions and includes parent (*Conners 3-P*), teacher (*Conners 3-T*), and self-report (*Conners 3-SR*). According to the examiner's manual, the full-length version provides for both initial evaluations and comprehensive reevaluations. The short version provides information for follow-up assessments in the following areas: inattention, hyperactivity/impulsivity, learning problems, aggression, and family relations. In addition to the full-length and short versions of the rating scales, two auxiliary scales may be used. The *Conners 3 ADHD Index* consists of 10 items that differentiate children with ADHD from those without this diagnosis. The ADHD index is used for screening students and to identify those who need further assessment. According to the examiner's manual, this index can be used to monitor the effectiveness of treatment plans and measure the child's response to intervention. The second auxiliary scale is the *Conners 3 Global Index*. This provides a measure of general psychopathology and can be used to monitor treatment and intervention.

ADMINISTRATION The full-length form takes approximately 20 minutes, whereas the short form takes 10 minutes. The ADHD index takes less than 5 minutes.

SCORING This assessment yields a total score and a symptom count score.

STANDARDIZATION The normative sample of 3,400 individuals included 50 boys and 50 girls from each age, with a racial/ethnic distribution that matched the 2000 U.S. Census. According to the examiner's manual, the sample included a spread of youth from various parental education levels and from various geographical regions in the United States and Canada.

RELIABILITY Various types of reliability are reported, including test-retest, interrater, and internal consistency. Both test-retest reliability and internal consistency were adequate. Interrater reliability ranged from .52 to .94. These scores represent a wide range in terms of consistency among scorers.

VALIDITY The test manual reports information regarding factorial validity, construct validity, and predictive validity. The latter type is the most useful because it provides evidence that the *Conners 3* differentiates between students with ADHD and those with a diagnosis.

SUMMARY The *Conners 3* consists of sets of rating scales for parents, teachers, and students to assist in gathering information about problem behaviors. This assessment assesses behavioral and emotional problems with a focus on ADHD. The instrument provides both a full-length form for initial evaluations and comprehensive reevaluations. The short version provides a measure for follow-up for monitoring progress or response to intervention. The *Conners 3* is available in both English and Spanish.

Summary

- Adaptive behaviors are important for functioning successfully from day to day. Limitations in adaptive behaviors, along with significantly below-average intellectual functioning, determine whether a student will be identified as having intellectual disabilities.
- The assessment of adaptive behaviors relates to age, gender, race, communication systems, home language, cultural and ethnic norms, and disability. As individuals develop, cultural expectations change.
- Positive behaviors allow students to be productive members of society. Assessment of problem behaviors involves a team of professionals, along with the parents and the student, who gather and examine information regarding behaviors and the functions that they serve.
- When a student's behavior continues to interfere significantly with participation, performance, or achievement, team members need to gather additional information to better understand the function of these behaviors.
- Together the team develops behavioral intervention plans that involve teaching new skills that students lack or replacement behaviors that are more appropriate, while providing positive behavior supports.

QUESTIONS FOR REFLECTION

1. How would you explain the term *adaptive behavior*? How does this differ from *problem behavior*? Provide examples of each.
2. Obtain a copy of the *Vineland II*, select one of the domains, and review the test items. How would the assessment information be helpful to the team? To a special educator?
3. If you were a member of Jean's IEP team (see page 168), what supports would you suggest for Jean? What additional questions might you ask Jean about her interests?
4. Make arrangements to visit a classroom and observe student behavior. Create an ABC form, and fill in the information that you observe. What classroom behaviors did you witness? What were the consequences that followed each behavior that occurred? Could you identify the antecedent conditions?
5. Examine two or more of the instruments for assessing problem behaviors described in this chapter. Compare the test items. Which of these two instruments would you recommend for Trish (the student we followed in the FBA)? Why?

REFERENCES

Achenbach, T. M. (2000). *Caregiver–teacher report form for ages 1½–5 (C–TRF/1½–5)*. Burlington, VT: ASEBA.

Achenbach, T. M. (2001a). *Child behavior checklist for ages 6–18 (CBC/6–18)*. Burlington, VT: ASEBA.

Achenbach, T. M. (2001b). *Teacher's report form for ages 6–18 (TRF)*. Burlington, VT: ASEBA.

Achenbach, T. M. (2001c). *Youth self-report for ages 11–18 (YSR)*. Burlington, VT: ASEBA.

Achenbach, T. M. (2003a). *Adult behavior checklist for ages 18–59 (ABCL/18-59)*. Burlington, VT: ASEBA.

Achenbach, T. M. (2003b). *Adult self-report for ages 18–59 (ASR/18–59)*. Burlington, VT: ASEBA.

Achenbach, T. M. (2009). *Direct observation form*. Retrieved April 4, 2009, from http://www.aseba.org/products/dof.html

Achenbach, T. M., & Rescorla, L. A. (2000). *Manual for the ASEBA preschool forms and profiles*. Burlington, VT: ASEBA.

Achenbach, T. M., & Rescorla, L. A. (2001). *Manual for the ASEBA school-age forms and profiles*. Burlington, VT: ASEBA.

Alberto, P. A., & Troutman, A. C. (2013). *Applied behavior analysis for teachers* (9th ed.). Boston: Pearson.

American Association on Intellectual and Developmental Disabilities (AAIDD). (2008). *Frequently asked questions on intellectual disability and the AAIDD definition*. Retrieved from http://www.aaidd.org/content_185.cfm

Benasich, A. A., & Fitch, R. (2012). *Developmental dyslexia: Early precursors, neurobehavioral markers, and biological substrates*. Baltimore, MD: Brookes.

Burks, H. F., & Gruber, C. P. (2006). *Burks' behavior rating scale, second edition (BBRS 2)*. Los Angeles, CA: Western Psychological Services.

Center for Effective Collaboration and Practice. (2001a). *A method for conducting a functional behavioral assessment*. Retrieved April 4, 2009, from http://cecp.air.org/fba/problembehavior2/appendixa.htm

Center for Effective Collaboration and Practice. (2001b). *A method for conducting a functional behavioral assessment*. Retrieved April 4, 2009, from http://cecp.air.org/fba/problembehavior2/direct2.htm

Center for Effective Collaboration and Practice. (2001c). *A method for conducting a functional behavioral assessment*. Retrieved April 4, 2009, from http://cecp.air.org/fba/problembehavior2/appendixf.htm

Cooper, J. O., Heron, T. E., & Heward, W. L. (2007). *Applied behavior analysis* (2nd ed.). Upper Saddle River, NJ: Merrill/Prentice Hall.

Conners, C. K. (2008). *Conners 3™ (Conners 3rd Edition™)*. San Antonio, TX: Pearson.

Gable, R. A., Hester, P. H., Rock, M. L., & Hughes, K. G. (2009). Back to basics: Rules, praise, ignoring, and reprimands revisited. *Intervention in School & Clinic, 44*(4), 195–205.

Harrison, P. L., & Oakland, T. (2003). *Adaptive behavior assessment system®, second edition (ABAS®, Second Edition)*. San Antonio, TX: Pearson.

McConaughy, S. H., & Achenbach, T. M. (2001a). *Semistructured clinical interview for children and adolescents (SCICA)*. Burlington, VT: ASEBA.

McConaughy, S. H., & Achenbach, T. M. (2001b). *Manual for the semistructured clinical interview for children and adolescents (SCICA; Second Edition)*. Burlington, VT: ASEBA.

McDonnell, J., Thorson, N., Disher, S., Mathot-Buckner, C., Mendel, J., & Ray, L. (2003). The achievement of students with developmental disabilities and their peers without disabilities in inclusive settings: An exploratory study. *Education and Treatment of Children, 26*(3), 224–236.

Palmer, S., Heyne, L., Montie, J., Abery, B., & University of Minnesota. (2011). Feature issue on supporting the social well-being of children and youth with disabilities. *Impact, 24*(1). Minneapolis: University of Minnesota, Institute on Community Integration.

Reynolds, C. R., & Kamphaus, R. W. (2005). *Behavior assessment system for children, second edition (BASC 2)*. San Antonio, TX: Pearson.

Rowe, K. S., Rowe, K. J., & Pollard, J. (2004). *Literacy, behaviour and auditory processing: Building "fences" at the top of the "cliff" in preference to "ambulance services" at the bottom*. Background paper to invited address presented at the ACER Research Conference, Adelaide, SA, 24–26 October 2004. Retrieved from http://www.acer.edu.au/research/programs/documents/Rowe-ACERResearchConf_2004Paper.pdf

Sparrow, S., Cicchetti, D., & Balla, D. (2005). *Vineland adaptive behavior scales* (2nd ed.). San Antonio, TX: Pearson.

PART IV
Achievement

 **CHAPTER 10** Achievement: Overall Performance

 **CHAPTER 11** Reading

 **CHAPTER 12** Written Language

 **CHAPTER 13** Oral Language

 **CHAPTER 14** Mathematics

 **CHAPTER 15** Performance-Based, Authentic, and Portfolio Assessments

10 Achievement: Overall Performance

Chapter Objectives

After completing this chapter, you should be able to:

- Describe assessment approaches related to the assessment of achievement.
- Explain the integral link among instruction, assessment, self-assessment, and peer assessment.
- Compare approaches to the assessment of achievement, curriculum-based assessment; criterion-referenced assessment; alternative assessments such as performance-based assessment, self-assessment, and peer assessment; and standardized assessments.
- Describe how the assessment of the physical, learning, and social environments influences achievement, including norm-referenced achievement.

Overview

Achievement testing is the assessment of past learning that is usually the result of formal and informal educational experiences. This chapter is concerned with approaches that assess the achievement of students. Several other chapters in this book also address aspects of the assessment of achievement. Chapters 11 and 12 examine the assessment of reading and written language; Chapter 13 addresses oral language. Chapter 14 examines the assessment of mathematics. Chapter 15 discusses performance-based, authentic, and portfolio assessments.

The assessment of achievement occurs regularly throughout students' school careers. Achievement tests are designed for groups of students or for individual students to assess their formal and informal learning experiences.

Responding to Diversity

The assessment of achievement must be sensitive to an individual's culture, ethnicity, race, language, geographic region of origin, gender, disability, and economic status. Assessment approaches, including standardized tests, performance-based assessment, and the other approaches this chapter describes, must be free from bias. Achievement tests can show bias in several ways (Salvia, Ysseldyke, & Bolt, 2010):

- In the format of the test
- If the test directions are too technical or do not translate easily into another language
- If the content of achievement tests differs in importance across cultures
- If the examinee test-taking behaviors vary from one culture to another
- If the examiner's personality characteristics influence the examinee's responses
- If the underlying psychological construct of the test is not universal
- If the individual examinee does not represent the norm group

There may be several flaws when assessing students who have limited English proficiency, so that testing them with standardized instruments is improper (Salvia et al., 2010). Here are some examples:

- Using nonverbal tests. There are several problems involved in using nonverbal tests with students who lack English-language competency. Some tests, such as the *Test of Nonverbal Intelligence 4*, are considered to be "nonverbal." When tests make assumptions about students' verbal comprehension and production, they may be invalid. Another problem with nonverbal tests is that many test items are not correlated with school success, so the results may not be pertinent to planning instruction.
- Testing as a cultural phenomenon. Although testing in the United States is pervasive, it may be used rarely in other countries. Doing well on tests may not be emphasized or experienced by students in some cultures. Students from other cultures may be unfamiliar with the expectations of testing and the competitive nature of testing. Unfamiliarity with testing and lack of test-taking skills can lead to poor test performance.
- Using translations. Some tests are available or in other languages. Simply translating test items does not render the test appropriate. Vocabulary, cultural expectations, background knowledge, test demands, and norms may not be appropriate for students whose primary language is not English. Similar problems result when an interpreter is used during the administration of tests.
- Relating to others. Cultural conventions may confound testing. For example, relations between males and females may be strictly prescribed by certain cultures. Relating to strangers or adults may influence rapport between test examiners and students. Some cultures emphasize cooperation, modesty, and respect. These values may have an effect on the quantity, quality, and types of responses that students make.

Using a variety of approaches when assessing achievement reflects sensitivity to the student as well as a thorough attempt to understand what the student has learned. The assessment of achievement includes a variety of approaches:

- Curriculum-based assessment
- Criterion-referenced assessment
- Alternative forms of assessment, such as systematic observations, anecdotal records, interviews with family members and the students themselves, samples of students' work, digital recordings, online media, performances, portfolios, and exhibitions
- Standardized tests, which are administered to individuals or groups

Curriculum-Based Assessment

Curriculum-based assessment (CBA) is an approach to linking instruction with assessment. CBA has three purposes: (1) to determine eligibility, (2) to develop the goals for instruction, and (3) to evaluate the student's progress in the curriculum. The consistent and frequent use of CBA can drive instruction. Based on the performance on a CBA instrument, teachers and other professionals can specify instructional goals. Because there is such a close link between assessment and instruction, it is possible to conduct CBA frequently to determine whether to make any changes in instruction or the curriculum. Data collection, interpretation, and intervention are all integral parts of CBA. Other terms for CBA are curriculum-referenced measurement, curriculum-embedded measurement, frequent measurement, continuous curriculum measurement, and therapeutic measurement. CBA is useful because it:

- Links curriculum and instruction.
- Provides information to teachers about what to teach.
- Can be administered frequently.
- Is sensitive to short-term academic gains.
- Drives instruction because of the direct linkage with curriculum.
- Assists in the evaluation of student progress and program evaluation.
- Can be reliable and valid.
- Assists in improving student achievement. (Stiggins, 2007; Wright, n.d.)

Developing a Curriculum-Based Assessment Instrument

There are many online sources for CBA instruments. However, in certain circumstances, some teachers may want to develop their own instruments. One important reason for developing a CBA instrument is that the curriculum may not correspond to the content of existing instruments. By constructing a CBA instrument using the steps listed next, teachers can specify goals, build into the instrument any special adaptations for test administration, and help to ensure that the CBA instrument is valid.

Step 1: Identify the Purpose(s)

Use the instrument to determine eligibility or entry into a curriculum, to develop the goals for intervention, or to evaluate the student's progress in the curriculum. Sometimes, one instrument can serve multiple purposes. For example, you can use the CBA instrument to develop goals and to evaluate the student's progress.

Step 2: Analyze the Curriculum

Determine what the curriculum teaches. Determine the specific tasks that the student should be learning.

Step 3: Develop Performance Objectives

Determine if a student has demonstrated progress in the curriculum. Specify behaviors that the student must demonstrate to indicate progress in the curriculum.

Step 4: Develop the Assessment Procedures

In this step, develop specific test items that correspond with the performance objectives. You can develop different types of items, for example, observing the student or requesting that the student perform specific actions or specific academic tasks, demonstrate particular behaviors, or answer particular questions. Make sure to delineate the scoring procedures. You will have to specify how you will determine how well the student performs. Considerations about reliability and validity are important. The CBA instrument must be valid and must have a close correspondence with the curriculum.

Step 5: Implement the Assessment Procedures

Once the assessment procedures have been developed, you can collect information. How you decide to record and keep track of the information is important. The way in which teachers assess students must be consistent each time. Recording sheets are helpful in keeping track of the information you collect. Piloting, or trying out, the CBA items before actual implementation is a good idea. Although a great deal of thought has gone into the development and construction of the items, it is always good practice to try out the items before using them to assess students. You should administer CBA items according to the procedures that have been developed.

Step 6: Organize the Information
Summarize the information that you have collected. Tables, graphs, or charts can be useful.

Step 7: Interpret and Integrate the Results
Integrate the CBA information with information from standardized tests, observations, anecdotal records, and other forms of assessment. This is the point in the assessment process where instruction and assessment link. The decision-making process continues as educators, along with the team, decide where, when, and how instruction should proceed.

Criterion-Referenced Tests

A **criterion-referenced test (CRT)** measures a student's performance with respect to a well-defined domain. Whereas **norm-referenced tests (NRTs)** discriminate among the performances of individual students on specific test items, CRTs provide a description of a student's knowledge, skills, or behavior in a specific range of well-defined instructional objectives. This specific range is referred to as a domain. CRTs, instead of using norms, provide information on the performance of a student with respect to specific test items. The results of criterion-referenced testing do not depend on the performance of other students, as they do with a NRT.

Several characteristics distinguish CRTs from NRTs. One of these is mastery. Performance on CRTs provides information on whether students have attained a predetermined level of competence or performance. Although it is possible to construct a test that is both norm-referenced and criterion-referenced, teachers and other professionals must use caution when interpreting the results of these tests because it is difficult to combine both types of tests in one instrument.

Another distinction between CRTs and NRTs is the breadth of the content domain that the test covers (Mehrens & Lehmann, 1991). Typical NRTs survey a broad domain, whereas CRTs usually have fewer domains but more items in each domain. CRTs typically sample the domain more thoroughly than do NRTs (Mehrens & Lehmann, 1991).

CRTs can also be very useful in helping to make instructional planning decisions. Because they frequently cover a more restricted range of content than NRTs, they can provide more information about a student's levels of performance.

Teacher-Developed Criterion-Referenced Tests

Teachers can develop CRTs. The advantage to developing your own CRT is that you can directly link the test items to the curriculum. Use the following steps when developing a CRT (Taylor, 2009).

Step 1: Identify the Knowledge, Processes, or Skills to Be Measured
Pinpoint the knowledge, processes, skills, and subskills that the student has been taught from the curriculum and from the student's individualized educational program (IEP).

Step 2: Develop Instructional Objectives or Subobjectives for the Skills

Break down each of the skills and subskills into smaller steps; these become the instructional objectives and subobjectives.

Step 3: Develop Test Items for Each Objective or Subobjective

To measure each skill, develop test items for each one.

Step 4: Determine the Performance Standards or Criteria for Performance

Give each of the objectives and subobjectives at least one criterion that indicates acceptable levels of performance.

Step 5: Administer the Test Items

Once you have developed the CRT, you can administer the items. An advantage to using CRTs is that, unlike NRTs, you can administer the items on a CRT frequently to document the student's progress.

Step 6: Score the Test Items and Present the Results in a Graph or Chart

Record the student's performance on the CRT. Graphing or charting the results can help both students and teachers in monitoring progress.

Step 7: Analyze and Interpret the Results

Knowledge about the student's level of performance facilitates the development of new instructional objectives and modifications.

Connecting Instruction With Assessment: Alternative and Informal Assessment

The terms **alternative assessment** and *informal assessment* are sometimes used interchangeably. A fundamental principle of alternative approaches is that assessment of achievement should link to the curriculum. Linking instruction to the assessment of achievement means that:

- Assessment occurs as a normal part of the student's work. Assessment activities should emerge from the curriculum and the teaching situation. The student does not stop work to do an assessment; the work and the assessment are linked. Examples of this type of assessment include the use of journals, notebooks, essays, oral reports, homework, classroom discussions, group work, and interviews. These assessment activities can occur individually or in small groups and can take place during one session or over multiple sessions.
- The conditions for assessment need to be similar to the conditions for doing meaningful tasks. Students should have sufficient time, have access to peers, be able to use appropriate tools (computers, tablets, books, calculators, manipulatives, etc.), and have the chance to revise their work.
- Assessment tasks should be meaningful and multidimensional. For example, they should provide students with the opportunity to demonstrate solving problems, drawing conclusions, understanding relationships, making inferences, and generating new questions.
- Feedback to students should be specific, meaningful, and prompt and should inform the students' thinking.
- Students participate in the assessment process. They help to generate and apply standards or rubrics. A rubric is an assessment scale that defines criteria for use in evaluating students. Self-assessment and peer assessment are part of the assessment process.

Assessment Approaches

Assessment activities and feedback from peers and teachers help promote student achievement. Ways in which the teacher can gather information and provide feedback to parents and students include the following:

- Probes
- Error analysis
- Oral descriptions
- Written descriptions
- Checklists and questionnaires
- Interviews
- Conferences
- Digital media, such as journals, blogs, tweets, and online communications
- Performance-based assessment
- Portfolios
- Exhibitions
- Self-assessment
- Peer assessment

Probes

A **probe** is a diagnostic technique that modifies instruction to determine whether an instructional strategy is effective. Probes can help diagnose student problems and assist in planning instruction. For example, suppose a teacher wants to determine whether a fourth-grade student who is engaged in science investigations is ready to proceed to the next investigation. The teacher can present a science problem to the student and observe the strategies that the student uses to solve it. The teacher probes with questions such as "What will happen if the temperature is increased?" The student in this case is able to successfully solve the problem but has difficulty understanding that an experiment may work under certain conditions but not under other conditions. The teacher then helps the student by further probing and guiding the student through the steps of the experiment.

The teacher can implement instructional probes during the process of instruction, using the following steps to design the probe:

1. The teacher identifies the targeted area of achievement and measures whether the student can perform the task. For example, in science, the student is studying how pushing or pulling affects moving objects.
2. The teacher probes by modifying the task. For example, the teacher adds weight to one of the objects. (See the next section for examples of other instructional modifications.)
3. The teacher measures whether the student can perform the task.

When conducting a diagnostic probe, the teacher should document the student's performance during step 1 (baseline), step 2 (instruction), and step 3 (baseline).

Types of Accommodations for Use With Probes

Types of accommodations that can apply to instruction include the following:

Instructional accommodations
- Change from a written presentation to an oral presentation.
- Combine verbal instruction with a written explanation.
- Require fewer problems to be completed.

- Provide additional practice.
- Slow the pace of instruction.
- Provide additional time to complete problems.

Material accommodations

- Use manipulatives.
- Place fewer questions, problems, or items on a page.
- Use color, word, or symbolic cues.
- Simplify the problem or the wording.
- Combine tactile mode with visual, oral, or kinesthetic modes.

Environmental accommodations

- Change the location of the instruction or the probe.
- Change the time of day for the instruction or the probe.
- Provide a work area that is quiet and free of distractions.
- Change the lighting of the work area.
- Change the seating arrangements.

Error Analysis

The purposes of **error analysis** are to (1) identify the patterns of errors or mistakes that students make in their work, (2) understand why students make the errors, and (3) provide targeted instruction to correct the errors. When conducting an error analysis, the teacher checks the student's work and categorizes the errors.

After conducting an error analysis, the teacher summarizes the error patterns. However, many errors that students make may not fall into a pattern. Alternatively, if a pattern emerges, it does not mean that the problem is serious. Teachers should view error analysis as a preliminary form of assessment and should always conduct further evaluation of the student's work.

Oral Descriptions

Verbal descriptions of a student's work provide immediate feedback to a student by a teacher or peer. Oral descriptions are especially useful because they are quick, efficient, and direct, and they integrate easily into instruction. They are effective for program planning and program evaluation.

Oral descriptions do have several drawbacks, however. They can be subjective, and because the descriptions are verbal, there is no permanent record. In addition, specific disabilities may limit the ability of the student to understand, remember, or reply to what has been said.

Written Descriptions

A written description is a brief narrative that records feedback about the student's work. The teacher can share the narrative with students, teachers, or parents. A written description, like an oral description, conveys an impression of important aspects of the student's work. Teachers can use written descriptions for program planning and program evaluation.

Before writing the narrative, the teacher should carefully review the student's work. The teacher writes the description, noting areas of strength as well as problem areas. A written description provides feedback to the student about the quality of the work. Because it is recorded, it becomes a reference as the student continues to work.

For example, a student who is engaged in environmental science has the following project: Investigate the migration patterns of killer bees. After developing graphs that depict migration patterns and studying the habitats of killer bees, the student develops conclusions and makes predictions about future migrations to new geographic areas. After examining the student's work, a teacher can comment on labeling, graphing, spelling, and use of language. In addition, the teacher can discuss the use of graphing and knowledge of geography to solve real-world problems, completeness of the results, the student's disposition toward science, the ability to plan ahead, work habits, and attention to detail. Two disadvantages of using written descriptions are that the parents may have difficulty reading or they may not have knowledge of written English.

Checklists and Questionnaires

Checklists and questionnaires are convenient ways to provide feedback about a student's work or attitudes. A checklist can be a quick and easy assessment approach. Figure 10.1 is an example of a checklist that provides feedback about student confidence, willingness, perseverance, and interest. Checklists are helpful for screening, diagnosis, program planning, and program evaluation.

Questionnaires provide an opportunity for teachers and students to collect information in more detail than checklists. Questionnaires can be open-ended, allowing respondents to express their attitudes, opinions, and knowledge in depth, or they can have a more structured format so that the respondents just need to fill in one or two words, circle responses, or indicate the appropriate picture or icon.

Interviews

The topic of conducting interviews was discussed in Chapter 8. Interviews help guide discussions, encourage students, determine motivation and enthusiasm, and identify work and study habits. One basic approach is to interview students individually about their likes and dislikes. Asking questions such as the following can be informative: "What do you like about social studies?" "What are your interests?" "What don't you like?" Interviews are useful for screening, diagnosis, program planning, and program evaluation.

My Beliefs About School

1. I like to go to school	most of the time	sometimes	never
2. My favorite subjects are	language arts social studies	mathematics health	science physical education
3. When I am at school, I like to	read use the computer	write use the library	do projects use the playground
4. I like to work	by myself	with one other person	with several peers
5. I do homework	most of the time	sometimes	never
6. If I need help doing homework, I usually ask	my parent no one	my brother or sister	a friend
7. Some things I like about my teacher are			

FIGURE 10.1 • Assessing Attitudes, Interests, and Habits

Structured interviews provide a more systematic way to assess achievement. A structured interview offers the opportunity to observe, question, and discuss areas of achievement.

An example of using a structured interview in science is to ask students to observe the sky several times during one evening, and the next day ask them the following questions:

1. What is the pattern of the stars as they move across the sky?
2. What is the pattern of the planets?
3. Do the planets follow the same pattern as the stars?
4. After showing students several pictures of the planets and stars, ask students to develop several hypotheses about their size, appearance, and motion.

Conferences

A conference is a conversation about the student's work that can include the student, educators, and parents. In a conference, participants share their views of the student's work with the goal of providing feedback and recommendations. Teacher–student conferences are helpful when assessing one piece of work or when summarizing the student's work over a period of time. The discussion in a conference can be strictly verbal, it can be recorded, or it can be written in summary form. Conferences can be useful for diagnosis, program planning, and program evaluation.

Digital Media, Such as Journals, Blogs, Tweets, Online Communications

Students can use digital media, such as journals, blogs, tweets, and other online communications, that allow them to record their work as well as their attitudes and feelings. A journal provides students the opportunity to record the steps to plan for an assignment, reflect on their own work, communicate about their learning, and document their progress. In a journal, students can indicate what they like and don't like and areas in which they have difficulty. Journals are effective for program planning and program evaluation. For example, a student could convey the following on a class blog:

> Today's topic: Blue Mountains of Australia
>
> Two important ideas: beautiful scenery, historic area
>
> What I understood best: geography
>
> What I need more work on: understanding aboriginal legends
>
> How this topic can be used in real life: tourism, climate change, legends

Performance-Based Assessment

When used to assess achievement, performance-based assessment is the demonstration of knowledge, skills, or behavior. Performance assessment requires students to develop a product or to demonstrate an ability or skill-based on an understanding of concepts and relationships. Chapter 15 describes performance-based assessment in detail.

Portfolios

A portfolio is a systematic collection of a student's work, assembled over a period of time. Many schools use electronic or digital portfolios to document progress over time. When documenting and assessing achievement, portfolios can provide information about conceptual understanding, problem solving, reasoning, communication abilities, habits, motivation, enthusiasm, creativity, work habits, and attitudes. Portfolios help students see that knowledge is interconnected. They are useful for program planning and program

Student's Name			Date		
After completing my social studies assignment, I can	1 Great!	2	3	4	5
1. make comparisons among different points of view.					
2. distinguish between fact and opinion.					
3. apply new skills in using information.					
4. understand new vocabulary.					
5. make inferences about events.					
6. integrate new information.					
7. discuss new concepts and theories.					

FIGURE 10.2 • Self-Assessment Checklist—Social Studies

evaluation. A more extensive discussion of the use of portfolios can be found in Chapter 15.

Exhibitions

An exhibition is a display of a student's work that demonstrates knowledge, abilities, skills, and attitudes. The displays can be in hard copy and/or electronic formats. Numerous types of technologies support the ongoing use of exhibitions of students' works. Exhibitions are discussed in Chapter 15.

Self-Assessment

Self-assessment provides students with an opportunity to review concepts and identify processes. It is an occasion for students to reflect on their learning. Figure 10.2 is an example of a checklist that students use when assessing their own learning.

Peer Assessment

Peer assessment allows students insight into the thinking and reasoning abilities of their peers. When conducting peer assessments, students have an opportunity to reflect on the learning processes of their peers as well as on their own. Figure 10.3 is an example of a checklist that students can use when conducting a peer assessment.

Student's Name _____ **Date** _____

Peer's Name _____

| | Yes | No | Somewhat |

1. My peer used new information to solve a problem.
2. My peer used new vocabulary.
3. My peer demonstrated the ability to think analytically.
4. My peer integrated and synthesized information.
5. My peer made several generalizations.

FIGURE 10.3 • Peer Assessment—Science

Observing the Student in Various Environments

Previous chapters discuss the importance of considering the student within the physical, learning, and social environments. The interactions between the student and the environment are important assessment considerations.

The physical environment can influence the student's performance. The temperature, lighting, and seating arrangements of teaching and learning spaces can affect how well the student performs. A comfortable and positive learning environment facilitates the acquisition of a positive disposition and contributes to achievement. The curriculum, instructional methods, materials, and assessment approaches are all areas of concern.

Relationships with students and teachers can affect achievement. The social environment is important to the development of self-concept and self-esteem. These, in turn, contribute to a positive disposition toward achievement. By observing the social environment, teachers can study the relationships students have with peers and adults.

Standardized Instruments

Standardized tests of achievement are tests that follow strict procedures for administration, scoring, and interpretation. A standardized test is usually norm-referenced. As discussed in Chapter 6, a NRT is a measure that compares a student's test performance with that of similar students who have taken the same test. In addition, scores from standardized tests can be used to make interpretations about an individual student's performance on several tests. The construction of a standardized test is often a lengthy and costly project that involves considerable research and development.

Steps in the Development of a Standardized Achievement Test

1. Test developers create specifications for the test.
2. Test items are written.
3. Test developers conduct an item tryout of initial draft items on a large group of individuals.

4. Test developers analyze the results of the item tryout, discard or modify some items, create new items, and develop methods of scoring and interpretation.
5. Test developers conduct a national standardization of the test. They select a national standardization sample representative of the United States, based on the results of the most recent census data. The sample participants represent balanced criteria for age, socioeconomic status, geographic region, urban/rural/suburban residence, race, ethnicity, and gender. The sample may include additional variables, depending on the purposes of the test.
6. Test developers analyze the data from the national tryout and develop norm tables. Norm tables help examiners compare the performance of individual students with the performance of the students' peers.
7. Final test materials, including test manuals, answer sheets, and scoring guides, result from these steps.

Benefits

The benefits of using standardized tests are that the test materials describe the development of the tests in detail, including the test content, administration, norms, reliability, validity, scoring, and interpretation. Because standardized tests are usually norm-referenced, testers can make comparisons among the performance of an individual student, the student's peers, and the students in the standardized sample group. In addition, the tests allow for comparisons between a student's performance on several subtests or his or her performance on several separate tests to identify relative strengths and weaknesses. Depending on the test, standardized achievement tests are helpful in screening, determining eligibility, program planning, monitoring progress, and program evaluation.

Disadvantages

Although standardized achievement tests have a number of advantages, they also have many disadvantages for students with special needs:

- The underlying assumptions of some tests is that all students have been exposed to the content that is tested. Teachers, test examiners, and administrators should check on the alignment of test items with the curriculum that is taught in classrooms.
- Another underlying assumption is that all students come from a homogeneous or similar culture. For example, some tests may use items that portray children in snowy or urban environments. Children who live in predominantly mild climates or in rural or suburban areas may be disadvantaged because of a lack of experience in these environments.
- Many tests may be biased against students with disabilities; females; and certain cultures, ethnic groups, and economic groups. For examples, females may be depicted as doing clerical work, whereas males may be portrayed as being managers or administrators.
- Many tests contain items that do not relate to the curriculum that is taught in classrooms. For example, a reading test may include items that test phonemic awareness, whereas the dominant approaches to teaching reading emphasize sight word recognition and vocabulary.
- Many tests do not measure or consider creativity, interest, initiative, motivation, and values.
- The emphasis on testing in schools may result in teachers teaching toward the test.
- An emphasis on testing may lead to competition among students, teachers, and schools.
- Test standards usually require that students be able to read and write independently.

Steps and Purposes of Standardized Achievement Testing

Screening

One frequent use of standardized achievement tests is to identify students who perform below, at the same level, or above their peers. That is, the utility of achievement test results in the screening process is in identifying students who need further assessment.

Determining Eligibility

Using standardized achievement tests in conjunction with other types of tests can help determine eligibility for services. For example, using the *Wechsler Individual Achievement Test, Second Edition (WIAT-II)* with a measure of cognitive ability can help determine eligibility for services.

Program Planning

Program planning and monitoring student progress connect instruction with assessment. Achievement tests can aid in instructional planning and can be helpful in identifying what the student knows and can do. Two useful tests for program planning are the *Peabody Individual Achievement Test—4* and the *KeyMath 3 Diagnostic Assessment*. The teacher can also utilize other assessment approaches discussed in this chapter to assist with program planning.

Monitoring Progress

Regularly monitoring students' progress in literacy, mathematics, and other academic content areas is important. NRTs may not be as useful in monitoring progress as are other assessment approaches because they are not sensitive to small changes in performance. Frequent monitoring assists the teacher in modifying instruction to meet the needs of the student. As with program planning, the teacher may also use other assessment approaches discussed in this chapter.

Program Evaluation

Teachers and other professionals employ achievement tests to conduct two types of program evaluation: individual student programs as specified in an IEP and, more broadly, the progress that a class, grade, school, or the school district itself has made over a period of time.

Group Tests

Group tests of achievement are usually administered to groups of students in classrooms. Students with special needs who are in regular classrooms frequently participate in group achievement testing. The purposes of group achievement tests are to (1) assist in screening students, (2) evaluate the relative performance of students when compared with their peers, (3) describe the relative effectiveness of methods of instruction, and (4) evaluate curricula. The Individuals with Disabilities Education Act (IDEA) requires that general state- and districtwide assessments include students with disabilities, using appropriate accommodations where necessary.

Most group tests require using scripted directions that the test publisher provides. Many tests are computer-based. Group tests report a variety of types of scores, including standard scores, percentiles, stanines, and age and grade equivalents. These scores can generate profiles, thus facilitating the comparison of students, classrooms, individual schools, and school districts.

Benefits

Group testing with standardized tests permits the testing of large groups of students using the same administration, scoring, and interpretation procedures. Although it is appropriate to administer group tests to individual students, it is not appropriate to administer individual tests to groups.

Disadvantages

Group testing has several disadvantages for students with special needs. The tests routinely require that students read and write independently. Many group achievement tests have separate test booklets that contain the test items and separate answer sheets. Some students may be able to correctly answer the questions but have difficulty transferring their answers to the answer sheet. Finally, many group achievement tests have multiple-choice answers. Students with disabilities as well as students from various cultures or ethnic groups may have difficulty using this format.

Individual Achievement Tests

When testing individual students, achievement tests provide the examiner with the opportunity to get to know students. The student and the test examiner can establish a rapport, and the examiner can help the student feel at ease. Individual testing allows the examiner to observe the student's appearance, adjustment to the testing, cooperation, effort, motivation, attitudes, speech patterns, anxiety level, activity level, flexibility, impulse control, fine and gross motor abilities, distractibility, and mood (Sattler, 2008). The examiner can individualize the test administration according to the needs of the student. For example, if a student is tired or hungry, the examiner can stop the test so that the student can take a break.

Kaufman Test of Educational Achievement, Second Edition

The *Kaufman Test of Educational Achievement, Second Edition (KTEA-II*; Kaufman & Kaufman, 2004) is an individually administered test of achievement for students in grades 1 through 12. The *KTEA-II* has two forms, the Comprehensive Form and the Brief Form. The age-based norms range from 4 years 6 months to 25 years for the Comprehensive Form and ages 4 years, 6 months through 90+ years for the Brief Form. Although the forms are not interchangeable, they do have overlapping uses. The applications listed for the Brief Form are contributing to a battery, screening, program planning, research, pretesting and posttesting, making placement decisions, student self-appraisal, use by government agencies, personnel selection, and measuring adaptive functioning. The Comprehensive Form has all these uses except screening. In addition, the Comprehensive Form is recommended for analyzing strengths and weaknesses and for analyzing errors. There is some overlap of items between the *KTEA-II* and the *Kaufman Assessment Battery for Children, Second Edition (KABC-II)*.

DESCRIPTION OF THE SUBTESTS IN THE COMPREHENSIVE FORM The Comprehensive Form consists of cover letter and word recognition, reading comprehension, phonological awareness, nonsense word decoding, word recognition fluency, decoding fluency, associational fluency, naming facility, mathematics concepts and applications, mathematics computation, written expression, listening, and oral expression.

ADMINISTRATION Persons who have had training in educational and psychological testing as well as persons who have had limited training in these areas can administer the *KTEA-II*. For children in grades 1 through 3, the Comprehensive Form takes from 20 minutes to 1 hour to administer; the Brief Form requires from 15 to 45 minutes to administer.

SCORING   Raw scores convert to standard scores, with a mean of 100 and a standard deviation of 15. Percentile ranks, stanines, normal curve equivalents, age equivalents, and grade equivalents are available. The manual describes the following methods of interpreting *KTEA-II* scores: the size of the difference and the significance of the difference between subtests and between composite scores, analysis of strengths and weaknesses, and identification of errors.

STANDARDIZATION   Test publishers renormed both the Comprehensive and the Brief Forms of the *KTEA-II*. Both age- and grade-based scores are available.

TECHNICAL ADEQUACY   Reliability and validity are acceptable. As with all standardized achievement tests, the teacher should evaluate the content validity.

VALIDITY   The validity results of the Comprehensive Form and the Brief Form were estimated using similar procedures. Content validity is determined through consultation with curriculum experts in each subject area.

> **TESTS-at-a-GLANCE**
>
> **Kaufman Test of Educational Achievement, Second Edition (KTEA-II)**
> http://www.pearsonclinical.com/education/products/100000665/kaufman-test-of-educational-achievement-second-edition-kteaii.html?Pid=PAa32215
>
> - **Publication Date:** 2004
> - **Purposes:** The Comprehensive Form measures reading decoding, spelling, reading comprehension, mathematics applications, and mathematics computation. The Brief Form consists of three subtests: Reading, Mathematics, and Spelling.
> - **Age/Grade Levels:** Grades 1 through 12; ages range from 6 years 0 months to 18 years 11 months.
> - **Time to Administer:** 20 minutes to approximately 1 hour.
> - **Technical Adequacy:** As with all achievement tests, educators must evaluate the content validity to determine how well it measures what has been taught.
> - **Suggested Uses:** The Comprehensive Form can be used to measure overall achievement, identify strengths and weaknesses, error analysis, and program planning. The Brief Form should be used for screening.

SUMMARY   The *Kaufman Test of Educational Achievement, Second Edition* is an individually administered test of achievement for students in whose ages range from 4 years 6 months to 25 years. The *KTEA-II* has two forms, the Comprehensive Form and the Brief Form. Although the forms overlap in content, they are not interchangeable. Evidence for the technical adequacy of the test is sufficient. The reliability is excellent, and the validity of both forms is adequate. As with all achievement tests, educators must evaluate the content validity to determine how well it measures what has been taught.

Wechsler Individual Achievement Test-III

The *Wechsler Individual Achievement Test, Third Edition* (*WIAT-III*) (Pearson, 2010) is an individually administered achievement test for students ages 4 years through 50 years, 11 months. The *WIAT-III* contains 19 subtests and yields a Total Achievement score and Composite Scores in the following areas: Oral Language, Total Reading, Basic Reading, Basic Comprehension and Fluency, Written Expression, Mathematics, and Math Fluency.

ADMINISTRATION   The *WIAT-III* is administered individually. It takes approximately 30 minutes to 2 hours to administer.

SCORING   Raw scores convert to grade-based standard scores. Percentiles, age and grade equivalents, normal curve equivalents, and stanines are also available. It is possible to determine the discrepancy between *WIAT-III* standard scores and *Wechsler Intelligence Scale for Children, Third Edition (WISC-III)* standard scores.

STANDARDIZATION   Sample stratification occurred according to age, grade, gender, race/ethnicity, geographic region, and the education of the parent(s) or guardian(s) based on data from the U.S. Census. The *WIAT-III* links with the *Wechsler Intelligence Scale for Children, Third*

> **TESTS-at-a-GLANCE**
>
> **Wechsler Individual Achievement Test, Second Edition (WIAT-III)**
> http://www.pearsonclinical.com/psychology/products/100000463/wechsler-individual-achievement-testthird-edition-wiatiii-wiatiii.html?Pid=015-8984-609
>
> - **Publication Date:** 2010
> - **Purposes:** Measures strengths and weaknesses in oral expression, listening comprehension, written expression, word reading skill, reading comprehension, spelling, and mathematics calculation or mathematics reasoning.
> - **Age/Grade Levels:** Ages 4 years through age 50 years, 11 months; Pre-Kindergarten through grade 12.
> - **Time to Administer:** Approximately 30 minutes to 2 hours.
> - **Technical Adequacy:** The standardization sample, reliability, and validity are very good.
> - **Suggested Uses:** Measuring overall achievement; achievement in reading, oral language, written expression, and mathematics.

Edition (WISC-III), and the *Wechsler Adult Intelligence Scale, Third Edition* (WAIS-III).

RELIABILITY Several types of reliability coefficients are reported. Overall, the reliability of the *WIAT-III* is adequate.

VALIDITY There is good evidence of construct validity.

SUMMARY The *WIAT-III* is an individually administered test that assesses achievement in students ages 4 through 50 years, 11 months. In the Snapshot, a special education teacher talks about the administration of the *WIAT-III* to Patricia, a student with reading difficulties.

Wide Range Achievement Test 4

The *Wide Range Achievement Test 4* (WRAT4; Wilkinson & Robertson, 2006) measures fundamental skills in word reading, sentence comprehension, spelling, and mathematics computation. The *WRAT4* has four subtests:

Word Reading. This subtest assesses letter identification and word recognition.

Sentence Comprehension. In this subtest, sentence comprehension is measured using a modified **cloze procedure**. The cloze procedure requires examinees to supply words that have been systematically deleted from sentences.

Spelling. Examinees are required to spell words that are dictated by the examiner.

Math Computation. The examinee is asked to solve problems through counting, recognizing numbers, figuring out oral problems presented by the examiner, and computing written mathematics problems.

> **TESTS-at-a-GLANCE**
>
> **Wide Range Achievement Test 4 (WRAT 4)**
> http://www4.parinc.com
>
> - **Publication Date:** 2006
> - **Purposes:** Measures word reading, sentence comprehension, spelling, and basic mathematics skills.
> - **Age/Grade Levels:** Ages 5 years through 94 years.
> - **Time to Administer:** 15 minutes to 45 minutes. The instrument can be administered to individual examinees or to small groups of up to approximately five individuals.
> - **Technical Adequacy:** Standardization and reliability are acceptable; validity is adequate for academic screening.
> - **Suggested Uses:** This instrument can be used as a screening instrument. An adaptation of this instrument, *Wide Range Achievement Test 4—Progress Monitoring Version* (WRAT4—PMV; Roid & Ledbetter, 2006), can be used for progress monitoring of students in kindergarten through grade 12.

ADMINISTRATION The *WRAT4* is individually administered and can be administered to individuals ages 5 years through 94 years. There are two forms: blue and green.

SCORING The *WRAT4* can be hand scored or computer scored. Scores can be reported for percentile ranks, normal curve equivalents, stanines, standard scores, and grade equivalents.

STANDARDIZATION The standardization sample of the *WRAT4* consisted of 3,000 individuals. The sample stratifications include age, region of the country, gender, ethnic group, geographic region, and parental education.

RELIABILITY Reliability appears to be adequate. Median internal consistency reliability coefficients for each form for the age-based and grade-based samples

> **SNAPSHOT**
>
> ### A Special Education Teacher's Comments
>
> My name is J. J. Auburn, and I recently evaluated Patricia, who is in fourth grade. She has received special education services since kindergarten because of speech and language difficulties. When she was in third grade, Patricia's teacher raised concerns about Patricia's behavior in the classroom and asked Patricia's parent to seek a medical opinion about the possibility that Patricia had an attention-deficit hyperactivity disorder. The parent did not follow this advice, and the school did not follow up. Her current fourth-grade teacher has raised these concerns again and referred Patricia for further evaluation.
>
> As part of the evaluation, I first observed Patricia in her classroom and during recess using a running record observation, which was described in Chapter 8. Next, I administered the *Wechsler Individual Achievement Test-III*. Patricia came willingly to the testing room. She seemed to listen carefully while I explained that some of the questions would be easy but they would get harder because this was a test for older children as well. We proceeded through the subtests.
>
> When we came to the Spelling subtest, I noticed an immediate change in her behavior and attitude. As soon as I gave her the Spelling sheet and a pencil and asked her to write the words given to her, she became restless. Her pencil grip seemed unsteady, and she wiggled in her seat. She repeated every word slowly and talked to herself throughout this subtest.
>
> After the Spelling subtest, we took a short break. Then I proceeded to administer the remaining subtests in the *WIAT-III*. The restlessness was still present. When we were finished, I thanked Patricia and walked her back to her classroom.
>
> I returned to my room and scored the test. An analysis of Patricia's performance showed that she had specific strengths and a number of weaknesses. I was very concerned about Patricia's behavioral changes when faced with tasks that involved writing.
>
> Patricia's literacy instruction emphasizes phonemic awareness, vocabulary development, and fluency. I wondered if Patricia's behavior was an attempt to hide her perceived discomfort with reading and writing. In preparation for the IEP meeting, I summarized the information from the observations that were conducted in the classroom and during recess and Patricia's test performance. I asked her teacher to bring samples of Patricia's classroom work and homework to the meeting. I also asked the teacher to bring work samples of students who were performing "typically" so that the team would be able to compare Patricia's performance with the performance of students who were performing at this standard.
>
> **Pause and consider:**
> - Why would J. J. request to see samples of other students' work?
> - Suggest specific areas for comparison (e.g., types of spelling errors, fluency)

range from .87 to .96. Alternate form immediate retest reliability coefficients range from .79 to .89 for the age-based sample and .86 to .90 for the grade-based sample.

VALIDITY Examiners should consider how well the test items assess the content areas of reading, mathematics, and spelling. Because the *WRAT4* is a relatively recent revision of a previous instrument, additional research studies are necessary to substantiate the construct validity of this instrument. Similarly, the adaptation of this instrument, *Wide Range Achievement Test 4—Progress Monitoring Version* (*WRAT4—PMV*; Roid & Ledbetter, 2006), can be used, with caution, for progress monitoring of students in kindergarten through grade 12. Progress monitoring is an essential activity of the response to intervention model.

SUMMARY The *Wide Range Achievement Test 4* can be administered to individuals or small groups as a screening measure in the areas of reading, spelling, and mathematics achievement. An adaptation of this instrument, *Wide Range Achievement Test 4—Progress Monitoring Version* (*WRAT4—PMV*; Roid & Ledbetter, 2006), is available for progress monitoring of students in kindergarten through grade 12.

Woodcock-Johnson Tests, Normative Update, Tests of Achievement

The *Woodcock-Johnson-III, Normative Update* (*WJ-III NU*; Woodcock, Schrank, McGrew, & Mather, 2007) is an individually administered battery that assesses cognitive and academic abilities in individuals ages 2 years through 90+ years. The battery consists of two tests: *Woodcock-Johnson-III Tests of Cognitive Ability* (*WJ-III COG*) and the *Woodcock-Johnson-III Tests of Achievement* (*WJ-III ACH*). Each part comprises a Standard Battery and a Supplemental Battery. Standard batteries can be administered alone or with the supplemental batteries. Chapter 16 describes the *WJ-III COG* and the *Batería-III Woodcock-Muñoz* (Woodcock & Muñoz-Sandoval, 2004), an achievement and cognitive battery for Spanish-speaking individuals, ages 2 through 90+ years.

The *WJ-III NU* can be used for (1) diagnosis, (2) determination of intra-ability and ability/achievement discrepancies, (3) program placement, (4) individual program planning, (5) guidance, (6) growth assessment, (7) program evaluation, and (8) research. The subtests measure reading, mathematics, written language, oral language, and knowledge (science, social studies). A description of the subtests can be found in Table 10.1. There are two parallel forms of the *WJ-III ACH* Standard Battery.

TABLE 10.1 • *Woodcock-Johnson-III NU*, Tests of Achievement

The *WJ-III NU* Standard Battery consists of 12 subtests.

1. *Letter–Word Identification.* Assesses the ability to identify letters and words in isolation.
2. *Reading Fluency.* Measures the ability to read statements rapidly and answer "yes" or "no."
3. *Story Recall.* Assesses the ability to listen to and recall details of stories.
4. *Understanding Directions.* Measures the ability to comprehend and follow directions.
5. *Calculation.* Assesses the ability to solve mathematical calculations using a booklet in which the student can respond in writing.
6. *Math Fluency.* Assesses the ability to add, subtract, and multiply rapidly.
7. *Spelling.* Measures the ability to spell orally presented words.
8. *Writing Fluency.* Measures the ability to write fluently.
9. *Passage Comprehension.* Measures the ability to read a short passage and to identify the missing word.
10. *Applied Problems.* Measures the ability to solve practical mathematical problems.
11. *Writing Samples.* Measures the ability to respond in writing to various response demands.
12. *Story Recall–Delayed.* Measures the ability to recall previously presented story.

The *WJ-III NU ACH* Extended Battery consists of 10 subtests.

1. *Word Attack.* Assesses the ability to apply the rules of phonic and structural analysis to read unfamiliar and nonsense words.
2. *Picture Vocabulary.* Measures the ability to identify objects.
3. *Oral Comprehension.* Assesses the ability to identify missing words in a passage that is presented orally.
4. *Editing.* Measures the ability to correct errors in written passages.
5. *Reading Vocabulary.* Assesses the ability to supply one-word synonyms and antonyms after reading words.
6. *Quantitative Concepts.* Assesses the ability to identify mathematics terms, formulas, and number patterns.
7. *Academic Knowledge.* Measures the ability to answer questions about science, social studies, and humanities.
8. *Spelling of Sounds.* Assesses knowledge of letter combinations that form regular patterns in written English.
9. *Sound Awareness.* Measures the ability to rhyme words and to remove, substitute, and reverse parts of words to make new words.
10. *Punctuation and Capitalization.* Assesses knowledge of punctuation and capitalization rules.

ADMINISTRATION. The time to administer the *WJ-III ACH* varies from approximately 20 minutes to over 1 hour, depending on whether examiners use both the Standard Battery and the Supplemental Battery. Raw scores can convert to age and grade equivalents, percentile ranks, and standard scores. Scoring can be accomplished only by using computer software.

STANDARDIZATION The *WJ-III NU* was standardized on more than 8,800 individuals in over 100 communities. The sample was stratified according to U.S. Census estimates.

RELIABILITY The test manual provides extensive information on reliability of the *WJ-III ACH*. The manual also provides information about standard errors of measurement for the subtests. Overall, the reliabilities of the subtests and the clusters are acceptable.

VALIDITY The manual reports a number of validity studies for the achievement battery. In general, there is evidence to support content, concurrent, and construct validity. The extent to which various subtests reflect students' abilities depends on the instructional orientation of the teacher and the school curriculum.

SUMMARY The Tests of Achievements of the *Woodcock-Johnson-III NU* assess academic abilities in individuals ages 24 months through adulthood. The battery is norm-referenced and individually administered. Reliability information is acceptable. A student's performance on the achievement subtests may be a reflection, in part, of the curriculum that has been taught.

TESTS-at-a-GLANCE

Woodcock-Johnson-III, Normative Update, Tests of Achievement (WJ-III ACH)
www.riverpub.com

- **Publication Date:** 2007
- **Purposes:** Measures overall achievement in reading, mathematics, written language, and general knowledge.
- **Age/Grade Levels:** Ages 2 years through 90+.
- **Time to Administer:** 20 minutes to over 1 hour.
- **Technical Adequacy:** Reliability information is acceptable. Validity is adequate; however, the teacher should determine content validity by comparing the test items with the curriculum that the student has been taught.
- **Suggested Uses:** Measuring overall achievement; may be used to indicate general areas of strength and weakness.

Research-Based Practices Testing Accommodations

To what extent do testing accommodations allow students with disabilities to be better able to demonstrate what they know and can do? Testing accommodations have been the subject of a great many research studies. The National Center for Educational Outcomes (NCEO) (http://www.cehd.umn.edu/nceo) has examined research on this topic. According to NCEO, accommodations can be grouped into the following categories:

- Presentation, such as repeating directions, reading items aloud, signing directions, and using visual cues.
- Response, such as using a computer or tablet, dictating responses, signing responses, and marking answers.
- Setting, such as individual, group, or specialized setting.
- Timing or scheduling, such as allowing extended time, providing frequent breaks, and allowing testing to occur over several days.

Allowing accommodations on tests can be controversial because there is uncertainty regarding the extent to which accommodations are beneficial to students with disabilities. Allowing extended time on tests is one of the most frequently allowed accommodations. Yet some researchers have found that students with disabilities who have been allowed extended time do not perform at a higher level than students who have not been allowed extended time. Do your own research, beginning with the Web site of the NCEO at http://www.education.umn.edu/nceo. What do recent research studies say about the benefits of allowing extended time on tests? What about other accommodations, such as test administration in small and large groups, use of a word processor, use of text-to-speech software to read test questions in mathematics and science, and use of a person who acts as scribe?

Summary

- School records and past and current classroom performance are important sources of information.
- Other sources of information about classroom performance include criterion-referenced assessment, curriculum-based assessment, journals, notebooks, blogs, essays, oral reports, homework, discussions, group work, interviews, alternative assessment, performance testing, self-assessment, peer assessment, systematic observations, anecdotal records, interviews with teachers and students, and samples of student's work.
- The information that teachers gather through the assessment process should inform and support learning and instruction.
- Achievement tests, when carefully chosen, can be important sources of information.

QUESTIONS FOR REFLECTION

The Buros Institute of Mental Measurements Web site provides online reviews and information about thousands of tests. The Web site is **http://www.unl.edu/buros**

1. Compare the test items of a group achievement test with an individual achievement test. What are the similarities? What are the differences? When would it be appropriate to use each of these tests?
2. Obtain a copy of a standardized achievement test. Review the test items in one curriculum area. What items represent the curriculum that is being taught in the local schools? What items differ? What conclusions and recommendations can you offer?
3. Identify a curriculum area for instruction. Can you develop two assessment tasks that link instruction to assessment?
4. Using a search engine, find four curriculum-based assessments. Compare and contrast the online resources. In what ways are they similar? Different?
5. Identify one topic about which you would like your students to learn. Develop two tasks for assessing students' learning of these tasks.

REFERENCES

Kaufman, A. S., & Kaufman, N. L. (2004). *Kaufman Test of Educational Achievement II*. Bloomington, MN: Pearson.

Mehrens, W. A., & Lehman, I. J. (1991). *Measurement and evaluation in education and psychology* (4th ed.). Orlando, FL: Holt, Rinehart and Winston.

Roid, G. H., & Ledbetter, M. F. (2006). *Wide Range Achievement Test 4—Progress Monitoring Version (WRAT4—PMV)*. Lutz, FL: Psychological Assessment Resources, Inc.

Salvia, J., Ysseldyke, J., & Bolt, S. (2010). *Assessment in special and inclusive education* (11th ed.). Belmont, CA: Wadsworth CENGAGE.

Sattler, J. (2008). *Assessment of children: Cognitive foundations* (5th ed.). La Mesa, CA: Author.

Stiggins, R. (2007). *Introduction to student-involved assessment for learning* (5th ed.). Upper Saddle River, NJ: Pearson.

Taylor, R. L. (2009). *Assessment of exceptional students* (8th ed.). Upper Saddle River, NJ: Pearson.

Tomlinson, C. (2008). Learning to love assessment. *Educational Leadership, 65*(4), 8–13.

Wilkinson, G. S., & Robertson G. J. (2006). *Wide Range Achievement test 4*. Lutz, FL: Psychological Assessment Resources, Inc.

Woodcock, R. W., & Muñoz-Sandoval, A. F. (2004). *Batería-III Woodcock-Muñoz*. Itasca, IL: Riverside.

Woodcock, R. W., Schrank, F. A., McGrew, K. S., & Mather, N. (2007). *Woodcock-Johnson III*. Itasca, IL: Riverside.

Wright, J. (n.d.). *Curriculum-based measurement: A manual for teachers*. Retrieved March 1, 2005, from http://www.interventioncentral.org

11 Reading

Chapter Objectives

After completing this chapter, you should be able to:

- Describe ways in which standardized achievement tests can be used in the assessment of literacy.
- Explain how the following approaches can be used to assess reading: curriculum-based assessment, curriculum-based measurement, and performance-based and informal approaches.

Overview

Literacy involves being able to read, write, think, and communicate. Probably no other subject receives as much emphasis in the early grades. As students progress through school, literacy is expected of all students. In school, literacy is linked to achievement. Once students leave school, being able to read and write is required in everyday life and is tied to success in many careers, to economic level, and to personal satisfaction.

The assessment of reading abilities and skills should involve a variety of approaches to reflect an understanding of what students know and are able to do. Assessment of reading and writing should reflect integrated activities that evaluate students' ability to think, rethink, construct, and interpret knowledge.

Assessment Principles

There is general consensus that the assessment of reading of students with special needs should consider the following (Bell & McCallum, 2008; International Reading Association, 2003):

- Assessments that include a variety of observations that consider the complexity of the processes involved in reading, in writing, and in using language. The assessment tasks must include high-quality texts, various genres, and authentic tasks.
- Assessment tasks that are age-appropriate.
- Assessment tools that are unbiased.
- A variety of assessment approaches, tools, and measures, including ongoing assessments and progress monitoring.

- Assessment approaches that consider background knowledge and prior experiences.
- Assessment tasks that are based on sound technical standards, including reliability, validity, norms, and scoring.
- Assessment tasks that consider reading and writing in various contexts and environments.
- Direct linkage between the curriculum that has been taught and assessment tasks.

Connecting Assessment With Instruction

Curriculum-based assessment (CBA) is a broad approach to linking assessment with instruction. CBA has three purposes: (1) to support response to intervention, (2) to develop the goals for instruction, and (3) to evaluate the student's progress in the curriculum.

Progress Monitoring

A fundamental principle of reading instruction is that instruction should be linked directly with assessment. Connecting instruction to assessment in reading means the following:

- Assessment occurs as a normal part of the student's work. Assessment activities emerge from the teaching situation. The student does not stop work to do an assessment; the work connects with the assessment. Examples of this type of assessment include the use of journals, notebooks, essays, oral reports, homework, classroom discussions, group work, and interviews. These assessment activities can occur individually or in small groups and can take place during one session or over multiple sessions.
- The conditions for assessment should be similar to the conditions for doing meaningful tasks. Students must have sufficient time, have access to peers, be able to use appropriate literacy materials, and have the chance to revise their work.
- Assessment tasks need to be meaningful and multidimensional. The tasks should provide students with the opportunity to demonstrate a variety of reading abilities and skills.
- Feedback to students is frequent, specific, meaningful, and prompt and assists students' acquisition of reading.
- Students participate in the assessment process. They help to generate and apply standards or rubrics. Self-assessment and peer assessment are part of the assessment process.
- Assessment results drive instructional planning and teaching.

There are two general approaches to progress monitoring in literacy: CBA instruments and CBM. We will examine these approaches, as well as more formal tools that are based on these approaches.

Curriculum-Based Assessment

CBA is directly linked to the students' curriculum. CBA requires testing students frequently, and the results are used to guide instruction (Hosp, Hosp, & Howell, 2007). CBA can be used to measure the rate of reading, reading errors, accuracy, and reading comprehension. The key assumption underlying CBA is that a reading curriculum or basal reading series has been implemented. Teachers can use instructional materials to construct the CBA and to establish levels of competence. The following steps describe how to develop and administer the CBA:

1. The teacher photocopies three 100-word passages from the first quarter of each of the basal readers for grades 1 through 6. For preprimers and primers, teachers select passages of 25 or 50 words, then label and arrange them in order of difficulty.

2. On three successive days, beginning with the easiest passage and proceeding to the more difficult ones, the student reads one of the passages orally. The teacher records the total number of seconds it took for the student to read the passage. From this, the teacher can determine the number of correct words the student reads per minute.
3. The teacher records errors made while the student is reading. Types of errors include omissions, substitutions, additions, repetitions, self-corrections, and pauses. To determine the percentage of reading accuracy, the number of words read correctly is divided by the total number of words in the passage. For example, Peter read a 100-word passage and made 5 errors. To calculate reading accuracy, his teacher followed these steps:

    - Subtracted total number of errors from number of words in the passage:

    $$100 - 5 = 95 \text{ words read correctly}$$

    - Divided the number of words read correctly by the total number of words in the passage:

    $$95/100 = 95 \text{ percent level of accuracy}$$

4. After each passage is read, the teacher asks the student six comprehension questions that the teacher has constructed. The acceptable level of performance is answering five of the six questions correctly. Teachers should construct the questions as follows:

    - Two text-explicit (TE) questions. These are questions with answers that the student can find precisely in the passage.

    Example: What is the name of the main character?

    - Two text-implicit (TI) questions. These are questions with answers that the passage implies.

    Example: What is a solar system?

    - Two script-implicit (SI) questions. These are questions that require the reader to combine prior knowledge with details from the passage.

    Example: What is the moral of the story?

Curriculum-Based Measurement

CBM (Hosp & Hosp, 2003; Hosp et al., 2007) is one type of CBA and involves the use of standardized procedures that directly measure student progress performance. A considerable research base supports the use of CBM. The features of CBM are (1) the direct link between the assessment and the student's curriculum; (2) brief, frequent assessments; (3) multiple forms of the assessment tool; (4) the low cost of developing assessment materials; and (5) a sensitivity to measuring the improvement of student performance. Repeated use of CBM, for example, once or twice a week, enables teachers to quickly document students' progress and target instruction.

Progress monitoring is essential to supporting students' advancement in literacy achievement and evaluating the benefits of instruction. Although teacher developed tools can be used to measure students' progress, more formal development measures can also be used. See Table 11.1 for a list of progress-monitoring measures.

The *Dynamic Indicators of Basic Early Literacy, Sixth Edition* (*DIBELS*; Good & Kaminski, 2006) is a CBM. It consists of seven individually administered subtests that assess phonological awareness, alphabetic understanding, and fluency. The purposes of *DIBELS* are to benchmark and monitor progress in literacy for students in kindergarten through third grade. The development of *DIBELS* is aligned with the research on reading reported by the National Reading Panel (National Institute of Child Health and Human Development, 2000).

TABLE 11.1 • Literacy Tools for Progress Monitoring

Measures	Areas	Psychometric Standards			Progress-Monitoring Characteristics			
		Reliability	Validity	Alternate Forms	Sensitivity to Students' Improvement	Curriculum Benchmarks	Improvement of Student Learning or Teacher Planning	Specification of Rates of Improvement
Accelerated Reader (AR)	Reading	○	•	•	•	•	•	•
AIMSweb	Early literacy	•	•	•	•	•	•	•
	Reading	•	•	•	•	•	•	•
Dynamic Indicators of Basic Early Literacy Skills (DIBELS)	Initial sound fluency	•	•	•	•	•	○	•
	Nonsense word fluency	•	•	•	•	•	•	•
	Oral reading fluency	•	•	•	•	•	•	•
	Phonemic reading fluency	•	•	•	•	•	•	•
	Retell fluency	•	•	•	○	○	○	○
	Word use fluency	•	•	•	○	○	○	•
EdCheckup	Maze reading	•	•	•	•	•	•	•
System to Enhance Educational Performance (STEEP)	Reading fluency	•	•	•	•	•	•	•
Monitoring Basic Skills Progress (MBSP)	Reading	•	•	•	•	•	•	•
PASeries	Reading	•	•	•	○	•	○	○
STAR	Early literacy	•	•	•	•	•	•	•
	Reading	•	•	•	•	•	•	•
Test of Word Reading Efficiency (TOWRE)	Phonemic decode efficiency	•	•	•	○	○	○	○
	Sight-word efficiency	•	•	•	○	○	○	○
Test of Silent Word Reading Fluency (TOSWRF)	Reading	•	•	•	○	○	○	○

TABLE 11.1 • (Continued)

Measures	Areas	Psychometric Standards		Progress-Monitoring Characteristics				
		Reliability	Validity	Alternate Forms	Sensitivity to Students' Improvement	Curriculum Benchmarks	Improvement of Student Learning or Teacher Planning	Specification of Rates of Improvement
Vital Indicators of Progress (VIP)	Initial sound fluency	•	•	•	•	•	o	•
	Letter naming fluency	•	•	•	•	•	o	•
	Nonsense word fluency	•	•	•	•	•	•	•
	Phoneme segmentation	•	•	•	•	•	•	•
Yearly Progress Pro	Reading	•	•	•	•	•	•	•

o Insufficient evidence
• Sufficient evidence
Source: Adapted from U.S. Department of Education, retrieved December 21, 2008, from http://www.studentprogress.org

The *DIBELS* benchmark assessments are administered three times a year, and the progress-monitoring materials can be administered more frequently. Not all subtests are administered at each grade level. The administration and scoring guide, as well as the photocopy masters for the standard, large-print, and Spanish versions can be downloaded, at no charge, from dibels.oregon.edu. The materials can also be downloaded for a handheld device and in print from Sopris West (**http://www.soprislearning.com/**). The Spanish version, *Indicadores Dinámicos del Éxito en la Lectura, 7a edición* (*IDEL*; Cummings, Baker, & Good, 2007), assesses early literacy skills of students who are learning to read Spanish. *IDEL* is not a translation of *DIBELS*. According to the authors, the development of *IDEL* considered the phonology, orthography, and syntax of the Spanish language.

The seven *DIBELS* subtests are as follows:

Initial Sound Fluency	Identification and production of beginning word sounds
Phonemic Sound Segmentation Fluency	Segmentation of words into phonemes
Letter Naming Fluency	Naming upper- and lowercase letters
Nonsense Word Fluency	Letter-sound matching and letter blending
Oral Reading Fluency	Reading text aloud
Retell Fluency	Reading comprehension
Word Use Fluency	Use of specific words in sentences

The number of correct responses per minute is calculated for every subtest except Word Use Fluency. The scores correspond to grade placement (kindergarten, first, second, or third) and levels of risk: at risk, at some risk, at low risk. *DIBELS* is designed to use local norms, and comparisons are made within districts.

The technical aspects of *DIBELS* are good. Reliability and validity coefficients are in the range of the .70s through .90s. Considerable research has been conducted on this measure.

However, there has been some controversy regarding the technical adequacy of the instrument (Bell & McCallum, 2008). Educators should examine the correspondence of DIBELS measures with local reading approaches. DIBELS can be most useful in screening and measuring progress.

Comparison of Progress-Monitoring Measures

The U.S. Department of Education established the following criteria for determining the adequacy of progress-monitoring measures: reliability, validity, alternate forms, sensitivity to students' improvement, alignment with curriculum standards or benchmarks, evidence for improvement of students' learning or teacher planning, and specification of rates of improvement. The extent to which formalized measures met these criteria are listed in Table 11.1 (U.S. Department of Education, 2008).

Criterion-Referenced Assessment

Instead of comparing a student's performance to a norm group, criterion-referenced assessments measure a student's performance with respect to a well-defined content domain (Salvia, Ysseldyke, & Bolt, 2010). Whereas norm-referenced tests in reading discriminate among the performances of individual students on specific test items, criterion-referenced tests provide a description of a student's curriculum-referenced knowledge, skills, or processes.

Informal Assessment Approaches

Formal assessment and feedback from peers and teachers encourage the development of reading abilities. Ways in which the teacher can gather information and provide feedback to parents and students include the following:

- Probes
- Error analysis
- Cloze procedures
- Think-alouds
- Retelling
- Oral descriptions
- Written descriptions
- Checklists and questionnaires
- Interviews
- Conferences
- Students' journals, notebooks, and blogs
- Performance-based assessments
- Portfolios
- Exhibitions
- Self-assessment
- Peer assessment

Probes

A probe is a diagnostic technique in which instruction is varied to examine whether an instructional schema is working. Probes are valuable for diagnosing student problems and assisting in planning instruction. For example, suppose a teacher wants to determine whether a student is ready to proceed to a more difficult reading book. The teacher can present the student with a selection from the book and observe the strategies that the student uses when reading. The student may be able to read the words on the page but perhaps needs some help learning new vocabulary. The teacher can then help the student by introducing the new vocabulary and providing background knowledge.

Teachers implement instructional probes during the process of instruction. When designing an instructional probe, we suggest the following steps:

1. The teacher identifies the area of reading that is to be the target and determines whether the student can do the tasks or use certain reading strategies. Examples include locating the title page, retelling a story, and recognizing common warning signs such as "Danger" and "Keep Out."
2. The teacher modifies the assignment. For example, to facilitate the recognition of warning signs, the teacher can have the student say, "Trace," "Recognize," and "Write the words." To assist in retelling, a teacher can ask: "What happened after? Tell me more about where the story takes place."
3. The teacher determines whether the student can read the words or retell the passage.

Error Analysis

The purposes of error analysis are to (1) identify the patterns of errors that students make in their work; (2) understand why students make the errors; and (3) provide instruction to help correct the errors. In an error analysis of reading skills, the student reads aloud, and the teacher categorizes the errors. Error analysis can facilitate the understanding of students' specific reading problems, such as word decoding, word prediction within the context of a reading passage, and sight-word recognition (McKenna & Pickard, 2006; Singleton, 2005).

After conducting an error analysis, the teacher should summarize the error patterns. However, many errors will not have a pattern, and a pattern of errors does not mean that there is a serious problem. Error analysis is only one form of assessment; teachers should always conduct further evaluation, such as CBM and progress monitoring, of the student's work.

Cloze Procedures

The cloze procedure is generally used to determine whether reading material is within a student's ability. The teacher selects a passage to be read and reproduces it, leaving out every fifth word. The assumption of the technique is that if the student can fill in the blanks, the reading is within the student's ability. Some alternatives to using the fifth-word rule are the following:

- The teacher decides which words to omit.
- The teacher can read orally and ask the student to fill in the missing word.
- Blanks can be left so that various parts of speech are omitted (Rhodes & Shanklin, 1993).

Think-Alouds

A think-aloud is the verbalization of a student's thoughts about a text before, during, or after reading. Think-alouds provide insight into the student's comprehension abilities and thinking processes. For example, before beginning to read a story about immigrants in the United States, the teacher could ask, "What do you think that this story will be about?" or "What do you already know about immigrants?" During the reading, the student might verbalize, "I don't know that word" or "My mother told me about that." After reading, the student might say, "I didn't understand that" or "That was hard."

When eliciting think-alouds, teachers can use the following procedures:

1. Ask students to think aloud while they are reading. Explain that thinking aloud will help students to understand the text.
2. Indicate where the student should stop reading to think aloud.
3. Model how a think-aloud is done.
4. While the student is thinking aloud, record the student's comments.
5. Analyze the think-aloud for patterns, such as the use of context clues, substitutions, misunderstandings, inferences, use of information, and the addition of information to the text.

Retelling

Retelling is a comprehension exercise in which the student retells as much of a text as can be remembered after reading it. Retelling provides considerable information about comprehension. The following procedures are useful in retelling:

1. Tell the student that you will request a retelling at the end of the reading.
2. Once the student has finished reading, request the retelling.
3. Record the retelling.
4. Once the student has finished the retelling, ask if there is anything else that the student would like to add.
5. At this point, you can choose to ask questions or use prompts to elicit additional information.
6. Use a checklist or record form to analyze the retelling for patterns and trends in knowledge of story structure, story elements, use of details, and use of language.

Oral Descriptions

Verbal descriptions of a student's work can provide immediate feedback to a student by a teacher or peer. Oral descriptions are useful because they are quick, efficient, and direct, and they integrate easily into instruction. They are adaptable for program planning and program evaluation. An example of providing oral feedback to a student who has just completed reading a passage is: "You did a nice job recognizing when words didn't make sense. You understood the events that occurred in the passage and retold the story with only two prompts." Oral descriptions do have several drawbacks, however. They are subjective, and because the descriptions are given verbally, there is no permanent record. In addition, specific disabilities may limit the ability of the student to understand, remember, or reply to what has been said.

Written Descriptions

A written description is a brief narrative that records feedback about the student's work, and teachers can share it with the student, other teachers, or parents. A written description, like an oral description, conveys an impression of important aspects of the student's work. Written descriptions are also useful for program planning and program evaluation.

Before writing the narrative, the teacher should carefully review what the student has accomplished. The teacher then writes the description, noting areas of strength as well as problem areas. Such written description provides feedback to the student about the quality of the student's reading. Because it is recorded, the student can refer to it and can also share it with other teachers or family. The disadvantage of using written descriptions arises when parents have difficulty reading or do not have knowledge of written English.

My Beliefs About Reading

1. I like to go to school	most of the time	sometimes	never
2. I like to read	books	magazines	newspapers
3. I like to read the following types of stories	fiction adventure	science science fiction	history/politics biography/autobiography
4. I like to read at home	most of the time	sometimes	never
5. I talk with my friends about what I read	most of the time	sometimes	never
6. I think I am a good reader	most of the time	sometimes	never
7. Some books that I like to read are:			

FIGURE 11.1 • Checklist for Assessing Attitudes, Interests, and Habits

Checklists and Questionnaires

Checklists and questionnaires are convenient ways to provide information about a student's work. A checklist is a procedure that a teacher can complete quickly. Figure 11.1 is an example of a checklist for students; it provides feedback to parents and teachers about students' reading habits and attitudes. Figure 11.2 is a checklist for gathering information about students' knowledge of books. Checklists are useful for screening, diagnosis, program planning, and program evaluation.

Student's Name _____ Date _____

Teacher's Name _____

Directions: Show a book that is unfamiliar to the student. Ask the student to tell you about the book.

Concept	Demonstrates	Does Not Demonstrate	Observations
1. front			
2. back			
3. title			
4. author			
5. letters			
6. words			
7. pictures			
8. page numbers			
9. punctuation			

FIGURE 11.2 • Checklist for Assessing Knowledge of Books

Name _____   Date _____

Child's Name _____   Grade _____

Parent Interview

1. How do you think your child is doing as a reader/writer? Why? (If a young child: What signs have you seen that your child is ready to learn to read/write?)

   _____
   _____
   _____
   _____

2. What would you like your child to do as a reader/writer that he or she isn't doing now?

   _____
   _____
   _____
   _____

3. Do you ever notice your child reading/writing at home? Tell me about it.

   _____
   _____
   _____
   _____

4. What do you think your child's attitude is toward reading/writing? What do you think has helped to create this attitude?

   _____
   _____
   _____
   _____

5. What sorts of questions about your role in helping your child become a better reader/writer might you like to ask me?

   _____
   _____
   _____
   _____

6. Because I like to help the children read and write about things they are interested in, it helps me to know each individual child's interests. What kinds of things does your child like to do in his or her free time?

   _____
   _____
   _____
   _____

7. Is there anything about the child's medical history that might affect his or her reading/writing? Is there anything else that might affect his or her reading/writing?

   _____
   _____
   _____
   _____

8. Is there anything else that you think would be helpful for me to know in teaching your child?

   _____
   _____
   _____
   _____

FIGURE 11.2 • *(Continued)*

Source: Based on "Parent Interview" by Lynn K. Rhodes. Reprinted by permission from *Literary Assessment: A Handbook of Instruments,* edited by Lynn K. Rhodes.

	Marking Period			
	First	Second	Third	Fourth
READING				
Level at which child is working				
Phonics and word attack skills				
Word recognition				
Comprehension				
Reference skills				
Oral reading				
Independent reading				
Completes assignments				
Demonstrates effort				
SPELLING				
Knowledge of spelling words				
Application of spelling skills in written work				
Completes assignments				
Demonstrates effort				
LANGUAGE				
Correctly uses language mechanics (punctuation, capitalization, etc.)				
Grammar (word usage/sentence structure)				
Demonstrates creative written expression				
Oral expression				
Completes assignments				
Demonstrates effort				
HANDWRITING				
Conforms to letter form, size, spacing, and slant				
Writes legibly and neatly in daily work				
Demonstrates effort				

FIGURE 11.2 • *(Continued)*

Source: Based on *Windows into Literacy: Assessing Learners K–8*. by Lynn K. Rhodes and Nancy L. Shanklin © 1993 by Lynn K. Rhodes and Nancy L. Shanklin.

Questionnaires provide an opportunity for teachers and students to collect information in more detail than they can with checklists. Open-ended questionnaires allow respondents to express their attitudes, opinions, and knowledge in depth. Structured questionnaires ask only that the student fill in one or two words or circle a response.

Interviews

There are special considerations when using interviews in reading assessment. Interviews are helpful when guiding discussions, encouraging students, and determining reading attitudes and habits. One basic approach is to interview students individually about their likes and dislikes. Asking questions such as "What do you like about reading?" "What are your interests?" or "What don't you like?" can be informative. Interviews are also useful for screening, diagnosis, program planning, and program evaluation.

Conferences

A conference is a conversation about the student's work that can include the student, educators, and parents. In a conference, participants share their views of the student's work with the goal of providing feedback and recommendations. Teacher–student conferences are helpful when assessing the student's reading ability. The discussion in a conference can be strictly verbal, or it can be recorded or summarized in written form. Conferences are useful for diagnosis, program planning, and program evaluation.

Students' Journals, Notebooks, and Blogs

Students can keep a notebook, journal, or blog that allows them to record their work as well as their attitudes and feelings about reading and what they have read. In a journal, students can indicate what they like and don't like about reading and list areas in which they have difficulty. A journal provides students the opportunity to reflect on their reading, to communicate about their learning, and to document their progress. Journals can be used for program planning and program evaluation. The following is a sample reading journal outline:

> What I read today: Antarctica and climate change (http://www.antarctica.ac.uk).
>
> Two important ideas: atmosphere is getting warmer; melting glaciers and ice sheets contribute to a rise in the sea level.
>
> What I liked best about the passage or story: resources for further study, including the work of scientists in Antarctica, videos, Web-based maps, images, and webcams about Antarctica.
>
> What I didn't like about the passage or story: I liked everything about the story.
>
> What the author was telling us: although a great deal of information is already known about Antarctica, there is much more that scientists need to learn.

Performance-Based Assessments

When measuring reading ability, performance-based assessment refers to the demonstration of reading and writing abilities, skills, and behavior. Performance-based assessment requires students to demonstrate that they can read a passage or story for a purpose; use one or more cognitive skills as they construct meaning from the text; and write about what they read, usually in response to a prompt or task. This assessment approach is useful in program planning and program evaluation. The following are examples of performance tasks teachers might ask students to undertake after reading a book or story:

- Write a poem.
- Use software to draw and caption pictures.

- Build a model.
- Develop a story map.
- Write a review for the class blog.
- Interview the author or a character in the story.
- Engage in a discussion with a peer, teacher, or other adult.
- Write a message about the book and send it to the teacher.
- Create a sculpture, diorama, or object that conveys an interpretation of a reading.
- Write a report about a subject related to the story.
- Adapt a nonfiction article or book to fiction.
- Write lyrics to a song.
- Write a play or a scenario.

Portfolios

A portfolio is a deliberate collection of a student's work that demonstrates the student's efforts, progress, and achievement. When documenting and assessing reading ability, portfolios provide information about reading, skills, comprehension, attitudes toward reading, work habits, and written communication abilities. Portfolios in literacy assessment are useful for program planning and program evaluation. Chapter 15 provides a more extensive discussion of the applications of portfolios.

A portfolio is not just a folder of worksheets or of all the work that the student has completed. Selecting the pieces to include in the portfolio requires careful consideration. The following are suggestions for inclusion in student portfolios:

- Writing samples collected over time
- Digital representations of student projects
- Student logs
- Projects that involve students in portraying characters or plot
- Blogs in which students record their thoughts about what they have read
- Written dialogues between the student and teacher
- Video or audio recordings of students reading
- Video recordings of students conferencing with each other
- Teacher-developed measures
- Anecdotal records
- Student think-alouds

Exhibitions

An exhibition is a display of a student's work that demonstrates knowledge, abilities, skills, and attitudes concerning one project or a unit of work. An exhibition offers an opportunity to summarize and to synthesize the student's accomplishments. In reading and writing assessment, exhibitions are valuable because students can realize that reading and writing involves integration, understanding, problem solving, and reasoning. This tool is useful for program planning and program evaluation. Examples of exhibitions in reading and writing include the following:

- Online exhibits
- Storyboards
- Series of messages to other children
- Diary of one of the characters in the story
- Reviews of related online sites, books, videos, images, and recordings
- Dialogues among the characters
- Maps depicting the travels of the characters

Student's Name _____			Date _____		
After reading the story, I:	1 Great!	2	3	4	5 Darn!
1. understand the assignment.					
2. believe that I can restate the assignment.					
3. feel that I can complete the assignment in a timely manner.					
4. feel that I am a usually successful reader.					

FIGURE 11.3 • Self-Assessment Checklist

Self-Assessment

Self-assessment provides students with an opportunity to analyze their own reading and writing. It is an occasion for students to reflect on their learning. Figure 11.3 is an example of a checklist that students use when assessing their own learning.

Peer Assessment

Peer assessment allows students insight into the reading and writing abilities of their peers. Students have an opportunity to reflect on others' learning processes and strategies as well as on their own. Figure 11.4 is an example of a checklist that students use when conducting a peer assessment.

Student's Name _____ Date _____

Peer's Name _____

	☹	😐	🙂
1. My peer understood the story.			
2. My peer understood the assignment.			
3. My peer completed the assignment.			
4. My peer conferenced with me.			
5. My peer's work is neat.			

FIGURE 11.4 L Peer Assessment Checklist

Standardized Instruments

Gray Oral Reading Tests–Fifth Edition

The *Gray Oral Reading Tests–Fifth Edition* (GORT-5; Wiederholt & Bryant, n.d.) is an individually administered norm-referenced test of reading comprehension and oral reading for individuals ages 6 years through 23 years, 11 months. The test assesses reading rate, accuracy, fluency, and comprehension.

ADMINISTRATION   For each passage, the examiner reads one or two sentences that provide motivation. After reading each passage orally, the student responds to five multiple-choice questions that the examiner reads aloud. The examiner records the student's responses.

TESTS-at-a-GLANCE

Gray Oral Reading Tests–Fifth Edition (GORT-5)
http://www.pearsonclinical.com/education/products/100000106/gray-oral-reading-test-fifth-edition-gort-5.html

- **Purpose:** Measures reading comprehension and oral reading.
- **Age/Grade Levels:** Ages 6 years through 23 years, 11 months.
- **Time to Administer:** 15 to 45 minutes.
- **Technical Adequacy:** Evidence of reliability and validity is adequate. Test items should be examined by the evaluator to determine congruence with reading instruction.
- **Suggested Use:** Measures oral reading skills. Caution should be used because many students attain higher reading comprehension scores when reading silently rather than aloud.

SCORING   The test reports scores as age and grade equivalents; percentiles; standard scores for the total scores for rate, accuracy, and comprehension; and an oral reading comprehension score.

STANDARDIZATION   Normative data were collected in 2008 through 2010.

SNAPSHOT

Assessment of Reading

Ravi is in fifth grade. He is a motivated student who wants to be engaged in learning. Ravi reads on the primer level. He cannot recall letter–sound associations. He has received support in the regular classroom and resource room since first grade. Despite this support, his reading and written language skills continue to lag considerably behind his peers.

At times, he may lose focus on schoolwork. Although Ravi can understand information that is given verbally and he can recall key concepts, he has so much difficulty reading that he is unable to keep up with other students. Ravi is embarrassed about not being able to read and write, and he is reluctant to ask for help.

The *Gray Oral Reading Test–Fifth Edition*, a standardized reading test, was administered to Ravi in two separate sessions to determine specific strengths and weaknesses. During the session, Ravi tried hard, but it was evident that he experiences frustration when asked to read.

Ravi has considerable difficulty in accuracy, fluency, and reading comprehension. Decoding is delayed, and he is unable to use context clues to figure out new words. He frequently confuses letters such as *b/d* and *m/w*. His reading comprehension has declined because he does not have the appropriate decoding skills. He guesses at words based on the context, but the guesses are not accurate.

Gray Oral Reading Test-Fifth Edition

Subtest	April 10, 2XXX		
	Standard Score	Percentile Rank	Grade Equivalent
Rate	4	2	3.4
Accuracy	2	<1	2.0
Fluency Score	1	<1	2.7
Comprehension Score	4	2	

Ravi's teachers determined that careful and close instruction and monitoring are required to build reading skills and abilities. Attention should be focused on a balanced approach that includes phonological awareness; phonics; reading and decoding strategies; sight-word development; practice with controlled reading materials; and integration of reading instruction into content areas, including mathematics, science, and social studies. Ravi's teachers should consider the integration of technology to support reading development and comprehension.

> **TESTS-at-a-GLANCE**
>
> **Test of Reading Comprehension–Fourth Edition (TORC-4)**
> www.pearsonclinical.com
> - **Publication Date:** 2004
> - **Purpose:** Measures vocabulary and reading comprehension.
> - **Age/Grade Levels:** Ages 7 years through 17 years 11 months.
> - **Time to Administer:** 1 to 3 hours, depending on the age of the student.
> - **Technical Adequacy:** Evidence of reliability and validity is adequate. Test items should be examined by the evaluator to determine congruence with reading instruction.
> - **Suggested Use:** Measuring vocabulary; indicates strengths and weaknesses in silent reading comprehension.
> - **Summary:** The *Test of Reading Comprehension–Fourth Edition*, is a norm-referenced test of vocabulary and reading comprehension. Evidence of reliability and validity is adequate. However, the teacher should examine the test items to determine congruence with the school curriculum.

RELIABILITY In general, the reliability coefficients are adequate.

VALIDITY For the most part, the *GORT-5* bases concurrent validity on the *GORT-4*.

SUMMARY The *GORT-5* is an individually administered norm-referenced test of reading comprehension and oral reading. The standardization is adequate. Although the reliability is acceptable, additional evidence of validity is needed.

Test of Reading Comprehension–Fourth Edition

The *Test of Reading Comprehension–Fourth Edition* (*TORC-4*; Brown, Hammill, & Wiederholt, 2009) is an individually administered, norm-referenced test of vocabulary and silent reading comprehension for students ages 7 years through 17 years 11 months. The *TORC-4* contains five subtests:

Relational Vocabulary. The student reads three words and then selects two other words that relate to the three words.

Sentence Completion. The student reads a sentence that contains two missing words and chooses the best word pair to complete the sentence.

Paragraph Construction. After reading sentences that are not in logical order, the student rearranges the sentences to form a sound paragraph.

Text Comprehension. The student reads a brief passage and answers multiple-choice questions.

Contextual Fluency. Students are asked to read as many words as possible within 3 minutes as the words increase in complexity.

ADMINISTRATION The *TORC-4* is individually administered. However, teachers can administer it to small groups of students.

SCORING Raw scores convert to age and grade equivalents, percentiles, and standard scores.

STANDARDIZATION *TORC-4* is the fourth edition of the *TORC*, originally published in 1968. This fourth edition was renormed during 2006–2007. The test manual reports demographic information about the students who participated in the standardization sample.

RELIABILITY The test reports test-retest and internal consistency reliability coefficients. Reliability for the *TORC-4* is adequate.

VALIDITY The test reports content and criterion-related validity. Teachers should examine the test items to determine alignment with instruction.

Woodcock Reading Mastery Test—Revised/Normative Update

The *Woodcock Reading Mastery Test–Revised/Normative Update* (*WRMT-R/NU*; Woodcock, 1998) is an individually administered test of reading skills and reading comprehension for individuals from age 5 (kindergarten) through age 75. The *WRMT-R/NU* consists of six tests arranged in clusters. The Visual-Auditory Learning and Letter Identification tests compose the Readiness Cluster. The Word Identification and Word Attack tests form the Basic Skills Cluster, and the Word Comprehension and Passage Comprehension tests constitute the Reading Comprehension Cluster. Form G of the test includes a Supplementary Letter Checklist. The following list describes each of the tests.

> *Visual-Auditory Learning.* The student looks at rebuses representing words and must "read" the rebuses.
>
> *Letter Identification.* The student looks at upper- and lowercase letters of the alphabet and must name each of the letters.
>
> *Supplementary Letter Checklist (Form G only).* The student must recognize and name letters in sans-serif type.
>
> *Word Identification.* The student must read single words that are in the test.
>
> *Word Attack.* The student must demonstrate a knowledge of phonics and word attack skills by pronouncing nonsense syllables.
>
> *Word Comprehension.* This subtest is composed of three parts: Antonyms, Synonyms, and Analogies. The student must connect words according to these categories.
>
> *Passage Comprehension.* The student reads a brief passage and supplies the missing words.

ADMINISTRATION   The *WRMT-R/NU* is administered individually.

SCORING   Raw scores are converted to standard scores, percentiles, and age and grade equivalents. In addition, there is a relative performance index (RPI) that provides an estimate of expected performance. The *WRMT-R/NU* scoring forms include visual profiles for describing performance.

STANDARDIZATION   For the 1998 edition, test publishers did not collect new norms, but they reanalyzed existing standardization data. The school-age sample data are from 1983 to 1985. The college and university sample data are from 1984 through 1985. Adult data are from 1984 through 1985. The standardization sample represents age, gender, region, race, ethnicity, and economic status as estimated by parental education. The standardization sample of the *WRMT-R/NU* forms a link with the standardization samples for the *Kaufman Test of Achievement (KTEA/NU)*, the *Peabody Individual Achievement Test-Revised/NU (PIAT-R/NU)*, and the *KeyMath-R*. The renorming sample for the *WRMT-R/NU* consisted of students age 5 (kindergarten) through age 22. There is no update for the sample of individuals over the age of 22. For the linking sample, the test examinees in the norm sample took one of the complete test batteries and one or more subtests from another battery. This linking approach permits the comparisons of test performance across batteries.

RELIABILITY   Test publishers report internal consistency reliability coefficients only for grades 1, 3, 5, 8, and

---

TESTS-at-a-GLANCE

Woodcock Reading Mastery Test-Revised/NU (WRMT-R/NU)

http://www.pearsonclinical.com/education/products/100000647/woodcock-reading-mastery-tests-revised-normative-update-wrmt-r-nu.html

- **Publication Date:** 1998
- **Purposes:** Measures reading readiness, reading skills, and reading comprehension.
- **Age/Grade Levels:** Age 5 (kindergarten) through adulthood.
- **Time to Administer:** 30 to 50 minutes.
- **Technical Adequacy:** For the 1998 edition, new norms were not collected. Existing standardization data were reanalyzed. Reliability is adequate. Validity is acceptable; however, teachers should examine the test items to determine the extent to which the items assess the curriculum taught. Many of the test items reflect a skills approach to learning to read.
- **Suggested Use:** As a limited measure of overall reading achievement. Examiners should evaluate the test items because the test does not reflect contemporary approaches to the teaching of literacy. The NU edition does not update the norms. There is some question about the validity of the test in view of current approaches to teaching literacy.

SNAPSHOT

Joseph

Joseph is in the ninth grade at the Creative Arts Charter School. Although he is a very capable student and a talented artist, his school achievement is considerably below expectations. Joseph and his family have moved several times, and this is the third school in which he has been enrolled in the past two years. At a recent parent–teacher meeting with Mr. Holmes, Joseph's teacher, and Kayla Smith, Joseph's mother, Mr. Holmes expressed concerns about Joseph's school performance.

Joseph's school attendance is a concern, and homework is rarely completed. Joseph appears to be reluctant to complete reading assignments for language arts, social studies, and science. A recent report by the school psychologist indicated that Joseph is experiencing difficulties in organization, concentration, attention, and self-esteem.

Mr. Holmes reviewed Joseph's performance on the *Woodcock Reading Mastery Tests-NU*, which the school's learning strategist had recently administered to Joseph. Joseph had difficulty with the Word Identification and Word Attack subtests. He often lost his place and added or omitted syllables. He was unable to apply common phonics rules. For some words, he pronounced them one syllable at a time.

On the Passage Comprehension subtest, Joseph responded acceptably when he was able to read the words in the passages. But he made errors when he was unable to decode words or determine the correct syntax for missing words.

Mr. Holmes commented that because Joseph struggles with reading, he is discouraged. Assignments in the content areas are frustrating, and Joseph's motivation has decreased. Mr. Holmes related that Joseph's team had met to identify interventions that would lead to school success. The interventions will concentrate on phonics, vocabulary building, fluency, and strategies for comprehending expository and narrative texts. Can you suggest other steps that should be explored?

11, and for adults. The coefficients are in the .80s and .90s. Test-retest reliability coefficients are not available.

VALIDITY The manual provides evidence of content validity. The test reports concurrent validity with the *Woodcock-Johnson Psychoeducational Battery–Revised*. The WRMT-R/NU uses a traditional, somewhat outdated approach to reading. Evidence to support the validity of the clusters is lacking. Examiners should carefully review the test to determine the correspondence between test items and the literacy curriculum.

SUMMARY The *WRMT-R/NU* is an individually administered test of reading skills and reading comprehension for individuals from kindergarten through adulthood, consisting of six tests in three clusters. The *NU* edition does not update the norms. There is some question about the validity of the test in view of current approaches to teaching literacy.

Summary

- The assessment of literacy must reflect the integral link between reading and written language and produce results useful in teaching and learning.
- Because reading and writing instruction varies considerably throughout the United States, it is important to select assessment instruments carefully that best match the curriculum.
- Progress in reading is achieved when key approaches—curriculum-based assessment, curriculum-based measurement, progress monitoring, and performance-based and informal measures and tools—are used.
- Evaluators should use the results of individual standardized tests of reading cautiously.
- Teachers should conduct assessments routinely and use multiple approaches. The slogan for the assessment of literacy is "multiple, multiple, and frequent"—use multiple approaches, use multiple instruments, and assess frequently!

QUESTIONS FOR REFLECTION

1. Can you suggest several technologies that you use frequently that provide access to electronic texts and media, communication, learning, and productivity? How should technological literacy be assessed?
2. The International Reading Association (IRA) has published resources on the assessment and teaching of reading. Visit IRA's Web site at **www.reading.org** and identify information on reading assessment.
3. Examine a norm-referenced standardized reading test. Explain how this test provides information about reading skills and abilities.
4. There are many Web-based resources on curriculum-based measurement. Using a Web browser, search for these resources using one or more of the following search terms: "curriculum-based assessment" and "curriculum-based measurement."
5. Develop two assessment tasks that link instruction in reading directly to assessment of reading.
6. As part of mandated statewide testing programs, many states allow school districts to submit alternative assessment portfolios for students with disabilities. Research the assessment guidelines that individual states require.
7. Develop guidelines for assembling portfolios that are used to assess student progress and communicate progress to parents. What should be included? Who should make the decision about contents? Teachers? Parents? Students?
8. Consider developing several guides that gather information about students. You can choose to develop a checklist or rating scale that assesses students' attitudes and habits in reading. A second choice is to develop an interview guide for use by parents to assess students' reading attitudes and habits at home.

REFERENCES

Bell, S., & McCallum, R. S. (2008). *Handbook of reading assessment*. Upper Saddle River, NJ: Pearson.

Brown, V. L., Hammill, D. D., & Wiederholt, J. L. (2009). *Test of reading comprehension 4*. Austin, TX: PRO-ED.

Cummings, K., Baker, D., & Good, R. (2007). *Indicadores Dinámicos del Éxito en la Lectura, 7a edición*. Eugene, OR: Institute of the Development of Educational Achievement.

Good, R. H., & Kaminski, R. A. (2006). *Dynamic indicators of basic literacy skills* (6th ed.). Eugene, OR: Institute for the Development of Educational Achievement. Available from http://dibels.uoregon.edu

Hosp, M., & Hosp, J. (2003). Curriculum-based measurement for reading, spelling, and math: How to do it and why. *Preventing School Failure, 48*(1), 10–17.

Hosp, M., Hosp, J., & Howell, K. (2007). *The ABCs of CBM: A practical guide to curriculum-based measurement*. New York: Guilford.

International Reading Association. (2003). *On literacy assessment*. Retrieved on June 17, 2009, from http://www.reading.org

McKenna, M., & Picard, M. (2006). Revisiting the role of miscue analysis in effective teaching. *The Reading Teacher, 60*(4), 378–380.

National Institute of Child Health and Human Development. (2000). *Report of the National Reading Panel. Teaching children to read: An evidence-based assessment of the scientific research literature on reading and its implications for reading instruction* (NIH Publication No. 00-4769). Washington, DC: U.S. Government Printing Office. Retrieved June 7, 2009, from http://www.nationalreadingpanel.org

Rhodes, L. K., & Shanklin, N. (1993). *Windows into literacy: Assessing learners K–8*. Portsmouth, NH: Heinemann.

Salvia, J., Ysseldyke, J., & Bolt, S. (2013). *Assessment in special and inclusive education*. Belmont, CA: Wadsworth, Cengage Learning.

Singleton, C. (2005). Dyslexia and oral reading errors. *Journal of Research in Reading, 28*(1), 4–14.

U.S. Department of Education. (2008). *National Center on Student Progress Monitoring*. Retrieved December 21, 2009, from http://www.studentprogress.org

Wiederholt, L., & Bryant, B. (n.d.). *Gray oral reading test–5*. San Antonio, TX: Pearson.

Woodcock, R. (1998). *Woodcock reading mastery tests—revised/normative update*. Circle Pines, MN: American Guidance Service.

12 Written Language

Chapter Objectives

After completing this chapter, you should be able to:

- Describe how the following approaches can be used to assess written language: curriculum-based assessment, curriculum-based measurement, performance-based approach, and informal approaches.
- Explain the use of standardized achievement tests in the assessment of written language.

Overview

Contemporary instructional practices stress the integral link between reading and writing for both instruction and assessment. In the previous chapter, we discussed approaches to the assessment of literacy, with an emphasis on the assessment of reading. This chapter continues this discussion and highlights the assessment of written language.

Communication is critical to human growth and development and is a prerequisite to academic learning. Communication involves the exchange of information between individuals and may involve written language, spoken language, gestures, signs, signals, or other behaviors.

Some teachers stress close association between the development of reading and writing and view the development of written language as a process. Other teachers may focus on topic development, organization, use of details, and language and writing style. Still other teachers may emphasize the development of specific skills such as correct spelling, punctuation, capitalization, and grammar. Assessment of written language can inform instruction by providing information on students' skills and abilities.

Assessing written language usually means making a direct connection between reading and writing and following these principles:

1. Assess reading and writing in various contexts. Reading and writing vary with the context. Contexts relate to the types of reading materials, the purpose of the writing, and

the strategies that students use. An understanding of students' reading and writing abilities must consider the contexts in which reading and writing occur.
2. Assess the literacy environment, instruction, and the students. Reading and writing assessment must consider environments in which reading and writing occur, types of instruction, and student factors.
3. Assess processes and products of writing. The assessment of writing processes as well as the products can provide a comprehensive understanding of students' abilities.
4. Analyze error patterns. Understanding the patterns of errors in writing improves student performance.
5. Include the assessment of background knowledge. Experience, prior learning, and background knowledge influence reading and writing performance.
6. Consider developmental patterns in reading and writing. Knowledge of typical developmental patterns in reading and writing contributes to our understanding of reading and writing abilities.
7. Use sound principles of assessment. Employ sound principles or standards when assessing students. These standards apply to reliability, validity, observation, and scoring, all of which were discussed in previous chapters.
8. Use triangulation. Triangulation signifies that conclusions about student performance are the result of multiple (here, at least three) sources of information. In turn, teachers should corroborate information about students by using several sources of data. Teachers must proceed with considerable caution when drawing conclusions about students and using only one source of information.
9. Include students, parents, teachers, and other school personnel in the assessment process. The involvement of students, parents, and other educators in the assessment process ensures the inclusion of multiple perspectives.
10. Assessment activities should be ongoing. Assessment activities can inform instruction best when they occur frequently and routinely.
11. Record, analyze, and use assessment information. Record assessment data frequently, analyze it, and use it on a routine basis to guide and drive instruction.

Connecting Assessment With Instruction

Most experts in literacy believe that standardized, norm-referenced tests of written language have a number of shortcomings, which are summarized in Table 12.1. Assessment of written language abilities and skills must form a direct link with instruction. Linking instruction to assessment in reading and written language means that:

- Assessment occurs as a normal part of the student's work. Assessment activities should emerge from the teaching and learning situation. Examples of this type of assessment include the use of journals, notebooks, essays, oral reports, homework, classroom discussions, group work, blogs, and interviews. These assessment activities can occur individually or in small groups and can take place during one session or over multiple sessions.
- The conditions for assessment are similar to the conditions for doing meaningful tasks. Students should have sufficient time, have access to peers, be able to use appropriate literacy materials, and have the chance to revise their work.
- Assessment tasks are meaningful and multidimensional. They should provide students with the opportunity to demonstrate a variety of writing abilities and skills.
- Feedback to students is specific, meaningful, and prompt and informs the students' work.

TABLE 12.1 • Shortcomings of Standardized, Norm-Referenced Tests

Norm-Referenced Tests of Written Language	Theories of Written Contemporary Language Assessment
Assess writing abilities separately from reading abilities	Link the assessment of writing with the reading abilities assessment of reading
Fail to tap background knowledge	Encourage the writer to use background knowledge while writing
Emphasize skills (spelling, punctuation, writing processes, capitalization, grammar, etc.)	Assess a variety of writing processes
May show bias in the questions	Demonstrate equitable assessment strategies
Present multiple-choice questions	Present open-ended questions
Do not assess writing attitudes and habits	Assess writing attitudes and habits
Show few or no direct links to instruction	Link assessment tools directly to instruction

- Students participate in the assessment process. They help to generate and apply standards or rubrics. Self-assessment and peer assessment are part of the assessment process.

Ways in which the teacher can gather information and provide feedback to parents and students include the following:

- Curriculum-based measurement
- Criterion-referenced assessment
- Probes
- Error analysis
- Oral descriptions
- Written descriptions
- Checklists and questionnaires
- Interviews
- Conferences
- Digital media
- Performance-based assessment
- Portfolios
- Exhibitions
- Self-assessment
- Peer assessment

Curriculum-Based Measurement

Curriculum-Based Measurement of Written Language

Curriculum-based measurement (CBM) of written language is consistent with the procedures described in the previous chapters on assessing overall achievement and assessing literacy. CBM is optimally used repeatedly and frequently to monitor teaching and learning. The teacher constructs or retrieves several writing prompts or story starters about which the student can choose to write. A different prompt is used for every repeated assessment. For example, the teacher may use one of the following story starters (or may search for others):

- "In the middle of the night, I was jolted awake by a sudden noise."
- "It's a beautiful day to start a new adventure."
- "Yesterday, I received an unusual message."
- "I enjoy using technology to connect with my friends."
- "As I walked down the path, I was startled to see a strange sight."

The teacher asks the student to select from three story-starter choices and allows 1 minute to think about the prompt. Next, the teacher asks the student to write, either using a pencil and paper or software, for 3 minutes in response to the story starter. Finally, the teacher collects the student's response and scores it.

Keeping track of students' performance can aid in evaluating progress and targeting instruction. By repeating this process over time, the teacher can document progress. Scoring of curriculum-based measures of written language can occur in several ways (Hessler & Konrad, 2008):

- *Total words written.* The teacher can count the number of total words written. Students may be asked to count the total words and graph them.
- *Total words spelled correctly.* The number of words spelled correctly can be counted and graphed.
- *Correct writing sequences.* The number of contextually correct two-word sequences can be identified and graphed.

Other items that can be assessed include punctuation marks, capitalization, grammar, organization, word choice, and sentence variety.

Curriculum-Based Measurement of Spelling

CBMs in spelling can be constructed (Hosp & Hosp, 2003); they can aid in tracking students' progress, and teachers can focus on specific areas for improvement. An example of CBM in spelling was described in Chapter 2. Here is another example that describes how a CBM can be constructed in spelling:

- The teacher estimates the level of difficulty of spelling words according to frustration, instruction, and mastery levels and constructs or identifies a spelling list of about 10 to 15 words. The time for dictation should be approximately 2 minutes.
- The teacher dictates one word at a time while the student writes each word.
- Scoring can be done in two ways: (1) count the number of words spelled correctly, or (2) count the number of correct letter sequences (CLSs; Hosp & Hosp, 2003). A CLS is when the correct letters are written in the accurate sequence. For example, the word *pretty* has six CLSs, as illustrated in the following example:

$$\char`^p \char`^r \char`^e \char`^t \char`^t \char`^y \char`^$$

As with other CBMs, administration should be frequently repeated and graphed to track progress.

Criterion-Referenced Assessment

Teachers can create criterion-referenced tests in written language. Such teacher-developed criterion-referenced tests are useful for screening, determining eligibility, diagnosing

TABLE 12.2 • Written Language Tools for Progress Monitoring

Measure	Areas	Psychometric Standards		Progress Monitoring Characteristics				
		Reliability	Validity	Alternate Forms	Sensitivity to Students' Improvement	Curriculum Benchmarks	Improvement of Student Learning or Teacher Planning	Specification of Rates of Improvement
AIMSweb	Spelling	•	•	o	•	•	•	•
	Written expression	•	o	•	•	•	•	•

o Insufficient evidence
• Sufficient evidence
Source: Adapted from the U.S. Department of Education, retrieved December 21, 2009, from http://www.studentprogress.org

strengths and needs, program planning, progress monitoring, and program evaluation. For example, a teacher can enumerate spelling words that the student must spell correctly, can identify punctuation that the student must use accurately, or can list words that require correct capitalization to develop a criterion-referenced test.

Formal Measures for Monitoring Progress

Progress monitoring is essential for supporting students' written language achievement and evaluating the benefits of instruction. Similar to the assessment of reading, the U.S. Department of Education established criteria for determining the adequacy of progress-monitoring measures: reliability, validity, alternate forms, sensitivity to students' improvement, alignment with curriculum standards or benchmarks, evidence for improvement of students' learning or teacher planning, and specification of rates of improvement (U.S. Department of Education, n.d.). The only formal progress-monitoring measure that meets the standards established by the U.S. Department of Education is the AIMSweb (see Table 12.2).

Informal Approaches

Probes

A probe is a diagnostic technique that can be especially useful in diagnosing student problems and in planning instruction in written language. For example, suppose a teacher wants to determine whether a student has considered feedback from peers when revising a writing sample. The teacher can review the student's written draft, inquire about the use of peer feedback (in this example, the probe, which allows the teacher to observe how the student responds to peer feedback), and assist the student in incorporating peer feedback into a revision of the draft.

Error Analysis

The purposes of error analysis are to (1) identify the patterns of errors or mistakes that students make in their work, (2) understand why students make the errors, and (3) provide instruction to correct the errors. A systematic approach to error analysis helps both the student and the teacher identify errors and correct them.

A checklist, developed by the teacher, the student, or through collaboration, can be helpful in identifying errors. Figure 12.1 is an example of a checklist that Toni, a sixth grader, developed with her teacher to help Toni with editing.

Spelling

Error analysis is important in the development of spelling. Spelling evaluation should be part of the process of developing written language rather than a finished product. Teachers should consider four principles in evaluating spelling (Wilde, 1989):

Checking and Correcting Work

Editing	Checked		Corrected	
	yes	no	yes	no
1. Grammar				
2. Periods				
3. Question marks				
4. Exclamation points				
5. Quotation marks				
6. Paragraphing				
7. Spelling				

FIGURE 12.1 • Toni's Editing Checklist

1. Evaluate spelling on the basis of natural writing rather than by tests of words in isolation.
2. Evaluate spelling analytically rather than as correct or incorrect.
3. Analyze spelling by discovering the strategies the student used in the context of writing.
4. As a matter of good professional practice in this area, learn about language development and about language disabilities and how they can affect the development of written language.

Questions to ask about a student's spelling include the following:

1. Is the word spelled as it sounds?
2. Is the spelling unusual?
3. Is the word a sight word?
4. Is the word a real word?
5. Is the word a "placeholder"?
6. Is a homophone used?
7. What strategies does a student use when the spelling is unknown?
   a. Writes down what it sounds like?
   b. Writes down what the student thinks the word looks like?
   c. Looks around the classroom to find the word?
   d. Thinks about parts of the word?
   e. Uses spelling rules?
   f. Uses a dictionary or spell checker?
   g. Asks someone for the correct spelling?
   h. Uses a personal spelling list?

Oral Descriptions

Verbal descriptions of a student's work provide immediate feedback to the student by a teacher or peer. Oral descriptions are quick, efficient, and direct, and they integrate easily into instruction. They should not be off-the-cuff expressions, however; they should be as well thought out as written descriptions. Oral descriptions are useful for program planning and program evaluation. An example of providing oral feedback to a student who has just completed writing a first draft is the following: "You did a nice job getting your ideas down. While developing your ideas, you consulted several sources and asked a peer for help with spelling."

Oral descriptions do have several drawbacks. They can be subjective, and there is no permanent record. In addition, specific disabilities may limit the ability of the student to understand, remember, or reply to them.

Written Descriptions

A written description is a brief narrative that records feedback about the student's work and that the student, other teachers, or parents can review. A written description, like an oral description or a conversation, conveys an impression of important aspects of students' work. When giving feedback, focus on the student's work and the processes used. Address strengths and areas for improvement. If possible, relate feedback to learning goals. Be descriptive, rather than judgmental. Stay positive and specific (Brookhart, 2007/2008).

Before writing the narrative, the teacher carefully reviews what the student has accomplished. The teacher should write the description, noting areas of strength as well as problem areas. A written description provides feedback to the student about the quality of the student's writing, and because it provides a record, the student can refer to it and share it with his or her family.

Checklists and Questionnaires

Checklists and questionnaires are convenient ways to provide feedback about a student's work. A checklist is fast and easy to complete. Questionnaires enable teachers and students to collect information in more detail than they can with checklists. Questionnaires can be open-ended, allowing respondents to express their attitudes, opinions, and knowledge in depth, or they can be structured so that the student just needs to fill in one or two words or to circle a response. Figure 12.3 is an example of an open-ended writing questionnaire.

Interviews

In Chapter 8 we discussed the topic of conducting interviews. There are special considerations when using this technique in the assessment of written language. Interviews are useful in developing ideas for writing, encouraging students, learning more about a student's written piece, and determining writing attitudes and habits. Asking questions such as the following can be informative: "What do you like about writing?" "Describe the process you use in developing a new piece of writing." "What are your interests?" "What don't you like?" Interviews are helpful for screening, diagnosis, program planning, and program evaluation.

Conferences

A conference is a conversation about the student's work that can include the student, educators, and/or parents. In a conference, participants share their views of the student's work with the goal of offering feedback and recommendations. Teacher–student conferences can be helpful when assessing the student's written language. The discussion can be strictly verbal, or it can be recorded electronically or summarized in written form. Conferences are useful for diagnosis, program planning, and program evaluation.

SNAPSHOT

Examples of Students' Written Work

Examining students' written work provides an opportunity to identify the skills, abilities, and processes that the student uses while developing the written piece. Figure 12.2 contains a checklist for use when providing feedback to students. The writing process breaks down into overlapping steps:

1. Writing authentic work. Students should have opportunities to engage in authentic writing. This means that when students write in school, they must write for the same reasons they write outside school. Students need to have control over their writing. They should have the necessary materials available, know how to use them, know the purposes for writing, and know how much time is available to them.

2. Rehearsing writing. Rehearsing means that students know what to expect and are able to choose the type of writing that is appropriate for the purpose. Rehearsing can involve drawing pictures, developing semantic webs, taking notes, and brainstorming.

3. Developing the first draft. Writing the first draft entails fluency, spelling, and rereading. Fluency is being able to put ideas into writing and having the thoughts flow. Spelling is a consideration in this step as well because, like writing, spelling is a process. Reading and rereading the draft are important because these steps allow the student to identify and correct errors and to elaborate ideas.

Writing Process

Student's Name _____ Date _____

Planning

To what extent does the writer think or plan before writing?

Does the writer use notes, mind maps, concept maps, outlines, or other tools during the planning process?

To what extent does the writer consult with others before writing?

To what extent does the writer use readings as a source of ideas?

To what extent does the writer help others develop ideas?

☐ Suggestions for improvement:

Developing the draft

To what extent is the writer able to put thoughts on paper?

Do the ideas flow?

Is the writer hindered due to punctuation, spelling, or grammar difficulties?

Does the writer's attitude support writing?

Does the writer proofread and make corrections to the written text?

To what extent does the writer use resources, such as grammar and spelling checkers, online dictionaries, thesaurus?

FIGURE 12.2 • Assessing the Writing Process

SNAPSHOT Continued

Revising and Finalizing the Draft

Does the writer elaborate or add information?

To what extent does the writer incorporate feedback?

Does the writer develop one or more introductions or endings to determine which is suitable?

To what extent is the writer able to edit:
   a. spelling
   b. capitalization
   c. punctuation
   d. grammar
   e. paragraphing

Is the writer willing to edit the draft?

To what extent have revisions and edits improved the written work?

☐ Suggestions for improvement:

FIGURE 12.2 • *(Continued)*

4. Conferencing with peers and/or teachers. Feedback from peers and/or teachers can yield important suggestions and ideas as the student develops the written piece.
5. Revising the written piece. Revising a piece of writing gives the student an opportunity to reflect on his or her own reading of it and on the feedback from peers and teachers. The student can choose to elaborate, clarify, take away information, make corrections, and change the sentence or paragraph structure.
6. Editing. Editing allows the student to make surface corrections to the written piece. This means making the piece conform to writing conventions. It also involves organization and ideas.
7. Producing and sharing the finished piece. The final piece can take various forms, depending on the purpose for writing. For example, the written piece may be a newspaper article, review of a story, poem, play, story, or report (Rhodes & Shanklin, 1993).
8. A potential problem with written descriptions is that parents who have difficulty reading or who do not have knowledge of written English are at a disadvantage.

Figure 12.3 is a checklist for use with students.

Pause and consider:
- Consider the checklist in Figure 12.3. Which items would you find most useful?
- What additional items can you suggest for inclusion in the checklist?
- In what ways could the checklist be used in combination with other forms of assessment?

What Kind of Writer I Am

1. Things I like to write at home (examples: notes, letters, poems, stories, etc.):
2. What other people think of my writing:
3. What I think of myself as a writer:
4. Things I like to write at school:
5. What I like about my writing:
6. What I don't like about my writing:

FIGURE 12.3 • Open-Ended Writing Questionnaire

Digital Media

Keeping a notebook, journal, online scrapbook, e-portfolio, or blog allows students to record their work as well as their attitudes and feelings about reading and writing. Journals, notebooks, blogs, and online communications can contain sample pieces the student has written as well as spontaneous types of entries. The following samples of written language can be part of a journal:

- Poems
- Short stories
- Writing fragments
- Student's comments about writing
- Log entries on specific topics
- Interdisciplinary writing
- Quotations from the student's readings
- Comments by peers or teachers

Performance-Based Assessment

Performance-based assessment of reading and writing abilities measures the integration of reading and writing and evaluates demonstrations of reading and writing abilities. Performance-based assessment requires students to read a passage or story for a purpose; use one or more cognitive skills as they construct meaning from the text; and write about what they read, usually in response to a prompt or task. Performance-based assessment can be used in program planning and program evaluation.

Portfolios

A portfolio, as we have discussed, is a deliberate collection of a student's work that demonstrates the student's efforts, progress, and achievement. When documenting and assessing written language ability, portfolios provide valuable information about reading, writing, spelling skills, comprehension, attitudes, and work habits. Portfolios in literacy assessment are useful for program planning and program evaluation. With the pervasiveness of technologies, there are many digital options available for collecting and displaying students' written works. See Chapter 15 for a more extensive discussion of portfolio use.

The following are suggestions for materials that students could include in student writing portfolios:

- Reports
- Student logs
- Plays
- Poems
- Lyrics to a song
- Creative writing
- Nonfiction writing
- Projects that involve students in portraying characters or plot

> **SNAPSHOT**
>
> **Pangea**
>
> Joy Kamena, a fifth-grade teacher, reviewed a writing sample developed by Yizhong, one of her students. Develop a checklist that she can use to analyze Yizhong's writing.
>
> **PANGEA**
>
> Pangea was the supercontinent that was made up of the seven other continents linked together. This explains how I think the continents dissembled themselves and how they got where they are today. South America, which was nestled in the curve of Africa, rotated 90° to the right and moved westward. North America above South America was connected to Europe with the middle part of Canada. This medium size continent made another 90° right turn and again moved to the west. After these continents unhooked themselves, Africa followed by moving southwest and detaching itself from Saudi Arabia and Europe. Now it was Australia's turn to slide out the Bengal bay and float southeast. Asia and Europe, which was the main link for Pangea, stayed where they were. This explains how continents moved with the continental drift.

- Journals in which students record their thoughts about what they have read
- Written dialogues between student and teacher

Exhibitions

An exhibition displays a student's work and demonstrates how the student combines knowledge, abilities, skills, and attitudes. This tool gives students the opportunity to summarize and synthesize their accomplishments. In reading and writing assessment, exhibitions are useful because students realize that reading and writing involves integration, understanding, problem solving, and reasoning. In this way, teachers have concrete information for program planning and program evaluation.

The elements of an exhibition that involve writing do not necessarily occur in a sequential order, but they are useful when thinking about the development of exhibitions:

- *Prompt:* A prompt is what teachers ask students to do. This can be as basic as "Write a research report about the city in which you live" or "Write a description of a new tool that would make a task easier," or it can be as comprehensive as "Develop an exhibition of your vision for the city of the future."
- *Vision:* A vision is what the exhibition will be like. For example, the exhibition on cities will include oral, written, and multimedia components that demonstrate students' skills and abilities to reflect on their learning, to analyze, to conduct research, and to synthesize. Teachers may ask students to integrate one or more disciplines, write reports, create multimedia presentations, and incorporate the arts.
- *Agreement on Standards:* Educators and students must agree on what makes an exhibition good. Various scoring systems or rubrics can assist in the evaluation of exhibitions.
- *Audience:* Students' work is exhibited to other students, educators, parents, and/or community members.
- *Coaching:* Peers and teachers should coach students toward the development of their exhibitions. Coaching, rather than evaluating, is important in the development phase of the exhibition.
- *Reflection:* All participants should reflect on their exhibitions. This allows the entire group of participants to develop an appreciation for what they have learned and accomplished. Reflection also provides an opportunity to think about how to do it better the next time.

Examples of exhibitions in reading and writing include the following:

- Storytelling
- Series of blog entries
- Journal entries by characters in the story
- Reviews of related books
- Dialogues among the characters
- Maps depicting the travels of the characters
- Videos

Self-Assessment

Self-assessment provides students with an opportunity to analyze their own writing and to reflect on their own learning. Figure 12.4 is an example of a questionnaire that students can use when assessing their own writing.

Peer Assessment

When conducting peer assessments, students have an opportunity to reflect on the writing processes, skills, and strategies of their peers as well as on their own writing processes, skills,

Student's Name _____ Date _____

Authentic Writing   **My Comments**
  1. I know my audience.
  2. I take risks when I write.

Rehearsal of Writing
  3. I think or plan ahead when I write.
  4. I consult with my peers.
  5. I use print and nonprint media as sources.
  6. I help others to write.

Developing the Draft
  7. I feel that I can put my thoughts down on paper.
  8. I have a good attitude toward writing.
  9. I am able to spell most words.
 10. I know which words to capitalize.
 11. I know how to use punctuation.
 12. I make changes to my text based on rereading.

Revising
 13. I incorporate feedback.
 14. I make changes, such as beginnings, transitions, and endings.

Editing
 15. I am willing to edit my draft.
 16. I am able to edit and correct spelling.
 17. I am able to edit and correct punctuation.
 18. I am able to edit and correct capitalization.
 19. I am able to edit and correct grammar.
 20. I am able to edit and correct paragraphing.

FIGURE 12.4 • Self-Assessment Checklist

and strategies. Figure 12.5 is an example of a checklist that students use when conducting a peer assessment.

Scoring

Teachers use two types of scoring, holistic and analytic, when evaluating writing samples, written products, portfolios, performance assessments, and exhibitions.

Holistic Scoring

Holistic scoring (see Figure 12.6) is a quick and efficient type of scoring. Holistic scoring produces one score that provides an impression of writing ability. Holistic scoring rests on the

	☹	😐	🙂
Student's Name _____ Date _____			
Peer's Name _____			
1. My peer writes for a purpose.			
2. My peer consulted me before writing.			
3. My peer made changes based on my feedback.			
4. My peer conferences with me.			
5. My peer uses transitions.			
6. My peer is able to edit the written text.			

FIGURE 12.5 • Peer Assessment Checklist

Holistic Scoring Guide—Writing

Score	Criteria
5	The paper is superb. The ideas are very well developed. If there are any errors in mechanics, grammar, or spelling, they are very minor. Sentence structure is very clear and varied. There is a clear sense of purpose and audience. Ideas are explained and very well supported.
4	The paper is very good. The ideas are very well developed. There are few errors in mechanics, grammar, or spelling. Sentence structure is clear and varied. There is a clear sense of purpose and audience. Ideas are explained and supported.
3	The paper is good. The ideas are well developed. There are some errors in mechanics, grammar, or spelling. Sentences follow a similar pattern. There is some sense of purpose or audience. Ideas are not always explained or supported.
2	The paper is moderate. Some ideas are developed. There are frequent errors in mechanics, grammar, or spelling. Sentences follow a similar pattern. There may be sentence fragments. There is little sense of purpose or audience. Ideas are infrequently explained or supported.
1	The paper is poor. Ideas are rarely developed. There are many errors in mechanics, grammar, or spelling. Sentences follow a similar pattern. There are sentence fragments. There is no sense of purpose or audience. Ideas are rarely explained or supported.

FIGURE 12.6 • Holistic Scoring

assumption that the entire elements of writing, such as organization, mechanics, and fluency, work together in the whole text. This type of scoring can be useful when the teacher is looking for one or two previously identified characteristics in a student's work. One important disadvantage of holistic scoring is that it does not provide detailed information about the success of the student in specific areas of writing.

Analytic Scoring

Analytic scoring (see Figure 12.7) is a type of scoring that produces a detailed analysis of the written text. The teacher uses a scale or rubric to assign points to different levels of performance in each of the assessed areas. For example, a teacher wants to describe the writing performance of students in organizing, using mechanics, and using paragraphing. The teacher rates the students' writing samples on a scale, from 1 to 5 or from 1 to 6, in each of these three areas, and the student receives three separate scores. Teachers should take care

Analytic Scoring—Writing

	1	2	3	4	5
Development of Ideas	Little understanding of audience; little elaboration of ideas	Some understanding of audience; some elaboration of ideas	Good understanding of audience; good elaboration of ideas	Very good understanding of audience; very good elaboration of ideas	Excellent understanding of audience; superb elaboration of ideas
Organization	No evidence of an organized plan for writing; ideas and paragraphs run together	Some evidence of an organized plan for writing; ideas and paragraphs are loosely organized	Good evidence of an organized plan for writing; ideas and paragraphs are organized	Very good evidence of an organized plan for writing; ideas and paragraphs are well organized	Excellent evidence of an organized plan for writing; ideas are original and paragraphs are well organized
Fluency	Language is very limited and repetitive; written text is very brief	Language is somewhat limited and repetitive; written text is brief	Language is good and there are few repetitions; written text has adequate elaboration	Language is very good and varied; there are no repetitions; written text has very good elaboration	Language is excellent and varied; there are no repetitions; written text has excellent elaboration
Spelling	Few words are spelled correctly	Most words are spelled phonetically; most sight words are spelled correctly	Most words are spelled correctly; some errors with homophones and endings	Words are spelled correctly; there are few errors	Words are spelled correctly; errors are minor
Capitalization and Punctuation	No capitalization or punctuation	Some evidence of correct capitalization and punctuation	Good evidence of capitalization and punctuation	Very good evidence of capitalization and punctuation; few errors	Excellent evidence of capitalization and punctuation; errors are rare

FIGURE 12.7 • Analytic Scoring

when scoring each of these areas not to let their impressions in one area—for example, organization—influence the impression in another area—such as mechanics in this example.

Analytic scoring is frequently done by two or more raters, working independently, who rate the same written text. When they have finished, comparisons are made between their ratings to determine their similarity. If the ratings are dissimilar, the two teachers can discuss why they gave certain ratings, or a third teacher can rate the text.

Anchor Papers

Anchor papers are students' papers that represent different writing levels of performance. They can be useful in the development of rubrics. For example, after a group of students completes a writing assignment, the teacher reviews the entire papers to determine which three represent, by degrees, high-quality performance, typical or average performance, and low performance. These are the anchor papers. Next, the teacher evaluates the entire set of student papers, using the anchor papers as guides to determine high, typical, or low performance.

Standardized Instruments

This section describes some of the commonly used individual, standardized tests of written language. All of these tests use standardized procedures for norm-referencing, administering, and scoring. The results of standardized tests of written language can be used to make interpretations and comparisons about an individual student's performance on several tests.

Content validity is a primary concern of any achievement test, including tests of written language. This type of validity measure relates the extent to which the test items reflect the instructional objectives of a test. An estimate of the content validity of a test results from thoroughly and systematically examining the test items to determine the extent to which they reflect the intended instructional objectives and content.

Although the test developer must describe the process that established the content validity of a test, the test examiner must make an independent determination. This is especially important when deciding on the content validity of written language tests. The test examiner has to compare the test objectives, format, number of responses or prompts, and types of responses or prompts with the curriculum that was taught.

Scoring tests of written language can be problematic for the test examiner. Students vary in their writing abilities, and many test manuals contain general directions, which are sometimes ambiguous, for scoring writing samples. Because test examiners must use judgment in scoring, there may be variations and inconsistencies between test scores.

Oral and Written Language Scales, Second Edition (OWLS-II™ LC/OE and RC/WE)

The *Oral and Written Language Scales, Second Edition* (*OWLS-II™ LC/OE and RC/WE*; Carrow-Woolfolk, 2011) assesses listening comprehension, oral expression, reading comprehension, and written expression in individuals ages 3 through 21 years. The four subscales can be

---

TESTS-at-a-GLANCE

Oral and Written Language Scales, Second Edition (OWLS-II™ LC/OE and RC/WE)

www.pearsonassesssments.com

- **Publication Date:** 2011
- **Purposes:** Assesses listening comprehension, oral expression, reading comprehension and written expression.
- **Age/Grade Levels:** Ages 3 years through 21 years.
- **Time to Administer:** 10 to 40 minutes
- **Technical Adequacy:** The standardization sample is adequate. Reliability is good; requires further evidence of construct validity.
- **Suggested Use:** The test can be used in combination with other measures and tools to assess learning difficulties, language disorders, and related problems.
- **Summary:** Evidence of reliability and validity is adequate. Teachers should examine the test items to determine congruence with the school curriculum as well as underlying assumptions about learning and language processing.

compared and, thus, allow comparisons to be made among the subscales regarding students' performance. The test is designed to assess four types of language processing: lexical/semantic, syntactic, pragmatic, and supralinguistic. The test can be used to identify students with learning difficulties, language disorders, and related problems; assist in monitoring progress; and provide information for intervention and program planning.

SCORING. Scores are reported as age-based and grade-based standard scores, test-age and grade equivalents, percentile ranks, and as an overall composite score.

STANDARDIZATION. The standardization sample for the *OWLS-II™ LC/OE and RC/WE* included 2,123 individuals from 31 states, ages 3 through 21. The sampling was stratified by age, ethnicity, gender, parental education level, and region of the United States.

RELIABILITY The reliability for the *OWLS-II™ LC/OE and RC/WE* is adequate.

VALIDITY The test has adequate validity. Teachers should examine the test items to determine the extent to which the *OWLS-II™ LC/OE and RC/WE* matches writing in the curriculum that was taught.

Test of Written Language, Fourth Edition

The *Test of Written Language, Fourth Edition* (*TOWL-4*; Hammill & Larsen, 2008) is the fourth edition of this test. The *TOWL-4* is intended for use with students ages 9 years through 17 years 11 months. It contains seven subtests organized into two formats: spontaneous and contrived. The spontaneous format assesses students' written essays, and the contrived format directly assesses specific skills associated with writing. Table 12.3 shows the subtests and abilities/skills measured.

ADMINISTRATION The *TOWL-4* is individually administered. However, it can be administered to small groups of students.

SCORING Raw scores convert to percentiles and standard scores.

STANDARDIZATION The *TOWL-4* is the fourth edition of the *TOWL*, originally published in 1978. It was revised in 1988. The test was renormed in 2006 and 2007 based on key demographic variables, such as age, gender, ethnicity, geographic region, parental education, and family income. Although the standardization sample approximates the characteristics of the 2005 U.S. Census, there are flaws in the alignment.

RELIABILITY The test reports test-retest and internal consistency reliability coefficients. The reliability for the *TOWL-4* is adequate.

VALIDITY The test reports content, criterion-related, and construct validity. Teachers should examine the test items to determine the extent to which the *TOWL-4* matches writing in the curriculum that was taught.

TESTS-at-a-GLANCE

Test of Written Language, Fourth Edition (TOWL-4)

www.pearsonassessments.com

- **Publication Date:** 2008
- **Purposes:** Assesses writing conventions, grammar, syntax, vocabulary, spelling, sentence construction, and story construction.
- **Age/Grade Levels:** Ages 9 years through 17 years 11 months.
- **Time to Administer:** 1 1/2 hours.
- **Technical Adequacy:** There are concerns about the standardization sample. Reliability is good; requires further evidence of validity.
- **Suggested Use:** Provides evidence of strengths and weaknesses in written language, spelling, and vocabulary. Examiners should evaluate the test items to determine the extent to which they reflect writing as it has been taught to the student. Caution should be used when making norm-referenced comparisons and interpretations of performance.
- **Summary:** The *Test of Written Language, Fourth Edition* is a norm-referenced test of skills and abilities associated with written language and the writing process. Evidence of reliability and validity is adequate. Teachers should examine the test items to determine congruence with the school curriculum.

TABLE 12.3 • Test of Written Language 4: Subtests

Subtest	Abilities/Skills Assessed
Spontaneous Format	
• Contextual Conventions	• Capitalization, punctuation, spelling, grammar
• Story Composition	• Plot, character development, general composition
Contrived Format	
• Vocabulary	• Word usage
• Spelling	• Correct spelling
• Punctuation	• Capitalization, punctuation
• Logical Sentences	• Rewriting of sentences so that they make sense
• Sentence Combining	• Rewriting of one sentence from two sentences

SNAPSHOT

Assessment of Written Expression

Sheri is 11 years old and is in the fourth grade. She enjoys being with her friends, and she loves playing with her dog.

Sheri's strengths include her ability to communicate verbally. Her weaknesses include visual fluency during reading, composing written material, and lack of organization.

The *Test of Written Language, Fourth Edition* was administered to Sheri to identify specific strengths and weaknesses. During the session, Sheri became fatigued, and a brief break was taken. Please see the following table for Sheri's results on this test.

Sheri has difficulty with capitalization, punctuation, forming words, word usage, writing conceptually sound sentences, and story construction. The gap between her performance and that of her peers continues to increase. Sheri is unable to correctly spell basic sight words, such as *the*, *she*, and *over*.

Subtest	April 2, 20xx		
	Standard Score	Percentile Rank	Grade Equivalent
Contextual Conventions	4	2	<2.0
Contextual Language	5	5	2.2
Story Construction	8	25	3.4

Sheri was observed after being asked to write about a picture of a child playing with several puppies. In the 15 minutes that she was allotted, she wrote:

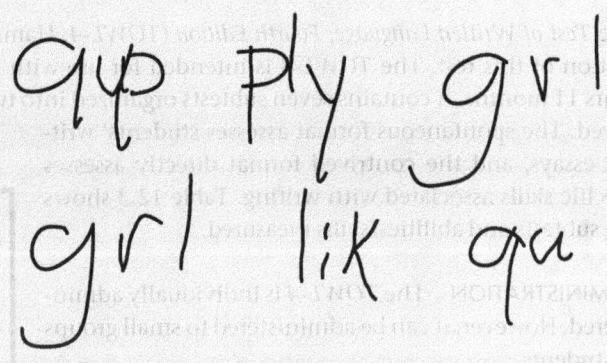

When asked to read what she had written, Sheri stated, "Puppies play with the girl. The girl likes the puppy."

When writing sentences, Sheri omits words and reverses letters, such as *p/q*.

After reviewing the results of standardized tests, observations, and work sample, Sheri's special education teacher recommended that written language instruction should address sounds in words, letter and symbol associations, spelling strategies, sentence development, and conventions of written language.

Pause and consider:
- Do you agree with the recommendations of Sheri's teacher? Why?
- What additional recommendations could you suggest?
- Based on your understanding of assessment, what other types of assessment could be useful in understanding Sheri's strengths and needs?

Test of Written Spelling, Fifth Edition

The *Test of Written Spelling, Fifth Edition* (*TWS-5*; Larsen, Hammill, & Moats, 2013) is for use with students in grades 1 through 12. The *TWS-5* assesses predictable words (words with spellings that are predictable using letter–sound patterns) and unpredictable words (words with spellings that are unpredictable, or are "word demons"). In administering the test, the examiner says a word, says a sentence that contains the word, and says the word again. The student writes the word only; words are not written in sentences.

Summary

- The assessment of literacy must reflect the close link between the development of reading and written language.
- Best practice requires that teachers conduct literacy assessments frequently and use the results to guide instruction.
- Assessment of literacy requires the use of multiple approaches, including standardized tests, curriculum-based measurement, criterion-referenced assessment, and alternative forms of assessment.

QUESTIONS FOR REFLECTION

1. Develop two assessment tasks that link the instruction in writing directly to assessment of writing.
2. Develop a checklist or rating scale that assesses students' attitudes and habits in writing.
3. Identify three assessment approaches this chapter discusses. Compare the purposes, advantages, and disadvantages of each approach.

REFERENCES

Brookhart, S. (2007/2008). Feedback that fits. *Educational Leadership, 65*(4), 54–59.

Carrow-Woolfolk, E. (2011). *Oral and written language scales, second edition*. Torrance, CA: Western Psychological Services.

Hammill, D. D., & Laren, S. C. (2008). *Test of written language* (4th ed.). Austin, TX: PRO-ED.

Hessler, T., & Konrad, M. (2008). Using curriculum-based measurement to drive IEPs and instruction in written expression. *Teaching Exceptional Children, 41*(2), 28–27.

Hosp, M., & Hosp, J. (2003). Curriculum-based measurement for reading, spelling, and math: How to do it and why. *Preventing School Failure, 48*(1), 10–13.

Larsen, S. C., Hammill, D. D., & Moats, D. (2013). *Test of written spelling* (5th ed.). Austin, TX: PRO-ED.

Rhodes, L. K., & Shanklin, N. (1993). *Windows into literacy: Assessing learners K–8*. Portsmouth, NH: Heinemann.

U.S. Department of Education. (n.d.). *National Center on Student Progress Monitoring*. Retrieved December 21, 2009, from http://www.studentprogress.org

Wilde, S. (1989). Looking at invented spelling: A kidwatcher's guide to spelling, Part 2. In K. S. Goodman, Y. M. Goodman, & W. J. Hood (Eds.), *The whole language evaluation book* (pp. 213–226). Portsmouth, NH: Heinemann.

13 Oral Language

Chapter Objectives

After completing this chapter, you should be able to:

- Describe several types of speech and language disorders.
- Discuss the three components of oral language assessment.
- Compare and contrast the use of language samples and language probes.
- Describe how the physical, learning, and social environments influence oral language.
- Describe the use of standardized tests for assessing oral language.
- Discuss best practice when assessing English language learners.

Overview

Language involves the use of symbols to communicate thoughts, feelings, ideas, and information. To **communicate** meaning, humans speak these symbols or produce them through digitized speech, write or input them by using the visual symbols of the language (letters and numerals), or express them through signing or gestures. Each of us uses these symbols of language every day.

This chapter focuses on one aspect of language: speaking and understanding oral language. We'll begin by examining common speech and language disorders and then turn our attention to the informal approaches that special educators use to assess oral language. This assessment information, coupled with data from standardized assessments, assists the individualized educational program (IEP) team in planning, implementing, and evaluating instruction. For some students with disabilities, the IEP team will need to consider a student's needs for contemporary technologies, such as a tablet or smart phone app, which allows the student to use augmentative or alternative communication. In this chapter, we'll learn more about that process.

Understanding Speech and Language Disorders

Teachers are often the first to notice a student's difficulties in understanding speech or expressing thoughts and ideas because they have considered questions such as: Does the student have a history of earaches, colds, or allergies? Does the student follow directions? Does the student ask to have directions repeated? Does the student speak clearly or demonstrate language difficulties?

Students with suspected speech and language disorders may be screened first for possible hearing loss. Often the school nurse conducts the screening or this person may organize a districtwide screening with trained volunteers. The hearing screening consists of listening to several tones within the speech range. If a student has difficulty hearing one or more of these tones, the examiner may refer the student to a medical clinic or recommend that the parents obtain a complete hearing assessment for their child.

More About Speech Disorders

A speech disorder is a broad term that covers a variety of conditions. **Speech disorders** include difficulties in articulation, such as the way words are pronounced and the fluency of speech, including rate and rhythm. Speech disorders also include conditions associated with pitch, volume, and voice quality, such as a voice that has a raspy tone. Stuttering, which occurs when words or sounds are repeated, is perhaps the most common speech disorder.

More About Language Disorders

A **language disorder** refers to a difficulty or inability in decoding or encoding the set of symbols used in language. Language disorders are typically divided into those associated with expressive language and receptive language.

Expressive language refers to the student's ability to use language to communicate information, thoughts, feelings, and ideas with others. Assessing expressive language involves examining the actual production of sound, speech, and language. For example, a special education teacher might record a small sample of a student's speech and then conduct an analysis of the number of words used, the grammatical structures, or the varied vocabulary.

Receptive language refers to the student's understanding of the language of others. Assessment of receptive language usually involves having the student listen to words or phrases and then demonstrate understanding. For example, a student might be asked to put the book on top of or under the table or to point to the picture that shows the boy putting on a jacket.

The Snapshot about Bethany describes some of the difficulties experienced by one student with a language disorder.

Oral Language Assessment

An assessment of oral language reflects, to some degree, the perspectives of the examiner who is gathering the information as well as the choice of the assessment approach. Many standardized instruments focus only on expressive and receptive language, whereas some authorities in the field (Semel, Wiig, & Secord, 2013) described oral language as consisting of three main areas or components: form, content, and use.

SNAPSHOT

Bethany

The teacher's words fell on Bethany's ears at an overwhelming rate. Bethany could hear what the teacher was saying but she has difficulty in understanding and remembering all the information that the teacher was explaining about the assignment for tomorrow.

Although Bethany has average intelligence, she is not able to comprehend every word that the teacher says. Before dismissing the class, Bethany's teacher handed her a written copy of the assignment, and Bethany smiled quickly as she gathered her books.

Bethany's teacher returned the smile as she reflected on the problems that Bethany had experienced earlier in the year. Through the referral and assessment process, the teacher was able to discover Bethany's difficulty in comprehending oral directions and in following class discussions.

It all began early in the year, after the school nurse had conducted a hearing screening for all the students in her classroom. The screening test consisted of identifying five different low and high tones that were presented loudly and then softly. Bethany passed the screening with no problems. However, as the first month of school passed, Bethany's teacher observed that even though Bethany seemed to be attentive, she had difficulty in following daily class discussions. Bethany frequently submitted incomplete homework assignments and, when questioned, would apologetically add that she didn't "know we had to do that." As the difficulty seemed to persist, the teacher decided to confer with Bethany's former teachers. Both teachers vaguely remembered that Bethany was not consistent in her work. Some of the assignments were done well, they remembered. One teacher felt that she did not seem to be motivated.

The following week, the teacher called Bethany's parents and asked them to come in for a conference. Both parents were surprised to hear about the teacher's concerns. When asked if Bethany needed to have the volume high on the television, her mother replied that Bethany seldom seemed to be interested in watching television or in going to the movies. Bethany's parents were concerned about her missing assignments. They tried to pinpoint some of their concerns: Why doesn't Bethany turn in complete assignments? Why doesn't she participate in class discussions? Is there a reason why Bethany does not like to watch television or go to the movies? They agreed that the teacher should make a referral to the assessment team. Perhaps the team might be able to provide some answers to these puzzling questions.

Through the assessment process, the team identified Bethany's problem. She had difficulty processing oral language. Usually difficulties in language processing involve one or more of three areas: auditory comprehension involves the construction of meaning by the listener; oral expression includes the ability to formulate and verbalize oral communication; and retrieval involves the ability to recover a word and its corresponding meaning from memory. Today she regularly works with the speech and language pathologist on auditory comprehension. In the classroom, her teacher uses several accommodations, such as written assignment slips and outlines of material covered in daily lessons, to help Bethany be more successful.

Pause and consider:

- What do you know about students who have speech and language disorders?
- What difficulties do they experience in the classroom, and what services do they receive?

Form

Form relates to the structural properties of language, including the sounds and written symbols of language and the letters that form a unit of meaning. The term **phonology** refers to the system of speech sounds of a language. The smallest units of sound are **phonemes**. For example, the English language makes use of about 44 different phonemes. The word *truck* consists of four phonemes (/t/r/u/k/). Students with articulation disorders often have difficulty in producing sounds. Substituting one phoneme for another and omitting phonemes are common mistakes that students make. Speech and language pathologists may describe this as a problem in articulation, for example, substituting letter(s) (*wabbit* for *rabbit*) or omitting letter(s) (*car* for *cars*).

Some students have difficulty in associating phonemes with their written equivalents, called **graphemes**. One of the reasons that English is such a difficult language is that (1) a single grapheme can represent more than one phoneme (for example, c—*cake*, c—*circus*) and (2) different graphemes can represent the same phoneme (for example, c—*cake*, k—*kite*)

(Polloway, Miller, & Smith, 2012). In teaching that a single grapheme can represent more than one phoneme, we say that a letter has different sounds. For example, how many sounds does the letter *a* have?

Morphology is the study of the units of letters that form a single unit of meaning. The basic unit of meaning is a **morpheme**. A morpheme can be a word such as *house* or *car* or a meaningful part of a word such as *re* in *renew*. Prefixes and suffixes, such as *re-*, *in-*, *-s*, and *-er* are morphemes.

Content

Content relates to the meaning of language and includes semantics and syntax.

Semantics

Semantics is the study of word meanings. Development of semantics begins with association of single concrete morphemes, for example, the association of *Mama* with a particular person. Development typically progresses to understanding complex utterances, for example, "Please get me the book," and more complex language, such as "It's raining cats and dogs."

Syntax

Syntax refers to the rules for arranging words into a sentence or phrase. In English, for example, adjectives are commonly placed before nouns. The combination of syntax and morphology is known as grammar.

Use

Use of language is important in social situations. **Pragmatics** refers to the ability to use language in functional ways, for example, the ability to use language in taking turns, to enter into a conversation or discussion with other children (or adults), to continue the

---

Research-Based Practices | **Understanding the Link Among Oral Language, Reading, and Writing**

Language is important for communicating thoughts and ideas; language is important to school success. Research findings indicate a complex relationship between oral language and developing skills in literacy. The National Institute of Child Health and Human Development (2005; **nichd.nih.gov**) conducted a longitudinal study that followed children from age 3 through third grade to examine the role of oral language in developing reading competence. The results suggest that oral language (form, content, and use) plays both indirect and direct roles in word recognition and serves as a better foundation for reading than vocabulary alone.

A number of recent studies involve young English language learners who are struggling to learn to read. Previously these students would have been referred to special education, but because schools now follow a response to intervention process, these students participate in a series of intensive instruction. Some researchers (D'Angiulli, Siegel, & Maggi, 2004; McMaster, Kung, Han, & Cao, 2008) have focused their investigations on Tier 1 response to intervention as they examine evidence-based reading instruction provided within general education. Their findings indicate that, given intervention, English language learners can achieve at the same rate as their peers. Overall, this research suggests that explicit, skills-based instruction delivered in the regular education classroom is effective in increasing achievement for young English language learners as well as non–English language learners who are experiencing difficulty in learning how to read.

In addition to reading, a child's difficulties in oral language also may affect written language, although the research is more limited in this area. Mackie and Dockrell (2004) examined the nature and extent of children's written language using two groups of 11-year-old children: one group of children with specific language impairments and a second group of children without disabilities. Their research found that children with specific language impairments wrote fewer words and produced more errors in syntax than children without disabilities.

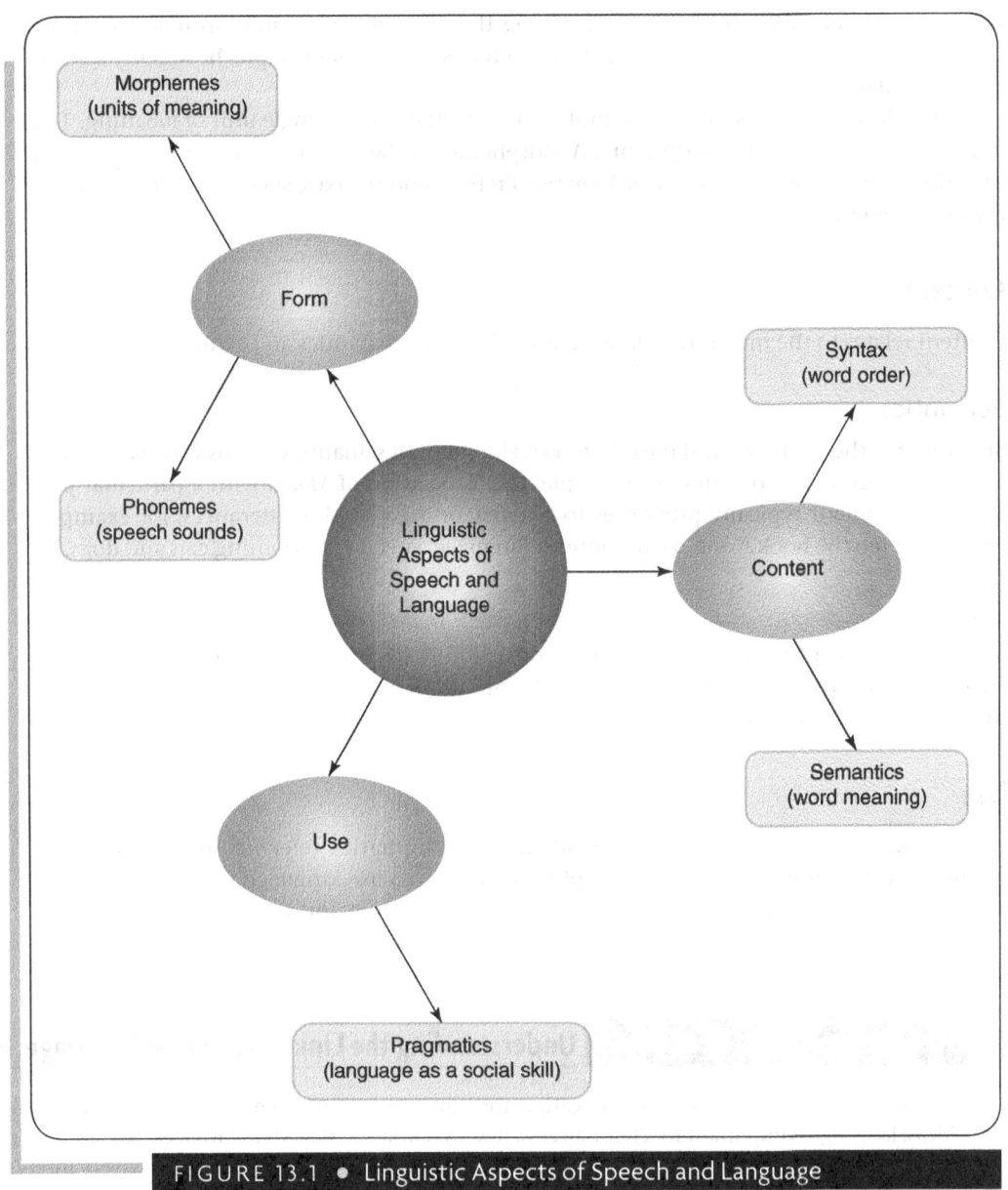

FIGURE 13.1 • Linguistic Aspects of Speech and Language

conversation, to interpret the meaning of the speaker, or to "read" the listener's nonverbal cues. Figure 13.1 illustrates the relationship among the aspects of speech and language we have discussed.

Assessment Questions, Purposes, and Approaches

Educators frequently have questions about a student's ability to use language to express wants, needs, concepts, and ideas. For example, an early elementary teacher may tell a child, "Use your words to tell your friend what you want." When a child is not able to use words in this fashion, the teacher may wonder if the child has a language delay and has not yet developed skills typical of same-aged peers. An educator at the middle school may observe that one of the students has difficulty in understanding new terms in the content areas, whereas another student may experience problems with knowing how to respond during a sharing of ideas.

To gather additional information about a student's skills, teachers often used informal assessments such as language samples and language probes. Teachers monitor student progress by collecting data on the use of oral language in the classroom as well as other settings at school or in the community. Frequently these assessment approaches can be very effective in connecting assessment with instruction. These approaches assist educators in determining where to start instruction and conduct individual progressing monitoring.

Language Samples

Language samples are examples of a student's use of language, such as explaining a topic of interest, telling a story, or stating and supporting an opinion. Language samples are considered to be one of the most effective ways of assessing oral language (Costanza-Smith, 2010; Heilmann, Nockerts, & Miller, 2010). The samples yield information about the student's vocabulary, use of syntax, understanding of semantics, proficiency in articulation, and the ability to use language in functional ways. Samples should also include examples of conversations with peers. Let's examine a language sample from 8-year-old Zachary as he looks at some toy cars with a friend.

Zachary: (Spinning the wheels of the car.)
Friend: "Hey, can I see the car?"
Zachary: no response.
Friend: HEY, Zachary, can I see your car?"
Zachary: "My car."
Friend: "It's actually my car. My dad brought it for me this weekend."
Zachary: "I want car."
Friend: "I let you play with it all during recess. Now I want it back."

Pause and consider:
- By examining this language sample, what can you learn about Zachary's vocabulary and how it compares to his same-age peer?
- What other information can you glean from this sample?

Teachers and parents collect samples of the student's language during various daily routines, activities, and assignments. Samples of the student's language can be recorded for further analysis. One research team (Heilmann et al., 2010) wondered if the length of the language utterance was critical in obtaining accurate data. They examined language samples of 1, 3, and 7 minutes and found that utterance length was most reliable when short samples were used. They further analyzed the results, comparing younger children (ages 2.8 to 5.11) with older children (6.0 to 13.3) and sample context (conversation or narrative). The findings indicated that the language sample measures were consistent across sample context and that length of the utterance was essential to obtaining accurate data.

Mean Length of Utterance

One way to analyze a language sample is by calculating a **mean length of utterance (MLU)**. Because morphemes are units of meaning, examiners frequently use them to measure expressive language development by obtaining a sample of the student's language and counting the individual morphemes per speech utterance. A speech utterance is the single phrase or sentence that the student expresses. Each utterance is comprised of individual morphemes, or units of meaning. To analyze the language sample, the number of morphemes is totaled and divided by the number of speech utterances to obtain the average MLU.

The following conversation was part of a 5-minute observation of Andre during free play in the kindergarten classroom:

Other Child:	My block... [2 morphemes]
Andre:	No, I want this. [4 morphemes]
Andre:	You can be the driver. [6 morphemes]

The total number of Andre's use of morphemes is 10, which is divided by the number of Andre's speech utterances (2). Although the MLU may be an oversimplification of the concept of spoken language, the MLU is useful in comparing levels of linguistic development and increases in individual mastery of expressive language (Polloway et al., 2012). Other considerations that will affect the MLU are (1) the length of the recording needed to obtain an adequate language sample of speech utterances and (2) the environment(s) that will be observed. Teachers who want a quick sample of a child's language sometimes gather several MLUs over the course of the day. MLUs are useful in monitoring a young child's progress in

SNAPSHOT

Chey

Chey is 15 years old and is a sophomore at Valley High. Her family came to the United States from Cambodia 10 years ago. At home, they still speak Chey's first language, Khmer. Chey loves horses and hopes to be a veterinary assistant when she finishes school. She has mild mental retardation and delays in receptive and expressive language skills in both English and Khmer, as noted in her IEP. Chey's IEP goals include using English to communicate in social settings and using appropriate style and tone for audience and occasion in conversation. Her teacher, Bri Wescott, is helping Chey work on initiating conversations, making friends, recognizing positive and negative peer pressure, and recognizing her own feelings and emotions.

Bri developed a series of four structured lessons to help Chey and the other students use expressive and receptive English language skills to participate in group discussions. These included starting a conversation, making friends, positive and negative peer pressure, and feelings and emotions. Bri used direct instruction along with pre- and posttests for each lesson to document students' progress. During the lessons, she used sensitive error correction (that is, accepting all answers in English) and also used a projector to display possible answers for all the students to see. Bri asked the students to read and respond to questions. She made sure that each student had enough time to compose the answers, and she carefully checked for understanding.

The pre- and posttests consisted of short realistic scenarios, such as the following example:

You are getting your books out of your locker when Joey, a popular boy at school, asks you to keep some cigarettes in your locker for him. Would you let Joey use your locker for this purpose? Why or why not? What would you say to him?

Chey and the other students were asked to record their responses to each scenario. Later Bri viewed the video informally noting appropriate style and tone. She also counted (MLUs). The pre- and posttest results showed that the lessons had assisted Chey and the other students in both receptive and expressive language skills. An unexpected outcome was that later Bri observed Chey volunteering to participate in role-play scenarios during their class session.

Pause and consider:

- After examining this scenario, what is one possible response that Chey may have given?
- Write down your answer and then count the MLUs. Share your findings with the class.

language development or an older student's progress in the increasing use of language for communication in functional life skills.

Language Probes

A **language probe** is a sampling of words or sounds that elicit specific information related to a receptive or expressive skill (Polloway et al., 2012). For example, the middle school special

SNAPSHOT

Juan

Maria Gomaz, a special educator, recently received a new student in the resource room. Juan is a 6-year-old native Spanish speaker who has bilingual language delays. His current IEP has goals relating to auditory memory and phonemic awareness, specifically relating to the ability to name letters and sounds. Maria observed that Juan tends to give up easily or takes a long time to recall information. For example, on a curriculum-based assessment, Juan was asked his address. Five minutes later, he blurted out the answer. Maria wonders if this makes it difficult to focus on what the teacher is saying during the time it takes him to recall an answer.

Maria began keeping detailed records of the CBM results so that she can measure his progress. In addition, by keeping a daily notebook of her observations, she was able to determine if the activities were actually affecting his learning. Following is an excerpt from her notebook.

Week of October 7
We did several activities in which Juan used an alphabet chart to help him put together an alphabet puzzle. After adding each piece of the puzzle, we reviewed the letter name and sound. I thought hooray! However, the next day, Juan could not remember the letter names or sounds. The repetition worked in the short term but he did not retain the information. Because I check for retention each day, I was able to determine that these particular activities with the alphabet were not effective for increasing Juan's retention of letter names and sounds.

Week of October 14
This week I decided to target instruction by focusing on the three letters that Juan knows and then adding a new one. We began with a letter-sorting activity with the three letters and then added the new letter. We practiced identifying capital and lowercase letters as well as letter sounds. I used a variety of kinesthetic strategies with him, such as forming the letters in sand and in play dough. By the end of the week, I found that Juan was able to recall the letter names and sounds for all four letters. This let me know that the kinesthetic strategies that I used worked well for him. I will continue to provide these targeted lessons in the future.

The error-correction procedure that Maria uses is immediate correction. If Juan incorrectly identifies a letter sound, she immediately corrects him, pointing out similar sounds. According to the daily CBM data, Maria decides if Juan is ready to add a new letter. Once Juan has recalled the letter name, sound, and symbol three days is a row, she introduces a new letter (see Figure 13.2). She will introduce a new letter when Juan is able to recall 90 percent of the information.

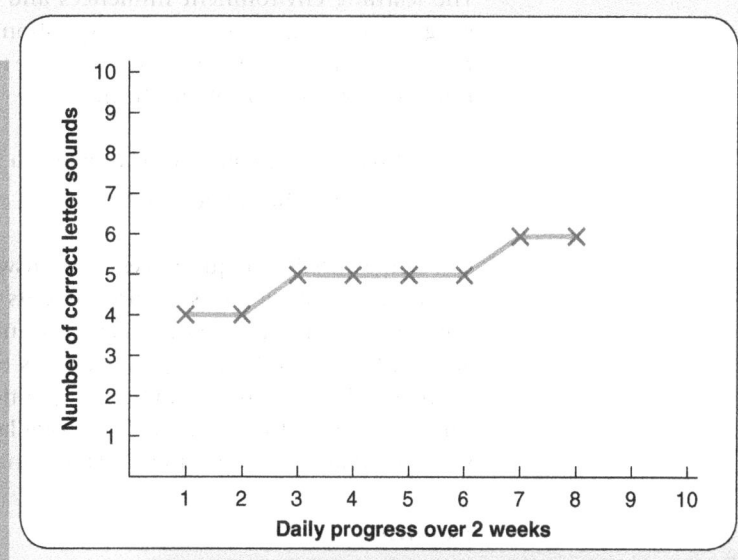

FIGURE 13.2 • Juan's Daily Progress in Phonemic Awareness

education teacher in an applied technology class selects four different tools from the introductory unit. The teacher presents each object to the student, and the teacher asks, "What is this? What is this used for?" The teacher sets the criteria for correct responses for each item. Because probes take advantage of the natural environment, they are helpful diagnostic techniques, assisting in assessing student knowledge and planning instruction.

Curriculum-Based Measurement

In Chapter 2, we learned that curriculum-based measurement (CBM) links instruction with assessment by emphasizing repeated, direct measurement of a student's performance. In the Snapshot of Juan, let's see how the special educator uses CBM to monitor his progress and the effectiveness of her instruction using an error correction procedure.

Observing the Student Within the Environment

In previous chapters, we discussed the importance of considering the student within the physical, learning, and social environments. The interactions between the student and the environment are important assessment considerations when assessing oral language.

Physical Environment

The physical setting can influence the student's development and use of language. Cooperative classroom activities and small-group work provide opportunities to use language in less-formal ways and possibly to enhance language acquisition. However, observations outside the regular classroom, such as in the hallways, in the cafeteria, and on the playground, may provide a more comprehensive understanding of the student's language.

Learning Environment

The learning environment influences and promotes the development of a student's language. For example, the types of questions a teacher asks directly influence the level of response that a student gives. Which of the following questions would encourage you to continue the conversation about the movie?

"What was the name of the movie you saw?"

"What was the movie about?"

Some questions require a yes or no answer; these are minimal-response (or closed-ended) questions. Some questions require students to think about the materials that they are using; these are thought-provoking questions and may require a phrase or a few sentences to answer. Other questions require students to think and weigh possible responses; they are open-ended questions. In addition to questioning techniques, there are other teaching strategies to promote the development of oral language. **Expansion** and modeling are two such strategies that are effective in the classroom.

Expansion

Expansion is a strategy that helps students learn syntax by supplying omitted structures. Billy, who is in kindergarten, told his teacher, "I want to use that thing." His teacher answered, "You want to use the scale at the science table?" The Snapshot about Nina describes how her teacher is helping Nina develop oral language skills.

Modeling

In addition to expansion, teachers can assist students in learning semantic features by **modeling** or by combining modeling with expansion. Peers can also be instrumental in modeling language. Let's listen in on two conversations.

Conversation one:

Agata: My brother got shot at the doctor's yesterday.

Teacher: Don't say, "got"; say, "had a shot."

Conversation two:

Agata: My brother got shot at the doctor's yesterday.

Teacher: Your brother had a shot at the doctor's yesterday? And did you get a shot at the doctor's, too?

Would you understand that Agata was describing a recent visit to the medical clinic where she received a vaccination? If you were Agata, which conversation would encourage you to continue telling about your experience? Teachers are more effective when they use expansion and modeling frequently and use correction sparingly. A checklist for supporting language can be found in Figure 13.3.

Social Environment

The social environment is important to the development of self-concept and self-esteem. These, in turn, contribute to skills in communicating effectively with others, communicating with a variety of audiences, and listening to others. By observing the social environment, teachers can study the relationships students have with peers and adults. Positive and supportive relationships influence language usage.

SNAPSHOT
Nina

Nina is in the 11th grade and enjoys all her classes in school. Nina also has mental retardation and receives special education and related services. Her IEP states that the speech-language pathologist will work individually with Nina and consult with her special education teacher. Her special education teacher has been collaborating with the speech-language pathologist to provide a rich language environment not only for Nina but also for all the students. Her classroom teacher encourages Nina to expand her vocabulary and to articulate clearly so that others can understand her. Various assessments focus on planning for instruction and evaluating progress.

Each week, the teacher invites the students to share a story or discuss current community and national events. During this time, she often creates a short video clip, recording a student's individual participation. The following segment reflects Nina's latest recording:

The School Boar (Board) is going to meet tonight. My father is going. They are going to vo (vote). Many people want low (lower) tax (taxes). I don't want them to cut the swim (swimming program). Everyone should vo (vote).

Nina's teacher will replay the sample video clip for Nina, and they will discuss whether to add it to Nina's records.

Pause and consider:
- How would you interpret Nina's results?
- How might the learning environment influence Nina's language sample? What steps could a special educator take to create a supportive learning environment?

Observation Setting

Physical Environment

1. How does the physical setting encourage conversations among students?

Learning Environment

2. Does the teacher provide materials and activities that encourage discussion?
3. Does the teacher create student groups during some learning activities?
4. Does the teacher use appropriate modeling of language?
5. Does the teacher provide opportunities for students to use language for different purposes?

   For example:

   ____ recalling a story or event

   ____ dictating directions

   ____ presenting facts or an opinion

   ____ other

6. Does the teacher provide opportunities for using language with different audiences?

   For example:

   ____ telling a fable to younger children

   ____ making a presentation to the parent–teacher association (PTA)

   ____ describing an exhibit to community members

   ____ taking a position on an issue and defending it to peers

   ____ other

7. Does the teacher employ techniques to enhance language opportunities?

   For example:

   ____ using expansion techniques

   ____ asking questions that are thought-provoking or open-ended

   ____ other

Social Environment

8. Does the school day provide for "free-time" socialization among students?

   For example:

   ____ informal time before classes begin

   ____ informal time before departure at end of day

   ____ other

9. Is lunchtime scheduled in such a way as to support socialization?

   ____ sufficient time to eat and socialize

   ____ students have choices where they may sit

   ____ students are allowed to talk

   ____ other

FIGURE 13.3 • Checklist for Observing a Language-Rich Environment

Mand modeling

For students with autism and other developmental disorders, teachers often use mand modeling or directives as part of the natural routines. **Mand modeling** is a systematic teaching strategy that involves the teacher observing the interests of the student during free time. The teacher then asks a question or gives the student a directive regarding this interest. If the student does not produce the targeted behavior, the teacher then models it for the student. Teachers usually begin by demonstrating what the student needs to say to obtain a desired object. For example, during lunch time, a teacher observes that a child is looking at the plate of cheese cubes. The teacher says, "More? More cheese?" and the child would respond "More." As soon as the child responds, the teacher follows through with providing the requested object. Mands are very effective for promoting language because they are closely associated with desired objects, and the child received immediate reinforcement.

Shaping

Language abilities become refined through the process of shaping the sounds or word as the vocalization more closely approximates the sound or word in the language. **Shaping** is a behavioral term that refers to reinforcing each progressive step as the child more closely articulates the sound. Eventually, children shape strings of sounds to approximate words.

For example, a teacher says to a young child, "Give the card to your friend." The child makes the response, "Car? Fren?" As time goes on, the child's responses approximate the actual word, "Give card to friend." The teacher smiles and responds, "Yes! Give the card to your friend!" Gradually, the child's responses duplicate the actual words.

Standardized Tests of Oral Language

This section highlights some of the commonly used individual, standardized tests of oral language. All the tests in this section are norm-referenced and use standardized procedures for administering and scoring. The tests yield a variety of scores, including standard scores, percentiles, stanines, age equivalents, and normal curve equivalents (NCEs).

Clinical Evaluation of Language Fundamentals, Fifth Edition

The *Clinical Evaluation of Language Fundamentals, Fifth Edition* (*CELF-5*; Semel et al., 2013) is designed for children ages 5 to 21 years. It uses a four-step process to assess a child's language and pinpoint areas of difficulty. By administering the core subtests, an examiner can obtain a Core Language Score to determine if a problem exists and whether the student qualifies for services. Additional assessment helps to determine the nature of the language disorder and the student's language strengths and weaknesses. Subtests include Receptive Language Score, Expressive Language Scores, Language Structure, and Language Content. The fifth edition includes assessment of pragmatics using observations and interactive activities. This new edition also includes assessment of Reading Comprehension and Structured Writing, allowing the examiner to compare skills to Oral Language.

CELF-4 Spanish (Wiig, Secord, & Semel, 2006) was developed to assess children, ages 5 to 21 years, who are Spanish speakers living in the United States. This assessment is not a translation of the *CELF-4* but rather a parallel test. According to the authors, this assessment incorporates grammatical forms appropriate for Spanish speakers and themes familiar to Spanish-speaking students.

ADMINISTRATION   The *CELF-5* and the *CELF-4 Spanish* are administered individually and take between 30 and 45 minutes for the Core Language Score.

Point Street School
Speech and Language Evaluation Report
Initial Evaluation

Name: Ashley Davis
Date of Evaluation: 1/11/xx
Primary Care Provider: Dr. John Simmons
Diagnosis: Speech Delay
Parents: Timothy and Donna Davis

Date of Birth: 6/11/xx
Age: 5.7 years

Referral Information:
Ashley Davis is a 5.7-year-old girl, who was referred for this communication evaluation by Dr. John Simmons due to his concerns with Ashley's delayed speech.

Background Information:
This information was gathered by interviewing Ashley's mother. Ashley is the younger of two children in the family and lives with her parents. Mrs. Davis indicated that Ashley has not been hospitalized and that her daughter has been a healthy child with no significant history of ear infections, allergies, asthma, seizures, or head injuries. It is unknown if Ashley's hearing was evaluated at birth. She stated that her daughter tends to talk "loud." The parent indicated that she has no concerns regarding Ashley's vision.

Mrs. Davis reported that Ashley primarily communicates using words on a sentence level. She indicated that she is able to understand most of her child's speech while nonfamily members have some difficulty. Ashley is reported to follow directions but might need adults to gesture to improve her understanding. The parent stated that Ashley has difficulty following 2-step directions. The parent added that Ashley's voice seems to be hoarse sometimes. Ashley can entertain herself well and tends to play by herself. Presently Ashley is home-schooled but her parents plan to enroll her in public school next year.

Methods of Evaluation:
Clinical Evaluation of Language Fundamentals, Fifth Edition (CELF-5)
Goldman Fristoe Test of Articulation, Second Edition (GFTA-2)
Parent interview
Observation

Receptive and Expressive Language Skills:
The *Clinical Evaluation of Language Fundamentals, Fifth Edition (CELF-5):*
This assessment is designed to measure receptive and expressive language skills by measuring selected processing and production abilities in the areas of syntax (sentence structure), semantics (word meaning), pragmatics (social language skills), and memory for linguistic information. It examines both receptive language (what a student understands) and expressive language (what a student can say). Scaled scores between 7 and 13 (for individual subtests) and standard scores of 85 to 115 (for core composites) are considered within average limits.

~~~~~~~~~~~~~~~~ (indicate that a portion of the report was omitted here)

In sum, on the *CELF-5*, Ashley achieved a standard score of 92 with subtests scaled scores all within the 7–10 range. Her percentile rank of 30 indicated that she did as well as or better than 30% of her peer group. Her voice quality was judged as hoarse. Her oral motor skills were observed to be within normal limits and functional for speech production at this time.

FIGURE 13.4 • Ashley's Speech and Language Evaluation Report

Articulation and Intelligibility Skills:
The *GFTA-2* is designed to assess a child's production of speech sounds in single words. Ashley received a standard score of 73, with a range of scores 66–80 (where 85–115 is considered within normal limits and 100 is the average.) She achieved a percentile rank of 7 indicating that she is performing as well as or better than 7% of the children in the normed sample. Her errors were characterized primarily by substitutions in the initial words positions, particularly initial blends, with other substitutions in the medial and final word position. Here errors were as follows:

Sound	Initial Position	Medial Position	Final Position
/p/	/t/ for /p/		/k/ for /p/
/m/			omitted
/n/			omitted
/w/	/d/ for /w/		
/b/			omitted
/g/	/d/	/d/	/d/
/k/	/t/	/t/	/t/
/j/	/l/	/j/	/j/
/t/, "ch"		"th"	omitted
/l/		omitted	
/r/		/w/	
"th" as in "thumb"	/t/	/s/	/s/
/v/	/b/		
/s/	th	th	th
/z/	/d/	/t/	omitted
"th" as in "that"	/d/	/v/	
Initial blends: /b/bl, br; d/drl; fw/fl, fr; d/gl, gr; t/kl, kr, kw; p/pl, sp; t/sp,tr, th, fw/sw			

An analysis of the types of errors found on this assessment revealed the presence of phonological processes of simplification patterns children apply when attempting to produce more difficult sounds. The presence of multiple errors impacted on Ashley's overall level of intelligibility or understandability on a conversational level. Her level of intelligibility was estimated at 75% by a trained observer who knew the context of the conversation.

Observation of Social Pragmatic Language Skills:
Ashley's social language skills also were informally assessed by observation. She engaged in appropriate levels of eye contact, took turns in conversation, and was able to initiate and maintain periods of conversation. She acknowledged the examiner's comments, answered simple questions, and was able to respond to the adult's conversation by providing comments that were contextually appropriate.

Clinical Observations:
Ashley came to this evaluation with her mother and sat close to her mother initially. After warming up to the new environment and the examiner, she conversed socially with the examiner. She was able to transition between structured and unstructured activities without difficulty. She was attentive and compliant during the evaluation, exhibiting

age-appropriate attending skills. The results of this evaluation are judged to be a reliable representation of her communication skills.

Summary:
Ashley Davis is a 5.7-year-old girl who is demonstrating age appropriate receptive and expressive language skills, based on the *Clinical Evaluation of Language Fundamentals, Fifth Edition (CELF-5)*, observations, and parent report.

Results of the *Goldman Fristoe Test of Articulation, Second Edition (GFTA-2)* revealed that the articulation skills exhibited are the result of phonological processes where children use immature speech sounds or speech patterns in their attempt to produce later-developing speech sounds. Her performance on this assessment indicated a high level of severity for a child of this age. Her level of intelligibility therefore is much lower than we would expect of same-age peers.

Recommendations:
1. Ashley should receive speech and language pathology services to address her articulation difficulty. Therapy should start at one time per week for up to 60 minutes. These services should be reevaluated in 3 months or sooner to assess the adequacy of this level of therapy.
2. She should continue to engage in literacy activities that will promote phonological or sound awareness.
3. She should receive an audiological assessment to determine present hearing acuity.
4. The family should discuss with Dr. Simmons a referral to an ear, nose, and throat specialist to evaluate Ashley's hoarse and raspy vocal quality.

It was a pleasure to meet with Ashley and her mother. Please feel free to contact this clinician with any further questions.

Gerald Parker, MS, CCC-SLP

Gerald Parker, MS, CCC-SLP
January 12, xxxx

FIGURE 13.4 • *(Continued)*

TESTS-at-a-GLANCE

Clinical Evaluation of Language Fundamentals, Fifth Edition (CELF-5)

http://www.pearsonclinical.com/language/products/100000705/clinical-evaluation-of-language-fundamentals-fifth-edition-celf5.html?Pid=CELF-5&Mode=summary

- **Publication Date:** 2013
- **Purposes:** Measures selected receptive and expressive skills in morphology, syntax, semantics, memory, and pragmatics. CELF-5 also includes reading comprehension and structured writing, allowing for a comparison of skills to oral language.
- **Age/Grade Levels:** Ages 5 through 21.
- **Time to Administer:** 30 to 45 minutes.
- **Technical Adequacy:** The fifth edition includes normative data based on the 2010 U.S. Census.
- **Suggested Use:** Identifying, diagnosing, and following up the evaluation of language skills. For Spanish-speaking individuals, the *CELF-4 Spanish Edition* is a parallel, not translated, version of the instrument.

SCORING Raw scores are converted to standard scores, percentile ranks, growth scale values, and age equivalents. Scoring options include hand scoring or Web-based on the publisher's Q-global platform. The Spanish Edition can be scored by hand or by using the *CELF-4 Scoring and Report Assistant*. This software provides scores and various reports, including Parent, Interpretive, Summary, and Graphical.

STANDARDIZATION The *CELF-5* standardization sample was representative of the U.S. population (as reported by the U.S. Bureau of the Census, 2010) and was stratified by age, sex, race/ethnicity, geographic region, and socioeconomic status (SES; based on parent education level).

RELIABILITY AND VALIDITY The examiner's manual reports reliability and validity studies, although additional research will add to our knowledge of these technical considerations.

SUMMARY The *Clinical Evaluation of Language Fundamentals, Fifth Edition (CELF-5)* provides information

> **SNAPSHOT**
>
> ### Ashley's Speech and Language Evaluation
>
> After discussing Ashley's evaluation with the school's speech and language pathologist (SLP), Ashley's parents decided to enroll her in their local community school, so that the recommendations of the report could be more easily implemented. The parents requested that the report be shared with Ashley's teachers.
>
> The speech and language pathologist offered to meet with the teachers to explain the assessment results and answer any questions that they might have. The teachers hoped that he would provide some suggestions for how to help Ashley. Let's sit in on their conversation:
>
> The speech and language pathologist began, "I assessed Ashley using both informal and formal measures. After interviewing the parent, I talked with Ashley about her interests, while conducting informal observations of her language."
>
> "I then administered two formal assessments. The first assessment, was the *Clinical Evaluation of Language Fundamentals*, often referred to as the 'CELF.' Her results indicated that she has age-appropriate receptive and expressive language skills. For example, she can take turns in conversation and initiate and maintain conversation."
>
> "The second assessment was the *Goldman Fristoe Test of Articulation-2*. I use this assessment to help identify articulation disorders. From the test results, I would estimate that her conversational level of intelligibility is about 75%. Typically we would expect a child to be 75% intelligible by 3 years of age and 90% or better by 4 years of age. So you can see that she has some significant articulation difficulties."
>
> "She received a standard score of 73, which is below the average range for children of her age. However, I find it is best not to rely on standard scores for this particular test because the distribution of articulation disorders is not a normal distribution, but rather skewed."
>
> "Instead, I use percentile ranks to discuss student articulation disorders. You can see by her evaluation report that she received a percentile rank of 7, which means that she performed the same as or better than 7% of same-aged peers; but that 93% of these peers did better."
>
> At this point, one of the teachers asked if they could talk about ways they could help Ashley in the classroom. Together, they talked at length about literacy activities and other language-rich experiences that would promote phonological awareness. The teachers and the speech and language pathologist planned how they could work together, so that the specific sounds that Ashley would be working on in speech therapy would be carried over to classroom activities. As they brainstormed, they thought about lyrics and melodies, limericks, and other rhymes that they could use.
>
> **Pause and consider:**
> - What information provided by the speech and language pathologist do you think was most helpful to the teachers?
> - If you were working with Ashley, what questions would you want to ask the speech and language pathologist?

regarding a student's language disorder and eligibility for services. The standardization sample was based on the 2010 census data. Scoring options include hand or Web-based scoring. The latter allows the examiner to generate various reports, including, for example, a summary report, an item analysis, or a pragmatics profile. This instrument is also available for young children. The *CELF—Preschool, Second Edition* measures a broad range of language skills for children ages 3 to 6 years. A Spanish edition, the *CELF-4—Spanish*, was developed to assess children, ages 5 to 21 years, who are Spanish speakers living in the United States.

Preschool Language Scales, Fifth Edition

The *Preschool Language Scales, Fifth Edition* (PLS™-5; Zimmerman, Steiner, & Pond, 2011) measures language acquisition and prelanguage skills in children ages birth through 7 years 11 months. The test has two subscales: auditory comprehension and expressive communication, which includes preverbal communication skills. This edition assesses children at 7 years on irregular plurals and synonyms, constructing sentences, and answering questions about a story. The test also has a Spanish-language version, the *Preschool Language Scales, Fifth Edition Spanish* (PLS-5™ *Spanish*; Zimmerman, Steiner, & Pond, 2012), which assesses receptive and

> **TESTS-at-a-GLANCE**
>
> **Preschool Language Scales, Fifth Edition**
> http://www.pearsonclinical.com/language/products/100000233/preschool-language-scales-fifth-edition-pls5.html?Pid=PLS-5
>
> - **Publication Date:** 2011
> - **Purposes:** Measures auditory comprehension and expressive communication that includes preverbal communication skills. For bilingual children, use of the English and Spanish Editions provide bilingual-conceptual language scores.
> - **Age/Grade Levels:** Ages birth through 7 years 11 months.
> - **Time to Administer:** 45 to 60 minutes.
> - **Technical Adequacy:** Norming sample is based on the U.S. Census (March 2008 update). This edition was carefully reviewed by experts in the field of assessment and bias issues. Split half reliabilities range from .80 to .97. Sensitivity and specificity fall in the low .80s.
> - **Suggested Use:** Assessing language acquisition and prelanguage skills in children. A Spanish edition is designed to test receptive and expressive language in Spanish.

expressive language in Spanish. According to the manual, this assessment provides bilingual-conceptual language scores for auditory comprehension, expressive communication, and a total language score.

ADMINISTRATION This instrument takes approximately 45 to 60 minutes to administer. Both English and Spanish versions use the same materials.

SCORING The test reports scores as standard scores, growth scores, and percentile ranks. Language age equivalents are also available.

STANDARDIZATION Approximately 1,400 children from over 45 states participated in the standardization sample. The sample approximated the U.S. Census (March 2008 update) and was stratified by race/ethnicity, caregiver education level, and geographic region. Spanish-speaking children from various regions in the United States participated in the standardization sample for the Spanish version.

RELIABILITY The examiner's manual reports split half reliabilities, sensitivity, and specificity. Split half reliabilities range from .80 to .97. Sensitivity for the total language score is .83, and specificity is .80.

VALIDITY According to the examiner's manual, nationally recognized experts in assessment and bias issues reviewed the test items and art.

SUMMARY The *Preschool Language Scales, Fifth Edition (PLS™-5)* is a standardized instrument for measuring preverbal and language skills in young children ages birth through 7 years 11 months. The standardization sample was based on the U.S. Census March 2008 update. The *Preschool Language Scales, Fifth Edition Spanish (PLS-5™ Spanish)*, assesses Spanish expressive and receptive language skills. For bilingual children, the examiner can obtain Spanish and English skills in one score.

Test of Adolescent and Adult Language, Fourth Edition

The *Test of Adolescent and Adult Language, Fourth Edition* (TOAL–4; Hammill, Brown, Larsen, & Wiederholt, 2007) assesses spoken and written language abilities in individuals ages 12 years through 24 years 11 months. The test consists of six subtests: word opposites, word derivations (after hearing the key word and the stimulus sentences, the individual says the missing word, which is a derivative of the key word), spoken analogies, word similarities, sentence combining, and orthographic usage (the individual writes all the correct words and punctuation marks).

ADMINISTRATION The TOAL-4 can be administered individually or to a small group. Administration time is approximately 60 minutes.

> **TESTS-at-a-GLANCE**
>
> **Test of Adolescent and Adult Language, Fourth Edition**
> www.pearsonassessments.com
>
> - **Publication Date:** 2007
> - **Purposes:** Assesses spoken language, written language, and general composite language.
> - **Age/Grade Levels:** Ages 12 years through 24 years 11 months.
> - **Time to Administer:** 60 minutes.
> - **Technical Adequacy:** The standardization sample, reliability, and validity studies are adequate.
> - **Suggested Use:** Assessing spoken and written language abilities in youth and young adults.

SCORING   Test results can be reported as percentile ranks or scaled scores. The scaled scores of the six subtests can be combined to form three composite scores: spoken language, written language, and general language. Composite scores can be reported as standard scores called *composite indexes* or as percentile ranks.

STANDARDIZATION   The *TOAL-4* was standardized on 1,671 individuals. The demographic characteristics of the standardization sample were derived from the census data projection for 2004 and were stratified by geographic region, gender, ethnicity, family income level, parental education, and age.

RELIABILITY   The examiner's manual reports three types of reliability: internal consistency, test-retest, and interscorer. In addition to describing general internal consistency, the manual describes internal consistency for selected subgroups of the population, including various ethnic subgroups and subgroups of children identified as having ADHD or learning disabilities. The authors present evidence that this assessment is reliable for each of these subgroups, suggesting that the test is not biased relative to these subgroups. The manual also presents information regarding test-retest reliability and interrater reliability. Correlation coefficients reported by the authors are relatively high.

VALIDITY   The examiner's manual provides detailed discussions regarding three types of validity: content-description validity, including rationale for selecting subtest formats and test items; criterion-prediction; and construct-identification. Although these terms differ from the standard terms of content validity, criterion-related validity, and construct validity, the concepts represented are the same according to the authors. Based on the information presented in the test manual, there is growing evidence of the validity of this assessment.

SUMMARY   The *TOAL-4* assesses language skills in individuals ages 12 years through 24 years 11 months. The test consists of six subtests: word opposites, word derivations, spoken analogies, word similarities, sentence combining, and orthographic usage. The manual presents evidence of the technical adequacy of this instrument.

Concerns About Standardized Tests of Oral Language

Receptive Language

The assessment of receptive language requires determining the students' understanding of language. Many standardized tests use symbols in test items to represent word meanings and then use symbol recognition as a key measure of receptive language. Therefore, teachers must examine these symbols for appropriateness, relevance, and clarity. We know that, during an individual's cognitive development, understanding of symbols moves from concrete to abstract levels. A test item that measures the student's understanding of common objects in the environment might include the task "Point to the ball." Test developers vary in how they represent the object "ball"; that is, some pictures provide a more abstract representation than others. In the following list of test materials, how would the items be ordered from most concrete to most abstract?

  Black-and-white line drawing of a ball
  Cartoon of a ball
  Photograph of a ball

The test should represent items in an appropriate way for the student. For example, items presented in abstract terms or items that are culture-bound may not be a true measure of the student's receptive language. The type of symbols, the inclusion of regional or cultural items familiar to the individual, and the response method that the student can use to indicate a choice are all particularly salient factors in the assessment of receptive language skills.

Expressive Language

An individual must have a reason for using language as well as for wanting to respond. Students may not care to perform, may be shy, or may not want to comply with the examiner's request. The student's need or desire to communicate directly affects the assessment results from standardized instruments. How can teachers engage reluctant students to participate in expressive language assessments?

Responding to Diversity

Today, many children in U.S. schools are English language learners; that is, English is not their home language. School personnel consider the home language to be the students' first language and regard them as culturally and linguistically diverse students. Some children come from homes in which the family's traditional language is spoken exclusively or nearly exclusively. Some children come from families where members speak more than one language at home, particularly when parents are from diverse backgrounds.

To benefit from their education program, many students who are culturally and linguistically diverse need second-language instruction. Some children need additional tutoring due to limited linguistic experiences, but most children who are culturally and linguistically diverse do not have a special need that requires a referral to special education services.

Some students are not linguistically competent, however, in their first language. This compounds the difficulties in assessing children. How can teachers distinguish language differences from speech and language disorders in linguistically and culturally diverse students? Assessment often begins with examining how the student communicates within the first-language setting. Are the characteristics of the student's language different from other students in that community who are of the same age? Response to intervention, which we discussed in Chapter 2, holds promise for providing both early intervention and more intensive instruction for English language learners.

In some schools, few teachers and other professionals are qualified to assess culturally and linguistically diverse students, and many standardized instruments are simply inadequate. Over the past few years, language sample analysis has been used to describe the language skills of children with language impairments. These samples now comprise large databases of language samples. One group of researchers (Heilmann, Miller, & Nockerts, 2011) compared conversational language samples with samples generated from a large database, the *Systematic Analysis of Language Transcripts* (**www.saltsoftware.com**). They found that the database samples correctly identified 78% of the children with language impairment and 85% of the children who were developing typically.

A Spanish/English version of this software can be used to identify language disorders among bilingual children whose native language is Spanish and who are learning English as a second language. Designed for children in kindergarten through third grade, the software presents the child the task of listening to a story and observing the story's picture sequence; then the child is asked to retell the story. The task is repeated so that the child listens and retells the story in Spanish and in English. The child's stories are transcribed using the software and then compared with English and Spanish story-retell narratives (which are stored in the software's database) from hundreds of native Spanish-speaking bilingual children.

From the data analysis, the child's language samples may be identified as delayed or may indicate the presence of one or more characteristics associated with a language disorder.

According to the authors (Miller & Iglesias, 2008), language sample analysis has long been considered a valid indicator of expressive language performance. The language sample analysis is the most accurate assessment because it uses real communication contexts (the same context for both Spanish and English), allows the examiner to track performance over time in each language, and uses databases of language samples from 789 bilingual children in grades K–3 for comparison of each language. Learn more about this large database and some case studies at: **www.saltsoftware.com/case-studies/**

Students With Severe Communication Disorders

Some students have severe communication disorders as a result of or in combination with other disabilities, such as physical and developmental disabilities. These disabilities affect the ability to communicate.

Augmentative or Alternative Communication (AAC) Systems

Students with severe communication disorders are not able to use oral language efficiently. For example, 10-year-old Felix is an honor-roll student who loves basketball games. He has cerebral palsy and uses a motorized wheelchair. The cerebral palsy has affected Felix's ability to use oral language. Although he can produce some sounds, his oral speech is not an effective way to communicate.

Felix, like many other students with severe physical disabilities, uses a tablet and a communication app as **augmentative or alternative communication (AAC)**. AAC, which the Individuals with Disabilities Education Act (IDEA) considers to be assistive technology (AT), is any method or device that assists communication. IDEA provides for the functional evaluation of a child with a disability and assistance in selecting, acquiring, and using an assistive technology (AT) device.

AAC enables students with severe communication disabilities to participate more fully with their peers without disabilities. Students may access communication devices in any number of ways: by pointing, by using a single switch, or by activating the device through eye gaze. The technology can store frequently used messages and allow the individual to access a prestored message with only one keystroke. However, it is important to remember that AAC is only one part of a student's communication system. Individuals who use AAC, as well as individuals who do not, employ a variety of communication forms, including gestures or eye gaze, eye blinks, and winks!

Assessment for AAC

The assessment and selection of AAC should be a team decision, including the individual (when possible), family members, a speech-language pathologist, an occupational therapist, and an educator, as well as other relevant team members. The assessment of an individual for AAC depends on a number of factors, including chronological age, imitative ability, motor control, cognitive ability, and visual needs. As members of the team, educators contribute information on classroom and academic performance. Educators and other team members then work to identify effective AAC technologies and appropriate apps or software. Then the team obtains one or more samples or trial technologies for the student to try. The student, family members, and other team members assess which one is most helpful to the student in interacting with classmates, participating in the classroom, completing academic coursework, and taking part in community activities. Some of the key questions for teachers, students, and family members to consider during an assessment are listed in Figure 13.5.

1. What are the environments where the student spends a portion of the day?
   _____ home
   _____ school
   _____ afterschool care
   _____ other (please specify)

2. What types of communication does the student presently use? How well do others understand?
   _____ points   poor good excellent
   _____ gestures   poor good excellent
   _____ eye gazes   poor good excellent
   _____ other (please specify) poor good excellent

3. During a typical day:
   a. with whom might the student interact?
   _____ _____ _____
   _____ _____ _____
   _____ _____ _____

   b. what are some messages that the student might use?
   To state a feeling:
   To make a request:
   To ask a question:
   To greet someone or say goodbye:

4. How could additional opportunities to communicate be provided:
   a. by modifying the present system?
   b. by using another device?

FIGURE 13.5 • Questionnaire for Assessment of an Augmentative/Alternative Communication Device for a Student

Summary

- Speech disorders include difficulties in articulation, fluency of speech, and quality of voice; language disorders include difficulties in understanding or using oral language.
- Educators must identify young students who are experiencing difficulties as soon as possible or early problems in oral language will develop into difficulties with written language and reading.
- Oral language assessment involves examining form, content, and use of oral language.
- Language samples and language probes are two valuable ways of assessing oral language.
- Educators should work closely with speech-language pathologists in assessing, planning, and implementing instruction for students with speech and language impairments.

QUESTIONS FOR REFLECTION

1. Interview a speech-language pathologist regarding assessment of speech and language skills. What assessment approaches does this individual use in gathering information about content, form, and use?

2. The assessment of oral language skills is important when assessing achievement, development, ability, and behavior. How might the assessment of language skills relate to assessment in one of these four areas?

3. Obtain two or more standardized tests for assessing oral language. Compare and contrast the content of the two instruments.

4. Create a checklist for assessing language in the physical, learning, or social environment. Visit two different classrooms and use your checklist. Evaluate the results.

REFERENCES

Costanza-Smith, A. (2010). The clinical utility of language samples. *Perspectives on Language Learning and Education, 17*(1) 9–15.

D'Angiulli, A., Siegel, L. S., & Maggi, S. (2004). Literacy instruction, SES, and word-reading achievement in English-language learners and children with English as a first language: A longitudinal study. *Learning Disabilities Research and Practice, 19*, 202–213.

Hammill, D. D., Brown, V. L., Larsen, S. C., & Wiederholt, J. L. (2007). *Test of adolescent and adult language, fourth edition.* Austin, TX: Pearson.

Heilmann, J., Miller, J. F., & Nockerts, A. (2011). Using language sample databases. *Language, Speech, and Hearing Services in Schools, 41*(91), 84–95.

Heilmann, J., Nockerts, A., & Miller, J. F. (2010). Language sampling: Does the length of the transcript matter? *Language, Speech & Hearing Services in Schools, 41*(4), 393–404. doi:10.1044/0161-1461(2009/09-0023)

Mackie, C., & Dockrell, J. E. (2004). The nature of written language deficits in children with specific language impairment. *Journal of Speech, Language, and Hearing Research 47*(6), 1469–1483.

McMaster, K. L., Kung, S. H., Han, I., & Cao, M. (2008). Peer-assisted learning strategies: A "Tier 1" approach to promoting English language learners' response to intervention. *Exceptional Children, 74*(2), 194–214.

Miller, J., & Iglesias, A. (2008). *Systematic analysis of language transcripts (SALT), Bilingual SE Version 2008* [Computer Software], SALT Software, LLC.

National Institute of Child Health and Human Development. (2005). Pathways to reading: The role of oral language in the transition to reading. *Developmental Psychology, 41*(2), 428–442.

Polloway, E. A., Miller, L., & Smith, T. E. C. (2012). *Language instruction for students with disabilities* (4th ed.). Denver, CO: Love.

Semel, E., Wiig, E. H., & Secord, W. (2013). *Clinical evaluation of language fundamentals®, fifth edition (CELF®-5).* San Antonio, TX: Pearson.

Wiig, E. H., Semel, E., & Secord, W. (2006) *Clinical evaluation of language fundamentals®, fourth edition Spanish (CELF®-4 Spanish).* San Antonio, TX: Pearson.

Zimmerman, I. L., Steiner, V. G., & Pond, R. E. (2011). *Preschool language scales, fifth edition (PLS™-5).* San Antonio, TX: Pearson.

Zimmerman, I. L., Steiner, V. G., & Pond, R. E. (2012). *Preschool language scales, fifth edition Spanish (PLS-5™ Spanish).* San Antonio, TX: Pearson.

14 Mathematics

Chapter Objectives

After completing this chapter, you should be able to:

- Explain how the following approaches can be used to assess mathematics performance: curriculum-based measurement, performance-based, and informal approaches.
- Describe ways in which standardized achievement tests can be used in the assessment of mathematics.

Overview

Mathematics assessment includes screening, identification of specific mathematics difficulties, program planning, progress monitoring, and program evaluation. The assessment questions determine the assessment approaches and tests that will be used. For example, teachers may ask questions such as these:

- Does the student have a disability in mathematics?
- What types of accommodations should be made?
- Where should mathematics instruction begin?
- Is the student making progress in mathematics?
- To what extent does instruction support mathematics achievement?

Today's mathematics standards emphasize mathematics problems that build on students' knowledge and prior experiences and actively engage students in accomplishing mathematics. For up-to-date information on principles and standards for mathematics, see the National Council for Teachers of Mathematics (NCTM) site **www.nctm.org/standards** and the Common Core Standards **www.corestandards.org/site**. According to the NCTM, knowing mathematics means doing mathematics. The doing of mathematics necessarily involves students in problems and tasks that:

- Are mathematically meaningful.
- Require students to think rather than to memorize.
- Require students to hypothesize and to generalize.
- Generate further mathematics questions or problems.

- Require that students learn while solving a task.
- Allow for more than one acceptable answer.

Connecting Assessment With Instruction

A fundamental principle is that assessment of mathematical abilities and skills forms a link that is integrally linked with mathematics instruction. Linking instruction with assessment in mathematics means that assessment occurs as a normal part of the student's schoolwork.

The conditions for assessment are similar to the conditions for doing meaningful tasks. Students should have sufficient time, have access to peers, be able to use appropriate tools (books, calculators, manipulatives, etc.), and have the chance to revise their work. Assessment tasks are meaningful and multidimensional. They should provide students with the opportunity to demonstrate mathematical abilities, including problem solving, drawing conclusions, understanding relationships, and generating new questions. Feedback to students is specific, meaningful, and prompt and informs the students' thinking about mathematics. Students can be actively involved in the assessment process.

Multiple forms of assessment should be used (Hong & Ehrensberger, 2007). These assessment activities can occur individually or in small groups and can take place during one session or over multiple sessions.

One of the most important aspects of assessment is feedback. Feedback from peers and teachers encourages the development of mathematical and scientific thinking. Ways in which the teacher can gather information and provide feedback to parents and students, in addition to standardized norm-referenced tests, include the following:

- Criterion-referenced assessment
- Probes
- Error analysis
- Oral descriptions
- Written descriptions
- Checklists and questionnaires
- Curriculum-based assessment
- Curriculum-based measurement
- Interviews
- Conferences
- Student journals, diaries, and blogs
- Performance-based assessment
- Portfolios
- Exhibitions (NCTM, 2006)

Probes

A probe is a diagnostic technique that can be especially useful in diagnosing students' difficulties and in planning instruction in mathematics. For example, suppose a teacher wants to determine whether a student understands the concepts of "less than" and "more than." The teacher can present the student with several objects, such as cubes or beads, and ask the student to identify which groups contain objects that are "less than" or "more than" those in the other group. Additional examples of probes include estimation of length, height, area, volume, money, and basic mathematical calculations.

Error Analysis

The purposes of error analysis are to (1) identify the patterns of errors or mistakes that students make in their work, (2) understand why students make the errors, and (3) provide targeted instruction to correct the errors. When conducting an error analysis, the teacher checks the student's mathematics problems and categorizes the errors. The following is a list of errors that students commonly make in various mathematical areas.

Addition and Subtraction

- Lack of understanding of regrouping.
- Confusion of 1s and 10s in carrying and writing.
- Forgetting to carry 10s and 100s.
- Forgetting to regroup when subtracting 10s and 100s.
- Regrouping when it is not required.
- Incorrect operation (the student subtracts instead of adding, or vice versa).
- Lack of knowledge of basic number facts.

Multiplication and Division

- Forgetting to carry in multiplication.
- Carrying before multiplying.
- Ignoring place value in division.
- Recording the answer from left to right in multiplication.
- Lack of alignment of work in columns.
- Lack of knowledge of basic number facts.

Fractions

- Incorrect cancellation.
- Failure to reduce to lowest common denominator.
- Ignoring the remainder.
- Incorrect conversion of mixed numbers to fractions.

Word Problems

- Difficulty in reading.
- Inability to relate to the context of the problem.
- Inability to understand the language and vocabulary of the problem.
- Difficulty in identifying the relevant and the irrelevant information.
- Difficulty in identifying the number of steps required to solve the problem.
- Trouble in doing mathematical operations (addition, subtraction, multiplication, division) (Ashlock, 1996; Tindal & Marston, 1990).

After conducting an error analysis, summarize the error patterns. Notice, however, that many errors that students make do not fall into a pattern, and some patterns that emerge do not indicate a serious problem. Teachers must view error analysis as a preliminary form of assessment and should conduct further evaluation of the student's work. Here are two examples. Can you identify the error pattern?

Example 1	Example 2
$100 \times 2 = 102$	$9 \times 9 = 89$
$200 \times 2 = 202$	$8 \times 8 = 68$
$300 \times 2 = 302$	$7 \times 7 = 77$

In the first example, the student used the incorrect operation. The student did not recognize the "×" as a multiplication symbol and added, rather than multiplied, the numbers. In the second example, the student did not know the multiplication facts.

Oral Descriptions

Verbal descriptions of a student's work provide immediate feedback to a student by a teacher or peer. Oral descriptions are quick, efficient, and direct, and they blend easily into instruction. They must not be off the cuff; oral descriptions should be as well thought out as written descriptions. Oral descriptions are helpful for program planning and program evaluation. Oral descriptions do have several drawbacks, however. They can be subjective, and because the descriptions are given verbally, there is no permanent record. In addition, specific disabilities limit the ability of the student to understand, remember, or reply to the description.

Written Descriptions

A written description is a brief narrative that records feedback about the student's work that the student, teachers, and/or parents can share. A written description, like an oral description, conveys an impression of important aspects of the student's work. Written descriptions are useful for program planning and program evaluation.

Before writing the narrative, the teacher carefully reviews the student's work. The teacher then writes the description, noting areas of strength as well as any problems. A written description provides information to the student about the quality of the work. Because it is a record, the student can refer to it as he or she continues to work.

For example, a student is asked to solve the following problem:

> Siti wants to paint a room in her home. She has to measure the width and height of the walls and find out how much paint is needed to cover all the walls. How would you advise Siti to figure out the cost of painting the room? Make a plan for Siti. What else does she need to consider?

After examining the student's solution, a teacher can comment on the organization, labeling, problem-solving processes, computations, spelling, and language use. The teacher can discuss the use of mathematics to solve real-world problems, the completeness of the solution, the student's disposition toward mathematics, the ability to plan ahead, work habits, and attention to detail (Kulm, 1994). Two disadvantages to using written descriptions are that the parents may have difficulty reading or they may not have knowledge of written English.

When providing either written or verbal feedback to students and parents, teachers may decide to use performance descriptors such as the following:

- *Awareness*—the student is aware of mathematics concepts and materials.
- *Emergent*—the student has a beginning understanding of mathematics concepts and needs some support and assistance when completing work.
- *Developing*—the student is developing an understanding of mathematics skills and understandings but continues to need support and practice.
- *Skilled*—the student is able to solve some problems independently and can produce accurate results.
- *Proficient*—the student uses various strategies, applies mathematical concepts, and works independently. GOOD!

Checklists and Questionnaires

Checklists and questionnaires are convenient and easy ways to provide feedback about a student's work. Figure 14.1 is an example of a checklist for teachers to provide feedback about the attitudes toward mathematics and student confidence, willingness, perseverance, and interest in doing mathematics. Checklists are useful for screening, diagnosis, instructional planning, progress monitoring, and program evaluation.

Attitudes	Ratings of Attitudes		
	Low	Medium	High
1. Interest			
2. Enjoyment			
3. Self-confidence			
4. Engagement			
5. Anxiety			
6. Motivation			
7. Persistence			

FIGURE 14.1 • Attitudes Toward Mathematics

Questionnaires allow teachers and students to collect information in more detail than they can with checklists. Open-ended questionnaires allow respondents to express their attitudes, opinions, and knowledge in depth; structured questionnaires allow respondents simply to fill in one or two words or circle a response.

Interviews

There are special considerations when using this technique in mathematics assessment. Interviews can guide discussions, encourage students, and determine disposition toward mathematics. One basic approach is to interview students individually about their likes and dislikes, asking questions such as "What do you like about mathematics?" "What are your interests?" and "What don't you like?" Interviews can help in screening, diagnosis, program planning, and program evaluation.

A structured interview is a more systematic way to assess mathematics performance. A structured interview is an opportunity to observe, question, and discuss mathematics and to elicit unexpected information about the student. Teachers can question students about a physical activity, such as measuring a room, determining the space requirements for a table, or estimating the size of a vegetable garden. Students who lack reading or communication skills can use pantomime or can manipulate objects to demonstrate what they know. For example, a teacher could pose the following questions about measuring:

How would you estimate the area of a vegetable garden?
Why is it important to know the area of a garden?
What is the perimeter of the garden?
Why is it important to estimate the perimeter?
How can this information be used?

Conferences

A conference is a conversation about the student's work and can include the student, educators, and/or parents. Participants in a conference share their views of the student's work with the goal of providing feedback and recommendations. Teacher–student conferences can be helpful when assessing one piece of work or when summarizing the student's work over a period of time. The discussion in a conference can be strictly verbal, or the teacher or evaluator may choose to record it, videotape it, or summarize it in written form. Conferences are effective for diagnosis, program planning, and program evaluation.

Student Journals, Diaries, and Blogs

Journals, diaries, and blogs encourage students to reflect on their own work, communicate about their learning, and document their progress. Students can keep a notebook, journal, electronic diary, or blog that allows them to record their work, attitudes, and feelings about mathematics. Students can indicate what they like and don't like about doing mathematics and which areas give them difficulty. These tools are effective for program planning and program evaluation. The following is a sample mathematics journal or blog template:

Mathematics topic:
Two examples of problems that I solved:
Two important ideas:
What I understand best:
What I want to improve:

Self-Assessment

Self-assessment provides students with an opportunity to analyze their own abilities and skills in mathematics and to reflect on their own learning. Students can keep track of topics in which they need further practice or clarification and seek assistance to achieve proficiency. Self-assessment provides students with an opportunity to review concepts and identify mathematical processes. Figure 14.2 is an example of a checklist that students use when assessing their own learning.

Student's Name _____ Date _____

After reading the mathematical word problem I can:	1 Great!	2	3	4	5 Darn!
1. draw a picture to help solve the problem.					
2. identify the operations to solve the problem.					
3. list the steps to solve the problem and explain why each step is necessary.					
4. use correct labeling.					
5. use numbers and symbols to write equation(s) to solve the problem.					
6. verify the results.					
7. interpret the results.					

FIGURE 14.2 • Self-Assessment Checklist

Figure 14.3 • Peer Assessment

Peer Assessment Checklist:

Student's Name _____ Date _____
Peer's Name _____

	☹	😐	☺
1. My peer used the data in the tables to solve the mathematical story problem.			
2. My peer used correct mathematical notation.			
3. My peer used pictures to illustrate the story problem.			
4. My peer used labeling.			
5. My peer's work is neat.			

Peer Assessment

When conducting peer assessments, students have an opportunity to check and consult with peers regarding skills and strategies. Peer assessment in mathematics provides rich opportunities for students to communicate with others about mathematics and to deepen their understanding of mathematical processes. Peer assessment allows students insight into the thinking and reasoning abilities of their peers. By engaging in collaborative learning and problem solving, students have an opportunity to reflect on the learning processes of their peers as well as their own. Figure 14.3 is an example of a checklist that students use when conducting a peer assessment.

Criterion-Referenced Assessment

Instead of comparing a student's performance to a norm group, criterion-referenced tests measure a student's performance with respect to a well-defined content domain. Although norm-referenced tests in mathematics allow for discrimination among the performance of individual students on specific test items, criterion-referenced tests provide a description of knowledge, skills, or behaviors in a specific range, or domain, of test items. For example, if a criterion is that students should be able to subtract single-digit numbers, then the assessment items could be:

$$9 - 2 = ?, 8 - 2 = ?, 5 - 3 = ?$$

Curriculum-Based Measurement

Curriculum-based measurement (CBM) is an approach that uses direct assessment to determine what students know and can do. Although there are several methods for constructing CBMs (Foegen, Jiban, & Deno, 2007; Fore, Boon, Lawson, & Martin, 2007; Hosp & Hosp,

2003), in general, the development and use are similar. When using CBMs in mathematics, students respond to questions, vocabulary, or carefully selected mathematics problems chosen from the students' mathematics curriculum. These carefully selected problems or questions are used to sample mathematics knowledge and skills. They are helpful in diagnosing and assisting with students' difficulties and assisting in planning, progress monitoring, and evaluating instruction.

Suppose a teacher wants to determine why a student seems to confuse basic mathematics operations. The student seems to be able to solve problems successfully, but still seems to be confused. The teacher presents the problems, but this time they are grouped according to the algorithm shown in Figure 14.4. The teacher then can help by showing the student how to organize the problems. Eventually, using another probe, the teacher is able to use fading to gradually lighten the lines that separate the problems until the student does not need them to complete the problem.

Teachers can implement CBM during the process of instruction. When administering a CBM, the teacher should document the student's performance during each of the following steps: step 1 (baseline), step 2 (instruction), and step 3 (new baseline). For example:

Step 1. *(Baseline).* The teacher identifies the area of mathematical performance that needs observation and measures whether the student can perform the task. Examples include number recognition, counting, addition, subtraction, and so on.
Step 2. *(Instruction).* The teacher probes the task. For example, to facilitate number recognition, the teacher asks the student to say, trace, recognize, and write a numeral.
Step 3. *(New Baseline).* The teacher measures whether the student can perform the task.

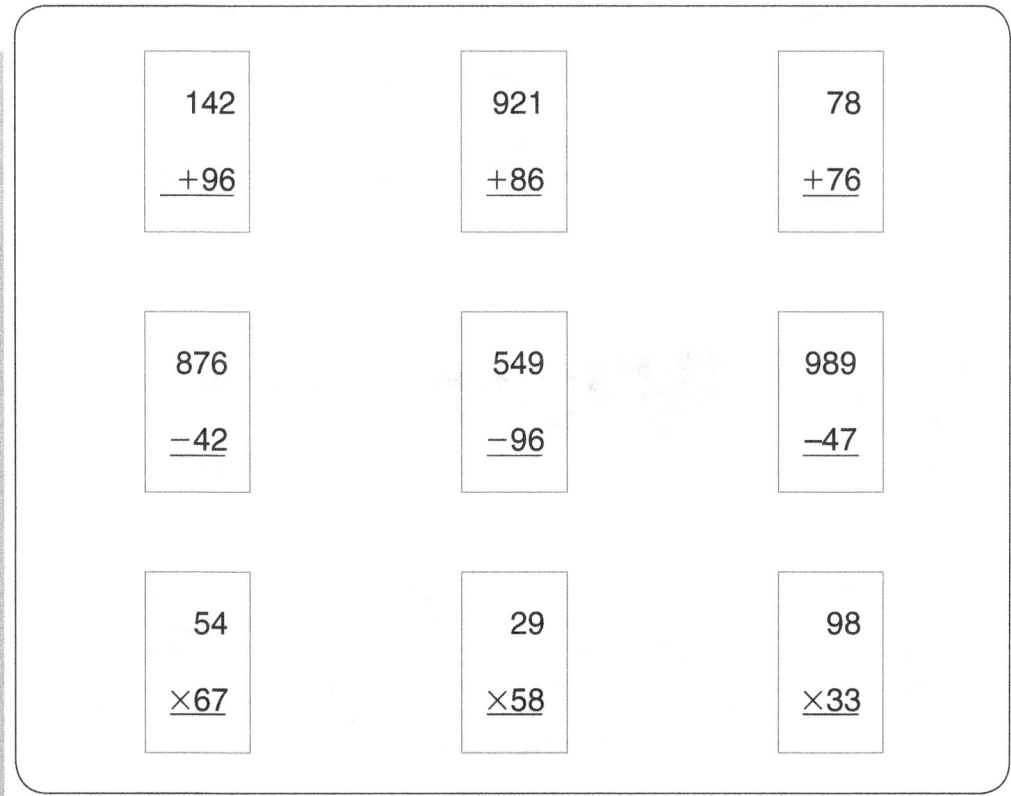

FIGURE 14.4 • Grouping Similar Problems on a Page

Suggestions for Accommodations When Using CBMs in Mathematics

Teachers may find that accommodations are useful when constructing and administering CBMs in mathematics. The following list contains three types of accommodations when considering CBM in mathematics instruction:

1. *Instructional accommodations*
   - Change from a written presentation to an oral presentation.
   - Combine verbal instruction with a written explanation.
   - Provide additional practice.
   - Slow the pace of instruction.
   - Provide additional time to complete problems.
   - Take tests orally.
2. *Material accommodations*
   - Use manipulatives.
   - Place fewer problems on a page.
   - Use color cues or other cues for mathematical operations.
   - Combine tactile mode with visual, oral, or kinesthetic modes.
3. *Environmental accommodations*
   - Change the location of instruction or the test.
   - Change the time of day for instruction or the test.
   - Provide a work area that is quiet and free of distractions.
   - Change the lighting in the work area.
   - Change the seating arrangement.

Formal Measures for Monitoring Progress

Progress monitoring is essential to supporting students' mathematics achievement and evaluating the benefits of instruction. Similar to what it did for the assessment of reading, the U.S. Department of Education established the following criteria for determining the adequacy of progress-monitoring measures: reliability, validity, alternate forms, sensitivity to students' improvement, alignment with curriculum standards or benchmarks, evidence for improvement of students' learning or teacher planning, and specification of rates of improvement. The extent to which formalized measures met these criteria is shown in Table 14.1 (U.S. Department of

---

Research-Based Practices | **Progress Monitoring Measures: Review of the Literature**

In a review of 578 research articles and reports (Foegen et al., 2007), researchers examined the technical characteristics of various measures that are used to assess performance and progress monitoring in mathematics. The researchers found that many studies have been conducted on elementary students, and a smaller number of studies were conducted in early education and middle school mathematics. Much more confidence can be placed in CBM measures of reading rather than mathematics to measure progress and growth. There is little consensus among researchers on the preferred approach to developing CBMs in mathematics. Researchers have various views on how to conduct CBMs in mathematics and the types of problems to include. There continues to be a great need for continued research on the development and implementation of robust measures of progress monitoring in mathematics.

TABLE 14.1 • Mathematics Tools for Progress Monitoring

		Psychometric Standards		Progress-Monitoring Characteristics				
Measures	Areas	Reliability	Validity	Alternate Forms	Sensitivity to Students' Improvement	Curriculum Benchmarks	Improvement of Student Learning or Teacher Planning	Specification of Rates of Improvement
Accelerated Reader (AR)	Math	•	•	•	•	•	•	•
AIMSweb	Early numeracy	•	•	•	•	•	o	•
	Math	•	•	•	•	•	o	•
Monitoring Basic Skills Progress (MBSP)	Math	•	•	o	•	o	•	•
PASeries	Math	•	•	•	•	•	•	o
STAR	Math	•	•	•	o	•	o	•
Yearly Progress Pro	Math	•	•	•	•	•	•	•

o Insufficient evidence
• Sufficient evidence
Source: Adapted from the U.S. Department of Education. Retrieved December 21, 2008, from http://www.studentprogress.org

Education, n.d.). In addition to the U.S. Department of Education ratings, other researchers (Foegen, 2008) are also studying the optimal uses of curriculum-based measurement.

Performance-Based Assessment

As a measure of mathematics instruction, performance-based assessment requires students to demonstrate mathematical abilities, skills, and dispositions, such as developing a product or demonstrating an understanding of concepts and relationships. This type of assessment is useful in program planning and program evaluation. The following are examples of performance tasks:

- Pretend that students own an electronics store. They need to know which types and brands of phones they could sell. What steps should they take?
- Use an electronic spreadsheet program to keep track of migrating birds, rainfall, sports team players, or the heart rates of students.
- Plan an exercise path or a nature walk. Calculate the distances between stops along the path. What should students consider when planning and constructing the path?

Portfolios

A portfolio is a deliberate collection of a student's work over time that demonstrates the student's efforts, progress, and achievement. If portfolios document and assess mathematical abilities, they provide information about conceptual understanding, problem solving, reasoning, communication abilities, disposition toward mathematics, creativity, work habits, and attitudes. Mathematics portfolios help students integrate new learning with prior learning. Portfolios in mathematics assessment aid in program planning and program evaluation.

A portfolio is not just a folder of practice worksheets or of all the work that the student has completed. The selection of the portfolio contents is always a carefully considered process. The following are suggestions for inclusion in student mathematics portfolios:

- Photographs of students' bridge-building projects, using components of different lengths.
- Projects that involve the students' use of software to design quilts or flags from squares and triangles.
- Experiments with statistics, such as tracking sports team results, Web site usage, or number and timing of text messages.
- Recordings of students collaborating on projects and demonstrations of learning.
- Recordings of students demonstrating what they have learned after analyzing data on rainfall, climate change, or endangered animal species.

Exhibitions

An exhibition is a display of a student's work that summarizes and synthesizes what the student has accomplished. Customarily, it demonstrates knowledge, abilities, skills, and attitudes concerning one project or a unit of work. In mathematics assessment, exhibitions are useful because students realize that doing mathematics is more than just a series of worksheets or exercises, that it involves conceptual understanding, problem solving, and reasoning. Exhibitions can be effective in program planning and program evaluation.

Observing the Student Within the Classroom Environment

In Chapter 8, you learned about the importance of considering the student within the physical, learning, and social environments. The interactions between the student and the environment are crucial assessment considerations.

Physical Environment

The physical environment can influence the student's mathematics performance. The temperature, lighting, and seating arrangement of the teaching and learning spaces affect how well the student performs.

Learning Environment

A comfortable learning environment can contribute to mathematics achievement. The curriculum, instructional methods, materials, and the assessment procedures are all areas of concern. The learning environment can promote a positive disposition toward mathematics. Students are willing to do mathematics when (1) mathematics problems are challenging, (2) students realize that mathematics problems are worth doing, (3) mathematics problems are accessible to a wide range of students, (4) a variety of instructional approaches are available, and (5) multiple assessment procedures check learning.

Social Environment

Relationships with students and teachers affect mathematics and achievement. The social environment is crucial to the development of self-concept and self-esteem. These, in turn, contribute to a positive disposition toward mathematics. By observing the social environment, teachers can study the relationships students have with peers and adults.

Standardized Instruments

This section describes the use of standardized, norm-referenced tests of mathematical abilities. Standardized, norm-referenced tests are effective for screening, determining eligibility, and conducting program evaluations. Evaluators may be able to compare scores from these tests with the performance of students of similar age or grade who are part of a standardization sample. Scores from standardized mathematics tests can be used to make interpretations about an individual student's performance on several tests.

KeyMath 3 Diagnostic Assessment

KeyMath 3 Diagnostic Assessment (KeyMath 3 DA; Connolly, 2007) is an individually or group administered test of mathematics skills, concepts, and operations. It is intended for use with individuals ages 4 years 6 months through 21 years and for kindergarten through grade 12. The instrument reflects the standards of the National Council of Teachers of Mathematics (NCTM, 2000) and is organized into 10 subjects, which are further organized into three areas: basic concepts (conceptual knowledge), operations (mathematical skills), and applications (problem solving).

ADMINISTRATION The *KeyMath 3 DA* can be administered by regular and special education teachers, aides, paraprofessionals, counselors, and school psychologists. Depending on the age of the student, it takes approximately 30 to 90 minutes to administer this test. The Snapshot about Kara describes how her teacher evaluated her performance on this test.

SCORING Raw scores are converted to scale scores, standard scores, percentile ranks, grade equivalents, age equivalents, and growth scale values, which can be used to monitor progress.

STANDARDIZATION The *KeyMath 3* was normed based on the 2004 U.S. Census estimates and was normed during 2006. The age and grade norm group samples included individuals ages 4 years 6 months through 21 years and kindergarten through grade 12. Stratification of the standardization sample reflects categories of age, gender, region, race, ethnicity, and economic status as estimated by parental education.

RELIABILITY The author determined alternate-form reliability by grade. For the areas, the correlations were ranged from .88 (applications) to .94 (basic concepts). The total test alternate reliability is .96. Internal consistency reliabilities ranged from .85 through .97.

VALIDITY According to the manual, test developers determined construct validity in several ways. The manual presents evidence demonstrating that knowledge about mathematics increases with age, that the subtests intercorrelate with the areas and the total test score, and that scores on the *KeyMath 3* correlate with scores on other tests of mathematical achievement. The revision of the measure involved the creation of a blueprint that is consistent with mathematics standards and considered experts' views on mathematics content, test development, and item bias.

SUMMARY The *KeyMath 3 Diagnostic Assessment* is an individually administered test of mathematics

---

TESTS-at-a-GLANCE

KeyMath 3 Diagnostic Assessment (KeyMath 3 DA)
www.pearsonclinical.com
- **Publication Date:** 2007
- **Purposes:** Measures mathematics concepts, skills, operations, and applications.
- **Age/Grade Levels:** 4 years 6 months through 21 years; kindergarten through grade 12.
- **Time to Administer:** Approximately 30 to 90 minutes.
- **Technical Adequacy:** Standardization sample is acceptable. Reliability and validity are acceptable.
- **Suggested Use:** Provides evidence of strengths and weaknesses in mathematics knowledge and skills. Can be used to monitor progress in mathematics.

SNAPSHOT

Kara

Kara is a 12-year-old in sixth grade. Her interests include drawing and soccer. Kara has an exuberant sense of humor and loves to play jokes on her friends and family. She has just finished making a book of her drawings that she intends to give to her grandmother, who lives with Kara, her 5-year-old brother John, and her mother and father. Kara was diagnosed as having a learning disability in mathematics when she was in third grade.

OBSERVATION: Kara was observed in her sixth-grade classroom. The 25 other students in the classroom were working in small groups solving problems that the teacher had assigned. The class was lively, and the students were engaging in their work—all except Kara. Kara sat with a small group of three other students. Kara appeared to be unsure of how she could contribute to the problem-solving activity. She was quiet, had a puzzled look on her face, and was listening to the students in the group.

TEACHER'S COMMENTS: Kara has lagged considerably behind her peers in mathematics. The rest of the class has been working on graphing, geometry, and probability. An examination of Kara's recent homework showed that she has trouble with basic number facts and that she reverses numbers when writing them.

SUMMARY OF TEST PERFORMANCE: At the end of the last school year, the individualized education program (IEP) team met to review Kara's program. The special education consultant reported that Kara's full-scale intelligence was well above average. On an individualized achievement test, Kara scored above average on the reading and spelling subtests but considerably below average on mathematical computation. On the *KeyMath 3* her scores in the areas of basic concepts, operations, and applications were all well below average.

PLANNING INSTRUCTION: Kara's teacher and the school's learning specialist met to discuss the assessment results. It was apparent that Kara was struggling with basic mathematics processes, but that she grasps mathematics concepts. Kara's teacher felt that instruction should emphasize basic mathematics processes, such as addition, subtraction, multiplication, and division, and that it was critically important to continue instruction on mathematics concepts. Curriculum materials were selected, and a guide was identified to track Kara's progress.

Pause and consider:

- What suggestions do you have for furthering pinpointing Kara's strengths and weaknesses in mathematics?
- How could you use CBM to identify weaknesses and develop instructional interventions?

---

achievement. The instrument has been updated to reflect contemporary views of mathematics instruction and assessment. Reliabilities and validity coefficients are well within the acceptable range. The standardization sample is representative of the U.S. population estimates for 2004.

Test of Mathematical Abilities, Third Edition

The *Test of Mathematical Abilities, Third Edition* (TOMA-3; Brown, Cronin, & Bryant, 2011) is a norm-referenced test of attitudes toward mathematics, mathematics vocabulary, computation, general information relating to mathematics, and mathematical story problems. The TOMA-3 can be individually administered or group administered to students ages 8 to 18 years, 11 months. It contains five subtests:

Mathematical Symbols and Concepts
Computation
Mathematics in Everyday Life
Word Problems

Attitude Toward Math

The Mathematical Ability Index is the overall composite score.

ADMINISTRATION The *TOMA-3* can be individually administered or group administered.

SCORING Raw scores convert to standard scores and percentile ranks. Subtest scores have a mean of 10 and a standard deviation of 3.

STANDARDIZATION The standardization sample for *TOMA-3* includes 1,456 students residing in 21 states.

RELIABILITY Reliability is acceptable.

VALIDITY Examiners should carefully compare the mathematics curriculum with the test items in order to determine content validity.

SUMMARY The *Test of Mathematical Abilities, Third Edition (TOMA-3)* is an individually administered or group administered test of various aspects of mathematical abilities. Information about reliability and validity is sketchy. Test examiners should evaluate the content validity of the test. The *TOMA-2* is most useful as a screening test.

TESTS-at-a-GLANCE

Test of Mathematical Abilities, Third Edition (TOMA-3)
www.proedinc.com/customer/productView.aspx?id=5151

- **Publication Date:** 2011
- **Purposes:** Measures attitudes toward mathematics, computation and understanding of word problems and identifies students' strengths and limitations in mathematics by comparing students' results to a norm-referenced sample.
- **Age/Grade Levels:** Ages 8 through 18 years, 11 months.
- **Time to Administer:** 60 to 90 minutes.
- **Technical Adequacy:** Information on reliability and validity is adequate. Test examiners are encouraged to evaluate the content validity of the test especially with regard to mathematics standards.
- **Suggested Use:** Provides some evidence of strengths and limitations in mathematics knowledge and skills. The *TOMA-3* should be used in combination with other instruments and measures.

Summary

- Contemporary views of mathematics stress that all children need to learn mathematics to function successfully in the world today.
- Equitable assessment of mathematical abilities and skills requires a variety of approaches to reflect an understanding of students' ability, culture, ethnicity, race, language, geographic region of origin, gender, disability, and economic level.
- Standardized norm-referenced tests of mathematics are effective for screening, determining eligibility, and conducting program evaluations.
- Mathematics assessment should be linked with instruction.
- Curriculum-based measurement uses direct assessment to determine what students know and can do.
- Mathematics assessment strategies include error analysis, oral descriptions, written descriptions, checklists and questionnaires, interviews, conferences, student journals, performance-based assessment, portfolios, exhibitions, self-assessment, and peer assessment.

QUESTIONS FOR REFLECTION

1. For information on mathematics learning standards, visit the Web site of the National Council of Teachers of Mathematics (**www.nctm.org**).
2. Search the Web to find additional resources on curriculum-based assessment. Share your results with others. What are the commonalities among approaches?
3. Develop and define descriptors that can be used to assess mathematics journals, diaries, and/or blog entries.
4. Reflect on the ways in which students' culture, ethnicity, or language influences attitudes, understanding, and assessment of mathematics.

REFERENCES

Ashlock, R. B. (1996). *Error patterns in computation: A semi-programmed approach* (5th ed.). Columbus, OH: Merrill.

Brown, V. L., Cronin, M. E., & Bryant, D. (2011). *Test of mathematical abilities* (3rd ed.). Austin, TX: PRO-ED.

Connolly, A. J. (2007). *KeyMath 3 Diagnostic Assessment.* Bloomington, MN: Pearson.

Foegen, A. (2008). Progress monitoring on middle school mathematics. *Remedial and Special Education, 29*(4), 195–207.

Foegen, A., Jiban, C., & Deno, S. (2007). Progress monitoring measures in mathematics. *Journal of Special Education, 41*(2), 121–139.

Fore, C., Boon, R., Lawson, C., & Martin, C. (2007). Using curriculum-based measurement for formative instructional decision-making in basic mathematics. *Education, 128*(2), 324–332.

Hong, B., & Ehrensberger, W. (2007). Assessing the mathematics skills of students with disabilities. *Preventing School Failure 52*(1), 41–47.

Hosp, M. K., & Hosp, J. L. (2003). Curriculum-based measurement for reading, spelling, and math: How to do it and why. *Preventing School Failure, 48*(11), 10–17.

Kulm, G. (1994). *Mathematics assessment.* San Francisco: Jossey-Bass.

National Council for Teachers of Mathematics (NCTM). (2000). *NCTM standards.* Retrieved January 2, 2007, from http://www.nctm.org

National Council for Teachers of Mathematics (NCTM). (2006). *Curriculum focal points for prekindergarten through grade 8 mathematics.* Reston, VA: Author.

Tindal, G. A., & Marston, D. B. (1990). *Classroom-based assessment.* Columbus, OH: Merrill.

U.S. Department of Education. (n.d.). National Center on Student Progress Monitoring. Retrieved December 21, 2008, from http://www.studentprogress.org

15 Performance-Based, Authentic, and Portfolio Assessments

Chapter Objectives

After completing this chapter, you should be able to:

- Describe performance-based assessment, authentic assessment, and portfolio assessment.
- Convey approaches to assessing performance-based assessments.
- Develop and implement performance-based assessment approaches.

Overview

This chapter examines alternatives to traditional assessment approaches. Each of these alternatives is evolving as educators search for improved practices and tools for linking instruction with assessment. Portfolios, performance tasks, exhibitions, or other documentation of students' achievement represent students' accomplishments. Although norm-referenced tests have their place in the assessment process, alternatives to norm-referenced tests provide a rich variety of methods for assessing students' progress, skills, and achievement.

Contemporary views of learning have influenced the development of alternative assessment approaches; now we know the following:

1. Students can construct knowledge by connecting new information and prior learning. Implications for assessment:
   - Students learn divergent thinking; rather than searching for one right answer, they can find multiple solutions.
   - Students use multiple forms of expression.
   - Students develop critical-thinking skills.
   - Students relate prior knowledge to new learning.
2. Students of all ages and abilities can solve problems. Implications for assessment:
   - All students participate in problem-solving activities.
   - Problem solving and critical thinking do not have to be contingent on mastery of basic skills.

285

3. Students approach learning with a multiplicity of learning styles, attention spans, motivations, and developmental and cognitive differences. Implications for assessment:
   - Multiple assessments should be available so that students can demonstrate what they know and can do.
   - Teachers must allot sufficient time to complete assessment tasks.
4. Students do better when they know the goals and understand how their performance will be evaluated. Implications for assessment:
   - Students participate in establishing goals.
   - Students discuss and describe criteria for performance.
   - Students routinely receive examples of acceptable levels of performance.
5. Students know when to use knowledge and how to direct their own learning. Implications for assessment:
   - Students have opportunities to monitor and evaluate their own learning.
   - Teachers utilize a range of assessment approaches.
6. Students' learning is affected by motivation, effort, and self-esteem. Implications for assessment:
   - Teachers consider motivation, self-esteem, and the promotion of best efforts in designing assessments.

Performance-Based Assessment

Performance-based assessment describes one or more approaches for measuring student progress, skills, and achievements. Performance-based assessment consists of portfolios, performance tasks, exhibitions, or other documentations of student accomplishments. One way of looking at performance assessment is to think of it as the ultimate form of linking instruction with assessment. Wiggins (1993) is a strong proponent of performance assessment. He urged educators to use "clear, apt, published, and consistently applied teacher criteria in grading work and published models of excellent work that exemplifies standards" and to create "ample opportunities [for students] to produce work that they can be proud of (thus, ample opportunity in the curriculum and instruction to monitor, self-assess, and self-correct their work)" (p. 28).

Performance-based assessment is particularly useful when students are engaging in learning and activities that take place over several days or when it is done at the completion of curriculum units. Students are able to bring into play a variety of resources and demonstrate mastery of various concepts and principles. For teachers of standards-based education, performance-based assessment serves several important functions (Arter & McTighe, 2001):

- Performance criteria help define the standards by specifying what one would look for as evidence of standards achievement.
- When made public, the performance criteria and scoring guides provide clear and consistent targets for students, parents, teachers, and others.
- Using performance-based assessment consistently across classrooms, schools, and districts makes the evaluation of student performance more reliable.
- Teaching criteria help students improve the very skills under assessment, thus integrating assessment and instruction (pp. 15–16).

The Three Gorges Dam project is an example of a performance assessment; see Figure 15.1.

> The Three Gorges Dam spans the Yangtze River, and it affects millions of people who live in southern China. The dam helps to control flooding, generates hydroelectric power, and decreases greenhouse carbon dioxide gas emissions through the reduction of coal as a power source. The construction of the dam was a giant engineering project. It created an enormous freshwater reservoir, which holds back the seasonal flooding of the Yangtze River onto villages and farmlands that are downstream. However, the construction of the dam has led to the forced relocation of several million people, burial of archeological artifacts and remains, endangerment of birds and fish that lived in the surrounding wetlands, and erosion of soil (Chetham, 2004; Wilkinson, 2007).
>
> Your objectives: Working as a team, you will use the available materials to build a dam, which demonstrates your understanding of the functions of dams and reservoirs. Explain several engineering principles used when building dams.
>
> Your tasks:
>
> 1. Find information about the construction of dams.
> 2. Obtain pictures of the Three Gorges Dam. Where is it located? Why was a dam needed?
> 3. Select from the available materials, and build a model of a dam that holds back water when it is poured into the reservoir: empty fish tank, metal baking pans, pebbles, clay or modeling materials, sand, toy building blocks, containers for pouring water, water, and duct tape.
> 4. Develop a visual presentation for other teams, using supporting details and evidence, in which you explain the principles your team learned when constructing the model of the dam and reservoir. The model and presentation should be neat and organized, convey new information about dams and reservoirs, include supporting details and evidence, be visually appealing, and relate what the team members learned as a result of their involvement in this project.
> 5. Critique the model construction and presentation. Explain how the model compares to a real dam. Provide suggestions for improving your presentation.

FIGURE 15.1 • China's Three Gorges Dam Project

Authentic Assessment

Authentic assessment is similar to performance assessment except that the student completes or demonstrates knowledge, skills, or behavior in a real-life context, and real-world standards measure the student's knowledge, skills, or behavior. Learning and performing daily living and job-related skills have been part of the functional life-skills curriculum for some time.

The conditions for authentic assessment are quite different from those of performance assessment. In performance assessment, the circumstances are often contrived or artificial, whereas in authentic assessment, the tasks are part of a real-world setting. For example, learning activities can focus on a student-run snack shop, where students plan and order materials and make and sell items. Just as with performance-based assessment, evaluators must develop the criteria for authentic assessment. Here are suggested characteristics of authentic performances:

Structure
- The activities are public.
- The activities involve an audience.

TABLE 15.1 • Examples of Authentic Assessment

Literacy	Science	Mathematics
Audio file of student reading	Experiment	Solving real-life problems
Video of peer conferencing	Original investigation	Banking activities
Blog postings	Model of a volcano	Designing community bicycle path
Book review	Using scientific databases	Designing and building a structure
Poster about a book	Wiki contributions	Development of a budget
Article for school Web site	Investigation of greenhouse gases	Teaching a buddy/peer
Job application	Designing and building a bridge	
Résumé	Developing an electric car	**Social Studies**
	Performing virtual experiments	Map of a nature trail
The Arts		Development of an interactive exhibit
Multimedia presentation	**Oral Expression**	Story board of a political campaign
Improvisational performance	Participating in a debate	Design for a local recycling center
Musical performance	Book talk	Producing an online video
Dance performance	Play reading	

- The activities require some collaboration.
- The activities require self-direction and motivation.

Design

- The activities are worth doing.
- The activities are motivating.
- The activities are contextualized.
- The activities involve complex processes, not isolated tasks or outcomes.
- The activities assess habits, attitudes, behaviors, motivation, and creativity

Scoring

- The activities involve criteria that are essential.
- The activities are graded according to performance standards.
- The activities involve self-assessment.
- The activities use multifaceted scoring, not one grade.

Equity

- The activities are fair.
- The activities involve multiple areas of learning.
- The activities are responsive to culture, gender, learning style, and language.

Table 15.1 presents examples of authentic assessments.

Portfolio Assessment

A **portfolio** is a systematic collection of a student's work covering an extended period of time. Portfolios can include works in progress, a student's best work, or work that the student is most proud of. Materials in the portfolio are a direct link to a student's **individualized education program (IEP)** and show growth toward the program's objectives.

Special educators find portfolios helpful in answering questions regarding what a student knows and can do. First, portfolios demonstrate a student's growth and progress over time. Students can develop portfolios over the course of a school year and share them during parent–teacher conferences and during annual reviews of the student's IEP. Portfolios may become part of the student's records, which move with the student from one grade or level to the next.

Second, portfolios present examples of the student's best work(s). Portfolios can reflect development over one or more years and can be part of graduation requirements, part of evaluations of individualized programs, or part of the student's résumé for potential employers to see the student's achievements.

Portfolio assessment provides benefits to students, teachers, and family members (Stiggins, 2007):

For students:
- Selecting items to include in the portfolios
- Engaging in a noncompetitive activity
- Experiencing a collaborative climate through peer collaboration activities
- Having ownership and tangible evidence of learning
- Building self-esteem
- Clarifying expectations
- Reflecting and judging their own work
- Receiving ongoing feedback regarding their work

For teachers:
- Connecting assessment and instruction
- Providing diagnostic information about a student's strengths and instructional needs
- Generating meaningful examples of student growth by constructing knowledge of what constitutes high-quality work
- Having concrete examples of student performance to discuss with family members

For family members:
- Viewing student progress over time
- Easy-to-understand examples

Contents of a Portfolio

The contents of a portfolio consist of product as well as process items. Product items include works such as papers, drawings, photographs, models, language samples, creative art, and other artifacts. Process items include successive drafts of a paper, works in progress, works in which students have cooperated with others, and self-reflections about a particular unit of study. Students' reflective statements are critical components of portfolios. Finally, a portfolio may include teacher and parent comments, scores from standardized tests, school attendance records, and records of school activities.

Organizing the Portfolio

Materials in the portfolio can be organized according to curriculum areas, skill areas, processes, themes, or chronological order. Because of their breadth and integrative format, portfolios are useful as part of curriculum and program evaluation.

Portfolios Support Students' Learning

Students learn a great deal from making selections, assembling and reviewing their materials, and refining their portfolios. Teachers support students during each step in the construction process and in refining their portfolios.

1. Deciding what they want to demonstrate in their portfolios. For portfolios to be valid, students must understand the performance they demonstrate. Teachers should discuss with students at the beginning of the year what to include in the portfolio and explain the evaluation process.
2. Incorporating self-reflections, which are important components of a portfolio. A self-reflection is a writing activity in which the student analyzes learning and accomplishments. In the written reflection, students describe their views of the learning process and the importance of the task. To help students become more familiar with the process of reflection, a teacher can use class discussions to encourage students to think about an activity or event. The teacher can model self-reflection or provide examples of student reflections. Students should also have opportunities to practice reflection with each other. Teachers can ask several questions to assist them:
    a. What do you like about this work?
    b. What steps and processes did you use to accomplish this task?
    c. How can you improve this task?
    d. What would you do next?
    e. What is your overall evaluation of your efforts and accomplishments?
3. Understanding portfolio evaluation. It is important that students understand how teachers will evaluate their portfolios. Teachers need to spend time discussing with the class the many ways of evaluating a work.
4. Choosing the pieces to include. Students learn a great deal in choosing and selecting the materials to include in the portfolio. Teachers help students by choosing assignments that require diverse skills and by keeping individual student ability and areas of interest in mind.
5. Determining how to present the pieces. Some content areas more readily lend themselves to one format than another. For example, a photograph may better represent the complexity or creativity of a model of a city or the construction of a sailboat than a written text could. A recording captures areas in which movements or interactions are important.

Using Technology

Teachers and students can organize and preserve student information, including text, sounds (talking, singing, music, and reading), images (pictures, drawings, videos, and photographs), and video (individual and group performances), Web pages, wikis, or blogs. Student- or teacher-developed Web sites can display the students' portfolios.

Incorporating the use of technology offers the capabilities of searching and combining information in meaningful ways. Preserving the contents of a portfolio electronically means that the portfolio can follow students from one grade to the next. After graduation, students can provide files to prospective employers or to college or university admissions officers to illustrate what they know and are able to do.

Exhibitions

An **exhibition** is a display of a student's work that demonstrates knowledge, abilities, skills, and attitudes concerning one project or a unit of work. An exhibition provides students with the opportunity to summarize and to synthesize what they have accomplished. Exhibitions are useful in a variety of academic content areas and in interdisciplinary studies because students can realize, by their own efforts, that learning is more than just a series of worksheets or exercises and that it involves conceptual understanding, problem solving, and reasoning. Exhibitions are useful for program planning and program evaluation.

SNAPSHOT

Linking Daryl's IEP With Systematic Assessment

Last year, when Daryl was in third grade, he was identified as having a learning disability. He had difficulties in reading, written language, and getting along with other students, and he was often argumentative. One of Daryl's IEP goals is that he will improve in reading.

Daryl's fourth-grade teacher, Mr. Tan, is interested in documenting students' progress in a systematic way. As part of his own professional development, Mr. Tan participated in a school workshop on developing, organizing, and maintaining students' portfolios. He learned about the following sites:

- Exemplars. This site contains examples of lessons and assessments that are aligned with standards and related to performance-based assessment
  - www.exemplars.com
- Smarter Balanced Assessment Consortium. A national consortium of states that is developing assessments that are aligned with Common Core State Standards.
  - www.smarterbalanced.org

Mr. Tan believes that Daryl can demonstrate progress in language and literacy by documenting activities in the portfolio. Daryl will keep a reading log that lists the books that he has read and a brief summary of each. Periodically, Daryl will complete more extensive book reports and add them to the portfolio. Various technologies will be used during assessments, record keeping, archiving, and displaying Daryl's progress. Daryl will use a device with a word prediction feature that will allow him to record his thoughts more efficiently. Daryl's teacher will share the portfolio of these materials with the IEP team during the annual review of Daryl's IEP.

Pause and consider:

- Develop suggestions for using various technologies for portfolios.
- How can portfolios integrate aspects of social media? Why should this be important or not important?
- Share ways in which you have created your own portfolio and whether the portfolio has been useful to you. If you have not kept your own portfolio, suggest ways in which a portfolio could be useful to yourself as an educational professional.

Daryl's portfolio will also include a section on working with others. This area relates directly to another IEP goal for building social skills. Daryl and his teacher discussed ways in which Daryl can make and keep friends, and they decided how they should document his progress. One of the ideas that they discussed was for Daryl to complete a daily self-assessment checklist. The teacher talked about his observations of Daryl on the playground that week and some examples of cooperating with others. They agreed that Mr. Tan will continue to share his observations with Daryl at the end of the day, and together they will record positive examples on a graph.

Responding to Diversity

Using performance-based, authentic, or portfolio assessment for students with disabilities requires teachers to be sensitive to the unique needs of these students. Portfolios allow students to highlight and contextualize their home culture, language, ethnicity, race, and even geographic diversity. For example, certain food preparations, such as rice pilaf, potato curry, or corn tortillas, and customs, such as Chinese New Year or Quinceañera (Latin American custom celebrating a girl's 15th birthday) may be specific to certain geographic locations.

Students who are experiencing difficulties in writing can be at a disadvantage when constructing a writing portfolio. For example, it may be difficult to determine whether an inadequate response results from poor writing skills, poor mastery of the content, poor problem-solving skills, lack of creativity, or a combination of these factors.

Portfolios have the potential of providing students with ways of demonstrating conceptual understandings beyond the ability to understand English. Much research is needed on the use of portfolios and the effects of this method on student learning. Questions to keep in mind include the following: Does the use of portfolios in the classroom increase student achievement? Are portfolios effective measures for meeting the goals of the IEPs for students with disabilities? What types of evidence show learning? How can motivation and engagement in learning be documented?

Developing Scoring Systems

Developing or selecting a scoring system is an important part of classroom-based assessment because effective systems provide valuable feedback to students, teachers, and parents regarding level of performance and progress in the curriculum. Using various technologies, teachers may make anecdotal notes, incorporate performance task checklists, or construct and share rubrics. Educators frequently use notes and checklists because they provide convenient ways of recording informal information. Yet anecdotal notes do not provide the student (or teacher and parents) with information about the evaluation process.

Checklists can list the components of what is to be evaluated during the performance. They are also easy to use, but they do not provide any detailed information about the quality of the achievement; they simply record whether one of the items in the performance was present or not. In the following section, we will discuss rubrics and how educators are using this scoring system in the classroom.

Rubrics

Rubrics are considered a very useful scoring system for performance-based, authentic, and portfolio assessments because they provide the greatest amount of detail regarding performance. A **rubric** is an assessment scale that identifies the area(s) of performance and defines various levels of achievement. Within each level, the rubric should include descriptors or detailed descriptions of each level of achievement. Descriptors provide specific information to students, teachers, and parents regarding what to expect at each achievement level (Tankersley, 2007). Descriptors also help teachers in scoring student performances consistently. Scoring systems generally fall into two main types: analytic and holistic. Rubrics have been readily shared on the Web, and many examples can be located. Archives of performance-based assessments and rubrics can be found at **www.exemplars.com** and other sites.

Analytic Scoring

An **analytic scoring** system reports an independent score for each of the criteria of the assessment scale. For a rubric developed for a writing portfolio, there might be four criteria: organization, details, voice, and grammar. An analytic scoring system reports separate scores for each of these criteria. Within each of these criteria, the various levels of achievement can be described either numerically or categorically. In an example of a writing portfolio, we might identify the following achievement levels of organization:

Criterion: Organization
4 = Extensive
3 = Moderate
2 = Slight
1 = Lacking

Notice that we have used both numerical and corresponding categorical descriptions of achievement in this rubric.

In our example, the rubric does not include descriptors of the levels of achievement. Thus, without further descriptions of the terms *moderate* and *slight*, one teacher might rank the organization of a student's paper a 3, whereas another teacher would rank 2. Detailed descriptors are helpful to teachers and others during evaluation procedures and serve to increase interrater reliability.

Descriptors are helpful to students and parents. Detailed information regarding levels of achievement assists students in understanding not only how teachers will evaluate their work but also how they can evaluate the work themselves. Descriptors are helpful to parents in understanding what their child can do. Depending on the richness and detail of the descriptors, analytic scoring can provide diagnostic information about the student's achievement. Teachers can examine scores on the individual criteria to identify areas of strengths and areas of improvement. Because this type of scoring system is an effective diagnostic tool, teachers should report student scores as categorical rather than numerical. By reporting analytic scores numerically, the result is a loss of rich analytic information, even if the scores show totals and averages.

Let's return to the Three Gorges Dam Project (Figure 15.1). The activity focuses on fifth-grade students creating and critiquing a model dam or reservoir. The students are asked to apply knowledge related to science, geography, and literacy and to use creative and critical thinking skills. The analytic scoring rubric (see Figure 15.2) provides detailed information for each level of achievement in content level, use of model or display, and critique of the model.

Scoring Rubric: China's Three Gorges Dam				
Scoring Criteria	**Attempted: 1**	**Partial: 2**	**Proficient: 3**	**Distinguished: 4**
Content knowledge	Students present a model and attempt to describe some principles or tasks that are needed to successfully construct the model. Major errors are apparent.	Students present the model and correctly describe at least three principles or tasks that are needed to successfully construct the model. Several errors are apparent.	Students present the model and correctly describe at least five principles or tasks that are needed to successfully construct the model. Minor errors are apparent.	Students present the model and correctly and comprehensively describe all major principles or tasks that are needed to successfully construct the model. Considerable details, insights, and evidence are used to support the presentation.
Presentation	Students attempt to explain the model and new understandings. The presentation contains considerable errors. The presentation is not well organized and/or visually appealing.	Students accurately explain the model and their understanding of at least three principles or tasks that are needed to construct the model. The presentation is neat and organized. Several errors are apparent.	Students correctly explain the model and demonstrate their understanding of at least five principles or tasks that are needed to construct the model. Minor errors are apparent. The presentation is neat, well organized, and visually appealing.	Students correctly and comprehensively communicate understanding of all major principles or tasks that are needed to construct the model. Considerable elaboration, details, insights, and evidence are used to support the presentation. The presentation is well organized and visually appealing.
Critique	Students attempt to explain how the model compares to a real dam. Minor suggestions are made for improving the presentation.	Students explain how the model compares to a real dam. Several suggestions for improvement are offered.	Students explain, using essential details, how the model compares to a real dam. Several substantive suggestions for improvement are offered.	Students provide a comprehensive explanation, using considerable details, how the model compares to a real dam. Comprehensive, substantive suggestions for improvement are offered.

FIGURE 15.2 • Analytic Scoring Rubric for the Three Gorges Dam Project

Description	Numerical Score
The paper is well organized, provides a sufficient number of explicit details in supporting statements, and contains no major grammatical errors.	4
The paper shows organization but may lack coherence, details are appropriate, and/or it contains some grammatical errors.	3
The paper lacks consistency in organization, details are not elaborate, and/or it contains many grammatical errors.	2
The paper has serious organizational problems, lacks details, and/or it contains numerous grammatical errors.	1

FIGURE 15.3 • Holistic Rubric for Scoring Student Writing

Holistic Scoring

Holistic scoring is a type of scoring in which the teacher assigns a single score to the student's work (see Figure 15.3). For example, the writing portfolio receives a single overall score. The teacher does not analyze the writing by separate criteria such as organization, details, voice, and grammar. Like analytic scoring, holistic scoring should include descriptors of each of the achievement levels. This type of scoring lacks the depth of information contained in analytic scoring; however, it tends to be easier to design and score than analytic scoring.

Benchmarks

Benchmarks are examples of student work that illustrate each scoring level on the rubric, either analytic or holistic. Teachers evaluate student work by using scoring standards and benchmarks. Benchmarks can be in the form of papers, such as example essays, or a small sample of student work, such as possible answers to a question. Student papers that represent writing at different levels of performance are sometimes called **anchor papers**. Figure 15.4 illustrates an example from a set of anchor papers developed by teachers.

Benchmarks can be helpful to students in understanding how teachers will assess their performance or portfolio. However, benchmarks should be shared carefully with students so that they will not think they must replicate the example, thus losing the individual nature of their work. Providing students with several different examples of benchmarks at various achievement levels can reduce this potential problem.

Ensuring Technical Adequacy

Reliability

The degree to which reliability is crucial depends on the purpose of the assessment. Some assessments are low-stakes assessments; that is, the consequences of the assessment do not have a major impact on the student's future. For example, an assessment designed to answer questions regarding student progress is a low-stakes assessment.

	5	4	3	2	1
PURPOSE	Clear, very consistent focus and intent	Clear focus; consistent	Focus and intent are somewhat clear	Focus and intent are not very clear	No focus; lacks coherence
ORGANIZATION	Clear, predictable presentation	Clear explanation	Organization somewhat confusing	Confusing	Little sense of organization
DETAILS	Abundant, sophisticated details that support and explain the content	Considerable details that support and explain the content	Some details that support and explain the content	Few details that support and explain the content	Little or no use of details
CONCLUSION	Excellent conclusion; provides synthesis of major points; insightful	Very good conclusion; synthesizes most major points	Good conclusion; synthesizes some points	Conclusion is attempted	No conclusion

FIGURE 15.4 • Rubric Used by Teachers for Scoring Anchor Papers of Students' Writing Assignments

Assessments that are part of graduation requirements have much higher stakes. High-stakes assessments refer to situations in which the collected information will have a direct and potentially adverse impact on the student. In high-stakes assessment, issues of reliability are critical.

Consistency and Stability

Reliability of performance-based assessments focuses on the consistency and the stability of the assessment. When using performance-based assessment, students frequently have multiple opportunities to perform individually. For example, a teacher can create a number of opportunities that require students to work together cooperatively; however, individual oral presentations on a unit of study occur infrequently because of the amount of class time these presentations require. In this case, consistency of student response is unknown due to low frequency of performance.

Multiple categories or points on the assessment scale affect the degree of interrater agreement. The more categories or points, the more difficult it may be to obtain interrater agreement, especially if the categories are vague. We have discussed one method of increasing consistency by including detailed descriptors in each of the achievement levels. We have examined how descriptors assist evaluators in making determinations regarding students' scores and help students evaluate their own work.

Teachers also want assurance that the performance will be stable. Stability is a function of the scoring system and environmental factors. Errors in the scoring systems affect stability, for example, when the teacher assigns an incorrect score or makes a calculation error. Environmental factors also affect stability. The learning and social environments of the classroom affect the student's motivation, attitude, self-esteem, confidence, and anxiety, which in turn can alter the student's performance.

Consequential Validity

Consequential validity is the extent to which an assessment instrument promotes the intended consequences (Linn & Baker, 1996). This type of validity can describe performance-based assessments. One of the primary reasons for using this type of assessment is to improve student learning, and the extent to which performance-based assessment improves student learning defines consequential validity. Factors that can affect student learning, and thus affect consequential validity, include school reform activities, instructional improvements, staff development activities, levels of student achievement, and accountability systems.

Both student and teacher perspectives can affect consequential validity:

From the student's perspective: For the assessment to be valid, students must know what to expect. Students must know what skills and knowledge are included in the assessment, what types of performance demonstrate these skills and knowledge, and what type of evaluation their performance will receive.

From the teacher's perspective: For the assessment to be valid, teachers must take care in designing tasks that accurately reflect achievement for students from nondominant cultures. For example, oral presentations may be difficult for students whose first language is not English. An oral presentation in science, for example, might be supplemented by information presented in another format, such as a detailed drawing to illustrate the concepts presented.

Fairness

Fairness of the assessment instrument is an important aspect of consequential validity. One of the driving forces behind the evolution of performance-based assessment has been the impetus to develop assessment instruments that are fair to students. Tests are opportunities for students to demonstrate learning regardless of culture, gender, race, socioeconomic status, or disability. Fairness means minimal bias, equitable assessment, and measures that are sensitive to diverse populations.

Improving Reliability and Validity

Peter Airasian (2005) suggested several guidelines for improving the reliability and validity of performance-based and portfolio assessments:

1. Know the purpose of the assessment.
2. Teach and give students practice on the assessment criteria.
3. State the criteria in observable behaviors.
4. Select criteria that are at an appropriate level of difficulty for the students.
5. Limit the number of criteria to a manageable number.
6. Maintain a written record.
7. Be sure the performance assessment is fair to all students (pp. 254–255).

Using Performance-Based, Authentic, and Portfolio Assessment

Careful design of performance, authentic, and portfolio assessments is important to ensure that educators, parents, and students draw appropriate conclusions. If we are unclear about our expectations, then we diminish the usefulness of the assessment. Several questions can guide us in using these assessment techniques:

Is the assessment representative of the student's work? For example, a performance task can demonstrate how a student develops a first draft of a book review, but not a finished one. Recordings might contain images of play rehearsals but not the opening-night production.

Are the criteria for assessment clear to all evaluators and students? Ambiguity, inconsistency in judging performance and authentic assessments, and subjectivity can be major problems. Both students and educators must be able to recognize the assessment tasks, the performance conditions, and the criteria for evaluation.

Have the criteria for evaluation changed over time? When designing an assessment, the educator may have specified the evaluation of all the student's creative writings. Later, it may be unclear whether this meant all the finished writing or all the writing, whether finished or not.

Who evaluates the contents? Depending on who evaluates the performance or authentic assessment tasks, interpretations can vary. Depending on the training of the educator, different conclusions can be reached.

Are performance assessments and authentic assessments fair? The use of performance and authentic assessments does not automatically mean that these assessments show no bias toward students with disabilities; certain cultural groups, minorities, and/or economic groups; and those for whom English is a second language.

Considerations About Using Performance-Based Assessments

The development and implementation of performance-based assessments present challenges to educators. Although they are not without problems, these assessment procedures have the potential of helping us develop valid and fair approaches to assessing students.

Educators in professional organizations and state departments of education have developed sets of standards that specify what students should know and achieve. Assessment procedures should assist educators and policymakers in improving instruction and learning. If assessment is to be beneficial, the procedures must provide useful information about the capabilities of students. We believe that performance-based, authentic, and portfolio assessment will continue to be valuable assessment approaches. If the purposes of assessment are not beneficial, then neither the assessment nor the assessment procedures are valid.

All assessment procedures should be fair to all students. Assessment procedures should contain no bias, and they should be attentive to differences in development and disabilities and to differences in culture, race, socioeconomic standing, and gender. Students must be given multiple opportunities to demonstrate what they know. A single test score cannot determine educational decisions.

The assessment tasks must be reliable and valid, and they should represent the standards that children are expected to achieve. Multiple-choice tests give children inadequate opportunities to demonstrate what they know. Alternatives to traditional assessment, such as performance-based assessment, portfolios, and exhibitions, are rich sources of information.

Educators should be involved in the development and implementation of assessment procedures. Because assessment forms a close link with instruction, educators must participate in the development, administration, scoring, and interpretation of assessment procedures. We need to continue to develop and revise effective authentic and performance tasks.

Teachers and other evaluators should use caution when applying portfolios to high-stakes testing. High-stakes testing is the use of assessments to make classification, retention, or promotion decisions about students. The pressure of such a situation can compromise student work.

Summary

- Performance-based assessments consist of portfolios, performance tasks, exhibitions, and other documentation of student accomplishments.
- Authentic assessment occurs when the student completes or demonstrates knowledge, skills, or behavior in a real-life context.
- A portfolio is a systematic collection of a student's work covering an extended period of time.
- Although not without concerns, performance-based assessment procedures have the potential of helping teachers implement reliable, valid, and fair approaches to assessment.

QUESTIONS FOR REFLECTION

1. Arrange an interview with a local special educator or administrator. How are educators in your local school using performance-based assessments for students with disabilities?
2. Identify Web sites and other resources that illustrate well-designed rubrics. Select a curriculum area, and use a search engine to narrow your search to five to eight sites that you would recommend in English language arts, science, mathematics, social studies, or other curriculum areas. Share your findings with others.
3. Compare the various methods of scoring performance-based assessments. What are the advantages and disadvantages of each?
4. Why are concerns relating to reliability and validity so important when using performance-based assessments?
5. Work with a small group of your peers to develop a set of questions for two or more chapters in this textbook. Your question sets should include multiple-choice, short-answer, and essay questions. Next, review the same chapters and identify how knowledge of the information could be demonstrated by either performance or portfolio assessment. Which method of assessment do you prefer? Why?

REFERENCES

Airasian, P. W. (2005). *Classroom assessment* (5th ed.). New York: McGraw-Hill.

Arter, J., & McTighe, J. (2001). Scoring rubrics in the classroom. In T. R. Guskey & R. J. Marzano (Eds.), *Experts in assessment*. Thousand Oaks, CA: Corwin Press.

Chetham, D. (2004). *Before the deluge: The vanishing world of the Yangtze's Three Gorges*. Hampshire, UK: Palgrave Macmillan.

Linn, R. L., & Baker, E. L. (1996). Can performance-based student assessments be psychometrically sound? In J. B. Baron & D. P. Wolf (Eds.), *Performance-based student assessment: Challenges and possibilities* (pp. 84–103). Chicago, IL: University of Chicago Press.

Stiggins, R. (2007). *Introduction to student-involved assessment for learning* (5th ed.). Upper Saddle River, NJ: Pearson.

Tankersley, K. (2007). *Tests that teach*. Reston, VA: Association for Supervision and Curriculum Development.

Wiggins, G. P. (1993). *Assessing student performance*. San Francisco, CA: Jossey-Bass.

Wilkinson, P. (2007). *Yangtze*. London: BBC Books.

PART V
Special Considerations

 **CHAPTER 16** Intelligence

 **CHAPTER 17** Young Children

 **CHAPTER 18** Youth in Transition

16 Intelligence

Chapter Objectives

After completing this chapter, you should be able to:

- Explain the concept of intelligence tests as samples of behavior.
- Discuss the stability of test performance.
- Describe specific tests of intelligence.

Overview

What is intelligence? What makes us intelligent? The nature of intelligence has received a great deal of attention over the years. One view of intelligence is that it is an arbitrary concept, impossible to define or quantify. Another view is that intelligence consists of multifaceted, complex, interrelated abilities associated with thinking, abstract thought, creativity, emotions, motivation, social interactions, and so on (Dai & Sternberg, 2004; Mayer, Salovey, & Caruso, 2008). The intelligence tests that are described in this chapter reflect the varied views of the construct of intelligence.

Intelligence Tests as Samples of Behavior

If intelligence could be assessed directly, we would be able to measure the neurochemical activities and neurobiological changes that occur in the brain. As educators, we rely instead on indirect measures or tests to estimate intelligence. Intelligence tests don't sample intelligence but rather the behaviors that can be associated with our conceptualizations of intelligence. We use intelligence tests to sample intelligent behavior. Our assumption is that the sample provides information about the intellectual abilities of individuals.

In addition to standardized tests, other sources of information are available about students' abilities (Sattler, 2008; Salvia, Ysseldyke, & Bolt, 2013). These information resources can be useful in confirming the results of standardized instruments; for students from diverse heritages and backgrounds, educators may need to rely on sources other than standardized tests for clues about cognitive abilities. Sources of information that can be gathered when determining intellectual abilities include school records; standardized results on achievement, behavior, and other tests; developmental histories; report card grades; observations of students; and parental reports.

There are many behaviors that intelligence tests do not sample or do not sample inadequately. These behaviors include mechanical, musical, artistic, motivational, and emotional behaviors (Mayer et al., 2008; Salvia et al., 2013). Recent research on the nature of intelligence has begun to explore the contribution of these behaviors to our understanding of intelligence.

Responding to Diversity

There has been much debate over the years about the value of intelligence testing. Arguments against the use of intelligence testing claim that testing limits opportunities, can be harmful to individuals from various cultural and ethnic groups, and facilitates the placement of students into categories. Advocates of intelligence testing have argued that it assists in diagnosis, helps to identify individuals who need specialized instruction or therapy, and promotes educational opportunities (Sattler, 2008). Membership in a cultural or ethnic group, socioeconomic status, educational attainment, language, and acculturation can affect intelligence test scores. Educators can reduce or prevent bias in the assessment of intelligence by being (1) aware of individual characteristics, (2) knowledgeable about test use and test selection, and (3) sensitive when administering tests, scoring, and interpreting performance.

Intelligence tests provide us with only part of what we want to know about an individual. The assessment of individuals should never depend on the results of one test; rather, good practice requires that we use the results of additional standardized tests, as well as observations, interviews, checklists, rating scales, samples of work, and other types of assessment, in appropriate combination, to gather information.

Standardized Instruments

As stated previously, a great many standardized tests of intelligence are on the market. This chapter highlights several, frequently used tests.

TESTS-at-a-GLANCE

Batería III Woodcock-Muñoz
www.riversidepublishing.com/products/bateriaIII/index.html

- **Publication Date:** 2007
- **Purposes:** The *Batería III Woodcock-Muñoz* is a Spanish version of the *Woodcock-Johnson III*. The *Batería III Woodcock-Muñoz* assesses cognitive, academic, and language abilities in Spanish-speaking individuals.
- **Age/Grade Levels:** 2 years through 90+, kindergarten through grade 16.9.
- **Time to Administer:** 10 minutes to more than 2 hours, depending on the scales that are administered.
- **Technical Adequacy:** Reliability and validity are adequate.
- **Suggested Use:** Measuring general cognitive abilities, aptitude, and achievement in Spanish-speaking students. This test should be used in combination with other measures to strengthen interpretation of results and suggest recommendations for individual students.

Batería III Woodcock-Muñoz

The *Batería III Woodcock-Muñoz* (Woodcock & Muñoz-Sandoval, 2007) forms a parallel Spanish version of the *Woodcock-Johnson Psychoeducational Battery III*. The *Batería III Woodcock-Muñoz* is an individually administered battery of tests that assesses intellectual, academic, and language abilities in Spanish-speaking individuals aged 2 years through 90+ years, kindergarten through grade 16.9.

Like the *Woodcock-Johnson Psychoeducational Battery III*, the *Batería III Woodcock-Muñoz* derives from the Horn-Cattell theory of cognitive processing, which we discuss later in this chapter in the description of the *Woodcock-Johnson Psychoeducational Battery III*.

ADMINISTRATION The *Batería III* takes from 10 minutes to more than 2 hours to administer, depending on which scales are administered. Raw scores convert to age and grade equivalents, percentile ranks, and standard scores.

TECHNICAL ADEQUACY Technical adequacy of the *Batería III Woodcock-Muñoz* derives from the *Woodcock-Johnson Psychoeducational Battery III*. The authors used the standardization sample of the *WJ III* to develop the scoring procedures and other technical information for the *Batería III Woodcock-Muñoz*. In general, there is evidence to support content, concurrent, and construct validity. The extent to which various subtests reflect students' abilities depends on the instructional orientation of the teacher and the school curriculum.

SUMMARY The *Batería III Woodcock-Muñoz* is a Spanish version of the *Woodcock-Johnson Psychoeducational Battery—Revised*. This norm-referenced, individually administered battery assesses cognitive, academic, and language abilities in Spanish-speaking individuals aged 2 years through adulthood, kindergarten through grade 16.9.

Comprehensive Test of Nonverbal Intelligence-II

The *Comprehensive Test of Nonverbal Intelligence-II* (*CTONI-2*; Hammill, Pearson, & Wiederholt, 2009) is a nonverbal measure of abstract/figural problem solving and reasoning for use with individuals aged 6 years through 89 years, 11 months. It is useful for assessing the performance of individuals who have language or motor problems that in some cases make it difficult for them to respond to more traditional tests. The test is made up of six subtests: Pictorial Analogies, Geometric Analogies, Pictorial Categories, Geometric Categories, Pictorial Sequences, and Geometric Sequences. For each of these subtests, the examinee must solve a visual problem that consists of either pictures (e.g., shoe, ball, cube) or geometric shapes (e.g., triangle, circle, diamond).

ADMINISTRATION The test items are contained in a stiff book that is set up like an easel. The examiner can pantomime the instructions or give them orally. If the examiner chooses to pantomime the instructions, he or she uses facial gestures, hand movements, and head movements. The student shows the correct response by pointing or by some other motor response. This nonverbal method of test administration does have several advantages. The examinee does not have to listen to directions, speak, read, or write. There is no time limit for the test.

SCORING Examiners score items as either correct or incorrect. Raw scores convert to standard scores, percentile ranks, and age equivalents.

STANDARDIZATION It is unclear whether the sample was stratified according to major demographic variables and the extent to which the sample is consistent with U.S. Census estimates.

RELIABILITY The test manual reports high reliabilities. Independent research is required to support the reliability of the subtests.

VALIDITY Validity determines whether a test measures what it purports to measure. Although the manual reports the results of several validity studies, more extensive research is necessary to determine whether this instrument measures the construct of intelligence and to determine its usefulness in measuring intellectual abilities of persons with disabilities.

SUMMARY The *CTONI-2* is a nonverbal measure that assesses visual problem solving and reasoning. Reliability is moderate. Teachers should use it cautiously until additional information relating to validity is available.

TESTS-at-a-GLANCE

Comprehensive Test of Nonverbal Intelligence-II

http://www.pearsonclinical.com/content/ani/clinicalassessments/us/en/psychology/products/100000624/comprehensive-test-of-nonverbal-intelligence-second-edition-ctoni-2-ctoni2.html?Pid=PAa19120&Mode=summary

- **Publication Date:** 2009
- **Purposes:** Measures nonverbal, abstract/figural problem solving and reasoning in individuals who have language or motor problems that may make it difficult for them to respond to more traditional tests.
- **Age/Grade Levels:** 6 years through 89 years 11 months.
- **Time to Administer:** 20 to 45 minutes.
- **Technical Adequacy:** Information about the standardization sample is sparse. Reliability is adequate, but additional information concerning validity is needed.
- **Suggested Use:** The *CTONI-2* may be useful as a screening instrument. It should be used cautiously until additional information relating to validity can be gathered.

Detroit Tests of Learning Aptitude, Fourth Edition

The *Detroit Tests of Learning Aptitude, Fourth Edition* (*DTLA-4*; Hammill, 1998) measures the intellectual aptitudes or abilities of students aged 6 through 17. According to the author, the *DTLA-4* measures intelligence, aptitude, and achievement. The *DTLA-4* consists of ten subtests:

Word Opposites: The student must verbalize the opposite of a word that the examiner says.

Design Sequences: The student must arrange cubes in a pattern from memory after being shown a picture of the pattern for 5 seconds.

Sentence Imitation: The student repeats a sentence after listening to the examiner say the sentence.

Reversed Letters: The examiner recites a series of letters. The student must record the letters, reversing their order of presentation.

Story Construction: After viewing three pictures, the student makes up three stories.

Design Reproduction: The student must draw a design from memory after being shown a design for 5 seconds.

Basic Information: The student responds to factual questions.

Symbolic Relations: The student views a design and must choose, from among six designs, the one that completes the pattern.

Word Sequences: The student repeats a series of unrelated words after listening to the examiner recite the words.

Story Sequences: The student arranges a series of cartoonlike pictures to make a story.

ADMINISTRATION Examiners should have some background in assessment. Directions for administration are provided on the test protocol. For some items, directions for administration are provided in the examiner's manual. Administration takes between 50 minutes and 2 hours.

SCORING Examiners score the responses as either correct or incorrect. The scores for each item make up the computation of the total score and the subtest scores. Raw scores can convert to age equivalents, percentiles, and quotients, which are standard scores that have a mean of 100 and a standard deviation of 15.

STANDARDIZATION The standardization sample of the *DTLA-4* consisted of 1,350 students in 37 states. In developing this instrument, the author used data from the standardization sample of the *DTLA-3* and selected additional samples. The standardization of the *DTLA-4* is confusing and ambiguous.

RELIABILITY Estimations of internal consistency reliability came from the standardization sample. The average reliabilities for the total score and the six subtests ranged from .82 to .93. Test-retest reliability derived from a sample of 98 students living in Austin, Texas. The coefficients ranged from .71 to .96.

VALIDITY The authors maintain that the *DTLA-4* has content validity because it measures behaviors that

---

TESTS-at-a-GLANCE

Detroit Tests of Learning Aptitude, Fourth Edition
www.proedinc.com/customer/productView.aspx?ID=1435

- **Publication Date:** 1998
- **Purposes:** Measures general intellectual aptitudes or abilities and achievement.
- **Age/Grade Levels:** 6 years through 17 years.
- **Time to Administer:** 50 minutes to 2 hours.
- **Technical Adequacy:** Questions remain about the appropriateness of the standardization sample, reliability, and validity.
- **Suggested Use:** May be helpful in determining areas of strength and weakness. Exercise caution when using test scores to make decisions regarding the identification of students and their eligibility for special services.
- **Summary:** The *Detroit Tests of Learning Aptitude, Fourth Edition*, is an individually administered test for students aged 6 through 17. Questions remain about the appropriateness of the standardization sample, reliability, and validity.

Salvia and Ysseldyke (2004) have developed and because it relates the subtests to the theories of intelligence. Although the authors present evidence of construct validity, additional validity studies are necessary.

Kaufman Assessment Battery for Children, Second Edition

The *Kaufman Assessment Battery for Children, Second Edition* (*KABC-II*; Kaufman & Kaufman, 2004), is a revision of the 1983 edition. This test assesses the intelligence and achievement of individuals aged 3 through 18 years. The test consists of 18 subtests that take from 30 minutes for young children to more than 1 hour for elementary and high school students. According to the manual, the *KABC-II* "measures a range of abilities including sequential and simultaneous processing, learning reasoning, and crystallized ability that are relevant to understanding children and adolescents from a variety of backgrounds" (Kaufman & Kaufman, 2004, p. 1).

The *KABC-II* is based on two theoretical models of mental processing. The first model was developed by Luria and others and holds that mental processing occurs in three blocks, which are the individual's ability to maintain arousal, code and store information, and plan and organize behavior. The Cattell-Horn-Carroll (CHC) theory, the second model, conceptualizes intelligence as fluid and crystallized. Fluid intelligence is the ability to solve problems using logical reasoning; crystallized intelligence is the ability that is closely related to the accumulation of knowledge, language development, information about one's culture, achievement, and communication abilities. Interpretation of test performance can be based on both models.

A unique feature of the *KABC-II* is that items on many subtests can be explained, demonstrated, administered a second time, and taught to students. Although a Spanish translation is included in the test kit, the manual cautions that the *KABC-II* "is not intended to be administered in Spanish" (Kaufman & Kaufman, 2004, p. 1). Depending on the age of the individual, examiners can combine various subtests to form the nonverbal scale. The nonverbal scale provides an estimate of intelligence for individuals who demonstrate communication problems and is useful for children who are deaf, hearing-impaired, speech or language disabled, or autistic, or who do not speak English. The examiner responds through movement.

ADMINISTRATION   The manual provides comprehensive directions for administering the *KABC-II*. The student's chronological age determines the starting point for each subtest, and each subtest has a designated stopping point to avoid administering too many items to any student. In addition, the test contains a discontinue rule if a student misses a number of items in a row.

STANDARDIZATION   The standardization sample of the *KABC-II* consisted of 3,025 individuals aged between 3 and 18 years. The standardization was conducted from September 2001 through January 2003 based on the March 2001 Current Population Survey. Students within each age group were included according to education level of the student's mother or female guardian, geographic region, and ethnic group. Students were included in the sample only if they spoke English, were noninstitutionalized, and did not have physical or perceptual difficulties that would prevent them from participating.

Subtest scores are reported as scaled scores with a mean of 10 and a standard deviation of 3. These subtest scores can be combined to yield standard scores (mean

---

TESTS-at-a-GLANCE

Kaufman Assessment Battery for Children, Second Edition

http://www.pearsonclinical.com/psychology/products/100000088/kaufman-assessment-battery-for-children-second-edition-kabc-ii.html

- **Publication Date:** 2004
- **Purposes:** Assesses sequential processing, planning, learning, simultaneous processing, knowledge, and nonverbal abilities.
- **Age/Grade Levels:** 3 years through 18 years.
- **Time to Administer:** 30 to 75 minutes.
- **Technical Adequacy:** The standardization sample is dated. Reliability is very good; validity is acceptable. However, additional evidence of validity is needed to support the theoretical bases of this test and its use with special populations.
- **Suggested Use:** Although the manual does report several "clinical validity" studies with special populations, the *KABC-II* should be used cautiously with students who have disabilities because students with disabilities were not systematically included in the standardization sample.

of 100, standard deviation of 15) for the indexes. Index scores can be derived for sequential processing, planning, learning, simultaneous processing, knowledge, and nonverbal abilities.

RELIABILITY The manual reports internal consistency and test-retest reliabilities. For the most part, the reliability coefficients are acceptable. Many coefficients exceed .90, and in general, the index scores are more reliable than the individual subtest scores.

VALIDITY The manual reports the results of studies examining the validity of the *KABC-II*. Concurrent validity of the *KABC-II* was investigated through correlations with other tests, including the *WISC-IV*. The *KABC-II* is a significant revision of the earlier version. The manual does provide evidence for the separate factor structure. However, additional research studies are necessary to add to our knowledge about the validity of the *KABC-II*.

Although not systematically included in the standardization sample, the manual reports "clinical validity" (Kaufman & Kaufman, 2004, p. 126) studies of students who have disabilities in reading, mathematics, and writing. Separate studies were conducted with students who had learning disabilities, emotional disturbance, and hearing loss, as well as with students who were gifted.

SUMMARY The *Kaufman Assessment Battery for Children, Second Edition (KABC-II)* assesses the abilities of individuals aged 3 through 18 years. According to the manual, the test measures sequential processing, planning, learning, simultaneous processing, knowledge, and nonverbal abilities. The manual presents evidence for the reliability and validity of the test. Additional research is advisable to confirm validity.

Stanford-Binet Intelligence Scale, Fifth Edition

The *Stanford-Binet Intelligence Scale, Fifth Edition* (Roid, 2003), is a revised edition of the *Stanford-Binet Intelligence Scale* (Thorndike, Hagen, & Sattler, 1986). The test was originally developed by Alfred Binet and Theodore Simon in France in 1905. Lewis M. Terman, a professor at Stanford University, revised the Binet-Simon test and introduced it to the United States in 1916. In 1937, Terman, along with Maud A. Merrill, standardized it again and created two revised forms, Form L and Form M. In 1960, the authors created Form L-M from the two forms but did not restandardize the test until 1972. The long-awaited fourth edition was published in 1986. The fifth edition has some similarities to previous editions: (1) It spans the same age range, (2) many of the item types are the same or adapted, and (3) it uses basal and ceiling levels.

The fifth edition of the Stanford-Binet assesses intellectual abilities in individuals aged 2 through 85 years and older. Like the fourth edition, the fifth edition uses a hierarchical model of intelligence with a global *g*, which includes both general intellectual ability factor and several broad factors. At the top level is *g*, general reasoning ability. The second level consists of broad factors titled Fluid Reasoning, Knowledge, Quantitative Processing, Visual-Spatial Processing, and Working Memory. The manual states that there are extensive high-end items for those who are gifted and low-end items for improved assessment of young children and individuals who are low functioning. The fifth edition contains 10 subtests that assess verbal and nonverbal abilities:

Verbal	**Nonverbal**
Verbal Fluid Reasoning	Nonverbal Fluid Reasoning
Verbal Knowledge	Nonverbal Knowledge
Verbal Quantitative Reasoning	Nonverbal Quantitative Reasoning
Verbal Visual-Spatial Processing	Nonverbal Visual-Spatial Processing
Verbal Working Memory	Nonverbal Working Memory

ADMINISTRATION   Administration of specific subtests depends on the age of the individual under assessment. The test provides specific instructions for each subtest.

SCORING   The manual provides clearly written directions for scoring. The scoring of the subtests varies from one subtest to another. Scores are calculated for full-scale IQ, verbal and nonverbal IQ, and composite indices spanning five factors, with a standard score mean of 100 and a standard deviation of 15. The subtest scores have a mean of 10 and a standard deviation of 3.

STANDARDIZATION   Five variables—geographic region, community size, ethnic group (white, African American, Hispanic, Asian/Pacific Islander), age, and gender—and data matches to the 2000 census formed the basis for the standardization sample. A total of 4,800 individuals aged between 2 and 85+ years participated in the standardization.

RELIABILITY   Reliabilities for the full-scale IQ, nonverbal IQ, and verbal IQ range from .95 to .98. Reliabilities for the factor indices range from .90 to .92. For the 10 subtests, reliabilities range from .84 to .89.

> **TESTS-at-a-GLANCE**
>
> **Stanford-Binet Intelligence Scale, Fifth Edition**
> www.riverpub.com/products/sb5/details.html
> - **Publication Date:** 2003
> - **Purposes:** Assesses general intellectual abilities (*g*) and intellectual abilities in five broad areas: Fluid Reasoning, Knowledge, Quantitative Processing, Visual-Spatial Processing, and Working Memory.
> - **Age/Grade Levels:** 2 through 85+ years.
> - **Time to Administer:** 1 to 2 hours.
> - **Technical Adequacy:** Well-normed, reliable instrument. Evidence of validity is adequate.
> - **Suggested Use:** Assessing intellectual ability and strengths and weaknesses. Can be used, in combination with other tests and forms of assessment, to identify students with special needs and determine eligibility for services; can be used when conducting a psychoeducational assessment and for clinical and neuropsychological assessment.

VALIDITY   The manual reports factor analyses of the subtest scores across all ages in the standardization sample to measure construct validity. Although the authors present evidence of validity, we recommend additional research over time with varied populations.

SUMMARY   The *Stanford-Binet Intelligence Scale, Fifth Edition* is a well-normed, reliable instrument. Evidence of validity is adequate. However, additional studies must be undertaken to investigate construct validity. One important strength of the instrument is that a broad age range of individuals can take the test, but all examinees do not take all subtests. Thus, comparisons among the performances of examinees over time is difficult. Another disadvantage is that administration of the fifth edition can be more time-consuming compared with other intelligence tests.

Test of Nonverbal Intelligence, Fourth Edition

The *Test of Nonverbal Intelligence, Fourth Edition* (TONI-4; Brown, Sherbenou, & Johnsen, 2010), is a nonverbal measure of abstract/figural problem solving for use with individuals aged 6 years to 89 years 11 months. It can assess the performance of individuals who have language or motor problems that make it difficult for them to respond to more traditional tests. The authors state that it can be useful when assessing persons who have aphasia, hearing impairments, lack of proficiency with spoken or written English, cerebral palsy, stroke, or head trauma. The test has two forms, each containing 45 items. The items consist of a series of abstract figures that require individuals to select the correct response by problem solving.

ADMINISTRATION   The test items sit on an easel, and the examiner pantomimes the instructions. The examiner begins the testing by pointing to a blank square in a pattern of figures, making a broad gesture to indicate the possible responses, pointing to the blank square again, and then looking questioningly at the individual. The student shows the correct response by pointing; using an eyeblink, head stick, light beam, or some other meaningful response. Throughout the administration of this instrument, neither the examiner nor the examinee

> **TESTS-at-a-GLANCE**
>
> **Test of Nonverbal Intelligence, Fourth Edition**
> http://www.pearsonclinical.com/psychology/products/100000612/test-of-nonverbal-intelligence-fourth-edition-toni4.html?Pid=TONI-4
>
> - **Publication Date:** 2010
> - **Purposes:** Nonverbal measure of abstract/figural problem solving that can be used when assessing the performance of individuals who have language or motor problems that may make it difficult for them to respond to more traditional tests.
> - **Age/Grade Levels:** 6 years to 89 years 11 months.
> - **Time to Administer:** 15 to 20 minutes.
> - **Technical Adequacy:** The standardization sample is just acceptable.
> - **Suggested Use:** The TONI-4 assesses one aspect of intelligence—problem solving. It is to be used with caution.
> - **Technical Adequacy:** Reliability coefficients are satisfactory. Validity is concerned with determining whether a test measures what it purports to measure. Because additional research on the construct and components of nonverbal intelligence is needed, interpretations should be made cautiously.
> - **Summary:** The TONI-4 is a nonverbal measure that assesses one aspect of intelligence, namely, problem solving. Reliability and validity coefficients are low to moderate. Caution is advisable when assessing young children, making interpretations, and developing recommendations.

speaks. This test is not timed and encourages the examiner to allow examinees sufficient time to respond to each test item. The total time to administer the TONI-4 is approximately 15 minutes. The advantage of this nonverbal method of test administration is that the examinee does not have to listen to directions, speak, read, or write.

According to the authors, teachers, psychologists, psychological associates, educational diagnosticians, and speech-language therapists can administer the TONI-4. Examiners should have sufficient training and knowledge in the area of assessment.

SCORING   Examiners score items as either correct or incorrect. Raw scores convert to deviation quotients (standard scores with a mean of 100 and a standard deviation of 15) and percentile ranks. Because there are no subtests, the TONI-4 reports only the total score.

STANDARDIZATION   The test manual of the TONI-4 describes the standardization sample. Additional information is needed to determine the extent to which the sample matches U.S. Census estimates.

RELIABILITY   The reported coefficients were in the moderate range. However, for the most part, the number of persons included in the special population samples is small, and additional research is advisable in this area.

VALIDITY   Because additional research on the construct and components of nonverbal intelligence is needed, interpretations should be made cautiously. Independent research studies should be conducted to determine the aspects of nonverbal intelligence that are sampled by this instrument.

Wechsler Intelligence Scale for Children, Fourth Edition Integrated

The *Wechsler Intelligence Scale for Children, Fourth Edition Integrated* (*WISC-IV Integrated*; Wechsler, 2004), is a major revision of the third edition of the *Wechsler Intelligence Scale for Children*, which was originally published in 1949. The *WISC-IV Integrated* incorporates the *WISC-IV* (2003) and is an individually administered test that assesses the intellectual ability of children aged 6 years through 16 years 11 months. The test measures intellectual abilities and problem-solving processes. According to the manual, the *WISC-IV* is useful for a number of purposes, including psychoeducational assessment, diagnosis of exceptional needs, and clinical and neuropsychological assessment.

Previous versions of this instrument have classified subtests into verbal and performance scales. However, the *WISC-IV* subtests are classified into four composites: Verbal Comprehension Index, Perceptual Reasoning Index, Working Memory Index, and Processing Speed Index. A description of the indexes and subtests can be found in Table 16.1.

ADMINISTRATION   The *WISC-IV Integrated* is administered individually by a skilled professional who is credentialed in school psychology. The manual clearly explains the directions for administration and scoring for each of the subtests. Each subtest has separate

TABLE 16.1 • WISC-IV Indexes and Subtests

Index	Subtest	Description
Verbal Comprehension Index	Similarities	The student explains the correspondence between pairs of words.
	Vocabulary	The examiner presents words orally, and the examinee defines them orally.
	Comprehension	The examiner presents oral questions that assess understanding of familiar problems and social concepts.
	Information (supplementary)	The student responds orally to general information questions.
	Word Reasoning (supplementary)	The student responds to one or more clues that are presented by the examiner.
Perceptual Reasoning Index	Block Design	The examinee reproduces a pattern using blocks.
	Picture Concepts	The examinee selects the correct drawing from several rows of drawings.
	Matrix Reasoning	The examinee selects the correct design from five choices.
	Picture Completion (supplementary)	The examinee observes a picture with a missing part and identifies the missing piece.
Working Memory Index	Digit Span	The student repeats a series of numbers forward in the Digits Forward section and a series of numbers in reverse order in the Digits Backward section.
	Letter-Number Sequencing	The student repeats a series of numbers and letters. The numbers are repeated, lowest to highest, and the letters are repeated in alphabetical order.
	Arithmetic (supplementary)	The student solves mathematical problems mentally and responds to them verbally.
Processing Speed Index	Coding	The student copies geometric symbols that are paired with either numbers or shapes.
	Symbol Search	The student searches two or three groups of paired shapes to locate the target shape.
	Cancellation (supplementary)	The student identifies target pictures that are presented.

starting points, and the rules for stopping vary among the subtests. Administration time is approximately 60 to 90 minutes.

SCORING The manual provides clearly written directions for scoring. The scoring of the subtests varies from one subtest to another. Raw scores convert to scaled scores, which are a form of standard score with a mean of 100 and a standard deviation of 15. Five composite scores are calculated: full-scale IQ, verbal comprehension index, perceptual processing speed index, working memory index, and processing speed index.

STANDARDIZATION The *WISC-IV* based its standardization sample on 2000 data from the U.S. Census. The standardization sample consisted of 2,200 children from 6 to 16 years and stratified according to age, gender, race/ethnicity, geographic region, and parental education. Students who were not fluent in English were excluded from the sample.

> **TESTS-at-a-GLANCE**
>
> **Wechsler Intelligence Scale for Children, Fourth Edition**
> http://www.pearsonclinical.com/psychology/products/100000310/wechsler-intelligence-scale-for-children-fourth-edition-wisciv.html?Pid=015-8979-044
>
> - **Publication Date:** 2004
> - **Purposes:** Intellectual abilities and problem solving.
> - **Age/Grade Levels:** 6 years through 16 years 11 months.
> - **Time to Administer:** 60 to 90 minutes.
> - **Technical Adequacy:** The standardization sample is excellent. Reliability is very good. Validity is excellent.
> - **Suggested Use:** Can be used when conducting a psychoeducational assessment, conducting a diagnosis of exceptional needs, determining eligibility for services, and performing a clinical and neuropsychological assessment.

The *WISC-IV* standardization sample did not include students with exceptional needs, nor does it provide separate norms for these children. However, the manual provides summaries of several studies conducted with special populations, including those with mental retardation, learning disabilities, autism, and attention-deficit hyperactivity disorder. The manual states that approximately 5.7 percent of students from these studies of special populations were added to the standardization sample. For the most part, these studies are few in number and contain small samples. However, they are encouraging. Additional research is needed in this area.

RELIABILITY Reliability refers to the consistency or stability of test performance. The manual reports split-half reliability coefficients for each of the subtests, for the three IQ scales, and for the four factor-based scales. Because the length of a test affects reliability, the highest reliability coefficient was .97 for full-scale IQ. For the subtests, reliability coefficients ranged from .79 to .90. Reliability coefficients for the index scores range from .88 to .94.

Test-retest reliability is an estimate of the stability of test scores over time. The test-retest reliabilities for the full-scale IQ and index scores is satisfactory. Interscorer reliability coefficients are .95 or higher.

SNAPSHOT
Intellectual Assessment

Hayley, who is 11 years old, was referred for special education services because her teachers observed that she has specific difficulties in reading, written language, and mathematics.

Emily Lauren Martinez, the school psychologist, is a member of the special services team. While the school's learning specialist focuses on Hayley's academic achievement, Emily concentrates on the assessment of intellectual abilities and problem-solving processes. She observed Hayley in several classes, examined work samples, and interviewed her.

Hayley told Emily that she feels she has difficulty completing assignments that require reading and writing. She enjoys participating in class discussions, especially when class discussions involve topics such as human rights and social justice. Hayley told Emily that she would like to be a social worker or lawyer when she grows up so that she can help people. Emily decided to administer an intelligence test to Hayley so that teachers have additional information about Hayley's potential.

After administering the *WISC-IV* to Hayley, Emily met with Hayley's teachers and explained the test's results to them. Hayley demonstrated overall average intelligence with a full-scale score of 101. When compared with her performance on other areas of this test, Hayley has relative strengths in Verbal Comprehension, with highest scaled scores in Vocabulary and Comprehension. Hayley seemed to have average Working Memory and relatively weak performance in Processing Speed and Perceptual Reasoning. Emily concluded that Hayley has relative difficulty with visual-perceptual and visual-motor activities, resulting in problems with planning and organization. Relative weaknesses in these areas may indicate that Hayley has difficulty figuring out how to begin activities and organize her work. She has difficulty keeping track of homework and long-term assignments. Hayley exhibits difficulty with impulse control, which affects her ability to reflect on school assignments and integrate new learning with prior learning. Emily wrote that there are a number of interventions that teachers can implement and strategies that Hayley can use to ameliorate these difficulties. These will be discussed at the upcoming planning meeting and incorporated into Hayley's individualized education program (IEP).

Pause and consider:
- What recommendations would you make based on the assessment results?
- In what ways do the results assist Hayley's team in developing and implementing a plan for her?

VALIDITY Concurrent validity of the *WISC-IV* was investigated with other tests, including the *WISC-II* and the *Wechsler Individual Achievement Test, Second Edition*. According to the manual, because the *WISC-III* is valid, the *WISC-IV* is also valid. Although it is true that there is considerable evidence for the validity of the *WISC-III*, the *WISC-IV* is a substantial revision of the earlier version. The manual does provide evidence for the separate factor structure with exceptional students. This evidence supports the validity of the *WISC-IV*. However, additional research studies are necessary to add to our knowledge about the validity of the *WISC-IV*.

SUMMARY The *WISC-IV* is an individually administered test of intelligence. Validity appears to be adequate. Although additional research is necessary to contribute to our understanding of it, this instrument is useful in the assessment of students.

SNAPSHOT

Andres

Andres is 11 years old and is in the fifth grade. He grew up in his neighborhood, and he has many friends there. When Andres arrives home after school, he has a snack and then races outdoors. Andres has disliked school ever since he can remember. He always had a hard time with reading, writing, and spelling, but he achieved somewhat better grades in mathematics.

Last week, there was a meeting at the school to discuss Andres's continuing academic difficulties. Andres attended the meeting with his parents. His teachers, while praising him for working hard, reported that Andres lags considerably behind his peers in academic areas. His teachers agreed that Andres is a delight to have in class. The participants in the meeting agreed that an assessment of Andres's intellectual abilities should be conducted to gain a better understanding of his learning needs.

After permission was obtained from Andres's family, the psychologist administered the *WISC-IV* to Andres. A standard score of 10 ± 3 falls within the average range. The following is a summary of the results of Andres's testing:

Verbal Scale	Standard Score
Information	6
Similarities	11
Arithmetic	8
Vocabulary	9
Comprehension	7
Digit Span	7
Verbal Scale Intelligence Quotient (VSIQ)	90

Performance Scale	Standard Score
Picture Completion	10
Coding	8
Picture Arrangement	15
Block Design	15
Object Assembly	8
Symbol Search	14
Performance Scale Intelligence Quotient (PSIQ)	108

Scale	Index
Verbal Comprehension Index	91
Perceptual Organization Index	113
Freedom from Distractibility Index	87
Processing Speed Index	106

The psychologist summarized Andres's performance on the *WISC-IV*. She wrote that Andres had significant strengths in both verbal and nonverbal concept formation, abstract reasoning, and visual sequencing, and relative weaknesses (although still within the average range) in using short-term memory and in visualizing the whole from the sum of its parts.

The psychologist recommended presenting new concepts globally first and then breaking them down into their components, taking into consideration the weaknesses in short-term memory when instructing in academic areas. Andres will need repetition in content areas when learning new concepts and help in organizing his thoughts to make connections with prior knowledge to retrieve information at a later time.

Wechsler Intelligence Scale for Children, Fourth Edition (WISC-IV Spanish)

A Spanish edition of the *WISC-IV* (PsychCorp, 2005) is available. This edition can be administered to children ages 6 through 16 years 11 months. According to the publisher, the Spanish edition represents the U.S. Spanish-speaking population, including those whose origins are Mexico, Cuba, Puerto Rico, the Dominican Republic, Central America, and South America. The norms allow comparison to English-language-speaking children who have similar educational experiences and parental educational levels.

In many instances, test items were directly translated from Spanish. For items in which no direct translation was possible, new items were generated. The Spanish edition includes the same 10 core subtests that can be found in the *WISC-IV* and four of the five supplemental subtests. The subtests are grouped into four indices: Verbal Comprehension, Perceptual Reasoning, Working Memory, and Processing Speed.

Woodcock-Johnson III, Normative Update, Tests of Cognitive Ability

The *Woodcock-Johnson III, Normative Update* (*WJ-III NU*; Woodcock, Schrank, McGrew, & Mather, 2007) is an individually administered battery that assesses general cognitive ability, specific cognitive abilities, scholastic aptitude, oral language, and academic achievement in individuals aged 2 years through adulthood. The battery consists of two tests, *Woodcock-Johnson III NU Tests of Cognitive Ability* (*WJ-III COG*) and the *Woodcock-Johnson III Tests of Achievement* (*WJ-III ACH*). The *WJ-III, Normative Update (NU)*, is discussed in Chapter 10.

The *WJ-III COG* is an application of the CHC theory of cognitive processing. According to the authors, the *WJ-III COG* measures General Intellectual Ability, Predicted Achievement, Intracognitive Discrepancies, Cognitive Categories (Verbal Ability, Thinking Ability, and Cognitive Efficiency), CHC Factors (Comprehension-Knowledge, Long-Term Retrieval, Visual-Spatial Thinking, Auditory Processing, Fluid Reasoning, Processing Speed, Short-Term Memory), and Clinical Clusters (Phonemic Awareness, Working Memory, Broad Attention, Cognitive Fluency, and Executive Processes). The *WJ-III COG* comprises two batteries, a Standard Battery and an Extended Battery. Teachers and other professionals can administer the Standard Battery alone or with the Extended Battery. Subtests 1 through 10 make up the Standard Battery, and subtests 11 through 20 make up the Extended Battery. Subtests combine to form clusters. Table 16.2 lists the subtests and the broad cognitive abilities that they measure.

> **TESTS-at-a-GLANCE**
>
> **Woodcock-Johnson III, Normative Update Tests of Cognitive Ability**
>
> www.riversidepublishing.com/products/wjIIIComplete/index.html
>
> - **Publication Date:** 2007
> - **Purposes:** Assesses cognitive abilities, general intellectual ability.
> - **Age/Grade Levels:** 2 years through adulthood.
> - **Time to Administer:** Approximately 1 to 2 hours.
> - **Technical Adequacy:** The standardization sample is appropriate. Reliability and validity are strong.
> - **Suggested Use:** Diagnosis; determining intra-individual, intra-cognitive, and intra-achievement discrepancies; determining predicted achievement; determining eligibility for services, program placement, individual program planning, and program evaluation.

ADMINISTRATION The time to administer the *WJ-III NU* varies from 20 minutes to several hours, depending on whether the examiner is administering both the *WJ-III COG* and the *WJ-III ACH* and whether the examiner includes the Extended Battery. The test is intended for individuals age 2 years through adulthood. A computer scoring program is necessary to ensure accurate scoring. Raw scores are converted to age and grade equivalents, percentile ranks, and standard scores. The manual reports confidence bands for standard scores for the 68 percent, 90 percent, and 95 percent confidence levels. It is possible to interpret intra-individual, intracognitive, and intra-achievement discrepancies, as well as predicted achievement.

NORMS The *WJ-III NU* was standardized on more than 8,800 individuals in over 100 communities. The sample was stratified according to U.S. Census estimates.

RELIABILITY The reliability of the *WJ-III NU* has greatly improved from the previous version of this test. The

TABLE 16.2 • Woodcock-Johnson III Cognitive Battery Subtests

The Standard Battery of the *WJ-III COG* consists of subtests 1 through 10. The Extended Battery consists of subtests 11 through 20.

Subtest	Narrow Ability	Broad Cognitive Factor
1 Verbal Comprehension	Lexical Knowledge	Comprehension Knowledge
11 General Information	Language Development General Information	
2 Visual-Auditory Learning	Associate Memory	Visual-Spatial Thinking
12 Retrieval Fluency	Ideational Fluency	
10 Visual-Auditory Learning—Delayed	Associate Memory	
3 Spatial Relations	Visualization Spatial Relations	Auditory Processing
13 Picture Recognition	Visual Memory	
19 Planning	Spatial Scanning	
4 Sound Blending	Phonetic Coding Analysis	Auditory Processing
14 Auditory Attention	Speech Sound Discrimination	
8 Incomplete Words	Phonetic Coding Synthesis	
5 Concept Formation	Induction	Fluid Reasoning
15 Analysis-Synthesis	Sequential Reasoning	
6 Visual Matching	Perceptual Speed	Processing Speed
16 Decision Speed	Semantic Processing	
18 Rapid Picture Naming	Naming Facility	
20 Pair Cancellation	Attention Concentration	
7 Numbers Reversed	Working Memory Memory Span	Short-Term Memory
17 Memory for Words	Memory Span	
9 Auditory Working Memory	Working Memory Memory Span	

authors provide extensive information on the reliability of the subtest scores, clusters, and the discrepancy scores. Reliabilities for the broad cognitive and achievement clusters are in the .90s.

VALIDITY   The manual reports a number of validity studies for both the cognitive and achievement batteries. In general, there is evidence to support content, concurrent, and construct validity. Evaluators should remember that the cognitive portion represents a single perspective, the CHC theory. The extent to which various subtests and interpretations reflect students' abilities depends on the orientation of the team to assessment.

SUMMARY   The *WJ-III NU COG* is a substantially improved version of its predecessor, the *Woodcock-Johnson Psychoeducational Battery—Revised (WJ—R;* (Woodcock & Johnson, 1989). It is a norm-referenced, individually administered battery that assesses cognitive and academic abilities in individuals age 2 years through adulthood. The cognitive battery consists of two parts, the Standard Battery and the Extended Battery. Documentation of reliability and validity are extensive.

Summary

- Our understanding of intelligence has developed and changed over the years.
- Variables that can affect performance on intelligence tests include the student's background, culture, primary language, environment, motivation, health, and emotional state, as well as the examiner's skills.
- Intelligence tests sample behaviors. Performance on a test helps us in our understanding of the student's approach to the demands of the tasks that are presented.
- Scores on an IQ test represent the examinee's performance at a given moment in time.

QUESTIONS FOR REFLECTION

1. When measuring intelligence, what special considerations do we need to make when testing students with diverse backgrounds?
2. What does the following statement mean? The results of intelligence tests should describe rather than explain behavior.
3. Examine several different intelligence tests. How do they differ in form and content?
4. What do you think intelligence tests will be like in the future?

REFERENCES

Brown, L., Sherbenou, R. J., & Johnsen, S. K. (2010). *Test of nonverbal intelligence 4*. Austin, TX: PRO-ED.

Dai, D. Y., & Sternberg, R. (Eds.). (2004). *Motivation, emotion, and cognition: Integrative perspectives on intellectual functioning and development*. Philadelphia, PA: Erlbaum.

Hammill, D. D. (1998). *Detroit tests of learning aptitude 4*. Itasca, IL: Riverside.

Hammill, D. D., Pearson, N. A., & Wiederholt, J. L. (2009). *Comprehensive test of nonverbal intelligence 2*. Austin, TX: PRO-ED.

Kaufman, A. S., & Kaufman, N. L. (2004). *Kaufman assessment battery for children, second edition*. Circle Pines, MN: American Guidance Service.

Mayer, J. D., Salovey, P., & Caruso, D. R. (2008). Emotional intelligence: New ability or eclectic traits? *American Psychologist, 63*(6), 503–517.

PsychCorp. (2005). *Wechsler intelligence scale for children IV, Spanish Edition*. San Antonio, TX: Author.

Roid, G. (2003). *The Stanford-Binet intelligence scale, fifth edition, Examiner's handbook*. Itasca, IL: Riverside.

Salvia, J., & Ysseldyke, J. (2004). *Assessment*. Boston, MA: Houghton-Mifflin.

Salvia, J., Ysseldyke, J., & Bolt, S. (2013). *Assessment in special and inclusive education* (11th ed.). Belmont, CA: Wadsworth Cengage.

Sattler, J. (2008). *Assessment of children: Cognitive foundations, fifth edition*. La Mesa, CA: Author.

Thorndike, R. L., Hagen, E. P., & Sattler, J. M. (1986). *Stanford-Binet intelligence scale: fourth edition*. Itasca, IL: Riverside.

Wechsler, D. (2004). *Wechsler intelligence scale for children IV—Integrated*. San Antonio, TX: PsychCorp.

Woodcock, R. W., & Johnson, H. B. (1989). *Woodcock-Johnson psychoeducational battery-revised*. Itasca, IL: Riverside.

Woodcock, R. W., & Muñoz-Sandoval, A. F. (2007). *Batería III Woodcock-Muñoz*. Itasca, IL: Riverside.

Woodcock, R. W., Schrank, F. A., McGrew, K. S., & Mather, N. (2007). *Woodcock-Johnson III*. Itasca, IL: Riverside.

17 Young Children

Chapter Objectives

After completing this chapter, you should be able to:

- Explain special considerations involved in assessing young children.
- Identify and describe how to select appropriate screening and developmental assessments.
- Describe developmental assessments and approaches for linking assessment with classroom activities.
- Discuss considerations for working with families and young children, including those whose home language is other than English.

Overview

Gathering information about the development of young children before they are enrolled in school is very different from the assessment of school-age children. Working with young children and their families can involve locating a mother and her preschool child in a homeless shelter, receiving a referral form from a community clinic, or working with a family recently arrived from another country where services for young children and families are not available. Assessment questions focus on the young child's general development in one or more areas. These areas, or **developmental domains**, focus on physical, cognitive, communication, social-emotional, and adaptive development. The focus on development differs in significant ways from the focus on the academic and achievement difficulties of school-age children and youth that we discussed in previous chapters. There are many excellent national and international resources for professionals who wish to learn more about working with young children (Table 17.1).

Teachers and administrators in public school programs usually define young children as students in kindergarten through grade 3; early childhood educators use the term "young children" to identify children between the ages of birth through 5 years or birth through 8 years. Thus, the definition of the term *young children* may imply different age ranges depending on the professional's frame of reference. Two national organizations of professionals, the Division of Early Childhood (DEC) of the Council for Exceptional Children (CEC) (**www.sped.org**) and the National Association for the Education of Young Children (NAEYC; **www.naeyc.org**),

TABLE 17.1 • Resources for Working With Young Children

Resources for Working With Young Children

Association for Childhood Education International (acei.org/) This international organization gathers and shares information about childhood education practices and policies in various countries to promote international and intercultural understanding.

Council for Exceptional Children, Division of Early Childhood (dec-sped.org/) This Division of the Council for Exceptional Children promotes policies and advance evidence-based practices to support the development of young children with special needs and their families.

National Association for the Education of Young Children (naeyc.org/) One of the world's largest organizations that works on behalf of young children and their families.

National Head Start Association (my.nhsa.org/) Created in 1965, this U.S. organization provides education, health, nutrition, and parent involvement services to low-income children and their families.

Zero to Three (zerotothree.org/) This U.S. organization informs, trains, and supports professionals, policymakers, and parents regarding the health and development of very young children, birth through 3 years.

---

define **young children** as children from birth through age 8. The Individuals with Disabilities Education Act (IDEA), Part C, describes eligibility and services for very young children from birth through 2 years of age and eligibility provisions for children from 3 through 9 years of age in Part B. We will focus on both age groups described in IDEA in our discussion of young children.

Professionals suggest that development, which is influenced by the child's interests, abilities, and opportunities in the natural environment, proceeds with individual variations during the early years. For example, 4-year-old Arron is interested in dinosaurs and can identify which are carnivores and which are herbivores. Will, who is also 4 years old, spends much of his time playing with his dump trucks. He speaks in two- to three-word phrases. The variations between Arron and Will may be due to genetic or biological factors, such as the child's temperament, or to prenatal factors, such as the mother's consumption of alcohol or drugs or use of tobacco during pregnancy. Social expectations and ways of caring for Arron and Will, or opportunity or its absence can influence both children's development. Most probably, according to many developmental theorists, two or more factors interact.

Today, tests can provide screening early in life for young children with special needs who can benefit from special services. Medical professionals identify many newborns with or at risk for a disability before leaving the hospital; visiting nurses and early intervention specialists screen infants in their homes; and early childhood special educators work with toddlers and preschoolers in their homes, child care centers, or early education programs. Professionals working with young children and their families represent a variety of disciplines, including audiology, family counseling, medicine, occupational therapy, physical therapy, psychology, social work, speech and language pathology, as well as education.

Screening

Screening is a process that identifies children who may have a disability and who need a comprehensive assessment. Some of the common questions raised by parents, caregivers, and early childhood teachers include: Is my child developing typically? Does the child have any problems that I need to know about?

Screening typically involves testing large numbers of young children, usually in a short amount of time. Screening does not identify children for services but rather pinpoints children who need further assessment. Using a comprehensive assessment process, evaluators may identify some children as needing early intervention or special education and related services.

In many cases, families are unaware of early childhood screenings and need to learn about the benefits of early intervention and the purposes of screening. These awareness activities are known as **Child Find**. Through Child Find, parents and caregivers become aware of screening activities, the first step in the process of identifying young children who fit the eligibility criteria for special services.

The community can sponsor screenings through the public school, through the state early intervention agency, or through community agencies. Customarily, a screening has several components, such as a physical examination by a doctor or nurse; a developmental history obtained by interviewing the parent or guardian; vision and hearing tests; and an assessment of the child's general development, including the physical, cognitive, communication, social-emotional, and adaptive domains. Professionals typically use a screening instrument to assist in making decisions regarding the screening outcome. Figure 17.1 illustrates the setup of a typical community screening program. You can read about one family's experience at a community screening in the Snapshot about Luiz and his mother.

Choosing Appropriate Standardized Screening Instruments

Generally, the purpose of screening tests is to evaluate large numbers of children to determine if further assessment is necessary; thus, these tests paint a broad picture and provide general information. Too narrow a focus can result in missing important aspects about the child and family. Communities can then devote valuable time and money to conducting comprehensive assessments on those children and their families who need further help.

FIGURE 17.1 • Typical Community Screening Program

Screening calls for norm-referenced tests, which compare a child's performance with the performance of other children who have taken the test. The norm sample must include children who have similar backgrounds and characteristics compared to the target child or children. For example, if the children under evaluation come from an inner-city area, then the screening instrument must have included children from urban areas for the norming sample.

Many different professionals and paraprofessionals administer and score screening tests. The administration of screening tests is standardized, as is their scoring. This means that the directions, calculation of scores, and determination of outcomes must contain clear explanations and must be the same for all children who come for screening. The outcomes of screening should not be subject to the judgment and biases of the many individual test examiners who administer and score the tests. In the following subsections, we examine screening instruments that are frequently used with young children. Some assessments, such as the *Battelle Developmental Inventory, Second Edition* and the *Bayley Scales of Infant and Toddler Development, Third Edition*, include both a screening test and a full developmental assessment. In the next chapter section, we will discuss those screens within the discussion of the complete developmental assessment.

Standardized Screening Instruments

Ages and Stages Questionnaires, Third Edition

The *Ages and Stages Questionnaires, Third Edition* (ASQ-3™; Squires & Bricker, 2009) is designed for children 2 months through 5 years of age. It consists of a set of parent questionnaires that focus on the following developmental areas: communication, gross motor, fine motor, problem solving, and personal-social skills. The set of questionnaires, available in both English and Spanish, includes a different questionnaire for each 2-month interval between 2 and 24 months and for 3-month intervals between 24 and 36 months of age. Beyond 3 years of age, questionnaires are available at 6-month intervals through 5 years of age. A user's guide includes suggested parent–child activities. A different tool that is similar to the ASQ-3™, *Ages and Stages Questionnaires: Social-Emotional* (ASQ:SE) (Squires, Bricker, & Twombly, 2009) is helpful when interests and concerns focus more specifically on social-emotional development.

ADMINISTRATION ASQ-3™ is administered individually and takes about 15 to 20 minutes. A parent can complete the questionnaire form individually, or the parent and early childhood educator or early intervention specialist can complete the form jointly.

SCORING The parent marks each item by indicating "yes," "sometimes," or "not yet." Afterward, the professional assigns scores for each item ("yes" = 10; "sometimes" = 5; "no" = 0), totals the scores, and compares the totals with the cutoff scores. Scores below the cutoff indicate that further assessment may be needed.

STANDARDIZATION The standardization sample included 12,695 children.

RELIABILITY The user's guide reports internal consistency and studies regarding test-retest and interobserver

---

TESTS-at-a-GLANCE

Ages and Stages Questionnaires, Third Edition

products.brookespublishing.com/Ages-Stages-Questionnaires-Third-Edition-ASQ-3-P569.aspx

- **Publication Date:** 2009
- **Purposes:** A parent-completed, first-level screening test that measures the following areas of development: communication, gross motor, fine motor, problem solving, and personal-social.
- **Age/Grade Level:** 2 months through 60 months.
- **Time to Complete:** 10 to 15 minutes.
- **Technical Adequacy:** The instrument has undergone extensive development with a large standardization sample. The authors present adequate evidence of reliability and validity.
- **Suggested Use:** Use as a first step in the screening process and to involve parents in monitoring their child's development.

reliability. Internal consistency correlations suggest moderate to strong internal consistency between the developmental areas and the overall score. In a test-retest study, parent agreement within a 2-week time period was strong. An interobserver reliability study comparing questionnaires completed by parents with questionnaires completed by trainer examiners on the same children indicated strong agreement.

VALIDITY Concurrent validity was measured by comparing children's performance on the *ASQ-3*™ with the *Battelle Developmental Inventory* (Newborg, 2005), an assessment often used in part to determine eligibility for early intervention or special education services. This study found moderate to high agreement, indicating that the *ASQ-3*™ can identify children who need further evaluation and not identify those children who are developing typically.

SUMMARY The *Ages and Stages Questionnaires, Third Edition,* is a set of parent-designed questionnaires for assessing their child's development in five main developmental areas. Scoring is conducted by an early childhood professional, with cutoff scores indicating when a child should be referred for further assessment. Several psychometric studies conducted on this edition provide emerging information regarding the technical characteristics of this instrument.

BRIGANCE® Early Childhood Screening III

The *BRIGANCE® Early Childhood Screening III* (Brigance, 2013) consists of a series of three screens across the following age levels: Birth to 35 months, 3 to 5 years, and K–1 (designed for 5- and 6-year-olds). According to the author, new content aligned with both early learning standards and Common Core Standards has been added to this revision. The *BRIGANCE® Early Childhood Screening* instruments assess content in the following areas:

- Physical development
- Language
- Academic/cognitive
- Self-help
- Social-emotional skills

ADMINISTRATION The *BRIGANCE® Early Childhood Screening III* is administered individually and takes about 10 to 15 minutes.

SCORING Raw scores are converted to a total screening score.

STANDARDIZATION The *BRIGANCE® Early Childhood Screening III* has been renormed.

RELIABILITY AND VALIDITY According to the Web site, additional research is currently underway.

Early Screening Inventory–Revised 2008 Edition

The *Early Screening Inventory–Revised (ESI-R), 2008 Edition* (Meisels, Wiske, & Henderson, 2008) consists of a brief developmental screening instrument. Designed for children from 3.0 to 5.11 years of age, the *ESI-R, 2008 Edition,* addresses the following developmental areas: visual, motor/adaptive, language and cognition, and gross motor skills.

TESTS-at-a-GLANCE

BRIGANCE® Early Childhood Screening III

www.curriculumassociates.com

- **Publication Date:** 2013
- **Purposes:** Screens development in the following areas: physical development, language, academic/cognitive, self-help, and social-emotional skills.
- **Age/Grade Levels:** Individual screens for children Birth–35 months, 3- to 5-year-olds, and K–1 for 5- to 6-year-olds.
- **Time to Administer:** 10 to 15 minutes.
- **Technical Adequacy:** This revision includes new norms. Additional information should be made available on the publisher's Web site to inform consumers.
- **Suggested Use:** Screening children and identifying those children who may have a disability and who need further assessment. Should be used with caution until information regarding technical adequacy is available.

> **TESTS-at-a-GLANCE**
>
> **Early Screening Inventory–Revised, 2008 Edition**
> http://www.pearsonclinical.com/childhood/products/100000382/early-screening-inventory-revised-2008-edition-esir.html?Pid=PAaESI&Mode=summary
>
> - **Publication Date:** 2008
> - **Purposes:** Screens development in the following areas: visual motor/adaptive, language and cognition, and gross motor.
> - **Age/Grade Levels:** 3.0 to 5.11 years.
> - **Time to Administer:** 15 to 20 minutes.
> - **Technical Adequacy:** The standardization sample needs to be updated to reflect changes in student demographics. The 2008 revision provides only minor changes in the test score sheet and examiner's manual.
> - **Suggested Use:** Screening children and identifying those children who may have a disability and who need further assessment. Should be used with caution until fully revised.

There are two forms of the test:

- *Early Screening Inventory–Preschool (ESI-P)* for ages 3.0 to 4.5 years
- *Early Screening Inventory–Kindergarten (ESI-K)* for ages 4.6 to 5.11 years

This screen also includes a parent questionnaire that includes information about the child's family, health history, self-help and social/emotional skills, and favorite activities. The questionnaire is available in English and Spanish. The minimal changes in the *ESI-R, 2008 Edition*, consist of changes in the score sheets to improve accuracy in scoring and a new examiner's manual that includes administration and scoring criteria for Spanish-speaking examiners.

ADMINISTRATION   The *ESI-R, 2008 Edition*, is administered individually and takes about 15 to 20 minutes.

SCORING   Raw scores are converted to a total screening score.

STANDARDIZATION   The *ESI-R, 2008 Edition*, was not restandardized. For the *ESI-K*, two sets of data were used in the standardization of the revised edition, *ESI-R*. The first set of data was collected from 1986 to 1990, and the second set was collected from 1992 to 1994. Combined data included 5,034 children across three different age groups (4.6 years to 4.11 years, 5.0 years to 5.5 years, and 5.6 years to 5.11 years). For the *ESI-P*, data was collected from 1993 to 1996 and included 977 children across three different age groups (3.0 years to 3.5 years, 3.6 years to 3.11 years, 4.0 years to 4.5 years).

RELIABILITY   No additional reliability studies were completed in this revision. Separate reliability studies were completed for the *ESI-R* published in 2003. For both age groups (*ESI-K* and *ESI-P*), high interrater reliability and test-retest data are reported in the examiner's manual.

VALIDITY   No additional validity studies were completed in this revision. Separate validity studies were completed for the *ESI-R* published in 2003. Small validity studies examined the performance of children who were assessed on the *ESI-K* or *ESI-P* with the McCarthy Scales of Children's Ability. The McCarthy was published in 1972 and is outdated today. The examiner's manual uses this data to provide evidence of predictive validity of the *ESI-R*.

SUMMARY   The *Early Screening Inventory–Revised (ESI-R), 2008 Edition*, provides a brief screening of a preschool child's development in three areas: visual motor/adaptive, language and cognition, and gross motor. A parent questionnaire, available in English and Spanish, provides additional information about the child's family and health history as well as self-help and social/emotional skills. The *ESI-R, 2008 Edition*, does not provide new norms or additional reliability and validity studies.

Greenspan Social-Emotional Growth Chart

The *Greenspan Social-Emotional Growth Chart* (Greenspan, 2004) is a screening tool for measuring social-emotional growth in young children from ages birth to 42 months. This assessment consists of a parent questionnaire that contains 35 items. The questionnaire items are ordered developmentally, according to the age at which a child usually masters the item.

Items are rated according to a 5-point scale. According to the author, typical developmental milestones in social emotional development can be indicated by age groups:

- *0–3 months:* Exhibits growing self-regulation and interest in the world.
- *4–5 months:* Engages in relationships.
- *6–9 months:* Uses emotions in an interactive, purposeful manner.
- *10–14 months:* Uses a series of interactive and emotional gestures to communicate.
- *15–18 months:* Uses a series of interactive and emotional gestures to solve problems.
- *19–30 months:* Uses ideas to convey feelings, wishes, or intentions.
- *31–42 months:* Creates logical bridges between emotions and ideas.

> **TESTS-at-a-GLANCE**
>
> **Greenspan Social-Emotional Growth Chart**
> http://www.pearsonclinical.com/childhood/products/100000214/greenspan-social-emotional-growth-chart.html?Pid=015-8280-229&Mode=summary
>
> - **Publication Date:** 2004
> - **Purposes:** Screens social-emotional development and allows comparison of the child's behavior with that typically expected of young children. Also yields a sensory processing score.
> - **Age/Grade Levels:** Birth to 42 months.
> - **Time to Administer:** 10 minutes.
> - **Technical Adequacy:** Additional information concerning reliability and validity would be helpful.
> - **Suggested Use:** Screening children in the area of social-emotional development.

In addition to the questionnaires, this tool comes with a manual and caregiver report. The report includes activities to encourage social-emotional development.

ADMINISTRATION   The questionnaire is completed by the parent or caregiver. The parent or caregiver responds to questions on a scale of 1 to 5 regarding behavior frequency from "All of the time" to "None of the time."

SCORING   The examiner calculates a total score based on the frequency of the behavior noted. For example, 1 point is awarded for "None of the time" and 5 points for "All of the time." The raw score is converted to a rating of full mastery, emerging mastery, or possible challenges. This assessment also yields a sensory processing score, which is calculated in the same fashion. The child's scores are plotted on a social-emotional growth chart that allows comparison of the child's growth to the expected normal growth curve for children.

STANDARDIZATION   The sample included 456 children from 15 days old to 42 months; it represented the population of children in the 2000 U.S. Census stratified according to race/ethnicity, region, and parent or guardian education level.

RELIABILITY   The manual presents evidence of internal consistency for the total growth chart. Alpha coefficients ranged from the mid-80s to the mid-90s, with higher scores at the older age levels. For the sensory processing score, internal consistency was low for children 4 to 18 months and adequate for other age groups.

VALIDITY   Evidence for construct validity is discussed in the manual, but additional information concerning criterion-related validity and concurrent validity would be helpful.

SUMMARY   The *Greenspan Social-Emotional Growth Chart* consists of a set of parent-designed questionnaires to assess their child's development. Scoring involves charting the child's growth and comparing it to an expected growth curve. Additional psychometric studies would lend evidence to the technical characteristics of this instrument.

The Ounce Scale

The *Ounce Scale* (Meisels, Marsden, Dombo, Weston, & Jewkes, 2003) is an observational tool for families and caregivers. Designed for children from birth through 42 months of age

> **TESTS-at-a-GLANCE**
>
> **The Ounce Scale**
> http://www.pearsonclinical.com/childhood/products/100000403/ounce-scale-the.html?Pid=PAaOunce
>
> - **Publication Date:** 2003
> - **Purposes:** Provides a structured method of tracking a child's growth and development as well as areas of difficulty.
> - **Age/Grade Levels:** Birth to 42 months.
> - **Time to Administer:** 10 to 20 minutes.
> - **Technical Adequacy:** Emerging studies indicate the effectiveness of this instrument.
> - **Suggested Use:** As a first step in the screening process and to involve parents in monitoring their child's development.

(3 years 6 months), this instrument focuses on the following developmental areas and associated questions:

- *Personal connections:* How does the child show that she trusts you?
- *Feelings about self:* How does the child express who he is?
- *Relationships with other children:* What does the child do around other children?
- *Understanding and communication:* How does the child understand and use gestures, vocalizations, and words to communicate?
- *Exploration and problem solving:* How does the child explore and figure things out?
- *Movement and coordination:* How does the child move his body and use his fingers, hands, and eyes to do things? (Pearson Education, 2008)

The *Ounce Scale* consists of three components: an observation record for observing and documenting a child's everyday behaviors, a family album for parents to use in recording and learning about their child's development, and a developmental profile for evaluating the child's development and progress over time. These components are available in both English and Spanish. These materials cover the following age ranges in months: 0–4, 4–8, 8–12, 12–18, 18–24, 24–30, 30–36, and 36–42. The instrument is designed to be used in the child's natural environment, such as the home, family child care, or center-based child care settings.

ADMINISTRATION Family members and others working with the child and family, such as Early Head Start visitors, visiting nurses, early intervention specialists, family child care providers, and teen parenting program staff, complete this observation tool.

STANDARDIZATION The *Ounce Scale* is a criterion-referenced instrument, based on developmental standards.

SCORING Observations recorded in the family album are used in ranking the child's progress on the developmental profile and summary report at each age level.

RELIABILITY AND VALIDITY The lead author of this instrument completed a 3-year study that involved 124 teachers and more than 250 children in seven Early Head Start programs in the Chicago area. This study found that the *Ounce Scale* had greater than 70 percent accuracy in discriminating between children who are at risk and those who are not (Erikson Institute, 2008).

SUMMARY The *Ounce Scale* provides information from multiple perspectives on six major developmental areas for children from birth to 42 months. Designed to be used in the child's natural environment, this instrument provides helpful information to parents, caregivers, and professionals working with the family. Additional studies that provide information about the technical characteristics of this instrument would be helpful.

Planning the Screening Procedure

In planning the screening procedure, the team must address several key areas. Each is discussed briefly in the following subsections.

Environment

The screening should typically take place in a setting that is quiet and free from distractions. The child should be in the company of a familiar caregiver during the assessment.

SNAPSHOT

Luiz and His Mother Visit the Community Screening Clinic

Recently Luiz's mother, Maria Hermetz, heard about a community screening clinic from a friend at the local convenience store. The clinic is held on the first Tuesday of each month at the community center and is free for all children in the community. Health and education professionals are available to answer questions about children's development.

Although Ms. Hermetz does not have any specific questions about 4-year-old Luiz, she decided that she would like to know if he is doing "what he should be doing" at this age. The following month she brought Luiz to the screening.

When Ms. Hermetz arrived at the community center, she observed that the large room had been separated into various areas (see Figure 17.1). The central area had a variety of toys and books for the children and chairs for the parents. "¡Buenos dias!" Ms. Hermetz was greeted by one of the clinic volunteers and asked to complete a brief form with questions regarding her son's development. Ms. Hermetz was relieved to learn that she could choose either an English or Spanish version of the form. Although she speaks English, she prefers to use her native Spanish. An early childhood special education teacher invited Luiz to join two other children who were playing with blocks nearby.

FIGURE 17.2 • Name Tag

Pause and consider:

- How might a parent feel upon entering a room where their child will be screened?
- What might you do to assist the parent and child?

As part of the screening process, the teacher will complete observations of the children as they play alone and together with other children in the waiting area. Earlier, during the planning of the screening program, the screening team identified the questions and the method that the teacher will use for recording the observation data, as discussed in Chapter 8. The teacher observed the children and noted important information to answer the following questions: How does the child approach the toys and other children? How does the child interact with the materials? How does the child communicate with adults? With other children?

An early childhood special educator gave Luiz a colorful name tag (Figure 17.2) and invited him to come with her to one of the four screening stations. Luiz liked pointing to various pictures in the examiner's book. After completing this station, Luiz moved to the next station to work with the speech-language pathologist. Later, he worked with the physical therapist at the motor development station. At the last station, a volunteer checked his hearing and vision. At each station, he received another colored sticker on his name tag. This procedure allowed the examiners to quickly determine which stations the child had completed.

After the screening, the nurse met with Ms. Hermetz to talk about the results and to answer any questions. Depending on the family's needs, the nurse may discuss various community resources. Today, she and Ms. Hermetz chatted about Luiz's development. About a week later, Ms. Hermetz received an e-mail that stated that the screening results had been completed and that no further assessment was indicated.

Rapport

Each examiner must allow time for the child to become familiar with the situation. Many children take time to "warm up" to strangers. If the child does not feel comfortable, the responses the child gives may not reflect the child's ability.

Physical Status

As routine practice, an examiner observes the child's current health status. Young children frequently have colds, leading to middle ear infections (a result of which is a temporary decrease in hearing). Can the child hear the directions? Does the child appear to be tired? If so, consider screening at another time. Does the child have difficulty meeting strangers? Does the child have a limited attention span? A child's attention will wander or be lost if the screening test has too many test items or the environment is noisy.

Development

Although educators define separate areas of development (physical, cognitive, communication, social-emotional, and adaptive), these areas are not independent but interact in complex ways. Screening procedures must be comprehensive in coverage and not focus on one or two developmental areas.

Parent Concerns

Some parents are very anxious about their children's screening tests. Parents may ask—or may not ask (even though it is a matter of primary concern)—"When will my child start talking?" or "Will this person find something wrong with my child?" Be sure that parents fully understand the reason for screening their children. An important component of any screening procedure is a time period for answering parents' questions, either before or after the testing.

Limitations of Screening

The screening process has several significant limitations. To gain a more comprehensive understanding, let's examine each of these in more detail.

Brief Picture

The results of a screening instrument, similar to those of other assessment approaches, show a snapshot of the child's development at one point in time. Many variables can affect screening results, including the child's physical, emotional, or motivational states; the examiner's familiarity with the screening tools; the examiner's understanding of child development and ability to establish rapport; the examiner's familiarity with children who are linguistically and culturally diverse; and the screening environment.

Because the results of screening present only a brief picture, best practices in screening suggest that a child receive periodic screening tests. The advantages of giving the child the same standardized instrument for each screening are the ease and usefulness of comparing the child's development on subsequent administrations. However, the cumulative effect of repeating items on periodic screenings and the tendency of some caregivers to "practice" the items with the child reduces the instrument's effectiveness.

Screening Tasks

Most standardized screening instruments include toys and test questions, which involve using or playing with the toys, such as cars, blocks, and a doll, in specific ways. For example, a common test item requires the examiner to tell the child to build a tower with a small pile of 1-inch cubes. Using toys in this way usually is a new experience for many young children. In fact, most early education programs encourage children to choose a toy, to explore its properties, and to use it in a way that they choose. Thus, when given several small cubes, a child may decide to make a train rather than a tower. However, for the examiner to score the test item as correct, the child must make a tower with the blocks. The young child may have no motivation or interest to comply with the examiner's request. Yet, because the screening test item is specific in defining a correct response, a child's score may be adversely affected when the child uses the material in a different way than stated.

SNAPSHOT
Special Challenges

Some families face special challenges that have an impact on Child Find activities and the screening and referral processes. We meet several families in the following snapshots:

- Fourteen-year-old Cheryl and her baby, Samantha, live on the streets of a large urban city. They occasionally sleep at a downtown shelter or in one of the vacant buildings on the waterfront.
- Sandy and her husband Brad commute long distances daily to their respective jobs. Baby James goes to his grandmother's home while his parents are at work. With their busy work schedules, Sandy and Brad don't have time to learn about James's development.
- Mindy and her 3-year-old son are immigrants living with her cousin in a small apartment house. Mindy worries that city officials will relocate her and return her and her child to their native country.
- Andreas graduated from college a few years ago and finds himself torn between the responsibilities of his job and his toddler. He often resents the demands that his child makes.
- Rita and Alexander and their three preschoolers live in a trailer at the end of a dirt road several miles from town. They have exhausted their meager savings since the mill closed and both parents lost their jobs. This rural family cannot readily access community resources and services.

False Negatives

A child who does, in fact, have a disability may pass through the screening without being identified for further assessment. The causes of **false negative** results are a lack of sensitivity of the screening instrument, a lack of training or limited clinical knowledge of the examiner(s), or other factors.

False Positives

A child who does not have a disability may be identified for further assessment. These **false positive** results increase parental anxiety and place an extra burden on the family until a comprehensive assessment is completed. The causes of false positives are a lack of specificity of the screening instrument, a lack of training or lack of clinical knowledge of the examiner(s), or other factors.

Special Challenges

Family situations can also present special challenges to the screening process. Families who are homeless or who have illegal immigrant status may be difficult to locate. You can read more about these special challenges in the Snapshot entitled Special Challenges.

Comprehensive Developmental Assessment

As a result of screening procedures, a young child may be referred to a multidisciplinary assessment team. The team addresses concerns about the child's development, and individual team members participate in planning and conducting a comprehensive assessment. Most states require that standardized instruments be part of the developmental assessment to determine eligibility for early intervention (services for children from birth through age 2) or special education and related services.

According to IDEA, assessment and program development for infants and toddlers must include the following:

- A multidisciplinary assessment of the unique strengths and needs of the infant or toddler and the identification of services appropriate to meet such needs.

- A family-directed assessment of the resources, priorities, and concerns of the family and the identification of the supports and services necessary to enhance the family's capacity to meet the developmental needs of the infant or toddler.
- A written individualized family service plan (IFSP) developed by a multidisciplinary team, including the parents.

IDEA also provides that the team, with the consent of the parents, can begin early intervention services before completion of the assessment. The IFSP includes information about the child's level of functioning, the goals or outcomes for the child, and the services that the child and family will receive. Figure 17.3 lists the required components of the IFSP related to assessment.

Early childhood special educators play a major role on the multidisciplinary team. They often conduct observations of the child in an early education setting, or they complete a developmental assessment on the child. Typically, developmental assessments cover a variety of developmental areas, including physical (gross and fine motor), cognitive, communication, social or emotional, and adaptive development. Best practice encourages professionals working with young children and their families to consider assessment a shared experience between families and professionals (Division of Early Childhood, 2007).

---

(1) A statement of the infant's or toddler's present levels of physical development, cognitive development, communication development, social or emotional development, and adaptive development, based on objective criteria.

(2) A statement of the family's resources, priorities, and concerns relating to enhancing the development of the family's infant or toddler with a disability.

(3) A statement of the measurable results or outcomes expected to be achieved for the infant or toddler and the family, including preliteracy and language skills, as developmentally appropriate for the child, and the criteria, procedures, and timelines used to determine the degree to which progress toward achieving the results or outcomes is being made and whether modifications or revisions of the results or outcomes or services are necessary.

(4) A statement of specific early intervention services based on peer-reviewed research, to the extent practicable, necessary to meet the unique needs of the infant or toddler and the family, including the frequency, intensity, and method of delivering services.

(5) A statement of the natural environments in which early intervention services will appropriately be provided, including a justification of the extent, if any, to which the services will not be provided in a natural environment.

(6) The projected dates for initiation of services and the anticipated length, duration, and frequency of the services.

(7) The identification of the service coordinator from the profession most immediately relevant to the infant's or toddler's or family's needs (or who is otherwise qualified to carry out all applicable responsibilities under this part) who will be responsible for the implementation of the plan and coordination with other agencies and persons, including transition services.

(8) The steps to be taken to support the transition of the toddler with a disability to preschool or other appropriate services.

FIGURE 17.3 • Assessment Information Required in the IFSP

Source: P.L. 108-446, 20 USC 1436, Sec. 636 (d).

Assessment practices should

- Answer the questions posed by the assessment team (including the family members).
- Integrate the child's everyday routines, interests, materials, caregivers, and play partners within the assessment process.
- Develop a system of shared partnerships with professionals and families for the communication and collection of ongoing information. (p. 10)

One of the purposes of a developmental assessment is to answer questions about the child's development using the referral and screening information. The developmental assessment results may indicate that the child's development is significantly behind and that the child has a developmental delay. Perhaps you'll remember from Chapter 1 that the term *developmental delay* is a term that describes eligibility for services for infants and toddlers. IDEA also includes the use of this eligibility term for children from 3 through 9 years of age (or a subset of this age group such as 3 to 5 years), if individual state departments of education choose to do so.

The developmental assessment is also helpful in answering questions about program planning. For children who are already receiving services, a developmental assessment provides a method of monitoring progress. Good practice dictates that assessment teams combine developmental assessment instruments with observations of the child and a parent report. Meisels and Atkins-Burnett (2000) emphasize that we cannot know the child in isolation from the family, and family members present evidence regarding the importance of incorporating environmental and familial information into the assessment process.

Arena Assessment

Sometimes professionals work across disciplines when assessing the development of young children. An **arena assessment** is a process in which the parent and two or more professionals first identify assessment questions and then meet in the same place, at the same time, to assess and gather information about the child. In planning an arena assessment, team members work closely with each other, first identifying one person to work with the child. This person may be someone who is most familiar with the child and family, such as an early childhood special educator or someone who has discipline-specific knowledge such as a physical therapist. The parent may be involved in cofacilitating or may sit with other team members. Based on the questions that the team wishes to answer, the facilitator asks the child to do various activities. As the facilitator works with the child, team members record notes of their observations. An arena assessment encourages sharing of information as team members become aware of others' goals and concerns for the child, and this process provides a common background for future team discussions.

Standardized Assessments

Early childhood special educators and early interventions use many different instruments to assist in the assessment process; some are norm-referenced, whereas others are criterion-referenced. Some of these assessments also come with a shorter version of the assessment that is designed for screening purposes. In the following subsections, we will examine the most common developmental assessments and how they are used.

Assessment, Evaluation, and Programming System for Infants and Children, Second Edition

The *Assessment, Evaluation, and Programming System (AEPS) for Infants and Children, Second Edition* (Bricker, 2002), designed for children from 1 month to 6 years of age, is a complete

TESTS-at-a-GLANCE

Assessment, Evaluation, and Programming System for Infants and Children, Second Edition

products.brookespublishing.com/Assessment-Evaluation-and-Programming-System-for-Infants-and-Children-AEPS-Second-Edition-4-Volume-Set-P471.aspx

- **Publication Date:** 2002
- **Purposes:** Criterion-referenced instrument for assessing skills, planning the program, monitoring, and evaluating a child's progress. The *AEPS* addresses the following areas: fine motor, gross motor, adaptive, cognitive, social-communication, and social.
- **Ages/Grade Levels:** Birth to 6 years.
- **Time to Administer:** Variable, depending on the number of areas assessed.
- **Technical Adequacy:** Criterion-referenced instrument; reliability and validity are adequate.
- **Suggested Use:** Useful for assisting in planning and monitoring a child's development across the five developmental domains addressed in IDEA. Volumes 3 and 4 provide excellent curriculum ideas for enhancing the child's development. The *AEPS* comes with a parent report, which allows parents to observe and record their child's progress, too.

system for assessing a child's skills, planning intervention activities, monitoring, and evaluating progress. The *AEPS* assesses the following developmental domains: fine (15 items) and gross motor (17 items), adaptive (35 items), cognitive (54 items), social-communication (49 items), and social (47 items). An unusual feature of this assessment is the lack of specific expected age levels. When a child has significant disabilities, families may appreciate this feature of the test because the focus is not on the amount of delay but rather on the skills that their child will be acquiring. The *AEPS* is comprised of a set of four manuals. Volume 1 is a guide to administration, Volume 2 focuses on assessment for children from birth to age 3 years and children 3 to 6 years of age, Volume 3 describes curriculum for children from birth to age 3 years, and Volume 4 describes curriculum for children 3 to 6 years of age. These latter two volumes link each assessment item with suggestions for embedding learning opportunities within the daily routine, using environmental arrangements, or providing intervention activities to assist children to meet their goals. The manuals cross-reference concurrent goals that the child may have in other domains. Additional materials available include the Child Observation Data Recording Form, which may be used for multiple assessments to follow the child's progress over time; a Family Report, which assists family members in participating in their child's assessment, goal development, intervention, and monitoring progress; and the Child Progress Record, which provides a visual representation of the child's skills in each developmental domain and the associated goals and objectives.

ADMINISTRATION The *AEPS* is administered individually, using test items that are appropriate for the child's developmental level. Information is collected by observation, teacher or parent/caregiver report, and direct assessment.

SCORING Test items are scored 2 if the child consistently meets criteria; 1 if the child inconsistently meets criteria, and 0 if the child does not meet criteria. Space is provided to include additional notes about other factors such as the assistance provided, interference of behavior, use of modification/adaptation, or the quality of performance.

STANDARDIZATION This is a criterion-related assessment. Separate test items are grouped for children from birth to 3 years of age and for children from 3 to 6 years of age.

RELIABILITY AND VALIDITY The Administration Guide includes a discussion of the psychometric properties and various small studies. Overall the evidence suggests that this assessment has adequate technical characteristics.

SUMMARY The *Assessment, Evaluation, and Programming System (AEPS) for Infants and Children, Second Edition,* designed for children from birth to 6 years of age, links assessment information to identifying a child's individual goals. Assessment information is gathered through observation, teacher/parent/caregiver report, and direct assessment. Ancillary materials include a curriculum book that could be helpful to educators in planning activities and embedding learning opportunities for children with disabilities in inclusive settings.

Battelle Developmental Inventory, Second Edition

The *Battelle Developmental Inventory, Second Edition* (*BDI-2*; Newborg, 2005), assesses development in young children from birth to 7 years 11 months. Each of the major domains assessed consist of several subdomains, including

- *Cognitive:* attention and memory, reasoning and academic skills, and perception and concepts
- *Communication:* receptive communication and expressive communication
- *Motor:* gross motor, fine motor, and perceptual motor
- *Personal-social:* adult interaction, peer interaction, and self-concept and social role
- *Adaptive:* self-care and personal responsibility

The *BDI-2* allows for flexibility in how information is gathered during the test administration. On many items, the examiner can choose the administrative procedure, including a structured test, observation, or interview. The test-item booklet describes specific instructions for each test item and what procedures are acceptable for that item. By using the interview procedure, the examiner can involve the parent or caregiver on items that may be difficult to assess directly.

The *BDI-2* also has a Spanish edition, the *Battelle Developmental Inventory, Spanish Edition (BDI-2 Spanish)*. This is an adaptation/translation of the English version of the *BDI-2*. According to the manual, this instrument is designed to be used by a bilingual examiner, by an English-speaking examiner and a Spanish-speaking colleague, or by a team of professionals. Both the Spanish and English editions include a screening test, the *BDI-2 Screening Test*, which consists of a subset of items from the complete *BDI-2*. This screen can be purchased separately.

ADMINISTRATION The *BDI-2* is administered individually and takes 1 to 2 hours, depending on the age of the child. The parent/caregiver can participate in this assessment by providing information through the interview on many items.

SCORING The test can be scored by hand or by using the *BDI-2 Data Manager* software. Scores convert to developmental quotients (mean of 100 and standard deviation of 15), percentile ranks, NCEs, *T*-scores, *z*-scores, and age equivalents for each of the subdomains. An overall *BDI-2* composite score can be reported as a developmental quotient or percentile rank. Confidence intervals are provided for each developmental quotient.

STANDARDIZATION The *BDI-2* was standardized using a sample of 2,500 children from birth to 7 years 11 months in 3- or 6-month intervals. The sample was stratified by age, gender, race/ethnicity, geographic area, and mother's educational level.

> **TESTS-at-a-GLANCE**
>
> **Battelle Developmental Inventory, Second Edition**
> www.riverpub.com/products/bdi2/index.html
>
> - **Publication Date:** 2005
> - **Purpose:** This comprehensive assessment is designed to identify delays or disabilities in one or more of the five developmental domains.
> - **Age/Grade Levels:** Birth to 7 years 11 months.
> - **Time to Administer:** 1 to 2 hours, depending on the age of the child.
> - **Technical Adequacy:** Normative sample closely matches the 2000 U.S. Census. Reliability and validity are adequate.
> - **Suggested Use:** This instrument can be used, in part, to determine eligibility for services and assessment process. The *BDI-2 Spanish* is an adaptation/translation of the English version of the *BDI-2*. Additional materials include scoring software and a screening test.

SNAPSHOT

Concerns About Bennie

Bennie Laurent is a shy, 4-year-old child who has frequent colds, earaches, and fevers. When he isn't sick, he likes to ride on the family tractor. At the urging of Grandmother, Bennie's father brought him to a well-baby and screening clinic in their rural community. Grandmother was concerned about Bennie's health and his slow development. Just recently he had begun to talk in complete sentences.

As part of the screening process, Bennie took the *Battelle Developmental Inventory-2* screening (Newborg, 2005), as did each child who came to the screening clinic. Based on observations conducted during the screening, the parent's report, and the *BDI-2* screening scores, Bennie was referred to the Developmental Evaluation Clinic for a comprehensive assessment.

At the Developmental Evaluation Clinic, the assessment team included a physician, a physical therapist, a speech-language pathologist, a psychologist, a special educator, and a social worker. Bennie's appointment lasted all morning and part of the afternoon. During this time, each member of the team observed or assessed Bennie and spoke with his dad. For Bennie and his family, the developmental assessment was helpful in answering questions about his development: Was there a developmental delay? Does he qualify for special services? What skills are developing? What are the child's needs?

When the individualized education program (IEP) team met to review the assessment results, they addressed the questions above. Bennie's developmental assessment indicated that he scored substantially below expected age levels in communication, cognitive, and social-emotional areas. The speech and language pathologist reported that his language assessments indicated delays in both expressive and receptive language skills. Bennie's father and grandmother discussed their concerns about his starting kindergarten next year and "being behind all the other children." The team came to the consensus that Bennie could benefit from the community pre-K program, where he would receive special education and speech and language services within the regular classroom setting.

Pause and consider:
- What types of concerns do you think Bennie's father and grandmother discussed with the team?
- How might various team members have responded to these concerns?

RELIABILITY   The manual reports detailed information including internal consistency and test-retest reliability. Overall internal consistency was high (.99), but age bands within some subdomains were relatively weak (.70 to .79). These included perception and concepts for infants 6 months to 23 months, fine motor for children 60 to 71 months, and adaptive for children in the 12- to 17-month age group. High test-retest reliability was reported for two groups of children: 2- and 4-year-olds. No other age-group studies were mentioned in the manual.

VALIDITY   Included in the manual is information regarding content, criterion-related, and construct validity. The author presents strong evidence regarding the validity of the *BDI-2*.

SUMMARY   The *Battelle Developmental Inventory, Second Edition,* is an easy-to-use instrument for measuring young children's development across the major developmental domains. The instrument provides some flexibility in administrative procedures, providing an opportunity for parent/caregiver input. Designed for children from birth to 7 years 11 months, this instrument provides a total composite standard score and scaled scores by subdomain.

Bayley Scales of Infant and Toddler Development®, Third Edition

The *Bayley Scales of Infant and Toddler Development, Third Edition* (*Bayley-III;* Bayley, 2005), for children from 1 to 42 months, measures development in the five major domains: cognitive, language (receptive and expressive), motor (fine and gross), social-emotional, and adaptive (conceptual, social, and practical) behavior. This assessment includes a screening test, the *Bayley Scales of Infant and Toddler Development, Third Edition* (*Bayley-III*) *Screening Test*, which consists of a subset of items and is designed to assess cognitive, language, and motor abilities of children from 1 to 42 months. This screen can be purchased separately.

ADMINISTRATION   The *Bayley-III* is administered individually and takes 30 to 90 minutes, depending on the age of the child. The parent/caregiver participates in aspects of the administration, and this assessment can be administered in the child's home.

SCORING   The test can be scored by hand or by using the *Bayley-III Scoring Assistant Software*. Scores convert to index scores, and subtest scaled scores correspond to individual domains. There is no global composite score because of the rationale that such a score could mask delays if one area is strong and another area is weak.

STANDARDIZATION   The normative sample for the cognitive, language, and motor scales consisted of 1,700 children between the ages of 16 days and 43 months 15 days. The sample was stratified by race/ethnicity, age, sex, parent educational level, and geographic location. The norms for the social-emotional scale were obtained from 456 children between the ages of 16 days and 42 months who participated in the normative sample of the *Greenspan Social-Emotional Growth Chart*. Norms for the adaptive behavior scale were obtained from 1,350 children from birth to 5 years 11 months who participated in the normative sample of the *Adaptive Behavior Assessment System, Second Edition (ABAS–II)*.

> **TESTS-at-a-GLANCE**
>
> **Bayley Scales of Infant and Toddler Development®, Third Edition**
>
> http://www.pearsonclinical.com/childhood/products/100000123/bayley-scales-of-infant-and-toddler-development-third-edition-bayley-iii.html
>
> - **Publication Date:** 2005
> - **Purpose:** This comprehensive assessment is designed to identify delays or disabilities in one or more of the five developmental domains.
> - **Age/Grade Levels:** 1 to 42 months.
> - **Time to Administer:** 30 to 90 minutes, depending on the age of the child.
> - **Technical Adequacy:** Normative sample closely matches the 2000 U.S. Census. Reliability and validity are strong.
> - **Suggested Use:** This instrument can be used, in part, to determine eligibility for services and to monitor development. Additional materials include scoring software and a screening test.

RELIABILITY   The manual reports adequate test-retest reliability and adequate internal consistency within each of the five domains. Reliability coefficients ranged from .86 to .91 for motor, cognitive, and expressive communication. Reliabilities for social-emotional and adaptive behavior scales were .83 to .94 and .79 to .98, respectively.

VALIDITY   The manual covers comprehensive validity information including content, concurrent, and construct validity for this instrument. The author presents strong evidence regarding the validity of the *Bayley-III*.

SUMMARY   The *Bayley Scales of Infant and Toddler Development, Third Edition*, is a well-developed instrument for measuring young children's development across the major developmental domains. Designed for children from 1 to 42 months, this assessment provides scaled scores. The technical characteristics of this instrument are strong.

Carolina Curriculum for Preschoolers With Special Needs, Second Edition

The *Carolina Curriculum for Preschoolers With Special Needs (CCPSN), Second Edition* (Johnson-Martin, Attermeier, & Hacker, 2004), is designed to guide a teacher or early interventionist in assessing a child's skills and planning the IEP. Organized by developmental domains, this assessment includes 22 test items in the following areas: personal-social, cognition, cognition/communication, communication, fine motor, and gross motor. For each test item, the curriculum manual contains a description of materials, procedures, and classroom and functional activities that can be used to help the child master the skill. Criteria for mastery are included.

TESTS-at-a-GLANCE

Carolina Curriculum for Preschoolers With Special Needs, Second Edition

products.brookespublishing.com/The-Carolina-Curriculum-CCITSN-CCPSN-Set-P489.aspx

- **Publication Date:** 2004
- **Purposes:** A criterion-referenced test that includes the following areas of development: personal-social, cognition, cognition/communication, communication, fine and gross motor.
- **Age/Grade Levels:** 2 through 5 years.
- **Time to Administer:** Varies because only areas of interest need to be assessed.
- **Technical Adequacy:** Criterion-referenced instrument; additional information regarding reliability and validity would be helpful.
- **Suggested Use:** Assessing a wide area of development in young children and providing suggestions for intervention activities.

Other materials included are an Assessment Log, which may be used for multiple assessments to follow the child's progress over time, and a Developmental Progress Chart, which provides a visual representation of the child's skills in each developmental domain and curriculum items that relate to promoting each skill. A similar assessment and materials for infants and toddlers is the *Carolina Curriculum for Infants and Toddlers With Special Needs (CCITSN), Third Edition.*

ADMINISTRATION The *CCPSN* is administered individually. Only test items appropriate for the child's developmental level are administered, and some items may be omitted because they are inappropriate, given the characteristics of a specific disability. Information is collected by observation and a short interview with the teacher or parent/caregiver. Additional information is collected by direct assessment.

SCORING Items that the child completes are marked with a + (plus sign), inconsistent or emerging skills are marked with ± (plus or minus), and items that the child is unable to do are marked with − (minus sign).

SNAPSHOT

The Hodgkin Family

The Hodgkin family consists of Sara (age 2), Joe (age 13 months), and their parents. Shortly after birth, Sara was identified as having a genetic disorder, trisomy 21, known as Down syndrome. Sara and her family have been involved in early intervention services since she was a baby. For the past 2 years, an early intervention specialist has conducted weekly home visits, helping Sara in her development. Recently, her parents have become increasingly concerned with Sara's progress in talking. An evaluation completed by a speech-language pathologist included a suggestion that the family begin to explore teaching Sara sign language because Sara was already using a number of natural gestures to communicate her wishes. Figure 17.4 illustrates a portion of Sara's IFSP, which provides an opportunity for parents to indicate the areas that are important to them.

Based on family concerns, priorities, and resources as they relate to Sara's development, the team will identify one or more outcome statements that describe what they would like to work on in the next 6 months. The outcome statements will guide the choice of services Sara will receive. In Sara's IFSP, the outcome statements reflect both child and family outcomes:

MAJOR OUTCOMES: CHILD Sara will learn to communicate in order to make her wishes known (such as to a have snack, a drink, or her favorite toy).

MAJOR OUTCOMES: FAMILY Mr. and Mrs. Hodgkin will receive information about parent groups in the community to meet other parents and receive peer parent support regarding issues of mutual interest, including learning more about using sign language.

Pause and consider:

- In what ways does the IFSP differ from what you know about IEPs?
- If you were an early interventionist specialist working with Sara and her family, how would you respond to these new IFSP outcomes?

> **SNAPSHOT** Continued
>
> **Individualized Family Service Plan: Family Considerations**
>
> Child's name: __Sara Hodgkin__   Person providing information __Mrs. Hodgkin (mother)__
>
> 1. Please describe your child (likes, dislikes, and strengths)
>
>   Sara is a happy, outgoing child. She has not been sick over the last 6 months. She seems to understand a lot that is said to her.
>
> 2. What are your concerns or how would you describe your child's needs?
>
>   We are worried about her lack of talking—and her slow progress in speech therapy.
>
> 3. What do you believe the strengths of your family are in meeting the child's needs?
>
>   My husband spends time playing with Sara and takes her shopping.
>
> 4. What would be helpful for your child and family?
>
>   To understand how to help Sara more. We want to understand what she wants and what she is trying to tell us.
>
> 5. Which of the following are concerns or areas about which you would like more information?
>
>   About the child
>   ___ feeding
>   _X_ communicating
>   _X_ learning
>   ___ vision or hearing
>   ___ problem behaviors
>   ___ equipment or supplies
>
>   About the family
>   _X_ meeting other families whose child has similar needs
>   _X_ finding out more about different services
>   ___ child care
>   _X_ transportation
>   ___ information about my child's disability
>   ___ information about SSI or Medicaid
>
> 6. Are there other concerns that you would like to discuss at the IFSP meeting?
>
>   We would like to meet families who use sign language with their children.
>
> **FIGURE 17.4** • **Excerpt From Sara's IFSP**

STANDARDIZATION This is a criterion-related assessment with an expected age range assigned to each test items.

RELIABILITY AND VALIDITY No information is provided in the manual.

SUMMARY The *Carolina Curriculum for Preschoolers With Special Needs (CCPSN), Second Edition,* is designed to link assessment information with activities to assist in developing skills across various developmental domains. Assessment information is gathered through observation, teacher or parent/caregiver interview, and direct assessment. The ancillary materials allow teachers or early interventionists to monitor child progress carefully. This assessment could be helpful to educators working with preschool children with mild to moderate disabilities.

Research-Based Practices | Individual Growth and Development Indicators

Ongoing assessment and progress monitoring inform early childhood educators, parents, and other IEP team members about children's progress. As early childhood educators implement response to intervention frameworks, these assessment measures must provide information for implementing and modifying instruction. For children with IFSPs and IEPs, these assessments should produce helpful information in monitoring progress, too. Thus, educators need measures that demonstrate instructional validity. Snyder and her colleagues (Snyder, Wixson, Talapatra, & Roach, 2008) summarized the writings of a number of professionals regarding recommendations that educators should follow:

- Use assessment approaches that have high treatment validity.
- Choose approaches that detect small increments of progress.
- Conduct repeated assessments.
- Report assessment results in ways that are immediately useful for program planning.

One area that shows promise is the use of a type of assessment known as individual growth and development indicators (IGDIs). This type of assessment approach differs from standardized, individual assessments such as norm-referenced or criterion-referenced assessments. Individual growth and development indicators provide helpful information about a child's development, even for children with significant disabilities, by using a set of key skill elements that are specifically linked to important outcomes and that represent specific domains (Carta, Greenwood, Walker, Kaminski, Good, McConnell, & McEvoy, 2002). For example, a team might identify a set of key skill elements linked to communication, or a set of key skill elements linked to early literacy. The set of key elements, known as the general outcomes measurement, is measured repeatedly over time. This approach of measuring a general outcome differs from most other assessments that focus on a specific set of subskills. Here, the focus is the child's rate of overall growth. Many Web sites provide information and training materials for professionals interested in this assessment approach, and there is a growing body of research that supports its effectiveness. A number of researchers (for example, Cadigan & Missall, 2007; Greenwood, Walker, Carta, & Higgins, 2006; Missall, Carta, McConnell, Walker, & Greenwood, 2008; Missall, Reschly, Betts, McConnell, Heistad, Pickart, et al., 2007; Nitsiou, 2006) explored the use of IGDIs associated with a general outcome measurement and found that the assessment measure provides both instructional and intervention validity.

Identifying individual growth and development indicators for measuring young children's early language and literacy assists teachers in monitoring interventions that are effective (Missall, Carta et al., 2008) and in providing information regarding predictive validity of early literacy skills of preschoolers and their oral reading fluency at the end of kindergarten and at the end of first grade (Missall, Reschly, et al., 2007). Individual growth and development indicators can be helpful in tracking language development in kindergarten children who are English language learners (Nitsiou, 2006) and in preschoolers who have autism spectrum disorders (Cadigan & Missall, 2007). Greenwood and his colleagues (Greenwood et al., 2006) focused on proficiency in problem solving among young children ages 1 to 4 years. They identified indicators that involved toy play behaviors that were sensitive to growth over time. The Juniper Gardens Children's Project has posted individual growth and development indicator materials for infants and toddlers online (**igdi.ku.edu/**); Educators interested in this approach can use these materials for assessing problem solving and other developmental areas. The Preschool Growth and Development Indicators from the University of Minnesota is an online resource for educators interested in early literacy (**ggg.umn.edu/**).

Considerations Regarding the Assessment of Young Children

Practitioners should be aware of a number of considerations regarding developmental assessment. First, standardized instruments that focus on screening and eligibility assessment of infants, toddlers, and preschoolers typically include the following developmental domains: cognitive, expressive and receptive language, fine and gross motor, and adaptive. Notice that these are not exactly the same as the domains included under the term *developmental delay*. In Chapter 1, we discussed that developmental delay refers to a delay in one or more of the following areas: physical development, including fine and gross motor; cognitive; communication; social or emotional; or adaptive development. Many commonly used instruments do not include the social-emotional domain. Yet this area is perhaps one of the most critical in increasing opportunities for young children of differing abilities to play and work together.

Another concern is the fact that criterion-referenced tests group items by the age at which children who are developing typically acquire a specific skill. However, development may not occur this way, particularly for children with special needs. For example, children who are blind can lag behind their peers in gross motor development. In addition, acquisition of certain other skills for these children may not follow the same sequence as for children with normal vision.

Teachers and therapists must guard against planning the child's program by looking solely at test performance. It is inappropriate for a planning team to identify items that the child fails as discrete items that the child needs to learn. For example, from the test item "Child stacks three blocks," an inappropriate objective would be "Randy will stack three blocks." A more appropriate programming activity would provide the child opportunities to manipulate a variety of materials in different ways, one of which might involve stacking.

In the classroom, early childhood educators use a variety of assessment approaches to provide information to plan and monitor individual and group progress. Educators also use assessment information to evaluate the program. In the following section, we will explore the critical link between assessment and the curriculum.

Responding to Diversity

By 2030, according to the National Association for the Education of Young Children (2009), 40 percent of schoolchildren will have a home language other than English. Today, for many children who are learning English, their language and learning needs are often misidentified. For example, their ability to speak and understand English may be overestimated, and their general cognitive and social abilities may be underestimated (Espinosa & López, 2007). This may occur because when young children are acquiring a second language, one language may be more dominant than the other; or children may experience a temporary plateau in language acquisition as they progress to bilingualism.

To meet the needs of these children and families, educators and other practitioners who assess young children will need to be well-prepared professionals (National Association for the Education of Young Children, 2009). In other words, in addition to knowing the child, they will be knowledgeable about language acquisition, including second and third language acquisition. They will be trained in and knowledgeable about assessment in general and about considerations in the assessment of young English language learners in particular (National Association for the Education of Young Children, 2009).

In a position paper, the Division of Early Childhood (2010) discussed several important recommendations when conducting observations and interviews. First, practitioners should conduct observations across environments, collecting information regarding what language(s) are used and by whom. Information collected should include how the child responds in each language. When conducting interviews, practitioners should include family members as well as service providers and cultural and linguistic informants (p. 5). Moreover, observation and interview information gathered in this way is helpful as educators link assessment information with classroom activities.

Linking Assessment With Classroom Activities

Beyond assessing for screening and eligibility purposes, early childhood educators use a variety of assessment approaches to:

- Monitor children's progress.
- Chart growth.
- Inform teaching practices.
- Evaluate the early childhood program.

Some educators may use criterion-referenced assessments, such as the *Carolina Curriculum for Preschool Children* or the *Assessment, Evaluation, Programming System for Infants and Children* discussed in the previous section. In this section, we'll examine other approaches, including documentation, observations, portfolios, and work samples. We'll also examine the influence of early childhood state standards on curriculum and assessment. Unlike more traditional assessments, these approaches encourage assessment results to be public and visible.

Reggio Emilia, originally developed in Italy, is an approach to curriculum planning, implementing, and assessing children's progress that places emphasis on public assessments. Using this approach, teachers set up documentation panels to record children's experiences and progress. Teachers display materials on the documentation panel that include some of the many ways children express their skills and knowledge: photographs, drawings, explanatory notes, and children's comments. Because the panels display documentation prominently in the classroom, children and teachers can refer to it during the day and share the children's work and progress with parents and other classroom visitors. Sometimes teachers use documentation panels in the classroom even though they are not following a Reggio Emilia approach to curriculum.

In the following subsections, we will examine other assessment approaches typically found in early childhood classrooms. These include *Teaching Strategies GOLD*, the *Work Sampling System*, and a teacher-made format for aligning curriculum and assessment with early childhood learning state standards.

Teaching Strategies GOLD

The *Teaching Strategies GOLD* (Teaching Strategies, GOLD® Assessment System: Technical summary, 2013) provides a way to assess individual child progress, birth through kindergarten, as well as group progress for programs that use a developmental curriculum. This strengths-based assessment is based on 38 objectives that include predictors of school success and are aligned with state early learning standards, the Common Core State Standards, and the Head Start Child Development and Early Learning Framework.

These objectives are organized into the following 10 areas of development:

- Social emotional
- Language
- Physical
- Cognitive
- Literacy
- Science and technology
- Social studies
- The arts
- Mathematics
- English language acquisition

For example, under social-emotional development, a child must regulate her own emotions: managing feelings and following limits and expectations. Using child assessment information from *Teaching Strategies GOLD*, teachers are able to plan learning experiences based on individual strengths and needs. A number of ancillary materials are included to assist teachers in organizing their observations and document facts. *Teaching Strategies GOLD* is available in hardcopy and online.

ADMINISTRATION Information is collected through recording observations, both short, informal notes and

---

TESTS-at-a-GLANCE

Teaching Strategies GOLD
https://teachingstrategies.com

- **Publication Date:** 2011
- **Purposes:** Closely linked to typical early childhood curriculum, the assessment monitors progress across social-emotional, language, physical, cognitive, literacy, science and technology, social studies, the arts, mathematics, and language acquisition for dual language learners (English and Spanish).
- **Age/Grade Levels:** Birth through Kindergarten.
- **Time to Administer:** Varies depending on observation period.
- **Technical Adequacy:** Limited information.
- **Suggested Use:** Monitoring children's progress and planning classroom activities. Could be very helpful for inclusive programs.

systematic observations, which were discussed in Chapter 8. Teachers also maintain a portfolio for each child to document progress.

SCORING   Individual child objectives are scored as emerging or accomplished. This information is reviewed frequently (at least once a week) to determine progress and guide program planning. Performance and growth reports allow teachers to identify children who are making progress and end-of-year expectations.

STANDARDIZATION   This assessment was not developed using a norm sample. Rather, it is based on objectives that research has shown to be predictors of school success, according to the publisher. The assessment is aligned with the Common Core State Standards, state early learning guidelines, and the Head Start Child Development and Early Learning Framework.

RELIABILITY AND VALIDITY   Assessment materials describe the process for observing and documenting information. Some attempt is made to encourage interrater reliability.

SUMMARY   The *Teaching Strategies GOLD* provides a structured approach for organizing and using teacher observations to gather information about children's progress and to inform instruction. This assessment is closely linked to state early childhood standards and the Common Core Curriculum. It is designed to include *all* children across a wide range of abilities.

The Work Sampling System®, Fifth Edition

The Work Sampling System®, Fifth Edition (Meisels, Marsden, Jablon, & Dichtelmiller, 2013), is based on national and state standards for early childhood and provides a way to assess individual and group progress for Pre-K to third-grade. This assessment focuses on personal and social development, language and literacy, mathematical thinking, scientific thinking, social studies, the arts, and physical development, health and safety. This assessment consists of the following materials: (1) Developmental Guidelines and Checklists and (2) Summary Reports. Using assessment information, teachers can build learning experiences and differentiate instruction.

ADMINISTRATION   Educators use observation to gather information and documentation about children's work. Results are recorded at three different points in the year (fall, winter, and spring).

SCORING   Three types of ratings are possible for skills, knowledge, or behavior: "not yet" indicates that it has not been demonstrated, "in process" indicates emerging but not consistent, and "proficient" indicates that it is firmly within the child's range of performance.

STANDARDIZATION   This is not a norm-referenced assessment but rather a performance-based assessment of children's skills and knowledge.

RELIABILITY AND VALIDITY   Meisels (2011) reports on various aspects of the technical quality of the original *Work Sampling System*, specifically for kindergarten through third grade. This report includes summaries of reliability and validity studies One study, completed by the Maryland State Department of Education, found

---

TESTS-at-a-GLANCE

The Work Sampling System®, Fifth Edition
http://www.pearsonclinical.com/childhood/products/100000755/the-work-sampling-system-5th-edition.html

- **Publication Date:** 2013
- **Purposes:** Closely linked to national and state early childhood standards, this assessment monitors progress in personal and social development, language and literacy, mathematical thinking, scientific thinking, social studies, the arts, and physical development, health, and safety.
- **Age/Grade Levels:** Preschool through third-grade
- **Time to Administer:** Varies depending on observation period.
- **Technical Adequacy:** Studies completed on the earlier edition suggest moderate to high reliability and validity.
- **Suggested Use:** Monitoring children's progress and planning classroom activities. Could be very helpful for inclusive programs.

high internal reliability (.966 p <.05) . Split-half reliability coefficients were .918 (Spearman-Brown) and .914 (Guttman). Validity studies by independent researchers examined literacy and mathematics and found moderate to strong concurrent and predictive validity. Future research will provide additional evidence to inform our understanding of this latest edition of the *Work Sampling System*.

SUMMARY Based on national and state guidelines for early childhood, *The Work Sampling System®, Fifth Edition* provides a structured assessment system for observing and documenting children's work, both at the individual and group level. Information collected could help inform instruction. By design, this assessment is closely linked to typical early childhood curricula and could be a helpful addition to inclusive classrooms.

Using Early Childhood State Standards

As a result of the standards movement, each state developed a set of early childhood standards that describe what young children should know and be able to do. Many early childhood teachers consider the standards to be helpful in planning and assessing classroom activities as well as monitoring children's development. These standards are available generally in print or Web-based format. Using these standards, an early childhood teacher can design a template for recording information about children's progress. For example, Monica Redlevske, a preschool teacher, developed a template that included each of the standard areas and enough room to note examples of the child's progress.

Monica and the other teachers record observations weekly during typical daily routines and special activities. Every week or two, they collect samples of children's work, photos of children's products, or evidence of their developing play skills. Then, on a regular basis, she and the other teachers organize the information for each child in file folders. Later they synthesize the information as developmental progress notes for parents and other team members for end-of-year reporting. The developmental progress notes for one child, Kassie, are illustrated in Figure 17.5.

Domain	Strengths	Goals
Personal and Social Development A) Self Control B) Self Concept C) Social Competence	• Seeks adult help when needed for emotional support • Demonstrates increased capacity to follow rules and routines • Developed a growing understating of how own actions affect others	• Increase ability to describe own and other's emotions • Increase ability to express feelings, needs, and opinions in difficult situations and conflicts • Increase expression of pride in accomplishments
Approaches to Learning A) Initiative & Curiosity B) Persistence & Reflection	• Engages in individual or group activities that express real-life experiences, ideas, knowledge, feelings, and fantasy • Seeks help appropriately from another child or adult when encountering a problem	• Increase the ability to find more than one solution to a question, task, or problem • Begin to demonstrate a capacity to maintain concentration for a meaningful period of time on a task, set of directions, or interactions, despite distractions or interruptions • Increase ability to persist in and complete an increasing variety of tasks, activities, projects, and experiences

FIGURE 17.5 • Kassie's Developmental Progress Notes

Domain	Strengths	Goals
Creative Arts A) Participates with increasing interest and enjoyment in a variety of music, movement, visual arts, drama activities	• Uses props to enhance role playing and dramatic play • Uses different art media and materials	• Increase the ability to create drawings, paintings, and other art creations that reflect more detail, creativity, and/or realism
Early Language and Literacy A) Communicating & Listening B) Book Knowledge & Appreciation C) Comprehension D) Sounds in Spoken Language E) Early Print Concepts F) Alphabet Knowledge G) Early Writing	• Handles and cares for books • Recognizes own written name • Identifies most letters of the alphabet • Copies and prints own name	• Increase ability to communicate clearly enough to be understood by familiar and unfamiliar listeners • Increase ability to retell information from a story
Health & Physical Education A) Healthy Habits B) Gross & Fine Motor Skills	• Regularly participates in active games, outdoor play, and other forms of exercise that enhance physical fitness • Uses basic personal hygiene practices and understands that those practices help maintain good health	• Moves with an awareness of personal space in relationship to others
Mathematics A) Number & Number Sense B) Shape & Size C) Mathematical Decision Making D) Patterns	• Demonstrates an increasing ability to count in sequence to 10 and beyond • Uses one-to-one correspondence in counting objects and matching groups of objects • Demonstrates increasing interest and awareness of numbers and counting as a means for solving problems and determining quality	• Increase ability to match, sort, put in a series, and regroup objects according to one or two attributes such as color, shape, or size • Increase ability to use nonstandard units of measurement (books, hands, blocks) to measure objects
Science A) Scientific Knowledge B) Scientific Process	• Explores and experiments with different material, objects and situations	• Increase ability to sort living things by characteristics such as movement, environment or body covering (hair, feathers, scales)
Social Studies A) Children develop understanding of the larger world through activities related to family and communities	• Dramatizes the ways people work and various aspects of their jobs	• Increase ability to identify tools and technology used at home, school, and work.

FIGURE 17.5 • *(Continued)*

Working With Families

For some parents, learning that their child has a disability comes as a surprise, but for other parents, the finding comes as a relief. These parents may have had questions and concerns for some time regarding their child's development. Figure 17.6 presents a number of general tips for sharing assessment information with family members.

In sharing knowledge and information, respect the point where the family is at any one period of time. One strategy is to offer choices. For example, in discussing the inconclusive results of a diagnostic assessment, the practitioner might ask, "Do you want to know the range of options or just the more likely?" Be honest. Say, "I don't know" when you don't, but also always follow up with "I'll find out" or "The field just doesn't know at this point."

Transition and Assessment

Children with special needs and their families usually become involved in transitions during three time periods: first, when the child turns 3 years old and moves from infant and toddler early intervention to preschool services; second, when the child turns 5 years old and moves from preschool to school-age services; and third, when the young adult leaves the education system and moves to the community, to work, or to further education. Transition is often a difficult time for children and families, perhaps because of a new school program, new teachers and therapists, or new procedures.

Transitions involve careful planning by the early childhood team so that the movement between programs can be successful. Assessment questions that the team addresses involve aspects of the new program and needs of the child. Here are some possible transition questions regarding any new program:

- What is the physical layout of the room, and what types of adaptations to the environment will the child need?
- What materials are available, and are they accessible to children?

- Provide family members with an opportunity to receive the assessment report in a one-to-one setting rather than during a large IFSP or IEP team meeting. This meeting allows the family time to ask questions with an empathetic practitioner and to reflect on the information prior to the larger, full-staff meeting.
- Share information with both parents (or major caregivers) at the same time.
- Be honest and straightforward regarding the disability.
- Be willing to say when you don't know.
- Allow time for families to express their feelings.
- Be sensitive to families if they are not ready to hear details.
- Offer to provide additional information.
- Suggest additional resources.
- Be available to the family for further discussions.
- Arrange to have a native-language interpreter available if families need assistance.

FIGURE 17.6 • Tips for Sharing Eligibility Information With Families

- What are the classroom routines and expectations of children? For example, do children have a designated place for their clothing and materials? Are the children permitted to carry materials from one center to other centers?
- What are the classroom procedures? For example, do children clean up after themselves? Do children obtain and return materials independently? Do some centers have a limit on the number of children who can be at them at any one time?

A teacher can collect information about the new program by means of a checklist or rating scale. By identifying this information early, teachers can complete adaptations to the environment and teach the child some of the routines or expose the child to new procedures before the child enters the new program.

Transition assessment also includes identifying the skills that will be helpful to the child in the new program. Transition activities provide opportunities for parents and teachers to work together, to exchange information, and to build common understandings before a child enters a new program. During transition activities, parents and early childhood teachers and caregivers have increased opportunities to facilitate the child's skills before the child enters kindergarten.

Transition assessment should never aim at excluding children from programs. Transition assessment does not mean assessing school readiness. Rather, it means identifying the needs and supports that will make entry into the new program as successful as possible.

Summary

- Assessment of young children involves a variety of assessment approaches for the purposes of screening, determining eligibility, monitoring children's progress, charting growth, informing teaching practices, and evaluating the early childhood program.
- Teachers and other professionals need to become familiar with the characteristics of good screening and developmental assessments. The use of observations and the careful recording of data must be integral aspects of assessing young children.
- Sensitivity to parent concerns and involvement of parents and caregivers throughout the assessment process are key components in working with young children.

QUESTIONS FOR REFLECTION

1. Research the position statements of two or more professional organizations such as Division of Early Childhood (DEC; dec-sped.org), a subdivision of the Council for Exceptional Children (CEC) (**sped.org**), or the National Association for the Education of Young Children (NAEYC). What are their positions regarding the assessment of young children? How do these positions compare? Develop your own position statement for assessing young children.
2. Make arrangements to visit a kindergarten or community screening program. After your visit, answer the following questions:
   - What are the components of the screening program?
   - What do the teachers feel are the strengths and limitations?
   - Synthesize the teachers' comments and provide a summary of their evaluation.
   - What other information could you add based on the information in this chapter?
3. Conduct a comprehensive review of several screening instruments. Compare their administration, standardization, and scoring procedures. What do the Web sites and manuals state about reliability and validity?
4. A young child received a referral for a comprehensive assessment as a result of the screening test. After examining the results of the comprehensive assessment, team members decided that the child was developing typically and there was no indication of delay. Explain several possible reasons why the child was referred as a result of the screening test.

5. Research the procedures at your state department of education regarding its eligibility system for young children. How does the system determine eligibility? What criteria does it use?
6. Review two or three developmental assessments. Compare the test items for a particular age group. What are the similarities? How are the items different? If you are assessing for the purpose of planning the child's program, which test items would provide the most helpful information?

REFERENCES

Bayley, N. (2005). *Bayley scales of infant and toddler development* (3rd ed.). New York, NY: Pearson Education.

Bricker, D. (Ed.). (2002). *Assessment, evaluation, and programming system (AEPS®) for infants and children* (2nd ed.). Baltimore, MD: Paul H. Brookes.

Brigance, A. H. (2013). *BRIGANCE® early childhood screens III*. North Billerica, MA: Curriculum Associates.

Cadigan, K., & Missall, K. N. (2007). Measuring expressive language growth in young children with autism spectrum disorders. *Topics in Early Childhood Special Education, 27*(2), 110–118.

Carta, J., Greenwood, C., Walker, D., & Buzhardt, J. (2010). *Using IGDIs: Monitoring progress and improving intervention for infants and young children*. Baltimore, MD: Brookes.

Division of Early Childhood. (2007). *Promoting positive outcomes for children with disabilities: Recommendations for curriculum, assessment, and program evaluation*. Missoula, MT: Author. Retrieved March 7, 2013, from http://www.dec-sped.org/uploads/docs/about_dec/position_concept_papers/Prmtg_Pos_Outcomes_Companion_Paper.pdf

Division of Early Childhood. (2010). Position statement: Responsiveness to ALL Children, Families, and Professionals: Integrating Cultural and Linguistic Diversity into Policy and Practice. Retrieved March 10, 2013 from: http://www.dec-sped.org/uploads/docs/about_dec/position_concept_papers/Position%20Statement_Cultural%20and%20Linguistic%20Diversity_updated_sept2010.pdf

Erikson Institute. (2008). *Ounce scale validation project*. Retrieved May 11, 2009, from http://www.erikson.edu/default/research/projects/projectdetail.aspx?c=399

Espinosa, L. M., & López, M.L. (2007). Assessment considerations for young English language learners across different levels of accountability. The National Early Childhood Accountability Task Force and First 5 LA. Retrieved March 7, 2013, from http://www.pewtrusts.org/uploadedFiles/wwwpewtrustsorg/Reports/Pre-k_education/Assessment%20for%20Young%20ELLs-Pew%208-11-07-Final.pdf

Greenspan, S. (2004). *Greenspan social-emotional growth chart*. San Antonio, TX: Pearson.

Greenwood, C. R., Walker, D., Carta, J. J., & Higgins, S. K. (2006). Developing a general outcome measure of growth in the cognitive abilities of children 1 to 4 years old: The early problem-solving indicator. *School Psychology Review, 35*(4), 55–551.

Individuals with Disabilities Education Improvement Act of 2004. (2004). Washington, DC: U.S. Government Printing Office. (P.L. 108-446, 20 USC 1400 et seq.).

Johnson-Martin, N. M., Attermeier, S. M., & Hacker, B. J. (2004). *The Carolina curriculum for preschoolers with special needs* (2nd ed.). Baltimore, MD: Paul H. Brookes.

Meisels, S. J. (2011). Using observational assessment to evaluate young children's learning: The technical quality of the *Work Sampling System*. Retrieved from http://www.erikson.edu/wp-content/uploads/AERA-FCD-WSS-summary.pdf

Meisels, S. J., & Atkins-Burnett, S. (2000). The elements of early childhood assessment. In J. P. Shonkoff & S. J. Meisels (Eds.), *Handbook of early childhood intervention* (2nd ed., pp. 231–257). Cambridge, UK: Cambridge University Press.

Meisels, S. J., Marsden, D. B., Dombo, A. L., Weston, D. R., & Jewkes, A. M. (2003). *The ounce scale*. San Antonio, TX: Pearson.

Meisels, S. J., Marsden, D. B., Jablon, J. R., Dorfman, A. B., & Dichtelmiller, M. K. (2013). *The work sampling system®* (5th ed.). San Antonio, TX: Pearson.

Meisels, S. J., Wiske, M. S., & Henderson, L. W. (2008). *Early screening inventory* (Rev. ed.). San Antonio, TX: Pearson.

Missall, K., Carta, J. J., McConnell, S. R., Walker, D., & Greenwood, C. R. (2008). Using individual growth and development indicators to measure early language and literacy. *Infants & Young Children: An Interdisciplinary Journal of Special Care Practices, 21*(3), 241–253.

Missall, K., Reschly, A., Betts, J., McConnell, S. R., Heistad, D., Pickart, M., et al. (2007). Examination of the predictive validity of preschool early literacy skills. *School Psychology Review, 36*(3), 433–452.

National Association for the Education of Young Children. (2009). *Where we stand on assessing young English language learners*. Retrieved March 7, 2013, from http://www.naeyc.org/files/naeyc/file/positions/WWSEnglishLanguageLearnersWeb.pdf

Newborg, J. (2005). *Battelle developmental inventory* (2nd ed.). Itasca, IL: Riverside Publishing.

Nitsiou, C. (2006). Tracking the status of language development in language-minority kindergartners. *Early Child Development & Care, 176*(8), 817–833.

Pearson Education. (2008). *The ounce scale*. Retrieved March 7, 2013, from http://www.pearsonassessments.com/ounce.aspx

Snyder, P. A., Wixson, C. S., Talapatra, D., & Roach, A. T. (2008). Assessment in early childhood: Instruction-focused strategies to support response-to-intervention frameworks. *Assessment for Effective Intervention, 34*(1), 25–34.

Squires, J., & Bricker, D. (2009). *Ages and stages questionnaires® (ASQ-3™)* (3rd ed.). Baltimore, MD: Paul H. Brookes.

Squires, J., Bricker, D., & Twombly, E. (2009). *Ages and stages qeustionnaires®: Social-emotional (ASQ:SE)*. Baltimore, MD: Paul H. Brookes.

Teaching Strategies, LLC. (2013). *Teaching strategies GOLD® assessment system: A technical report*. Retrieved from http://www.teachingstrategies.com/content/pageDocs/TS-GOLD-Technical-Summary-2013.pdf

18 Youth in Transition

Chapter Objectives

After completing this chapter, you should be able to:

- Define the concept of transition.
- Explain the purposes of transition assessment.
- Describe the ways in which students' transition needs and preferences are assessed.

Overview

The provision of transition services is critical when preparing students with disabilities for adult life. Although students with disabilities continue to fall behind their typical peers in postschool employment, wages, postsecondary education, and residential independence, they are making gains. The federal government mandates that students with disabilities be provided with services that facilitate their transition from school to postschool activities, including postsecondary education, integrated employment (including supported employment), continuing and adult education, adult services, independent living, and community participation.

In order to prepare young people for future productive and fulfilling lives in our communities, they should develop knowledge, skills, and competencies that will prepare them for work in the 21st century (Pellegrino & Hilton, 2012). These skills include problem solving, critical thinking, communication, self-management, and intrapersonal and intrapersonal skills. Key contributors to the development of young people are teachers, appropriate curricula, sound assessment approaches, and support from families and their communities.

Considerable research has been conducted on transition and employment outcomes for students with disabilities (Trainor, 2008; Wehman, 2006), with mixed results. Disparities exist for students who have certain racial or ethnic backgrounds, are associated with low socioeconomic backgrounds, are from immigrant families, and whose dominant language is not English. High school completion rates are also influenced by these demographic characteristics.

Cooperation between experts and interagency collaboration are essential to the assessment process. Professionals who come from a variety of disciplines and incorporate input from parents, caregivers, and the student should conduct the assessment of transition needs and preferences. Collaboration is important to the success of a student's transition.

Various assessment tools are available to conduct transition assessment, including standardized instruments, curriculum-based assessment, performance-based assessment, direct observation, checklists, and other approaches. Much more experimentation with various assessment methods, especially in how and when to use them, is necessary to develop assessment tools that educators can apply with confidence.

Although transitions occur across an individual's life span, the transition from the school setting to adult life is one that requires careful assessment and planning. The effects of this transition have a great impact on the individual with a disability.

Legal Requirements

U.S. legislation mandates that transition services be provided to students with disabilities. The focus is on assisting the individual with a disability to make a smooth transfer from the school to independent adult life. The legislation requires the individualized education program (IEP) team to begin school transition planning early, update transition plans annually, and include a statement of individual needs for transition services as a component of the IEP. Federal legislation requires that secondary transition services be implemented by age 16.

Federal legislation requires that schools base individual transition planning on present levels of performance. Transition planning is an outcome-oriented process in which the focus is on the attainment of prespecified performance objectives. Assessment of students' transition needs and preferences is an important part of the transition process and should include assessment of vocational, career, academic, personal, social, and living needs. This requires a variety of approaches and (because transition planning is a process that occurs over a long period of time) periodic transition assessments. Monitoring of transition plans is essential.

Transition services means a coordinated set of activities for a student, designed with an outcome-oriented process, that promotes movement from school to postschool activities, including postsecondary education, vocational training, integrated employment (including supported employment), continuing and adult education, adult services, independent living, and community participation.

A coordinated set of activities means that all transition activities must meet the student's needs and complement, not duplicate, each other. The transition process involves many individuals and agencies. The coordinated set of activities must be based on the individual student's needs, taking into account the student's preferences and interests.

Although progress has been made, many challenges remain (National Council on Disability, 2008), including (1) increasing secondary-age students' access to relevant and rigorous curricula while at the same time increasing the numbers of students who successfully complete high school; (2) expanding the range of options for students who enter employment after graduation from high school; (3) improving access to higher education opportunities; (4) ensuring that there is a wide range of opportunities for vocational and educational opportunities for individuals with disabilities who do not complete a high school program; (5) increasing research and information about age-appropriate transition assessments; (6) increasing the understanding of transition planning, self-determination, and self-advocacy by students with disabilities; (7) improving the involvement of vocational rehabilitation counselors in transition activities; and (8) decreasing the rate at which students with disabilities drop out of school (Flexer, Baer, Luft, & Simmons, 2008; National Council on Disability, 2008).

Transition Assessment

Beginning at age 16 (or sooner if determined by the pupil evaluation team) and updated annually, the IEP team must develop a statement of transition services needs of the student that focuses on the student's courses of study. When the student is age 16, the IEP team must discuss and document transition services at every IEP meeting until the student leaves school. Assessment for transition can include questions related to the types of employment in which the student is interested; future educational needs and aspirations; personal, social, and community resources and supports; and independent living needs and aspirations. Methods of collecting information can include interviews with the student, family, school personnel, job counselors, and employers; review of educational records; surveys of the student's interests and needs; functional assessments; and observations.

As individuals with disabilities transition from school to adult life, assessment is crucial in career and vocational education and in life-skill development. Transition assessment can be defined as follows: the ongoing process of collecting data on the individual's strengths, needs, preferences, and interests as they relate to the demands of current and future working, educational, living, and personal and social environments. Assessment data serve as the common thread in the transition process and form the basis for defining goals and services that will make up the individualized education program.

Transition assessment relates to the life roles of individuals with disabilities and the supports they need before, during, and after the transition to adult life. The data collected during transition assessment is vital in assisting individuals with disabilities and their families to make choices that take into account the individual's strengths, needs, and preferences about postsecondary education, career development, vocational training, community living, and personal and social goals.

Purposes of Transition Assessment

Transition focuses on facilitating improved postsecondary outcomes for persons with disabilities. Transition assessment assists individuals with disabilities, their families, educators, specialists, employers, and community members to develop, implement, and evaluate the transition process. Transition assessment is integral to instruction and program planning.

Research-Based Practices | Education and Employment

Research on U.S. youth has yielded disturbing findings relating to education and employment. When compared with all Americans, almost twice as many students with disabilities do not complete high school. Students with disabilities are much less likely to complete postsecondary education. Of those students who do participate in postsecondary education, many have poor self-concept and socialization skills and experience stress and anxiety. These students are reluctant to let instructors know that they need accommodations because they fear that they will be stigmatized. One of the most disturbing findings is that students with disabilities are much less likely to be employed than students without disabilities. A growing number of students apply for Supplemental Security Income (SSI), a federal program that assists persons with disabilities by providing funds to meet basic needs for food, clothing, and shelter each year. Thus, there is an ever-widening gap between persons with and without disabilities relating to education and income (Greene & Kochbar-Bryant, 2003; Sitlington, Neubert, & Clark, 2009).

Because transition planning can begin as early as the elementary years, transition assessment is an ongoing process. Although the purposes of transition change as the student gets older, the major purposes are to

- Identify the person's level of career development.
- Determine the individual's strengths, abilities, interests, and preferences regarding postsecondary education, employment, independent living, community involvement, and personal and social goals.
- Identify the individuals who exhibit interests and skills.
- Identify the accommodations, modifications, supports, and services that the individual will need in order to be a responsible and contributing community member (Sitlington et al., 2009).

Involving Families

Parental and family involvement and support are integral to the transition process. Beginning in the early elementary years, parental involvement throughout the process is important. Educators should periodically interview parents about their aspirations for their children. As children progress through school, parents' views of their children's abilities change. Educators should welcome parents as partners throughout the transition process (Wehman, 2006). Questions that can be discussed with parents include the following:

Expectations

- What are your expectations for your child?
- What are your perspectives on your child's motivation, preferences, and interests?
- What are your expectations regarding employment?
- What are your child's daily responsibilities at home?
- In what types of tasks or jobs do you think that your child will be successful?
- What are your goals for your child's future?
- In what types of jobs do you think your child will be successful

Transportation

- Does your child have access to transportation?
- Does your child use public transportation? If so, are there any problems?
- What are your expectations for your child's transportation to and from work?

Education and Experiences

- Do you feel that your child will need further education and/or training after completing high school? If so, what types of education and/or training would be beneficial?
- What steps have you taken to obtain additional information on this education and/or training?
- Has your child participated as a volunteer in community activities?
- What experiences has your child had with your family that could prepare your child for independent living?

Person-Centered Planning

Person-centered planning means that the student with the disability engages in an active, meaningful way with parents, educators, community members, and others during the assessment, planning, and service delivery processes. Person-centered planning is focused on self-determination and on the student's hopes, dreams, and desires. Natural supports—the individuals and supports that the general population uses, rather than specialized services—are emphasized. Examples of natural supports include neighbors, employers, clergy, and other community members.

Person-centered planning encourages students with disabilities to take a leadership role during the transition activities. Person-centered planning should result in a comprehensive plan that addresses educational opportunities, employment opportunities, financial and income needs, friendship and socialization needs, transportation needs, health and medical needs, and legal and advocacy needs (Wehman, 2006). Person-centered planning has several characteristics:

- Person-centered planning focuses on abilities, rather than disabilities.
- It encourages planning that is oriented toward the future.
- Involvement of community members and organizations is integral.
- It emphasizes supports, connections, and commitment rather than programs and services.
- Person-centered approaches are individualized according to each student's needs and desires. The student with the disability and family members provide strong direction for transition planning and implementation activities.

When developing IEPs that are person-centered, individuals who are part of the student's personal network should be identified. Along with the student and the family, this personal network develops a vision or dream of the student's future. These individuals can include the student, family members, special educators, general educators, vocational educators, vocational rehabilitation counselors, providers of adult services, and other community members. Each major transition should connect to part of the student's dream.

The IEP team should identify the experiences, supports, and services that need to be in place to achieve the dream. Achieving the IEP goals and objectives should move the student closer to the dream and to inclusion in the community. A variety of instruments can be useful in person-centered planning:

- Learning styles inventories
- Classroom observation instruments
- Curriculum-based assessments
- Learning environment assessments
- Physical environment assessments
- Social environment assessments
- Future planning questionnaires
- Interviews with students
- Interviews with parents and family members
- Adaptive behavior instruments
- Behavioral and functional assessments
- Technology evaluations
- Self-determination checklists (Sitlington et al., 2009)

Self-Determination Skills

Student self-determination is at the center of transition planning. Self-determination is considered to be the attitudes and behaviors that influence individuals to set goals, take actions in pursuit of the goals, and assess progress toward the goals (Trainor, 2008). All activities in the transition process, including assessment, planning, implementation, and evaluation, must involve the individual with the disability as an active participant to the maximum extent

Strengths and Preferences What skills have I learned that will help me reach my dreams? Things I like to do are . . .	**Needs** What do I still need to learn to do to reach my dreams? What skills do I have trouble with? What do I need help with?
Opportunities What is helping me now to reach my dreams? Who can assist me concerning my dreams?	**Worries** What worries me when I think about reaching my dreams?

FIGURE 18.1 • Self-Determination Skills Guide

possible. **Self-determination** means that the individual's hopes, dreams, and desires influence the types of assessments that the team implements. Figure 18.1 is a guide that can be used by students and teachers to express students' hopes and dreams. Transition assessment should include and document self-determination skills. Parents' involvement should also be encouraged. Various instruments assist in this process, including one or more interviews with the individual, interviews with parents and family members, checklists, and observations (Sitlington

SNAPSHOT

Lee

Lee is a 14-year-old in the sixth grade. He has been identified as having mild mental retardation and an emotional disability. Lee's language abilities are well below the range of an average 14-year-old. Lee often gets frustrated when he is unable to communicate effectively and sometimes responds inappropriately by striking out at others.

In a conversation with his special education teacher, Shauna Moore, Lee talked about feeling different from his classmates. He stated that this made him angry and sad. When asked what he likes to do, he responded, "I like to play video games." Shauna asked Lee what he would like to do for a career when he was older. Lee indicated that he would like to be a "vet" (veterinarian). When asked why he wanted to be a veterinarian he said, "Animals can understand me."

In an interview, Lee's mother expressed concerns about his future. She worries that he will not be able to do the things that other students are going to be doing, like "travel independently" or "have a girlfriend." She stated that he prefers to play alone or with his dog but has "no friends." She does not have many problems understanding her son, but she knows that he does get easily frustrated when he is unable to communicate well with others. When asked about Lee's future after high school, she thought that he might be able to work as a building custodian as long as he was supervised.

Pause and consider:

- What are the next steps for Lee's transition team?
- How would you advise the team to proceed with further assessments and planning?
- Provide specific suggestions for monitoring progress.

Shauna suggested that the IEP team should begin to plan for Lee's transition by first assessing Lee's interests, preferences, and aptitudes. Once these are shared with the team, the team will set goals with Lee for his life after school and develop a plan of action that will enable him to reach his goals.

et al., 2009). As teachers learn to understand their students' views of self-determination, teachers' practices and expectations will change. Suggested questions to ask are listed in Figure 18.1.

- Does the individual understand the transition planning process? Does the person demonstrate self-advocacy skills?
- Can the individual explain his or her role in the transition planning process? Can the person identify interests and preferences?
- Can the individual describe personal transition goals?
- What are the individual's strengths, needs, interests, preferences, and worries?

Assessment Instruments

This chapter describes published instruments that provide information on transition assessment. For *all* assessment instruments, users should carefully review technical aspects and administration procedures and consider how to use the tools appropriately.

Job and Career Interests

The team that is helping to plan for a student's transition may need to gather information about the student's job and career interests. These interest inventories can assist individuals in investigating educational and occupational alternatives, learning about careers, and setting goals for the future.

Reading-Free Vocational Interest Inventory 2

The *Reading-Free Vocational Interest Inventory 2* (*RF-II*; Becker, 2000) is a vocational interest inventory for students who have mental retardation or learning disabilities. The test consists of 55 sets of three pictures. The pictures are black-and-white drawings that depict women and men in work activities.

ADMINISTRATION   The *RF-VII* can be administered to individuals or to groups of students. The examiner reads the directions to students, and the students circle the drawings that depict the work that they prefer to do. The test requires no reading by students.

SCORING   The consumable student booklets are hand-scored. Raw scores transform to *T*-scores, percentiles, and stanines. Scores that fall above the 75th percentile indicate areas of high interest; scores falling below the 25th percentile indicate areas of low interest.

SNAPSHOT

Transition Assessment

Brita, who is almost 16 years old, has been thinking about her future. When she has time in her busy schedule, she thinks about what she would like to do when she leaves high school. Ever since she can remember, Brita has enjoyed cooking. She loves to bake breads and cook soups and stews. Her recent successful placement as an apprentice chef has reinforced her desire to enter the cooking field. Her dream is to become a restaurant chef.

Brita's transition team is meeting in a few weeks to plan transition activities that support her as she leaves high school and enters the next phase of her life. Brita's team includes her mom, special education teacher, vocational rehabilitation counselor, worksite coordinator, and transition specialist. In preparation for the meeting with her team, Brita has completed the strengths, needs, opportunities, and worries worksheet with her special education teacher. Here is Brita's form.

SNAPSHOT Continued

Strengths and Preferences	**Needs**
What skills have I learned that will help me reach my dreams? Things I like to do are . . . measure ingredients read recipes follow directions work with others	What do I still need to learn to do to reach my dreams? What skills do I have trouble with? What do I need help with? finding new recipes doing math completing college applications
Opportunities	**Worries**
What is helping me now to reach my dreams? Who can assist me concerning my dreams? How can they help? my mom my teacher	What worries me when I think about reaching my dreams? How can I pay for school? Do I need help finishing high school classes?

Mr. Kane, Brita's special education teacher, will be discussing Brita's performance on recent tests, including achievement and cognitive ability assessments. Mr. Kane will report that Brita is very motivated and has experienced success in her apprenticeship. She continues to experience difficulty in reading and mathematics, but the introduction of assistive software has enabled Brita to keep up with her academic classes.

Brita's worksite coordinator, Ms. Kerem, will share her impressions of Brita's performance in the cooking apprenticeship. Brita has been working in a natural foods restaurant during the past two months. When she started the apprenticeship, Brita helped to set up the ingredients for making breakfast muffins. Now, she is able to set up the ingredients, mix them in the commercial mixer, and put the trays in the ovens. Ms. Kerem believes that Brita has been very successful and is enthusiastic about her progress.

The transition specialist, Ms. Barker, will be assessing Brita's skills for leaving high school. Ms. Barker knows that Brita and her family would like Brita to continue her education at the community college, where she can earn a certificate as a chef. Transition skills that should be considered include completing school applications, living independently, self-advocacy, organizational abilities, study skills, and interpersonal skills. In preparation for the transition assessment, Ms. Barker and Brita met to discuss the supports that are already in place to help Brita fulfill her dream. Figure 18.2 shows the circle of supports that Brita and Ms. Barker developed.

> **Pause and consider:**
> - What are the next steps that Brita and her team can take in planning for Brita's transition?
> - Develop a strengths, needs, opportunities and worries chart for yourself. How does this analysis help you develop a plan for yourself?

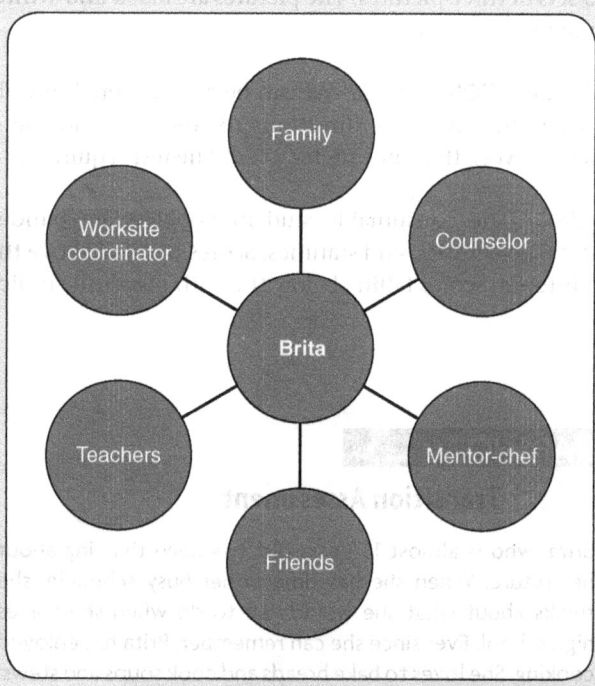

FIGURE 18.2 • Brita's Circle of Supports

STANDARDIZATION   The *RF-VII* was standardized on over 8,000 students with mild mental retardation or learning disabilities in grades 7 through 12. In addition, adult norms were derived from the test performance of over 3,000 adults with mental retardation and economic or environmental disadvantages. Although the test manual describes a study of students in grades 7 through 12 who showed moderate mental retardation, the norm tables do not incorporate this information. However, the manual suggests that the norms are appropriate for students who show moderate mental retardation.

RELIABILITY   Test-retest and internal consistency reliability is adequate, with coefficients generally in the .70s and .80s.

VALIDITY   Although the manual states that experts reviewed the items, the description of content validity is sketchy. Concurrent validity was determined by comparing the *RFVII* with the 1964 revision of the *Geist Picture Interest Inventory* (Geist, 1964). The description of construct validity is limited.

SUMMARY   The *Reading-Free Vocational Interest Inventory 2* measures the vocational interests of students with mild mental retardation or learning disabilities who are in grades 7 through 12. The norms need updating to reflect recent census figures. Reliability is adequate; validity is limited. The author should provide evidence of predictive validity so that users can make predictions about vocational interests and actual vocations that are pursued.

Adaptive Behavior and Life Skills

Chapter 9 describes several assessment tools that can be used to evaluate adaptive behavior and life skills. These instruments can be utilized when conducting transition assessments.

Connecting Assessment With Instruction: Performance-Based Assessment

Chapter 15 describes performance-based assessments as documentation of the student's efforts, progress, and achievement. When applied to transition assessment, performance-based assessments can be used to document the transition needs and preferences of students. Evidence of a student's transition needs can include work samples, audio and video recordings, inventories, checklists, observations, and self-reports.

A portfolio that documents transition needs and preferences produces a rich, detailed portrait of the student. It depicts the student in natural work and living environments and provides continuous information, feedback, and growth toward transition needs and goals. Portfolio assessment can also link interventions directly to the student's activities.

In addition to the assessment tools this chapter describes, the assessment of transition needs can include many of the procedures that previous chapters described, including

- Oral descriptions
- Written descriptions
- Checklists and questionnaires
- Interviews
- Conferences
- Student journals and notebooks
- Discussions among students, parents, and teachers.

Summary

- The overall intent of transition assessment is to assist students in making a transition from school to post-school activities, including postsecondary education, vocational training, integrated employment (including supported employment), continuing and adult education, adult services, independent living, and community participation.
- Transition assessment must include the evaluation of vocational, career, academic, personal, social, and living needs.
- Transition assessment is an outcome-oriented process that begins when the child is young and takes place over a period of time.
- Transition assessment involves person-centered planning. This means that the student with the disability engages in an active meaningful way with parents, educators, community members, and others during the assessment, planning, and service delivery processes. Person-centered planning focuses on self-determination and on the students' hopes, dreams, and desires.

QUESTIONS FOR REFLECTION

1. Interview a school counselor or a rehabilitation counselor regarding transition services and assessment approaches that the school offers to students. Share your findings with others.
2. After reviewing the purposes of transition assessment, identify specific assessment tools and approaches that fit these purposes.
3. The American Association of Intellectual and Developmental Disabilities (AAIDD) has made resources on person-centered planning available at its Web site: aaidd.org. Can you explain the importance of this approach?
4. The American Association of Intellectual and Developmental Disabilities (AAIDD) has made resources on self-determination available at its Web site: aaidd.org. Can you explain the importance of this approach and its relationship to person centered-planning?
5. Visit a local school and interview a special education teacher who provides transition services. Consider the types of assessment instruments and approaches that are used.
6. www.youthhood.org is an interactive Web site that has been developed for individuals who are preparing for the transition after high school. The site contains resources for planning future educational activities, entering the workforce, and independent living. Demonstrate one or more features of this site to a young adult, and ask them to comment on the usefulness of the features. To what extent can the site be useful to educators as they support students' transition plans?
7. How can performance-based assessment contribute to the assessment of transition needs and preferences?

REFERENCES

Becker, R. L. (2000). *Reading-free vocational interest, inventory 2.* Lutz, FL: Psychological Assessment Resources.

Flexer, R., Baer, R., Luft, P., & Simmons, T. (2008). *Transition planning for secondary students with disabilities.* Upper Saddle River, NJ: Pearson.

Geist, H. (1964). *Geist picture interest inventory.* Los Angeles, CA: Western Psychological Corporation.

Greene, G., & Kochbar-Bryant, C. A. (2003). *Pathways to successful transition for youth with disabilities.* Columbus, OH: Merrill Prentice-Hall.

National Council on Disability. (2008). *The Rehabilitation Act: Outcomes for Transition-Age Youth.* Retrieved December 15, 2008, from http://www.ncd.gov

Pellegrino, J. W., & Hilton, M. (2012). *Education for life and work: Developing transferable knowledge and skills in the 21st century.* Washington, DC: National Research Council.

Sitlington, P. L., Neubert, D. A., & Clark, G. (2009). *Transition education and services for students with disabilities* (5th ed.). Upper Saddle River, NJ: Pearson.

Trainor, A. (2008). Using cultural and social capital to improve postsecondary outcomes and expand transition models for youth with disabilities. *Journal of Special Education, 42*(3), 148–162.

Wehman, P. (2006). *Life beyond the classroom: Transition strategies for young people with disabilities.* Baltimore, MD: Paul H. Brookes.

Glossary

accommodations Changes to the education program and assessment procedures and materials that do not substantially alter the instructional level, the content of the curriculum, or the assessment criteria.

achievement testing The assessment of past learning.

adaptive behavior The collection of conceptual, social, and practical skills that individuals learn to function in their everyday lives.

adverse effect Once the IEP team determines that the child or youth has a disability, the team must determine if the disability has led to deficits that prevent the child from accessing and progressing in the general education curriculum.

alternate assessments Assessments that allow students with persistent academic problems and students with severe or significant disabilities who are working toward modified or alternative achievement standards to participate in general large-scale assessments.

alternate form reliability An estimate of the correlation of scores between two forms of the same test.

AIM line See goal line.

analytic scoring A type of scoring in which an independent score is reported for each area of the scoring rubric. This type of scoring provides diagnostic information. Individual scores indicate areas of strengths and areas that need improvement.

anchor papers Student papers that represent writing at different levels of performance.

anecdotal record A brief narrative description of an event or events that the observer felt was important to record.

antecedents The events that happen before the behavior occurs.

arena assessment A process in which the parent and two or more professionals first identify assessment questions and then meet in the same place to assess and gather information about the child.

assessment A global term for observing, collecting, recording, and interpreting information to answer questions and make instructional decisions about students.

assessment approach A term used to describe the way information is collected for making an educational decision.

assessment strategies Individualized activities or routines that the teacher follows and that help students demonstrate their best effort.

assistance team A school team consisting of the parents (or caregivers), teachers, counselors, specialists, administrators, other individuals, such as community members, who may be important to the student, and when possible, the student. The purpose of the team is to help the student be successful by engaging in problem-solving, identifying, and monitoring intervention(s).

assistive technology (AT) Assistive technology helps individuals with disabilities to learn, be independent, communicate, and lead productive lives.

assistive technology services Services that assist students with disabilities in selecting, acquiring, and using assistive technology devices.

augmentative or alternative communication (AAC) A method or device used by a person with a communication disability to communicate.

authentic assessment An assessment during which the student completes or demonstrates knowledge, skills, or behavior in a real-life context.

basal level The point below which the examiner assumes that the student could obtain all correct responses and at which the examiner begins testing.

benchmarks Examples of student work that illustrate each scoring level on the assessment scale.

category recording A system of recording behavior by discrete groupings.

ceiling level The point above which the examiner assumes that the student would obtain all incorrect responses if the testing were to continue and the point at which the examiner stops testing.

checklist A list of characteristics or behaviors arranged in a consistent manner that allows the evaluator to record the presence or absence of individual characteristics, events, or behaviors.

Child Find A series of activities that increase public awareness and provide information about screening, programs, and early intervention or special education services. These services and activities help in locating children with special needs.

chronological age The precise age of a person in years, months, and days.

cloze procedure An assessment that uses a word passage in which words are deleted according to a word-count formula.

collaborating A process that involves a commitment to working cooperatively with others to address common interests and issues.

communicate To use oral symbols, written symbols, or manual signs or gestures to express meaning.

composite score A score that is derived by combining the results of two or more contributing tests according to a specific formula. The composite score represents the student's overall performance.

concurrent validity The extent to which two different tests administered at about the same time correlate with each other.

conferencing A process conducted by two or more individuals for the purpose of sharing information, concerns, and ideas regarding common issues.

confidence interval The range within which the true score can be found; frequently called the band of error or confidence level.

consequences Events that follow the behavior.

consequential validity The extent to which an assessment instrument promotes the intended consequences.

construct validity The extent to which a test measures a particular construct or concept.

content validity The extent to which the test items reflect the content they are designed to cover.

correlation The extent to which two or more scores vary together.

correlation coefficient A statistic that measures the correlation, or relationship, among tests, test items, scoring procedures, observations, or behavior ratings. A correlation coefficient quantifies a relationship and provides information about whether there is a relationship, the strength of the relationship, and the direction of the relationship. The symbol for correlation coefficient is a lowercase r.

criterion-referenced test (CRT) A test that measures a student's test performance with respect to a well-defined content domain.

criterion-related validity The extent that test scores obtained on one test or another measure are related to scores obtained on another test or another outcome.

cultural broker An individual within the community, typically identified by community members because of the individual's knowledge, skills, and wisdom concerning ethnic, racial, or cultural matters.

curriculum-based assessment (CBA) A broad approach to linking curriculum, instruction, and assessment.

curriculum-based measurement (CBM) A type of curriculum-based assessment that emphasizes repeated, direct measurement of student performance.

cut score A prespecified score established to select or classify students.

data-driven decision making A process that involves systematically collecting and analyzing data to guide practices that will improve student progress and achievement.

derived scores The result of transforming raw scores to other types of scores.

descriptors Written descriptions used in a rating scale or in a rubric to explain and provide more detail about each of the levels of achievement.

determining eligibility A process used to determine if a student meets the eligibility criteria for services according to federal and state definitions.

developmental delay A delay in one or more of the following areas of development: physical, including fine and gross motor; cognitive; communication; social or emotional; or adaptive development. The term is used to identify infants and toddlers so that they can receive early intervention services without being labeled for a specific disability. The Individuals with Disabilities Education Improvement Act (IDEA) of 2004 states that, at the discretion of an individual state, the term *developmental delay* may be used with children ages 3 through 9 so that young children can receive special education services without being labeled for a specific disability category.

developmental domains Areas associated with the young child's general development. These areas include physical, cognitive, communication, social, emotional, and adaptive development.

developmental quotient An estimate of the rate of development.

developmental score Raw score that has been transformed to reflect the average performance at age and grade levels.

deviation IQ score A standard score with a mean of 100 and a standard deviation of 15 or 16.

due process A set of safeguards to be followed during the assessment process and the delivery of services described in Individuals with Disabilities Education Improvement Act (IDEA) of 2004. Due process ensures that the rights of families and their children are not violated.

duration recording A method of recording that measures the length of time a specific event or behavior persists.

early childhood team (ECT) A team that consists of the parents, the family service coordinator, and representatives of various disciplines who assess, plan, implement and evaluate early intervention services. The team makes decisions regarding eligibility and services for children birth through age 2 and, in some states, for children ages 3 to 5.

ecological assessment Approach that allows teachers to gather information about a student in more than one setting and to determine how the setting affects student behaviors or student functioning.

error analysis A technique that identifies patterns of errors in students' work.

error of commission Including information that did not actually occur.

error of omission Leaving out information that is helpful or important to understanding a student's behavior.

error of transmission Recording behaviors in an improper sequence.

evaluation The process of establishing a value judgment based on the collection of actual data.

event recording The recording of a behavior each time it occurs during an observation period. Also called frequency recording.

examiner bias Personal or professional perspectives that can interfere with the interpretation of assessment results.

exhibition A display of a student's work that demonstrates knowledge, abilities, skills, and attitudes.

expansion A restatement of the student's verbal language that adds words or more complex phrases.

expressive language The ability to use language to communicate information, thoughts, feelings, and ideas.

externalizing behaviors A broad array of behaviors directed outward that include disruptive and antisocial behaviors.

extrapolation The process of estimating the performance of students outside the ages and grades of the normative sample.

false negative The type of error that is made when a student is not referred by the screening but should have been.

false positive The type of error that is made when a student is referred by the screening but should not have been.

family A unit of two or more individuals who may or may not be related but who have extended commitments to each other.

family-centered practices An approach to working with families that emphasizes the importance of enabling family members to mobilize their own resources in order to promote child and family functioning.

Family Educational Rights and Privacy Act (FERPA) A law (PL 93–380) that states that no educational agency may release student information without written consent from the student's parents. FERPA also gives the family the right to review all records kept on its child as well as the right to challenge any of the information within the records.

frequency distribution A way of organizing test scores based on how often they occur.

functional behavioral assessment A systematic process of gathering information that identifies the causes of and interventions for addressing problem behaviors.

goal line A line represented on a graph that shows the rate of progress that a student must make to meet the level of expected performance. Also referred to as an AIM line.

grapheme The written equivalent of a phoneme.

growth rate Represents the average performance of the student over time and is represented by a slope on a graph.

holistic scoring A type of scoring in which the teacher assigns a single score based on a scoring rubric. This type of scoring lacks the depth of information found in analytic scoring; however, it may be easier to design and conduct than analytic scoring.

hypothesis generation A process used in interpreting the results of testing that provides an explanation of a student's performance and behavior based on the collected assessment data.

IEP team A multidisciplinary team consisting of the parents; school personnel; and when possible, the student. It is responsible for planning, developing, monitoring, and evaluating specialized instruction and related services for a student with a disability.

individualized education program (IEP) The Individuals with Disabilities Education Improvement Act (IDEA) of 2004 mandates that all students with disabilities ages 3 through 21 have an individualized education program (IEP). This written plan specifies the special education and related services that must be provided.

individualized family service plan (IFSP) The Individuals with Disabilities Education Improvement Act (IDEA) of 2004 mandates that all young children (birth through 2 years) and their families have an individualized family service plan (IFSP). Children ages 3 to 5 may receive services provided by an IFSP or an IEP. The IFSP is a written document that specifies the plan for services and is guided by the family's concerns, priorities, and resources.

Individuals with Disabilities Education Improvement Act (IDEA) of 2004 A federal law that focuses on the education of children and youth with disabilities. IDEA mandates specific requirements relating to the assessment process that teachers and test examiners must know and understand.

informed consent A process that involves (1) presenting information so that it can be easily understood, (2) providing alternatives, (3) identifying risks and benefits, and (4) accepting or consenting to the information proposed.

intensity recording A measure of the strength of a behavior.

internal consistency reliability An estimate of the homogeneity or interrelatedness of responses to test items.

internalizing behaviors Behaviors that are inner-directed and include social withdrawal, anxious or inhibited behaviors, or somatic problems.

interpolation The process of estimating the scores of students within the ages and grades of the norming sample.

interscorer/interrater/interobserver reliability An estimate of the extent to which two or more scorers, observers, or raters agree on how to score a test or how to observe behaviors.

interval recording A recording of specific events or behaviors during a prespecified time interval.

interval scale A scale in which the items are the same distance apart; the scale does not have an absolute zero.

intervention fidelity Intervention that was implemented as planned and delivered consistently to all students over time

item response theory (IRT) A statistical calculation that determines how well the instrument differentiates between individuals at various levels of measured abilities or characteristics.

language Symbols used to communicate thoughts, feelings, ideas, and information.

language disorder A difficulty or inability in decoding or encoding the set of symbols used in language or an inability to effectively use inner language. *See also* speech disorder.

language dominance An individual's preferred language.

language probe A diagnostic technique in which instruction is modified to elicit specific information about a student's receptive or expressive language.

language proficiency An individual's level of expertise in a language.

language sample A recording of a student's oral language that yields information regarding vocabulary, syntax, semantics, articulation, and the ability to use language in functional ways.

latency recording A measure of the amount of time elapsed between a behavior or event (or request to begin the behavior) and the beginning of the prespecified behavior.

literacy The ability to read, write, think, and communicate.

makerspaces Spaces designed by children or youth to enhance the ability to create, invent, or learn.

maladaptive behaviors Behaviors that include antisocial behaviors, aggression, withdrawal behaviors, delayed social skills, and difficulties with interpersonal relationships.

mand modeling A systematic teaching strategy that involves the teacher observing the interest of the child, then asking a question or giving the child a directive regarding this interest. If the child does not produce the targeted behavior, the teacher then models it for the child.

mean The average score.

mean length of utterance (MLU) The average number of individual units of meaning that the student expresses using phrases or sentences during the observation period. MLU can be used to assess the amount of spoken language.

median The point on a scale above which and below which 50 percent of the cases occur. A point or score that separates the top 50 percent of students who took the test from the bottom 50 percent of students who took the same test.

mode The score that occurs most often in a group of scores; the most commonly occurring test score.

modeling Teaching by performing the behavior to be learned.

modifications Changes or adaptations made to the educational program or assessment that alter the level, content, and/or assessment criteria.

monitoring individual progress A process used to determine if the student is making progress by examining the student's work, accomplishments, and achievements.

morpheme The single unit of letters that comprise a unit of meaning. A morpheme may be a whole word, prefix, or a suffix.

morphology The study of the single units of letters that represent a unit of meaning.

multitiered intervention system A continuum of support that allows educators to provide academic and behavior intervention to meet the needs of all learners.

No Child Left Behind Act (NCLB) of 2001 A federal law that created many changes with the goals of improving academic performance for *all* students. This act stressed accountability through scientifically based research practices and regular and ongoing assessment of student progress.

nominal scale The items on the scale represent names; the values assigned to the names do not have any innate meaning or value.

normal curve A symmetrical bell-shaped curve.

normal curve equivalent (NCE) A standard score with a mean of 50 and a standard deviation of 21.06.

norm-referenced test A test that compares a student's test performance with that of similar students who have taken the same test.

observation A systematic process of gathering information by looking at students and their environments.

observer drift Changes in observation resulting from the observer's shifting away from the original objectives of the observation.

ordinal scale The items on the scale are listed in rank order.

percentage duration rate The percentage of time that a behavior or event occurs. To calculate the percentage duration rate, the observer divides the total duration of the behavior or event by the total time of the observation and multiplies this answer by 100 to obtain a percentage.

percentage score The percentage of test items that were answered correctly.

percentile rank The point in a distribution at or below which the scores of a given percentage of students fall.

performance-based assessment The demonstration of knowledge, skills, or behavior.

person-centered planning The student with the disability engages in an active meaningful way with parents, educators, community members, and others during the assessment, planning, and service delivery processes.

phoneme The smallest unit of sound that has meaning in a language.

phonemic awareness The skills of recognizing, separating, blending, and manipulating phonemes.

phonics Knowledge of how specific spoken sounds relate to particular written letters.

phonology The study of speech sounds.

population The large group from which the sample of individuals is selected and to which individual comparisons are made regarding test performance.

portfolio A systematic collection of a student's work, assembled over a period of time, that demonstrates the student's efforts, progress, and achievement.

pragmatics The study of the use of language in social situations.

probe A diagnostic technique that modifies instruction in order to determine whether an instructional strategy is effective.

program evaluation A process used to assess (1) the progress that the student has made in the individualized education program and (2) the overall quality of the school program.

program planning The process of determining the student's current level of functioning and planning the instructional program.

progress monitoring A process of regularly assessing student performance on general outcomes measures during RTI and making instructional decisions based on the data.

questionnaire A set of questions designed to gather information.

rating scale An instrument that measures the degree of the response.

ratio scale A scale where the items on the scale are the same distance apart; the scale does have an absolute zero.

raw score The number of items correct without adjustment for guessing.

reactivity The adjustments that individuals make in behaviors during an observation.

reading comprehension Being able to obtain meaning from a text, understand what is read, connect information within the context of a text, and relate what is being read to what is already known.

reading fluency Being able to read letters, sounds, words, and text passages quickly, automatically, accurately, and smoothly.

receptive language The ability to understand spoken language.

referral A process in which questions and concerns about a student are raised and referred to the IEP team. The referral may come from a teacher, parent, or the student.

reliability The consistency or stability of test performance. The 1999 edition of *Standards for Educational and Psychological Testing* describes reliability and provides a departure from more traditional thinking about reliability. In this edition, reliability refers to the scoring procedure that enables the examiner to quantify, evaluate, and interpret behavior or work samples and the consistency of such measurements when the testing procedure is repeated on a population of individuals or groups.

response to intervention (RTI) A process of identifying students who are experiencing difficulties and providing specific interventions to address areas of concern before children fail.

rubric An assessment scale that identifies the area(s) of performance and defines various levels of achievement.

running record A description of the events that is written as the events occur.

sample A subgroup of a large group that is representative of the large group. This subgroup is the group that is actually tested.

scaled score A score that is derived from raw scores according to a scaling process. Scaled scores enhance test interpretation because scaled scores from one test may be compared with those from a second test.

scatter plot A type of interval recording form that the observer uses to record single behaviors or a series of behaviors during the observation period.

screening A process used to identify students who may have a disability and who will be referred for further assessment.

self-determination When an individual's hopes, dreams, and desires influence the types of assessments that the transition team implements.

semantics The study of word meanings.

shaping The technique of reinforcing successive approximations of the target or goal behavior. In reference to the development of language, the verbal response is reinforced as the sound or word being produced more and more closely approximates the sound or word in the language.

skewed distribution A curve in which most of the scores are at either the low end or the high end of the curve.

speech The production of oral language for the purpose of expression.

speech disorder A difficulty in articulation, such as the way words are pronounced; the fluency of speech, including rate and rhythm; or the pitch, volume, and quality of the voice.

split-half reliability An estimate of the correlation of scores between two halves of a test.

standard deviation (SD) A measure of the degree to which various scores deviate from the mean, or average score.

standard error of measurement (SEM) The amount of error associated with individual test scores, test items, item samples, and test times.

standardization sample The individuals who are actually tested during the process of test development.

standardized test A test in which the administration, scoring, and interpretation procedures are prescribed in the test manual and must be strictly followed. A standardized test is usually norm-referenced.

standard scores Raw scores that have been transformed so that they have the same mean and the same standard deviation.

stanine A type of standard score that has a mean of 5 and a standard deviation of 2; the distribution of scores can be divided into 9 stanines.

stimulus An environmental condition, event, teacher, or other individual that can affect behavior.

student assistance team (SAT) *See* assistance team.

supports Educational, behavioral or other habilitative strategies that promote the development and interests of a person with an intellectual disability and are consistent with a high quality and personal satisfaction with life.

syntax A system of rules that dictates how words are combined into meaningful phrases and sentences.

target behavior A behavior that is acquired or eliminated by manipulating the antecedents and consequences.

test-retest reliability An estimate of the correlation between scores when the same test is administered two times.

transition Moving from one system of services to another.

transition services A coordinated set of activities for a student, designed within an outcome-oriented process, that promotes movement from school to postschool activities, including postsecondary education, career and technical skills, integrated employment (including supported employment), continuing and adult education, adult services, independent living, and community participation.

triangulation Conclusions about student performance that are based on multiple sources of information.

trend line Represents the average performance of the student over time and is represented by a slope on a graph.

true score The score an individual would obtain on a test if there were no measurement errors.

universal design "[A] concept or philosophy for designing and delivering products and services that are usable by people with the widest possible range of functional capabilities, which include products and services that are directly usable (without requiring assistive technologies) and products and services that are made usable with assistive technologies." (20 USC Sec. 602(35); 29 USC Sec. 3002)

universal screening A process that occurs two or three times during the year to identify students who are experiencing difficulties with age appropriate skills.

validity The extent to which a test measures what it says it measures.

young children Children ages birth through age 8.

Name Index

A
Abery, B., 165
Achenbach, T. M., 184–85
Airasian, P. W., 296
Alberto, P. A., 168
Alonzo, J., 31
Anderson, D., 31
Anderson, M. E., 46
Arter, J., 286
Artiles, A. J., 53
Ashlock, R. B., 272
Atkins-Burnett, S., 327
Attermeier, S. M., 331

B
Baer, R., 344
Baker, D., 215
Baker, E. L., 82, 295
Bal, A., 53
Balla, D., 166
Barboza, G. E., 152
Barry, C. T., 107
Bayley, N., 330
Beaty, J. J., 135–36, 138, 144
Becker, R. L., 349
Beebe-Frankenberger, M. E., 19
Bell, S., 211, 216
Benasich, A. A, 170
Bender, W. N., 23
Benner, G. J., 108
Bentzen, W. R., 108
Bergstrom, M., 31
Betts, J., 334
Bolt, S., 87, 192, 216, 301
Boon, R., 276
Boutot, A., 53
Bricker, D., 318, 327
Brigance, A. H., 319
Brookhart, S. M., 76–77, 79, 159, 236
Brown, V. L., 226, 264, 282, 307
Bryant, B., 225
Bryant, D., 282
Bunch, G. C., 44
Burks, H. F., 183
Burns, M. K., 19

C
Cadigan, K., 334
Cao, M., 251
Cardarelli, A., 25
Carrow-Woolfolk, E., 244

Carta, J. J., 334
Caruso, D. R., 301
Chen, D., 55–56
Cheng-Fei, L., 31
Chetham, D., 287
Christ, T. J., 31
Cicchetti, D., 166
Clark, G., 345
Compton, D. L., 19, 33, 108
Conners, C. K., 186
Connolly, A. J., 281
Cook, L., 65, 160
Cooper, J. O., 176
Costanza-Smith, A., 253
Craddock, G., 47
Cronin, M. E., 282
Cummings, K., 215
Cusumano, D. L., 31

D
Dai, D. Y., 301
D'Angiulli, A., 251
Deno, S., 276
Dichtelmiller, M. K., 337
Disher, S., 165
Dockrell, J. E., 251
Dombo, A. L., 321
Dorfman, A. B., 337

E
Ehrensberger, W., 271
Erwin, E. J., 52, 55, 67
Espinosa, L. M., 335

F
Fitch, R., 170
Flanagan, D. P., 107
Flexer, R., 344
Foegen, A., 276, 278–79
Ford, D. Y., 108
Fore, C., 276
Freeman, E., 25
Frick, P. J., 107
Friend, M., 65, 160
Froiland, J., 108
Fuchs, D., 19, 27, 31, 108
Fuchs, L. S., 19, 27, 31, 108

G
Gable, R. A., 171
Garcia, S. B., 25

Geaney, E. R., 44
Geist, H., 351
Gipps, C., 82
Good, R. H., 213, 215
Graney, S. B., 31
Greene, G., 345
Greenfield, R., 25
Greenspan, S., 320
Greenwood, C. R., 19, 334
Griffiths, A. J., 19, 27
Gronlund, N. E., 135
Gruber, C. P., 183

H
Hacker, B. J., 331
Hagen, E. P., 306
Hammill, D. D., 226, 245, 247, 264, 303–4
Han, I., 251
Harris, L., 67
Harrison, P. L., 165
Harry, B., 25
Heick, P. F., 161
Heilmann, J., 253, 266
Heistad, D., 334
Helms, J. E., 108
Henderson, L. W., 319
Heraux, C. G., 152
Heron, T. E., 176
Hessler, T., 233
Hester, P. H., 171
Heward, W. L., 160, 176
Heyne, L., 165
Higgins, S. K., 334
Hilton, M., 343
Hong, B., 271
Hosp, J. L., 212–13, 233, 276
Hosp, M. K., 212–13, 233, 276
Howell, K., 212–13
Hughes, K. G., 171

I
Iglesias, A., 267

J
Jablon, J. R., 337
Jewkes, A. M., 321
Jiban, C., 276
Johnsen, S. K., 307
Johnson, H. B., 313
Johnson-Martin, N. M., 331
Johnstone, C. J., 46

360

K

Kaminski, R. A., 213
Kamphaus, R. W., 107, 182
Kaufman, A. S., 107, 204, 305–6
Kaufman, N. L., 204, 305–6
Klingner, J., 25
Kochbar-Bryant, C. A., 345
Konrad, M., 233
Korzeniewski, S. J., 152
Kulm, G., 273
Kung, S. H., 251

L

Laren, S. C., 245
Larsen, S. C., 247, 264
Lawson, C., 276
Ledbetter, M. F., 206–7
Lehman, I. J., 194
Lesaux, N. K., 45
Linan-Thompson, S., 25, 45
Linn, R. L., 82, 135, 295
Lo, L., 53
Long, J. D., 31
Long, L., 108
López, M.L., 335
Luft, P., 344
Lyman, H. B., 123

M

Mackeogh, T., 47
Mackie, C., 251
Maggi, S, 251
Mahdavi, J. N., 19
Mandell, D. S., 53
Marsden, D. B., 321, 337
Marston, D. B., 272
Martin, C., 276
Martinez, R. S., 31
Mather, N., 208, 312
Mathot-Buckner, C., 165
Mayer, J. D., 301
McBride, Y. Y., 97
McCallum, R. S., 211, 216
McClarty, K. L., 97
McConaughy, S. H., 184–85
McConnell, S. R., 334
McGrew, K. S., 208, 312
McKenna, M., 217
McMaster, K. L., 251
McTighe, J., 286
Mehrens, W. A., 194
Meisels, S. J., 319, 321, 327, 337
Mendel, J., &, 165
Merrell, K. W., 159
Miller, D. N., 108
Miller, J. F., 253, 266–67
Miller, L., 251
Miller, M. D., 135

Miller, N. A., 46
Missall, K. N., 31, 334
Moats, D., 247
Monaghen, B. D., 31
Montie, J., 165
Muñoz-Sandoval, A. F., 208, 302
Murphy, D., 97
Murphy, S., 97

N

Nelson, J., 108
Neubert, D. A., 345
Newborg, J., 319, 329–30
Nitko, A. J., 76–77, 79, 159
Nitsiou, C., 334
Nockerts, A., 253, 266

O

Oakland, T., 165
O'Connor, E. P., 25
O'Donnell, P. S., 108
Oehmke, J., 152
O'Malley, K. J., 97
Ortiz, A. A., 25, 45

P

Palmer, S., 165
Parson, L. B., 19
Pearson, N. A., 303
Pellegrino, J. W., 343
Picard, M., 217
Pickart, M., 334
Pollard, J., 170
Polloway, E. A., 251, 254–55
Pond, R. E., 263
Post, L. A., 152
Proctor, C., 25

R

Ralston, N. C., 108
Ray, L., 165
Reschly, A., 334
Rescorla, L. A., 184
Reynolds, C. R., 182
Rhodes, L. K., 217, 238
Rinaldi, C., 25
Roach, A. T., 334
Robertson G. J., 206
Rock, M. L., 171
Roid, G. H., 206–7, 306
Rowe, K. J., 170
Rowe, K. S., 170

S

Sabatini, J., 45
Salovey, P., 301
Salvia, J., 87, 159, 192, 216, 301, 305
Samson, J. F., 45

Sanders, E. A., 108
Sattler, J. M., 92–93, 100, 135, 138, 144, 204, 301–2, 306
Scherer, M. J., 47
Schiamberg, L. B., 152
Schrank, F. A., 208, 312
Secord, W., 249, 259
Semel, E., 249, 259
Shanklin, N., 217, 238
Shapiro, E. S., 161
Shaw, J. M., 44
Sherbenou, R. J., 307
Shogren, K. A., 52
Shore, J. R., 45
Shores, C., 23
Siegel, L. S., 251
Simmons, T., 344
Singleton, C., 217
Sitlington, P. L., 345–48
Smith, T. E. C., 251
Snyder, P. A., 334
Soodak, L. C., 52
Sparrow, S., 166
Squires, J., 318
Stecker, P. M., 31
Steiner, V. G., 263
Sternberg, R., 301
Stiggins, R., 193, 289
Stobart, G., 82
Sullivan, A. L., 108

T

Talapatra, D., 334
Tankersley, K., 292
Taylor, R. L., 194
Thompson, S. J., 46
Thorndike, R. L., 306
Thorson, N., 165
Tilly, W. D., 19
Tincani, M., 53
Tindal, G. A., 31, 272
Trainor, A., 343, 347
Travers, J., 53
Troutman, A. C., 168
Turnbull, A. P., 52
Turnbull, H. R., 52
Twombly, E., 318

V

Vallas, R., 108
VanDerHeyden, A., 19
VanDerHeyden & Burns, 2005, 31

W

Walker, D., 334
Wechsler, D., 308
Wehman, P., 343, 346–47

Weston, D. R., 321
Whitcomb, S., 159
Wiederholt, J. L., 225–26, 264, 303
Wiggins, G. P., 286
Wiig, E. H., 249, 259
Wilde, S., 235
Wilkinson, G. S., 206
Wilkinson, P., 287
Wiske, M. S., 319

Wixson, C. S., 334
Woodcock, R. W., 208, 226, 302, 312–13
Wright, J., 193

Y
Ysseldyke, J., 87, 159, 192, 216, 301, 305

Z
Zimmerman, I. L., 263
Zopluoglu, C., 31

Subject Index

A

Accelerated Reader (AR), 214
Accommodations, 6–7
  environmental, 197, 278
  frequently used, 7
  instructional, 197, 278
  material, 197, 278
  with probes, 196–97
  when using CBMs in mathematics, 278
Achievement testing
  CBA *See* Curriculum-based assessment (CBA)
  CRT *See* Criterion-referenced tests (CRT)
  defined, 191
  responding to diversity, 191–92
Adaptive behavior, 164–65
  and achievement of students with developmental disabilities, 165
Adaptive Behavior Assessment System Second Edition (ABAS II)
  administration, 165–66
  at-a-glance, 165
  confidence intervals, 166
  interrater reliability coefficients, 166
  norm-referenced scaled scores, 166
  reliability, 166
  scoring, 166
  standardization, 166
  summary, 166
  test-retest reliability coefficients, 166
  validity, 166
Administration
  ABAS II, 165–66
  AEPS, 328
  BASC 2, 182
  Batería III Woodcock-Muñoz, 302
  Bayley-III, 331
  BBRS 2, 183
  BDI-2, 329
  BRIGANCE® Early Childhood Screening III, 319
  CBCL System, 185
  CCPSN, 332
  CELF-5, 259
  Conners 3™, 186
  DTLA-4, 304
  ESI-R, 2008 Edition, 320
  GORT-5, 225
  Greenspan Social-Emotional Growth Chart, 321
  KABC-II, 305
  KeyMath 3 DA, 281
  KTEA-II, 204–5
  Ounce Scale, 322
  PLS™ -5, 264
  Stanford-Binet Intelligence Scale, Fifth Edition, 307
  Teaching Strategies GOLD, 336–37
  TOAL-4, 264
  TOMA-3, 283
  TONI-4, 308–9
  TORC-4, 226
  TOWL-4, 245
  Vineland II, 167
  WIAT-III, 205
  WISC-IV Integrated, 308–9
  WJ III NU, 209, 312
  WRAT4, 206
  WRMT—R/NU, 227
Administration
  The Work Sampling System®, Fifth Edition, 337
Adult Behavior Checklist for Ages 18–59, 185
Adult Self-Report Form for Ages 18–59, 185
Adverse consequences, 82–83
Adverse effects of disability, 60
Ages and Stages Questionnaires, Third Edition (ASQ-3™)
  administration, 318
  at-a-glance, 318
  reliability, 318–19
  scoring, 318
  standardization, 318
  summary, 319
  validity, 319
Aggression, 168
AIM line, 28
AIMSweb, 31, 214
Alternate assessments, 8, 13–14, 195
Alternate form reliability, 77
American Association on Intellectual and Developmental Disabilities (AAIDD), 164
American Educational Research Association, 46, 74, 82–83, 86
American Psychological Association, 46, 74, 86, 110
Analytic scoring, 243–44, 292–93
Anchor papers, 294
  written language, assessment of, 244
Anecdotal record, 134–35
Antisocial behavior, 168
Arena assessment, 327
Assessment, 161. *See also* Alternate assessments; Curriculum-based assessment (CBA); Special education assessment
  alternate, 8
  arena, 327
  augmentative or alternative communication (AAC), 267–68
  comprehensive developmental, 325–27
  consideration of adverse consequences, 83
  defined, 4
  ecological, 171
  evaluation of approaches, 101–2
  functional behavioral assessment (FBA), 174–82
  informed written consent for, 11–12
  national and statewide, 123–24
  nonbiased, 83
  parents' and children's rights and, 11
  of students' performance, 4
  teacher's use of, 4
Assessment, Evaluation, and Programming System (AEPS) for Infants and Children, Second Edition
  administration, 328
  areas of developmental domains, 328
  at-a-glance, 328
  manuals, 328
  reliability, 328
  scoring, 328
  standardization, 328
  summary, 328–29
  validity, 328
Assessment approach, 4
  checklists and questionnaires, 198
  conferences, 199
  error analysis, 197
  exhibitions, 200
  interviews, 198–99
  under NCLB Act, 11–13
  oral descriptions, 197

363

Subject Index

Assessment approach (*Continued*)
  peer assessment, 200
  performance-based assessment, 199
  portfolios, 199–200
  probes, 196–97
  self-assessment, 200
  use of digital media, 199
  written descriptions, 197–98
Assessment data, 11
Assessment for Effective Intervention, 102
Assessment reports
  family members and, 123
  individual test reports, 119–22
  of observations, 116
  progress reports, 116
  sharing of, 122–23
  students and, 123
  technology-generated reports, 119–22
Assessment strategies, 85
Assistance team, 134
Assistive Technology Act of 2004, 46
Assistive technology needs
  approaches to, 48–49
  classroom expectations and student needs for, 47
  IEP plan and, 49
Assistive technology service, 47
ASSISTments, 37
Attention-seeking behaviors, 170
Augmentative or alternative communication (AAC), 267
  assessment for, 267–68
Authentic assessment
  considerations about using, 297
  design, 288
  equity, 288
  examples, 288
  scoring, 288
  structure, 287–88

B

Band of error, 98
Bar graphs, 110
  data presentation in, 113
Basal level, 96–97
BASC 2 ASSIST™ Plus software, 183
Batería III Woodcock-Muñoz
  administration, 302
  at-a-glance, 302
  summary, 303
  technical adequacy, 303
Battelle Developmental Inventory, 319
Battelle Developmental Inventory, Second Edition (BDI-2), 96, 318
  administration, 329
  at-a-glance, 329

  reliability, 329
  scoring, 329
  Spanish edition, 329
  standardization, 329
  subdomains, 329
  summary, 329
  validity, 329
Bayley Scales of Infant and Toddler Development, Third Edition (Bayley-III), 318
  administration, 331
  at-a-glance, 331
  items, 330
  reliability, 331
  scoring, 331
  standardization, 331
  summary, 331
  validity, 331
Behavioral observations, 100
Behavior Assessment System for Children, Second Edition (BASC 2), 182–83
  administration, 182
  at-a-glance, 182
  reliability, 183
  scoring, 182–83
  standardization, 182
  summary, 183
  validity, 183
Behavior problems
  preventive measures for, 31
  RTI implementation for, 31–32
Behaviors
  adaptive, 164–65
  attention-seeking, 170
  cultural expectations and, 168
  externalizing, 168
  internalizing, 168
  problem, 168–69
  responding to diversity, 169–70
Benchmarks, 294
Bias
  examiner, 108
  nonbiased assessment, 83
  test, and fairness, 108
Biographical information, 98
Blogs, 199, 222, 275
Braille literacy, 4
Brainstorm technology ideas, 48
BRIGANCE® Early Childhood Screening III
  administration, 319
  at-a-glance, 319
  reliability, 319
  scoring, 319
  standardization, 319
  validity, 319
BRIGANCE series, 87
Buckley amendment, 122–23

Burks Behavior Rating Scales, Second Edition (BBRS 2)
  administration, 183
  at-a-glance, 183
  relaibility, 183
  scoring, 183
  standardization, 183
  summary, 183–84
  validity, 183

C

Calculating raw scores, 98
Caregiver–Teacher Report Form/1 1/2 – 5 (C–TRF), 184
Carolina Curriculum for Preschoolers with Special Needs (CCPSN), Second Edition
  administration, 332
  Assessment Log, 332
  at-a-glance, 332
  Developmental Progress Chart, 332
  reliability, 333
  scoring, 332
  standardization, 333
  summary, 333
  test items, 331
  validity, 333
Category recording, 141–42
Cattell-Horn-Carroll theory, 305
Ceiling level, 96–97
Center for Effective Collaboration and Practice, 178
Checklists, 144, 198, 292
  for assessing attitudes, interests, and habits, 219
  for assessing knowledge of books, 219–21
  mathematical abilities and skills, assessment of, 273–74
  written language, assessment of, 236
Child Behavior Checklist System (CBCL System)
  administration, 185
  age levels, 184–85
  at-a-glance, 185
  Child Behavior Checklist for Ages 1 1/2 –5, 184
  Child Behavior Checklist for Ages 6–18, 184
  reliability, 185
  scoring, 185
  standardization, 185
  summary, 185–86
  validity, 185
Child Find, 58, 317
Chronological age, 98
Classroom Assessment Techniques (CATS), 37

Classroom-based assessment cycle, 35–38
  approaches to gather information, 37
Clinical Evaluation of Language Fundamentals-Fifth Edition (CELF-5)
  administration, 259
  at-a-glance, 262
  CELF—Preschool, Second Edition, 263
  Core Language Score, 259
  reliability, 262
  scoring, 262
  Spanish version, 259
  standardization, 262
  summary, 262–63
  validity, 262
Cloze procedure, 206, 216–17
Coaching, 240
Collaborating, 161
Common Core Standards, 124
Communicate, 248
Composite score, 105, 115
Comprehensive developmental assessment, 325–27
Comprehensive Test of Nonverbal Intelligence-II (CTONI-2)
  administration, 303
  at-a-glance, 303
  reliability, 303
  scoring, 303
  standardization, 303
  summary, 303
  validity, 303
Concurrent validity, 80–81
Conferencing, 199
  defined, 160
  reading assessment, 222
  written language, assessment of, 236
Confidence intervals, 97–98, 105
Confidentiality, 15
Conners' Rating Scales, 185
Conners 3™ (*Conners 3rd Edition*™)
  administration, 186
  reliability, 186
  scoring, 186
  standardization, 186
  summary, 186
  validity, 186
Consequences, 82–83, 174, 176, 294
Consequential validity, 82, 295–96
  student's perspective, 296
  teacher's perspective, 296
Consistency of assessment, 295
Construct validity, 81, 281
  OWLS-II™ LC/OE and RC/WE, 245
Content validity, 80
Core State Standards, 11
Correlation, 75
Correlation coefficient, 75

Council for Exceptional Children (CEC), 15
  Initial Preparation Standards for Special Educators, 15
Council of Chief State School Officers, 11
Criterion-referenced assessments
  reading, 216
  written language, 233–34
Criterion-referenced assessments (CRT), 194–95
Criterion-referenced test (CRT), 86–87, 194–95
  administering test items, 195
  analyzing and interpreting of results, 195
  developing skills and subskills, 195
  distinguishing with norm-referenced test, 87
  graphing or charting of results, 195
  performance standards, 195
  teacher-developed, 194–95
  usefulness, 194
  vs norm-referenced tests, 194
Criterion-related validity, 80–81
Cultural broker, 175
Curriculum-based assessment (CBA), 192–94
  analyzing curriculum, 193
  assessment procedures, 193–94
  development of, 193–94, 212–13
  interpreting and integrating results, 194
  organizing information, 194
  performance objectives, 193
  purposes, 193
  reading, 212–13
  usefulness, 193
Curriculum-based measurement (CBM), 27–28, 31
  mathematical abilities and skills, assessment of, 276–79
  in mathematics, 30
  oral language assessment, 256
  reading, 213–16
  spelling, 233
  written language, 232–33
Cut scores, 79

D
Data-based decision making (DBDM), 21
Data-driven decision making, 11
Data triangulation chart, 180–81
Degrees of involvement, 139–40
  high, 139
  low, 140
  medium, 140
  no involvment, 140

Derived score, 92
Descriptors, 141–44
Determining eligibility for special education services, 41–43
Detroit Tests of Learning Aptitude, Fourth Edition (DTLA-4)
  administration, 304
  at-a-glance, 304
  Basic Information subtest, 304
  Design Reproduction subtest, 304
  Design Sequences subtest, 304
  reliability, 304
  Reversed Letters subtest, 304
  scoring, 304
  Sentence Imitation subtest, 304
  standardization, 304
  Story Construction subtest, 304
  Story Sequences subtest, 304
  Symbolic Relations subtest, 304
  validity, 304–35
  Word Opposites subtest, 304
  Word Sequences subtest, 304
Developmental delay, 10, 327, 334
Developmental domains, 315
Developmental quotients, 93
Developmental score, 92–93
  criticism of, 93
Deviation IQ score, 96
Diagnostique, 102
Digital media, 199
  written language, assessment of, 239
Disruptive behavior, 140
Division of Early Childhood (DEC), 315–16, 326, 335, 341
Domain, 87
Draw-A-Person, 161
Due process requirements, 10–11
Duration recording, 138–39
  percentage of time for, 139
Dynamic Indicators of Basic Early Literacy, Sixth Edition (DIBELS), 213–16
  benchmark assessments, 215
  development of, 213
  subtests, 215
  technical aspects of, 215–16

E
Early childhood state standards, 338
Early childhood team, 59, 340
Early intervention services, eligibility for, 10
Early Screening Inventory–Kindergarten (ESI-K), 320
Early Screening Inventory–Preschool (ESI-P), 320

Early Screening Inventory–Revised (ESI-R), 2008 Edition
  administration, 320
  at-a-glance, 320
  reliability, 320
  scoring, 320
  standardization, 320
  summary, 320
  validity, 320
Ecological assessment, 171
EdCheckup, 214
Effective interpersonal skills, 161
Elementary and Secondary Education Act, 1965, 11, 13
English language learners, 25
  assessment requirements for students with disability, 45
  special education and, 45
Environmental accommodations, 197
Equity, 83
ERIC/OSEP Special Project, 16
Erikson Institute, 322
Error analysis, 197
  mathematical abilities and skills, assessment of, 271–72
  reading, 213, 217
  written language, assessment of, 234–35
Error of commission, 145
Error of omission, 144–45
Error of transmission, 145
Errors in measurement, 73
  sources, 74
  standard error of measurement, 97
  variances or standard deviations of measurement, 78–79
Event recording, 136–38
Evidence-based practices, 16
Examiner bias, 108
Exceptional Children, 102
Exhibitions, 200
  mathematical abilities and skills, assessment of, 280
  reading assessment, 223
  student benefits, 290
  written language, assessment of, 240
Expansion, 256
Expressive language, 249
Externalizing behaviors, 168
Extrapolation, 93

F
Face-to-face meetings, 160
Fairness in assessment, 296
  responding to diversity, 82–83
False negative, 325
False positive, 325
Family
  addressing parent questions and concerns, 59–60
  approach to child rearing, 55
  aspirations, 53–55
  assessment process for, 59–64
  assistance, 55
  characteristics, 52
  communication styles, 55
  conducting interview with, 65–67
  defined, 52
  education programs, evaluation of, 64
  federal legislation and, 57
  functions, 52
  guaranteed rights, 57
  language skills, 56
  legal status, 56
  listening to and understanding parent perspectives, 64–68
  literacy skills, 56
  meeting in interviews, 56
  parental roles, 56–57
  parent–teacher conferences, 67–68
  perceptions of disability, 55–56
  responding to diversity, 53–57
  rights of, 57
  school authority and, 55
  stories, 67
  structure, 56
  support groups, 56
  transient status, 57
Family-centered practices, 57–59
  neighborhood screening activities and, 58
  screening questions and decisions for, 59
Family Educational Rights and Privacy Act (FERPA), 14–15, 122
Family life cycle frame, 52
Fluid reasoning, 306
Formative assessment, 37
Formative evaluation, 26–27
Frequency distribution, 88
  normal curve, 89
  skewed distribution, 89
Functional behavioral assessment (FBA), 32, 174–82
  conducting, 174–82
  rubrics, 178–80

G
Goal line, 28
Grammar, 251
Graphemes, 250–51
Graphing of scores, 99
Gray Oral Reading Tests–Fifth Edition (GORT-5)
  administration, 225
  at-a-glance, 225
  reliability, 226
  scoring, 225
  standardization, 225
  summary, 226
  validity, 226
Greenspan Social-Emotional Growth Chart
  administration, 321
  at-a-glance, 321
  developmental milestones in, 321
  reliability, 321
  scoring, 321
  standardization, 321
  summary, 321
  validity, 321
Group tests of achievement
  benefits, 204
  disadvantages, 204
Growth rate, 28
Growth scores, 97

H
High-quality evidence-based instruction, 19, 21
Holistic scoring, 241–43, 294
Hypothesis generation, 107

I
IEP team, 6, 248
  alternate assessment decision-making process, 13–14
  evaluation of student gains, 63
  function of, 6
  person-centered planning, 347
  purpose of making accommodations and modifications, 6–7
  reevaluation and, 8
  referral and decisions, 60
  three-year evaluation program, 63
Indicadores Dinámicos del Éxito en la Lectura, 7a edición (IDEL), 215
Individual achievement tests
  Kaufman Test of Educational Achievement, Second Edition (KTEA-II), 204–5
  Wechsler Individual Achievement Test-Third Edition (WIAT-III), 205–6
  Wide Range Achievement Test 4 (WRAT4), 206–7
  Woodcock-Johnson III, Normative Update (WJ III NU), 208–9
Individual growth and development indicators, 334
Individualized education program (IEP), 6, 8, 25, 40–41, 43–44
  assessment information required, 8
  scaled scores, 106
  transition services, 10

Subject Index

Individualized family service plan (IFSP), 10, 44
Individual progress monitoring, 43
Individuals with Disabilities Education Act (IDEA), 5–6, 21, 41, 44–46, 57, 130, 316, 325
  protection of parents' and children's rights, 10–11
  rights of parents and guardians, 58
Individuals with Disabilities Education Improvement Act, 21, 41
Individual test reports, 119–22
Informal assessments, 4, 195, 216–24
Informed consent, 11–12
Instructional accommodations, 196–97
Intellectual disabilities, 9
Intelligence, defined, 301
Intelligence quotient (IQ) scores, 75
Intelligence tests
  responding to diversity, 302
  as samples of behavior, 301–2
  standardized tests, 302–13
Intensity recording, 139–40
Internal consistency reliability, 77–78
Internalizing behaviors, 168
International Reading Association, 211
Interpersonal skills
  collaborating and, 161
Interpolation, 93
Interscorer/interobserver/interrater reliability, 78
Interstate New Teacher Assessment and Support Consortium (InTASC), 15
Interval-event recording, 140–41
Interval-only recording, 140–41
Interval recording, 140–41
Interval scale, 88
Intervention fidelity, 19, 33
Interviews/interviewing, 198–99
  completing, 66–67
  establishing rapport with the individual, 159
  mathematical abilities and skills, assessment of, 274
  meeting family, 66
  parents, 65–67
  planning, 65–66
  questionnaires, 159–60
  reading assessment, 222
  structured, 274
  with students, 159
  written language, assessment of, 236
Iris Center, 31
Item response theory (IRT), 74, 79

J

Journal of Early Intervention, 102
Journal of Learning Disabilities, 102
Journal of Reading, 102
Journal of School Psychology, 102
Journal of Special Education, 102

K

Kaufman Assessment Battery for Children, Second Edition (KABC-II)
  administration, 305
  at-a-glance, 305
  features of, 305
  reliability, 306
  standardization, 305–6
  subtests, 305
  summary, 306
  theoretical models of mental processing, 305
  validity, 306
Kaufman Test of Educational Achievement, Second Edition (KTEA-II), 204–5
  administration, 204–5
  at-a-glance, 205
  Comprehensive Form, 204
  content validity, 205
  reliability, 205
  scoring, 205
  standardization, 205
  summary, 205
  technical adequacy, 205
  validity, 205
KeyMath 3 Diagnostic Assessment (KeyMath 3 DA)
  administration, 281
  at-a-glance, 281
  reliability, 281
  scoring, 281
  standardization, 281
  summary, 281–82
  validity, 281
Kuder-Richardson formulas, 77

L

Labeling, detrimental effects of, 9
Language
  aspects of, 248
  disorders, 249
  dominance, 83
  and literacy, 56
  probe, 253, 255–56
  proficiency, 83
  samples, 253
Latency recording, 140
Learning classroom environment
  mathematics assessment, 280
  observations, 151–54, 256–57, 280
  oral language assessment, 256–57
  problem behavior and, 170–71
Literacy, 25, 28, 203, 211, 231
  authentic assessment, 288
  language and, 56
  portfolios in assessment, 223, 239

M

Makerspaces, 151
Maladaptive behaviors, 165
Mand modeling, 259
Material accommodations, 197
Math computation, 206
Mathematical abilities and skills, assessment of
  addition, 272
  checklists and questionnaires, 273–74
  criterion-referenced tests, 276
  curriculum-based measurement (CBM), 276–79
  division, 272
  error analysis, 271–72
  exhibitions, 280
  feedback, 271
  fractions, 272
  interview approach, 274
  multiplication, 272
  observing a student in classroom, 280
  oral descriptions, 273
  peer assessment, 276
  performance-based assessment, 279–80
  performance descriptors, 273
  portfolios, 279–80
  probes, 271
  progress monitoring, 203, 278–79
  RTI evaluation of, 30
  self-assessment, 275
  standardized, norm-referenced tests, 281–83
  student journals, diaries, and blogs, 275
  subtraction, 272
  teacher–student conferences, 274–75
  verbal descriptions, 273
  word problems, 272
  written descriptions, 273
MCLASS, 31
Mean, 89–91
Mean length of utterance (MLU), 253–55
Measurement scales
  interval, 88
  nominal, 87
  ordinal, 87
  ratio, 88

Measures of central tendency
　mean, 89–91
　median, 91
　mode, 91
　standard deviation (SD), 91
Median, 91
Minneapolis Public Schools' Problem-Solving Model, 19
Mode, 91
Modeling language, 257
Modifications, 6–7
　frequently used, 7
Monitoring Basic Skills Progress (MBSP), 214
Monitoring student performance, 32
Morphemes, 251
Morphology, 251
Multidisciplinary team, 6–7
Multiple-choice tests, 297
Multiple observations, 132
Multitiered intervention system, 21–25

N
National assessment, 123–24
National Association for the Education of Young Children (NAEYC), 315–16, 335, 341
National Center for Research on Evaluation, Assessment, and Student Testing, 16
National Council for Teachers of Mathematics (NCTM), 270
National Council on Disability, 344
National Council on Measurement in Education, 46, 74, 86
National Forum on Assessment, 83
National Governors Association Center for Best Practices, 11
National Institute of Child Health and Human Development, 213, 251
National percentile rank (NPR), 124
Negatively skewed distribution, 89
Negative relationship, 76
No Child Left Behind (NCLB) Act of 2001, 11
Nominal scale, 87
Nonbiased assessment, 83
Normal curve, 89
　position of percentiles in, 94
Normal curve equivalents (NCEs), 96, 205–6, 259
Normative sample, 86
Norm-referenced test (NRT), 86, 108, 201
　distinguishing criterion-referenced test with, 87
Norms, defined, 86
Norm sample, 86

Northwest Evaluation Association (NWEA), 124
Nudges, 33

O
Observations
　accuracy in, 132
　assessment questions and type of, 133
　body movements, 133
　checklists for, 144
　defined, 130
　developing informal norms, 145–46
　facial expressions/affect, 133
　IDEA and, 130
　integrating assessment information with, 132
　interactions, 132
　learning environment, 151–54, 256–57, 280
　mathematics performance, 280
　multiple, 132
　oral language assessment, 256–59
　participation in play and games, 133
　physical classroom environment, 149–51, 155–57, 256, 280
　planning, 130–32
　reliability of, 144
　social environment, 152, 154, 257–59, 280
　sources of error, 144–45
　of student in various environments, 132–33, 201
　types (See Recording techniques)
　validity of, 145
　work habits, 132
Observations of environment, 100
Observer drift, 145
Occupational therapy, 6, 62, 164, 316
Off-task behavior, 141–42
Ohio's Intervention-Based Assessment Model, 19
One-Minute Paper question, 37
Online communications, 199
On-task behavior, 141–42, 145
Oral and Written Language Scales, Second Edition (OWLS-II™ LC/OE and RC/WE)
　at-a-glance, 244
　reliability, 245
　scoring, 245
　standardization, 245
　subscales, 244–45
　validity, 245
Oral descriptions, 197
　mathematical abilities and skills, assessment of, 273

　reading, 218
　written language, assessment of, 235–36
Oral language assessment
　content, 251
　curriculum-based measurement (CBM), 256
　examiner perspectives, 249
　form, 250–51
　language probe, 255–56
　language samples for, 253
　in learning classroom environment, 256–57
　link with reading and writing, 251
　mean length of utterance (MLU), 253–55
　in physical classroom environment, 256
　in social environment, 257–59
　standardized tests for, 259–65
　use, 251–52
Ordinal scale, 87
Ounce Scale
　administration, 322
　at-a-glance, 322
　components, 322
　developmental areas and associated questions, 322
　reliability, 322
　scoring, 322
　standardization, 322
　summary, 322
　validity, 322

P
Paraphrasing, 37
Parent Rating Scales (PRS), 182
Parents. *See also* Family
　federal legislation and, 57
　guaranteed rights, 57
　parent–teacher conferences, 67–68
Parent–teacher conferences, 67–68
　conference planning, 67–68
　postconference activities, 68
　time for conference, 68
Partnership for Assessment of Readiness for College and Careers (PARCC), 124
PASeries, 214
Pearson Education, 322
Peer assessment, 200
　of mathematical abilities and skills, 276
　reading, 223
　written language, 240–41
Pennsylvania's Instructional Support Teams, 19
People-first language, 109
Percentage duration rate, 138

Percentage score, 92
Percentile rank, 94, 106
Performance-based assessments, 199, 286–87
   analytic scoring, 292–93
   anchor papers, 294
   benchmarks, 294
   considerations about using, 297
   consistency, 295
   exhibitions, 290
   fairness, 296
   guidelines for improving reliability and validity, 296
   holistic scoring, 294
   mathematical abilities and skills, assessment of, 279–80
   reading, 222–23
   reliability, 294–95
   rubrics, 292–93
   stability, 295
   Three Gorges Dam project example, 287
   transition assessment, 351
   written language, 239–40
Person-centered planning, 346–47
Phonemes, 250
Phonemic awareness, 28, 202
   tier 2 intervention for, 22
Phonology, 250
Physical classroom environment
   observations, 149–51, 155–57, 256, 280
   oral language assessment, 256
   problem behavior in classroom, 170
   problem behavior in classroom and, 170
Physical space and student functioning, 150
Physical therapy, 6, 62, 164, 316
Pie charts, 110
Population, 85
Portfolios, 199–200
   considerations about using, 297
   contents of, 289
   family benefits, 289
   IEP and, 288–89
   learning supported by, 289–90
   in literacy assessment, 223, 239
   mathematics, 279–80
   organizing, 289
   in reading assessment, 223
   responding to diversity, 291
   student benefits, 289
   teacher benefits, 289
   technology for, 290
   transition assessment, 351
Positively skewed distribution, 89
Positive relationship, 75–76

Pragmatics, 251
Predictive validity, 81
Prefixes, 251
Preschool Language Scales, Fifth Edition (PLS ™ -5)
   administration, 264
   at-a-glance, 264
   auditory comprehension subscale, 263
   expressive communication subscale, 263
   reliability, 264
   scoring, 264
   Spanish-language version, 263
   standardization, 264
   subscales, 263
   summary, 264
   validity, 264
Probes, 196–97
   language, 255–56
   mathematical abilities and skills, assessment of, 271
   reading, 216–17
   testing accommodations, 196–97
   written language, assessment of, 234
Problem behavior in classroom. *See also* Recording techniques
   assessment of, 171
   learning environments and, 170–71
   physical classroom environment and, 170
   social environments and, 171
   standardized instruments for assessing, 182–86
Problem behaviors, 168–69
Professional judgment, 122
Professional knowledge, 108–9
Professional Learning Community (PLC), 26
Professional standards of special educators, 15
   InTASC standards, 15
Program evaluation, 43–44, 197–99, 202–3, 218–19, 222–23, 234, 236, 239, 273–75, 279–81, 289–90
Program planning, 43
Progress monitoring, 20–21
   individual, 43
   literacy tools for, 214–15
   mathematical abilities and skills, assessment of, 278–79
   mathematics tools for, 279
   reading, 212
   reading assessment, 212
   response to intervention (RTI), 20–21

   special education assessment, 43
   in written language, 234
   written language, assessment of, 234
Progress report, 116
Prompt, 240

Q
Quantitative processing, 306
Questionnaires, 159–60, 198
   mathematical abilities and skills, assessment of, 273–74
   for reading assessment, 219–22
   written language, assessment of, 236
Questions and decisions
   in determining eligibility for special education services, 60
   in evaluating services, 63–64
   in monitoring services, 62–63
   in planning services, 62

R
Rating scale, 141–43
Ratio scale, 88
Raw score, 91–92, 205, 226–27, 245, 262, 281, 283, 319–21, 349
Reactivity, 145
Reading assessment
   assessment principles, 211–12
   checklist for assessing attitudes, interests, and habits, 219
   checklist for assessing knowledge of books, 219–21
   cloze procedures, 217
   comparison of progress-monitoring measures, 216
   criterion-referenced assessments, 216
   curriculum-based assessment (CBA), 212–13
   curriculum-based measurement (CBM), 213–16
   error analysis, 213, 217
   exhibitions, 223
   informal assessments, 216–24
   oral descriptions, 218
   peer assessment, 223
   performance-based assessments, 222–23
   portfolios, 223
   probes, 216–17
   progress monitoring, 212
   questionnaires for, 219–22
   retelling, 218
   RTI evaluation of, 28
   self-assessment, 223
   standardized instruments for, 225–28

370 Subject Index

Reading assessment (*Continued*)
   students' journals, notebooks, and blogs, 222
   teacher–student conferences, 222
   think-alouds, 217–18
   using interviews, 222
   written descriptions, 218
Reading comprehension, 28, 81, 204, 212, 215
Reading fluency, 28, 214
Reading-Free Vocational Interest Inventory 2 (RFVII), 349–51
   administration, 349
   reliability, 351
   scoring, 349
   standardization, 351
   summary, 351
   validity, 351
Receptive language, 249
Recording techniques
   anecdotal record, 134–35
   category recording, 141
   duration recording, 138–39
   event recording, 136–38
   intensity recording, 139–40
   interval-event recording, 140–41
   interval-only recording, 140–41
   interval recording, 140–41
   latency recording, 140
   rating scales, 141–43
   running record, 135–36
   scan-check technique, 146
Reevaluation, 8
Referral, 40–41
Reflection, 240
Relationship
   direction of a, 75
   between IQ and, 75
   negative, 76
   positive, 75–76
   strength of a, 75
   zero, 76
Reliability, 294–95
   ABAS II, 166
   AEPS, 328
   alternate form, 77
   ASQ-3™, 318–19
   of assessment instruments, 74
   BASC 2, 183
   Bayley-III, 331
   BBRS 2, 183
   BDI-2, 329
   BRIGANCE® Early Childhood Screening III, 319
   CBCL System, 185
   CCPSN, 333
   CELF-5, 262
   Conners 3 ™ (*Conners 3rd Edition* ™), 186
   correlation coefficient of, 76
   CTONI-2, 303
   defined, 73
   DTLA-4, 304
   ESI-R, 2008 Edition, 320
   factors influencing, 79
   GORT-5, 226
   Greenspan Social-Emotional Growth Chart, 321
   guidelines for improving, 296
   internal consistency, 77–78
   interscorer/interobserver/interrater, 78
   KABC-II, 306
   KeyMath 3 DA, 281
   KTEA-II, 205
   of observations, 144
   Ounce Scale, 322
   OWLS-II™ LC/OE and RC/WE, 245
   PLS ™ -5, 264
   reported in test manuals, 74
   RFVII, 351
   split-half, 77–78
   Stanford-Binet Intelligence Scale, Fifth Edition, 307
   Teaching Strategies GOLD, 337
   testing using correlation coefficients, 74–78
   test-retest, 77
   TOAL-4, 265
   TOMA-3, 283
   TONI-4, 309
   TORC-4, 226
   TOWL-4, 245
   Vineland II, 167
   WIAT-III, 206
   WISC-IV Integrated, 310
   WJ III NU, 209, 312–13
   The Work Sampling System ®, Fifth Edition, 337
   WRAT4, 206–7
   WRMT—R/NU, 227–28
   zero relationship, 76
Remedial and Special Education, 102
Report writing
   accuracy in, 109
   avoiding technical jargon, 110
   background information, 114
   behavioral observations, 114–15
   checklist for evaluating an assessment report, 111
   clear writing, 110
   environment observations, 114
   evaluation form, 119
   evaluation of report, 115
   general principles for, 109–10
   identifying data, 114
   including essentials, 109
   organizing information, 109
   recommendations for, 115
   referral reason, 114
   relating facts, 109
   reservations in, 109–10
   synthesizing information, 110
Research-based interventions, 16
Responding to diversity
   behaviors, 169–70
   fairness in assessment, 82–83
   portfolios, 291
Response to intervention (RTI), 5, 38, 41
   benefits, 19
   defined, 18
   emerging issues, 33
   high-quality instruction, 19
   implementing, 26–32
   as multitiered intervention system, 21–25
   overrepresentation, role in minimizing, 25
   progress monitoring, 20–21
   questions and decisions in, 24
   responding to diversity, 25–26
   school–parent interactions, 19–20
   for students with problem behaviors, 31
   tier 1 of intervention, 21–22
   tier 2 of intervention, 22–24
   tier 3 of intervention, 25
   universal screening procedure, 19
Retelling, 218
Revised Behavior Problem Checklist, 185
Right of consent, 57
Right of evaluation, 57
Right of notice, 57
Right to an independent evaluation, 57
Rubrics, 178–80, 292–93
Running record, 135–36

S
Sample, 85–86
Scaled scores, 106
Scan-check technique, 146
Scatter plot, 76, 178
Schoolwide assessments, 4
Science achievement, 11
Scores/scoring
   AEPS, 328
   analytic, 243–44, 292–93
   anchor papers, 294
   ASQ-3™, 318
   basal level, 96–97
   BASC 2, 182–83
   Bayley-III, 331
   BBRS 2, 183
   BDI-2, 329
   benchmarks, 294

Subject Index

BRIGANCE® Early Childhood Screening III, 319
calculating raw, 98
categories, 124
CBCL System, 185
CCPSN, 332
ceiling level, 96–97
checklists, 292
composite, 105
confidence intervals, 97–98
Conners 3 ™ (*Conners 3rd Edition* ™), 186
CTONI-2, 303
derived, 92
developmental, 92–93
deviation IQ, 96
DTLA-4, 304
ESI-R, 2008 Edition, 320
GORT-5, 225
graphing, 99
Greenspan Social-Emotional Growth Chart, 321
growth, 97
guidelines, 98
holistic, 241–43, 294
information from, 124
KeyMath 3 DA, 281
KTEA-II, 205
normal curve equivalents (NCEs), 96
Ounce Scale, 322
OWLS-II™ LC/OE and RC/WE, 245
percentage, 92
PLS ™ -5, 264
raw, 91–92
of relative standing, 94–96
RFVII, 349
rubrics, 292–93
scaled, 106
standard, 115
standard error of measurement, 97
Stanford-Binet Intelligence Scale, Fifth Edition, 307
stanines, 96
Teaching Strategies GOLD, 337
TOAL-4, 265
TOMA-3, 283
TONI-4, 309
TORC-4, 226
TOWL-4, 245
transforming raw scores to derived scores, 98–99
true, 97
Vineland II, 167
WIAT-III, 205
WISC-IV Integrated, 309
The Work Sampling System ®, Fifth Edition, 337
WRAT4, 206
WRMT—R/NU, 227
Screening
 areas of development, 324
 environment, 322
 false negative, 325
 false positive, 325
 health status of child, 323–24
 limitations of, 324–25
 parent concerns, 324
 purpose of, 40–41
 rapport with examiner, 323
 special challenges, 325
 standardized achievement tests, 203
 tasks, 324
 universal, 19
 of young children, 322–24
Script-implicit (SI) questions, 213
Self-assessment, 200
 mathematical abilities and skills, assessment of, 275
 reading, 223
 written language, 240
Self-determination, 164, 344, 347–49
Self-Report of Personality (SRP), 182
Semantics, 251
Sensitivity, 16
Shaping process, 259
Skewed distribution, 89
Social classroom environment
 mathematics assessment, 280
 observations, 152, 154, 257–59, 280
 oral language assessment, 257–59
 problem behavior in classroom, 171
Special education
 disabilities related to qualifying children and youth for, 6
 eligibility for, 5–6
 identifying students for, 5
 parent involvement in and perception of, 53
Special education assessment, 38–39
 assessment questions, 39–40
 of assistive technology needs, 46–49
 connecting assessment with instruction, 43
 for determining student eligibility, 41–43
 framework, 39
 program evaluation, 43–44
 program planning for, 43
 progress monitoring, 43
 purposes and approaches, 40–44
 referral for, 38
 response to diversity, 44–46
 student evaluation, 43–44
 for universally designed test items, 46
Special educators
 professional standards of, 15
 response to diversity, 15–16
Special services team. *See* IEP team
Speech and language pathology, 6, 316
Speech disorders, 249
Speech utterance, 254
Spelling, 206
 curriculum-based measurement (CBM), 233
 RTI evaluation of, 30
 Test of Written Spelling 5 (TWS-5), 247
Spelling evaluation, 235
Split-half reliability, 77–78
Stability of assessment, 295
Standard deviation (SD), 91
Standard error of measurement (SEM), 78–79, 97, 105
Standard hearing test, 80
Standardization sample, 85–86
Standardized achievement tests, 105, 201
 benefits, 202
 construction of, 201–2
 determining eligibility for services, 203
 disadvantages, 202
 monitoring students' progress, 203
 program evaluation, 203
 program planning, 203
 screening process, 203
 steps and purposes, 203
Standardized assessments, 105–7
Standardized instruments, 201–2
 for evaluating adaptive behavior, 165–68
 intelligence, assessment of, 302–13
 mathematical abilities, assessment of, 281–83
 oral language assessment, 259–65
 problem behavior in classroom, 182–86
 reading assessment, 225–28
 written language, assessment of, 244–47
Standardized tests, 16, 85
 criterion-referenced tests, 86–87
 norm-referenced, 86
Standard scores, 94–96
Standards for Educational and Psychological Testing, 74, 79
Stanford-Binet Intelligence Scale, Fifth Edition
 administration, 307

Stanford-Binet Intelligence Scale (*Continued*)
  at-a-glance, 307
  reliability, 307
  scoring, 307
  standardization, 307
  subtests, 306
  summary, 307
  validity, 307
Stanford-Binet Intelligence Scale—V, 96
Stanines, 96
STAR, 214
STAR Math, 31
Statewide assessment, 123–24
Stimulus behavior, 140
Structured Developmental History (SDH), 182
Structured interviews, 199, 274
Student achievement, 11
Student assistance team, 134
Student diaries, 275
Student interviews, 159
Student journals, 199, 222, 275
Student notebooks, 222
Student Observation System (SOS), 182
Student's performance, 32
  in mathematics, 30
  represented on the graph, 28
  RTI and, 20
  tier 2 interventions, 23
Students with disabilities
  alternate assessment options, 14
  arrangement of physical space for, 150
  assistive technology service, 47
  attention-seeking behaviors, 170
  bias towards, 202, 297
  event recording, 136
  group testing, 203–4
  interviews and, 159
  norm-referenced test for, 86
  person-centered planning, 347
  portfolio assessment for, 291
  research practices with, 16
  RTI process, 25
  special education services, 63
  teaching, 15
  testing accommodations, 209
  transition services, 343–45
Stuttering, 249
Suffixes, 251
Summary
  ABAS II, 166
  AEPS, 328–29
  ASQ-3™, 319
  BASC 2, 183
  Batería III Woodcock-Muñoz, 303

Bayley-III, 331
BBRS 2, 183–84
BDI-2, 329
CBCL System, 185–86
CCPSN, 333
CELF-5, 262–63
Conners 3 ™ (*Conners 3rd Edition* ™), 186
CTONI-2, 303
ESI-R, 2008 Edition, 320
GORT-5, 226
Greenspan Social-Emotional Growth Chart, 321
KABC-II, 306
KeyMath 3 DA, 281–82
KTEA-II, 205
Ounce Scale, 322
PLS ™ -5, 264
RFVII, 351
Stanford-Binet Intelligence Scale, Fifth Edition, 307
Teaching Strategies GOLD, 337
TOAL-4, 265
TOMA-3, 283
Vineland II, 167
WIAT-III, 206
WISC-IV Integrated, 311
WJ III NU, 209, 313
The Work Sampling System ®, *Fifth Edition*, 338
WRAT4, 207
WRMT—R/NU, 228
Supports, 164–65
Syntax, 251
System to Enhance Educational Performance (STEEP), 214

T
Target behavior, 140, 176
Teacher-Developed Program Evaluation Form, 64
Teacher Rating Scales (TRS), 182
Teacher's Report Form for Ages 6–18, 184
Teacher–student conferences
  mathematical abilities and skills, assessment of, 274–75
  reading assessment, 222
  written language, assessment of, 236
Teaching Strategies GOLD
  administration, 336–37
  at-a-glance, 336
  objectives, 336
  reliability, 337
  scoring, 337
  standardization, 337
  summary, 337
  validity, 337

Technical adequacy
  Batería III Woodcock-Muñoz, 303
  Kaufman Test of Educational Achievement, Second Edition (KTEA-II), 205
Technology-generated reports, 119–22
Testing accommodations, 209
Testing environment, 73
Test interpretation
  assessment information, 103–4
  classroom assessment, 104
  examiner bias, 108
  hypothesis generation, 107
  observations of student behaviors, 104
  overall test performance, 107
  overview, 103
  of standardized assessments, 105–7
  student's relative strengths and needs, 107
  subtest performance, 107
  using professional knowledge, 108–9
Test of Adolescent and Adult Language, Fourth Edition (TOAL–4)
  administration, 264
  at-a-glance, 264
  reliability, 265
  scoring, 265
  standardization, 265
  summary, 265
  validity, 265
Test of Mathematical Abilities-3 (TOMA-3)
  administration, 283
  at-a-glance, 283
  reliability, 283
  scoring, 283
  standardization, 283
  subtests, 282–83
  summary, 283
  validity, 283
Test of Nonverbal Intelligence, Fourth Edition (TONI-4)
  administration, 308–9
  at-a-glance, 309
  reliability, 309
  scoring, 309
  standardization, 309
  validity, 309
Test of Reading Comprehension–Fourth Edition (TORC-4)
  administration, 226
  at-a-glance, 226
  Contextual Fluency subtest, 226
  Paragraph Construction subtest, 226
  Relational Vocabulary subtest, 226

reliability, 226
scoring, 226
Sentence Completion subtest, 226
standardization, 226
Text Comprehension subtest, 226
validity, 226
Test of Silent Word Reading Fluency (TOSWRF), 214
Test of Word Reading Efficiency (TOWRE), 214
Test of Written Language-Fourth Edition (TOWL-4)
administration, 245
at-a-glance, 245
reliability, 245
scoring, 245
standardization, 245
subtests, 246
validity, 245
Test of Written Spelling 5 (TWS-5), 247
Test Record Form, completing
behavioral observations, 100
biographical information, 98
calculating raw scores, 98
chronological age, 98
discussion of results, 100
graphing of scores, 99
interpreting test performance, 99–100
observations of environment, 100
transforming raw scores to derived scores, 98–99
Test-retest reliability, 77
Tests/testing. *See also* Authentic assessment; Criterion-referenced assessments; Criterion-referenced test (CRT); Functional behavioral assessment (FBA); Standardized achievement tests; Standardized tests
achievement, 191–95
criterion-referenced test (CRT), 86–87, 194–95
equity, 83
National Center for Research on Evaluation, Assessment, and Student Testing, 16
norm-referenced test (NRT), 86–87, 108, 201
Text-explicit (TE) questions, 213
Text-implicit (TI) questions, 213
Think-alouds, 217–18
Three-year evaluation program, 63
Topics in Early Childhood Special Education, 102
Tourette's syndrome, 169
Transition assessment
instruments for, 349–51
involving families, 346
person-centered planning, 346–47
purposes, 345–46
self-determination skills, 347–49
Transition assessment
performance-based assessments, 351
portfolios, 351
Transition needs, 10
Transition process, 344
Transition services, 10
legal mandates, 344
Trend line, 28
Triangulation, 180
True score, 97
Tweets, 199

U
Universal design, 46
Universal screening, 19
University of Delaware, 37
University of Minnesota, 165
U.S. Department of Education, 215–16, 234, 278–79

V
Validity
ABAS II, 166
AEPS, 328
ASQ-3™, 319
BASC 2, 183
Bayley-III, 331
BBRS 2, 183
BDI-2, 329
BRIGANCE® Early Childhood Screening III, 319
CBCL System, 185
CCPSN, 333
CELF-5, 262
concurrent, 80–81
Conners 3 ™ (Conners 3rd Edition ™), 186
consequential, 82, 295–96
construct, 81
content, 80
criterion-related, 80–81
CTONI-2, 303
DTLA-4, 304–35
ESI-R, 2008 Edition, 320
GORT-5, 226
Greenspan Social-Emotional Growth Chart, 321
guidelines for improving, 296
KABC-II, 306
KeyMath 3 DA, 281
KTEA-II, 205
of observational measures, 145
Ounce Scale, 322
OWLS-II™ LC/OE and RC/WE, 245
PLS™ -5, 264
predictive, 81
RFVII, 351
Stanford-Binet Intelligence Scale, Fifth Edition, 307
Teaching Strategies GOLD, 337
of a test and of test interpretations, 79
of test interpretations, 82
TOAL-4, 265
TOMA-3, 283
TONI-4, 309
TORC-4, 226
TOWL-4, 245
Vineland II, 167
WIAT-III, 206
WISC-IV Integrated, 311
WJ III NU, 209, 313
The Work Sampling System ®, Fifth Edition, 337–38
WRAT4, 207
WRMT—R/NU, 228
Verbal descriptions, 197, 235, 273
Verbal knowledge, 306
Vineland Adaptive Behavior Scales, Second Edition (Vineland II)
administration, 167
at-a-glance, 167
domains and subdomains, 167
Expanded Interview, 166
four forms of, 166
Parent/Caregiver Rating Form, 166
reliability, 167
scores, 167
standardization, 167
subdomain scores, 167
summary, 167
Survey Interview, 166
Teacher Rating Form, 166
validity, 167
Vision, 240
Visual-spatial processing, 306
Vital Indicators of Progress (VIP), 215
Vocabulary achievement, relationship between IQ and, 75

W
Web sites
ASSISTments, 37
Buros Center for Testing, 101
NCEO, 209
NCLB Act, 11
OSEP Ideas that Work, 46
research-based practices, 16
RTI Action Network, 19
Supreme Court, 16
Test Reviews Online, 101

Web sites (*Continued*)
  universally designed test items, 46
  What Works Clearing House, 19
Wechsler Adult Intelligence Scale-Third Edition (WAIS-III), 206
Wechsler Individual Achievement Test, Second Edition (WIAT II), 96, 203
Wechsler Individual Achievement Test-Third Edition (WIAT-III)
  administration, 205
  at-a-glance, 206
  reliability, 206
  scoring, 205
  standardization, 205–6
  summary, 206
validity, 206
Wechsler Intelligence Scale for Children, Fourth Edition Integrated (WISC-IV Integrated)
  administration, 308–9
  at-a-glance, 310
  Perceptual Reasoning Index, 308–9
  Processing Speed Index, 308–9
  reliability, 310
  scoring, 309
  standardization, 309–10
  subtests, 308–9
  summary, 311
  validity, 311
  Verbal Comprehension Index, 308–9
  Working Memory Index, 308–9
Wechsler Intelligence Scale for Children, Fourth Edition (WISC IV Spanish), 312
Wechsler Intelligence Scale for Children—IV, 96
Wechsler Intelligence Scale for Children-Third Edition (WISC-III), 205–6
What Works Clearinghouse, 16
Whole-class instruction, 22
Wide Range Achievement Test 4 (WRAT4)
  administration, 206
  at-a-glance, 206
  math computation, 206
  reliability, 206–7
  scoring, 206
  sentence comprehension, 206
  spelling, 206
  standardization, 206
  summary, 207
  validity, 207
Withdrawal behavior, 168
Woodcock-Johnson III, Normative Update Tests of Cognitive Ability (WJ III NU)
  administration, 312
  at-a-glance, 312
  norms, 312
  reliability, 312–13
  subtests, 313
  summary, 313
  validity, 313
Woodcock-Johnson III, Normative Update (WJ III NU)
  administration, 209
  application, 208
  at-a-glance, 209
  Extended Battery, 208
  reliability, 209
  Standard Battery, 208
  standardization, 209
  summary, 209
  validity, 209
Woodcock-Johnson Psychoeducational Battery III, 302
Woodcock Reading Mastery Test—Revised/Normative Update (WRMT—R/NU), 226–28
  administration, 227
  at-a-glance, 227
  Letter Identification test, 227
  Passage Comprehension test, 227
  reliability, 227–28
  scoring, 227
  standardization, 227
  summary, 228
  Supplementary Letter Checklist (Form G only) test, 227
  validity, 228
  Visual-Auditory Learning test, 227
  Word Attack test, 227
  Word Comprehension test, 227
  Word Identification test, 227
Working memory, 306
The Work Sampling System ®, Fifth Edition
  administration, 337
  at-a-glance, 337
  reliability, 337
  scoring, 337
  standardization, 337
  summary, 338
  validity, 337–38
Written descriptions, 197–98
  reading, assessment of, 218
  written language, assessment of, 236
Written language, assessment of
  analytic scoring, 243–44
  anchor papers, 244
  checklists and questionnaires for, 236
  connection between reading and writing, 230–31
  criterion-referenced tests, 233–34
  curriculum-based measurement (CBM), 232–33
  digital media, 239
  error analysis, 234–35
  exhibitions, 240
  holistic scoring, 241–43
  interviews, 236
  link with instruction, 231–32
  oral descriptions, 235–36
  peer assessment, 240–41
  performance-based assessment, 239–40
  progress monitoring, 234
  RTI evaluation of, 28–30
  self-assessment, 240
  shortcomings of standardized, norm-referenced tests, 232
  spelling evaluation, 235
  standardized tests, 264–65
  teacher–student conferences, 236
  using probes, 234
  written descriptions, 236

Y

Yearly Progress Pro, 215
Young children, assessment of
  arena assessment, 327
  comprehensive developmental assessment, 325–27
  considerations regarding the assessment of, 334–35
  limitations of screening, 324–25
  planning the screening procedure, 322–24
  progress in classroom, 335–38
  resources for working with, 316
  responding to diversity, 335
  screening for special needs, 316–17
  standardized assessment tests, 327–34
  standardized screening instruments for assessing, 317–22
  standards movement and, 338
  working with families, 340–41
Young children, defined, 315–16
Youth Self-Report for Ages 11–18, 184–85

Z

Zero relationship, 76